Matthew Henry's Commentary

on the

New Testament

with preface by
C. H. Spurgeon

Volume 9

Colossians to James

Baker Book House

Grand Rapids, Michigan 49506

Reprinted 1983 by
Baker Book House Company
from an edition
originally published
under the title
An Exposition of the New Testament
by
William Mackenzie, London
in 1886-1888

Ten-volume Set
ISBN: 0-8010-4277-1

Printed and Bound
in
The United States of America

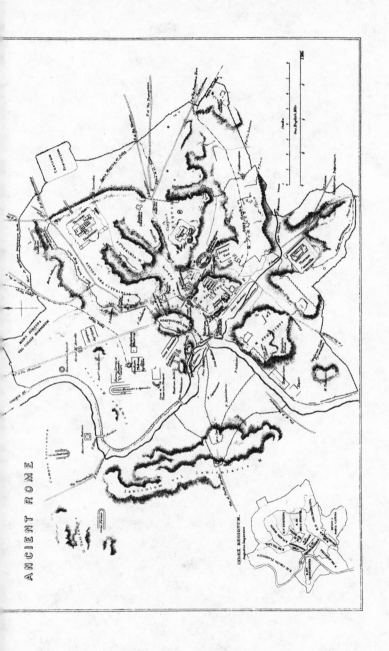

ANCIENT ROME

INDEX REGIONUM.

EXPOSITION OF THE EPISTLE OF ST. PAUL TO THE COLOSSIANS

COLOSSE was a considerable city of Phrygia, and probably not far from Laodicea and Hierapolis ; we find these mentioned together, *ch.* iv. 13. It is now buried in ruins, and the memory of it chiefly preserved in this epistle. The design of the epistle is to warn them of the danger of the Jewish zealots, who pressed the necessity of observing the ceremonial law ; and to fortify them against the mixture of the Gentile philosophy with their Christian principles. He professes a great satisfaction in their stedfastness and constancy, and encourages them to perseverance. It was written about the same time with the epistles to the Ephesians and Philippians, A.D. 62, and in the same place, while he was now a prisoner at Rome. He was not idle in his confinement, and the word of God was not bound.

This epistle, like that to the Romans, was written to those he had never seen, nor had any personal acquaintance with. The church planted at Colosse was not by Paul's ministry, but by the ministry of Epaphras or Epaphroditus, an evangelist, one whom he delegated to preach the gospel among the Gentiles ; and yet, I. There was a flourishing church at Colosse, and one which was eminent and famous among the churches. One would have thought none would have come to be flourishing churches but those which Paul himself had planted ; but here was a flourishing church planted by Epaphras. God is sometimes pleased to make use of the ministry of those who are of less note, and lower gifts, for doing great service to his church. God uses what hands he pleases, and is not tied to those of note, that the *excellence of the power may appear to be of God and not of men,* 2 Cor. iv. 7. II. Though Paul had not the planting of this church, yet he did not therefore neglect it ; nor, in writing his epistles, does he make any difference between that and other churches. The Colossians, who were converted by the ministry of Epaphras, were as dear to him, and he was as much concerned for their welfare, as the Philippians, or any other who were converted by his ministry. Thus he put an honour upon an inferior minister, and teaches us not to be selfish, nor think all that honour lost which goes beside ourselves. We learn, in his example, not to think it a disparagement to us, to water what others have planted, or build upon the foundation which others have laid; as he himself, as a *wise masterbuilder, laid the foundation, and another built thereon*, 1 Cor. iii. 10.

CHAPTER I

We have here, I. The inscription, as usual, ver. 1, 2. II. His thanksgiving to God for what he had heard concerning them—their faith, love, and hope, ver. 3-8. III. His prayer for their knowledge, fruitfulness, and strength, ver. 9-11. IV. An admirable summary of the Christian doctrine concerning the operation of the Spirit, the person of the Redeemer, the work of redemption, and the preaching of it in the gospel, ver. 12-29.

PAUL, an apostle of Jesus Christ by the will of God, and Timotheus *our* brother, ²To the saints and faithful brethren in Christ which are at Colosse: Grace *be* unto you, and peace, from God our Father and the Lord Jesus Christ.

I. The inscription of this epistle is much the same with the rest; only it is observable that, 1. He calls himself an *apostle of Jesus Christ by the will of God*. An apostle is a prime-minister in the kingdom of Christ, immediately called by Christ, and extraordinarily qualified; his work was peculiarly to plant the Christian church, and confirm the Christian doctrine. He attributes this not to his own merit, strength, or sufficiency; but to the free grace and good-will of God. He thought himself engaged to do his utmost, as an apostle, because he was made so by the will of God. 2. He joins Timothy in commission with himself, which is another instance of his humility; and, though he elsewhere calls him his son (2 Tim. ii. 1), yet here he calls him his brother, which is an example to the elder and more eminent ministers to look upon the younger and more obscure as their brethren, and to treat them accordingly with kindness and respect. 3. He calls the Christians at Colosse *saints, and faithful brethren in Christ*. As all good ministers, so all good Christians, are brethren one to another, who stand in a near relation and owe a mutual love. Towards God they must be saints, consecrated to his honour and sanctified by his grace, bearing his image and aiming at his glory. And in both these, as saints to God and as brethren to one another, they must be faithful. Faithfulness runs through every character and relation of the Christian life, and is the crown and glory of them all.

II. The apostolical benediction is the same as usual: *Grace be unto you, and peace, from God our Father, and the Lord Jesus Christ*. He wishes them *grace and peace*, the free favour of God and all the blessed fruits of it; every kind of spiritual blessings, and that *from God our Father, and the Lord Jesus Christ;* jointly from both, and distinctly from each; as in the former epistle.

³ We give thanks to God and the Father of our Lord Jesus Christ, praying always for you, ⁴ Since we heard of your faith

in Christ Jesus, and of the love *which ye have* to all the saints,
⁵ For the hope which is laid up for you in heaven, whereof ye
heard before in the word of the truth of the gospel; ⁶ Which is
come unto you, as *it is* in all the world; and bringeth forth
fruit, as *it doth* also in you, since the day ye heard *of it,*
and knew the grace of God in truth: ⁷ As ye also learned of
Epaphras our dear fellow-servant, who is for you a faithful
minister of Christ; ⁸ Who also declared unto us your love in
the Spirit.

Here he proceeds to the body of the epistle, and begins with thanksgiving to God for what he had heard concerning them, though he had no
personal acquaintance with them, and knew their state and character only
by the reports of others.

I. He gave thanks to God for them, that they had embraced the gospel
of Christ, and given proofs of their fidelity to him. Observe, In his prayers
for them he gave thanks for them. Thanksgiving ought to be a part of
every prayer; and whatever is the matter of our rejoicing ought to be the
matter of our thanksgiving. Observe, 1. Whom he gives thanks to: *To
God, even the Father of our Lord Jesus Christ.* In our thanksgiving we
must have an eye to God as God (he is the object of thanksgiving as well
as prayer), and as the Father of our Lord Jesus Christ, in and through
whom all good comes to us. He is the Father of our Lord Jesus Christ as
well as our Father; and it is matter of encouragement, in all our addresses
to God, that we can look to him as Christ's Father and our Father,
as his God and our God, John xx. 17. Observe, 2. What he gives
thanks to God for—for the graces of God in them, which were evidences
of the grace of God towards them: *Since we heard of your faith in Christ
Jesus, and of the love you have to all the saints; for the hope which is laid
up for you in heaven, v.* 4, 5. Faith, hope, and love, are the three principal graces in the Christian life, and proper matter of our prayer and
thanksgiving. (1.) He gives thanks for their faith in Christ Jesus, that
they were brought to believe in him, and take upon them the profession
of his religion, and venture their souls upon his undertaking. (2.) For
their love. Besides the general love which is due to all men, there is a
particular love owing to the saints, or those who are of the Christian
brotherhood, 1 Pet. ii. 17. We must love all the saints, bear an extensive
kindness and good-will to good men, notwithstanding smaller points of
difference, and many real weaknesses. Some understand it of their charity
to the saints in necessity, which is one branch and evidence of Christian
love. (3.) For their hope: *The hope which is laid up for you in heaven, v.*
5. The happiness of heaven is called their hope, because it is the *thing
hoped for; looking for the blessed hope,* Tit. ii. 13. What is laid out upon
believers in this world is much; but what is laid up for them in heaven is
much more. And we have reason to give thanks to God for the hope of
heaven which good Christians have, or their well-grounded expectation of
the future glory. Their faith in Christ, and love to the saints, had an eye
to the *hope laid up for them in heaven.* The more we fix our hopes on the
recompense of reward in the other world, the more free and liberal shall
we be of our earthly treasure upon all occasions of doing good.

II. Having blessed God for these graces, he blesses God for the means of grace which they enjoyed : *Wherein you heard before in the word of the truth of the gospel.* They had heard in the word of the truth of the gospel concerning this *hope laid up for them in heaven.* Observe, 1. The gospel is the word of truth, and what we may safely venture our immortal souls upon : it proceeds from the God of truth and the Spirit of truth, and is a faithful saying. He calls it *the grace of God in truth, v.* 6. 2. It is a great mercy to hear this word of truth ; for the great thing we learn from it is the happiness of heaven. Eternal life is brought to light by the gospel, 2 Tim. i. 10. They heard of the hope laid up in heaven in the word of the truth of the gospel. " *Which has come unto you, as it hath to all the world, and bringeth forth fruit, as it doth also in you, v.* 6. This gospel is preached and brings forth fruit in other nations ; it has come to you, *as it hath to all the world,* according to the commission, *Go preach the gospel in all the nations,* and to *every creature.*" Observe, (1.) All who hear the word of the gospel ought to bring forth the fruit of the gospel, that is, be obedient to it, and have their principles and lives formed according to it. This was the doctrine first preached : *Bring forth therefore fruits meet for repentance,* Matt. iii. 8. And our Lord says, *If you know these things, happy are you if you do them,* John xiii. 17. Observe, (2.) Wherever the gospel comes, it will bring forth fruit to the honour and glory of God : *It bringeth forth fruit, as it doth also in you.* We mistake, if we think to monopolise the comforts and benefits of the gospel to ourselves. Does the gospel bring forth fruit in us ? So it does in others.

III. He takes this occasion to mention the minister by whom they believed (*v.* 7, 8) : *As you also learned of Epaphras, our dear fellow-servant, who is for you a faithful minister of Christ.* He mentions him with great respect, to engage their love to him. 1. He calls him his fellow-servant, to signify not only that they served the same Master, but that they were engaged in the same work. They were fellow-labourers in the work of the Lord, though one was an apostle and the other an ordinary minister. 2. He calls him his dear fellow-servant : all the servants of Christ ought to love one another, and it is an endearing consideration that they are engaged in the same service. 3. He represents him as one who was a faithful minister of Christ to them, who discharged his trust and fulfilled his ministry among them. Observe, Christ is our proper Master, and we are his ministers. He does not say who is your minister ; but *who is the minister of Christ for you.* It is by his authority and appointment, though for the people's service. 4. He represents him as one who gave them a good word : *Who also declared unto us your love in the Spirit, v.* 8. He recommends him to their affection, from the good report he made of their sincere love to Christ and all his members, which was wrought in them by the Spirit, and is agreeable to the spirit of the gospel. Faithful ministers are glad to be able to speak well of their people.

9 For this cause we also, since the day we heard *it*, do not cease to pray for you, and to desire that ye might be filled with the knowledge of his will in all wisdom and spiritual understanding ; 10 That ye might walk worthy of the Lord unto all pleasing, being fruitful in every good work, and increasing in the knowledge of God ; 11 Strengthened with all might

according to his glorious power, unto all patience and long-suffering with joyfulness;

The apostle proceeds in these verses to pray for them. He heard that they were good, and he prayed that they might be better. He was constant in this prayer : *We do not cease to pray for you.* It may be he could hear of them but seldom, but he constantly prayed for them.—*And desire that you may be filled with the knowledge,* &c. Observe what it is that he begs of God for them.

I. That they might be knowing intelligent Christians : *filled with the knowledge of his will, in all wisdom and spiritual understanding.* Observe, . The knowledge of our duty is the best knowledge. A mere empty notion of the greatest truths is insignificant. Our knowledge of the will of God must be always practical : we must know it, in order to do it. 2. Our knowledge is then a blessing indeed when it is in wisdom, when we know how to apply our general knowledge to our particular occasions, and to suit it to all emergencies. 3. Christians should endeavour to be filled with knowledge ; not only to know the will of God, but to know more of it, and to *increase in the knowledge of God* (as it is *v.* 10), and to *grow in grace, and in the knowledge of our Lord and Saviour,* 2 Pet. iii. 18.

II. That their conversation might be good. Good knowledge without a good life will not profit. Our understanding is then a spiritual understanding when we exemplify it in our way of living : *That you may walk worthy of the Lord unto all pleasing* (*v.* 10), that is, as becomes the relation we stand in to him and the profession we make of him. The agreeableness of our conversation to our religion is pleasing to God as well as to good men. We walk unto all well-pleasing when we walk in all things according to the will of God. *Being fruitful in every good work.* This is what we should aim at. Good words will not do without good works. We must abound in good works, and in every good work : not in some only, which are more easy, and suitable, and safe, but in all, and every instance of them. There must be a regular uniform regard to all the will of God. And the more fruitful we are in good works the more we shall *increase in the knowledge of God. He who doeth his will shall know of the doctrine, whether it be of God,* John vii. 17.

III. That they might be strengthened : *Strengthened with all might, according to his glorious power* (*v.* 11), fortified against the temptations of Satan and furnished for all their duty. It is a great comfort to us that he who undertakes to give strength to his people is a God of power and of glorious power. Where there is spiritual life there is still need of spiritual strength, strength for all the actions of the spiritual life. To be strengthened is to be furnished by the grace of God for every good work, and fortified by that grace against every evil one : it is to be enabled to do our duty, and still to hold fast our integrity. The blessed Spirit is the author of this strength ; for we are *strengthened with might by his Spirit in the inward man,* Eph. iii. 16. The word of God is the means of it, by which he conveys it ; and it must be fetched in by prayer. In was in answer to earnest prayer that the apostle obtained sufficient grace. In praying for spiritual strength we are not straitened in the promises, and therefore should not be straitened in our own hopes and desires. Observe, 1. He prayed that they might be strengthened with might : this seems a tautology ; but he means, that they might be mightily strengthened, or strengthened with might derived from another. 2. It is with all might.

It seems unreasonable that a creature should be strengthened with all might, for that is to make him *almighty ;* but he means, with all that might which we have occasion for, to enable us to discharge our duty or preserve our innocence, that grace which is sufficient for us in all the trials of life and able to help us in time of need. 3. It is *according to his glorious power.* He means, according to the grace of God : but the grace of God in the hearts of believers is the power of God ; and there is a glory in this power ; it is an excellent and sufficient power. And the communications of strength are not according to our weakness, to whom the strength is communicated, but according to his power, from whom it is received. When God gives he gives like himself, and when he strengthens he strengthens like himself. 4. The special use of this strength was for suffering work : *That you may be strengthened unto all patience and long-suffering with joyfulness.* He prays not only that they may be *supported* under their troubles, but *strengthened* for them, the reason is there is work to be done even when we are suffering. And those who are strengthened *according to his glorious power* are strengthened, (1.) To all patience. When patience *hath its perfect work* (Jam. i. 4) then we are strengthened to all patience—when we not only bear our troubles patiently, but receive them as gifts from God, and are thankful for them. To you *it is given to suffer,* Phil. i. 29. When we bear our troubles well, though ever so many, and the circumstances of them ever so aggravating, then we bear them with all patience. And the same reason for bearing one trouble will hold for bearing another, if it be a good reason. All patience includes all the kinds of it; not only bearing patience, but waiting patience. (2.) This is even unto long-suffering, that is, drawn out to a great length : not only to bear trouble awhile, but to bear it as long as God pleases to continue it. (3.) It is with joyfulness, to rejoice in tribulation, to take joyfully the spoiling of our goods, and rejoice that we are counted worthy to suffer for his name, to have joy as well as patience in the troubles of life. This we could never do by any strength of our own, but as we are strengthened by the grace of God.

12 Giving thanks unto the Father, which hath made us meet to be partakers of the inheritance of the saints in light : 13 Who hath delivered us from the power of darkness, and hath translated *us* into the kingdom of his dear Son : 14 In whom we have redemption through his blood, *even* the forgiveness of sins : 15 Who is the image of the invisible God, the firstborn of every creature : 16 For by him were all things created, that are in heaven, and that are in earth, visible and invisible, whether *they be* thrones, or dominions, or principalities, or powers : all things were created by him, and for him : 17 And he is before all things, and by him all things consist. 18 And he is the head of the body, the church : who is the beginning, the firstborn from the dead ; that in all *things* he might have the pre-eminence. 19 For it pleased *the Father* that in him should all fulness dwell ; 20 And, having made peace through the blood of his cross, by him to reconcile all things unto himself ; by him,

I say, whether *they be* things in earth, or things in heaven. [21] And you, that were sometimes alienated and enemies in *your* mind by wicked works, yet now hath he reconciled [22] In the body of his flesh through death, to present you holy and un-blameable and unreproveable in his sight : [23] If ye continue in the faith grounded and settled, and *be* not moved away from the hope of the gospel, which ye have heard, *and* which was preached to every creature [in all creation] which is under heaven; whereof I Paul am made a minister; [24] Who now rejoice in my sufferings for you, and fill up that which is behind of the afflictions of Christ in my flesh for his body's sake, which is the church : [25] Whereof I am made a minister, according to the dispensation of God which is given to me for you, to fulfil the word of God; [26] *Even* the mystery which hath been hid from ages and from generations, but now is made manifest to his saints : [27] To whom God would [was pleased to] make known what *is* the riches of the glory of this mystery among the Gentiles; which is Christ in you, the hope of glory : [28] Whom we preach, warning every man, and teaching every man in all wisdom ; that we may present every man perfect in Christ Jesus : [29] Whereunto I also labour, striving according to his working, which worketh in me mightily.

Here is a summary of the doctrine of the gospel concerning the great work of our redemption by Christ. It comes in here not as the matter of a sermon, but as the matter of a thanksgiving ; for our salvation by Christ furnishes us with abundant matter of thanksgiving in every view of it : *Giving thanks unto the Father, v.* 12. He does not discourse of the work of redemption in the natural order of it ; for then he would speak of the purchase of it first, and afterwards of the application of it. But here he inverts the order, because, in our sense and feeling of it, the application goes before the purchase. We first find the benefits of redemption in our hearts, and then are led by those streams to the original and fountain-head. The order and connection of the apostle's discourse may be considered in the following manner :—

I. He speaks concerning the operations of the Spirit of grace upon us. We must give thanks for them, because by these we are qualified for an interest in the mediation of the Son : *Giving thanks to the Father,* &c. *v.* 12, 13. It is spoken of as the work of the Father, because the Spirit of grace is the Spirit of the Father, and the Father works in us by his Spirit. Those in whom the work of grace is wrought must give thanks unto the Father. If we have the comfort of it, he must have the glory of it. Now what is it which is wrought for us in the application of redemption? 1. "He hath *delivered us from the power of darkness, v.* 13. He has rescued us from the state of heathenish darkness and wickedness. He hath saved us from the dominion of sin, which is darkness (1 John i. 6), from the dominion of Satan, who is the *prince of darkness* (Eph. vi. 12), and from the damnation of hell, which is *utter darkness,*" Matt. xxv. 30. They are

called out of darkness, 1 Pet. ii. 9. 2. "He hath *translated us into the
kingdom of his dear Son,* brought us into the gospel-state, and made us
members of the church of Christ, which is a state of light and purity."
You were once darkness, but now are you light in the Lord, Eph. v. 8. *Who
hath called you out of darkness into his marvellous light,* 1 Pet. ii. 9. Those
were made willing subjects of Christ who were the slaves of Satan. The
conversion of a sinner is the translation of a soul into the kingdom of Christ
out of the kingdom of the devil. The power of sin is shaken off, and the
power of Christ submitted to. The law of the Spirit of life in Christ Jesus
makes them free from the law of sin and death ; and it is the kingdom of
his dear Son, or the Son of his peculiar love, his beloved Son (Matt. iii. 17),
and eminently the beloved, Eph. i. 6. 3. "He hath not only done this,
but hath *made us meet to partake of the inheritance of the saints in light,*
v. 12. He hath prepared us for the eternal happiness of heaven, as the
Israelites divided the promised land by lot ; and has given us the earnest
and assurance of it." This he mentions first because it is the first indication of the future blessedness, that by the grace of God we find ourselves
in some measure prepared for it. God gives *grace and glory,* and we are
here told what they both are. (1.) What that glory is. It is the *inheritance of the saints in light.* It is an inheritance, and belongs to them
as children, which is the best security and the sweetest tenure : *If
children, then heirs,* Rom. viii. 17. And it is an inheritance of the saints
—proper to sanctified souls. Those who are not saints on earth will never
be saints in heaven. And it is an inheritance in light ; the perfection of
knowledge, holiness, and joy, by communion with God, who is light, and
the Father of lights, Jam. i. 17 ; 1 John i. 5. (2.) What this grace is.
It is a meetness for the inheritance : "*He hath made us meet to be partakers,*
that is, suited and fitted us for the heavenly state by a proper temper and
habit of soul ; and he makes us meet by the powerful influence of his
Spirit." It is the effect of the divine power to change the heart, and
make it heavenly. Observe, All who are designed for heaven hereafter,
are prepared for heaven now. As those who live and die unsanctified go
out of the world with their hell about them, so those who are sanctified
and renewed go out of the world with their heaven about them. Those
who have the inheritance of sons have the education of sons and the disposition of sons : they *have the Spirit of adoption, whereby they cry, Abba,
Father,* Rom. viii. 15. *And, because you are sons, God hath sent forth the
Spirit of his Son into your hearts, crying, Abba, Father,* Gal. iv. 6. This
meetness for heaven is the earnest of the Spirit in our heart, which is part
of payment, and assures the full payment. Those who are sanctified shall
be glorified (Rom. viii. 30), and will be for ever indebted to the grace of
God, which hath sanctified them.

II. Concerning the person of the Redeemer. Glorious things are here
said of him ; for blessed Paul was full of Christ, and took all occasions to
speak honourably of him. He speaks of him distinctly as God, and as
Mediator. 1. As God he speaks of him, *v.* 15–17. (1.) He is the *image
of the invisible God.* Not as man was made *in the image of God* (Gen.
i. 27), in his natural faculties and dominion over the creatures : no, he is
the *express image of his person,* Heb. i. 3. He is so the image of God as
the son is the image of his father, who has a natural likeness to him ; so
that he who has seen him has *seen the Father,* and his *glory was the glory
of the only-begotten of the Father,* John i. 14 ; xiv. 9. (2.) He is the *first-
born of every creature.* Not that he is himself a creature ; for it is

πρωτότοκος πάσης κτίσεως—*born* or *begotten before all the creation*, or before any creature was made, which is the scripture way of representing eternity, and by which the eternity of God is represented to us : *I was set up from everlasting, from the beginning, or ever the earth was ; when there was no depth, before the mountains were settled, while as yet he had not made the earth*, Prov. viii. 23–26. It signifies his dominion over all things, as the first-born in a family is heir and lord of all, so he is the *heir of all things*, Heb. i. 2. The word, with only the change of the accent, πρωτοτόκος, signifies actively the first begetter or producer of all things, and so it well agrees with the following clause. *Vid. Isidor. Peleus. epist.* xxx. *lib.* 3. (3.) He is so far from being himself a creature that he is the Creator : *For by him were all things created, which are in heaven and earth, visible and invisible, v.* 16. He made all things out of nothing, the highest angel in heaven, as well as men upon earth. He made the world, the upper and lower world, with all the inhabitants of both. *All things were made by him, and without him was not any thing made which was made*, John i. 3. He speaks here as if there were several orders of angels : *Whether thrones, or dominions, or principalities, or powers*, which must signify either different degrees of excellence or different offices and employments. *Angels, authorities, and powers*, 1 Pet. iii. 22. Christ is the eternal wisdom of the Father, and the world was made in wisdom. He is the eternal Word, and the world was made by the word of God. He is the *arm of the Lord*, and the world was made by that arm. *All things are created by him and for him ;* δι' αὐτοῦ καὶ εἰς αὐτὸν. Being created by him, they were created for him ; being made by his power, they were made according to his pleasure and for his praise. He is the end, as well as the cause of all things. *To him are all things*, Rom. xi. 36 ; εἰς αὐτὸν τὰ πάντα. (4.) He *was before all things*. He had a being before the world was made, before the beginning of time, and therefore from all eternity. Wisdom was with the Father, and possessed by him in the beginning of his ways, before his works of old, Prov. viii. 22. And in the beginning the word was with God and was God, John i. 1. He not only had a being before he was born of the virgin, but he had a being before all time. (5.) *By him all things consist.* They not only subsist in their beings, but consist in their order and dependences. He not only created them all at first, but it is by the word of his power that they are still upheld, Heb. i. 3. The whole creation is kept together by the power of the Son of God, and made to consist in its proper frame. It is preserved from disbanding and running into confusion.

2. The apostle next shows what he is as Mediator, *v.* 18, 19. (1.) He is the *head of the body the church :* not only a head of government and direction, as the king is the head of the state and has right to prescribe laws, but a head of vital influence, as the head in the natural body : for all grace and strength are derived from him ; and the church is his body, *the fulness of him who filleth all in all*, Eph. i. 22, 23. (2.) He is the *beginning, the first-born from the dead*, ἀρχὴ, πρωτότοκος—the principle, the first-born from the dead ; the principle of our resurrection, as well as the first-born himself. All our hopes and joys take their rise from him who is the author of our salvation. Not that he was the first who ever rose from the dead, but the first and only one who rose by his own power, and was *declared to be the Son of God, and Lord of all things*. And he is the head of the resurrection, and has given us an example and evidence of our resurrection from the dead. He rose as the first-fruits, 1 Cor. xv. 20. (3.) He hath in *all things the pre-eminence.* It was the will of the Father

that he should have *all power in heaven and earth*, that he might be preferred above angels and all the powers in heaven (he has *obtained a more
excellent name than they*, Heb. i. 4), and that in all the affairs of the kingdom of God among men he should have the pre-eminence. He has the
pre-eminence in the hearts of his people above the world and the flesh;
and by giving him the pre-eminence we comply with the Father's will,
That *all men should honour the Son even as they honour the Father*, John v.
23. (4.) All fulness dwells in him, and it pleased the Father it should do
so (*v.* 19), not only a fulness of abundance for himself, but redundance for
us, a fulness of merit and righteousness, of strength and grace. As the
head is the seat and source of the animal spirits, so is Christ of all graces
to his people. *It pleased the Father* that all fulness should dwell in him;
and we may have free resort to him for all that grace for which we have
occasion. He not only intercedes for it, but is the trustee in whose hands
it is lodged to dispense to us : *Of his fulness we receive, and grace for grace,*
grace in us answering to that grace which is in him (John i. 16), and *he
fills all in all*, Eph. i. 23.

III. Concerning the work of redemption He speaks of the nature of it,
or wherein it consists ; and of the means of it, by which it was procured.

1. Wherein it consists. It is made to lie in two things :—(1.) In the
remission of sin : *In whom we have redemption, even the forgiveness of sins,
v.* 14. It was sin which sold us, sin which enslaved us : if we are redeemed,
we must be redeemed from sin ; and this is by forgiveness, or remitting
the obligation to punishment. So Eph. i. 7, *In whom we have redemption,
the forgiveness of sins, according to the riches of his grace.* (2.) In reconciliation to God. God by him *reconciled all things to himself, v.* 20. He is the
Mediator of reconciliation, who procures peace as well as pardon for sinners,
who brings them into a state of friendship and favour at present, and will
bring all holy creatures, angels as well as men, into one glorious and blessed
society at last : *things in earth, or things in heaven.* So Eph. i. 10, *He will
gather together in one all things in Christ, both which are in heaven and which
are on earth.* The word is ἀνακεφαλαιώσασθαι—*he will bring them all under
one head.* The Gentiles, who were alienated, and *enemies in their minds
by wicked works, yet now hath he reconciled, v.* 21. Here see what was their
condition by nature, and in their Gentile state—estranged from God, and
at enmity with God : and yet this *enmity is slain*, and, notwithstanding
this distance, we are now reconciled. Christ has laid the foundation for
our reconciliation ; for he has paid the price of it, has purchased the proffer
and promise of it, proclaims it as a prophet, applies it as a king. Observe,
The greatest enemies to God, who have stood at the greatest distance and
bidden him defiance, may be reconciled, if it be not their own fault.

2. How the redemption is procured : *it is through his blood* (*v.* 14) ; he
has *made peace through the blood of his cross* (*v.* 20), and it is *in the body of
his flesh through death, v.* 22. It was the *blood which made an atonement,
for the blood is the life ; and without the shedding of blood there is no
remission*, Heb. ix. 22. There was such a value in the blood of Christ that,
on account of Christ's shedding it, God was willing to deal with men upon
new terms to bring them under a covenant of grace, and *for his sake*, and
in consideration of his death upon the cross, to pardon and accept to favour
all who comply with them.

IV. Concerning the preaching of this redemption. Here observe,

1. To whom it was preached : *To every creature under heaven* (*v.* 23),
that is, it was ordered to be preached to every creature, Mark xvi. 15. It

may be preached to every creature ; for the gospel excludes none who do not exclude themselves. More or less it has been or will be preached to every nation, though many have sinned away the light of it and perhaps some have never yet enjoyed it.

2. By whom it was preached : *Whereof I Paul am made a minister.* Paul was a great apostle : but he looks upon it as the highest of his titles of honour to be a minister of the gospel of Jesus Christ. Paul takes all occasions to speak of his office ; for he *magnified his office*, Rom. xi. 13. And again in *v. 25, Whereof I am made a minister.* Observe here,

(1.) Whence Paul had his ministry : it was *according to the dispensation of God which was given to him* (*v.* 25), the economy or wise disposition of things in the house of God. He was steward and master-builder, and this was given to him : he did not usurp it, nor take it to himself ; and he could not challenge it as a debt. He received it from God as a gift, and took it as a favour.

(2.) For whose sake he had his ministry : " *It is for you*, for your benefit : *ourselves your servants for Jesus' sake*, 2 Cor. iv. 5. We are Christ's ministers for the good of his people, to *fulfil the word of God* (that is, fully to preach it), of which you will have the greater advantage. The more we fulfil our ministry, or fill up all the parts of it, the greater will be the benefit of the people ; they will be the more filled with knowledge, and furnished for service."

(3.) What kind of preacher Paul was. This is particularly represented.

[1.] He was a suffering preacher : *Who now rejoice in my sufferings for you, v.* 24. He suffered in the cause of Christ, and for the good of the church. He suffered for preaching the gospel to them. And, while he suffered in so good a cause, he would rejoice in his sufferings, *rejoice that he was counted worthy to suffer*, and esteem it an honour to him. *And fill up that which is behind of the afflictions of Christ in my flesh.* Not that the afflictions of Paul, or any other, were expiations for sin, as the sufferings of Christ were. There was nothing wanting in them, nothing which needed to *be filled up.* They were perfectly sufficient to answer the intention of them, the satisfaction of God's justice, in order to the salvation of his people. But the sufferings of Paul and other good ministers made them conformable to Christ ; and they followed him in his suffering state : so they are said to fill up what was behind of the sufferings of Christ, as the wax fills up the vacuities of the seal, when it receives the impression of it. Or it may be meant not of Christ's sufferings, but of his suffering for Christ. He *filled that which was behind.* He had a certain rate and measure of suffering for Christ assigned him ; and, as his sufferings were agreeable to that appointment, so he was still filling up more and more what was behind, or remained of them to his share.

[2.] He was a close preacher : he preached not only in public, but *from house to house*, from person to person. *Whom we preach, warning every man, and teaching every man in all wisdom, v.* 28. Every man has need to be warned and taught, and therefore let every man have his share. Observe, *First*, When we warn people of what they do amiss, we must teach them to do better : warning and teaching must go together. *Secondly*, Men must be warned and taught in all wisdom. We must choose the fittest seasons, and use the likeliest means, and accommodate ourselves to the different circumstances and capacities of those we have to do with, and teach them as they are able to bear. That which he aimed at was to *present every man perfect in Christ Jesus*, τελείος, either perfect in the knowledge of the Christian doctrine (*Let us therefore, as many as are perfect, be thus minded*, Phil. iii. 15 ; 2 Tim. iii. 17), or else crowned with a glorious reward hereafter, when he will *present to himself a glorious church* (Eph. v. 27), and bring them to the *spirits of just men made perfect*, Heb. xii. 23. Observe, Ministers ought to aim at the improvement and salvation of every particular person who hears them. *Thirdly*, He was a laborious preacher, and one who took pains : he was no loiterer, and did not do his work negligently (*v.* 29) : *Whereunto I also labour, striving according to his working, which worketh in me mightily*. He laboured and strove, used great diligence and contended with many difficulties, according to the measure of grace afforded to him and the extraordinary presence of Christ which was with him. Observe, As Paul laid out himself to do much good, so he had this favour, that the power of God wrought in him the more effectually. The more we labour in the work of the Lord the greater measure of help we may expect from him in it (Eph. iii. 7) : *According to the gift of the grace of God given unto me, by the effectual working of his power*.

3. The gospel which was preached. We have an account of this : *Even the mystery which hath been hid from ages, and from generations, but is now made manifest to his saints, v.* 26, 27. Observe, (1.) The mystery of the gospel was long hidden : it was concealed from ages and generations, the several ages of the church under the Old-Testament dispensation. They were in a state of minority, and training up for a more perfect state of things, and could not look to the end of those things which were ordained, 2 Cor. iii. 13. (2.) This mystery now, in the fulness of time, is made manifest to the saints, or clearly revealed and made apparent. The veil which was over Moses's face is done away in Christ, 2 Cor. iii. 14. The meanest saint under the gospel understands more than the greatest prophets under the law. He who is least in the kingdom of heaven is greater than they. The *mystery of Christ, which in other ages was not made known unto the sons of men, is now revealed unto his holy apostles and prophets by the Spirit*, Eph. iii. 4, 5. And what is this mystery ? It is the riches of God's glory among the Gentiles. The peculiar doctrine of the gospel was a mystery which was before hidden, and is now made manifest and made known. But the great mystery here referred to is the breaking down of the partition-wall between the Jew and Gentile, and preaching the gospel to the Gentile world, and making those partakers of the privileges of the gospel state who before lay in ignorance and idolatry : *That the Gentiles should be fellow-heirs, and of the same body, and partakers together of his promise in Christ by the gospel*, Eph. iii. 6. This mystery, thus made known, *is Christ in you* (or among you) *the hope of glory*. Observe, Christ is the hope of glory. The ground of our hope is Christ in the word, or the gospel revelation, declaring the nature and methods of obtaining it. The evidence of our hope is Christ in the heart, or the sanctification of the soul, and its preparation for the heavenly glory.

4. The duty of those who are interested in this redemption : *If you continue in the faith, grounded and settled, and be not moved away from the hope of the gospel which you have heard, v.* 23. We must continue in the faith grounded and settled, and not be moved away from the hope of the gospel ; that is, we must be so well fixed in our minds as not to be moved from it by any temptations. We must be stedfast and immovable (1 Cor. xv. 58) and *hold fast the profession of our faith without wavering*, Heb. x. 23. Observe, We can expect the happy end of our faith only when we continue in the faith, and are so far grounded and settled in it as not to be moved

from it. We must not *draw back unto perdition*, but *believe unto the saving of the soul*, Heb. x. 39. We must be faithful to death, through all trials. that we may receive the *crown of life and receive the end of our faith, the salvation of our souls*, 1 Pet. i. 9.

CHAPTER II.

I. The apostle expresses concern for the Colossians, ver. 1-3. II. He repeats it again, ver. 5. III. He cautions them against false teachers among the Jews (ver. 4, 6, 7), and against the Gentile philosophy, ver. 8-12. IV. He represents the privileges of Christians, ver. 13-15. And, V. Concludes with a caution against the judaising teachers, and those who would introduce the worship of angels, ver. 16-23.

FOR I would that ye knew what great conflict I have for you and *for* them at Laodicea, and *for* as many as have not seen my face in the flesh; ² That their hearts might be comforted, being knit together in love, and unto all riches of the full assurance of understanding, to the acknowledgment of [**that they may know**] the mystery of God, and of the Father, and of Christ; ³ In whom are hid all the treasures of wisdom and knowledge.

We may observe here the great concern which Paul had for these Colossians and the other churches which he had not any personal knowledge of. The apostle had never been at Colosse, and the church planted there was not of his planting; and yet he had as tender a care of it as if it had been the only people of his charge (*v.* 1) : *For I would that you knew what great conflict I have for you, and for those at Laodicea, and for as many as have not seen my face in the flesh.* Observe, 1. Paul's care of the church was such as amounted to a conflict. He was in a sort of agony, and had a constant fear respecting what would become of them. Herein he was a follower of his Master, who was in an agony for us, and was *heard in that he feared*. (2.) We may keep up a communion by faith, hope, and holy love, even with those churches and fellow christians of whom we have no personal knowledge, and with whom we have no conversation. We can think, and pray, and be concerned for one another, at the greatest distance; and those we never saw in the flesh we may hope to meet in heaven. But,

I. What was it that the apostle desired for them ? *That their hearts may be comforted, being knit together in love*, &c., *v.* 2. It was their spiritual welfare about which he was solicitous. He does not say that they may be healthy, and merry, and rich, and great, and prosperous; but that their *hearts may be comforted.* Note, The prosperity of the soul is the best prosperity, and what we should be most solicitous about for ourselves and others. We have here a description of soul-prosperity.

1. When our knowledge grows to an understanding of the mystery of God, and of the Father, and of Christ,—when we come to have a more

clear, distinct, methodical knowledge of the truth as it is in Jesus, then the soul prospers : *To understand the mystery,* either what was before concealed, but is now made known concerning the Father and Christ, or the mystery before mentioned, of calling the Gentiles into the Christian church, as the Father and Christ have revealed it in the gospel ; and not barely to speak of it by rote, or as we have been taught it by our catechisms, but to be led into it, and enter into the meaning and design of it. This is what we should labour after and then the soul prospers.

2. When our faith grows to a full assurance and bold acknowledgment of this mystery. (1.) To a full assurance, or a well-settled judgment, upon their proper evidence, of the great truths of the gospel, without doubting, or calling them in question, but embracing them with the highest satisfaction, as faithful sayings and worthy of all acceptation. (2.) When it comes to a free acknowledgment, and we not only believe with the heart, but are ready, when called to it, to make confession with our mouth, and are not ashamed of our Master and our holy religion, under the frowns and violence of their enemies. This is called the *riches of the full assurance of understanding.* Great knowledge and strong faith make a soul rich. This is being rich towards God, and rich in faith, and having the true riches, Luke xii. 21 ; xvi. 11 ; Jam. ii. 5.

3. It consists in the abundance of comfort in our souls : *That their hearts might be comforted.* The soul prospers when it is filled with joy and peace (Rom. xv. 13), and has a satisfaction within which all the troubles without cannot disturb, and is able to joy in the Lord when all other comforts fail, Hab. iii. 17, 18.

4. The more intimate communion we have with our fellow-christians the more the soul prospers : *Being knit together in love.* Holy love knits the hearts of Christians one to another ; and faith and love both contribute to our comfort. The stronger our faith is, and the warmer our love, the greater will our comfort be. Having occasion to mention Christ (*v.* 2), according to his usual way, he makes this remark to his honour (*v.* 3) : *In whom are hidden all the treasures of wisdom and knowledge.* He had said (*ch.* i. 19) *that all fulness dwells in him :* here he mentions particularly the *treasures of wisdom and knowledge.* There is a fulness of wisdom in him, as he has perfectly revealed the will of God to mankind. Observe, The treasures of wisdom are hidden not from us, but for us, in Christ. Those who would be wise and knowing must make application to Christ. We must spend upon the stock which is laid up for us in him, and draw from the treasures which are hidden in him. He is the wisdom of God, and is *of God made unto us wisdom,* &c., 1 Cor. i. 24, 30.

II. His concern for them is repeated (*v.* 5) : *Though I am absent in the flesh, yet am I with you in the spirit, joying, and beholding your order, and the stedfastness of your faith in Christ.* Observe, 1. We may be present in spirit with those churches and Christians from whom we are absent in body ; for the communion of saints is a spiritual thing. Paul had heard concerning the Colossians that they were orderly and regular ; and though he had never seen them nor was present with them, he tells them he could easily think himself among them, and look with pleasure upon their good behaviour. 2. The order and stedfastness of Christians are matter of joy to ministers ; they joy when they behold their order, their regular behaviour and stedfast adherence to the Christian doctrine. 3. The more stedfast our faith in Christ is, the better order there will be in our whole conversation ; for we live and walk by faith, 2 Cor. v. 7 : Heb. x. 38.

⁴ And this I say, lest any man should beguile you with enticing words [**delude you with persuasiveness of speech**]. ⁵ For
though I be absent in the flesh, yet am I with you in the
spirit, joying and beholding your order, and the stedfastness of
your faith in Christ. ⁶ As ye have therefore received Christ
Jesus the Lord, *so* walk ye in him: ⁷ Rooted and built up in
him, and stablished in the faith, as ye have been taught,
abounding therein with thanksgiving. ⁸ Beware lest any man
spoil you through philosophy and vain deceit, after the tradition
of men, after the rudiments of the world, and not after Christ.
⁹ For in him dwelleth all the fulness of the Godhead bodily.
¹⁰ And ye are complete [**made full**] in him, which is the head
of all principality and power : ¹¹ In whom also ye are circumcised with the circumcision made without hands, in putting off
the body of the sins of the flesh by [**in the putting off of the
body of the flesh in**] the circumcision of Christ : ¹² Buried with
him in baptism, wherein also ye are risen with *him* through
the faith of the operation [**faith in the working**] of God, who
hath raised him from the dead.

The apostle cautions the Colossians against deceivers (*v.* 4): *And this I
say lest any man beguile you with enticing words;* and *v.* 8, *Lest any man
spoil you.* He insists so much upon the perfection of Christ and the gospel
revelation, to preserve them from the ensnaring insinuations of those who
would corrupt their principles. Note, 1. The way in which Satan spoils
souls is by beguiling them. He deceives them, and by this means slays
them. He is the *old serpent who beguiled Eve through his subtlety,* 2 Cor.
xi. 3. He could not ruin us if he did not cheat us ; and he could not cheat
us but by our own fault and folly. 2. Satan's agents, who aim to spoil
them, beguile them with enticing words. See the danger of enticing words ;
how many are ruined by the flattery of those who lie in wait to deceive,
and by the false disguises and fair appearances of evil principles and wicked
practices. *By good words, and fair speeches, they deceive the hearts of the
simple,* Rom. xvi. 18. "You ought to stand upon your guard against
enticing words, and be aware and afraid of those who would entice you to
any evil ; for that which they aim at is to spoil you." *If sinners entice
thee consent thou not,* Prov. i. 10. Observe,

I. A sovereign antidote against seducers (*v.* 6, 7): *As you have therefore
received Christ Jesus the Lord, so walk you in him, rooted and built up,* &c.
Here note, 1. All Christians have, in profession at least, *received Jesus
Christ the Lord,* received him as Christ, the great prophet of the church,
anointed by God to reveal his will ; as Jesus the great high priest, and
Saviour from sin and wrath by the expiatory sacrifice of himself ; and as
Lord, or sovereign and king, whom we are to obey and be subject to.—
Received him, consented to him, taken him for ours in every relation and
every capacity, and for all the purposes and uses of them. 2. The great
concern of those who have received Christ is *to walk in him*—to make their
practices conformable to their principles and their conversation agreeable
to their engagements. As we have received Christ, or consented to be his,

so we must walk with him in our daily course and keep up our communion with him. 3. The more closely we walk with Christ the more we are *rooted and established in the faith.* A good conversation is the best establishment of a good faith. If we walk in him, we shall be rooted in him ; and the more firmly we are rooted in him the more closely we shall walk in him : *Rooted and built up.* Observe, We cannot be built up in Christ, unless we be first rooted in him. We must be united to him by a lively faith, and heartily consent to his covenant, and then we shall *grow up in him in all things.—As you have been taught—*"according to the rule of the Christian doctrine, in which you have been instructed." Observe, A good education has a good influence upon our establishment. We must be *established in the faith, as we have been taught, abounding therein.* Observe, Being established in the faith, we must abound therein, and improve in it more and more ; and this with thanksgiving. The way to have the benefit and comfort of God's grace is to be much in giving thanks for it. We must join thanksgiving to all our improvements, and be sensible of the mercy of all our privileges and attainments. Observe,

II. The fair warning given us of our danger : *Beware lest any man spoil you through philosophy and vain deceit, after the tradition of men, after the rudiments of the world, and not after Christ, v.* 8. There is a philosophy which is a noble exercise of our reasonable faculties, and highly serviceable to religion, such a study of the works of God as leads us to the knowledge of God and confirms our faith in him. But there is a philosophy which is vain and deceitful, which is prejudicial to religion, and sets up the wisdom of man in competition with the wisdom of God, and while it pleases men's fancies ruins their faith ; as nice and curious speculations about things above us, or of no use and concern to us ; or a care of words and terms of art, which have only an empty and often a cheating appearance of knowledge. *After the tradition of men, after the rudiments of the world :* this plainly reflects upon the Jewish pedagogy or economy, as well as the Pagan learning. The Jews governed themselves by the traditions of their elders and the rudiments or elements of the world, the rites and observances which were only preparatory and introductory to the gospel state ; the Gentiles mixed their maxims of philosophy with their Christian principles ; and both alienated their minds from Christ. Those who pin their faith on other men's sleeves, and walk in the way of the world, have turned away from following after Christ. The deceivers were especially the Jewish teachers, who endeavoured to keep up the law of Moses in conjunction with the gospel of Christ, but really in competition with it and contradiction to it. Now here the apostle shows,

1. That we have in Christ the substance of all the shadows of the ceremonial law ; for example, (1.) Had they then the Shechinah or special presence of God, called the glory, from the visible token of it ? So have we now in Jesus Christ (*v.* 9) : *For in him dwelleth all the fulness of the Godhead bodily.* Under the law, the presence of God dwelt between the cherubim, in a cloud which covered the mercy-seat ; but now it dwells in the person of our Redeemer, who partakes of our nature, and is bone of our bone and flesh of our flesh, and has more clearly declared the Father to us. It dwells in him bodily ; not as the body is opposed to the spirit, but as the body is opposed to the shadow. The fulness of the Godhead dwells in Christ really, and not figuratively ; for he is both God and man. (2.) Had they circumcision, which was the seal of the covenant ? In Christ we are *circumcised with the circumcision made without hands* (*v.* 11),

by the work of regeneration in us, which is the spiritual or Christian circumcision. *He is a Jew who is one inwardly, and circumcision is that of the heart,* Rom. ii. 29. This is owing to Christ, and belongs to the Christian dispensation. *It is made without hands;* not by the power of any creature, but by the power of the blessed Spirit of God. We are *born of the Spirit,* John iii. 5. And it is *the washing of regeneration, and renewing of the Holy Spirit,* Tit. iii. 5. It consists *in putting off the body of the sins of the flesh,* in renouncing sin and reforming our lives, not in mere external rites. It is not the *putting away of the filth of the flesh, but the answer of a good conscience towards God,* 1 Pet. iii. 21. And it is not enough to put away some one particular sin, but we must put off the whole body of sin. The *old man must be crucified, and the body of sin destroyed,* Rom. vi. 6. Christ was circumcised, and, by virtue of our union to him, we partake of that effectual grace which puts off the *body of the sins of the flesh.* Again, The Jews thought themselves complete in the ceremonial law; but we are *complete in Christ, v.* 10. That was imperfect and defective; *if the first covenant had been faultless, there would no place have been sought for the second* (Heb. viii. 7), and the *law was but a shadow of good things, and could never, by those sacrifices, make the comers thereunto perfect,* Heb. x. 1. But all the defects of it are made up in the gospel of Christ, by the complete sacrifice for sin and revelation of the will of God. *Which is the head of all principality and power.* As the Old-Testament priesthood had its perfection in Christ, so likewise had the kingdom of David, which was the eminent principality and power under the Old Testament, and which the Jews valued themselves so much upon. And he is the Lord and head of all the powers in heaven and earth, of angels and men. *Angels, and authorities, and powers are subject to him,* 1 Pet. iii. 22.

2. We have communion with Christ in his whole undertaking (*v.* 12): *Buried with him in baptism, wherein also you have risen with him.* We are both buried and rise with him, and both are signified by our baptism; not that there is anything in the sign or ceremony of baptism which represents this burying and rising, any more than the crucifixion of Christ is represented by any visible resemblance in the Lord's supper: and he is speaking of the *circumcision made without hands;* and says it is *through the faith of the operation of God.* But the thing signified by our baptism is that we are buried with Christ, as baptism is the seal of the covenant and an obligation to our dying to sin; and that we are raised with Christ, as it is a seal and obligation to our living to righteousness, or newness of life. God in baptism engages to be to us a God, and we become engaged to be his people, and by his grace to die to sin and to live to righteousness, or put off the old man and put on the new.

¹³ And you, being dead in your sins and the uncircumcision of your flesh, hath he quickened together with him, having forgiven you all trespasses; ¹⁴ Blotting out the handwriting of [**bond written in**] ordinances that was against us, which was contrary to us, and took it out of the way, nailing it to his cross; ¹⁵ *And* having spoiled [**put off from himself**] principalities and powers, he made a show of them openly, triumphing over them in it.

The apostle here represents the privileges we Christians have above the Jews, which are very great.

I. Christ's death is our life : *And you, being dead in your sins and the uncircumcision of your flesh, hath he quickened together with him, v.* 13. A state of sin is a state of spiritual death. Those who are in sin are dead in sin. As the death of the body consists in its separation from the soul, so the death of the soul consists in its separation from God and the divine favour. As the death of the body is the corruption and putrefaction of it, so sin is the corruption or depravation of the soul. As a man who is dead is unable to help himself by any power of his own, so an habitual sinner is morally impotent : though he has a natural power, or the power of a reasonable creature, he has not a spiritual power, till he has the divine life or a renewed nature. It is principally to be understood of the Gentile world, who *lay in wickedness.* They were *dead in the uncircumcision of their flesh,* being *aliens to the covenant of promise, and without God in the world,* Eph. ii. 11, 12. By reason of their uncircumcision they were dead in their sins. It may be understood of the spiritual uncircumcision or corruption of nature ; and so it shows that we are dead in law, and dead in state. Dead in law, as a condemned malefactor is called a dead man because he is under a sentence of death ; so sinners by the guilt of sin are under the sentence of the law and *condemned already,* John iii. 18. And dead in state, by reason of the *uncircumcision of our flesh.* An unsanctified heart is called an *uncircumcised heart :* this is our state. Now through Christ we, who were dead in sins, are quickened ; that is, effectual provision is made for taking away the guilt of sin, and breaking the power and dominion of it. *Quickened together with him*—by virtue of our union to him, and in conformity to him. Christ's death was the death of our sins ; Christ's resurrection is the quickening of our souls.

II. Through him we have the remission of sin : *Having forgiven you all trespasses.* This is our quickening. The pardon of the crime is the life of the criminal : and this is owing to the resurrection of Christ, as well as his death ; for, as he *died for our sins,* so he *rose again for our justification,* Rom. iv. 25.

III. Whatever was in force against us is taken out of the way. He has obtained for us a legal discharge from the *hand-writing of ordinances, which was against us (v.* 14), which may be understood, 1. Of that obligation to punishment in which consists the guilt of sin. The curse of the law is the hand-writing against us, like the hand-writing on Belshazzar's wall. *Cursed is every one who continues not in every thing.* This was a hand-writing which was *against us, and contrary to us;* for it threatened our eternal ruin. This was removed when he *redeemed us from the curse of the law, being made a curse for us,* Gal. iii. 13. He cancelled the obligation for all who repent and believe. "Upon me be the curse, my father." He vacated and disannulled the judgment which was against us. When he was nailed to the cross, the curse was as it were nailed to the cross. And our indwelling corruption is crucified with Christ, and by virtue of his cross. When we remember the dying of the Lord Jesus, and see him nailed to the cross, we should see the hand-writing against us taken out of the way. Or rather, 2. It must be understood of the ceremonial law, the *hand-writing of ordinances,* the ceremonial institutions or *the law of commandments contained in ordinances* (Eph. ii. 15), which was a yoke to the Jews and a partition-wall to the Gentiles. The Lord Jesus *took it out of the way, nailed it to his cross;* that is, disannulled the obligation of it, that all might see and be satisfied that it was no more binding. When the substance came, the shadows fled away. It is abolished (2 Cor. iii. 13), and *that which decayeth and waxeth old is ready to vanish away,* Heb. viii. 13. The expressions are in allusion to the ancient methods of cancelling a bond, either by crossing the writing or striking it through with a nail.

IV. He has obtained a glorious victory for us over the powers of darkness: *And, having spoiled principalities and powers, he made a show of them openly, triumphing over them in it, v.* 15. As the curse of the law was against us, so the power of Satan was against us. He treated with God as the Judge, and redeemed us out of the hands of his justice by a price ; but out of the hands of Satan the executioner he redeemed us by power and with a high hand. *He led captivity captive.* The devil and all the powers of hell were conquered and disarmed by the dying Redeemer. The first promise pointed at this ; the bruising of the heel of Christ in his sufferings was the breaking of the serpent's head, Gen. iii. 15. The expressions are lofty and magnificent : let us turn aside and see this great sight. The Redeemer conquered by dying. See his crown of thorns turned into a crown of laurels. He *spoiled them,* broke the devil's power, and conquered and disabled him, and *made a show of them openly*—exposed them to public shame, and made a show of them to angels and men. Never had the devil's kingdom such a mortal blow given to it as was given by the Lord Jesus. He tied them to his chariot-wheels, and rode forth conquering and to conquer—alluding to the custom of a general's triumph, who returned victorious. *Triumphing over them in it;* that is, either in his cross and by his death : or, as some read it, in himself, by his own power ; for he *trod the wine-press alone, and of the people there was none with him.*

16 Let no man therefore judge you in meat, or in drink, or in respect of an holyday, or of the new moon, or of the sabbath *days :* 17 Which are a shadow of things to come ; but the body *is* of Christ. 18 Let no man beguile [**rob**] you of your reward in [**prize by**] a voluntary humility and worshipping of angels, intruding into those things which he hath not seen [**dwelling in the things which he hath seen**], vainly puffed up by his fleshly mind, 19 And not holding the Head, from which all the body by joints and bands having nourishment ministered, and knit together [**from whom all the body, being supplied and knit together through the joints and bands**], increaseth with the increase of God. 20 Wherefore if ye be dead with Christ from the rudiments of the world, why, as though living in the world, are ye subject to ordinances, 21 (Touch not ; taste not ; handle not ; 22 Which all are to perish with the using ;) after the commandments and doctrines of men ? 23 Which things have indeed a show of wisdom in will worship, and humility, and neglecting of the body ; not in any honour to the satisfying [**not of any value against the indulgence**] of the flesh.

The apostle concludes the chapter with exhortations to proper duty, which he infers from the foregoing discourse.

I. Here is a caution to take heed of judaising teachers, or those who would impose upon Christians the yoke of the ceremonial law : *Let no man therefore judge you in meat or in drink,* &c., *v.* 16. Much of the ceremonies of the law of Moses consisted in the distinction of meats and days. It appears by Rom. xiv. that there were those who were for keeping up those distinctions : but here the apostle shows that since Christ has come, and has cancelled the ceremonial law, we ought not to keep it up. " Let no man impose those things upon you, for God has not imposed them : if God has made you free, be not you again *entangled in that yoke of bondage."* And this the rather because these things *were shadows of things to come (v.* 17), intimating that they had no intrinsic worth in them and that they are now done away. *But the body is of Christ :* the body, of which they were shadows, has come ; and to continue the ceremonial observances, which were only types and shadows of Christ and the gospel, carries an intimation that Christ has not yet come and the gospel state has not yet commenced. Observe the advantages we have under the gospel, above what they had under the law ; they had the shadows, we have the substance.

II. He cautions them to take heed of those who would introduce the worship of angels as mediators between God and them, as the Gentile philosophers did : *Let no man beguile you of your reward, in a voluntary humility and worshipping of angels, v.* 18. It looked like a piece of modesty to make use of the mediation of angels, as conscious to ourselves of our unworthiness to speak immediately to God ; but, though it has a show of humility, it is a voluntary, not a commanded humility ; and therefore it is not acceptable, yea, it is not warrantable : it is taking that honour which is due to Christ only and giving it to a creature. Besides, the notions upon which this practice was grounded were merely the inventions of men and not by divine revelation,—the proud conceits of human reason, which make a man presume to dive into things, and determine them, without sufficient knowledge and warrant : *Intruding into those things which he hath not seen, vainly puffed up by his fleshly mind*—pretending to describe the order of angels, and their respective ministries, which God has hidden from us ; and therefore, though there was a show of humility in the practice, there was a real pride in the principle. They advanced those notions to gratify their own carnal fancy, and were fond of being thought wiser than other people. Pride is at the bottom of a great many errors and corruptions, and even of many evil practices, which have a great show and appearance of humility. Those who do so do *not hold the head, v.* 19. They do in effect disclaim Christ, who is the only Mediator between God and man. It is the highest disparagement to Christ, who is the head of the church, for any of the members of it to make use of any intercessors with God but him. When men let go their hold of Christ, they catch at that which is next them and will stand them in no stead.—*From which all the body, by joints and bands, having nourishment ministered, and knit together, increaseth with the increase of God.* Observe, 1. Jesus Christ is not only a head of government over the church, but a head of vital influence to it. They are knit to him by joints and bands, as the several members of the body are united to the head, and receive life and nourishment from him. 2. The body of Christ is a growing body : *it increaseth with the increase of God.* The new man is increasing, and the nature of grace is to grow, where there is not an accidental hindrance.— *With the increase of God,* with an increase of grace which is from God as its author ; or, in a usual Hebraism, with a large and abundant increase.—*That you may be filled with all the fulness of God*, Eph. iii. 19. See a parallel expression, *Which is the head, even Christ, from whom the whole body, fitly joined together, maketh increase of the body*, Eph. iv. 15, 16.

III. He takes occasion hence to warn them again : " *Wherefore, if you be dead with Christ from the rudiments of the world, why, as though living in the world, are you subject to ordinances?* v. 20. If as Christians you are dead to the observances of the ceremonial law, why are you subject to them ? Such observances as, *Touch not, taste not, handle not,*" v. 21, 22. Under the law there was a ceremonial pollution contracted by touching a dead body, or any thing offered to an idol ; or by tasting any forbidden meats, &c., *which all are to perish with the using*, having no intrinsic worth n themselves to support them, and those who used them saw them perishng and passing away ; or, which tend to corrupt the Christian faith, having no other authority than the traditions and injunctions of men.— *Which things have indeed a show of wisdom in will-worship and humility.* They thought themselves wiser than their neighbours, in observing the law of Moses together with the gospel of Christ, that they might be sure in the one, at least, to be in the right ; but, alas ! it was but a show of wisdom, a mere invention and pretence. So they seem to neglect the body, by abstaining from such and such meats, and mortifying their bodily pleasures and appetites ; but there is nothing of true devotion in these things, for the gospel teaches us to worship God in spirit and truth and not by ritual observances, and through the mediation of Christ alone and not of any angels. Observe, 1. Christians are freed by Christ from the ritual observances of Moses's law, and delivered from that yoke of bondage which God himself had laid upon them. 2. Subjection to ordinances, or human appointments in the worship of God, is highly blamable, and contrary to the freedom and liberty of the gospel. The apostle requires Christians *to stand fast in the liberty with which Christ hath made them free, and not to be entangled again with the yoke of bondage*, Gal. v. 1. And the imposition of them is invading the authority of Christ, the head of the church, and *introducing another law of commandments contained in ordinances*, when Christ has abolished the old one, Eph. ii. 15. 3. Such things have only a show of wisdom, but are really folly. It is true wisdom to keep close to the appointments of the gospel, and an entire subjection to Christ, the only head of the church.

CHAPTER III

I. The apostle exhorts us to set our hearts upon heaven and take them off from this world, ver. 1-4. II. He exhorts to the mortification of sin, in the various instances of it, ver. 5-11. III. He earnestly presses to mutual love and compassion, ver. 12-17. And concludes with exhortations to relative duties, of wives and husbands, parents and children, masters and servants, ver. 18-25.

IF ye then be risen with Christ, seek those things which are above, where Christ sitteth on the right hand of God. 2 Set your affection [mind] on things above, not on things on the earth. 3 For ye are dead, and your life is hid with Christ in

God. ⁴ When Christ, *who is* our life, shall appear [be **mani-fested**], then shall ye also appear [be **manifested**] with him in glory.

The Apostle, having described our privileges by Christ in the former part of the epistle, and our discharge from the yoke of the ceremonial law, comes here to press upon us our duty as inferred thence. Though we are made free from the obligation of the ceremonial law, it does not therefore follow that we may live as we list. We must walk the more closely with God in all the instances of evangelical obedience. He begins with exhorting them to set their hearts on heaven, and take them off from this world : *If you then have risen with Christ.* It is our privilege that we have risen with Christ ; that is, have benefit by the resurrection of Christ, and by virtue of our union and communion with him are justified and sanctified, and shall be glorified. Hence he infers that we must *seek those things which are above.* We must mind the concerns of another world more than the concerns of this. We must make heaven our scope and aim, seek the favour of God above, keep up our communion with the upper world by faith, and hope, and holy love, and make it our constant care and business to secure our title to and qualifications for the heavenly bliss. And the reason is because *Christ sits at the right hand of God.* He who is our best friend and our head is advanced to the highest dignity and honour in heaven, and has gone before to secure to us the heavenly happiness ; and therefore we should seek and secure what he has purchased at so vast an expense, and is taking so much care about. We must live such a life as Christ lived here on earth and lives now in heaven, according to our capacities.

I. He explains this duty (*v.* 2): *Set your affections on things above, not on things on the earth.* Observe, To seek heavenly things is to set our affections upon them, to love them and let our desires be towards them. Upon the wings of affection the heart soars upwards, and is carried forth towards spiritual and divine objects. We must acquaint ourselves with them, esteem them above all other things, and lay out ourselves in preparation for the enjoyment of them. David gave this proof of his *loving the house of God,* that he diligently sought after it, and prepared for it, Ps. xxvii. 4. This is to be spiritually minded (Rom. viii. 6), and to *seek and desire a better country, that is, a heavenly,* Heb. xi. 14, 16. *Things on earth* are here set in opposition to *things above.* We must not dote upon them, nor expect too much from them, that we may set our affections on heaven ; for heaven and earth are contrary one to the other, and a supreme regard to both is inconsistent ; and the prevalence of our affection to one will proportionably weaken and abate our affection to the other.

II. He assigns three reasons for this, *v.* 3, 4.

1. That we are dead ; that is, to present things, and as our portion. We are so in profession and obligation ; for we are *buried with Christ, and planted into the likeness of his death.* Every Christian is *crucified unto the world,* and *the world is crucified unto him,* Gal. vi. 14. And if we are dead to the earth, and have renounced it as our happiness, it is absurd for us to *set our affections* upon it, and *seek* it. We should be like a dead thing to it, unmoved and unaffected towards it.

2. Our true life lies in the other world : *You are dead and your life is hid with Christ in God v.* 3. The new man has its livelihood thence. It is born and nourished from above ; and the perfection of its life is reserved

for that state. It is *hid with Christ :* not hid from us only, in point of secrecy, but hid for us, denoting security. The life of a Christian *is hid with Christ. Because I live you shall live also,* John xiv. 19. Christ is at present a hidden Christ, or one *whom we have not seen;* but this is our comfort, that our *life is hid with him,* and laid up safely with him. As we have reason to *love him whom we have not seen* (1 Pet. i. 8), so we may take the comfort of a happiness out of sight, and *reserved in heaven for us.*

3. Because at the second coming of Christ we hope for the perfection of our happiness. If we live a life of Christian purity and devotion now, *when Christ, who is our life, shall appear we shall also appear with him in glory, v.* 4. Observe, (1.) Christ is a believer's life. *I live, yet not I, but Christ lives in me,* Gal. ii. 20. He is the principle and end of the Christian's life. He lives *in* us by his Spirit, and we live to him in all we do. *To me to live is Christ,* Phil. i. 21. (2.) Christ will appear again. He is now *hid;* and the *heavens must contain* him ; but he will appear in all the pomp of the upper world, with his *holy angels,* and in *his own glory and his Father's glory,* Mark viii. 38; Luke ix. 26. (3.) We shall then appear with him in glory. It will be his glory to have his redeemed with him ; he will come to be glorified in his saints (2 Thess. i. 10); and it will be their glory to come with him, and be with him for ever. At the second coming of Christ there will be a general meeting of all the saints ; and those whose life is now *hid with Christ* shall then appear with Christ in that glory which he himself enjoys, John xvii. 24. Do we look for such a happiness, and should we not set our affections upon that world, and live above this ? What is there here to make us fond of it ? What is there not there to draw our hearts to it ? Our head is there, our home is there, our treasure is there, and we hope to be there for ever.

⁵ Mortify therefore your members which are upon the earth ; fornication, uncleanness, inordinate affection, evil concupiscence, [**desire**] and covetousness, which is idolatry : ⁶ For which things sake the wrath of God cometh on the children of disobedience ; ⁷ In the which ye also walked some time, when ye lived in them.

The apostle exhorts the Colossians to the mortification of sin, the great hindrance to seeking the things which are above. Since it is our duty to set our affections upon heavenly things, it is our duty to mortify our *members which are upon the earth,* and which naturally incline us to the things of the world : "Mortify them, that is, subdue the vicious habits of mind which prevailed in your Gentile state. Kill them, suppress them, as you do weeds or vermin which spread and destroy all about them, or as you kill an enemy who fights against you and wounds you."— *Your members which are upon the earth;* either the members of the body, which are the earthly part of us, and were *curiously wrought in the lower parts of the earth* (Ps. cxxxix. 15), or the corrupt affections of the mind, which lead us to earthly things, the members of the body of death, Rom. vii. 24. He specifies,

I. The lusts of the flesh, for which they were before so very remarkable : *Fornication, uncleanness, inordinate affection, evil concupiscence*—the various workings of the carnal appetites and fleshly impurities, which they indulged in their former course of life, and which were so contrary to the Christian state and the heavenly hope.

II. The love of the world : *And covetousness, which is idolatry ;* that is, an inordinate love of present good and outward enjoyments, which proceeds from too high a value in the mind, puts upon too eager a pursuit, hinders the proper use and enjoyment of them, and creates anxious fear and immoderate sorrow for the loss of them. Observe, Covetousness is spiritual idolatry : it is the giving of that love and regard to worldly wealth which are due to God only, and carries a greater degree of malignity in it, and is more highly provoking to God than is commonly thought.—And it is very observable that among all the instances of sin which good men are recorded in the scripture to have fallen into (and there is scarcely any but some or other, in one or other part of their life, have fallen into), there is no instance in all the scripture of any good man charged with covetousness. He proceeds to show how necessary it is to mortify sins, *v.* 6. 7. 1. Because, if we do not kill them, they will kill us : *For which things' sake the wrath of God cometh on the children of disobedience, v.* 6. See what we are all by nature more or less : we are *children of disobedience :* not only disobedient children, but under the power of sin and naturally prone to disobey. The *wicked are estranged from the womb ; they go astray as soon as they are born, speaking lies,* Ps. lviii. 3. And, being children of disobedience, we are *children of wrath,* Eph. ii. 3. The wrath of God comes upon all the children of disobedience. Those who do not obey the precepts of the law incur the penalties of it. The sins he mentions were their sins in their heathen and idolatrous state, and they were then especially the children of disobedience ; and yet these sins brought judgments upon them, and exposed them to the wrath of God. 2. We should mortify these sins because they have lived in us : *In which you also walked some time when you lived in them, v.* 7. Observe, The consideration that we have formerly lived in sin is a good argument why we should now forsake it. We have walked in by-paths, therefore let us walk in them no more. *If I have done iniquity, I will do no more,* Job xxxiv. 32. The time past of our lives may suffice us to have wrought the will of the Gentiles, when we walked in lasciviousness, 1 Pet. iv. 3.—*When you lived among those who did such things* (so some understand it, then you walked in those evil practices. It is a hard thing to live among those who do the works of darkness and not have fellowship with them, as it is to walk in the mire and contract no soil. Let us keep out of the way of evil-doers.

8 But now ye also put off [**now put ye also away**] all these ; anger, wrath, malice, blasphemy, filthy communication [**railing, shameful speaking**] out of your mouth. 9 Lie not one to another, seeing that ye have put off the old man with his deeds ; 10 And have put on the new *man,* which is [**is being**] renewed in knowledge after the image of him that created him : 11 Where there is neither Greek nor Jew, circumcision nor uncircumcision; Barbarian, Scythian, bond *nor* free : but Christ *is* all, and in all.

As we are to mortify inordinate appetites, so we are to mortify inordinate passions (*v.* 8) : *But now you also put off all these, anger, wrath, malice ;* for these are contrary to the design of the gospel, as well as grosser impurities ; and, though they are more spiritual wickedness, have not less malignity in them. The gospel religion introduces a change of the higher as well as the lower powers of the soul, and supports the dominion of right reason and conscience over appetite and passion. Anger and wrath are bad, but malice is worse, because it is more rooted and deliberate ; it is anger heightened and settled. And, as the corrupt principles in the heart must be cut off, so the product of them in the tongue ; as *blasphemy*, which seems there to mean, not so much speaking ill of God as speaking ill of men, giving ill language to them, or raising ill reports of them, and injuring their good name by any evil arts,—*filthy communication*, that is, all lewd and wanton discourse, which comes from a polluted mind in the speaker and propagates the same defilements in the hearers,—and lying : *Lie not one to another,* (*v.* 9), for it is contrary both to the law of truth and the law of love, it is both unjust and unkind, and naturally tends to destroy all faith and friendship among mankind. Lying makes us like the devil (who is the *father of lies*), and is a prime part of the devil's image upon our souls ; and therefore we are cautioned against this sin by this general reason : Seeing *you have put off the old man with his deeds, and have put on the new man, v.* 10. The consideration that we have by profession put away sin and espoused the cause and interest of Christ, that we have renounced all sin and stand engaged to Christ, should fortify us against this sin of lying. Those who have put off the old man have put it off with its deeds ; and those who have put on the new man must put on all its deeds—not only espouse good principles but act them in a good conversation. The new man is said to be *renewed in knowledge,* because an ignorant soul cannot be a good soul. Without knowledge the heart cannot be good, Prov. xix. 2. The grace of God works upon the will and affections by renewing the understanding. Light is the first thing in the new creation, as it was in the first : *after the image of him who created him.* It was the honour of man in innocence that he was made after the image of God ; but that image was defaced and lost by sin, and is renewed by sanctifying grace : so that a renewed soul is something like what Adam was in the day he was created. In the privilege and duty of sanctification *there is neither Greek nor Jew, circumcision nor uncircumcision, Barbarian, Scythian, bond nor free, v.* 11. There is now no difference arising from different country or different condition and circumstance of life : it is as much the duty of the one as of the other to be holy, and as much the privilege of the one as of the other to receive from God the grace to be so. Christ came to take down all partition-walls, that all might stand on the same level before God, both in duty and privilege. And for this reason, because *Christ is all in all.* Christ is a Christian's all, his only Lord and Saviour, and all his hope and happiness. And to those who are sanctified, one as well as another and whatever they are in other respects, he is *all in all,* the *Alpha and Omega,* the *beginning and the end :* he is all in all things to them.

¹² Put on therefore, as the elect of God, holy and beloved, bowels of mercies [**a heart of compassion**], kindness, humbleness of mind, meekness, longsuffering ; ¹³ Forbearing one another, and forgiving one another, if any man have a quarrel [**complaint**] against any : even as Christ forgave you, so also *do* ye. ¹⁴ And

above all these things *put on* charity [**love**], which is the bond of perfectness. · ¹⁵ And let the peace of God rule in your hearts, to the which also ye are called in one body; and be ye thankful. ¹⁶ Let the word of Christ dwell in you richly in all wisdom ; teaching and admonishing one another in psalms and hymns and spiritual songs, singing with grace in your hearts to the Lord. ¹⁷ And whatsoever ye do in word or deed, *do* all in the name of the Lord Jesus, giving thanks to God and the Father by him.

The apostle proceeds to exhort to mutual love and compassion : *Put on therefore bowels of mercy, v.* 12. We must not only put off anger and wrath (as *v.* 8), but we must put on compassion and kindness ; not only cease to do evil, but learn to do well ; not only not do hurt to any, but do what good we can to all.

I. The argument here used to enforce the exhortation is very affecting : *Put on as the elect of God, holy and beloved.* Observe, 1. Those who are holy are the elect of God ; and those who are the elect of God, and holy, are beloved—beloved of God, and ought to be so of all men. 2. Those who are the elect of God, holy and beloved, ought to conduct themselves in everything as becomes them, and so as not to lose the credit of their holiness, nor the comfort of their being chosen and beloved. It becomes those who are holy towards God to be lowly and loving towards all men. Observe, what we must put on in particular. (1.) Compassion towards the miserable : *Bowels of mercy,* the tenderest mercies. Those who owe so much to mercy ought to be merciful to all who are proper objects of mercy. *Be you merciful as your Father is merciful,* Luke vi. 36. (2.) *Kindness* towards our friends, and those who love us. A courteous disposition becomes the elect of God ; for the design of the gospel is not only to soften the minds of men, but to sweeten them, and to promote friendship among men as well as reconciliation with God. (3.) *Humbleness of mind,* in submission to those above us, and condescension to those below us. There must not only be a humble demeanour, but a humble mind. *Learn of me, for I am meek and lowly in heart,* Matt. xi. 29. (4.) *Meekness* towards those who have provoked us, or been any way injurious to us. We must not be transported into any indecency by our resentment of indignities and neglects ; but must prudently bridle our own anger, and patiently bear the anger of others. (5.) *Long-suffering* towards those who continue to provoke us. *Charity suffereth long,* as well *as is kind,* 1 Cor. xiii. 4. Many can bear a short provocation who are weary of bearing when it grows long. But we must suffer long both the injuries of men and the rebukes of divine Providence. If God is long-suffering to us, under all our provocations of him, we should exercise long-suffering to others in like cases. (6.) Mutual forbearance, in consideration of the infirmities and deficiencies under which we all labour : *Forbearing one another.* We have all of us something which needs to be borne with, and this is a good reason why we should bear with others in what is disagreeable to us. We need the same good turn from others which we are bound to show them. (7.) A readiness to forgive injuries : *Forgiving one another, if any man have a quarrel against any.* While we are in this world, where there is so much corruption in our hearts, and so much occasion of difference and contention, quarrels will sometimes happen, even among the elect of God, who are holy and beloved, as Paul and Barnabas had a *sharp contention which parted them asunder one from the other* (Acts xv. 39), and Paul and Peter, Gal. ii. 14. But it is our duty to forgive one another in such cases; not to bear any grudge, but put up with the affront and pass it by. And the reason is: *Even as Christ forgave you, so also do ye.* The consideration that we are forgiven by Christ so many offences is a good reason why we should forgive others. It is an argument of the divinity of Christ that he had *power on earth to forgive sins;* and it is a branch of his example which we are obliged to follow, if we ourselves would be forgiven. *Forgive us our trespasses, as we forgive those who trespass against us,* Matt. vi. 12.

II. In order to all this, we are exhorted here to several things:—1. To clothe ourselves with love (*v.* 14): *Above all things put on charity: ἐπὶ πᾶσι δὲ τούτοις—over all things.* Let this be the upper garment, the robe, the livery, the mark of our dignity and distinction. Or, Let this be principal and chief, as the whole sum and abstract of the second table. *Add to faith virtue, and to brotherly-kindness charity,* 2 Pet. i. 5–7. He lays the foundation in faith, and the top-stone in charity, *which is the bond of perfectness,* the cement and centre of all happy society. Christian unity consists of unanimity and mutual love. 2. To submit ourselves to the government of the *peace of God* (*v.* 15): *Let the peace of God rule in your hearts,* that is, God's being at peace with you, and the comfortable sense of his acceptance and favour: or, a disposition to peace among yourselves, a peaceable spirit, that keeps the peace, and makes peace. This is called the *peace of God,* because it is of his working in all who are his. The *kingdom of God is righteousness and peace,* Rom. xiv. 17. "Let this peace *rule in your heart*—prevail and govern there, or as an umpire decide all matters of difference among you."—*To which you are called in one body.* We are called to this peace, to peace with God as our privilege and peace with our brethren as our duty. Being united in one body, we are called to be at peace one with another, as the members of the natural body; *for we are the body of Christ, and members in particular,* 1 Cor. xii. 27. To preserve in us this peaceful disposition, we must be thankful. The work of thanksgiving to God is such a sweet and pleasant work that it will help to make us sweet and pleasant towards all men. "Instead of envying one another upon account of any particular favours and excellence, be thankful for his mercies, which are common to all of you." 3. To let the *word of Christ dwell in us richly, v.* 16. The gospel is the word of Christ, which has come to us; but that is not enough, it must dwell in us, or *keep house* —ἐνοικείτω, not as a servant in a family, who is under another's control, but as a master, who has a right to prescribe to and direct all under his roof. We must take our instructions and directions from it, and our portion of meat and strength, of grace and comfort, in due season, as from the *master of the household.* It must dwell in us; that is, be always ready and at hand to us in everything, and have its due influence and use. We must be familiarly acquainted with it, and *know it for our good,* Job. v. 27. It must dwell in us richly: not only keep house in our hearts, but keep a good house. Many have the word of Christ dwelling in them, but it dwells in them but poorly; it has no mighty force and influence upon them. Then the soul prospers when the word of God *dwells in us richly,* when we have abundance of it in us, and are full of the scriptures and of the grace of Christ. And this in all wisdom. The proper office of wisdom is to apply what we know to ourselves, for our own direction. The word of Christ must dwell in us, not in all notion and speculation, to make us doctors, but in all wisdom, to make us good Christians, and enable us to conduct ourselves in everything as becomes Wisdom's children. 4. To teach and admonish one another. This would contribute very much to our furtherance in all grace; for we sharpen ourselves by quickening others, and improve our knowledge by communicating it for their edification. We must *admonish one another in psalms and hymns*. Observe, Singing of psalms is a gospel ordinance; ψαλμοῖς καὶ ὕμνοις καὶ ᾠδαῖς—the Psalms of David, and spiritual hymns and odes, collected out of the scripture, and suited to special occasions, instead of their lewd and profane songs in their idolatrous worship. Religious poesy seems countenanced by these expressions and is capable of great edification. But, when we sing psalms, we make no melody unless we sing with grace in our hearts, unless we are suitably affected with what we sing and go along in it with true devotion and understanding. Singing of psalms is a teaching ordinance as well as a praising ordinance; and we are not only to quicken and encourage ourselves, but to *teach and admonish one another*, mutually excite our affections, and convey instructions. 5. All must be done in the name of Christ (*v.* 17): *And whatsoever you do in word or deed, do all in the name of the Lord Jesus*, according to his command and in compliance with his authority, by strength derived from him, with an eye to his glory, and depending upon his merit for the acceptance of what is good and the pardon of what is amiss, *Giving thanks to God and the Father by him*. Observe, (1.) We must give thanks in all things whatsoever we do, we must still give thanks, Eph. v. 20, *Giving thanks always for all things*. (2.) The Lord Jesus must be the Mediator of our praises as well as of our prayers. *We give thanks to God and the Father in the name of the Lord Jesus Christ*, Eph. v. 20. Those who do all things in Christ's name will never want matter of thanksgiving to God, even the Father.

18 Wives, submit yourselves unto your own husbands, as it is fit in the Lord. 19 Husbands, love *your* wives, and be not bitter against them. 20 Children, obey *your* parents in all things: for this is wellpleasing unto the Lord. 21 Fathers, provoke not your children *to anger*, lest they be discouraged. 22 Servants, obey in all things *your* masters according to the flesh; not with eyeservice, as menpleasers; but in singleness of heart, fearing God: 23 And whatsoever ye do, do *it* heartily, as to the Lord, and not unto men; 24 Knowing that of the Lord ye shall receive the reward of the inheritance: for ye serve the Lord Christ. 25 But he that doeth wrong shall receive for the wrong which he hath done: and there is no respect of persons.

The apostle concludes the chapter with exhortations to relative duties, as before in the epistle to the Ephesians. The epistles which are most taken up in displaying the glory of divine grace, and magnifying the Lord Jesus, are the most particular and distinct in pressing the duties of the several relations. We must never separate the privileges and duties of the gospel religion.

I. He begins with the duties of wives and husbands (*v.* 18) : *Wives, submit yourselves unto your own husbands, as it is fit in the Lord.* Submission is the duty of wives, ὑποτάσσεσθε. It is the same word which is used to express our duty to magistrates (Rom. xiii. 1, *Let every soul be subject to the higher powers*), and is expressed by subjection and reverence, Eph. v. 24, 33. The reason is that *Adam was first formed, then Eve: and Adam was not deceived, but the woman, being deceived, was in the transgression,* 1 Tim. ii. 13, 14. He was first in the creation and last in the transgression. The *head of the woman is the man;* and the *man is not of the woman, but the woman of the man; neither was the man created for the woman, but the woman for the man,* 1 Cor. xi. 3, 8, 9. It is agreeable to the order of nature and the reason of things, as well as the appointment and will of God. But then it is submission, not to a rigorous lord or absolute tyrant, who may do his will and is without restraints, but to a husband, and to her own husband, who stands in the nearest relation, and is under strict engagements to proper duty too. And *this is fit in the Lord,* it is becoming the relation, and what they are bound in duty to do, as an instance of obedience to the authority and law of Christ. On the other hand, *husbands must love their wives and not be bitter against them, v.* 19. They must love them with tender and faithful affection, as Christ loved the church, and as their own bodies, and even as themselves (Eph. v. 25, 28, 33), with a love peculiar to the nearest relation and the greatest comfort and blessing of life. And they must not be bitter against them, not use them unkindly, with harsh language or severe treatment, but be kind and obliging to them in all things ; for the *woman was made for the man, neither is the man without the woman,* and the *man also is by the woman,* 1 Cor. xi. 9, 11, 12.

II. The duties of children and parents. *Children, obey your parents in all things, for this is well-pleasing unto the Lord, v.* 20. They must be willing to do all their lawful commands, and be at their direction and disposal ; as those who have a natural right and are fitter to direct them than themselves. The apostle (Eph. vi. 2) requires them to honour as well as obey their parents ; they must esteem them and think honourably of them, as the obedience of their lives must proceed from the esteem and opinion of their minds. And this is *well-pleasing to God,* or acceptable to him ; for it is the *first commandment with promise* (Eph. vi. 2), with an explicit promise annexed to it, namely, *That it shall be well with them, and they shall live long on the earth.* Dutiful children are the most likely to prosper in the world and enjoy long life. And parents must be tender, as well as children obedient (*v.* 21) : " *Fathers, provoke not your children to anger, lest they be discouraged.* Let not your authority over them be exercised with rigour and severity, but with kindness and gentleness, lest you raise their passions and discourage them in their duty, and by holding the reins too tight make them fly out with the greater fierceness." The bad temper and example of imprudent parents often prove a great hindrance to their children and a stumbling-block in their way ; see Eph. vi. 4. And it is by the tenderness of parents, and dutifulness of children, that God ordinarily furnishes his church with a seed to serve him, and propagates religion from age to age.

III. Servants and masters : *Servants, obey your masters in all things according to the flesh, v.* 22. Servants must do the duty of the relation in which they stand, and obey their master's commands in *all things* which are consistent with their duty to God their heavenly Master. *Not with eye-service as men pleasers*—not only when their master's eye is upon them, but when they are from under their master's eye. They must be both just and diligent. *In singleness of heart fearing God*—without selfish designs, or hypocrisy and disguise, as those who fear God and stand in awe of him. Observe, The fear of God ruling in the heart will make people good in every relation. Servants who fear God will be just and faithful when they are from under their master's eye, because they know they are under the eye of God. See Gen. xx. 11, *Because I thought, Surely the fear of God is not in this place.* Neh. v. 15, *But so did not I because of the fear of God.* "And *whatsoever you do, do it heartily* (*v.* 23), with diligence, not idly and slothfully :" or, "Do it cheerfully, not discontented at the providence of God which put you in that relation."—*As to the Lord and not as to men.* It sanctifies a servant's work when it is done as unto God—with an eye to his glory and in obedience to his command, and not merely as unto men, or with regard to them only. Observe, We are really doing our duty to God when we are faithful in our duty to men. And, for servants' encouragement, let them know that a good and faithful servant is never the further from heaven for his being a servant : "*Knowing that of the Lord you shall receive the reward of the inheritance, for you serve the Lord Christ, v.* 24. Serving your masters according to the command of Christ, you serve Christ, and he will be your pay-master : you will have a glorious reward at last. Though you are now servants, you will receive the inheritance of sons. But, on the other hand, *He who does wrong will receive for the wrong which he has done," v.* 25. There is a righteous God, who, if servants wrong their masters, will reckon with them for it, though they may conceal it from their master's notice. And he will be sure to punish the unjust as well as reward the faithful servant : and so if masters wrong their servants.—*And there is no respect of persons with him.* The righteous Judge of the earth will be impartial, and carry it with an equal hand towards master and servant ; not swayed by any regard to men's outward circumstances and condition of life. The one and the other will stand upon a level at his tribunal.

It is probable that the apostle has a particular respect, in all these instances of duty, to the case mentioned 1 Cor. vii. of relations of a different religion, as a Christian and heathen, a Jewish convert and an uncircumcised Gentile, where there was room to doubt whether they were bound to fulfil the proper duties of their several relations to such persons. And, if it hold in such cases, it is much stronger upon Christians one towards another, and where both are of the same religion, And how happy would the gospel religion make the world, if it everywhere prevailed ; and how much would it influence every state of things and every relation of life !

CHAPTER IV

I. He continues his account of the duty of masters, from the close of the former chapter, ver. 1. II. He exhorts to the duty of prayer (ver. 2-4), and to a prudent and decent conduct towards those with whom we converse, ver. 5, 6. III. He closes the epistle with the mention of several of his friends, of whom he gives an honourable testimony, ver. 7-18.

MASTERS, give unto *your* servants that which is just and equal ; knowing that ye also have a Master in heaven.

The apostle proceeds with the duty of masters to their servants, which might have been joined to the foregoing chapter, and is a part of that discourse. Here observe, 1. Justice is required of them : *Give unto your servants that which is just and equal* (*v.* 1), not only strict justice, but equity and kindness. Be faithful to your promises to them, and perform your agreements ; not defrauding them of their dues, nor *keeping back by fraud the hire of the labourers,* Jam. v. 4. Require no more of them than they are able to perform ; and do not lay unreasonable burdens upon them, and beyond their strength. Provide for them what is fit, supply proper food and physic, and allow them such liberties as may fit them the better for cheerful service and make it the easier to them, and this though they be employed in the meanest and lowest offices, and of another country and a different religion from yourselves. 2. A good reason for this regard : "*Knowing that you also have a Master in heaven.* You who are masters of others have a Master yourself, and are servants of another Lord. You are not lords of yourselves, and are accountable to one above you. Deal with your servants as you expect God should deal with you, and as those who believe they must give an account. You are both servants of the same Lord in the different relations in which you stand, and are equally accountable to him at last. *Knowing that your Master also is in heaven, neither is there respect of persons with him,*" Eph. vi. 9.

2 Continue in prayer, and watch in the same with thanksgiving ; 3 Withal praying also for us, that God would open unto us a door of utterance [**door for the word**], to speak the mystery of Christ, for which I am also in bonds : 4 That I may make it manifest, as I ought to speak.

If this be considered as connected with the foregoing verse, then we may observe that it is part of the duty which masters owe their servants to pray with them, and to pray daily with them, or *continue in prayer.* They must not only do justly and kindly by them, but act a Christian and religious part, and be concerned for their souls as well as their bodies : "As parts of your charge, and under your influence, be concerned for the blessing of God upon them, as well as the success of your affairs in their hands." And this is the duty of every one—to *continue in prayer.* "Keep up your constant times of prayer, without being diverted from it by other business ; keep your hearts close to the duty, without wandering or deadness, and even to the end of it : *Watching in the same.*" Christians should lay hold of all opportunities for prayer, and choose the fittest seasons, which are least liable to disturbance from other things, and keep their minds lively in the duty, and in suitable frames.— *With thanksgiving,* or solemn acknowledgment of the mercies received. Thanksgiving must have a part in every prayer.— *Withal praying also for us, v.* 3. The people must pray particularly for their ministers, and bear them upon their hearts at all times at the throne of grace. As if he had said, "Do not forget us, whenever you pray for yourselves," Eph. vi. 19; 1 Thess. v. 25; Heb. xiii. 18. *That God would open to us a door of utterance,* that is, either afford opportunity to preach the gospel (so he says, *a great door and effectual is opened to me,* 1 Cor. xvi. 9), or else give me ability and courage, and enable me with freedom and faithfulness; so Eph. vi. 19, *And for me, that utterance may be given to me, that I may open my mouth boldly, to speak the mystery of Christ, for which I am also in bonds;* that is, either the deepest doctrines of the gospel with plainness, of which Christ is the principal subject (he calls it the *mystery of the gospel,* Eph. vi. 19), or else he means the preaching of the gospel to the Gentile world, which he calls the *mystery hidden from ages* (*ch.* i. 26) and the *mystery of Christ,* Eph. iii. 4. For this he was now in bonds. He was a prisoner at Rome, by the violent opposition of the malicious Jews. He would have them pray for him, that he might not be discouraged in his work, nor driven from it by his sufferings : *That I may make it manifest as I ought to speak, v.* 4. That I may make this mystery known to those who have not heard of it, and make it plain to their understanding, in such a manner as I ought to do." He had been particular in telling them what he prayed for on their behalf, *ch.* i. Here he tells them particularly what he would have them pray for on his behalf. Paul knew as well as any man how to speak; and yet he begged their prayers for him, that he might be taught to speak. The best and most eminent Christians need the prayers of meaner Christians, and are not above asking them. The chief speakers need prayer, that God would give them a door of utterance, and that they may speak as they ought to speak.

⁵ Walk in wisdom toward them that are without, redeeming the time. ⁶ Let your speech *be* alway with grace, seasoned with salt, that ye may know how ye ought to answer every man.

The apostle exhorts them further to a prudent and decent conduct towards all those with whom they conversed, towards the heathen world, or those out of the Christian church among whom they lived (*v.* 5) : *Walk in wisdom towards those who are without.* Be careful, in all your converse with them, to get no hurt by them, or contract any of their customs; for *evil communications corrupt good manners;* and to do no hurt to them, or increase their prejudices against religion, and give them an occasion of dislike. Yea, do them all the good you can, and by all the fittest means and in the proper seasons recommend religion to them.—*Redeeming the time;* that is, either "improving every opportunity of doing them good, and making the best use of your time in proper duty" (diligence in redeeming time very much recommends religion to the good opinion of others), or else "walking cautiously and with circumspection, to give them no advantage against you, nor expose yourselves to their malice and ill-will," Eph. v. 15, 16. *Walk circumspectly, redeeming the time, because the days are evil,* that is, dangerous, or times of trouble and suffering. And towards others, or those who are within as well as those who are without, "Let *your speech be always with grace, v.* 6. Let all your discourse be as becomes Christians, suitable to your profession—savoury, discreet, seasonable." Though it be not always of grace, it must be always with grace ; and, though the matter of our discourse be that which is common, yet there must be an air of piety upon it and it must be in a Christian manner ; *seasoned with salt.* Grace is the salt which seasons our discourse, makes it savoury, and keeps it from corrupting. *That you may know how to answer every man.* One answer is proper for one man, and another for another man, Prov. xxvi. 4, 5. We have need of a great deal of wisdom and grace to give proper answers to every man, particularly in answering the questions and objections of adversaries against our religion, giving the reasons of our faith, and show-ing the unreasonableness of their exceptions and cavils to the best advan-tage for our cause and least prejudice to ourselves. *Be ready always to give an answer to every man who asketh you a reason of the hope that is in you, with meekness and fear,* 1 Pet. iii. 15.

[7] All my state [affairs] shall Tychicus declare unto you, *who* is a beloved brother, and a faithful minister and fellow-servant in the Lord : [8] Whom I have sent unto you for the same pur-pose, that he [ye] might know your [our] estate, and comfort your hearts ; [9] With Onesimus, a faithful and beloved brother, who is *one* of you. They shall make known unto you all things which *are done* here. [10] Aristarchus my fellow-prisoner saluteth you, and Marcus, sister's son to [Mark, the cousin of] Barnabas, (touching whom ye received commandments : if he come unto you, receive him ;) [11] And Jesus, which is called Justus, who are of the circumcision. These only *are my* fellow-workers unto the kingdom of God, which have been a comfort unto me. [12] Epaphras, who is *one* of you, a servant of Christ, saluteth you, always labouring fervently for you in prayers, that ye may stand perfect and complete [fully assured] in all the will of God. [13] For I bear him record, that he hath a great zeal for you, and them *that are* at Laodicea, and them in Hierapolis. [14] Luke, the beloved physician, and Demas, greet you. [15] Salute the brethren which are in Laodicea, and Nymphas, and the church which is in his house. [16] And when this epistle is read among you, cause that it be read also in the church of the Laodiceans ; and that ye likewise read the *epistle* from Laodicea. [17] And say to Archippus, Take heed to the ministry which thou hast received in the Lord, that thou fulfil it. [18] The salutation by the hand of me Paul. Remember my bonds. Grace *be* with you. Amen.

In the close of this epistle the apostle does several of his friends the honour to leave their names upon record, with some testimony of his re-spect, which will be spoken of wherever the gospel comes, and last to the end of the world.

I. Concerning **Tychicus,** *v.* 7. By him this epistle was sent ; and he does not give them an account in writing of his present state, because Tychicus would do it by word of mouth more fully and particularly. He knew they would be glad to hear how it fared with him. The churches cannot but be concerned for good ministers and desirous to know their state. He gives him this character, *A beloved brother and faithful minister.* Paul, though a great apostle, owns a faithful minister for a brother and a beloved brother. Faithfulness in any one is truly lovely, and renders him worthy our affection and esteem. *And a fellow-servant in the Lord.* Ministers are servants to Christ, and fellow-servants to one another. They have one Lord, though they have different stations and capacities of service. Observe, It adds much to the beauty and strength of the gospel ministry when ministers are thus loving and condescending one to another, and by all just means support and advance one another's reputation. Paul sent him not only to tell them of his affairs, but to bring him an account of theirs ; *Whom I have sent unto you for the same purpose, that he might know your estate, and comfort your hearts, v.* 8. He was as willing to hear from them as they could be to hear from him, and thought himself as much obliged to sympathise with them as he thought them obliged to sympathise with him. It is a great comfort, under the troubles and difficulties of life, to have the mutual concern of fellow-christians.

II. Concerning Onesimus (*v.* 9) : *With Onesimus, a faithful and beloved brother, who is one of you.* He was sent back from Rome along with Tychicus. This was he whom Paul had begotten in his bonds, Phflem. 10. He had been servant to Philemon, and was a member, if not a minister, of their church. He was converted at Rome, whither he had fled from his master's service ; and was now sent back, it is probable, with the epistle to Philemon, to introduce him again into his master's family. Observe, Though he was a poor servant, and had been a bad man, yet being now a convert, Paul calls him a *faithful and beloved brother.* The meanest circumstance of life, and greatest wickedness of former life, make no difference in the spiritual relation among sincere Christians : they partake of the same privileges, and are entitled to the same regards. The *righteousness of God by faith of Jesus Christ is unto all and upon all those that believe ; for there is no difference* (Rom. iii. 22) : and *their is neither Jew nor Greek, neither bond nor free, for you are all one in Christ Jesus,* Gal. iii. 28. Perhaps this was sometime after he was converted and sent back to Philemon, and by this time he had entered into the ministry, because Paul calls him a brother.

III. *Aristarchus, a fellow-prisoner.* Those who join in services and sufferings should be thereby engaged to one another in holy love. Paul had a particular affection for his fellow-servants and his fellow-prisoners.

IV. *Marcus, sister's son to Barnabas.* This is supposed to be the same who wrote the gospel which bears his name. *If he come unto you, receive him.* Paul had a quarrel with Barnabas upon the account of this Mark, who was his nephew, and *thought not good to take him with them, because he departed from them from Pamphylia, and went not with them to the work,* Acts xv. 38. He would not take Mark with him, but took Silas, because Mark had deserted them ; and yet Paul is not only reconciled to him himself, but recommends him to the respect of the churches, and gives a great example of a truly Christian and forgiving spirit. If men have been guilty of a fault, it must not be always remembered against them. We must forget as well as forgive. *If a man be overtaken in a fault, you who are spiritual restore such a one in the spirit of meekness,* Gal. vi. 1.

V. Here is one who is called *Jesus*, which is the Greek name for the Hebrew *Joshua*. *If Jesus had given them rest, then would he not afterwards have spoken of another day*, Heb. iv. 8. *Who is called Justus.* It is probable that he changed his name for that of Justus, in honour to the name of the Redeemer. Or else Jesus was his Jewish name, for he was of the circumcision ; and Justus his Roman or Latin name. *These are my fellow labourers unto the kingdom of God, who have been a comfort unto me.* Observe, What comfort the apostle had in the communion of saints and ministers ! One is his fellow servant, another his fellow prisoner, and all his fellow workers, who were working out their own salvation and endeavouring to promote the salvation of others. Good ministers take great comfort in those who are their fellow-workers unto the kingdom of God. Their friendship and converse together are a great refreshment under the sufferings and difficulties in their way.

VI. *Epaphras* (v. 12), the same with *Epaphroditus*. He is *one of you*, one of your church ; *he salutes you*, or sends his service to you, and his best affections and wishes. *Always labouring fervently for you in prayers.* Epaphras had learned of Paul to be much in prayer for his friends. Observe, **1.** In what manner he prayed for them. He laboured in prayer, laboured fervently, and always laboured fervently for them. Those who would succeed in prayer must take pains in prayer ; and we must be earnest in prayer, not only for ourselves, but for others also. It is the effectual fervent prayer which is the prevailing prayer, and availeth much (Jam. v. 16), and *Elias prayed earnestly that it might not rain, v.* 17. **2.** What is the matter of this prayer : *That you may stand perfect and complete in all the will of God.* Observe, To stand perfect and complete in the will of God is what we should earnestly desire both for ourselves and others. We must stand complete in all the will of God ; in the will of his precepts by a universal obedience, and in the will of his providence by a cheerful submission to it : and we stand perfect and complete in both by constancy and perseverance unto the end. The apostle was witness for Epaphras that he had a great zeal for them : "*I bear him record ;* I can testify for him that he has a great concern for you, and that all he does for you proceeds from a warm desire for your good." And his zeal extended to all about them : to *those who are in Laodicea and Hierapolis.* He had a great concern for the Christian interest in the neighbouring places, as well as among them.

VII. *Luke* is another here mentioned, whom he calls the *beloved physician.* This is he who wrote the Gospel and Acts, and was Paul's companion. Observe, He was both a physician and an evangelist. Christ himself both taught and healed, and was the great physician as well as prophet of the church. He was the beloved physician ; one who recommended himself more than ordinary to the affections of his friends. Skill in physic is a useful accomplishment in a minister, and may be improved to more extensive usefulness and greater esteem among Christians.

VIII. *Demas.* Whether this was written before the second epistle to Timothy or after is not certain. There we read (2 Tim. iv. 10), *Demas hath forsaken me, having loved this present world.* Some have thought that this epistle was written after ; and then it is an evidence that, though Demas forsook Paul, yet he did not forsake Christ ; or he forsook him but for a time, and recovered himself again, and Paul forgave him and owned him as a brother. But others think more probably that this epistle was written before the other ; this in *anno* 62, that in 66, and then it is an evidence how considerable a man Demas was, who yet afterwards revolted. Many who have made a great figure in profession, and gained a great name among Christians, have yet shamefully apostatised : *They went forth from us, because they were not of us,* 1 John ii. 19.

IX. The *brethren in Laodicea* are here mentioned, as living in the neighbourhood of Colosse : and Paul sends salutations to them, and orders that this epistle should be read in the church of the Laodiceans (*v.* 16), that a copy of it should be sent thither, to be read publicly in their congregation. And some think Paul sent another epistle at this time to Laodicea, and ordered them to send for that from Laodicea, and read it in their church : *And that you likewise read the epistle from Laodicea.* If so, that epistle is now lost, and did not belong to the canon : for all the epistles which the apostles ever wrote were not preserved, any more than the words and actions of our blessed Lord. *There are many other things which Jesus did, which if they should be written every one, I suppose the world itself could not contain the books which would be written,* John xxi. 25. But some think it was the epistle to the Ephesians, which is still extant.

X. *Nymphas* is mentioned (*v.* 15) as one who lived at Colosse, and had a church in his house ; that is, either a religious family, where the several parts of worship were daily performed ; or some part of the congregation met there, when they had no public places of worship allowed, and they were forced to assemble in private houses for fear of their enemies. *The disciples were assembled for fear of the Jews* (John xx. 19), and the apostle preached in his *own lodging and hired house,* Acts xxviii. 23, 30. In the former sense it showed his exemplary piety ; in the latter his zeal and public spirit.

XI. Concerning *Archippus,* who was one of their ministers at Colosse. They are bidden to admonish him to mind his work as a minister, to *take heed to it and to fulfil it*—to be diligent and careful of all the parts of it, and to persevere in it unto the end. They must attend to the main design of their ministry, without troubling themselves or the people with things foreign to it, or of less moment. Observe, (1.) The ministry we have received is a great honour ; for it is *received in the Lord,* and is by his appointment and command. (2.) Those who have received it must fulfil it, or do the full duty of it. Those betray their trust, and will have a sad account at last, who *do this work of the Lord negligently.* (3.) The people may put their ministers in mind of their duty, and excite them to it : *Say to Archippus, Take heed to the ministry,* though no doubt with decency and respect, not from pride and conceit.

XII. Concerning himself (*v.* 18) : *The salutation of me Paul. Remember my bonds.* He had a scribe to write all the rest of the epistle, but these words he wrote with his own hand : *Remember my bonds.* He does not say, "Remember I am a prisoner, and send me supply ; " but, "Remember I am in bonds as the apostle of the Gentiles, and let this confirm your faith in the gospel of Christ : " it adds weight to this exhortation : *I therefore, the prisoner of the Lord, beseech you to walk worthy,* Eph. iv. 1. " *Grace be with you.* The favour of God, and all good, the blessed fruits and effects of it, be with you, and be your portion."

EXPOSITION OF THE FIRST EPISTLE OF ST. PAUL TO THE THESSALONIANS

THESSALONICA was formerly the metropolis of Macedonia; it is now called *Salonichi*, and is the best peopled, and one of the best towns for commerce, in the Levant. The apostle Paul, being diverted from his design of going into the provinces of Asia, properly so called, and directed after an extraordinary manner to preach the gospel in Macedonia (Acts xvi. 9, 10), in obedience to the call of God went from Troas to Samothracia, thence to Neapolis, and thence to Philippi, where he had good success in his ministry, but met with hard usage, being cast into prison with Silas his companion in travel and labour, from which being wonderfully delivered, they comforted the brethren there, and departed. Passing through Amphipolis and Apollonia, they came to Thessalonica, where the apostle planted a church that consisted of some believing Jews and many converted Gentiles, Acts xvii. 1-4. But a tumult being raised in the city by the unbelieving Jews, and the lewd and baser sort of the inhabitants, Paul and Silas, for their safety, were sent away by night unto Berea, and afterwards Paul was conducted to Athens, leaving Silas and Timotheus behind him, but sent directions that they should come to him with all speed. When they came, Timotheus was sent to Thessalonica, to enquire after their welfare and to establish them in the faith (1 Thess. iii. 2), and, returning to Paul while he tarried at Athens, was sent again, together with Silas, to visit the churches in Macedonia. So that Paul, being left at Athens alone (1 Thess. iii. 1), departed thence to Corinth, where he continued a year and a half, in which time Silas and Timotheus returned to him from Macedonia (Acts xviii. 5), and then he wrote this epistle to the church of Christ at Thessalonica, which, though it is placed after the other epistles of this apostle, is supposed to be first in time of all Paul's epistles, and to be written about A.D. 51. The main scope of it is to express the thankfulness of this apostle for the good success his preaching had among them, to establish them in the faith, and persuade them to a holy conversation.

CHAPTER I

After the introduction (ver. 1) the apostle begins with a thanksgiving to God for the saving benefits bestowed on them, ver. 2-5. And then mentions the sure evidences of the good success of the gospel among them, which was notorious and famous in several other places, ver. 6-10.

PAUL, and Silvanus, and Timotheus, unto the church of the Thessalonians *which is* in God the Father and *in* the Lord Jesus Christ : Grace *be* unto you, and peace, from God our Father, and the Lord Jesus Christ.

In this introduction we have,

I. The inscription, where we have, 1. The persons from whom this epistle came, or by whom it was written. Paul was the inspired apostle and writer of this epistle, though he makes no mention of his apostleship, which was not doubted of by the Thessalonians, nor opposed by any false apostle among them. He joins Silvanus (or Silas) and Timotheus with himself (who had now come to him with an account of the prosperity of the churches in Macedonia), which shows this great apostle's humility, and how desirous he was to put honour upon the ministers of Christ who were of an inferior rank and standing. A good example this is to such ministers as are of greater abilities and reputation in the church than some others. 2. The persons to whom this epistle is written, namely, the church of the Thessalonians, the converted Jews and Gentiles in Thessalonica ; and it is observable that this church is said to *be in God the Father and in the Lord Jesus Christ :* they had fellowship with the Father, and his Son Jesus Christ, 1 John i. 3. They were a Christian church, because they believed in God the Father and in the Lord Jesus Christ. They believed the principles both of natural and revealed religion. The Gentiles among them were turned to God from idols, and the Jews among them believed Jesus to be the promised Messias. All of them were devoted and dedicated to God the Father and the Lord Jesus Christ : to God as their chief good and highest end, to Jesus Christ as our Lord and Mediator between God and man. God the Father is the original and centre of all natural religion ; and Jesus Christ is the author and centre of all revealed religion. *You believe in God,* says our Saviour, *believe also in me,* John xiv. 1.

II. The salutation or apostolical benediction : *Grace be with you, and peace from God our Father and the Lord Jesus Christ.* This is the same for substance as in the other epistles. Grace and peace are well joined together ; for the free grace or favour of God is the spring or fountain of all the peace and prosperity we do or can enjoy ; and where there are gracious dispositions in us we may hope for peaceful thoughts in our own breasts ; both grace and peace, and all spiritual blessings, come to us from God the Father and the Lord Jesus Christ ; from God the original of all good, and from the Lord Jesus Christ the purchaser of all good for us ; from God in Christ, and so our Father in covenant, because he is the God and Father of our Lord Jesus Christ. Note, As all good comes from God, so no good can be hoped for by sinners but from God in Christ. And the best good may be expected from God, as our Father for the sake of Christ.

² We give thanks to God always for you all, making mention of you in our prayers; ³ Remembering without ceasing your work of faith, and labour of love, and patience of hope in our Lord Jesus Christ, in the sight of God and our Father; ⁴ Knowing, brethren beloved, your election of God. ⁵ For our gospel came not unto you in word only, but also in power, and in the Holy Ghost, and in much assurance; as ye know what manner of men we were among you for your sake.

I. The apostle begins with thanksgiving to God. Being about to mention the things that were matter of joy to him, and highly praiseworthy in them, and greatly for their advantage, he chooses to do this by way of thanksgiving to God, who is the author of all that good that comes to us, or is done by us, at any time. God is the object of all religious worship, of prayer and praise. And thanksgiving to God is a great duty, to be performed always or constantly; even when we do not actually give thanks to God by our words, we should have a grateful sense of God's goodness upon our minds. Thanksgiving should be often repeated; and not only should we be thankful for the favours we ourselves receive, but for the benefits bestowed on others also, upon our fellow-creatures and fellow-christians. The apostle gave thanks not only for those who were his most intimate friends, or most eminently favoured of God, but for them all.

II. He joined prayer with his praise or thanksgiving. When we in every thing by prayer and supplication make our requests known to God, we should join thanksgiving therewith, Phil. iv. 6. So when we give thanks for any benefit we receive we should join prayer. We should pray always and without ceasing, and should pray not only for ourselves, but for others also, for our friends, and should make mention of them in our prayers. We may sometimes mention their names, and should make mention of their case and condition; at least we should have their persons and circumstances in our minds, remembering them without ceasing. Note, As there is much that we ought to be thankful for on the behalf of ourselves and our friends, so there is much occasion of constant prayer for further supplies of good.

III. He mentions the particulars for which he was so thankful to God; namely,

1. The saving benefits bestowed on them. These were the grounds and reasons of his thanksgiving. (1.) Their faith and their work of faith. Their faith he tells them (v. 8) was very famous, and spread abroad. This is the radical grace; and their faith was a true and living faith, because a working faith. Note, Wherever there is a true faith, it will work: it will have an influence upon heart and life; it will put us upon working for God and for our own salvation. We have comfort in our own faith and the faith of others when we perceive the work of faith. *Show me thy faith by thy works,* Jam. ii. 18. (2.) Their love and the labour of love. Love is one of the cardinal graces; it is of great use to us in this life and will remain and be perfected in the life to come. *Faith works by love;* it shows itself in the exercise of love to God and love to our neighbour; as love will show itself by labour, it will put us upon taking pains in religion. (3.) Their hope and the patience of hope. *We are saved by hope.* This grace is compared to the soldier's helmet and sailor's anchor, and is of great use

in times of danger. Wherever there is a well-grounded hope of eternal life, it will appear by the exercise of patience ; in a patient bearing of the calamities of the present time and a patient waiting for the glory to be revealed. *For, if we hope for that we see not, then do we with patience wait for it,* Rom. viii. 25.

2. The apostle not only mentions these three cardinal graces, faith, hope, and love, but also takes notice, (1.) Of the object and efficient cause of these graces, namely, our Lord Jesus Christ. (2.) Of the sincerity of them : being in the *sight of God even our Father.* The great motive to sincerity is the apprehension of God's eye as always upon us ; and it is a sign of sincerity when in all we do we endeavour to approve ourselves to God, and that is right which is so in the sight of God. Then is the work of faith, or labour of love, or patience of hope, sincere, when it is done as under the eye of God. (3.) He mentions the fountain whence these graces flow, namely God's electing love : *Knowing, brethren beloved, your election of God, v.* 4. Thus he runs up these streams to the fountain, and that was God's eternal election. Some by their election of God would understand only the temporary separation of the Thessalonians from the unbelieving Jews and Gentiles in their conversion ; but this was according to the *eternal purpose of him who worketh all things according to the counsel of his own will,* Eph. i. 11. Speaking of their election, he calls them, *brethren beloved ;* for the original of the brotherhood that is between Christians and the relation wherein they stand one to another is election. And it is a good reason why we should *love one another,* because we are all beloved of God, and were beloved of him in his counsels when there was not any thing in us to merit his love. The election of these Thessalonians was known to the apostles, and therefore might be known to themselves, and that by the fruits and effects thereof—their sincere faith, and hope, and love, by the successful preaching of the gospel among them. Observe, [1.] All those who in the fulness of time are effectually called and sanctified were from eternity elected and chosen to salvation. [2.] The election of God is of his own good pleasure and mere grace, not for the sake of any merit in those who are chosen. [3.] The election of God may be known by the fruits thereof. [4.] Whenever we are giving thanks to God for his grace either to ourselves or others, we should run up the streams to the fountain and give thanks to God for his electing love, by which we are made to differ.

3. Another ground or reason of the apostle's thanksgiving is the success of his ministry among them. He was thankful on his own account as well as theirs, that he had not laboured in vain. He had the seal and evidence of his apostleship hereby, and great encouragement in his labours and sufferings. Their ready acceptance and entertainment of the gospel he preached to them were an evidence of their being elected and beloved of God. It was in this way that he knew their election. It is true he had been in the third heavens ; but he had not searched the records of eternity, and found their election there, but knew this by the success of the gospel among them (*v.* 5), and he takes notice with thankfulness, (1.) That the gospel came to them also not in word only, but in power ; they not only heard the sound of it, but submitted to the power of it. It did not merely tickle the ear and please the fancy, not merely fill their heads with notions and amuse their minds for awhile, but it affected their hearts : a divine power went along with it for convincing their consciences and amending their lives. Note, By this we may know our election, if we not only

speak of the things of God by rote as parrots, but feel the influence of these things in our hearts, mortifying our lusts, weaning us from the world, and raising us up to heavenly things. (2.) It came in the Holy Ghost, that is, with the powerful energy of the divine Spirit. Note, Wherever the gospel comes in power, it is to be attributed to the operation of the Holy Ghost; and unless the Spirit of God accompany the word of God, to render it effectual by his power, it will be to us but as a dead letter; and the letter killeth, it is the Spirit that giveth life. (3.) The gospel came to them in much assurance. Thus did they entertain it by the power of the Holy Ghost. They were fully convinced of the truth of it, so as not to be easily shaken in mind by objections and doubts; they were willing to leave all for Christ, and to venture their souls and everlasting condition upon the verity of the gospel revelation. The word was not to them, like the sentiments of some philosophers about matters of opinion and doubtful speculation, but the object of their faith and assurance. Their *faith was the evidence of things not seen;* and the Thessalonians thus knew what manner of men the apostle and his fellow-labourers were among them, and what they did for their sake, and with what good success.

⁶ And ye became followers of us, and of the Lord, having received the word in much affliction, with joy of the Holy Ghost: ⁷ So that ye were ensamples to all that believe in Macedonia and Achaia. ⁸ For from you sounded out the word of the Lord not only in Macedonia and Achaia, but also in every place your faith to God-ward is spread abroad; so that we need not to speak anything. ⁹ For they themselves show of us what manner of entering in we had unto you, and how ye turned to God from idols to serve the living and true God; ¹⁰ And to wait for his Son from heaven, whom he raised from the dead, *even* Jesus, which delivered us from the wrath to come.

In these words we have the evidence of the apostle's success among the Thessalonians, which was notorious and famous in several places. For,

I. They were careful in their holy conversation to imitate the good examples of the apostles and ministers of Christ, *v.* 6. As the apostle took care to demean himself well, not only for his own credit's sake, but for the benefit of others, by a conversation suitable to his doctrine, that he might not pull down with one hand what he built up with the other, so the Thessalonians, who observed what manner of men they were among them, how their preaching and living were all of a piece, showed a conscientious care to be followers of them, or to imitate their good example. Herein they became also followers of the Lord, who is the perfect example we must strive to imitate; and we should be followers of others no further than they are followers of Christ, 1 Cor. xi. 1. The Thessalonians acted thus, notwithstanding that much affliction which the apostles and themselves also were exposed to. They were willing to share in the sufferings that attended the embracing and professing of Christianity. They entertained the gospel, notwithstanding the troubles and hardships which attended the preachers and professors of it too. Perhaps this made the word more precious, being dear-bought; and the examples of the apostles shone very bright under their afflictions; so that the Thessalonians embraced the word cheerfully, and followed the example of the suffering apostles joy fully *with joy in the Holy Ghost*—such solid and spiritual and lasting joy as the Holy Ghost is the author of, who, when our afflictions abound, makes our consolations much more to abound.

II. Their zeal prevailed to such a degree that they were themselves examples to all about them, *v.* 7, 8. Observe here,

1. Their example was very effectual to make good impressions upon many others. They were τυποὶ—*stamps*, or instruments to make impression with. They had themselves received good impressions from the preaching and conversation of the apostles, and they made good impressions, and their conversation had an influence upon others. Note, Christians should be so good as by their example to influence others.

2. It was very extensive, and reached beyond the confines of Thessalonica, even to the believers of all Macedonia, and further, in Achaia ; the Philippians, and others who received the gospel before the Thessalonians, were edified by their example. Note, Some who were last hired into the vineyard may sometimes outstrip those who come in before them, and become examples to them.

3. It was very famous. The word of the Lord, or its wonderful effects upon the Thessalonians, sounded, or was famous and well known, in the regions round about that city, and *in every place ;* not strictly every where, but here and there, up and down in the world : so that, from the good success of the gospel among them, many others were encouraged to entertain it, and to be willing, when called, to suffer for it. Their faith was spread abroad. (1.) The readiness of their faith was famed abroad. These Thessalonians embraced the gospel as soon as it was preached to them ; so that every body took notice what manner of entering in among them the apostles had, that there were no such delays as at Philippi, where it was a great while before much good was done. (2.) The effects of their faith were famous. [1.] They quitted their idolatry ; they turned from their idols, and abandoned all the false worship they had been educated in. [2.] They gave themselves up to God, to the living and true God, and devoted themselves to his service. [3.] They set themselves to wait for the Son of God from heaven, *v.* 10. And this is one of the peculiarities of our holy religion, to wait for Christ's second coming, as those who believe he will come and hope he will come to our joy. The believers under the Old Testament waited for the coming of the Messiah, and believers now wait for his second coming ; he is yet to come. And there is good reason to believe he will come, because God has raised him from the dead, which is a full assurance unto all men that he will come to judgment, Acts xvii. 31. And there is good reason to hope and wait for his coming, because he has delivered us from the wrath to come. He came to purchase salvation, and will, when he comes again, bring salvation with him, full and final deliverance from sin, and death, and hell, from that wrath which is yet to come upon unbelievers, and which, when it has once come, will be yet to come, because it is *everlasting fire* prepared for the devil and his angels, Matt. xxv. 41.

CHAPTER II

In this chapter the apostle puts the Thessalonians in mind of the manner of his preaching among them, ver. 1-6. Then of the manner of his conversation among them, ver. 7-12. Afterwards of the success of his ministry, with the effects both on himself and on them (ver. 13-16), and then apologises for his absence, ver. 17-20.

FOR yourselves, brethren, know our entrance in unto you, that it was not in vain : ² But even after that we had suffered before, and were shamefully entreated, as ye know, at Philippi, we were bold in our God to speak unto you the gospel of God with much contention. ³ For our exhortation *was* not of deceit [error], nor of uncleanness, nor in guile : ⁴ But as we were allowed [approved] of God to be put in trust with the gospel, even so we speak ; not as pleasing men, but God, which trieth our hearts. ⁵ For neither at any time used we flattering words, as ye know, nor a cloak of covetousness; God *is* witness : ⁶ Nor of men sought we glory, neither of you, nor *yet* of others, when we might have been burdensome, as the apostles of Christ.

Here we have an account of Paul's manner of preaching, and his comfortable reflection upon his entrance in among the Thessalonians. As he had the testimony of his own conscience witnessing to his integrity, so he could appeal to the Thessalonians how faithfully he, and Silas, and Timotheus, his helpers in the work of the Lord, had discharged their office. *You yourselves, brethren, know our entrance in unto you.* Note, It is a great comfort to a minister to have his own conscience and the consciences of others witnessing for him that he set out well, with good designs and from good principles ; and that *his preaching was not in vain*, or, as some read it, *was not vain.* The apostle here comforts himself either in the success of his ministry, that it was not fruitless or in vain (according to our translation), or, as others think, reflecting upon the sincerity of his preaching, that it was not vain and empty, or deceitful and treacherous. The subject-matter of the apostle's preaching was not vain and idle speculations about useless niceties and foolish questions, but sound and solid truth, such as was most likely to profit his hearers. A good example this is, to be imitated by all the ministers of the gospel. Much less was the apostle's preaching vain or deceitful. He could say to these Thessalonians what he told the Corinthians (2 Cor. iv. 2) : *We have renounced the hidden things of dishonesty, not walking in craftiness, nor handling the word of God deceitfully.* He had no sinister or worldly design in his preaching, which he puts them in mind to have been,

I. With courage and resolution : *We were bold in our God to speak unto you the gospel of God, v. 2.* The apostle was inspired with a holy boldness, nor was he discouraged at the afflictions he met with, or the opposition that was made against him. He had met with ill usage at Philippi, as these Thessalonians well knew. There it was that he and Silas were shamefully treated, being put in the stocks; yet no sooner were they set at liberty than they went to Thessalonica, and preached the gospel with as much boldness as ever. Note, Suffering in a good cause should rather sharpen than blunt the edge of holy resolution. The gospel of Christ, at its first setting out in the world, met with much opposition; and those who preached it preached it *with contention*, with great agony, which denoted either the apostles' striving in their preaching or their striving against the opposition they met with. This was Paul's comfort; he was neither daunted in his work, nor driven from it.

II. With great simplicity and godly sincerity: *Our exhortation was not of deceit, nor of uncleanness, nor in guile, v.* 3. This, no doubt, was matter of the greatest comfort to the apostle—the consciousness of his own sincerity; and was one reason of his success. It was the sincere and un-corrupted gospel that he preached and exhorted them to believe and obey. His design was not to set up a faction, to draw men over to a party, but to promote *pure religion and undefiled before God and the Father*. The gospel he preached was without deceit, it was true and faithful; it was not fallacious, nor a cunningly-devised fable. Nor was it of uncleanness. His gospel was pure and holy, worthy of its holy author, tending to dis-countenance all manner of impurity. *The word of God is pure.* There should be no corrupt mixtures therewith; and, as the matter of the apostle's exhortation was thus true and pure, the manner of his speaking was without guile. He did not pretend one thing and intend another. *He believed, and therefore he spoke.* He had no sinister and secular aims and views, but was in reality what he seemed to be. The apostle not only asserts his sincerity, but subjoins the reasons and evidences thereof. The reasons are contained, *v.* 4.

1. They were stewards, *put in trust* with the gospel: and it is required of a steward that he be faithful. The gospel which Paul preached was not his own, but the gospel of God. Note, Ministers have a great favour shown them, and honour put upon them, and trust committed to them. They must not dare to corrupt the word of God: they must diligently make use of what is entrusted with them, so as God hath allowed and commanded, knowing they shall be called to an account, when they must be no longer stewards.

2. Their design was to please God and not men. God is a God of truth, and requires truth in the inward parts; and, if sincerity be wanting, all that we do cannot please God. The gospel of Christ is not accommodated to the vain fancies and lusts of men, to gratify their appetites and pas-sions; but, on the contrary, it was designed for the mortifying of their corrupt affections, and delivering them from the power of fancy that they might be brought under the power of faith. *If I yet pleased men, I should not be the servant of Christ,* Gal. i. 10.

3. They acted under the consideration of God's omniscience, as in the sight of him who *tries our hearts*. This is indeed the great motive to sincerity, to consider that God not only seeth all that we do, but knoweth our thoughts afar off, and searcheth the heart. He is well acquainted with all our aims and designs, as well as our actions. And it is from this God who trieth our hearts that we must receive our reward. The evi-dences of the apostle's sincerity follow; and they are these :—(1.) He avoided flattery : *Neither at any time used we flattering words, as you know, v.* 5. He and his fellow-labourers preached Christ and him crucified, and did not aim to gain an interest in men's affections for themselves, by

glorying, and fawning and wheedling them. No, he was far from this; nor did he flatter men in their sins ; nor tell them, if they would be of his party, they might live as they listed. He did not flatter them with vain hopes, nor indulge them in any evil work or way, promising them life, and *so daubing with untempered mortar.* (2.) He avoided covetousness. He did not make the ministry *a cloak,* or a covering, for *covetousness, as God was witness, v.* 5. His design was not to enrich himself by preaching the gospel, so far from this, he did not stipulate with them for bread. He was not like the false apostles, who, *through covetousness, with feigned words made merchandise* of the people, 2 Pet. ii. 3. (3.) He avoided ambition and vain-glory : *Nor of men sought we glory, neither of you nor yet of others, v.* 6. They expected neither people's purses nor their caps, neither to be enriched by them nor caressed, and adored, and called Rabbi by them. This apostle exhorts the Galatians (*ch.* v. 26) *not to be desirous of vainglory ;* his ambition was to obtain *that honour which comes from God,* John v. 44. He tells them that they might have used greater authority as apostles, and expected greater esteem, and demanded maintenance, which is meant by the phrase of *being burdensome,* because perhaps some would have thought this too great a burden for them to bear.

⁷ But we were gentle among you, even as a nurse cherisheth her children : ⁸ So being affectionately desirous of you, we were willing to have imparted unto you, not the gospel of God only, but also our own souls, because ye were dear unto us. ⁹ For ye remember, brethren, our labour and travail : for labouring night and day, because we would not be chargeable unto [that we might not burden] any of you, we preached unto you the gospel of God. ¹⁰ Ye *are* witnesses, and God *also,* how holily and justly and unblameably we behaved ourselves among you that believe : ¹¹ As ye know how we exhorted and comforted and charged every one of you, as a father *doth* his children, ¹² That ye would walk worthy of God, who hath called you unto his kingdom and glory.

In these words the apostle reminds the Thessalonians of the manner of his conversation among them. And,

1. He mentions the gentleness of their behaviour : *We were gentle among you, v.* 7. He showed great mildness and tenderness who might have acted with the authority of an apostle of Christ. Such a behaviour greatly recommends religion, and is most agreeable to God's gracious dealing with sinners, in and by the gospel. This great apostle, though he abhorred and avoided flattery, was most condescending to all men. He accommodated himself to all men's capacities, *and became all things to all men.* He showed the kindness and care of a nurse that cherishes her children. This is the way to win people, rather than to rule with rigour. The word of God is indeed powerful ; and as it comes often with awful authority upon the minds of men, as it always has enough in it to convince every impartial judgment, so it comes with the more pleasing power, when the ministers of the gospel recommend themselves to the affections of the people. And as a nursing mother bears with frowardness in a child, and

condescends to mean offices for its good, and draws out her breast, cherishing it in her bosom, so in like manner should the ministers of Christ behave towards their people. The *servant of the Lord must not strive, but be gentle unto all men, and patient,* 2 Tim. ii. 24. This gentleness and goodness the apostle expressed several ways. 1. By the most affectionate desire of their welfare : *Being affectionately desirous of you, v.* 8. The apostle had a most affectionate love to their persons, and sought them, not theirs ; themselves, not their goods ; and to gain them, not to be a gainer by them, or to make a merchandise of them : it was their spiritual and eternal welfare and salvation that he was earnestly desirous of. 2. By great readiness to do them good, willingly imparting to them, *not the gospel of God only, but also our own souls, v.* 8. See here the manner of Paul's preaching. He spared no pains therein. He was willing to run hazards, and venture his soul, or life, in preaching the gospel. He was willing to spend and be spent in the service of men's souls ; and, as those who give bread to the hungry from a charitable principle are said to impart their souls in what they give (Isa. lviii. 10), so did the apostles in giving forth the bread of life ; so dear were these Thessalonians in particular to this apostle, and so great was his love to them. 3. By bodily labour to prevent their charge, or that his ministry might not be expensive and burdensome to them : *You remember our labour and travail ; for, labouring night and day, &c., v.* 9. He denied himself the liberty he had of taking wages from the churches. To the labour of the ministry he added that of his calling, as a tent-maker, that he might get his own bread. We are not to suppose that the apostle spent the whole night and day in bodily labour, or work, to supply the necessities of his body ; for then he would have had no time for the work of the ministry. But he spent part of the night, as well as the day, in this work ; and was willing to forego his rest in the night, that he might have an opportunity to do good to the souls of men in the day time. A good example is here set before the ministers of the gospel, to be industrious for the salvation of men's souls, though it will not follow that they are always obliged to preach freely. There is no general rule to be drawn from this instance, either that ministers may at no time work with their hands, for the supply of their outward necessities, or that they ought always to do so. 4. By the holiness of their conversation, concerning which he appeals not only to them, but to God also (*v.* 10): *You are witnesses and God also.* They were observers of their outward conversation in public before men, and God was witness not only of their behaviour in secret, but of the inward principles from which they acted. Their behaviour was holy towards God, just towards all men, and unblameable, without giving cause of scandal or offence ; and they were careful to give no offence either to those who were without, or to those who believed, that they might give no ill example ; that their preaching and living might be all of a piece. Herein, said this apostle, *do I exercise myself, to have always a conscience void of offence towards God, and towards men,* Acts xxiv. 16.

II. He mentions their faithful discharge of the work and office of the ministry, *v.* 11, 12. Concerning this also he could appeal to them as witnesses. Paul and his fellow-labourers were not only good Christians, but faithful ministers. And we should not only be good as to our general calling as Christians, but in our particular callings and relations. Paul exhorted the Thessalonians, not only informing them in their duty, but exciting and quickening them to the performance of it, by proper motives and arguments. And he comforted them also, endeavouring to cheer and support their spirits under the difficulties and discouragements they might meet with. And this he did not only publicly, but privately also, and from house to house (Acts xx. 20), *and charged every one* of them by personal addresses : this, some think, is intended by the similitude of a father's charging his children. This expression also denotes the affectionate and compassionate counsels and consolations which this apostle used. He was their spiritual father ; and, as he cherished them like a nursing mother, so he charged them as a father, with a father's affection rather than a father's authority. As *my beloved sons, I warn you,* 1 Cor. iv. 14. The manner of this apostle's exhortation ought to be regarded by ministers in particular for their imitation, and the matter of it is greatly to be regarded by them and all others ; namely, that *they would walk worthy of God, who hath called them to his kingdom and glory, v.* 12. Observe, 1. What is our great gospel privilege—that God has called us to his kingdom and glory. The gospel calls us into the kingdom and state of grace here and unto the kingdom and state of glory hereafter, to heaven and happiness as our end and to holiness as the way to that end. 2. What is our great gospel duty—that we walk worthy of God, that the temper of our minds and tenour of our lives be answerable to this call and suitable to this privilege. We should accommodate ourselves to the intention and design of the gospel, and live suitably to our profession and privileges, our hopes and expectations, as becomes those who are called with such a high and holy calling.

¹³ For this cause also thank we God without ceasing, because, when ye received the word of God which ye heard of us, ye received *it* not *as* the word of men, but as it is in truth, the word of God, which effectually worketh also in you that believe. ¹⁴ For ye, brethren, became followers of the churches of God which in Judæa are in Christ Jesus : for ye also have suffered like things of your own countrymen, even as they *have* of the Jews : ¹⁵ Who both killed the Lord Jesus, and their own prophets, and have persecuted us ; and they please not God, and are contrary to all men : ¹⁶ Forbidding us to speak to the Gentiles that they might be saved, to fill up their sins alway : for [but] the wrath is come upon them to the uttermost.

Here observe, I. The apostle makes mention of the success of his ministry among these Thessalonians (*v.* 13), which is expressed,

1. By the manner of their receiving the word of God : *When you received the word of God, which you heard of us, you received it not as the word of men, but (as it is in truth) the word of God.* Where note, (1.) The word of the gospel is preached by men like ourselves, men of like passions and infirmities with others : *We have this treasure in earthen vessels.* The word of God, which these Thessalonians received, they heard from the apostles. (2.) However, it is in truth the word of God. Such was the word the apostles preached by divine inspiration, and such is that which is left upon record, written in the scriptures by divine inspiration ; and such is that word which in our days is preached, being either contained in, or evidently founded on, or deduced from, these sacred oracles. (3.) Those are greatly

to blame who give out their own fancies or injunctions for the word of God. This is the vilest way of imposing upon a people, and to deal unfaithfully. (4.) Those are also to blame who, in hearing the word, look no further than to the ministry of men, or the words of men, who are only, or chiefly, pleased with the elegance of the style, or the beauty of the composition, or the voice and manner in which the word is preached, and expect to receive their advantage herein. (5.) We should receive the word of God as the word of God, with affections suitable to the holiness, wisdom, verity, and goodness thereof. The words of men are frail and perishing, like themselves, and sometimes false, foolish, and fickle : but God's word is holy, wise, just, and faithful ; and, like its author, lives and abides for ever. Let us accordingly receive and regard it.

2. By the wonderful operation of this word they received : *It effectually worketh in those that believe, v.* 13. Those who by faith receive the word find it profitable. *It does good to those that walk uprightly,* and by its wonderful effects evidences itself to be the word of God. This converts their souls, and enlightens their minds, and rejoices their hearts (Ps. xix.) ; and such as have this inward testimony of the truth of the scriptures, the word of God, by the effectual operations thereof on their hearts, have the best evidence of their divine original to themselves, though this is not sufficient to convince others who are strangers thereto.

II. He mentions the good effects which his successful preaching had,

1. Upon himself and fellow-labourers. It was a constant cause of thankfulness : *For this cause thank we God without ceasing, v.* 13. The apostle expressed his thankfulness to God so often upon this account that he seemed to think he never could be sufficiently thankful that God had counted him faithful, and put him into the ministry, and made his ministrations successful.

2. Upon them. The word wrought effectually in them, not only to be examples unto others in faith and good works (which he had mentioned before), but also in constancy and patience under sufferings and trials for the sake of the gospel : *You became followers of the churches of God, and have suffered like things as they have done* (*v.* 14), and with like courage and constancy, with like patience and hope. Note, The cross is the Christian's mark, if we are called to suffer we are called only to be followers of the churches of God ; *so persecuted they the prophets that were before you,* Matt. v. 12. It is a good effect of the gospel when we are enabled to suffer for its sake. The apostle mentions the sufferings of the churches of God, which *in Judea were in Christ Jesus.* Those in Judea first heard the gospel, and they first suffered for it : for the Jews were the most bitter enemies Christianity had, and were especially enraged against their countrymen who embraced Christianity. Note, Bitter zeal and fiery persecution will set countrymen at variance, and break through all the bonds of nature, as well as contradict all the rules of religion. In every city where the apostles went to preach the gospel the Jews stirred up the inhabitants against them. They were the ringleaders of persecution in all places ; so in particular it was at Thessalonica : Acts xvii. 5, *The Jews that believed not, moved with envy, took unto them certain lewd fellows of the baser sort, and gathered a company, and set all the city in an uproar.* Upon this occasion, the apostle gives a character of the unbelieving Jews (*v.* 15), enough to justify their final rejection and the ruin of their place, and church, and nation, which was now approaching. (1.) They *killed the Lord Jesus,* and impudently and presumptuously wished that his blood might be on them

and their children. (2.) They killed *their own prophets:* so they had done all along ; their fathers had done so : they had been a persecuting generation. (3.) They hated the apostles, and did them all the mischief they could. They persecuted them, and drove and chased them from place to place : and no marvel, if they killed the Lord Jesus, that they persecuted his followers. (4.) They *pleased not God.* They had quite lost all sense of religion, and due care to do their duty to God. It was a most fatal mistake to think that they did God service by killing God's servants. Murder and persecution are most hateful to God and cannot be justified on any pretence ; they are so contrary to natural religion that no zeal for any true or only pretended institution of religion can ever excuse them. (5.) They were *contrary to all men.* Their persecuting spirit was a perverse spirit ; contrary to the light of nature, and contrary to humanity, contrary to the welfare of all men, and contrary to the sentiments of all men not under the power of bigotry. (6.) They had *an implacable enmity to the Gentiles,* and envied them the offers of the gospel : *Forbidding the apostles to speak to the Gentiles, that they might be saved.* The means of salvation had long been confined to the Jews. *Salvation is of the Jews,* says our Saviour. And they were envious against the Gentiles, and angry that they should be admitted to share in the means of salvation. Nothing provoked them more than our Saviour's speaking to them at any time concerning this matter ; this enraged the Jews at Jerusalem, when, in his defence, Paul told them, *he was sent unto the Gentiles,* Acts xxii. 21. They heard him patiently till he uttered these words, but then could endure no longer, but *lifted up their voices, and said, Away with such a fellow from the earth, for it is not fit that he should live.* Thus did the Jews fill up their sins ; and nothing tends more to any person or people's filling up the measure of their sins than opposing the gospel, obstructing the progress of it, and hindering the salvation of precious souls. For the sake of these things *wrath has come upon them to the uttermost ;* that is, wrath was determined against them, and would soon overtake them. It was not many years after this that Jerusalem was destroyed, and the Jewish nation cut off by the Romans. Note, When the measure of any man's iniquity is full, and he has sinned to the uttermost, then comes wrath, and that to the uttermost.

17 But we, brethren, being taken from you a short time in presence, not in heart, endeavoured the more abundantly to see your face with great desire. 18 Wherefore we would have come unto you, even I Paul, once and again ; but Satan hindered us. 19 For what *is* our hope, or joy, or crown of rejoicing ? *Are* not even ye in the presence of our Lord Jesus Christ at his coming ? 20 For ye are our glory and joy.

In these words the apostle apologises for his absence. Here observe, 1. He tells them they were involuntarily forced from them : *We, brethren, were taken from you, v.* 17. Such was the rage of his persecutors. He was unwillingly sent away by night to Berea, Acts xvii. 10. 2. Though he was absent in body, yet he was present in heart. He had still a remembrance of them, and great care for them. 3. Even his bodily absence was but for a short time, the time of an hour. Time is short, all our time on earth is short and uncertain, whether we are present with our friends or absent from them. This world is not a place where we are always, or long, to be together. It is in heaven that holy souls shall meet, and never part more. 4. He earnestly desired and endeavoured to see them again : *We endeavoured more abundantly to see your face with great desire, v.* 17. So that the apostle at least intended his absence should be but for a short time. His desire and endeavour were to return again very soon to Thessalonica. But men of business are not masters of their own time. Paul did his endeavour, and he could do no more, *v.* 18. 5. He tells them that Satan hindered his return (*v.* 18), that is, either some enemy or enemies, or the great enemy of mankind, who stirred up opposition to Paul, either in his return to Thessalonica, when he intended to return thither, or stirred up such contentions or dissensions in those places whither he went as made his presence necessary. Note, Satan is a constant enemy to the work of God, and does all he can to obstruct it. 6. He assures them of his affection and high esteem for them, though he was not able, as yet, to be present with them according to his desire. They were his *hope, and joy, and crown of rejoicing ; his glory and joy.* These are expressions of great and endeared affection, and high estimation. And it is happy when ministers and people have such mutual affection and esteem of each other, and especially if they shall thus rejoice, if those that sow and those that reap shall rejoice together, *in the presence of our Lord Jesus Christ at his coming.*

The apostle here puts the Thessalonians in mind that though he could not come to them as yet, and though he should never be able to come to them, yet our Lord Jesus Christ will come, nothing shall hinder this. And further, when he shall come, all must appear in his presence, or before him. Ministers and people must all appear before him, and faithful people will be the glory and joy of faithful ministers in that great and glorious day.

CHAPTER III

In this chapter the apostle gives further evidence of his love to the Thessalonians, reminding them of his sending Timothy to them, with the mention of his design therein and his inducements so to do, ver. 1-5. He acquaints them also with his great satisfaction at the return of Timothy, with good tidings concerning them, ver. 6-10. And concludes with fervent prayer for them, ver. 11, to the end.

WHEREFORE when we could no longer forbear, we thought it good to be left at Athens alone ; ² And sent Timotheus, our brother, and minister of God, and our fellow-labourer in the gospel of Christ, to establish you, and to comfort you concerning your faith : ³ That no man should be moved by these afflictions : for yourselves know that we are appointed thereunto. ⁴ For verily, when we were with you, we told you before that we should suffer tribulation ; even as it came to pass, and ye know. ⁵ For this cause, when I could no longer forbear, I sent to know your faith, lest by some means the tempter have tempted you, and our labour be in vain.

In these words the apostle gives an account of his sending Timothy to the Thessalonians. Though he was hindered from going to them himself, yet his love was such that he could not forbear sending Timothy to them. Though Timothy was very useful to him, and he could not well spare him, yet Paul was content, for their good, *to be left alone at Athens.* Note, Those ministers do not duly value the establishment and welfare of their people who cannot deny themselves in many things for that end. Observe,

I. The character he gives of Timothy (*v.* 2): *We sent Timotheus, our brother.* Elsewhere he calls him his son; here he calls him brother. Timothy was Paul's junior in age, his inferior in gifts and graces, and of a lower rank in the ministry: for Paul was an apostle, and Timothy but an evangelist; yet Paul calls him brother. This was an instance of the apostle's humility, and showed his desire to put honour upon Timothy and to recommend him to the esteem of the churches. He calls him also a minister of God. Note, Ministers of the gospel of Christ are ministers of God, to promote the kingdom of God among men. He calls him also his fellow-labourer in the gospel of Christ. Note, Ministers of the gospel must look upon themselves as labourers in the Lord's vineyard; they have an honourable office and hard work, yet a good work. *This is a true saying, If any man desire the office of a bishop, he desires a good work,* 1 Tim. iii. 1. And ministers should look upon one another, and strengthen one another's hands, not strive and contend one with another (which will hinder their work), but strive together to carry on the great work they are engaged in, namely, to preach and publish the gospel of Christ, and to persuade people to embrace and entertain it and live suitably thereto.

II. The end and design why Paul sent Timothy: *To establish you and to comfort you concerning your faith, v.* 2. Paul had converted them to the Christian faith, and now he was desirous that they might be confirmed and comforted, that they might be confirmed in the choice they had made of the Christian religion, and be comforted in the profession and practice of it. Note, The more we are comforted, the more we shall be confirmed, because, when we find pleasure in the ways of God, we shall thereby be engaged to continue and persevere therein. The apostle's design was to establish and comfort the Thessalonians concerning their faith—concerning the object of their faith, namely, the truths of the gospel, and particularly that Jesus Christ was the Saviour of the world, and so wise and good, so powerful and faithful, that they might rely upon him,—concerning the recompence of faith, which was more than sufficient to balance all their losses and reward all their labours.

III. The motive inducing Paul to send Timothy for this end, namely, a godly fear or jealousy, lest they should be moved from the faith of Christ, *v.* 3. He was desirous that no man, no one among them, should be moved or shaken in mind, that they should not apostatise or waver in the faith. And yet,

I. He apprehended there was danger, and feared the consequence.

(I.) There was danger, [I.] By reason of *affliction* and persecution for the sake of the gospel, *v.* 3. These Thessalonians could not but perceive what afflictions the apostles and preachers of the gospel met with, and this might possibly stumble them ; and also those who made profession of the gospel were persecuted, and without doubt these Thessalonians themselves were afflicted. [2.] By reason of the tempter's subtlety and malice. The apostle was afraid lest by any means the tempter had tempted them, *v.* 5. The devil is a subtle and unwearied tempter, who seeks an opportunity to beguile and destroy us, and takes all advantages against us, both in a time of prosperity and adversity; and he has often been successful in his attacks upon persons under afflictions. He has often prejudiced the minds of men against religion on account of the sufferings its professors are exposed to. We have reason therefore to be jealous over ourselves and others, lest we be ensnared by him.

(2.) The consequence the apostle feared was lest his labour should be in vain. And thus it would have been, if the tempter had tempted them, and prevailed against them, to move them from the faith. They would have lost what they had wrought, and the apostle would have lost what he laboured for. Note, It is the devil's design to hinder the good fruit and effect of the preaching of the gospel. If he cannot hinder ministers from labouring in the word and doctrine, he will, if he be able, hinder them of the success of their labours. Note also, Faithful ministers are much concerned about the success of their labours. No one would willingly labour in vain; and ministers are loth to spend their strength, and pains, and time, for nought.

2. To prevent this danger, with its bad consequence, the apostle tells them what care he took in sending Timothy, (1.) To put them in mind of what he had told them before concerning suffering tribulation (*v.* 4), he says (*v.* 3), *We are appointed thereunto*, that is, unto afflictions. So is the will and purpose of God that *through many afflictions we must enter into his kingdom.* Their troubles and persecutions did not come by chance, not merely from the wrath and malice of the enemies of religion, but by the *appointment of God.* The event only came to pass according as God had determined, and they knew he had told them before it would be; so that they should not think it strange, and, being fore-warned, they should be fore-armed. Note, The apostles were so far from flattering people with an expectation of worldly prosperity in religion that, on the contrary, they told them plainly they must count upon trouble in the flesh. And herein they followed the example of their great Master, the author of our faith. Besides, it might prove a confirmation of their faith, when they perceived that it only happened to them as was predicted before. (2.) To know their faith, that so he might inform the apostles whether they remained stedfast under all their sufferings, whether their faith failed or not, because, if their faith did not fail, they would be able to stand their ground against the tempter and all his temptations: their faith would be a *shield, to defend them against all the fiery darts of the wicked,* Eph. vi. 16.

6 But now when Timotheus came from you unto us, and brought us good tidings of your faith and charity [love], and that ye have good remembrance of us always, desiring greatly to see us, as we also *to see* you : 7 Therefore, brethren, we were comforted over you in all your affliction and distress by your faith : 8 For now we live, if ye stand fast in the Lord. 9 For what thanks can we render to God again for you, for all the joy wherewith we joy for your sakes before our God ; 10 Night and day praying exceedingly that we might see your face, and might perfect that which is lacking in your faith ?

Here we have Paul's great satisfaction upon the return of Timothy with good tidings from the Thessalonians, in which we may observe,

I. The good report Timothy made concerning them, *v.* 6. Without question, he was a willing messenger of these good tidings. *Concerning their faith*, that is, concerning their stedfastness in the faith, that they were not shaken in mind, nor turned aside from the profession of the gospel. *Their love* also continued ; their love to the gospel and the ministers of the gospel. For they had a good and a kind remembrance of the apostles, and that constantly, or always. The names of the apostles were very dear to them, and the thoughts of them, and what they themselves had received from them, were very precious, insomuch that they *desired greatly to see them again*, and receive some spiritual gift from them ; and there was no love lost, for the apostle was as desirous to see them. It is happy where there is such mutual love between minister and people. This tends to promote religion, and the success of the gospel. The world hates them, and therefore they should love one another.

II. The great comfort and satisfaction the apostle had in this good report concerning them (*v.* 7, 8) : *Therefore, brethren, we were comforted in all our affliction and distress.* The apostle thought this good news of them was sufficient to balance all the troubles he met with. It was easy to him to bear affliction, or persecution, or fightings from without, when he found the good success of his ministry and the constancy of the converts he had made to Christianity ; and his distress of mind on account of his fears within, lest he had laboured in vain, was now in a good measure over, when he understood their faith and the perseverance of it. This put new life and spirit into the apostle and made him vigorous and active in the work of the Lord. Thus he was not only comforted, but greatly rejoiced also : *Now, we live, if you stand fast in the Lord, v.* 8. It would have been a killing thing to the apostles if the professors of religion had been unsteady, or proved apostates ; whereas nothing was more encouraging than their constancy.

III. The effects of this were thankfulness and prayer to God on their behalf. Observe, 1. How thankful the apostle was, *v.* 9. He was full of joy, and full of praise and thanksgiving. When we are most cheerful we should be most thankful. What we rejoice in we should give thanks for. This is to rejoice before our God, to spiritualise our joy. Paul speaks as if he could not tell how to express his thankfulness to God, or his joy and rejoicing for their sakes. But he was careful God should not lose the glory of the comfort he received in the welfare of his friends. His heart was enlarged with love to them and with thanksgiving to God. He was willing to express the one and the other as well as he could. As to thankfulness to God, this especially is very imperfect in the present state ; but, when we come to heaven, we shall do this work better than now we can. 2. He prayed for them night and day (*v.* 10), evening and morning, or very frequently, in the midst of the business of the day or slumber of the night lifting up his heart to God in prayer. Thus we should pray always. And Paul's prayer was fervent prayer. He prayed exceedingly, and was earnest in his supplication. Note, When we are most thankful we should always give ourselves to prayer ; and those we give thanks for have yet need to be prayed for. Those whom we most rejoice in, and who are our greatest comforts, must be our constant care, while in this world of temptation and imperfection. There was something still lacking in their faith ; Paul desired that this might be perfected, and to see their face in order thereunto. Note, (1.) The best of men have something wanting in their faith, if not as to the matter of it, there being some mysteries or doctrines not sufficiently known or believed by them, yet as to the clearness and certainty of their faith, there being some remaining darkness and doubtings, or at least as to the effects and operations of it, these being not so conspicuous and perfect as they should be. And (2.) The ministry of the word and ordinances is helpful, and to be desired and used for the perfecting of that which is lacking in our faith.

11 Now God himself and our Father, and our Lord Jesus Christ, direct our way unto you. 12 And the Lord make you to increase and abound in love one toward another, and toward all *men*, even as we *do* toward you: 13 To the end he may stablish your hearts unblameable in holiness before God, even our Father, at the coming of our Lord Jesus Christ with all his saints.

In these words we have the earnest prayer of the apostle. He desired to be instrumental in the further benefit of the Thessalonians; and the only way to be so while at a distance was by prayer for them, together with his writing or sending to them. He desired that their faith might be perfected, which he could not be the proper cause or author of; for he pretended no to dominion over their faith, nor to have the donation of it, and he therefore concludes with prayer for them. Observe,

I. Whom he prays to, namely, God and Christ. Prayer is a part of religious worship, and all religious worship is due unto God only. Prayer is here made to God, even the Father and our Father; and also to Christ, even our Lord Jesus Christ. Therefore Jesus Christ our Lord is God even as God our Father is God. Prayer is to be offered to God as our Father. So Christ taught his disciples to pray; and so the Spirit of adoption prompts them to pray, to cry, *Abba, Father.* Prayer is not only to be offered in the name of Christ, but offered up to Christ himself, as our Lord and our Saviour.

II. What he prays for, with respect to himself and his fellow-labourers, and on behalf of the Thessalonians.

1. He prays that himself and fellow-labourers might have a prosperous journey to them by the will of God, that their way might be directed to them, *v.* 11. The taking of a journey to this or that place, one would think, is a thing depending so much on a man's own will, and lies so much in his own power, that Paul needed not by prayer to go to God about it. But the apostle knew that *in God we live, and move, and have our being*, that we depend upon God in all our motions and actions, as well as for the continuance of life and being, that divine Providence orders all our affairs and that it is owing thereto if we prosper therein, that God our Father directs and orders his children whither they shall go and what they shall do, that our Lord Jesus Christ in a particular manner directs the motions of his faithful ministers, those stars which he holds in his right hand. Let us acknowledge God in all our ways, and he will direct our paths.

2. He prays for the prosperity of the Thessalonians. Whether he should have an opportunity of coming to them or not, yet he earnestly prayed for the prosperity of their souls. And there are two things he desired for them, which we should desire for ourselves and friends:—(1.) That they

might increase and abound in love (*v.* 12), in love to one another and in love to all men. Note, Mutual love is required of all Christians, and not only that they love one another, but that they also have a charitable disposition of mind and due concern for the welfare of all men. Love is of God, and is the fulfilling of the gospel as well as of the law. Timothy brought good tidings of their faith, yet something was lacking therein ; and of their charity, yet the apostle prays that this might increase and abound. Note, We have reason to desire to grow in every grace, and have need of the Spirit's influence in order to growth in grace ; and the way to obtain this is by prayer. We are beholden to God not only for the stock put into our hands at first, but for the improvement of it also. And to our prayer we must add endeavour. To excite this in the Thessalonians the apostle again mentions his love, his abounding love, towards them. The more we are beloved, the more affectionate we should be. (2.) That they might be established unblamable in holiness, *v.* 13. This spiritual benefit is mentioned as an effect of increasing and abounding love : *To the end that he* (the Lord) *may establish your hearts.* Note, The more we grow and abound in grace, and particularly in the grace of love, the more we are established and confirmed in it. Note also, Holiness is required of all those who would go to heaven, and therein we must be unblamable ; that is, we must act in everything so that we may not in the least contradict the profession we make of holiness. Our desire should be to have our hearts established in holiness before God, and be preserved safe, to the coming of the Lord Jesus Christ ; and that we may be unblamable before God, even the Father, now, and be presented blameless before the throne of his glory, when the Lord Jesus shall come with all his saints. Note, [1.] The Lord Jesus will certainly come, and come in his glory. [2.] When he comes his saints will come with him : *They shall appear with him in glory.* [3.] Then the excellency as well as the necessity of holiness will appear, because without this no hearts shall be established at that day, nor shall any one be unblamable, or avoid everlasting condemnation.

CHAPTER IV

In this chapter the apostle gives earnest exhortations to abound in holiness, with a caution against uncleanness, enforced with several arguments, ver. 1-8. He then mentions the great duties of brotherly love, and quietness with industry in our callings, ver. 9-12. And concludes with comforting those who mourned for their relations and friends that died in the Lord, ver. 13-18.

FURTHERMORE then we beseech you, brethren, and exhort *you* by the Lord Jesus, that as ye have received of us how ye ought to walk and to please God [*add* even as ye do walk—] *so* ye would abound more and more. ² For ye know what commandments we gave you by the Lord Jesus. ³ For this is the will of God, *even* your sanctification, that ye should abstain from fornication : ⁴ That every one of you should know how to

possess his vessel in sanctification and honour;   ⁵ Not in the
lust of concupiscence [**passion of lust**], even as the Gentiles
which know not God :   ⁶ That no *man* go beyond [**transgress**]
and defraud his brother in *any* matter : because that the Lord
is the avenger of all such, as we also have forewarned you and
testified.   ⁷ For God hath not called us unto [**for**] uncleanness,
but unto holiness [**in sanctification**].   ⁸ He therefore that
despiseth, despiseth [**rejecteth, rejecteth**] not man, but God,
who hath also given unto us his holy Spirit.

Here we have,

I. An exhortation to abound in holiness, to *abound more and more* in
that which is good, *v.* 1, 2. We may observe,

1. The manner in which the exhortation is given—very affectionately.
The apostle entreats them as brethren ; he calls them so, and loved them
as such. Because his love to them was very great, he exhorts them very
earnestly : *We beseech and exhort you.* The apostle was unwilling to take
any denial, and therefore repeats his exhortation again and again.

2. The matter of his exhortation—that they would abound more and
more in holy walking, or excel in those things that are good, in good
works. Their faith was justly famed abroad, and they were already
examples to other churches : yet the apostle would have them yet further
to excel others, and to make further progress in holiness. Note, (1.) Those
who most excel others fall short of perfection. The very best of us should
*forget those things which are behind, and reach forth unto those things which
are before.* (2.) It is not enough that we abide in the faith of the gospel,
but we must abound in the work of faith. We must not only persevere to
the end, but we should grow better, and walk more evenly and closely with
God.

3. The arguments with which the apostle enforces his exhortation.
(1.) They had been informed of their duty. They knew their Master's
will, and could not plead ignorance as an excuse. Now as faith, so knowledge is dead without practice. They had received of those who had converted them to Christianity, or been taught of them, *how they ought to walk.*
Observe, The design of the gospel is to teach men not only what they should
believe, but also how they ought to live ; not so much to fill men's minds
with notions as to regulate their temper and behaviour. The apostle taught
them how to walk, not how to talk. To talk well without living well will
never bring us to heaven : for the character of those who are in Christ
Jesus is this : *They walk not after the flesh, but after the Spirit.* (2.)
Another argument is that the apostle taught and exhorted them in the
name, or by the authority, of the Lord Jesus Christ. He was Christ's
minister and ambassador, declaring to them what was the will and command of the Lord Jesus. (3.) Another argument is this. Herein they
would please God. Holy walking is most pleasing to the holy God, *who is
glorious in holiness.* This ought to be the aim and ambition of every
Christian, to please God and to be accepted of him. We should not be
men-pleasers, nor flesh-pleasers, but should walk so as to please God. (4.)
The rule according to which they ought to walk and act—*the commandments they had given them by the Lord Jesus Christ,* which were the commandments of the Lord Jesus Christ himself, because given by authority

and direction from him and such as were agreeable to his will. The apostles of our Lord Jesus Christ were only commissioned by him to teach men to observe all things *whatsoever he had commanded them*, Matt. xxviii. 20. Though they had great authority from Christ, yet that was to teach men what Christ had commanded, not to give forth commandments of their own. They did not act as lords over God's heritage (1 Pet. v. 3), nor should any do so that pretend to be their successors. The apostle could appeal to the Thessalonians, who knew what commandments he gave them, that they were no other than what he had received from the Lord Jesus.

II. A caution against uncleanness, this being a sin directly contrary to sanctification, or that holy walking to which he so earnestly exhorts them. This caution is expressed, and also enforced by many arguments.

1. It is expressed in these words: *That you should abstain from fornication* (v. 3), by which we are to understand all uncleanness whatsoever, either in a married or unmarried state. Adultery is of course included, though fornication is particularly mentioned. And other sorts of uncleanness are also forbidden, of which it is a shame even to speak, though they are done by too many in secret. All that is contrary to chastity in heart, speech, and behaviour, is contrary to the command of God in the decalogue, and contrary to that holiness which the gospel requires.

2. There are several arguments to enforce this caution. As, (1.) This branch of sanctification in particular is the will of God, v. 3. It is the will of God in general that we should be holy, because *he that called us is holy*, and because we are *chosen unto salvation through the sanctification of the Spirit;* and not only does God require holiness in the heart, but also purity in our bodies, and that we should cleanse ourselves from all *filthiness both of flesh and spirit*, 2 Cor. vii. 1. Wherever the body is, as it ought to be, devoted to God, and dedicated and set apart for him, it should be kept clean and pure for his service ; and, as chastity is one branch of our sanctification, so this is one thing which God commands in his law, and what his grace effects in all true believers. (2.) This will be greatly for our honour : as much is plainly implied, v. 4. Whereas the contrary will be a great dishonour. *And his reproach shall not be wiped away*, Prov. vi. 33. The body is here called the vessel of the soul, which dwells therein (so 1 Sam. xxi. 5), and it must be kept pure from defiling lusts. Every one should be careful in this matter, as he values his own honour and will not be contemptible on this account, that his inferior appetites and passions gain not the ascendant, tyrannizing over his reason and conscience, and enslaving the superior faculties of his soul. What can be more dishonourable than for a rational soul to be enslaved by bodily affections and brutal appetites ? (3.) To indulge the lust of concupiscence is to live and act like heathens ? *Even as the Gentiles who know not God, v.* 5. The Gentiles, and especially the Grecians, were commonly guilty of some sins of uncleanness which were not so evidently forbidden by the light of nature. But they did not know God, nor his mind and will, so well as Christians know, and should know, this his will, namely *our sanctification* in this branch of it. It is not so much to be wondered at, therefore, if the Gentiles indulge their fleshly appetites and lusts ; but Christians should not walk as unconverted Gentiles, *in lasciviousness, lusts, excess of wine, revellings, banquetings,* &c. (1 Pet. iv. 3), because those who are in Christ *have crucified the flesh with its affections and lusts.* (4.) The sin of uncleanness, especially adultery, is a great piece of injustice that God will be the avenger of ; so we may

understand those words, *That no man go beyond or defraud his brother* (*v.* 6) *in any matter*—ἐν τῷ πράγματι, in *this* matter of which the apostle is speaking in the preceding and following verses, namely, the sin of uncleanness. Some understand these words as a further warning and caution against injustice and oppression, all fraud and deceit in our dealings with men, which are certainly criminal, and contrary to the gospel. And Christians should not impose upon the ignorance and necessity of those they deal with, and so go beyond them, nor should they by equivocations or lying arts defraud them; and although this may be practised by some and lie long undiscovered, and so go unpunished among men, yet the righteous God will render a recompence. But the meaning may rather be to show the injustice and wrong that in many cases are done by the sin of uncleanness. Not only are fornication and other acts of uncleanness sins against his own body who commits them (1 Cor. vi. 18), not only are they very injurious to the sinner himself both in soul and body, but sometimes they are very injurious, and no less than defrauding, acts of injustice to others, particularly to those who are joined together in the marriage covenant and to their posterity. And, as this sin is of such a heinous nature, so it follows that God will be the avenger of it. *Whoremongers and adulterers God will judge*, Heb. xiii. 4. This the apostle had forewarned and testified by his gospel, which, as it contained exceedingly great and precious promises, so also it *revealed from heaven the wrath of God against all ungodliness and unrighteousness among men*, Rom. i. 18. (5.) The sin of uncleanness is contrary to the nature and design of our Christian calling: *For God hath called us not unto uncleanness, but unto holiness, v.* 7. The law of God forbids all impurity, and the gospel requires the greatest purity; it calls us from uncleanness unto holiness. (6.) The contempt therefore of God's law and gospel is the contempt of God himself: *He that despises despises God, not man* only. Some might possibly make light of the precepts of purity and holiness, because they heard them from men like themselves; but the apostle lets them know that they were God's commands, and to violate them was no less than to despise God. He adds, *God hath given Christians his Spirit*, intimating that all sorts of uncleanness do in an especial manner grieve the Holy Spirit, and will provoke him to withdraw from us; and also the Holy Spirit is given unto us to arm us against these sins, and to help us to mortify these deeds of the body, that we may live, Rom. viii. 13.

⁹ But as touching brotherly love ye need not that I write unto you: for ye yourselves are taught of God to love one another. ¹⁰ And indeed ye do it toward all the brethren which are in all Macedonia: but we beseech you, brethren, that ye increase more and more; ¹¹ And that ye study to be quiet, and to do your own business, and to work with your own hands, as we commanded you; ¹² That ye may walk honestly toward them that are without, and *that* ye may have lack of nothing.

In these words the apostle mentions the great duties,

I. Of brotherly love. This he exhorts them to increase in yet more and more. The exhortation is introduced, not with a compliment, but with a commendation, because they were remarkable in the exercise of it, which made it less needful that he should write to them about it, *v.* 9. Thus by his good opinion of them he insinuated himself into their affections, and so made way for his exhortation to them. Note, We should take notice of that in others which is good to their praise, that by so doing we may lay engagements upon them to abound therein more and more. Observe,

I. What it is that the apostle commends in them. It was not so much their own virtue as God's grace; yet he takes notice of the evidence they gave of the grace of God in them. (1.) It was God's grace that he took special notice of: that God had taught them this good lesson: *You your-selves are taught of God to love one another, v.* 9. Whoever does that which is good is taught of God to do it, and God must have the glory. All who are savingly taught of God are taught this lesson, to love one another. This is the livery of Christ's family. Note also, The teaching of the Spirit exceeds the teaching of men; and, as no man should teach contrary to what God teaches, so none can teach so effectually as he teaches; and men's teaching is vain and useless unless God teach also. (2.) The Thessalonians gave good evidence of their being taught of God by *their love to the brethren in all Macedonia, v.* 10. They not only loved those of their own city and society, or such as were near them and just of their own senti-ments, but their love was extensive. And a true Christian's is so to all the saints, though distant from him in place, and differing from him in some opinions or practices of less moment.

2. The exhortation itself is to increase more and more in this great grace and duty of brotherly love, *v.* 10. Though these Thessalonians had in some sense no need of an exhortation to brotherly love, as if it were wholly want-ing, yet they must be exhorted to pray for more, and labour for more. There are none on this side heaven who love in perfection. Those who are eminent in this or any other grace have need of increase therein as well as of perseverance unto the end.

II. Of quietness and industry in their callings. Observe, I. The apostle exhorts to these duties: that they should *study to be quiet, v.* 11. It is the most desirable thing to have a calm and quiet temper, and to be of a peaceable and quiet behaviour. This tends much to our own and others' happiness; and Christians should study how to be quiet. We should be ambitious and industrious how to be calm and quiet in our minds, in patience to possess our own souls, and to be quiet towards others; or of a meek and mild, a gentle and peaceable disposition, not given to strife, contention, or division. Satan is very busy to disquiet us; and we have that in our own hearts that disposes us to be disquiet; therefore let us study to be quiet. It follows, *Do your own business.* When we go beyond this, we expose ourselves to a great deal of inquietude. Those who are busy-bodies, meddling in other men's matters, generally have but little quiet in their own minds and cause great disturbances among their neighbours; at least they seldom mind the other exhortation, to be diligent in their own call-ing, *to work with their own hands;* and yet this was what the apostle com-manded them, and what is required of us also. Christianity does not dis-charge us from the work and duty of our particular callings, but teaches us to be diligent therein. 2. The exhortation is enforced with a double argument; namely, (1.) So we shall live creditably. Thus we shall walk honestly, or decently and creditably, towards those that are without, *v.* 12. This will be to act as becomes the gospel, and will gain a good report from those that are strangers, yea, enemies to it. Note, It is a great ornament to religion when the professors of it are of meek and quiet spirits, diligent to do their own business, and not busy-bodies in other men's matters.

(2.) We shall live comfortably, and have lack of nothing, *v.* 12. People often by their slothfulness bring themselves into narrow circumstances, and reduce themselves to great straits, and are liable to many wants, when such as are diligent in their own business live comfortably and have lack of nothing. They are not burdensome to their friends, nor scandalous to strangers. They earn their own bread, and have the greatest pleasure in so doing.

13 But I would not have you to be ignorant, brethren, concerning them which are asleep, that ye sorrow not, even as others which have no hope. 14 For if we believe that Jesus died and rose again, even so them also which sleep in Jesus will God bring with him. 15 For this we say unto you by the word of the Lord, that we which are alive *and* remain unto the coming of the Lord shall not prevent [**precede**] them which are asleep. 16 For the Lord himself shall descend from heaven with a shout, with the voice of the archangel, and with the trump of God : and the dead in Christ shall rise first : 17 Then we which are alive *and* remain shall be caught up together with them in the clouds, to meet the Lord in the air : and so shall we ever be with the Lord. 18 Wherefore comfort one another with these words.

In these words the apostle comforts the Thessalonians who mourned for the death of their relations and friends that died in the Lord. His design is to dissuade them from excessive grief, or inordinate sorrow, on that account. *All* grief for the death of friends is far from being unlawful ; we may weep at least for ourselves if we do not weep for them, weep for own loss, though it may be their gain. Yet we must not be immoderate in our sorrows, because,

I. This looks as if we had no hope, *v.* 13. It is to act too much like the Gentiles, who had no hope of a better life after this ; whereas we Christians, who have a most sure hope, the hope of eternal life after this, *which God who cannot lie hath promised us,* should moderate all our joys and our sorrows on account of any worldly thing. This hope is more than enough to balance all our griefs upon account of any of the crosses of the present time.

II. This is an effect of ignorance concerning those who are dead, *v.* 13. There are some things which we cannot but be ignorant of concerning those that are asleep ; for the land they are removed to is a land of darkness, which we know but little of and have no correspondence with. To go among the dead is to go among we know not whom, and to live we know not how. Death is an unknown thing, and the state of the dead, or the state after death, we are much in the dark about ; yet there are some things concerning those especially who die in the Lord that we need not, and ought not, to be ignorant of ; and, if these things be really understood and duly considered, they will be sufficient to allay our sorrow concerning them.

1. They sleep in Jesus. They are asleep, *v.* 13. They have *fallen asleep in Christ,* 1 Cor. xv. 18. Death does not annihilate them. It is

but a sleep to them. It is their rest, and undisturbed rest. They have retired out of this troublesome world, to rest from all their labours and sorrows, and they sleep in Jesus, *v.* 14. Being still in union with him, they sleep in his arms and are under his special care and protection. Their souls are in his presence, and their dust is under his care and power; so that they are not lost, nor are they losers, but great gainers by death, and their removal out of this world is into a better.

2. They shall be raised up from the dead, and awakened out of their sleep, for *God will bring them with him, v.* 14. They then are with God, and are better where they are than when they were here; and when God comes he will bring them with him. The doctrine of the resurrection and the second coming of Christ is a great antidote against the fear of death and inordinate sorrow for the death of our Christian friends; and this doctrine we have a full assurance of, because we *believe that Jesus died and rose again, v.* 14. It is taken for granted that as Christians they knew and believed this. The death and resurrection of Christ are fundamental articles of the Christian religion, and give us hope of a joyful resurrection; for *Christ, having risen from the dead, has become the first fruits of those that slept;* and therefore *those who have fallen asleep in him have not perished nor are lost,* 1 Cor. xv. 18, 20. His resurrection is a full confirmation of all that is said in the gospel, or by the word of the Lord, which has *brought life and immortality to light.*

3. Their state and condition shall be glorious and happy at the second coming of Christ. This the apostle informs the Thessalonians of *by the word of the Lord* (*v.* 15), by divine revelation from the Lord Jesus; for though the resurrection of the dead, and a future state of blessedness, were part of the creed of the Old-Testament saints, yet they are much more clearly revealed in and by the gospel. By this word of the Lord we know, (1.) That the Lord Jesus will come down from heaven in all the pomp and power of the upper world (*v.* 16): *The Lord himself shall descend from heaven with a shout.* He ascended into heaven after his resurrection, and passed through these material heavens into the third heaven, which must retain him till the restitution of all things; and then he will come again, and appear in his glory. He will descend from heaven into this our air, *v.* 17. The appearance will be with pomp and power, *with a shout*—the shout of a king, and the power and authority of a mighty king and conqueror, with *the voice of the archangel;* an innumerable company of angels will attend him. Perhaps *one,* as general of those hosts of the Lord, will give notice of his approach and the glorious appearance of this great Redeemer and Judge will be proclaimed and ushered in by the *trump of God. For the trumpet shall sound,* and this will awaken those that sleep in the dust of the earth, and will summon all the world to appear. For, (2.) The dead shall be raised: *The dead in Christ shall rise first* (*v.* 16), before those who are *found alive at Christ's coming shall be changed;* and so it appears that those who shall then *be found alive shall not prevent those that are asleep, v.* 15. The first care of the Redeemer in that day will be about his dead saints; he will raise them before the great change passes on those that shall be found alive: so that those who did not sleep in death will have no greater privilege or joy at that day than those who fell asleep in Jesus. (3.) Those that shall be found alive will then be changed. They shall *be caught up together with them in the clouds, to meet the Lord in the air, v.* 17. At, or immediately before, this rapture into the clouds, those who are alive will undergo a mighty change, which will be equivalent to

dying. This change is so mysterious that we cannot comprehend it : we know little or nothing of it, 1 Cor. xv. 51. Only, in the general, *this mortal must put on immortality*, and these bodies will be made fit to inherit the kingdom of God, which flesh and blood in its present state are not capable of. This change will be *in a moment, in the twinkling of an eye* (1 Cor. xv. 52), in the very instant, or not long after the raising up of those that sleep in Jesus. And those who are raised and thus changed, shall meet together in the clouds, and there meet with their Lord, to congratulate him on his coming, to receive the crown of glory he will then bestow upon them, and to be assessors with him in judgment, approving and applauding the sentence he will then pass upon the prince of the power of the air, and all the wicked, who shall be doomed to destruction with the devil and his angels. (4.) Here is the bliss of the saints at that day : they shall *be ever with the Lord, v.* 17. It will be some part of their felicity that all the saints shall meet together, and remain together for ever ; but the principal happiness of heaven is this, *to be with the Lord*, to see him, live with him, and enjoy him, for ever. This should comfort the saints upon the death of their friends, that, although death has made a separation, yet their souls and bodies will meet again ; we and they shall meet together again : we and they with all the saints shall meet our Lord, and be with him for ever, no more to be separated either from him or from one another for ever. And the apostle would have us *comfort one another with these words, v.* 18. We should endeavour to support one another in times of sorrow, not deaden one another's spirits, nor weaken one another's hands, but should comfort one another ; and this may be done by serious consideration and discourse on the many good lessons to be learned from the doctrine of the resurrection of the dead, the second coming of Christ, and the glory of the saints in that day.

CHAPTER V

The apostle, having spoken in the end of the foregoing chapter concerning the resurrection, and the second coming of Christ, proceeds to speak concerning the uselessness of enquiring after the particular time of Christ's coming, which would be sudden and terrible to the wicked, but comfortable to the saints, ver. 1-5. He then exhorts them to the duties of watchfulness, sobriety, and the exercise of faith, love, and hope, as being suitable to their state, ver. 6-10. In the next words he exhorts them to several duties they owed to others, or to one another (ver. 11-15), afterwards to several other Christian duties of great importance (ver. 16-22), and then concludes this epistle, ver. 23-28.

BUT of the times and the seasons, brethren, ye have no need that I write unto you. ² For yourselves know perfectly that the day of the Lord so cometh as a thief in the night. ³ For when they shall say, Peace and safety ; then sudden destruction cometh upon them, as travail upon a woman with child ; and they shall not escape. ⁴ But ye, brethren, are not in darkness, that that day should overtake you as a thief. ⁵ Ye are all the children of light, and the children of the day: we are not of the night, nor of darkness.

In these words observe,

I. The apostle tells the Thessalonians it was needless or useless to enquire about the particular time of Christ's coming: *Of the times and seasons you need not that I write unto you, v.* 1. The thing is certain that Christ will come, and there is a certain time appointed for his coming; but there was no need that the apostle should write about this, and therefore he had no revelation given him; nor should they or we enquire into this secret, *which the Father has reserved in his own power. Of that day and hour knoweth no man.* Christ himself did not reveal this while upon earth; it was not in his commission as the great prophet of the church: nor did he reveal this to his apostles; there was *no need* of this. There are times and seasons for us to do our work in : these it is our duty and interest to know and observe, but the time and season when we must give up our account we know not, nor is it needful that we should know them. Note, There are many things which our vain curiosity desires to know which there is no necessity at all of our knowing, nor would our knowledge of them do us good.

II. He tells them that the coming of Christ would be sudden, and a great surprise to most men, *v.* 2. And this is what they knew perfectly, or might know, because our Lord himself had so said : *In such an hour as you think not, the Son of man cometh,* Matt. xxiv. 44. So Mark xiii. 35, 36, *Watch you therefore, for you know not when the master of the house cometh; lest, coming suddenly, he find you sleeping.* And no doubt the apostle had told them, as of the coming of Christ, so also of his coming suddenly, which is the meaning of his coming *as a thief in the night,* Rev. xvi. 15. As the thief usually cometh in the dead time of the night, when he is least expected, such a *surprise* will the day of the Lord be ; so sudden and surprising will be his appearance. The knowledge of this will be more useful than to know the exact time, because this should awaken us to stand upon our watch, that we may be ready whenever he cometh.

III. He tells them how terrible Christ's coming would be to the ungodly, *v.* 3. It will be to their destruction in that day of the Lord. The righteous God will bring ruin upon his and his people's enemies; and this their destruction, as it will be total and final, so, 1. It will be sudden. It will overtake them, and fall upon them, in the midst of their carnal security and jollity, when they say in their hearts, *Peace and safety,* when they dream of felicity and please themselves with vain amusements of their fancies or their senses, and think not of it,—*as travail cometh upon a woman with child,* at the set time indeed, but not perhaps just then expected, nor greatly feared. 2. It will be unavoidable destruction too : *They shall not escape;* they shall in no wise escape. There will be no means possible for them to avoid the terror nor the punishment of that day. There will be *no place where the workers of iniquity shall be able to hide themselves,* no shelter from the storm, nor shadow from the burning heat that shall consume the wicked.

IV. He tells them how comfortable this day will be to the righteous, *v.* 4, 5. Here observe, 1. Their character and privilege. They are not in darkness; they are the children of the light, &c. This was the happy condition of the Thessalonians as it is of all true Christians. They are not in a state of sin and ignorance as the heathen world. They were *some time darkness, but were made light in the Lord.* They were favoured with the divine revelation of things that are unseen and eternal, particularly concerning the coming of Christ, and the consequences thereof. They were the *children of the day,* for the day-star had risen upon them ; yea, the Sun of righteousness had arisen on them with healing under his wings. They were no longer under the darkness of heathenism, nor under the shadows of the law, but under the gospel, which brings life and immortality to light, 2 Tim. i. 10. 2. Their great advantage on this account : that *that day should not overtake them as a thief, v.* 4. It was at least their own fault if they were surprised by that day. They had fair warning, and sufficient helps to provide against that day, and might hope to stand with comfort and confidence before the Son of man. This would be a time of *refreshing to them from the presence of the Lord,* who to *those that look for him will appear without sin unto their salvation,* and will come to them as a friend in the day, not as a thief in the night.

⁶ Therefore, let us not sleep, as *do* others ; but let us watch and be sober. ⁷ For they that sleep sleep in the night ; and they that be drunken are drunken in the night. ⁸ But let us, who are of the day, be sober, putting on the breastplate of faith and love ; and, for an helmet, the hope of salvation. ⁹ For God hath not appointed us to wrath, but to obtain salvation by our Lord Jesus Christ, ¹⁰ Who died for us, that, whether we wake or sleep, we should live together with him.

On what had been said, the apostle grounds seasonable exhortations to several needful duties.

I. To watchfulness and sobriety, *v.* 6. These duties are distinct, yet they mutually befriend one another. For, while we are compassed about with so many temptations to intemperance and excess, we shall not keep sober, unless we be upon our guard, and, unless we keep sober, we shall not long watch. 1. Then *let us not sleep as do others, but let us watch ;* we must not be secure and careless, nor indulge spiritual sloth and idleness. We must not be off our watch, but continually upon our guard against sin, and temptation to it. The generality of men are too careless of their duty and regardless of their spiritual enemies. They say, *Peace and safety,* when they are in the greatest danger, doze away their precious moments on which eternity depends, indulging idle dreams, and have no more thoughts nor cares about another world than men that are asleep have about this. Either they do not consider the things of another world at all, because they are asleep ; or they do not consider them aright, because they dream. But let us watch, and act like men that are awake, and that stand upon their guard. 2. Let us also *be sober,* or temperate and moderate. Let us keep our natural desires and appetites after the things of this world within due bounds. Sobriety is usually opposed to excess in meats and drinks, and here particularly it is opposed to drunkenness ; but it also extends to all other temporal things. Thus our Saviour warned his disciples to *take heed lest their hearts should be overcharged with surfeiting and drunkenness, and cares of this life, and so that day come on them unawares,* Luke xxi. 34.

Our moderation then, as to all temporal things, *should be known to all men, because the Lord is at hand.* Besides this, watchfulness and sobriety are most suitable to the Christian's character and privilege, as being *children of the day ;* because *those that sleep sleep in the night, and those that are drunken are drunken in the night, v. 7.* It is a most reproachful thing for men to sleep away the day-time, which is for work and not for sleep, to be drunken in the day, when so many eyes are upon them to behold their shame. It was not so strange if those who had not the benefit of divine revelation suffered themselves to be lulled asleep by the devil in carnal security, and if they laid the reins upon the neck of their appetites, and indulged themselves in all manner of riot and excess ; for it was night-time with them. They were not sensible of their danger, therefore they *slept ;* they were not sensible of their duty, therefore they were drunk : but it ill becomes Christians to do thus. What! shall Christians, who have the light of the blessed gospel shining in their faces, be careless about their souls, and unmindful of another world ? Those who have so many eyes upon them should conduct themselves with peculiar propriety.

II. To be well armed as well as watchful : to put on the whole armour of God. This is necessary in order to such sobriety as becomes us and will be a preparation for the day of the Lord, because our spiritual enemies are many, and mighty, and malicious. They draw many to their interest, and keep them in it, by making them careless, secure, and presumptuous, by making them drunk—drunk with pride, drunk with passion, drunk and giddy with self-conceit, drunk with the gratifications of sense : so that we have need to arm ourselves against their attempts, by putting on the spiritual breast-plate to keep the heart, and the spiritual helmet to secure the head ; and this spiritual armour consists of the three great graces of Christians, faith, love, and hope, *v.* 8. 1. We must live by faith, and this will keep us watchful and sober. If we believe that the eye of God (who is a spirit) is always upon us, that we have spiritual enemies to grapple with, that there is a world of spirits to prepare for, we shall see reason to watch and be sober. Faith will be our best defence against the assaults of our enemies. 2. We must get a heart inflamed with love ; and this also will be our defence. True and fervent love to God, and the things of God, will keep us watchful and sober, and hinder our apostasy in times of trouble and temptation. 3. We must make salvation our hope, and should have a lively hope of it. This good hope, through grace of eternal life, will be as a helmet to defend the head, and hinder our being intoxicated with the pleasures of sin, which are but for a season. If we have hope of salvation, let us take heed of doing anything that shall shake our hopes, or render us unworthy of or unfit for the great salvation we hope for. Having mentioned salvation and the hope of it, the apostle shows what grounds and reasons Christians have to hope for this salvation, as to which observe, He says nothing of their meriting it. No, the doctrine of our merits is altogether unscriptural and anti-scriptural ; there is no foundation of any good hope upon that account. But our hopes are to be grounded, (1.) Upon God's appointment : because *God hath not appointed us to wrath, but to obtain salvation, v.* 9. If we would trace our salvation to the first cause, that is God's appointment. Those who live and die in darkness and ignorance, who sleep and are drunken as in the night, are, it is but too plain, *appointed to wrath ;* but as for those who are of the day, if they watch and be sober, it is evident that they are *appointed to obtain salvation.* And the sureness and firmness of the divine appointment are the great support and encouragement of our hope. Were we to obtain salvation by our own merit or power, we could have but little or no hope of it; but seeing we are to obtain it by virtue of God's appointment, which we are sure cannot be shaken (*for his purpose according to election shall stand*), on this we build unshaken hope, especially when we consider, (2.) Christ's merit and grace, and that salvation is by our Lord Jesus Christ, who died for us. Our salvation therefore is owing to, and our hopes of it are grounded on, Christ's atonement as well as God's appointment: and, as we should think on God's gracious design and purpose, so also on Christ's death and sufferings, for this end, *that whether we wake or sleep* (whether we live or die, for death is but a sleep to believers, as the apostle had before intimated), *we should live together with Christ*, live in union and in glory with him forever. And, as it is the salvation that Christians hope for to *be forever with the Lord*, so one foundation of their hope is their union with him. And if they are united with Christ, and live in him, and live to him, here, the sleep of death will be no prejudice to the spiritual life, much less to the life of glory hereafter. On the contrary, Christ died for us, that, living and dying, we might be his ; that we might live to him while we are here and live with him when we go hence.

¹¹ Wherefore comfort yourselves together, and edify one another, even as also ye do. ¹² And we beseech you, brethren, to know them which labour among you, and are over you in the Lord, and admonish you ; ¹³ And to esteem them very highly in love for their work's sake. *And* be at peace among yourselves. ¹⁴ Now we exhort you, brethren, warn them that are unruly [**disorderly**], comfort the feeble-minded [**encourage the fainthearted**], support the weak, be patient toward all *men*. ¹⁵ See that none render evil for evil unto any *man*; but ever follow that which is good, both among yourselves, and to all *men.*

In these words the apostle exhorts the Thessalonians to several duties.

I. Towards those who were nearly related one to another. Such should comfort themselves, or exhort one another, and edify one another, *v.* 11. 1. They must comfort or exhort themselves and one another ; for the original word may be rendered both these ways. And we may observe, As those are most able and likely to comfort others who can comfort themselves, so the way to have comfort ourselves, or to administer comfort to others, is by compliance with the exhortation of the word. Note, We should not only be careful about our own comfort and welfare, but to promote the comfort and welfare of others also. He was a Cain that said, *Am I my brother's keeper ?* We *must bear one another's burdens, and so fulfil the law of Christ.* 2. They must edify one another, by *following after those things whereby one may edify another*, Rom. xiv. 19. As Christians are lively stones built up together a spiritual house, they should endeavour to promote the good of the whole church by promoting the work of grace in one another. And it is the duty of every one of us to study that which is for the edification of those with whom we converse, *to please all men for their* real *profit.* We should communicate our knowledge and experiences one to another. We should join in prayer and praise one with another,

We should set a good example one before another. And it is the duty of those especially who live in the same vicinity and family thus to comfort and edify one another ; and this is the best neighbourhood, the best means to answer the end of society. Such as are nearly related together and have affection for one another, as they have the greatest opportunity, so they are under the greatest obligation, to do this kindness one to another. This the Thessalonians did (*which also you do*), and this is what they are exhorted to continue and increase in doing. Note, Those who do that which is good have need of further exhortations to excite them to do good, to do more good, as well as continue in doing what they do.

II. He shows them their duty towards their ministers, *v.* 12, 13. Though the apostle himself was driven from them, yet they had others who laboured among them, and to whom they owed these duties. The apostle here exhorts them to observe,

1. How the ministers of the gospel are described by the work of their office ; and they should rather mind the work and duty they are called to than affect venerable and honourable names that they may be called by. Their work is very weighty, and very honourable and useful. (1.) Ministers must labour among their people, labour with diligence, and unto weariness (so the word in the original imports) ; *they must labour in the word and doctrine,* 1 Tim. v. 17. They are called labourers, and should not be loiterers. They must labour with their people, to instruct, comfort, and edify them. And, (2.) Ministers are to rule their people also, so the word is rendered, 1 Tim. v. 17. They must rule, not with rigour, but with love. They must not exercise dominion as temporal lords ; but rule as spiritual guides, by setting a good example to the flock. They are over the people in the Lord, to distinguish them from civil magistrates, and to denote also that they are but ministers under Christ, appointed by him, and must rule the people by Christ's laws, and not by laws of their own. This may also intimate the end of their office and all their labour ; namely, the service and honour of the Lord. (3.) They must also admonish the people, and that not only publicly, but privately, as there may be occasion. They must instruct them to do well, and should reprove when they do ill. It is their duty not only to give good counsel, but also to give admonition, to give warning to the flock of the dangers they are liable to, and reprove for negligence or what else may be amiss.

2. What the duty of the people is towards their ministers. There is a mutual duty between ministers and people. If ministers should labour among the people, then (1.) The people must know them. As the shepherd should know his flock, so the sheep must know their shepherd. They must know his person, hear his voice, acknowledge him for their pastor, and pay due regard to his teaching, ruling, and admonitions. (2.) They must esteem their ministers highly in love ; they should greatly value the office of the ministry, honour and love the persons of their ministers, and show their esteem and affection in all proper ways, and this for their work's sake, because their business is to promote the honour of Christ and the welfare of men's souls. Note, Faithful ministers ought to be so far from being lightly esteemed because of their work that they should be highly esteemed on account of it. The work of the ministry is so far from being a disgrace to those who upon other accounts deserve esteem, that it puts an honour upon those who are faithful and diligent, to which otherwise they could lay no claim, and will procure them that esteem and love among good people which otherwise they could not expect.

III. He gives divers other exhortations touching the duty Christians owe to one another. 1. *To be at peace among themselves, v.* 13. Some understand this exhortation (according to the reading in some copies) as referring to the people's duty to their ministers, to live peaceably with them, and not raise nor promote dissensions at any time between minister and people, which will certainly prove a hindrance to the success of a minister's work and the edification of the people. This is certain, that ministers and people should avoid everything that tends to alienate their affections one from another. And the people should be at peace among themselves, doing all they can to hinder any differences from rising or continuing among them, and using all proper means to preserve peace and harmony. 2. *To warn the unruly, v.* 14. There will be in all societies some who walk disorderly, who go out of their rank and station; and it is not only the duty of ministers, but of private Christians also, to warn and admonish them. Such should be reproved for their sin, warned of their danger, and told plainly of the injury they do their own souls, and the hurt they may do to others. Such should be put in mind of what they should do, and be reproved for doing otherwise. 3. *To comfort the feeble-minded, v.* 14. By these are intended the timorous and faint-hearted, or such as are dejected and of a sorrowful spirit. Some are cowardly, afraid of difficulties, and disheartened at the thought of hazards, and losses, and afflictions; now, such should be encouraged; we should not despise them, but comfort them; and who knows what good a kind and comfortable word may do them? 4. *To support the weak, v.* 14. Some are not well able to perform their work, nor bear up under their burdens; we should therefore support them, help their infirmities, and lift at one end of the burden, and so help to bear it. It is the grace of God, indeed, that must strengthen and support such; but we should tell them of that grace, and endeavour to minister of that grace to them. 5. *To be patient towards all men, v.* 14. We must bear and forbear. We must be long-suffering, and suppress our anger, if it begin to rise upon the apprehension of affronts or injuries; at least we must not fail to moderate our anger: and this duty must be exercised towards all men, good and bad, high and low. We must not be high in our expectations and demands, nor harsh in our resentments, nor hard in our impositions, but endeavour to make the best we can of everything, and think the best we can of everybody. 6. *Not to render evil for evil to any man, v.* 15. This we must look to, and be very careful about, that is, we must by all means forbear to avenge ourselves. If others do us an injury, this will not justify us in returning it, in doing the same, or the like, or any other injury to them. It becomes us to forgive, as those that are, and that hope to be, forgiven of God. 7. *Ever to follow that which is good, v.* 15. In general, we must study to do what is our duty, and pleasing to God, in all circumstances, whether men do us good turns or ill turns; whatever men do to us, we must do good to others. We must always endeavour to be beneficent and instrumental to promote the welfare of others, both among ourselves (in the first place to those that *are of the household of faith*), and then, *as we have opportunity unto all men,* Gal. vi. 10.

[16] Rejoice evermore. [17] Pray without ceasing. [18] In every thing give thanks: for this is the will of God in Christ Jesus concerning you. [19] Quench not the Spirit. [20] Despise not

prophesyings. ²¹ Prove all things; hold fast that which is good. ²² Abstain from all appearance [**every form**] of evil.

Here we have divers short exhortations, that will not burden our memories, but will be of great use to direct the motions of our hearts and lives; for the duties are of great importance, and we may observe how they are connected together, and have a dependence upon one another. 1. *Rejoice evermore, v.* 16. This must be understood of spiritual joy; for we must rejoice in our creature-comforts as if we rejoiced not, and must not expect to live many years, and rejoice in them all; but, if we do rejoice in God, we may do that evermore. In him our joy will be full; and it is our fault if we have not a continual feast. If we are sorrowful upon any worldly account, yet still we may always rejoice, 2 Cor. vi. 10. Note, A religious life is a pleasant life, it is a life of constant joy. 2. *Pray without ceasing, v.* 17. Note, The way to rejoice evermore is to pray without ceasing. We should rejoice more if we prayed more. We should keep up stated times for prayer and continue instant in prayer. We should pray always, and not faint: pray without weariness, and continue in prayer, till we come to that world where prayer shall be swallowed up in praise. The meaning is not that men should do nothing but pray, but that nothing else we do should hinder prayer in its proper season. Prayer will help forward and not hinder all other lawful business, and every good work. 3. *In every thing give thanks, v.* 18. If we pray without ceasing, we shall not want matter for thanksgiving *in every thing*. As we must in every thing make our requests known to God by supplications, so we must not omit thanksgiving, Phil. iv. 6. We should be thankful in every condition, even in adversity as well as prosperity. It is never so bad with us but it might be worse. If we have ever so much occasion to make our humble complaints to God, we never can have any reason to complain of God, and have always much reason to praise and give thanks : the apostle says, This is the *will of God in Christ Jesus concerning us, that we give thanks,* seeing God is reconciled to us in Christ Jesus; in him, through him, and for his sake, he allows us to rejoice evermore, and appoints us in every thing to give thanks. It is pleasing to God. 4. *Quench not the Spirit* (*v.* 19), for it is this Spirit of grace and supplication that helpeth our infirmities, that assisteth us in our prayers and thanksgiving ; Christians are said to *be baptized with the Holy Ghost and with fire.* He worketh as fire, by enlightening, enlivening, and purifying the souls of men. We must be careful not to quench this holy fire. As fire is put out by withdrawing fuel, so we quench the Spirit if we do not stir up our spirits, and all that is within us, to comply with the motions of the good Spirit ; and as fire is quenched by pouring water, or putting a great quantity of dirt upon it, so we must be careful not to quench the Holy Spirit by indulging carnal lusts and affections, or minding only earthly things. 5. *Despise not prophesyings* (*v.* 20); for, if we neglect the means of grace, we forfeit the Spirit of grace. By *prophesyings* here we are to understand the preaching of the word, the interpreting and applying of the scriptures ; and this we must not despise, but should prize and value, because it is the ordinance of God, appointed of him for our furtherance and increase in knowledge and grace, in holiness and comfort. We must not despise preaching, though it be plain, and not with enticing words of men's wisdom, and though we be told no more than what we knew before. It is useful, and many times needful, to have our minds stirred up, our affections and resolutions excited, to those things that we knew before to be our interest and our duty. 6. *Prove all things ; hold fast that which is good, v.* 21. This is a needful caution, to prove all things ; for, though we must put a value on preaching, we must not take things upon trust from the preacher, but try them by the law and the testimony. We must search the scriptures, whether what they say be true or not. We must not believe every spirit, but must try the spirits. But we must not be always trying, always unsettled ; no, at length we must be settled, and hold fast that which is good. When we are satisfied that any thing is right, and true, and good, we must hold it fast, and not let it go, whatever opposition or whatever persecution we meet with for the sake thereof. Note, The doctrines of human infallibility, implicit faith, and blind obedience, are not the doctrines of the Bible. Every Christian has, and ought to have, the judgment of discretion, and should have *his senses exercised in discerning between good and evil,* truth and falsehood, Heb. v 13, 14. And proving all things must be in order to holding fast that which is good. We must not always be seekers, or fluctuating in our minds, *like children tossed to and fro with every wind of doctrine.* 7. *Abstain from all appearance of evil, v.* 22. This is a good means to prevent our being deceived with false doctrines, or unsettled in our faith ; for our Saviour has told us (John vii. 17), *If a man will do his will, he shall know of the doctrine whether it be of God.* Corrupt affections indulged in the heart, and evil practices allowed of in the life, will greatly tend to promote fatal errors in the mind ; whereas purity of heart, and integrity of life, will dispose men to receive the truth in the love of it. We should therefore abstain from evil, and all appearances of evil, from sin, and that which looks like sin, leads to it, and borders upon it. He who is not shy of the appearances of sin, who shuns not the occasions of sin, and who avoids not the temptations and approaches to sin, will not long abstain from the actual commission of sin.

23 And the very God of peace sanctify you wholly ; and I *pray God* your whole spirit and soul and body be preserved blameless unto [preserved entire, without blame at] the coming of our Lord Jesus Christ. 24 Faithful *is* he that calleth you, who also will do *it.* 25 Brethren, pray for us. 26 Greet all the brethren with a holy kiss. 27 I charge you by the Lord that this epistle be read unto all the holy brethren. 28 The grace of our Lord Jesus Christ *be* with you. Amen.

In these words, which conclude this epistle, observe,

I. Paul's prayer for them, *v.* 23. He had told them, in the beginning of this epistle, that he always made mention of them in his prayers ; and, now that he is writing to them, he lifts up his heart to God in prayer for them. Take notice, 1. To whom the apostle prays, namely, *The very God of peace.* He is the God of grace, and the God of peace and love. He is the author of peace and lover of concord ; and by their peaceableness and unity, from God as the author, those things would best be obtained which he prays for. 2. The things he prays for on behalf of the Thessalonians are their sanctification, that *God would sanctify them wholly ;* and their preservation, that they might be *preserved blameless.* He prays that they may be wholly sanctified, that the whole man may be sanctified, and then that the whole man, spirit, soul, and body, may be preserved : or, he prays that they may be wholly sanctified, that is, more perfectly, for the best are sanctified but in part while in this world ; and therefore we should pray for and press towards complete sanctification. Where the good work of grace is begun, it shall be carried on, be protected and preserved ; and all those who are sanctified in Christ Jesus shall be preserved to the coming of our Lord Jesus Christ. And because, if God did not carry on his good work in the soul, it would miscarry, we should pray to God to perfect his work, and *preserve us blameless,* free from sin and impurity, till at length we are *presented faultless before the throne of his glory with exceeding joy.*

II. His comfortable assurance that God would hear his prayer : *Faithful is he who calleth you, who will also do it, v.* 24. The kindness and love of God had appeared to them in calling them to the knowledge of his truth, and the faithfulness of God was their security that they should persevere to the end ; and therefore, the apostle assures them, God would do what he desired ; he would effect what he had promised ; he would accomplish all the good pleasure of his goodness towards them. Note, Our fidelity to God depends upon his faithfulness to us.

III. His request of their prayers : *Brethren, pray for us, v.* 25. We should pray for one another ; and brethren should thus express brotherly love. This great apostle did not think it beneath him to call the Thessalonians brethren, nor to request their prayers. Ministers stand in need of their people's prayers ; and the more people pray for their ministers the more good ministers may have from God, and the more benefit people may receive by their ministry.

IV. His salutation : *Greet all the brethren with a holy kiss, v.* 26. Thus the apostle sends a friendly salutation from himself, and Silvanus, and Timotheus, and would have them salute each other in their names ; and thus he would have them signify their mutual love and affection to one another by the kiss of charity (1 Pet. v. 14), which is here called a holy kiss, to intimate how cautious they should be of all impurity in the use of this ceremony, then commonly practised ; as it should not be a treacherous kiss like that of Judas, so not a lascivious kiss like that of the harlot, Prov. vii. 13.

V. His solemn charge for the reading of this epistle, *v.* 27. This is not only an exhortation, but an adjuration by the Lord. And this epistle was to be read to all the holy brethren. It is not only allowed to the common people to read the scriptures, and what none should prohibit, but it is their indispensable duty, and what they should be persuaded to do. In order to this, these holy oracles should not be kept concealed in an unknown tongue, but translated into the vulgar languages, that all men, being concerned to know the scriptures, may be able to read them, and be acquainted with them. The public reading of the law was one part of the worship of the sabbath among the Jews in their synagogues, and the scriptures should be read in the public assemblies of Christians also.

VI. The apostolical benediction that is usual in other epistles. *The grace of our Lord Jesus Christ be with you. Amen, v.* 28. We need no more to make us happy than to know that grace which our Lord Jesus Christ has manifested, be interested in that grace which he has purchased, and partake of that grace which dwells in him as the head of the church. This is an ever-flowing and overflowing fountain of grace to supply all our wants.

EXPOSITION OF THE SECOND EPISTLE OF ST. PAUL TO THE THESSALONIANS

THIS Second Epistle was written soon after the former, and seems to have been designed to prevent a mistake, which might arise from some passages in the former epistle, concerning the second coming of Christ, as if it were near at hand. The apostle in this epistle is careful to prevent any wrong use which some among them might make of those expressions of his that were agreeable to the dialect of the prophets of the Old Testament, and informs them that there were many intermediate counsels yet to be fulfilled before that day of the Lord should come, though, because it is sure, he had spoken of it as near. There are other things that he writes about for their consolation under sufferings, and exhortation and direction in duty.

CHAPTER I

After the introduction (ver. 1, 2), the apostle begins this epistle with an account of his high esteem for these Thessalonians, ver. 3, 4. He then comforts them under their afflictions and persecutions, ver. 5-10, and tells them what his prayers were to God for them, ver. 11, 12.

PAUL, and Silvanus, and Timotheus, unto the church of the Thessalonians in God our Father and the Lord Jesus Christ: ² Grace unto you, and peace, from God our Father and the Lord Jesus Christ. ³ We are bound to thank God always for you, brethren, as it is meet, because that your faith groweth exceedingly, and the charity [love] of every one of you all toward each other aboundeth; ⁴ So that we ourselves glory in you in the churches of God for your patience and faith in all your persecutions and tribulations that ye endure—

Here we have,

I. The introduction (*v.* 1, 2), in the same words as in the former epistle, from which we may observe that as this apostle did not count it grievous to him to write the same things (Phil. iii. 1) in his epistles that he had delivered in preaching, so he willingly wrote the same things to one church that he did to another. The occurrence of the same words in this epistle as in the former shows us that ministers ought not so much to regard the variety of expression and elegance of style as the truth and usefulness of the doctrines they preach. And great care should be taken lest, from an affectation of novelty in method and phrases, we advance new notions or doctrines, contrary to the principles of natural or revealed religion, upon which this church of the Thessalonians was built, as all true churches are ; namely, *in God our Father and the Lord Jesus Christ.*

II. The apostle's expression of the high esteem he had for them. He not only had a great affection for them (as he had expressed in his former epistle, and now again in his pious wish of grace and peace for them), but he also expresses his great esteem for them, concerning which observe,

1. How his esteem of them is expressed. (1.) He glorified God on their behalf : *We are bound to thank God always for you, brethren, as it is meet, v.* 3. He chose rather to speak of what was praiseworthy in them in a way of thanksgiving to God than by commendation of them ; and, as what he mentions was matter of his rejoicing, he accounted it matter of thanksgiving, and it was meet or fit it should be so, for we are bound, and it is our duty, to be thankful to God for all the good that is found in us or others : and it not only is an act of kindness to our fellow-christians, but our duty, to thank God on their behalf. (2.) He also *glories in them before the churches of God, v.* 4. The apostle never flattered his friends, but he took pleasure in commending them, and speaking well of them, to the glory of God and for the excitement and encouragement of others. Paul did not glory in his own gifts, nor in his labour among them, but he gloried in the grace of God which was bestowed upon them, and so his glorying was good, because all the commendation he gave to them, and the pleasure he took himself, centred in the praise and glory of God.

2. For what he esteemed them and thanked God ; namely, the increase of their faith, and love, and patience. In his former epistle (*ch.* i. 3) he gave thanks for their faith, love, and patience ; here he gives thanks for the increase of all those graces, that they were not only true Christians, but growing Christians. Note, Where there is the truth of grace there will be increase of it. *The path of the just is as the shining light, which shines more and more unto the perfect day.* And where there is the increase of grace God must have all the glory of it. We are as much indebted to him for the improvement of grace, and the progress of that good work, as we are for the first work of grace and the very beginning of it. We may be tempted to think that though when we were bad we could not make ourselves good, yet when we are good we can easily make ourselves better ; but we have as much dependence on the grace of God for increasing the grace we have as for planting grace when we had it not. The matter of the apostle's thanksgiving and glorying on behalf of the Thessalonians was, (1.) That their faith grew exceedingly, *v.* 3. They were more confirmed in the truth of gospel-revelations, confided in gospel-promises, and had lively expectations of another world. The growth of their faith appeared by the works of faith ; and, where faith grows, all other graces grow proportionably. (2.) Their charity abounded (*v.* 3), their love to God and

man. Note, Where faith grows love will abound, for faith works by love ; and not only the charity of some few of them, but of every one to each other, did abound. There were no such divisions among them as in some other churches. (3.) Their patience as well as faith increased in all their persecutions and tribulations. And patience has then its perfect work when it extends itself to all trials. There were many persecutions which the Thessalonians endured for the sake of righteousness, as well as other troubles which they met with in this calamitous life ; yet they endured all these, by faith *seeing him that is invisible*, and looking to the *recompense of reward ;* and endured them with patience, not with an insensibility under them, but with patience arising from Christian principles, which kept them quiet and submissive, and afforded them inward strength and support.

5 *Which is* a manifest token of the righteous judgment of God, that ye may be counted worthy of the kingdom of God, for which ye also suffer : 6 Seeing [If so be] *it is* a righteous thing with God to recompense tribulation to them that trouble you ; 7 And to you who are troubled rest with us, when the Lord Jesus shall be revealed from heaven with his mighty angels, 8 In flaming fire, taking vengeance on them that know not God, and that obey not the gospel of our Lord Jesus Christ : 9 Who shall be punished with everlasting destruction from the presence [face] of the Lord, and from the glory of his power ; 10 When he shall come to be glorified in his saints, and to be admired [marvelled at] in all them that believe (because our testimony among you was believed) in that day.

Having mentioned their persecutions and tribulations, which they endured principally for the cause of Christ, the apostle proceeds to offer several things for their comfort under them ; as,

I. He tells them of the present happiness and advantage of their sufferings, *v.* 5. Their faith being thus tried, and patience exercised, they were improved by their sufferings, insomuch that they were *counted worthy of the kingdom of God.* Their sufferings were a manifest token of this, that they were worthy or meet to be accounted Christians indeed, seeing they could suffer for Christianity. And the truth is, Religion, if it is worth any thing, is worth every thing ; and those either have no religion at all, or none that is worth having, or know not how to value it, that cannot find in their hearts to suffer for it. Besides, from their patient suffering, it appeared that, according to the righteous judgment of God, they should be counted worthy of the heavenly glory : not by worthiness of condignity, but of congruity only ; not that they could merit heaven, but they were made meet for heaven. We cannot by all our sufferings, any more than by our services, merit heaven as a debt ; but by our patience under our sufferings we are qualified for the joy that is promised to patient sufferers in the cause of God.

II. He tells them next of the future recompense that shall be given to persecutors and persecuted.

1. In this future recompense there will be, (1.) A punishment inflicted on persecutors : God will *recompense tribulation to those that trouble you,*

v. 6. And there is nothing that more infallibly marks a man for eternal ruin than a spirit of persecution, and enmity to the name and people of God : as the faith, patience, and constancy of the saints are to them an earnest of everlasting rest and joy, so the pride, malice, and wickedness of their persecutors are to them an earnest of everlasting misery; for every man carries about with him, and carries out of the world with him, either his heaven or his hell. God will render a recompense, and will trouble those that trouble his people. This he has done sometimes in this world, witness the dreadful end of many persecutors ; but especially this he will do in the other world, where the portion of the wicked must be *weeping, and wailing, and gnashing of teeth.* (2.) A reward for those that are persecuted : God will recompense their trouble with rest, *v.* 7. There is a rest that remains for the people of God, a rest from sin and sorrow. Though many may be the troubles of the righteous now, yet God will deliver them out of them all. The future rest will abundantly recompense all their present troubles. The sufferings of this present time are not worthy to be compared with the glory that shall be revealed. There is enough in heaven to countervail all that we may lose or suffer for the name of Christ in this world. The apostle says, *To you who are troubled rest with us.* In heaven, ministers and people shall rest together, and rejoice together, who suffer together here; and the meanest Christian shall rest with the greatest apostle : nay, what is far more, if we suffer for Christ, we shall also reign with him, 2 Tim. ii. 12.

2. Concerning this future recompense we are further to observe,

(1.) The certainty of it, proved by the righteousness and justice of God : *It is a righteous thing with God* (*v.* 6) to render to every man according to his works. The thought of this should be terrible to wicked men and persecutors, and the great support of the righteous and such as are persecuted ; for, seeing there is a righteous God, there will be a righteous recompense. God's suffering people will lose nothing by their sufferings, and their enemies will gain nothing by their advantages against them.

(2.) The time when this righteous recompense shall be made : *When the Lord Jesus shall be revealed from heaven, v.* 7. That will be the day of the *revelation of the righteous judgment of God;* for then will God judge the world in righteousness by that man whom he hath appointed, even Jesus Christ the righteous Judge. The righteousness of God does not so visibly appear to all men in the procedure of his providence as it will in the process of the great judgment-day. The scripture has made known to us the judgment to come, and we are bound to receive the revelation here given concerning Christ. As,

[1.] That the Lord Jesus will in that day appear from heaven. Now the heavens retain him, they conceal him ; but then he will be revealed and made manifest. He will come in all the pomp and power of the upper world, *whence we look for the Saviour.*

[2.] He will be revealed with his mighty angels (*v.* 7), or the angels of his power : these will attend upon him, to grace the solemnity of that great day of his appearance ; they will be the ministers of his justice and mercy in that day ; they will summon the criminals to his tribunal, and gather in the elect, and be employed in executing his sentence.

[3.] He will come in flaming fire, *v.* 8. A fire goeth before him, which shall consume his enemies. The earth, and all the works that are therein, shall be burnt up, and the elements shall melt with fervent heat. This will be a trying fire, to try every man's work,—a refining fire, to purify the saints, who shall share in the purity, and partake of the felicity, of the new heaven and the new earth,—a consuming fire to the wicked. His light will be piercing, and his power consuming, to all those who in that day shall be found as chaff.

[4.] The effects of this appearance will be terrible to some and joyful to others.

First, They will be terrible to some ; for he will then take vengeance on the wicked. 1. On those that sinned against the principles of natural religion, and rebelled against the light of nature, *that knew not God* (*v.* 8.), though the invisible things of him are manifested in the things that are seen. 2. On those that rebel against the light of revelation, that *obey not the gospel of our Lord Jesus Christ.* And this is the condemnation, that light is come into the world, and men love darkness rather than light. This is the great crime of multitudes—the gospel is revealed to them, and they will not believe it ; or, if they pretend to believe it, they will not obey it. Note, Believing the truths of the gospel is in order to our obeying the precepts of the gospel : there must be the obedience of faith. To such persons as are here mentioned the revelation of our Lord Jesus Christ will be terrible, because of their doom, which is mentioned, *v.* 9. Here observe, (1.) They will then be punished. Though sinners may be long reprieved, yet they will be punished at last. Their misery will be a proper punishment for their crimes, and only what they have deserved. They did sin's work, and must receive sin's wages. (2.) Their punishment will be no less than destruction, not of their being, but of their bliss ; not that of the body alone, but both as to body and soul. (3.) This destruction will be everlasting. They shall be always dying, and yet never die. Their misery will run parallel with the line of eternity. The chains of darkness are everlasting chains, and the fire is everlasting fire. It must needs be so, since the punishment is inflicted by an eternal God, fastening upon an immortal soul, set out of the reach of divine mercy and grace. (4.) This destruction shall come from the *presence of the Lord,* that is, immediately from God himself. Here God punishes sinners by creatures, by instruments ; but then he will take the work into his own hands. It will be destruction from the Almighty, more terrible than the consuming fire which consumed Nadab and Abihu, which came from before the Lord. (5.) It shall come from the *glory of his power,* or from his glorious power. Not only the justice of God, but his almighty power, will be glorified in the destruction of sinners ; and who knows the power of his anger ? He is able to cast into hell.

Secondly, It will be a joyful day to some, even to the saints, unto those that believe and obey the gospel. And then the apostle's testimony concerning this day will be confirmed and *believed* (*v.* 10) ; in that bright and blessed day, 1. Christ Jesus will be glorified and admired by his saints. They will behold his glory, and admire it with pleasure ; they will glorify his grace, and admire the wonders of his power and goodness towards them, and sing hallelujahs to him in that day of his triumph, for their complete victory and happiness. 2. Christ will be glorified and admired in them. His grace and power will then be manifested and magnified, when it shall appear what he has purchased for, and wrought in, and bestowed upon, all those who believe in him. As his wrath and power will be made known in and by the destruction of his enemies, so his grace and power will be magnified in the salvation of his saints. Note, Christ's dealings with those who believe will be what the world one day shall wonder at. Now, they are a wonder to many; but how will they be wondered at in this great and glorious day; or, rather, how will Christ, whose name is Wonderful, be admired, when the mystery of God shall be finished ! Christ will not be so much admired in the glorious esteem of angels that he will bring from heaven with him as in the many saints, *the many sons*, that he will bring to glory.

11 Wherefore also we pray always for you, that our God would count you worthy of *this* calling, and fulfil all the good pleasure of *his* [every desire of] goodness, and the work of faith with power : 12 That the name of our Lord Jesus Christ may be glorified in you, and ye in him, according to the grace of our God and the Lord Jesus Christ.

In these verses the apostle again tells the Thessalonians of his earnest and constant prayer for them. He could not be present with them, yet he had a constant remembrance of them ; they were much upon his thoughts ; he wished them well, and could not express his good-will and good wishes to them better than in earnest constant prayer to God for them : *Wherefore also we pray*, &c. Note, The believing thoughts and expectation of the second coming of Christ should put us upon prayer to God for ourselves and others. We should watch and pray, so our Saviour directs his disciples (Luke xxi. 36), *Watch therefore, and pray always, that you may be counted worthy to stand before the Son of man.* Observe,

I. What the apostle prayed for, *v.* 11. It is a great concern to be well instructed what to pray for ; and without divine instruction we know not what to pray for, as without divine assistance we shall not pray in such a manner as we ought. Our prayers should be suitable to our expectations. Thus the apostle prays for them, 1. That God would begin his good work of grace in them ; so we may understand this expression : *That our God would count you* (or, as it might be read, *make you*) *worthy of this calling.* We are called with a high and holy calling ; we are called to God's kingdom and glory ; and no less than the inheritance of the saints is the hope of our calling, nothing less than the enjoyment of that glory and felicity which shall be revealed when Christ Jesus shall be revealed from heaven. Now, if this be our calling, our great concern should be to be worthy of it, or meet and prepared for this glory : and because we have no worthiness of our own, but what is owing purely to the grace of God, we should pray that he would make us worthy, and then count us worthy, of this calling, or that he would make us meet to partake of the inheritance of the saints in light, Col. i. 12. 2. That God would carry on the good work that is begun, and *fulfil all the good pleasure of his goodness.* The good pleasure of God denotes his gracious purposes towards his people, which flow from his goodness, and are full of goodness towards them ; and it is thence that all good comes to us. If there be any good in us, it is the fruit of God's good-will to us, it is owing to the good pleasure of his goodness, and therefore is called grace. Now, there are various and manifold purposes of grace and good-will in God towards his people ; and the apostle prays that all of them may be fulfilled or accomplished towards these Thessalonians. There are several good works of grace begun in the hearts of God's people, which proceed from this good pleasure of God's goodness, and we should desire that they may be completed and perfected. In particular, the apostle prays that God would fulfil in them the *work of faith with power*. Note, (1.) The fulfilling of the work of faith is in order to the fulfilling of every other good work. And, (2.) It is the power of God that not only begins, but that carries on and perfects the work of faith.

II. Why the apostle prayed for these things (*v.* 12): *That the name of the Lord Jesus may be glorified;* this is the end we should aim at in everything we do and desire, that God and Christ in all things may be glorified. Our own happiness and that of others should be subordinate to this ultimate end. Our good works should so shine before men that others may glorify God, that Christ may be glorified in and by us, and then we shall be glorified in and with him. And this is the great end and design of the grace of our God and the Lord Jesus Christ, which is manifested to us and wrought in us. Or thus : it is according to the grace of God and Christ, that is, it is an agreeable thing, considering the grace that is manifested to us and bestowed on us, by God and Christ, that we direct all we do to the glory of our Creator and Redeemer.

CHAPTER II

The apostle is very careful to hinder the spreading of an error into which some among them had fallen concerning the coming of Christ, as being very near, ver. 1-3. Then he proceeds to confute the error he cautioned them against, by telling them of two great events that were antecedent to the coming of Christ—a general apostasy, and the revelation of antichrist, concerning whom the apostle tells them many remarkable things, about his name, his character, his rise, his fall, his reign, and the sin and ruin of hi. subjects, ver. 4-12. He then comforts them against the terror of this apostasy, and exhorts them to stedfastness, ver. 13-15. And concludes with a prayer for them, ver. 16, 17.

NOW we beseech you, brethren, by [touching] the coming of our Lord Jesus Christ, and *by* our gathering together unto him, ² That ye be not soon shaken in mind, or be troubled, neither by spirit, nor by word, nor by letter as from us, as that the day of Christ is at hand [now present]. ³ Let no man deceive you by any means—

From these words it appears that some among the Thessalonians had mistaken the apostle's meaning, in what he had written in his former epistle about the coming of Christ, by thinking that it was near at hand, —that Christ was just ready to appear and come to judgment. Or, it may be, some among them pretended that they had the knowledge of this by particular revelation from the Spirit, or from some words they had heard from the apostle, when he was with them, or some letter he had written or they pretended he had written to them or some other person : and hereupon the apostle is careful to rectify this mistake, and to prevent the spreading of this error. Observe, If errors and mistakes arise among Christians, we should take the first opportunity to rectify them, and hinder the spreading thereof ; and good men will be especially careful to suppress errors that may arise from a mistake of their words and actions, though that which was spoken or done was ever so innocent or well. We have a subtle adversary, who watches all opportunities to do mischief, and will sometimes promote errors even by means of the words of scripture. Observe,

I. How very earnest and solicitous this apostle was to prevent mistakes : *We beseech you, brethren,* &c., *v.* 1. He entreats them as brethren who might have charged them as a father charges his children : he shows great kindness and condescension, and insinuates himself into their affections. And this is the best way to deal with men when we would preserve or recover them from errors, to deal gently and affectionately with them : rough and rigorous treatment will but exasperate their spirits, and prejudice them against the reasons we may offer. He obtests and even conjures them in the most solemn manner : *By the coming of Christ,* &c. The words are in the form of an oath ; and his meaning is that if they believed Christ would come, and if they desired he would come, and rejoiced in the hope of his coming, they should be careful to avoid the error, and the evil consequences of it, against which he was now cautioning them. From this form of obtestation used by the apostle, we may observe,

1. It is most certain that the Lord Jesus Christ will come to judge the world, that he will come in all the pomp and power of the upper world in the last day, to execute judgment upon all. Whatever uncertainty we are at, or whatever mistakes may arise about the time of his coming, his coming itself is certain. This has been the faith and hope of all Christians in all ages of the church ; nay, it was the faith and hope of the Old Testament saints, ever since Enoch the seventh from Adam, who said, *Behold, the Lord cometh,* &c., Jude 14.

2. At the second coming of Christ all the saints will be gathered together to him ; and this mention of the gathering of the saints together unto Christ at his coming shows that the apostle speaks of Christ's coming to judgment at the last day, and not of his coming to destroy Jerusalem. He speaks of a proper, and not a metaphorical advent : and, as it will be part of Christ's honour in that day, so it will be the completing of the happiness of his saints. (1.) That they all shall be gathered together. There will then be a general meeting of all the saints, and none but saints ; all the Old-Testament saints, who got acquaintance with Christ by the dark shadows of the law, and saw this day at a distance ; and all the New-Testament saints, to whom life and immortality were brought to light by the gospel ; they will all be gathered together. There will then come from the four winds of heaven all that are, or ever were, or ever shall be, from the beginning to the end of time. All shall be gathered together. (2.) That they shall be gathered *together to Christ.* He will be the great centre of their unity. They shall be gathered together to him, to be attendants on him, to be assessors with him, to be presented by him to the Father, to be with him for ever, and altogether happy in his presence to all eternity. (3.) The doctrine of Christ's coming and our gathering together to him is of great moment and importance to Christians ; otherwise it would not be the proper matter of the apostle's obtestation. We ought therefore not only to believe these things, but highly to account of them also, and look upon them as things we are greatly concerned in and should be much affected with.

II. The thing itself against which the apostle cautions the Thessalonians is that they should not be deceived about the time of Christ's coming, and so *be shaken in mind, or be troubled.* Note, Errors in the mind tend greatly to weaken our faith, and cause us trouble ; and such as are weak in faith and of troubled minds are oftentimes apt to be deceived, and fall a prey to seducers. 1. The apostle would not have them be deceived : *Let no man deceive you by any means, v.* 3. There are many who lie in wait to deceive, and they have many ways of deceiving ; we have reason therefore to be cautious and stand upon our guard. Some deceivers will pretend new revelations, others misinterpret scripture, and others will be guilty of gross forgeries ; divers means and artifices of deceit men will use ; but we must be careful that no man deceive us by any means. The particular matter in which the apostle cautions them not to be deceived is about the near approach of Christ's coming, as if it was to have been in the apostle's days ; and harmless as this error might seem to many, yet because it was indeed an error, it would have proved of bad consequence to many persons. Therefore, 2. He gives them warning, and would not have them be soon shaken in mind, nor be troubled. (1.) He would not have their faith weakened. We should firmly believe the second coming of Christ, and be settled and established in the faith of this ; but there was danger lest the Thessalonians, if they apprehended the coming of Christ was just at hand, upon finding that they, or others whom they too much regarded, were mistaken as to the time, should thereupon question the truth or certainty of the thing itself ; whereas they ought not to waver in their minds as to this great thing, which is the faith and hope of all the saints. False doctrines are like the winds, that toss the water to and fro, and they are apt to unsettle the minds of men, who are sometimes as unstable as water. Then, (2.) He would not have their comforts lessened, that they should not be troubled nor affrighted with false alarms. It is probable that the coming of Christ was represented in so much terror as to trouble many serious Christians among them, though in itself it should be matter of the believer's hope and joy ; or else many might be troubled with the thought how surprising this day would be, or with the fear of their unpreparedness, or upon the reflection on their mistake about the time of Christ's coming : we should always watch and pray, but must not be discouraged nor uncomfortable at the thought of Christ's coming.

³ —For *that day shall not come*, except there come a falling away first, and that man of sin be revealed, the son of perdition ; ⁴ Who opposeth and exalteth himself above all that is called God, or that is worshipped ; so that he as God sitteth in the temple of God, showing himself that he is [**setting himself forth as**] God. ⁵ Remember ye not, that, when I was yet with you, I told you these things ? ⁶ And now ye know what withholdeth [**that which restraineth**] that he might be revealed in his time. ⁷ For the mystery of iniquity doth already work only he who now letteth *will let* [**only there is one who restraineth now**], until he be taken out of the way. ⁸ And then shall that Wicked [**the lawless one**] be revealed, whom the Lord shall consume with the spirit of his mouth, and shall destroy with the brightness of his coming : ⁹ *Even him*, whose coming is after the working of Satan with all power and signs

and lying wonders, [10] And with all deceivableness of unrighteousness in [for] them that perish ; because they received not
the love of the truth, that they might be saved. [11] And for
this cause God shall send them strong delusion [a working of
error], that they should believe a lie : [12] That they all might
be damned [judged] who believed not the truth, but had pleasure
in unrighteousness.

In these words the apostle confutes the error against which he had
cautioned them, and gives the reasons why they should not expect the
coming of Christ as just at hand. There were several events previous to
the second coming of Christ ; in particular, he tells them there would be
I. A general apostasy, *there would come a falling away first, v. 3.* By
this apostasy we are not to understand a defection in the state, or from
civil government, but in spiritual or religious matters, from sound doctrine,
instituted worship and church government, and a holy life. The apostle
speaks of some very great apostasy, not only of some converted Jews or
Gentiles, but such as should be very general, though gradual, and should
give occasion to the revelation or rise of *antichrist,* that *man of sin.* This,
he says (*v. 5*), he had told them of when he was with them, with design,
no doubt, that they should not take offence nor be stumbled at it. And
let us observe that no sooner was Christianity planted and rooted in the
world than there began to be a defection in the Christian church. It was
so in the Old-Testament church ; presently after any considerable advance
made in religion there followed a defection : soon after the promise there
was revolting ; for example, soon after men began to call upon the name
of the Lord all flesh corrupted their way,—soon after the covenant with
Noah the Babel-builders bade defiance to heaven,—soon after the covenant
with Abraham his seed degenerated in Egypt,—soon after the Israelites
were planted in Canaan, when the first generation was worn off, they forsook God and served Baal,—soon after God's covenant with David his
seed revolted, and served other gods,—soon after the return out of captivity
there was a general decay of piety, as appears by the story of Ezra and
Nehemiah ; and therefore it was no strange thing that after the planting
of Christianity there should come a falling away.
II. A revelation of that man of sin, that is (*v. 3*), antichrist would take
his rise from this general apostasy. The apostle afterwards speaks of the
revelation of that wicked one (*v. 8*), intimating the discovery which should
be made of his wickedness, in order to his ruin : here he seems to speak of
his rise, which should be occasioned by the general apostasy he had mentioned, and to intimate that all sorts of false doctrines and corruptions
should centre in him. Great disputes have been as to who or what is intended by this man of sin and son of perdition : and, if it be not certain
that the papal power and tyranny are principally or only intended, yet
this is plain. What is here said does very exactly agree thereto. For
observe,
    1. The names of this person, or rather the state and power here spoken
of. He is called the man of sin, to denote his egregious wickedness ; not
only is he addicted to, and practises, wickedness himself, but he also promotes, countenances, and commands sin and wickedness in others ; and he
is the son of perdition, because he himself is devoted to certain destruc-

tion, and is the instrument of destroying many others both in soul and body. These names may properly be applied, for these reasons, to the papal state ; and thereto agree also,

2. The characters here given, *v.* 4. (1.) That he *opposes and exalts him-self above all that is called God, or is worshipped ;* and thus have the bishops of Rome not only opposed God's authority, and that of the civil magistrates, who are called gods, but have exalted themselves above God and earthly governors, in demanding greater regard to their commands than to the commands of God or the magistrate. (2.) *As God, he sits in the temple of God, showing himself that he is God.* As God was in the temple of old, and worshipped there, and is in and with his church now, so the antichrist here mentioned is some usurper of God's authority in the Christian church, who claims divine honours ; and to whom can this better apply than to the bishops of Rome, to whom the most blasphemous titles have been given, as *Dominus Deus noster papa—Our Lord God the pope ; Deus alter in terrâ—Another God on earth ; Idem est dominium Dei et papœ—The dominion of God and the pope is the same ?*

3. His rise is mentioned, *v.* 6, 7. Concerning this we are to observe two things :—(1.) There was something that hindered or withheld, or *let, until it was taken away.* This is supposed to be the power of the Roman empire, which the apostle did not think fit to mention more plainly at that time ; and it is notorious that, while this power continued, it prevented the advances of the bishops of Rome to that height of tyranny to which soon afterwards they arrived. (2.) This mystery of iniquity was gradually to arrive at its height ; and so it was in effect that the universal corruption of doctrine and worship in the Romish church came in by degrees, and the usurpation of the bishops of Rome was gradual, not all at once ; and thus the mystery of iniquity did the more easily, and almost insensibly, prevail. The apostle justly calls it a *mystery of iniquity,* because wicked designs and actions were concealed under false shows and pretences, at least they were concealed from the common view and observation. By pretended devotion, superstition and idolatry were advanced ; and, by a pretended zeal for God and his glory, bigotry and persecution were promoted. And he tells us that this mystery of iniquity did even then begin, or did *already work.* While the apostles were yet living, *the enemy came, and sowed tares ;* there were then the *deeds of the Nicolaitans,* persons who pretended zeal for Christ, but really opposed him. Pride, ambition, and worldly interest of church-pastors and church-rulers, as in Diotrephes and others, were the early working of the mystery of iniquity, which, by degrees, came to that prodigious height which has been visible in the church of Rome.

4. The fall or ruin of the antichristian state is declared, *v.* 8. The head of this antichristian kingdom is called *that wicked one,* or that lawless person who sets up a human power in competition with, and contradiction to, the divine dominion and power of the Lord Jesus Christ ; but, as he would thus manifest himself to be the man of sin, so the revelation or discovery of this to the world would be the sure presage and the means of his ruin. The apostle assures the Thessalonians that the Lord would consume and destroy him ; the consuming of him precedes his final destruction, and that is by the *Spirit of his mouth,* by his word of command ; the pure word of God, accompanied with the Spirit of God, will discover this mystery of iniquity, and make the power of antichrist to consume and waste away ; and in due time it will be totally and finally destroyed, and this will be by the brightness of Christ's coming. Note, The coming of

Christ to destroy the wicked will he with peculiar glory and eminent lustre and brightness.

5. The apostle further describes the reign and rule of this man of sin. Here we are to observe, (1.) The manner of his coming, or ruling, and working : in general, that it is after the example of Satan, the grand enemy of souls, the great adversary of God and man. He is the great patron of error and lies, the sworn enemy of the truth as it is in Jesus and all the faithful followers of Jesus. More particularly, it is with Satanical power and deceit. A divine power is pretended for the support of this kingdom, but it is only after the working of Satan. Signs and wonders, visions and miracles, are pretended ; by these the papal kingdom was first set up, and has all along been kept up, but they have false signs to support false doctrines ; and lying wonders, or only pretended miracles that have served their cause, things false in fact, or fraudulently managed, to impose upon the people : and the diabolical deceits with which the antichristian state has been supported are notorious. The apostle calls it *all deceivableness of unrighteousness, v.* 10. Others may call them pious frauds, but the apostle called them unrighteous and wicked frauds ; and, indeed, all fraud (which is contrary to truth) is an impious thing. Many are the subtle artifices the man of sin has used, and various are the plausible pretences by which he has beguiled unwary and unstable souls to embrace false doctrines, and submit to his usurped dominion. (2.) The persons are described who are his willing subjects, or most likely to become such, *v.* 10. They are such as *love not the truth that they may be saved.* They heard the truth (it may be), but they did not love it ; they could not bear sound doctrine, and therefore easily imbibed false doctrines ; they had some notional knowledge of what was true, but they indulged some powerful prejudices, and so became a prey to seducers. Had they loved the truth, they would have persevered in it, and been preserved by it ; but no wonder if they easily parted with what they never had any love to. And of these persons it is said that they perish or are lost ; they are in a lost condition, and in danger to be lost for ever. For,

6. We have the *sin and ruin of the subjects* of antichrist's kingdom declared, *v.* 11, 12. (1.) Their sin is this : *They believed not the truth, but had pleasure in unrighteousness :* they did not love the truth, and therefore they did not believe it ; and, because they did not believe the truth, therefore they had pleasure in unrighteousness, or in wicked actions, and were pleased with false notions. Note, An erroneous mind and vicious life often go together and help forward one another. (2.) Their ruin is thus expressed : *God shall send them strong delusions, to believe a lie.* Thus he will punish men for their unbelief, and for their dislike of the truth and love to sin and wickedness ; not that God is the author of sin, but in righteousness he sometimes withdraws his grace from such sinners as are here mentioned ; he gives them over to Satan, or leaves them to be deluded by his instruments ; he gives them up to their own hearts' lusts, and leaves them to themselves, and then sin will follow of course, yea, the worst of wickedness, that shall end at last in eternal damnation. God is just when he inflicts spiritual judgments here, and eternal punishments hereafter, upon those who have no love to the truths of the gospel, who will not believe them, nor live suitably to them, but indulge false doctrines in their minds, and wicked practices in their lives and conversations.

13 But we are bound to give thanks alway to God for you

brethren beloved of the Lord, because God hath from the
beginning chosen you to salvation through sanctification of the
Spirit and belief of the truth :   14 Whereunto he called you by
our gospel to the obtaining of the glory of our Lord Jesus
Christ.   15 Therefore, brethren, stand fast, and hold the traditions which ye have been taught, whether by word, or our
epistle.

Here observe, I. The consolation the Thessalonians might take against
the terrors of this apostasy, v. 13, 14. For they were chosen to salvation,
and called to the obtaining of glory. Note, When we hear of the apostasy
of many, it is matter of great comfort and joy that there is a remnant
according to the election of grace which does and shall persevere ; and
especially we should rejoice if we have reason to hope that we are of that
number. The apostle reckoned himself bound in duty to be thankful to
God on this account : *We are bound to give thanks to God always for you.*
He had often given thanks on their behalf, and he is still abounding in
thanksgiving for them ; and there was good reason, because they were
beloved by the Lord, as appeared in this matter—their security from
apostatizing. This preservation of the saints is owing,

1. To the stability of the election of grace, v. 13. Therefore were they
beloved of the Lord, because God had chosen them from the beginning.
He had loved them with an everlasting love. Concerning this election of
God we may observe, (1.) The eternal date of it—it is from the beginning ;
not the beginning of the gospel, but the beginning of the world, before the
foundation of the world, Eph. i. 4. Then, (2.) The end to which they were
chosen—salvation, complete and eternal salvation from sin and misery, and
the full fruition of all good. (3.) The means in order to obtaining this end
—*sanctification of the spirit and belief of the truth.* The decree of election
therefore connects the end and the means, and these must not be separated.
We are not elected of God because we were holy, but that we might be
holy. Being chosen of God, we must not live as we list ; but, if we are
chosen to salvation as the end, we must be prepared for it by sanctification
as the necessary means to obtain that end, which sanctification is by the
operation of the Holy Spirit as the author, and by faith on our part. There
must be the belief of the truth, without which there can be no true sanctification, nor perseverance in grace, nor obtaining of salvation. Faith and
holiness must be joined together, as well as holiness and happiness ; therefore our Saviour prayed for Peter that his faith might not fail (Luke xxii.
32), and for his disciples (John xvii. 17), *Sanctify them by thy truth ; thy
word is truth.*

2. To the efficacy of the gospel call, v. 14. As they were chosen to
salvation, so they were called thereunto by the gospel. Whom he did
predestinate those he also called, Rom. viii. 30. The outward call of God
is by the gospel ; and this is rendered effectual by the inward operation of
the Spirit. Note, Wherever the gospel comes it calls and invites men to
the obtaining of glory : it is a call to honour and happiness, even the *glory
of our Lord Jesus Christ,* the glory he has purchased, and the glory he is
possessed of, to be communicated unto those who believe in him and obey
his gospel ; such shall be with Christ, to behold his glory, and they shall
be glorified with Christ and partake of his glory. Hereupon there follows,

II. An exhortation to stedfastness and perseverance : *Therefore, brethren, stand fast, v.* 15. Observe, He does not say, "You are chosen to salvation, and therefore you may be careless and secure;" but *therefore stand fast.* God's grace in our election and vocation is so far from superseding our diligent care and endeavour that it should quicken and engage us to the greatest resolution and diligence. So the apostle John having told those to whom he wrote that they had received the anointing which should abide in them, and that they should abide in him (in Christ), subjoins this exhortation, *Now abide in him,* 1 John ii. 27, 28. The Thessalonians are exhorted to stedfastness in their Christian profession, to *hold fast the traditions which they had been taught,* or the doctrine of the gospel, which had been delivered by the apostle, by word or epistle. As yet the canon of scripture was not complete, and therefore some things were delivered by the apostles in their preaching, under the guidance of the infallible Spirit, which Christians were bound to observe as coming from God; other things were afterwards by them committed to writing, as the apostle had written a former epistle to these Thessalonians; and these epistles were written as the writers were moved by the Holy Ghost. Note, There is no argument hence for regarding oral traditions in our days, now that the canon of scripture is complete, as of equal authority with the sacred writings. Such doctrines and duties as were taught by the inspired apostles we must stedfastly adhere to; but we have no certain evidence of any thing delivered by them more than what we find contained in the holy scriptures.

16 Now our Lord Jesus Christ himself, and God, even our Father, which hath loved us, and hath given *us* everlasting consolation and good hope through grace, 17 Comfort your hearts, and stablish you in every good word and work.

In these words we have the apostle's earnest prayer for them, in which observe,

I. To whom he prays: *Our Lord Jesus Christ himself, and God, even our Father.* We may and should direct our prayers, not only to God the Father, through the mediation of our Lord Jesus Christ, but also *to our Lord Jesus Christ himself;* and should pray in his name unto God, not only as his Father but as our Father in and through him.

II. From what he takes encouragement in his prayer—from the consideration of what God had already done for him and them: *Who hath loved us, and given us everlasting consolation and good hope through grace, v.* 16. Here observe, 1. The love of God is the spring and fountain of all the good we have or hope for; our election, vocation, justification, and salvation, are all owing to the love of God in Christ Jesus. 2. From this fountain in particular all our consolation flows. And the consolation of the saints is an everlasting consolation. The comforts of the saints are not dying things; they shall not die with them. The spiritual consolations God gives none shall deprive them of; and God will not take them away: because he loves them with an everlasting love, therefore they shall have everlasting consolations. 3. Their consolation is founded on the hope of eternal life. They rejoice in hope of the glory of God, and are not only patient, but joyful, in tribulations; and there is good reason for these strong consolations, because the saints have good hope: their hope is grounded on the love of God, the promise of God, and the experience they have had of the power, the goodness, and the faithfulness of God, and it is good hope through grace; the free grace and mercy of God are what they hope for, and what their hopes are founded on, and not on any worth or merit of their own.

III. What it is that he asks of God for them—that *he would comfort their hearts, and establish them in every good word and work, v.* 17. God had given them consolations, and he prayed that they might have more abundant consolation. There was good hope, through grace, that they would be preserved, and he prayed that they might be established: it is observable how comfort and establishment are here joined together. Note therefore, 1. Comfort is a means of establishment; for the more pleasure we take in the word, and work, and ways of God, the more likely we shall be to persevere therein. And, 2. Our establishment in the ways of God is a likely means in order to comfort; whereas, if we are wavering in faith, and of a doubtful mind, or if we are halting and faltering in our duty, no wonder if we are strangers to the pleasures and joys of religion. What is it that lies at the bottom of all our uneasiness, but our unsteadiness in religion? We must be established in every good word and work, in the word of truth and the work of righteousness: Christ must be honoured by our good works and good words; and those who are sincere will endeavour to do both, and in so doing they may hope for comfort and establishment, till at length their holiness and happiness be completed.

CHAPTER III

In the close of the foregoing chapter, the apostle had prayed earnestly for the Thessalonians, and now he desires their prayers, encouraging them to trust in God, to which he subjoins another petition for them, ver. 1-5. He then proceeds to give them commands and directions for correcting some things he was informed were amiss among them, ver. 6-15, and concludes with benedictions and prayers, ver. 16-18.

FINALLY, brethren, pray for us, that the word of the Lord may have *free* course, [may run] and be glorified, even as *it is* with you: ² And that we may be delivered from unreasonable and wicked men; for all *men* have not faith. ³ But the Lord is faithful, who shall stablish you, and keep *you* from evil. ⁴ And we have confidence in the Lord touching you, that ye both do and will do the things which we command you. ⁵ And the Lord direct your hearts into the love of God, and into the patient waiting for [patience of] Christ.

In these words observe,

I. The apostle desires the prayers of his friends. *Finally, brethren, pray for us, v.* 1. He always remembered them in his prayers, and would not have them forget him and his fellow-labourers, but bear them on their hearts at the throne of grace. Note, 1. This is one way by which the communion of saints is kept up, not only by their praying together, or with one another, but by their praying for one another when they are absent one from another. And thus those who are at a great distance may meet together at the throne of grace ; and thus those who are not capable of doing or receiving any other kindness may yet this way do and receive real and very great kindness. 2. It is the duty of people to pray for their ministers ; and not only for their own pastors, but also for all good and faithful ministers. And, 3. Ministers need, and therefore should desire, the prayers of their people. How remarkable is the humility, and how engaging the example, of this great apostle, who was so mighty in prayer himself, and yet despised not the prayers of the meanest Christian, but desired an interest in them. Observe, further, what they are desired and directed to pray for ; namely, (1.) For the success of the gospel ministry : *That the word of the Lord may have free course, and be glorified, v.* 1. This was the great thing that Paul was most solicitous about. He was more solicitous that God's name might be sanctified, his kingdom advanced, and his will done, than he was about his own daily bread. He desired that the word of the Lord might run (so it is in the original) that it might get ground, that the interest of religion in the world might go forward and not backward, and not only go forward, but go apace. All the forces of hell were then, and still are, more or less, raised and mustered to oppose the word of the Lord, to hinder its publication and success. We should pray, therefore, that oppositions may be removed, that so the gospel may have free course to the ears, the hearts, and the consciences of men, that it may be glorified in the conviction and conversion of sinners, the confutation of gainsayers, and the holy conversation of the saints. God, who magnified the law, and made it honourable, will glorify the gospel, and make that honourable, and so will glorify his own name ; and good ministers and good Christians may very well be contented to be little, to be any thing, to be nothing, if Christ be magnified and his gospel be glorified. Paul was now at Athens, or as some think, at Corinth, and would have the Thessalonians pray that he might have as good success there as he had at Thessalonica, that it might be as well with others even as it was with them. Note, If ministers have been successful in one place, they should desire to be successful in every place where they may preach the gospel. (2.) For the safety of gospel ministers. He asks their prayers, not for preferment, but for preservation : *That we may be delivered from unreasonable and wicked men, v.* 2. Note, Those who are enemies to the preaching of the gospel, and persecutors of the faithful preachers of it, are unreasonable and wicked men. They act against all the rules and laws of reason and religion, and are guilty of the greatest absurdity and impiety. Not only in the principles of atheism and infidelity, but also in the practice of vice and immorality, and especially in persecution, there is the greatest absurdity in the world, as well as impiety. There is need of the spiritual protection, as well as the assistance, of godly and faithful ministers, for these are as the standard-bearers, who are most struck at, and therefore all who wish well to the interest of Christ in the world should pray for them. *For all men have not faith ;* that is, many do not believe the gospel ; they will not embrace it themselves, and no wonder if such are restless and malicious in their endeavours to oppose the gospel, decry the ministry, and disgrace the ministers of the word ; and too many have not common faith or honesty; there is no confidence that we can safely put in them, and we should pray to be delivered from those who have no conscience nor honour, who never regard what they say or do. We may sometimes be in as much or more danger from false and pretended friends as from open and avowed enemies.

II. He encourages them to trust in God. We should not only pray to God for his grace, but also place our trust and confidence in his grace, and humbly expect what we pray for. Observe,

1. What the good is which we may expect from the grace of God—establishment, and preservation from evil; and the best Christians stand in need of these benefits. (1.) That God would establish them. This the apostle had prayed for on their behalf (*ch.* ii. 17), and now he encourages them to expect this favour. We stand no longer than God holds us up ; unless he *hold up our goings in his paths, our feet will slide,* and we shall fall. (2.) That God will keep them from evil. We have as much need of the grace of God for our perseverance to the end as for the beginning of the good work. The evil of sin is the greatest evil, but there are other evils which God will also preserve his saints from—the evil that is in the world, yea, from all evil, to his heavenly kingdom.

2. What encouragement we have to depend upon the grace of God : *The Lord is faithful.* He is faithful to his promises, and is the Lord who cannot lie, who will not alter the thing that has gone out of his mouth. When once the promise therefore is made, performance is sure and certain. He is faithful to his relation, a faithful God and a faithful friend ; we may depend upon his filling up all the relations he stands in to his people. Let it be our care to be true and faithful in our promises, and to the relations we stand in to this faithful God. He adds,

3. A further ground of hope that God would do this for them, seeing they did and would do the things they were commanded, *v.* 4. The apostle had this confidence in them, and this was founded upon his confidence in God ; for there is otherwise no confidence in man. Their obedience is described by doing what he and his fellow-labourers had commanded them, which was no other thing than the commandments of the Lord ; for the apostles themselves had no further commission than to teach men *to observe and to do what the Lord had commanded,* Matt. xxviii. 20. And as the experience the apostle had of their obedience for the time past was one ground of his confidence that they would do the things commanded them for the time to come, so this is one ground to hope that *whatsoever we ask of God we shall receive of him, because we keep his commandments, and do those things that are pleasing in his sight,* 1 John iii. 22.

III. He makes a short prayer for them, *v.* 5. It is a prayer for spiritual blessings. Two things of the greatest importance the apostle prays for :—
1. That their hearts may be brought into the love of God, to be in love with God as the most excellent and amiable Being, the best of all beings ; and this is not only most reasonable and necessary in order to our happiness, but is our happiness itself ; it is a great part of the happiness of heaven itself, where this love shall be made perfect. We can never attain to this unless God by his grace direct our hearts aright, for our love is apt to go astray after other things. Note, We sustain a great deal of damage by misplacing our affections ; it is our sin and our misery that we place our affections upon wrong objects. If God direct our love aright upon himself, the rest of the affections will thereby be rectified. 2. That a *patient waiting for Christ* may be joined with this love of God. There is no true love of God without faith in Jesus Christ. We must wait for Christ, which supposes our faith in him, that we believe he came once in flesh and will come again in glory : and we must expect this second coming

of Christ, and be careful to get ready for it ; there must be a patient waiting, enduring with courage and constancy all that we may meet with in
the meantime : and we *have need of patience,* and need of divine grace to
exercise Christian patience, the *patience of Christ* (as some read the word),
patience for Christ's sake and after Christ's example.

⁶ Now we command you, brethren, in the name of our Lord
Jesus Christ, that ye withdraw yourselves from every brother that
walketh disorderly, and not after the tradition which he received
of us.   ⁷ For yourselves know how ye ought to follow us : for
we behaved not ourselves disorderly among you ; ⁸ Neither did
we eat any man's bread for nought ; but wrought with labour
and travail night and day, that we might not be chargeable to
any of you : ⁹ Not because we have not power, but to make
ourselves an ensample unto you to follow us.   ¹⁰ For even when
we were with you, this we commanded you, that if any would
not work, neither should he eat.   ¹¹ For we hear that there are
some which walk among you disorderly, not working at all, but
are busybodies.   ¹² Now them that are such we command and
exhort by our Lord Jesus Christ, that with quietness they work,
and eat their own bread.   ¹³ But ye, brethren, be not weary in
well doing.   ¹⁴ And if any man obey not our word by this
epistle, note that man, and have no company with him, that he
may be ashamed.   ¹⁵ Yet count *him* not as an enemy, but
admonish *him* as a brother.

The apostle having commended their obedience for the time past, and
mentioned his confidence in their obedience for the time to come, proceeds
to give them commands and directions to some who were faulty, correcting
some things that were amiss among them. Observe, The best society of
Christians may have some faulty persons among them, and some things
that ought to be reformed.   Perfection is not to be found on this side
heaven : but evil manners beget good laws ; the disorders that Paul heard
of as existing among the Thessalonians occasioned the good laws we find
in these verses, which are of constant use to us, and all others whom they
may concern. Observe,

I. That which was amiss among the Thessalonians, which is expressed,

1. More generally.   There were some who *walked disorderly, not after the
tradition they received* from the apostle, *v.* 6.   Some of the brethren were
guilty of this disorderly walking ; they did not live regularly, nor govern
themselves according to the rules of Christianity, nor agreeably to their
profession of religion ; not according to the precepts delivered by the
apostle, which they had received, and pretended to pay a regard to.   Note,
It is required of those who have received the gospel, and who profess a
subjection to it, that they live according to the gospel.   If they do not,
they are to be counted disorderly persons.

2. In particular, there were among them some *idle persons and busy-
bodies, v.* 11.   This the apostle was so credibly informed of that he had
sufficient reason to give commands and directions with relation to such

persons, how they ought to behave, and how the church should **act** towards them. (1.) There were some among them who were idle, *not working at all*, or doing nothing. It does not appear that they were gluttons or drunkards, but idle, and therefore disorderly people. It is not enough for any to say they do no hurt, for it is required of all persons that they do good in the places and relations in which Providence has placed them. It is probable that these persons had a notion (by misunderstanding some passages in the former epistle) concerning the near approach of the coming of Christ, which served them for a pretence to leave off the work of their callings, and live in idleness. Note, It is a great error, or abuse of religion, to make it a cloak for idleness or any other sin. If we were sure that the day of judgment were ever so near, we must, notwithstanding, do the work of the day in its day, that when our Lord comes he may find us so doing. The servant who waits for the coming of his Lord aright must be working as his Lord has commanded, that all may be ready when he comes. Or, it may be, these disorderly persons pretended that the liberty wherewith Christ had made them free discharged them from the services and business of their particular callings and employments in the world : whereas they were *to abide in the same calling wherein they were called of God, and therein abide with God*, 1 Cor. vii. 20, 24. Industry in our particular callings as men is a duty required of us by our general calling as Christians. Or perhaps the general charity there was then among Christians to their poor brethren encouraged some to live in idleness, as knowing the church would maintain them : whatever was the cause, they were much to blame. (2.) There were busy-bodies among them : and it should seem, by the connection, that the same persons who were idle were busy-bodies also. This may seem to be a contradiction ; but so it is, that most commonly those persons who have no business of their own to do, or who neglect it, busy themselves in other men's matters. If we are idle, the devil and a corrupt heart will soon find us something to do. The mind of man is a busy thing ; if it be not employed in doing good, it will be doing evil. Note, Busy-bodies are disorderly walkers, such as are guilty of vain curiosity, and impertinent, meddling with things that do not concern them, and troubling themselves and others with other men's matters. The apostle warns Timothy (1 Tim. v. 13) to beware of such *as learn to be idle, wandering about from house to house and are not only idle, but tatlers also and busy-bodies, speaking things which they ought not*.

II. The good laws which were occasioned by these evil manners, concerning which we may take notice,

1. Whose laws they are : they are commands of the apostles of our Lord, given in the name of their Lord and ours, that is, the commands of our Lord himself. *We command you, brethren, in the name of the Lord Jesus Christ, v. 6.* Again, *We command and exhort you by our Lord Jesus Christ, v. 12.* The apostle uses words of authority and entreaty : and, where disorders are to be rectified or prevented, there is need of both. The authority of Christ should awe our minds to obedience, and his grace and goodness should allure us.

2. What the good laws and rules are. The apostle gives directions to the whole church, commands to those disorderly, persons, and an exhortation to those in particular who did well among them.

(1.) His commands and directions to the whole church regard, [1.] Their behaviour towards the disorderly, persons who were among them, which is thus expressed (*v. 6*), to *withdraw themselves from such*, and afterwards to *mark that man, and have no company with him, that he may be ashamed; yet not to count him as an enemy, but to admonish him as a brother.* The directions of the apostle are carefully to be observed in our conduct towards disorderly persons. We must be very cautious in church-censures and church-discipline. We must, *First,* Note that man who is suspected or charged with not obeying the word of God, or walking contrary thereto, that is, we must have sufficient proof of his fault before we proceed further. We must, *Secondly,* Admonish him in a friendly manner; we must put him in mind of his sin, and of his duty; and this should be done privately (Matt. xviii. 15); then, if he will not hear, we must, *Thirdly,* Withdraw from him, and not keep company with him, that is, we must avoid familiar converse and society with such, for two reasons, namely, that we may not learn his evil ways; for he who follows vain and idle persons, and keeps company with such, is in danger of becoming like them. Another reason is for the shaming, and so the reforming, of those that offend, that when idle and disorderly persons see how their loose practices are disliked by all wise and good people they may be ashamed of them, and walk more orderly. Love therefore to the persons of our offending brethren, even when we hate their vices, should be the motive of our withdrawing from them; and even those who are under the censures of the church must not be accounted as enemies (*v.* 15); for, if they be reclaimed and reformed by these censures, they will recover their credit and comfort, and right to church-privileges as brethren. [2.] Their general conduct and behaviour ought to be according to the good example the apostle and those who were with him had given them: *Yourselves know how you ought to follow us, v.* 7. Those who planted religion among them had set a good example before them; and the ministers of the gospel should be ensamples to the flock. It is the duty of Christians not only to walk according to the traditions of the apostles, and the doctrines they preached, but also according to the good example they set before them, *to be followers of them so far as they were followers of Christ.* The particular good example the apostle mentions was their diligence, which was so different from what was found in the disorderly walkers he takes notice of: " *We behaved not ourselves disorderly among you* (*v.* 7), we did not spend our time idly, in idle visits, idle talk, idle sports." They took pains in their ministry, in preaching the gospel, and in getting their own living. *Neither did we eat any man's bread for nought, v.* 8. Though he might justly have demanded a maintenance, because those who preach the gospel may of right expect to live by the gospel. This is a just debt that people owe to their ministers, and the apostle had power or authority to have demanded this (*v.* 9); but he waived his right from affection to them, and for the sake of the gospel, and that he might be an example for them to follow (*v.* 9), that they might learn how to fill up time, and always be employed in something that would turn to good account.

(2.) He commands and directs those that lived idle lives to reform, and set themselves to their business. He had given commandments to this purport, as well as a good example of this, when he was among them, *Even when we were with you, this we commanded you, that if any man would not work neither should he eat, v.* 10. It was a proverbial speech among the Jews, *He who does not labour does not deserve to eat.* The labourer is worthy of his meat; but what is the loiterer worthy of? It is the will of God that every man should have a calling, and mind his calling, and make a business of it, and that none should live like useless drones in the world. Such persons do what in them lies to defeat the sentence, *In the sweat of thy face shalt thou eat thy bread.* It was not the mere humour of the apostle, who was an active stirring man himself and therefore would have everybody else to be so too, but it was the command of our Lord Jesus Christ, that *with quietness we work and eat our own bread, v. 12.* Men ought some way or other to earn their own living, otherwise they do not eat their own bread. Observe, There must be work or labour, in opposition to idleness ; and there must be quietness, in opposition to being busy-bodies in other men's matters. We must study to be quiet, and do our own business. This is an excellent but rare composition, to be of an active yet quiet spirit, active in our own business and yet quiet as to other people's.

(3.) He exhorts *those that did well not* to be *weary in well-doing (v. 13)* ; as if he had said, " Go on and prosper. The Lord is with you while you are with him. See that whatever you do, that is good, you persevere therein. Hold on your way, and hold out to the end. You must never give over, nor tire in your work. It will be time enough to rest when you come to heaven, that *everlasting rest which remains for the people of God.*"

16 Now the Lord of peace himself give you peace always by all means [in all ways]. The Lord *be* with you all.   17 The salutation of Paul with mine own hand, which is the token in every epistle : so I write.   18 The grace of our Lord Jesus Christ *be* with you all.   Amen.

In this conclusion of the epistle we have the apostle's benediction and prayers for these Thessalonians. Let us desire them for ourselves and our friends. There are three blessings pronounced upon them, or desired for them :

I. That God would give them peace. Note, 1. Peace is the blessing pronounced or desired. By peace we may understand all manner of prosperity ; here it may signify, in particular, peace with God, peace in their own minds and consciences, peace among themselves, and peace with all men. 2. This peace is desired for them always, or in every thing ; and he desired they might have all good things at all times. 3. Peace by all means : that, as they enjoyed the means of grace, they might with success use all the means and methods of peace too ; for peace is often difficult, as it is always desirable. 4. That God would give them peace, who is the Lord of peace. If we have any peace that is desirable, God must give it, who is the *author of peace and lover of concord.* We shall neither have peaceable dispositions ourselves nor find men disposed to be at peace with us, unless the God of peace give us both.

II. That the presence of God might be with them : *The Lord be with you all.* We need nothing more to make us safe and happy, nor can we desire any thing better for ourselves and our friends, than to have God's gracious presence with us and them. This will be a guide and guard in every way that we may go, and our comfort in every condition we may be in. It is the presence of God that makes heaven to be heaven, and this will make this earth to be like heaven. No matter where we are if God be with us, nor who is absent if God be present with us.

III. That the *grace of our Lord Jesus Christ might be with them.* So this apostle concluded his first epistle to these Thessalonians ; and it is through the grace of our Lord Jesus Christ that we may comfortably hope to have peace with God and enjoy the presence of God, for he has made those nigh that were afar off. It is this grace that is all in all to make us happy. This is what the apostle admired and magnified on all occasions, what he delighted and trusted in ; and by this salutation or benediction, written with his own hand, as the token of every epistle (when the rest was written by an amanuensis), he took care lest the churches he wrote to should be imposed on by counterfeit epistles, which he knew would be of dangerous consequence.

Let us be thankful that we have the canon of scripture complete, and by the wonderful and special care of divine Providence preserved pure and uncorrupt through so many successive ages, and not dare to add to it, nor diminish from it. Let us believe the divine original of the sacred scriptures, and conform our faith and practice to this our sufficient and only rule, *which is able to make us wise unto salvation, through faith which is in Christ Jesus.* Amen.

EXPOSITION OF THE FIRST EPISTLE
OF ST. PAUL TO TIMOTHY

HITHERTO Paul's epistles were directed to churches; now follow some to
particular persons: two to Timothy, one to Titus, and another to
Philemon—all three ministers. Timothy and Titus were evangelists,
an inferior order to the apostles, as appears by Eph. iv. 11, *Some prophets, some apostles, some evangelists.* Their commission and work was
much the same with that of the apostles, to plant churches, and water
the churches that were planted; and accordingly they were itinerants,
as we find Timothy was. Timothy was first converted by Paul, and
therefore he calls him his *own son in the faith:* we read of his conversion,
Acts xvi. 3.

The scope of these two epistles is to direct Timothy how to discharge his duty
as an evangelist at Ephesus, where he now was, and where Paul ordered
him for some time to reside, to perfect the good work which he had
begun there. As for the ordinary pastoral charge of that church, he
had very solemnly committed it to the presbytery, as appears from
Acts xx. 28, where he charges the presbyters *to feed the flock of God,
which he had purchased with his own blood.*

CHAPTER I

After the inscription (ver. 1, 2) we have, I. The charge given to Timothy, ver. 3, 4. II. The
true end of the law (ver. 5-11), where he shows that it is entirely agreeable to the gospel.
III. He mentions his own call to be an apostle, for which he expresses his thankfulness,
ver. 12-16. IV. His doxology, ver. 17. V. A renewal of the charge to Timothy, ver. 18.
And of Hymeneus and Alexander, ver. 19, 20.

PAUL, an apostle of Jesus Christ by the commandment of
God our Saviour, and Lord Jesus Christ, *which is* our
hope; ² Unto Timothy, *my* own son in the faith: Grace, mercy,
and peace, from God our Father and Jesus Christ our Lord.
³ As I besought thee to abide still at Ephesus, when I went

into Macedonia, that thou mightest charge some that they teach no other doctrine, ⁴ Neither give heed to fables and endless genealogies, which minister questions, rather than godly edifying [a dispensation of God], which is in faith: *so do.*

Here is, I. The inscription of the epistle, from whom it is sent: *Paul an apostle of Jesus Christ,* constituted an apostle *by the commandment of God our Saviour, and Lord Jesus Christ.* His credentials were unquestionable. He had not only a commission, but a commandment, not only from God our Saviour, but from Jesus Christ: he was a preacher of the gospel of Christ, and a minister of the kingdom of Christ. Observe, God is our Saviour.—*Jesus Christ, who is our hope.* Observe, Jesus Christ is a Christian's hope; our hope is in him, all our hope of eternal life is built upon him; Christ is in us the hope of glory, Col. i. 27. He calls Timothy his own son, because he had been an instrument of his conversion, and because he had been a son that served him, served with him in the gospel, Phil. ii. 22. Timothy had not been wanting in the duty of a son to Paul, and Paul was not wanting in the care and tenderness of a father to him.

II. The benediction is, *grace, mercy, and peace, from God our Father.* Some have observed that whereas in all the epistles to the churches the apostolical benediction is *grace and peace,* in these two epistles to Timothy and that to Titus it is *grace, mercy, and peace:* as if ministers had more need of God's mercy than other men. Ministers need more grace than others, to discharge their duty faithfully; and they need more mercy than others, to pardon what is amiss in them: and if Timothy, so eminent a minister, must be indebted to the mercy of God, and needed the increase and continuance of it, how much more do we ministers, in these times, who have so little of his excellent spirit!

III. Paul tells Timothy what was the end of his appointing him to this office: *I besought thee to abide at Ephesus.* Timothy had a mind to go with Paul, was loth to go from under his wing, but Paul would have it so; it was necessary for the public service: *I besought thee,* says he. Though he might assume an authority to command him, yet for love's sake he chose rather to beseech him. Now his business was to take care to fix both the ministers and the people of that church: *Charge them that they teach no other doctrine* than what they have received, that they do not add to the Christian doctrine, under pretence of improving it or making up the defects of it, that they do not alter it, but cleave to it as it was delivered to them. Observe, 1. Ministers must not only be charged to preach the true doctrine of the gospel, but charged to preach no other doctrine. *If an angel from heaven preach any other doctrine let him be anathema,* Gal. i. viii. 2. In the times of the apostles there were attempts made to corrupt Christianity (*we are not as many, who corrupt the word,* 2 Cor. ii. 17), otherwise this charge to Timothy might have been spared. 3. He must not only see to it that he did not preach any other doctrine, but he must charge others that they might not add any thing of their own to the gospel, or take any thing from it, but that they preach it pure and uncorrupt. He must also take care to prevent their regarding *fables and endless genealogies,* and strifes of words. This is often repeated in these two epistles (as *ch.* iv. 7; vi. 4; 2 Tim. ii. 23), as well as in the epistle to Titus. As among the Jews there were some who brought Judaism into Christianity; so among the Gentiles there were some who brought paganism into Christianity. "Take heed of these," says he, " watch against them, or they will be the corrupting and ruining of religion among you, for *they minister questions rather than edifying.*" That which ministers questions is not for edifying ; that which gives occasion for doubtful disputes pulls down the church rather than builds it up. And I think, by a parity of reason, everything else that ministers questions rather than godly edifying should be disclaimed and disregarded by us, such as an uninterrupted succession in the ministry from the apostles down to these times, the absolute necessity of episcopal ordination, and of the intention of the minister to the efficacy and validity of the sacraments he ministers. These are as bad as Jewish fables and endless genealogies, for they involve us in inextricable difficulties, and tend only to shake the foundations of a Christian's hope and to fill his mind with perplexing doubts and fears. Godly edifying is the end ministers should aim at in all their discourses, that Christians may be improving in godliness and growing up to a greater likeness to the blessed God. Observe, further, Godly edifying must be in faith : the gospel is the foundation on which we build ; it is by faith that we come to God at first (Heb. xi. 6), and it must be in the same way, and by the same principle of faith, that we must be edified. Again, Ministers should avoid, as much as may be, what will occasion disputes ; and would do well to insist on the great and practical points of religion, about which there can be no disputes ; for even disputes about great and necessary truths draw off the mind from the main design of Christianity, and eat out the vitals of religion, which consist in practice and obedience as well as in faith, that we may not hold the truth in unrighteousness, but may keep the mystery of the faith in a pure conscience.

[5] Now the end of the commandment is charity [**love**] out of a pure heart, and *of* a good conscience, and *of* faith unfeigned : [6] From which some having swerved have turned aside unto vain jangling [**vain talking**]; [7] Desiring to be teachers of the law ; understanding neither what they say, nor whereof they affirm. [8] But we know that the law *is* good, if a man use it lawfully ; [9] Knowing this, that the law is not made for a righteous man, but for the lawless and disobedient [**unruly**], for the ungodly and for sinners, for unholy and profane, for murderers of fathers and murderers of mothers, for manslayers, [10] For whoremongers, for them that defile themselves with mankind, for menstealers, for liars, for perjured persons [**false swearers**], and if there be any other thing that is contrary to sound doctrine ; [11] According to the glorious gospel of the blessed God, which was committed to my trust.

Here the apostle instructs Timothy how to guard against the judaizing teachers, or others who mingled fables and endless genealogies with the gospel. He shows the use of the law, and the glory of the gospel.

I. He shows the end and uses of the law : it is intended to promote love, *for love is the fulfilling of the law,* Rom. xiii. 10.

1. *The end of the commandment is charity,* or love, Rom. xiii. 8. The main scope and drift of the divine law are to engage us to the love of God and one another ; and whatever tends to weaken either our love to God

or love to the brethren tends to defeat the end of the commandment : and surely the gospel, which obliges us to love our enemies, to do good to those who hate us (Matt. v. 44), does not design to lay aside or supersede a commandment the end whereof is love ; so far from it that, on the other hand, we are told that though we had all advantages, and wanted charity, we are but as sounding brass and a tinkling cymbal, 1 Cor. xiii. 1. *By this shall all men know that you are my disciples, if you love one another,* John xiii. 35. Those therefore who boasted of their knowledge of the law, but used it only as a colour for the disturbance that they gave to the preaching of the gospel (under pretence of zeal for the law, dividing the church and distracting it), defeated that which was the very end of the commandment, and that is love, love *out of a pure heart,* a heart purified by faith, purified from corrupt affections. In order to the keeping up of holy love our hearts must be cleansed from all sinful love ; our love must arise *out of a good conscience,* kept without offence. Those answer the end of the commandment who are careful to keep a good conscience, from a real belief of the truth of the word of God which enjoins it, here called a *faith unfeigned.* Here we have the concomitants of that excellent grace charity ; they are three :—(1.) A pure heart ; there it must be seated, and thence it must take its rise. (2.) A good conscience, in which we must exercise ourselves daily, that we may not only get it, but that we may keep it, Acts xxiv. 16. (3.) Faith unfeigned must also accompany it, for it is love without dissimulation : the faith that works by it must be of the like nature, genuine and sincere. Now some who set up for teachers of the law swerved from the very end of the commandment : they set up for disputers, but their disputes proved vain jangling ; they set up for teachers, but they pretended to teach others what they themselves did not understand. If the church be corrupted by such teachers, we must not think it strange, for we see from the beginning it was so. Observe, [1.] When persons, especially ministers, swerve from the great law of charity—the end of the commandment, they will turn aside to vain jangling ; when a man misses his end and scope, it is no wonder that every step he takes is out of the way. [2.] Jangling, especially in religion, is vain ; it is unprofitable and useless as to all that is good, and it is very pernicious and hurtful : and yet many people's religion consists of little else but vain jangling. [3.] Those who deal much in vain jangling are fond and ambitious to be teachers of others ; they desire (that is, they affect) the office of teaching. [4.] It is too common for men to intrude into the office of the ministry when they are very ignorant of those things about which they are to speak : they understand neither what they say nor whereof they affirm ; and by such learned ignorance, no doubt, they edify their hearers very much.

2. The use of the law (v. 8) : *The law is good, if a man use it lawfully.* The Jews used it unlawfully, as an engine to divide the church, a cover to the malicious opposition they made to the gospel of Christ ; they set it up for justification, and so used it unlawfully. We must not therefore think to set it aside, but use it lawfully, for the restraint of sin. The abuse which some have made of the law does not take away the use of it ; but, when a divine appointment has been abused, call it back to its right use and take away the abuses, for the law is still very useful as a rule of life ; though we are not under it as under a covenant of works, yet it is good to teach us what is sin and what is duty. It is not made for a righteous man, that is, it is not made for those who observe it ; for, if we could keep the law, righteousness would be by the law (Gal. iii. 21) : but it is made for wicked

persons, to restrain them, to check them, and to put a stop to vice and profaneness. It is the grace of God that changes men's hearts; but the terrors of the law may be of use to tie their hands and restrain their tongues. A righteous man does not want those restraints which are necessary for the wicked; or at least the law is not made primarily and principally for the righteous, but for sinners of all sorts, whether in a greater or less measure, v. 9, 10. In this black roll of sinners, he particularly mentions breaches of the second table, duties which we owe to our neighbour; against the fifth and sixth commandments, *murderers of fathers and mothers, and manslayers;* against the seventh, *whoremongers, and those that defile themselves with mankind;* against the eighth, *men-stealers;* against the ninth, *liars and perjured persons;* and then he closes his account with this, *and if there be any other thing that is contrary to sound doctrine.* Some understand this as an institution of a power in the civil magistrate to make laws against such notorious sinners as are specified, and to see those laws put in execution.

II. He shows the glory and grace of the gospel. Paul's epithets, are expressive and significant; and frequently every one is a sentence: as here (*v.* 11), *According to the glorious gospel of the blessed God.* Let us learn hence, 1. To call God the blessed God, infinitely happy in the enjoyment of himself and his own perfections. 2. To call the gospel the glorious gospel, for so it is: much of the glory of God appears in the works of creation and providence, but much more in the gospel, where it shines in the face of Jesus Christ. Paul reckoned it a great honour put upon him, and a great favour done him, that this glorious gospel was committed to his trust; that is, the preaching of it, for the framing of it is not committed to any man or company of men in the world. The settling of the terms of salvation in the gospel of Christ is God's own work; but the publishing of it to the world is committed to the apostles and ministers. Note here, (1.) The ministry is a trust, for the gospel was committed unto this apostle; it is an office of trust as well as of power, and the former more than the latter; for this reason ministers are called stewards, 1 Cor. iv. 1. (2.) It is a glorious trust, because the gospel committed to them is a glorious gospel; it is a trust of very great importance. God's glory is very much concerned in it. Lord, what a trust is committed to us! How much grace do we want, to be found faithful in this great trust!

12 And I thank Christ Jesus our Lord, who hath enabled me, for that he counted me faithful, putting me into the ministry [appointing me to his service]. 13 Who was before a blasphemer, and a persecutor, and injurious: but I obtained mercy, because I did *it* ignorantly, in unbelief. 14 And the grace of our Lord was exceeding abundant with faith and love which is in Christ Jesus. 15 This *is* a faithful saying, and worthy of all acceptation, that Christ Jesus came into the world to save sinners; of whom I am chief. 16 Howbeit for this cause I obtained mercy, that in me first [as chief] Jesus Christ might show forth all [all his] longsuffering, for a pattern to them which should hereafter believe on him to life everlasting. 17 Now

unto the King eternal, immortal, invisible, the only wise God, be honour and glory for ever and ever. Amen.

Here the apostle, I. Returns thanks to Jesus Christ for putting him into the ministry. Observe, 1. It is Christ's work to put men into the ministry, Acts xxvi. 16, 17. God condemned the false prophets among the Jews in these words, *I have not sent these prophets, yet they ran : I have not spoken to them, yet they prophesied,* Jer. xxiii. 21. Ministers, properly speaking, cannot make ministers, much less can persons make themselves ministers: for it is Christ's work, as king and head, prophet and teacher, of his church. 2. Those whom he puts into the ministry he fits for it ; whom he calls he qualifies. Those ministers who are no way fit for their work, nor have ability for it, are not of Christ's putting into the ministry, though there are different qualifications as to gifts and graces. 3. Christ gives not only ability, but fidelity, to those whom he puts into the ministry : He *counted me faithful ;* and none are counted faithful but those whom he makes so. Christ's ministers are trusty servants, and they ought to be so, having so great a trust committed to them. 4. A call to the ministry is a great favour, for which those who are so called ought to give thanks to Jesus Christ : *I thank Christ Jesus our Lord, who hath put me into the ministry.*

II. The more to magnify the grace of Christ in putting him into the ministry, he gives an account of his conversion.

1. What he was before his conversion : *A blasphemer, a persecutor, and injurious.* Saul breathed out threatenings and slaughter against the disciples of the Lord, Acts ix. 1. He made havoc of the church, Acts viii. 3. He was a blasphemer of God, a persecutor of the saints, and injurious to both. Frequently those who are designed for great and eminent services are left to themselves before their conversion, to fall into great wickedness, that the mercy of God may be the more glorified in their remission, and the grace of God in their regeneration. The greatness of sin is no bar to our acceptance with God, no, nor to our being employed for him, if it be truly repented of. Observe here, (1.) Blasphemy, persecution, and injuriousness, are very great and heinous sins, and those who are guilty of them are sinners before God exceedingly. To blaspheme God is immediately and directly to strike at God ; to persecute his people is to endeavour to wound him through their sides ; and to be injurious is to be like Ishmael, whose hand was against every one, and every one was against him ; for such invade God's prerogative, and encroach upon the liberties of their fellow-creatures. (2.) True penitents, to serve a good purpose, will not be backward to own their former condition before they were brought home to God : this good apostle often confessed what his former life had been, as Acts xxii. 4 : xxvi. 10, 11.

2. The great favour of God to him : *But I obtained mercy.* This was a blessed *but* indeed, a great favour, that so notorious a rebel should find mercy with his prince.

(1.) If Paul had persecuted the Christians wilfully, knowing them to be the people of God, for aught I know he had been guilty of the unpardonable sin ; but, because he did it ignorantly and in unbelief, he obtained mercy. Note, [1.] What we do ignorantly is a less crime than what we do knowingly ; yet a sin of ignorance is a sin, for he that knew not his Master's will, but did commit things worthy of stripes, shall be beaten with few stripes, Luke xii. 48. Ignorance in some cases will extenuate a crime, though it do not take it away. [2.] Unbelief is at the bottom of what sinners do ignorantly ; they do not believe God's threatenings, otherwise they could not do as they do. [3.] For these reasons Paul obtained mercy : *But I obtained mercy, because I did it ignorantly, in unbelief.* [4.] Here was mercy for a blasphemer, a persecutor, and an injurious person : "*But I obtained mercy,* I a blasphemer," &c.

(2.) Here he takes notice of the abundant grace of Jesus Christ, *v.* 14. The conversion and salvation of great sinners are owing to the grace of Christ, his exceedingly abundant grace, even that grace of Christ which appears in his glorious gospel (*v.* 15) : *This is a faithful saying,* &c. Here we have the sum of the whole gospel, *that Jesus Christ came into the world.* The Son of God took upon him our nature, was made flesh, and dwelt among us, John i. 14. He came into the world, *not to call the righteous, but sinners to repentance,* Matt. ix. 13. His errand into the world was to seek and find, and so save, *those that were lost,* Luke xix. 10. The ratification of this is *that it is a faithful saying, and worthy of all acceptation.* It is good news, worthy of all acceptation ; and yet not too good to be true, for it is a faithful saying. It is a faithful saying, and therefore worthy to be embraced in the arms of faith : it is worthy of all acceptation, and therefore to be received with holy love, which refers to the foregoing verse, where the grace of Christ is said to abound in faith and love. In the close of the verse Paul applies it to himself : *Of whom I am chief.* Paul was a sinner of the first rank ; so he acknowledges himself to have been, for he breathed out threatenings and slaughter against the disciples of the Lord, &c., Acts ix. 1, 2. Persecutors are some of the worst of sinners : such a one Paul had been. Or, *of whom I am chief,* that is, of pardoned sinners I am chief. It is an expression of his great humility ; he that elsewhere calls himself the *least of all saints* (Eph. iii. 8) here calls himself the chief of sinners. Observe, [1.] Christ Jesus has come into the world ; the prophecies concerning his coming are now fulfilled. [2.] He came to save sinners ; he came to save those who could not save and help themselves. [3.] Blasphemers and persecutors are the chief of sinners, so Paul reckoned them. [4.] The chief of sinners may become the chief of saints ; so this apostle was, for he was not a whit behind the very chief apostles (2 Cor. xi. 5), for Christ came to save the chief of sinners. [5.] This is a very great truth, it is a faithful saying ; these are true and faithful words, which may be depended on. [6.] It deserves to be received, to be believed by us all, for our comfort and encouragement.

(3.) The mercy which Paul found with God, notwithstanding his great wickedness before his conversion, he speaks of,

[1.] For the encouragement of others to repent and believe (*v.* 16) : *For this cause I obtained mercy, that in me first Jesus Christ might show forth all long-suffering, for a pattern to those who should hereafter believe.* It was an instance of the long-suffering of Christ that he would bear so much with one who had been so very provoking ; and it was designed for a pattern to all others, that the greatest sinners might not despair of mercy with God. Note here, *First,* Our apostle was one of the first great sinners converted to Christianity. *Secondly,* He was converted, and obtained mercy, for the sake of others as well as of himself ; he was a pattern to others. *Thirdly,* The Lord Jesus Christ shows great long-suffering in the conversion of great sinners. *Fourthly,* Those who obtain mercy believe on the Lord Jesus Christ ; for without faith it is impossible to please God, Heb. xi. 6. *Fifthly,* Those who believe on Christ believe on him to life everlasting; they believe to the saving of the soul, Heb. x. 39.

[2.] He mentions it to the glory of God: having spoken of the mercy he had found with God, he could not go on with his letter without inserting a thankful acknowledgment of God's goodness to him: *Now unto the King eternal, immortal, invisible, the only wise God, be honour and glory for ever and ever. Amen.* Observe, *First*, That grace which we have the comfort of, God must have the glory of. Those who are sensible of their obligations to the mercy and grace of God will have their hearts enlarged in his praise. Here is praise ascribed to him, as *the King eternal, immortal, invisible. Secondly*, When we have found God good we must not forget to pronounce him great: and his kind thoughts of us must not at all abate our high thoughts of him, but rather increase them. God had taken particular cognizance of Paul, and shown him mercy, and taken him into communion with himself, and yet he calls him the King eternal, &c. God's gracious dealings with us should fill us with admiration of his glorious attributes. He is eternal, without beginning of days, or end of life, or change of time. He is the Ancient of days, Dan. vii. 9. He is immortal, and the original of immortality; he only has immortality (1 Tim. vi. 16), for he cannot die. He is invisible, for he cannot be seen with mortal eyes, dwelling in the light to which no man can approach, whom no man hath seen nor can see, 1 Tim. vi. 16. He is *the only wise God* (Jude 25); he only is infinitely wise, and the fountain of all wisdom. "*To him be glory for ever and ever*," or, "Let me be for ever employed in giving honour and glory to him, as the thousands of thousands do," Rev. v. 12, 13.

18 This charge I commit unto thee, son Timothy, according to the prophecies which went before on thee, that thou by them mightest war a [the] good warfare; 19 Holding faith, and a good conscience; which some having put away concerning faith have made shipwreck [thrust from them made shipwreck concerning the faith]. 20 Of whom is Hymenæus and Alexander; whom I have delivered unto Satan, that they may learn not to blaspheme.

Here is the charge he gives to Timothy to proceed in his work with resolution, *v.* 18. Observe here, The gospel is a charge committed to the ministers of it; it is committed to their trust, to see that it be duly applied according to the intent and meaning of it, and the design of its great Author. It seems, there had been prophecies before concerning Timothy, that he should be taken into the ministry, and should prove eminent in the work of the ministry; this encouraged Paul to commit this charge to him. Observe, 1. The ministry is a warfare, it is a good warfare against sin and Satan: and under the banner of the Lord Jesus, who is the Captain of our salvation (Heb. ii. 10), and in his cause, and against his enemies, ministers are in a particular manner engaged. 2. Ministers must war this good warfare, must execute their office diligently and courageously, notwithstanding oppositions and discouragements. 3. The prophecies which went before concerning Timothy are here mentioned as a motive to stir him up to a vigorous and conscientious discharge of his duty; so the good hopes that others have entertained concerning us should excite us to our duty: *That thou by them mightest war a good warfare.* 4. We must hold both faith and a good conscience : *Holding faith and a good conscience, v.* 19. Those that put away a good conscience will soon make shipwreck of faith. Let us live up to the directions of a renewed enlightened conscience, and keep conscience void of offence (Acts xxiv. 16), a conscience not debauched by any vice or sin, and this will be a means of preserving us sound in the faith ; we must look to the one as well as the other, for the mystery of the faith must be held in a pure conscience, *ch.* iii. 9. As for those who had made shipwreck of the faith, he specifies two, *Hymeneus and Alexander,* who had made a profession of the Christian religion, but had quitted that profession ; and Paul had delivered them to Satan, had declared them to belong to the kingdom of Satan, and, as some think, had, by an extraordinary power, delivered them to be terrified or tormented by Satan, *that they might learn not to blaspheme,* not to contradict or revile the doctrine of Christ and the good ways of the Lord. Observe, The primary design of the highest censure in the primitive church was to prevent further sin and to reclaim the sinner. In this case it was for the destruction of the flesh, that the spirit might be saved in the day of the Lord Jesus, 1 Cor. v. 5. Observe, (1.) Those who love the service and work of Satan are justly delivered over to the power of Satan : *Whom I have delivered over to Satan.* (2.) God can, if he please, work by contraries : Hymeneus and Alexander are delivered to Satan, that they may learn not to blaspheme, when one would rather think they would learn of Satan to blaspheme the more. (3.) Those who have put away a good conscience, and made shipwreck of faith, will not stick at any thing, blasphemy not excepted. (4.) Therefore let us hold faith and a good conscience, if we would keep clear of blasphemy ; for, if we once let go our hold of these, we do not know where we shall stop.

CHAPTER II

In this chapter Paul treats, I. Of prayer, with many reasons for it, ver. 1-8. II. Of women's apparel, ver. 9, 10. III. Of their subjection, with the reasons of it, ver. 11-14. IV. A promise given for their encouragement in child-bearing, ver. 15.

I EXHORT therefore, that, first of all, supplications, prayers, intercessions, *and* giving of thanks, be made for all men ; 2 For kings, and *for* all that are in authority [high place], that we may lead a quiet and peaceable life in all godliness and honesty [gravity] ; 3 For this *is* good and acceptable in the sight of God our Saviour ; 4 Who will have all men to [willeth that all men should] be saved, and to come unto the knowledge of the truth. 5 For *there is* one God, and one mediator between God and men, the man [*himself* man] Christ Jesus ; 6 Who gave himself a ransom for all, to be testified in due time. 7 Whereunto I am ordained a preacher, and an apostle, (I speak the truth in Christ, *and* lie not ;) a teacher of the Gentiles in faith and verity.   8 I will therefore that men pray every where, lifting up holy hands, without wrath and doubting [disputing].

Here is, I. A charge given to Christians to pray for all men in general, and particularly for all in authority. Timothy must take care that this be done. Paul does not send him any prescribed form of prayer, as we have reason to think he would if he had intended that ministers should be tied to that way of praying ; but, in general, that they should make *supplications, prayers, intercessions, and giving of thanks :* supplications for the averting of evil, prayers for the obtaining of good, intercessions for others, and thanksgivings for mercies already received. Paul thought it enough to give them general heads ; they, having the scripture to direct them in prayer and the Spirit of prayer poured out upon them, needed not any further directions. Observe, The design of the Christian religion is to promote prayer ; and the disciples of Christ must be praying people. *Pray always with all prayer,* Eph. vi. 18. There must be prayers for ourselves in the first place ; this is implied here. We must also pray *for all men,* for the world of mankind in general, for particular persons who need or desire our prayers. See how far the Christian religion was from being a sect, when it taught men this diffusive charity, to pray, not only for those of their own way, but for all men. Pray for kings, (*v.* 2) ; though the kings at this time were heathens, enemies to Christianity, and persecutors of Christians, yet they must pray for them, because it is for the public good that there should be civil government, and proper persons entrusted with the administration of it, for whom therefore we ought to pray, yea, though we ourselves suffer under them. *For kings, and all that are in authority,* that is, inferior magistrates : we must pray for them, and we must give thanks for them, pray for their welfare and for the welfare of their kingdoms, and therefore must not plot against them, that in the peace thereof we may have peace, and give thanks for them and for the benefit we have under their government, that *we may lead a quiet and peaceable life in all godliness and honesty.* Here see what we must desire for kings, that God will so turn their hearts, and direct them and make use of them, that we under them may lead a quiet and peaceable life. He does not say, "that we may get preferments under them, grow rich, and be in honour and power under them ;" no, the summit of the ambition of a good Christian is to lead a quiet and peaceable life, to get through the world unmolested in a low private station. We should desire that we and others may lead a peaceable life *in all godliness and honesty,* implying that we cannot expect to be kept quiet and peaceable unless we keep in all godliness and honesty. Let us mind our duty, and then we may expect to be taken under the protection both of God and the government. *In all godliness and honesty.* Here we have our duty as Christians summed up in two words : godliness, that is, the right worshipping of God ; and honesty, that is, a good conduct towards all men. These two must go together ; we are not truly honest if we are not godly, and do not render to God his due ; and we are not truly godly if we are not honest, for God hates robbery for burnt-offering. Here we may observe, 1. Christians are to be men much given to prayer : they ought to abound herein, and should use themselves to prayers, supplications, &c.   2. In our prayers we are to have a generous concern for others as well as for ourselves ; we are to pray for all men, and to give thanks for all men ; and must not confine our prayers nor thanksgivings to our own persons or families.   3. Prayer consists of various parts, of supplications, intercessions, and thanksgivings; for we must pray for the mercies we want, as well as be thankful for mercies already received; and we are to deprecate the judgments which our own sins or the sins of others have deserved. 4. All men, yea, kings themselves, and those who are in authority, are to be prayed for. They want our prayers, for they have many difficulties to encounter, many snares to which their exalted stations expose them. 5. In praying for our governors, we take the most likely course to lead a peaceable and quiet life. The Jews at Babylon were commanded to seek the peace of the city whither the Lord had caused them to be carried captives, and to pray to the Lord for it; for in the peace thereof they should have peace, Jer. xxix. 7. 6. If we would lead a peaceable and quiet life, we must live in all godliness and honesty; we must do our duty to God and man. *He that will love life, and see good days, let him refrain his tongue from evil, and his lips that they speak no guile; let him eschew evil, and do good; let him seek peace and pursue it,* 1 Pet. iii. 10, 11. Now the reason he gives for this is *because this is good in the sight of God our Saviour;* that is, the gospel of Christ requires this. That which is acceptable in the sight of God our Saviour we should do, and should abound in.

II. As a reason why we should in our prayers concern ourselves for all men, he shows God's love to mankind in general, *v.* 4.

1. One reason why all men are to be prayed for is because there is one God, and that God bears a good will to all mankind. There is one God (*v.* 5), and one only, there is no other, there can be no other, for there can be but one infinite. This one God *will have all men to be saved;* he desires not the death and destruction of any (Ezek. xxxiii. 11), but the welfare and salvation of all. Not that he has decreed the salvation of all, for then all men would be saved; but he has a good will to the salvation of all, and none perish but by their own fault, Matt. xxiii. 37. He will have all to be saved, *and to come to the knowledge of the truth,* to be saved in the way that he has appointed and not otherwise. It concerns us to get the knowledge of the truth, because that is the way to be saved; *Christ is the way and the truth, and so he is the life.*

2. There is one Mediator, and that Mediator gave himself a ransom for all. As the mercy of God extends itself to all his works, so the mediation of Christ extends itself thus far to all the children of men that he paid a price sufficient for the salvation of all mankind; he brought mankind to stand upon new terms with God, so that they are not now under the law as a covenant of works, but as a rule of life. They are under grace; not under the covenant of innocence, but under a new covenant: *He gave himself a ransom.* Observe, The death of Christ was a ransom, a counter-price. We deserved to have died. Christ died for us, to save us from death and hell; he gave himself a ransom voluntarily, a ransom for all; so that all mankind are put in a better condition than that of devils. He died to work out a common salvation: in order hereunto, he put himself into the office of Mediator between God and man. A mediator supposes a controversy. Sin had made a quarrel between us and God; Jesus Christ is a Mediator who undertakes to make peace, to bring God and man together, in the nature of an umpire or arbitrator, a days-man who lays his hand upon us both, Job ix. 33. He is a ransom that *was to be testified in due time;* that is, in the Old-Testament times, his sufferings and the glory that should follow were spoken of as things to be revealed in the last times, 1 Pet. i. 10, 11. And they are accordingly revealed, Paul himself

having been ordained a preacher and an apostle, to publish to the Gentiles the glad tidings of redemption and salvation by Jesus Christ. This doctrine of Christ's mediation Paul was entrusted to preach to every creature, Mark xvi. 15. He was appointed to be a teacher of the Gentiles; besides his general call to the apostleship, he was commissioned particularly to preach to the Gentiles, *in faith and truth,* or faithfully and truly. Note, (1.) It is good and acceptable in the sight of God our Saviour that we pray for kings and for all men, and also that we lead a peaceable and quiet life; and this is a very good reason why we should do the one as well as the other. (2.) God has a good will to the salvation of all; so that it is not so much the want of a will in God to save them as it is a want of will in themselves to be saved in God's way. Here our blessed Lord charges the fault: *You will not come unto me that you may have life,* John v. 40. *I would have gathered you, and you would not.* (3.) Those who are saved must come to the knowledge of the truth, for this is God's appointed way to save sinners. Without knowledge the heart cannot be good; if we do not know the truth, we cannot be ruled by it. (4.) It is observable that the unity of God is asserted, and joined with the unity of the Mediator; and the church of Rome might as well maintain a plurality of gods as a plurality of mediators. (5.) He that is a Mediator in the New-Testament sense, gave himself a ransom. Vain then is the pretence of the Romanists that there is but one Mediator of satisfaction, but many of intercession; for, according to Paul, Christ's giving himself a ransom was a necessary part of the Mediator's office; and indeed this lays the foundation for his intercession. (6.) Paul was ordained a minister, to declare this to the Gentiles, that Christ is the one Mediator between God and men, who gave himself a ransom for all. This is the substance of which all ministers are to preach, to the end of the world; and Paul magnified his office, as he was the apostle of the Gentiles, Rom. xi. 13. (7.) Ministers must preach the truth, what they apprehend to be so, and they must believe it themselves; they are, like our apostle, to preach in faith and verity, and they must also be faithful and trusty.

III. A direction how to pray, *v.* 8. 1. Now, under the gospel, prayer is not to be confined to any one particular house of prayer, but men must pray everywhere: no place is amiss for prayer, no place more acceptable to God than another, John iv. 21. *Pray everywhere.* We must pray in our closets, pray in our families, pray at our meals, pray when we are on journeys, and pray in the solemn assemblies, whether more public or private. 2. It is the will of God that in prayer we should lift up holy hands: *Lifting up holy hands,* or pure hands, pure from the pollution of sin, washed in the fountain opened for sin and uncleanness. *I will wash my hands,* &c., Ps. xxvi. 6. 3. We must pray in charity: *Without wrath,* or malice, or anger at any person. 4. We must pray in faith *without doubting* (Jam. i. 6), or, as some read it, *without disputing,* and then it falls under the head of charity.

9 In like manner also, that women adorn themselves in modest apparel, with shamefacedness and sobriety; not with broidered hair, or gold, or pearls, or costly *array* [raiment], 10 but (which becometh women professing godliness) with good works. 11 Let the woman learn in silence [quietness] with all subjection. 12 But I suffer not a woman to teach, nor to usurp

authority [**have dominion**] over the man, but to be in silence
[**quietness**].   13 For Adam was first formed, then Eve.   14 And
Adam was not deceived, but the woman being deceived was in
the transgression.   15 Notwithstanding she shall be saved in
childbearing, if they continue in faith and charity [**love**] and
holiness with sobriety.

I. Here is a charge, that women who profess the Christian religion
should be modest, sober, silent, and submissive, as becomes their place.
1. They must be very modest in their apparel, not affecting gaudiness,
gaiety, or costliness (you may read the vanity of a person's mind in the
gaiety and gaudiness of his habit), because they have better ornaments
with which they should *adorn themselves, as becometh women professing
godliness, with good works.* Note, Good works are the best ornament ;
these are, in the sight of God, of great price. Those that profess godliness should, in their dress, as well as other things, act as becomes their
profession ; instead of laying out their money on fine clothes, they must
lay it out in works of piety and charity, which are properly called good
works. 2. Women must learn the principles of their religion, learn Christ,
learn the scriptures ; they must not think that their sex excuses them from
that learning which is necessary to salvation. 3. They must be silent,
·ubmissive, and subject, and not usurp authority. The reason given is
because *Adam was first formed, then Eve* out of him, to denote her subordination to him and dependence upon him ; and that she was made for
him, to be a help-meet for him. And as she was last in the creation,
which is one reason for her subjection, so she was first in the transgression, and that is another reason. *Adam was not deceived*, that is, not first;
the serpent did not immediately set upon him, but the woman was first in
the transgression (2 Cor. xi. 3), and it was part of the sentence, *Thy
desire shall be to thy husband, and he shall rule over thee*, Gen. iii. 16. But
it is a word of comfort (v. 15), that those who continue in sobriety shall be
saved in child-bearing, or *with* child-bearing—the Messiah who was born
of a woman, should break the serpent's head (Gen. iii. 15) ; or the sentence
which they are under for sin shall be no bar to their acceptance with
Christ, *if they continue in faith and charity, and holiness, with sobriety.*
II. Here observe, 1. The extensiveness of the rules of Christianity ;
they reach not only to men, but to women, not only to their persons, but
also to their dress, which must be modest, like their sex ; and to their
outward deportment and behaviour, it must be in silence, with all subjection. 2. Women are to profess godliness as well as men ; for they are
baptized, and thereby stand engaged to exercise themselves to godliness :
and, to their honour be it spoken, many of them were eminent professors
of Christianity in the days of the apostles, as the book of Acts will inform
us. 3. Women being more in danger of exceeding in their apparel, it was
more necessary to caution them in this respect. 4. The best ornaments
for professors of godliness are good works. 5. According to Paul, women
must be learners, and are not allowed to be public teachers in the church ;
for teaching is an office of authority, and the woman must not usurp
authority over the man, but is to be in silence. But, notwithstanding
this prohibition, good women may and ought to teach their children at
home the principles of religion. Timothy from a child had known the
holy scriptures ; and who should teach him but his mother and grand-

mother ? 2 Tim. iii. 15. Aquilla and his wife Priscilla expounded unto
Apollos the way of God more perfectly ; but then they did it privately, for
they took him unto them, Acts xviii. 26. 6. Here are two very good
reasons given for the man's authority over the woman, and her subjection
to the man, *v.* 13, 14. Adam was first formed, then Eve ; she was created
for the man, and not the man for the woman (1 Cor. xi. 9) ; then she was
deceived, and brought the man into the transgression. 7. Though the
difficulties and dangers of child-bearing are many and great, as they are
part of the punishment inflicted on the sex for Eve's transgression, yet
here is much for her support and encouragement : *Notwithstanding she
shall be saved*, &c. Though in sorrow, yet she shall bring forth, and be a
living mother of living children ; with this proviso, that they continue in
faith, and charity, and holiness, with sobriety : and women, under the
circumstance of child-bearing should by faith lay hold of this promise for
their support in the needful time.

CHAPTER III

In this chapter our apostle treats of church-officers. He specifies, I. The qualifications of
a person to be admitted to the office of a bishop, ver. 1-7. II. The qualifications of
deacons (ver. 8-10), and of their wives (ver. 11), again of the deacons, ver. 12, 13. III.
The reasons of his writing to Timothy, whereupon he speaks of the church and the
foundation-truth professed therein, ver. 14, to the end.

THIS *is* a true saying, If a man desire the office of a bishop,
he desireth a good work. ² A bishop then must be
blameless [**without reproach**], the husband of one wife,
vigilant, sober, of good behaviour [**temperate, sober-minded,
orderly**], given to hospitality, apt to teach ; ³ Not given to
wine, no striker, not greedy of filthy lucre ; but patient, not a
brawler, not covetous ; [**no brawler, no striker : but gentle,
not contentious, no lover of money** ;] ⁴ One that ruleth well
his own house, having his children in subjection with all
gravity ; ⁵ (For if a man know not how to rule his own house,
how shall he take care of the church of God ?) ⁶ Not a novice,
lest being lifted up with pride he fall into the condemnation of
the devil. ⁷ Moreover he must have a good report of [**testimony from**] them which are without ; lest he fall into reproach
and the snare of the devil.

The two epistles to Timothy, and that to Titus, contain a scripture-plan
of church-government, or a direction to ministers. Timothy, we suppose,
was an evangelist who was left at Ephesus, to take care of those whom the
Holy Ghost had made bishops there, that is, the presbyters, as appears by
Acts xx. 28, where the care of the church was committed to the presbyters,
and they were called bishops. It seems they were very loth to part with

Paul, especially because he told them they should *see his face no more* (Acts xx. 38) ; for their church was but newly planted, they were afraid of undertaking the care of it, and therefore Paul left Timothy with them to set them in order. And here we have the character of a gospel minister, whose office it is, as a bishop, to preside in a particular congregation of Christians : *If a man desires the office of a bishop, he desires a good work, v.* 1. Observe,

I. The ministry is a work. However the office of a bishop may be now thought a good preferment, then it was thought a good work. 1. The office of a scripture-bishop is an office of divine appointment, and not of human invention. The ministry is not a creature of the state, and it is a pity that the minister should be at any time the tool of the state. The office of the ministry was in the church before the magistrate countenanced Christianity, for this office is one of the great gifts Christ has bestowed on the church, Eph. iv. 8–11. 2. This office of a Christian bishop is a work, which requires diligence and application : the apostle represents it under the notion and character of a work ; not of great honour and advantage, for ministers should always look more to their work than to the honour and advantage of their office. 3. It is a good work, a work of the greatest importance, and designed for the greatest good : the ministry is conversant about no lower concerns than the life and happiness of immortal souls ; it is a good work, because designed to illustrate the divine perfections in bringing many sons to glory ; the ministry is appointed to open men's eyes, and to turn them from darkness to light, and from the power of Satan unto God, &c., Acts xxvi. 18. 4. There ought to be an earnest desire of the office in those who would be put into it ; if a man desire, he should earnestly desire it for the prospect he has of bringing greater glory to God, and of doing the greatest good to the souls of men by this means. This is the question proposed to those who offer themselves to the ministry of the church of England : "Do you think you are moved by the Holy Ghost to take upon you this office ?"

II. In order to the discharge of this office, the doing of this work, the workman must be duly qualified. 1. A minister must be blameless, he must not lie under any scandal ; he must give as little occasion for blame as can be, because this would be a prejudice to his ministry and would reflect reproach upon his office. 2. He must be the husband of one wife ; not having given a bill of divorce to one, and then taken another, or not having many wives at once, as at that time was too common both among Jews and Gentiles, especially among the Gentiles. 3. He must be vigilant and watchful against Satan, that subtle enemy ; he must watch over himself, and the souls of those who are committed to his charge, of whom having taken the *oversight*, he must improve all opportunities of doing them good. A minister ought to be vigilant, because our adversary the devil goes about like a roaring lion, seeking whom he may devour, 1 Pet. v. 8. 4. He must be sober, temperate, moderate in all his actions, and in the use of all creature-comforts. Sobriety and watchfulness are often in scripture put together, because they mutually befriend one another : *Be sober, be vigilant.* 5. He must be of good behaviour, composed and solid, and not light, vain, and frothy. 6. He must be given to hospitality, open-handed to strangers, and ready to entertain them according to his ability, as one who does not set his heart upon the wealth of the world, and who is a true lover of his brethren. 7. Apt to teach. Therefore this is a preaching bishop whom Paul describes, one who is both able and willing to communicate to others the knowledge which God has given him, one who is fit to teach and ready to take all opportunities of giving instruction, who is himself *well instructed in the things of the kingdom of heaven*, and is communicative of what he knows to others. 8. No drunkard : *Not given to wine.* The priests were not to drink wine when they went in to minister (Lev. x. 8, 9), lest they should drink and pervert the law. 9. No striker ; one who is not quarrelsome, nor apt to use violence to any, but does every thing with mildness, love, and gentleness. The servant of the Lord must not strive, but be gentle towards all, &c., 2 Tim. ii. 24. 10. One who is not greedy of filthy lucre, who does not make his ministry to truckle to any secular design or interest, who uses no mean, base, sordid ways of getting money, who is dead to the wealth of this world, lives above it, and makes it appear he is so. 11. He must be patient, and not a brawler, of a mild disposition. Christ, the great Shepherd and Bishop of souls, is so. Not apt to be angry or quarrelsome : as not a striker with his hands, so not a brawler with his tongue ; for how shall men teach others to govern their tongues who do not make conscience of keeping them under good government themselves ? 12. Not covetous. Covetousness is bad in any, but it is worst in a minister, whose calling leads him to converse so much with another world. 13. He must be one who keeps his family in good order : *That rules well his own house*, that he may set a good example to other masters of families to do so too, and that he may thereby give a proof of his ability to take care of the church of God : *For, if a man know not how to rule his own house, how shall he take care of the church of God.* Observe, The families of ministers ought to be examples of good to all other families. Ministers must have their children in subjection ; then it is the duty of ministers' children to submit to the instructions that are given them.— *With all gravity.* The best way to keep inferiors in subjection, is to be grave with them. Not having his children in subjection with all austerity, but with all gravity. 14. He must not be a novice, not one newly brought to the Christian religion, or not one who is but meanly instructed in it, who knows no more of religion than the surface of it, for such a one is apt to be lifted up with pride : the more ignorant men are the more proud they are : *Lest being lifted up with pride, he fall into the condemnation of the devil.* The devils fell through pride, which is a good reason why we should take heed of pride, because it is a sin that turned angels into devils. 15. He must be of good reputation among his neighbours, and under no reproach from former conversation ; for the devil will make use of that to ensnare others, and work in them an aversion to the doctrine of Christ preached by those who have not had a good report.

III. Upon the whole, having briefly gone through the qualifications of a gospel-bishop, we may infer, 1. What great reason we have to cry out, as Paul does, *Who is sufficient for these things?* 2 Cor. ii. 16. *Hic labor, hoc opus—This is a work indeed.* What piety, what prudence, what zeal, what courage, what faithfulness, what watchfulness over ourselves, our lusts, appetites, and passions, and over those under our charge ; I say, what holy watchfulness is necessary in this work ! 2. Have not the best qualified and the most faithful and conscientious ministers just reason to complain against themselves, that so much is requisite by way of qualification, and so much work is necessary to be done ? And alas ! how far short do the best come of what they should be and what they should do ! 3. Yet let those bless God, and be thankful, whom the Lord has enabled, and counted faithful, putting them into the ministry : if God is pleased to make any in some degree able and faithful, let him have the praise and glory of it. 4. For the encouragement of all faithful ministers, we have Christ's gracious word of promise, *Lo, I am with you always even unto the end of the world*, Matt. xxviii. 20. And, if he be with us, he will fit us for our work in some measure, will carry us through the difficulties of it with comfort, graciously pardon our imperfections, and reward our faithfulness with a crown of glory that fadeth not away, 1 Pet. v. 4.

⁸ Likewise *must* the deacons *be* grave, not double-tongued, not given to much wine, not greedy of filthy lucre; ⁹ Holding the mystery of the faith in a pure conscience. ¹⁰ And let these also first be proved; then let them use the office of a deacon, being *found* [serve as deacons, if they be] blameless. ¹¹ Even so *must their* wives [women in like manner must] *be* grave, not slanderers, sober [temperate], faithful in all things. ¹² Let the deacons be the husbands of one wife, ruling their children and their own houses well. ¹³ For they that have used the office of a deacon well purchase to themselves a good degree [standing] and great boldness in the faith which is in Christ Jesus.

We have here the character of deacons: these had the care of the temporal concerns of the church, that is, the maintenance of the ministers and provision for the poor: they served tables, while the ministers or bishops gave themselves only to the ministry of the word and prayer, Acts vi. 2, 4. Of the institution of this office, with that which gave occasion to it, you have an account in Acts vi. 1–7. Now it was requisite that deacons should have a good character, because they were assistants to the ministers, appeared and acted publicly, and had a great trust reposed in them. They must be *grave*. Gravity becomes all Christians, but especially those who are in office in the church. *Not double-tongued :* that will say one thing to one and another thing to another, according as their interest leads them : a double-tongue comes from a double heart; flatterers and slanderers are double-tongued. *Not given to much wine;* for this is a great disparagement to any man, especially to a Christian, and one in office, unfits men for business, opens the door to many temptations. *Not greedy of filthy lucre;* this would especially be bad in the deacons, who were entrusted with the church's money, and, if they were covetous and greedy of filthy lucre, would be tempted to embezzle it, and convert that to their own use which was intended for the public service. *Holding the mystery of faith in a pure conscience, v.* 9. Note, The mystery of faith is best held in a pure conscience. The practical love of truth is the most powerful preservative from error and delusion. If we keep a pure conscience (take heed of everything that debauches conscience, and draws us away from God), this will preserve in our souls the mystery of faith. *Let these also first be proved, v.* 10. It is not fit that the public trusts should be lodged in the hands of any, till they have been first proved, and found fit for the business they are to be entrusted with; the soundness of their judgments, their zeal for Christ, and the blamelessness of their conversation, must be proved. Their wives likewise must have a good character (*v.* 11); they must be of a grave behaviour, not slanderous tale-bearers, carrying stories to make mischief and sow discord; they must be *sober and faithful in all things,* not given to any excess, but trusty in all that is committed to them. All who are related to ministers must double their care to walk as becomes the gospel of Christ, lest, if they in any thing walk disorderly, the ministry be blamed. As he said before of the bishops or ministers, so here of the deacons, they must be *the husband of one wife,* such as had not put away their wives, upon dislike, and married others ; they must *rule their children and their own houses well :* the families of deacons should be examples to other families. And the reason why the deacons must be thus qualified is (*v.* 13) because, though the office of a deacon be of an inferior degree, yet it is a step towards the higher degree ; and those who had served tables well the church might see cause afterwards to discharge from that service, and prefer to serve in preaching the word and in prayer. Or it may be meant of the good reputation that a man would gain by his fidelity in this office : *they will purchase to themselves great boldness in the faith that is in Christ Jesus.* Observe, 1. In the primitive church there were but two orders of ministers or officers, *bishops* and *deacons,* Phil. i. 1. After-ages have invented the rest. The office of the bishop, presbyter, pastor, or minister, was confined to prayer and to the ministry of the word ; and the office of the deacon was confined to, or at least principally conversant about, serving tables. Clemens Romanus, in his epistle to the Christians (*cap.* 42, 44), speaks very fully and plainly to this effect, that the apostles, foreknowing, by our Lord Jesus Christ, that there would arise in the Christian church a controversy about the name *episcopacy,* appointed the forementioned orders, bishops and deacons. 2. The scripture-deacon's main employment was to serve tables, and not to preach or baptize. It is true, indeed, that Philip did preach and baptize in Samaria (Acts viii.), but you read that he was an evangelist (Acts xxi. 8), and he might preach and baptize, and perform any other part of the ministerial office, under that character ; but still the design of the deacon's office was to mind the temporal concerns of the church, such as the salaries of the ministers and providing for the poor. 3. Several qualifications were very necessary, even for these inferior officers : *The deacons must be grave,* &c. 4. Some trial should be made of persons' qualifications before they are admitted into office in the church, or have any trust committed to them : *Let these also first be proved.* 5. Integrity and uprightness in an inferior office are the way to be preferred to a higher station in the church : *They purchase to themselves a good degree.* 6. This will also give a man great boldness in the faith, whereas a want of integrity and uprightness will make a man timorous, and ready to tremble at his own shadow. *The wicked fleeth when no man pursueth, but the righteous are bold as a lion,* Prov. xxviii. 1.

¹⁴ These things write I unto thee, hoping to come unto thee shortly : ¹⁵ But if I tarry long, that thou mayest know how thou oughtest to behave thyself in the house of God, which is the church of the living God, the pillar and ground of the truth. ¹⁶ And without controversy great is the mystery of godliness : God [He who] was manifest in the flesh, justified in the Spirit, seen of angels, preached unto the Gentiles, believed on in the world, received up into glory.

He concludes the chapter with a particular direction to Timothy. He hoped shortly to come to him, to give him further directions and assistance in his work, and to see that Christianity was well planted, and took root well, at Ephesus; he therefore wrote the more briefly to him. But he wrote *lest he should tarry long, that* Timothy *might know how to behave himself in the house of God,* how to conduct himself as became an evangelist, and the apostle's substitute. Observe,

I. Those who are employed in the house of God must see to it that they behave themselves well, lest they bring reproach upon the house of God, and that worthy name by which they are called. Ministers ought to behave themselves well, and to look not only to their praying and preaching, but to their behaviour: their office binds them to their good behaviour, for any behaviour will not do in this case. Timothy must know how to behave himself, not only in the particular church where he was now appointed to reside for some time, but being an evangelist, and the apostle's substitute, he must learn how to behave himself in other churches, where he should in like manner be appointed to reside for some time; and therefore it is not the church of Ephesus, but the catholic church, which is here called *the house of God, which is the church of the living God.* Observe here,
1. God is the living God; he is the fountain of life, he is life in himself, and he gives life, breath, and all things to his creatures; in him we live, and move, and have our being, Acts xvii. 25, 28. 2. The church is the house of God, he dwells there; the Lord has chosen Zion, to dwell there, "This is my rest, here will I dwell, for I have chosen it;" there may we see God's power and glory, Ps. lxiii. 2.

II. It is the great support of the church that it is the church of the living *God,* the true God in opposition to false gods, dumb and dead idols.
1. As the church of God, it is *the pillar and ground of truth;* that is, either, (1.) The church itself is the pillar and ground of truth. Not that the authority of the scriptures depends upon that of the church, as the papists pretend, for truth is the pillar and ground of the church; but the church holds forth the scripture and the doctrine of Christ, as the pillar to which a proclamation is affixed holds forth the proclamation. *Even to the principalities and powers in heavenly places is made known by the church the manifold wisdom of God,* Eph. iii. 10. (2.) Others understand it of Timothy. He, not he himself only, but he as an evangelist, he and other faithful ministers, are the pillars and ground of truth; it is their business to maintain, hold up, and publish, the truths of Christ in the church. It is said of the apostles that *they seemed to be pillars,* Gal. ii. 9. [1.] Let us be diligent and impartial in our own inquiries after truth; let us buy the truth at any rate, and not think much of any pains to discover it. [2.] Let us be careful to keep and preserve it. *"Buy the truth, and sell it not"* (Prov. xxiii. 23), do not part with it on any consideration." [3.] Let us take care to publish it, and to transmit it safe and uncorrupted unto posterity. [4.] When the church ceases to be the pillar and ground of truth, we may and ought to forsake her; for our regard to truth should be greater than our regard to the church; we are no longer obliged to continue in the church than she continues to be the pillar and ground of truth.

2. But what is the truth which the churches and ministers are the pillars and grounds of? He tells us (*v.* 16) that *without controversy great is the mystery of godliness.* The learned Camero joins this with what goes before, and then it runs thus: "The pillar and ground of the truth, and *without controversy great is the mystery of godliness.*" He supposes this mystery to be the pillar, &c. Observe,

(1.) Christianity is a mystery, a mystery that could not have been found out by reason or the light of nature, and which cannot be comprehended by reason, because it is above reason, though not contrary thereto. It is a mystery, not of philosophy or speculation; but of godliness, designed to promote godliness; and herein it exceeds all the mysteries of the Gentiles. It is also a revealed mystery, not shut up and sealed; and it does not cease to be a mystery because now in part revealed. But,

(2.) What is the mystery of godliness? It is Christ; and here are six things concerning Christ, which make up the mystery of godliness. [1.] That he is God manifest in the flesh : *God was manifest in the flesh.* This proves that he is God, the eternal Word, that was made flesh and was manifest in the flesh. When God was to be manifested to man he was pleased to manifest himself in the incarnation of his own Son : *The Word was made flesh,* John i. 14. [2.] He is *justified in the Spirit.* Whereas he was reproached as a sinner, and put to death as a malefactor, he was raised again by the Spirit, and so was justified from all the calumnies with which he was loaded. *He was made sin for us, and was delivered for our offences;* but, being raised again, he was justified in the Spirit; that is, it was made to appear that his sacrifice was accepted, and so he rose again for our justification, as he was delivered for our offences, Rom. iv. 25. He was put to death in the flesh, but quickened by the Spirit, 1 Pet. iii. 18. [3.] He was *seen of angels.* They worshipped him (Heb. i. 6); they attended his incarnation, his temptation, his agony, his death, his resurrection, his ascension ; this is much to his honour, and shows what a mighty interest he had in the upper world, that angels ministered to him, for he is the Lord of angels. [4.] He is *preached unto the Gentiles.* This is a great part of the mystery of godliness, that Christ was offered to the Gentiles a Redeemer and Saviour ; that whereas, before, salvation was of the Jews, the partition-wall was now taken down, and the Gentiles were taken in. *I have set thee to be a light of the Gentiles,* Acts xiii. 47. [5.] That he was *believed on in the world,* so that he was not preached in vain. Many of the Gentiles welcomed the gospel which the Jews rejected. Who would have thought that the world, which lay in wickedness, would believe in the Son of God, would take him to be their Saviour who was himself crucified at Jerusalem ? But, notwithstanding all the prejudices they laboured under, he was believed on, &c. [6.] He was *received up into glory,* in his ascension. This indeed was before he was believed on in the world ; but it is put last, because it was the crown of his exaltation, and because it is not only his ascension that is meant, but his sitting at the right hand of God, where he ever lives, making intercession, and has all power, both in heaven and earth, and because, in the apostasy of which he treats in the following chapter, his remaining in heaven would be denied by those who pretend to bring him down on their altars in the consecrated wafers. Observe, *First,* He who was manifest in flesh was God, really and truly God, God by nature, and not only so by office, for this makes it to be a mystery. *Secondly,* God was manifest in flesh, real flesh. *Forasmuch as the children are partakers of flesh and blood, he also himself likewise took part of the same,* Heb. ii. 14. And, what is more amazing, he was manifest in the flesh after all flesh had corrupted his way, though he himself was holy from the womb. *Thirdly,* Godliness is a mystery in all its parts and branches, from the beginning to the end, from Christ's incarnation to his ascension. *Fourthly,* It being a great mystery, we should rather humbly adore it and piously believe it, than curiously pry into it, or be too positive in our explications of it and determinations about it, further than the holy scriptures have revealed it to us.

CHAPTER IV

Paul here foretells, I. A dreadful apostasy, ver. 1-3. II. He treats of Christian liberty, ver. 4, 5. III. He gives Timothy divers directions with respect to himself, his doctrine, and the people under his care, ver. 6, to the end.

NOW the Spirit speaketh expressly, that in the latter times some shall depart from the faith, giving heed to seducing spirits, and doctrines of devils; ² Speaking lies in hypocrisy [through the hypocrisy of men that speak lies]; having their conscience seared with a hot iron; ³ Forbidding to marry, *and commanding* to abstain from meats, which God hath created to be received with thanksgiving of them which believe and know the truth. ⁴ For every creature of God *is* good, and nothing to be refused [rejected] if it be received with thanksgiving : ⁵ For it is sanctified by the word of God and prayer.

We have here a prophecy of the apostasy of the latter times, which he had spoken of as a thing expected and taken for granted among Christians, 2 Thess. ii.

I. In the close of the foregoing chapter, we had the mystery of godliness summed up ; and therefore very fitly, in the beginning of this chapter, we have the mystery of iniquity summed up : *The Spirit speaks expressly that in the latter times some shall depart from the faith;* whether he means the Spirit in the Old Testament, or the Spirit in the prophets of the New Testament, or both. The prophecies concerning antichrist, as well as the prophecies concerning Christ, came from the Spirit. The Spirit in both spoke expressly of a general apostasy from the faith of Christ and the pure worship of God. This should come in the *latter times*, during the Christian dispensation, for these are called the latter days ; in the following ages of the church, for the mystery of iniquity now began to work. *Some shall depart from the faith*, or there shall be an apostasy from the faith. Some, not all ; for in the worst of times God will have a remnant, according to the election of grace. *They shall depart from the faith*, the faith delivered to the saints (Jude 3), which was delivered at once, the sound doctrine of the gospel. *Giving heed to seducing spirits*, men who pretended to the Spirit, but were not really guided by the Spirit, 1 John iv. 1, *Beloved, believe not every spirit*, every one who pretends to the Spirit. Now here observe,

1. One of the great instances of the apostasy, namely, giving heed to doctrines of demons, or concerning demons ; that is, those doctrines which teach the worship of saints and angels, as a middle sort of deities, between the immortal God and mortal men, such as the heathen called demons, and

worshipped under that notion. Now this plainly agrees to the church of Rome, and it was one of the first steps towards that great apostasy, the enshrining of the relics of martyrs, paying divine honours to them, erecting altars, burning incense, consecrating images and temples, and making prayers and praises to the honour of saints departed. This demon-worship is paganism revived, the image of the first beast.

2. The instruments of promoting and propagating this apostasy and delusion. (1.) It will be done by hypocrisy of those that speak lies, the agents and emissaries of Satan, who promote these delusions by lies and forgeries and pretended miracles, v. 2. It is done by their hypocrisy, professing honour to Christ, and yet at the same time fighting against all his anointed offices, and corrupting or profaning all his ordinances. This respects also the hypocrisy of those who have *their consciences seared with a red-hot iron*, who are perfectly lost to the very first principles of virtue and moral honesty. If men had not their consciences seared as with a hot iron, they could never maintain a power to dispense with oaths for the good of the catholic cause, could never maintain that no faith is to be kept with heretics, could never divest themselves of all remains of humanity and compassion, and clothe themselves with the most barbarous cruelty, under pretence of promoting the interest of the church. (2.) Another part of their character is that they forbid to marry, forbid their clergy to marry, and speak very reproachfully of marriage, though an ordinance of God ; and that they command *to abstain from meats*, and place religion in such abstinence at certain times and seasons, only to exercise a tyranny over the consciences of men.

3. On the whole observe, (1.) The apostasy of the latter times should not surprise us, because it was expressly foretold by the Spirit. (2.) The Spirit is God, otherwise he could not certainly foresee such distant events, which as to us are uncertain and contingent, depending on the tempers, humours, and lusts of men. (3.) The difference between the predictions of the Spirit and the oracles of the heathen is remarkable ; the Spirit speaks expressly, but the oracles of the heathen were always doubtful and uncertain. (4.) It is comfortable to think that in such general apostasies all are not carried away, but only some. (5.) It is common for seducers and deceivers to pretend to the Spirit, which is a strong presumption that all are convinced that this is the most likely to work in us an approbation of what pretends to come from the Spirit. (6.) Men must be hardened, and their consciences seared, before they can depart from the faith, and draw in others to side with them. (7.) It is a sign that men have departed from the faith when they will command what God has forbidden, such as saint and angel or demon-worship ; and forbid what God has allowed or commanded, such as marriage and meats.

II. Having mentioned their hypocritical fastings, the apostle takes occasion to lay down the doctrine of the Christian liberty, which we enjoy under the gospel, of using God's good creatures,—that, whereas under the law there was a distinction of meats between clean and unclean (such sorts of flesh they might eat, and such they might not eat), all this is now taken away ; and we are to call nothing common or unclean, Acts x. 15. Here observe, 1. We are to look upon our food as that which God has created ; we have it from him, and therefore must use it for him. 2. God, in making those things, had a special regard to *those who believe and know the truth*, to good Christians, who have a covenant right to the creatures, whereas others have only a common right. 3. What God has created is to be *received with thanksgiving.* We must not refuse the gifts of God's bounty, nor be scrupulous in making differences where God has made none ; but receive them, and be thankful, acknowledging the power of God the Maker of them, and the bounty of God the giver of them : *Every creature of God is good, and nothing to be refused, v.* 4. This plainly sets us at liberty from all the distinctions of meats appointed by the ceremonial law, as particularly that of swine's flesh, which the Jews were forbidden to eat, but which is allowed to us Christians, by this rule, *Every creature of God is good,* &c. Observe God's good creatures are then good, and doubly sweet to us, when they are received with thanksgiving.—*For it is sanctified by the word of God and prayer, v.* 5. It is a desirable thing to have a sanctified use of our creature-comforts. Now they are sanctified to us, (1.) By the word of God ; not only his permission, allowing us the liberty of the use of these things, but his promise to feed us with food convenient for us. This gives us a sanctified use of our creature-comforts. (2.) By prayer, which blesses our meat to us. The word of God and prayer must be brought to our common actions and affairs, and then we do all in faith. Here observe, [1.] Every creature is God's, for he made all. *Every beast in the forest is mine* (says God), *and the cattle upon a thousand hills. I know all the fowls of the mountains, and the wild beasts of the field are mine,* Ps. l. 10, 11. [2.] Every creature of God is good : when the blessed God took a survey of all his works, God saw all that was made, and behold it was very good, Gen. i. 31. [3.] The blessing of God makes every creature nourishing to us ; man lives not by bread alone, but by every word that proceeds out of the mouth of God (Matt. iv. 4), and therefore nothing ought to be refused. [4.] We ought therefore to ask his blessing by prayer, and so to sanctify the creatures we receive by prayer.

⁶ If thou put the brethren in remembrance of these things, thou shalt be a good minister of Jesus Christ, nourished up in the words of faith and of good doctrine, whereunto thou hast attained [**the good doctrine which thou hast followed until now**]. ⁷ But refuse profane and old wives' fables, and exercise thyself *rather* unto godliness. ⁸ For bodily exercise profiteth little [**for a little time**]: but godliness is profitable unto all things, having promise of the life that now is, and of that which is to come. ⁹ This *is* a faithful saying and worthy of all acceptation. ¹⁰ For therefore we both labour and suffer reproach [**strive**], because we trust in the living God, who is the Saviour of all men, especially of those that believe. ¹¹ These things command and teach. ¹² Let no man despise thy youth ; but be thou an example of the believers, in word, in conversation, in charity, in spirit [**in word, in manner of life, in love**], in faith, in purity. ¹³ Till I come, give attendance to reading, to exhortation, to doctrine [**teaching**]. ¹⁴ Neglect not the gift that is in thee, which was given thee by prophecy, with the laying on of the hands of the presbytery. ¹⁵ Meditate upon [**be diligent in**

these things ; give thyself wholly to them ; that thy profiting may appear to [that thy progress may be manifest unto] all. [16] Take heed unto thyself, and unto the doctrine [thy teaching], continue in them [these things] : for in doing this thou shalt both save thyself, and them that hear thee.

The apostle would have Timothy to instil into the minds of Christians such sentiments as might prevent their being seduced by the judaizing teachers. Observe, Those are good ministers of Jesus Christ who are diligent in their work ; not that study to advance new notions, but that *put the brethren in remembrance of those things which they have received and heard. Wherefore I will not not be negligent to put you always in remembrance of these things, though you knew them,* 2. Pet. i. 12. And elsewhere, *I stir up your pure minds by way of remembrance,* 2. Pet. iii. 1. And, says the apostle Jude, *I will therefore put you in remembrance,* Jude 5. You see that the apostles and apostolical men reckoned it a main part of their work to put their hearers in remembrance ; for we are apt to forget, and slow to learn and remember, the things of God—*Nourished up in the words of faith and good doctrine whereunto thou has attained.* Observe, 1. Even ministers themselves have need to be growing and increasing in the knowledge of Christ and his doctrine : they must be nourished up in the words of faith. 2. The best way for ministers to grow in knowledge and faith is to put the brethren in remembrance ; while we teach others, we teach ourselves. 3. Those whom ministers teach are brethren, and are to be treated like brethren ; for ministers are not lords of God's heritage.

I. Godliness is here pressed upon him and others : *Refuse profane and old wives' sayings, v.* 7, 8. The Jewish traditions, which some people fill their heads with, have nothing to do with them. *But exercise thyself rather unto godliness ;* that is, mind practical religion. Those who would be godly must exercise themselves unto godliness ; it requires a constant exercise. The reason is taken from the gain of godliness ; *bodily exercise profits little,* or for a little time. Abstinence from meats and marriage, and the like, though they pass for acts of mortification and self-denial, yet profit little, they turn to little account. What will it avail us to mortify the body if we do not mortify sin ? Observe, 1. There is a great deal to be got by godliness ; it will be of use to us in the whole of our life, for it has *the promise of the life that now is and of that which is to come.* 2. The gain of godliness lies much in the promise : and the promises made to godly people relate to the life that now is, but especially they relate to the life that is to come. Under the Old Testament the promises were mostly of temporal blessings, but under the New Testament of spiritual and eternal blessings. If godly people have but little of the good things of the life that now is, yet it shall be made up to them in the good things of the life that is to come. 3. There were profane and old wives' fables in the days of the apostles ; and Timothy, though an excellent man, was not above such a word of advice, *Refuse profane, &c.* 4. It is not enough that we refuse profane and old wives' fables, but we must exercise ourselves to godliness ; we must not only cease to do evil, but we must learn to do well (Isa. i. 16, 17), and we must make a practice of exercising ourselves to godliness. And, 5. Those who are truly godly shall not be losers at last, whatever becomes of those who content themselves with bodily exercise, for godliness has the promise, &c.

II. The encouragement which we have to proceed in the ways of godliness, and to exercise ourselves to it, notwithstanding the difficulties and discouragements that we meet with in it. He had said (*v.* 8) that it *is profitable for all things, having the promise of the life which now is.* But the question is, Will the profit balance the loss? For, if it will not it is not profit. Yes, we are sure it will. Here is another of Paul's faithful sayings, worthy of all acceptation—that all our labours and losses in the service of God and the work of religion will be abundantly recompensed, so that though we lose for Christ we shall not lose by him. *Therefore we labour and suffer reproach, because we trust in the living God, v.* 10. Observe,

1. Godly people must labour and expect reproach; they must do well, and yet expect at the same time to suffer ill: toil and trouble are to be expected by us in this world, not only as men, but as saints.

2. Those who labour and suffer reproach in the service of God and the work of religion may depend upon the living God that they shall not lose by it. Let this encourage them, *We trust in the living God.* The consideration of this, that the God who has undertaken to be our pay-master is the living God, who does himself live for ever and is the fountain of life to all who serve him, should encourage us in all our services and in all our sufferings for him, especially considering that he is *the Saviour of all men.* (1.) By his providences he protects the persons, and prolongs the lives, of the children of men. (2.) He has a general good-will to the eternal salvation of all men thus far that he is not willing that any should perish, but that all should come to repentance. He desires not the death of sinners; he is thus far the Saviour of all men that none are left in the same desperate condition that fallen angels are in. Now, if he be thus the Saviour of all men, we may hence infer that much more he will be the rewarder of those who seek and serve him; if he has such a good-will for all his creatures, much more will he provide well for those who are new creatures, who are born again. He is the Saviour of all men, but *especially of those that believe;* and the salvation he has in store for those that believe is sufficient to recompense them for all their services and sufferings. Here we see, [1.] The life of a Christian is a life of labour and suffering: *We labour and suffer.* [2.] The best we can expect to suffer in the present life is reproach for our well-doing, for our work of faith and labour of love. [3.] True Christians trust in the living God; for cursed is the man that trusts in man, or in any but the living God; and those that trust in him shall never be ashamed. *Trust in him at all times.* [4.] God is the general Saviour of all men, as he has put them into a salvable state; but he is in a particular manner the Saviour of true believers; there is then a general and a special redemption.

III. He concludes the chapter with an exhortation to Timothy,

1. To *command and teach these things* that he had now been teaching him. "Command them to exercise themselves unto godliness, teach them the profit of it, and that if they serve God they serve one who will be sure to bear them out."

2. To conduct himself with that gravity and prudence which might gain him respect, notwithstanding his youth: "*Let no man despise thy youth;* that is, give no man an occasion to despise thy youth." Men's youth will not be despised if they do not by youthful vanities and follies make themselves despicable; and this men may do who are old, who may therefore thank themselves if they be despised.

3. To confirm his doctrine by a good example: *Be thou an example of*

the believers, &c. Observe, Those who teach by their doctrine must teach
by their life, else they pull down with one hand what they build up with
the other : they must be examples both *in word and conversation.* Their
discourse must be edifying, and this will be a good example : their conversation must be strict, and this will be a good example : they must be
examples *in charity,* or love to God and all good men, examples *in spirit,*
that is, in spiritual-mindedness, in spiritual worship,—*in faith,* that is, in
the profession of Christian faith,—and *in purity* or chastity.

4. He charges him to study hard : *Till I come, give attendance to reading,
to exhortation, to doctrine, to meditation upon these things, v.* 13. Though
Timothy had extraordinary gifts, yet he must use ordinary means. Or it
may be meant of the public reading of the scriptures ; he must *read and
exhort,* that is, read and expound, read and press what he read upon them ;
he must expound it both by way of exhortation and by way of doctrine ;
he must teach them both what to do and what to believe. Observe, (1.)
Ministers must teach and command the things that they are themselves
taught and commanded to do ; they must teach people to observe all things
whatsoever Christ has commanded, Matt. xxviii. 20. (2.) The best way
for ministers to avoid being despised is to teach and practise the things
that are given them in charge. No wonder if ministers are despised who
do not teach these things, or who, instead of being examples of good to
believers, act directly contrary to the doctrines they preach ; for ministers
are to be ensamples of their flock. (3.) Those ministers that are the best
accomplished for their work must yet mind their studies, that they may be
improving in knowledge ; and they must mind also their work ; they are
to give attendance to reading, to exhortation, to doctrine.

5. He charges him to beware of negligence : *Neglect not the gift that is
in thee, v.* 14. The gifts of God will wither if they be neglected. It may
be understood either of the office to which he was advanced, or of his
qualifications for that office ; if of the former, it was ordination in an
ordinary way ; if of the latter, it was extraordinary. It seems to be the
former, for it was by *laying on of hands,* &c. Here see the scripture-way
of ordination : it was by the laying on of hands, and the laying on of the
hands of the presbytery. Observe, Timothy was ordained by men in office.
It was an extraordinary gift that we read of elsewhere as being conferred
on him by the laying on of Paul's hands, but he was invested in the office
of the ministry by the laying on of the hands of the presbytery. (1.) We
may note, The office of the ministry is a gift, it is the gift of Christ ; when
he ascended on high, he received gifts for men, and he gave some apostles,
and some pastors and teachers (Eph. iv. 8, 11), and this was a very kind
gift to his church. (2.) Ministers ought not to neglect the gift bestowed
upon them, whether by gift we are here to understand the office of the
ministry or the qualifications for that office ; neither the one nor the other
must be neglected. (3.) Though there was prophecy in the case of
Timothy (the gift was given by prophecy), yet this was accompanied by
the laying on of the hands of the presbytery, that is, a number of presbyters ; the office was conveyed to him this way ; and I should think here
is a sufficient warrant for ordination by presbyters, since it does not appear
that Paul was concerned in Timothy's ordination. It is true, extraordinary gifts were conferred on him by the laying on of the apostle's hands
(2 Tim. 1. 6), but, if he was concerned in his ordination, the presbytery
was not excluded, for that is particularly mentioned, whence it seems
pretty evident that the presbytery have the inherent power of ordination.

6. Having this work committed to him, he must *give himself wholly to it*: "Be wholly in those things, *that thy profiting may appear*." He was a wise knowing man, and yet must still be profiting, and make it appear that he improved in knowledge. Observe, (1.) Ministers are to be much in meditation. They are to consider beforehand how and what they must speak. They are to meditate on the great trust committed to them, on the worth and value of immortal souls, and on the account they must give at the last. (2.) Ministers must be wholly in these things, they must mind these things as their principal work and business: *Give thyself wholly to them.* (3.) By this means their profiting will appear in all things, as well as to all persons; this is the way for them to profit in knowledge and grace, and also to profit others.

7. He presses it upon him to be very cautious : "*Take heed to thyself and to the doctrine*, consider what thou preachest ; *continue in them*, in the truths that thou hast received ; and this will be the way to *save thyself, and those that hear thee*." Observe, (1.) Ministers are engaged in saving work, which makes it a good work. (2.) The care of ministers should be in the first place to save themselves. "Save thyself in the first place, so shalt thou be instrumental to save those that hear thee." (3.) Ministers in preaching should aim at the salvation of those that hear them, next to the salvation of their own souls. (4.) The best way to answer both these ends is to take heed to ourselves, &c.

CHAPTER V.

Here the apostle, I. Directs Timothy how to reprove, ver. 1, 2. II. Adverts to widows, both elder and younger, ver. 3-16. III. To elders, ver. 17-19. IV. Treats of public reproof, ver. 20. V. Gives a solemn charge concerning ordination, ver. 21, 22. VI. Refers to his health (ver. 23), and states men's sins to be very different in their effects, ver. 24, 25.

REBUKE not an elder, but intreat *him* as a father; *and* the younger men as brethren; ² The elder women as mothers; the younger as sisters, with all purity.

Here the apostle gives rules to Timothy, and in him to other ministers, in reproving. Ministers are reprovers by office; it is a part, though the least pleasing part, of their office ; they are to preach the word, to reprove and rebuke, 2 Tim. iv. 2. A great difference is to be made in our reproofs, according to the age, quality, and other circumstances of the persons rebuked ; thus, an elder in age or office must be entreated as a father ; *on some have compassion, making a difference*, Jude 22. Now the rule is, 1. To be very tender in rebuking elders—elders in age, elders by office. Respect must be had to the dignity of their years and place, and therefore they must not be rebuked sharply nor magisterially ; but Timothy himself, though an evangelist, must entreat them as fathers, for this would be the likeliest way to work upon them, and to win upon them. 2. The younger must be rebuked as brethren, with love and tenderness ; not as desirous to spy faults or pick quarrels, but as being willing to make the best of them.

There is need of a great deal of meekness in reproving those who deserve reproof. 3. The elder women must be reproved, when there is occasion. as mothers. Hos. ii. 2, *Plead with your mother, plead.* 4. The younger women must be reproved, but reproved as *sisters, with all purity.* If Timothy, so mortified a man to this world and to the flesh and the lusts of it, had need of such a caution as this, much more have we.

3 Honour widows that are widows indeed. 4 But if any widow have children or nephews [**grandchildren**], let them learn first to show piety at home, and to requite their parents: for that is good and acceptable before God. 5 Now she that is a widow indeed, and desolate, trusteth in God, and continueth in supplications and prayers night and day. 6 But she that liveth in [**giveth herself to**] pleasure is dead while she liveth. 7 And these things give in charge, that they may be blameless. 8 But if any provide not for his own, and specially for those of his own house, he hath denied the faith, and is worse than an infidel [**unbeliever**]. 9 Let not a widow be taken into the number under threescore years old, having been the wife of one man, 10 Well reported of for good works; if she have brought up children, if she have lodged strangers, if she have washed the saints' feet, if she have relieved the afflicted, if she have diligently followed every good work. 11 But the younger widows refuse: for when they have begun to wax wanton against Christ, they will marry; 12 Having damnation [**condemnation**], because they have cast off their first faith. 13 And withal they learn *to be* idle, wandering about from house to house; and not only idle, but tattlers also and busybodies, speaking things which they ought not. 14 I will therefore that the younger women [**widows**] marry, bear children, guide the house, give none occasion to the adversary to speak reproachfully. 15 For some are already turned aside after Satan. 16 If any man or woman [**any woman**] that believeth have widows, let them relieve them, and let not the church be charged; that it may relieve them that are widows indeed.

Directions are here given concerning the taking of widows into the number of those who were employed by the church and had maintenance from the church : *Honour widows that are widows indeed.* Honour them, that is, maintain them, admit them into office. There was in those times an office in the church in which widows were employed, and that was to tend the sick and the aged, to look to them by the direction of the deacons. We read of the care taken of widows immediately upon the first forming of the Christian church (Acts vi. 1), where the Grecians thought their widows were neglected in the daily ministration and provision made for poor widows. The general rule is to *honour widows that are widows indeed,* to maintain them, to relieve them with respect and tenderness.

I. It is appointed that those widows only should be relieved by the charity of the church who were pious and devout, and not wanton widows that *lived in pleasure, v.* 5, 6. She is to be reckoned a widow indeed, and fit to be maintained at the church's charge, who, being *desolate, trusteth in God.* Observe, It is the duty and comfort of those who are desolate to trust in God. *Therefore* God sometimes brings his people into such straits that they have nothing else to trust to, that they may with more confidence trust in him. Widowhood is a desolate estate ; but *let the widows trust in me* (Jer. xlix. 11), and rejoice that they have a God to trust to. Again, Those who trust in God must *continue in prayer.* If by faith we confide in God, by prayer we must give glory to God and commit ourselves to his guidance. Anna was a widow indeed, who *departed not from the temple* (Luke ii. 37), *but served God with fasting and prayer night and day.* But she is not a widow indeed *that lives in pleasure* (v. 6), or who lives licentiously. A jovial widow is not a widow indeed, not fit to be taken under the care of the church. *She that lives in pleasure is dead while she lives,* is no living member of the church, but as a carcase in it, or a mortified member. We may apply it more generally ; those who live in pleasure are dead while they live, spiritually dead, *dead in trespasses and sins ;* they are in the world to no purpose, buried alive as to the great ends of living.

II. Another rule he gives is that the church should not be charged with the maintenance of those widows who had relations of their own that were able to maintain them. This is mentioned several times (v. 4) : *If any widow have children or nephews,* that is grandchildren or near relations, let them maintain them, and let not the church be burdened. So v. 16. This is called showing *piety at home* (v. 4), or showing piety towards their own families. Observe, The respect of children to their parents, with their care of them, is fitly called piety. This is requiting their parents. Children can never sufficiently requite their parents for the care they have taken of them, and the pains they have taken with them ; but they must endeavour to do it. It is the indispensable duty of children, if their parents be in necessity, and they in ability to relieve them, to do it to the utmost of their power, *for this is good and acceptable before God.* The Pharisees taught that a gift to the altar was more acceptable to God than relieving a poor parent, Matt. xv. 5. But here we are told that this *is better than all burnt-offerings and sacrifices ; this is good and acceptable,* &c. He speaks of this again (v. 8), *If any provide not for his own,* &c. If any men or women do not maintain their own poor relations who belong to them, they do in effect *deny the faith ;* for the design of Christ was to confirm the law of Moses, and particularly the law of the fifth commandment, which is, *Honour thy father and mother ;* so that those deny the faith who disobey that law, much more if they provide not for their wives and children, who are parts of themselves ; if they spend that upon their lusts which should maintain their families, they have denied the faith *and are worse than infidels.* One reason why this care must be taken that those who are rich should maintain their poor relations, and not burden the church with them is (v. 16) *that it may relieve those who are widows indeed.* Observe, Charity misplaced is a great hindrance to true charity ; there should be prudence in the choice of the objects of charity, that it may not be thrown away upon those who are not properly so, that there may be the more for those who are real objects of charity.

III. He gives directions concerning the characters of the widows that were to be taken into the number to receive the church's charity : not under sixty years old, nor any who have divorced their husbands or been divorced from them and have married again ; she must have been *the wife of one man,* such as had been a housekeeper, had a good name for hospitality and charity, *well reported of for good works.* Observe, Particular care ought to be taken to relieve those, when they fall into decay, who, when they had wherewithal, were ready to every good work. Here are instances of such good works as are proper to be done by good wives : *If she have brought up children :* he does not say, If she have borne children (*children are a heritage of the Lord*), that depends on the will of God ; but, if she had not children of her own, yet if she had brought up children. *If she have lodged strangers,* and *washed the saints' feet* ; if she have been ready to give entertainment to good Christians and good ministers, when they were in their travels for the spreading of the gospel. Washing of the feet of their friends was a part of their entertainments. *If she have relieved the afflicted* when she had ability, let her be relieved now. Observe, Those who would find mercy when they are in distress must show mercy when they are in prosperity.

IV. He cautions them to take heed of admitting into the number those who are likely to be no credit to them (*v.* 11) : *The younger widows refuse ;* they will be weary of their employments in the church, and of living by rule, as they must do ; so they *will marry, and cast off their first faith.* You read of a first love (Rev. ii. 4), and here of a first faith, that is, the engagements they gave to the church to behave well, and as became the trust reposed in them : it does not appear that by their first faith is meant their vow not to marry, for the scripture is very silent on that head ; besides the apostle here advises the younger widows to marry (*v.* 14), which he would not if hereby they must have broken their vows. Dr. Whitby well observes, "If this faith referred to a promise made to the church not to marry, it could not be called their first faith." *Withal they learn to be idle, and not only idle, but tattlers,* &c., *v.* 13. Observe, It is seldom that those who are idle are idle only, they learn *to be tattlers and busybodies,* and to make mischief among neighbours, and sow discord among brethren. Those who had not attained to such a gravity of mind as was fit for the deaconesses (or the widows who were taken among the church's poor), let them *marry, bear children,* &c., *v.* 14. Observe, If housekeepers do not mind their business, but are tattlers, they give occasion to the adversaries of Christianity to reproach the Christian name, which, it seems, there were some instances of, *v.* 15. We learn hence, 1. In the primitive church there was care taken of poor widows, and provision made for them ; and the churches of Christ in these days should follow so good an example, as far as they are able. 2. In the distribution of the church's charity, or alms, great care is to be taken that those share in the public bounty who most want it and best deserve it. A widow was not to be taken into the primitive church that had relations who were able to maintain her, or who was not well reported of for good works, but lived in pleasure : *But the younger widows refuse, for, when they have begun to wax wanton against Christ, they will marry.* 3. The credit of religion, and the reputation of Christian churches, are very much concerned in the character and behaviour of those that are taken into any employment in the church, though of a lower nature (such as the business of deaconesses), or that receive alms of the church ; if they do not behave well, but are tattlers and busy-bodies, they will give occasion to the adversary to speak reproachfully. 4. Christianity obliges its professors to relieve their indigent friends, particularly poor widows, that the church may not be charged with them, that it may relieve those that are widows indeed : rich people should be ashamed to burden the church with their poor relations, when it is with difficulty that those are supplied who have no children or nephews, that is, grand-children, who are in a capacity to relieve them.

¹⁷ Let the elders that rule well be counted worthy of double honour, especially they who labour in the word and doctrine. ¹⁸ For the scripture saith, Thou shalt not muzzle the ox that [when he] treadeth out the corn. And, the labourer *is* worthy of his reward. ¹⁹ Against an elder receive not an accusation, but before two or three witnesses. ²⁰ Them that sin rebuke before all, that others also may fear. ²¹ I charge *thee* before God, and the Lord Jesus Christ, and the elect angels, that thou observe these things without preferring one before another [without prejudice], doing nothing by partiality. ²² Lay hands suddenly [hastily] on no man, neither be partaker of other men's sins : keep thyself pure. ²³ Drink no longer water, but use a little wine for thy stomach's sake and thine often infirmities. ²⁴ Some men's sins are open beforehand, going before to judgment; and some *men* they follow after. ²⁵ Likewise also the good works *of some* are manifest beforehand ; and they that are otherwise cannot be hid.

Here are directions,

I. Concerning the supporting of ministers. Care must be taken that they be honourably maintained (*v.* 17) : *Let the elders that rule well be counted worthy of double honour* (that is, of double maintenance, double to what they have had, or to what others have), *especially those who labour in the word and doctrine,* those who are more laborious than others. Observe, The presbytery ruled, and the same that ruled were those *who laboured in the word and doctrine:* they had not one to preach to them and another to rule them, but the work was done by one and the same person. Some have imagined that by the *elders that rule well* the apostle means lay-elders, who were employed in ruling but not in teaching, who were concerned in church-government, but did not meddle with the administration of the word and sacraments ; and I confess this is the plainest text of scripture that can be found to countenance such an opinion. But it seems a little strange that mere ruling elders should be accounted worthy of double honour, when the apostle preferred preaching to baptizing, and much more would he prefer it to ruling the church ; and it is more strange that the apostle should take no notice of them when he treats of church-officers ; but, as it is hinted before, they had not, in the primitive church, one to preach to them and another to rule them, but ruling and teaching were performed by the same persons, only some might labour more in the word and doctrine than others. Here we have, 1. The work of ministers ; it consists principally in two things : ruling well and labouring in the word and doctrine. This was the main business of elders or presbyters in the days of the apostles. 2. The honour due to those who were not idle, but laborious in this work ; they were worthy of double honour, esteem, and maintenance. He quotes a scripture to confirm this command concerning the maintenance of ministers that we might think foreign ; but it intimates what a significancy there was in many of the laws of Moses, and particularly in this, *Thou shalt not muzzle the ox that treads out the corn*, Deut. xxv. 4. The beasts that were employed in treading out the corn (for that way they took instead of threshing it) were allowed to feed while they did the work, so that the more work they did the more food they had ; therefore let the elders that labour in the word and doctrine be well provided for ; *for the labourer is worthy of his reward* (Matt. x. 10), and there is all the reason in the world that he should have it. We hence learn, (1.) God, both under the law, and now under the gospel, has taken care that his ministers be well provided for. Does God take care for oxen, and will he not take care of his own servants ? The ox only treads out the corn of which they make the bread that perishes ; but ministers break the bread of life which endures for ever. (2.) The comfortable subsistence of ministers, as it is God's appointment that those who preach the gospel should live of the gospel (1 Cor. ix. 14), so it is their just due, as much as the reward of the labourer ; and those who would have ministers starved, or not comfortably provided for, God will require it of them another day.

II. Concerning the accusation of ministers (*v.* 19) : *Against an elder receive not an accusation, but before two or three witnesses.* Here is the scripture-method of proceeding against an elder, when accused of any crime. Observe, 1. There must be an accusation ; it must not be a flying uncertain report, but an accusation, containing a certain charge, must be drawn up. Further, He is not to be proceeded against by way of enquiry ; this is according to the modern practice of the inquisition, which draws up articles for men to purge themselves of such crimes, or else to accuse themselves ; but, according to the advice of Paul, there must be an accusation brought against an elder. 2. This accusation is not to be received unless supported by two or three credible witnesses ; and the accusation must be received before them, that is, the accused must have the accusers face to face, because the reputation of a minister is, in a particular manner, a tender thing ; and therefore, before any thing be done in the least to blemish that reputation, great care should be taken that the thing alleged against him be well proved, that he be not reproached upon an uncertain surmise ; "but (*v.* 20) *those that sin rebuke before all ;* that is, thou needest not be so tender of other people, but rebuke them publicly." Or "those that sin before all rebuke before all, that the plaster may be as wide as the wound, and that those who are in danger of sinning by the example of their fall may take warning by the rebuke given them for it, *that others also may fear.*" Observe, 1. Public scandalous sinners must be rebuked publicly : as their sin has been public, and committed before many, or at least come to the hearing of all, so their reproof must be public, and before all. (2.) Public rebuke is designed for the good of others, that they may fear, as well as for the good of the party rebuked ; hence it was ordered under the law that public offenders should receive public punishment, that *all Israel* might *hear, and fear, and do no more wickedly.*

III. Concerning the ordination of ministers (*v.* 22) : *Lay hands suddenly on no man ;* it seems to be meant of the ordaining of men to the office of the ministry, which ought not to be done rashly and inconsiderately, and before due trial made of their gifts and graces, their abilities and qualifications for it. Some understand it of absolution : "Be not too hasty in lay-ing hands on any ; remit not the censure of the church to any, till time be first taken for the proof of their sincerity in their repentance, *neither be partakers of other men's sins,* implying that those who are too easy in re-mitting the censures of the church encourage others in the sins which are thus connived at, and make themselves thereby guilty. Observe, We have great need to watch over ourselves at all times, that we do not make our-selves partakers of other men's sins. "Keep thyself pure, not only from doing the like thyself, but from countenancing it, or being any way acces-sary to it in others." Here is, 1. A caution against the rash ordination of ministers, or absolution of those who have been under church-censures : *Lay hands suddenly on no man.* 2. Those who are rash, either in the one case or the other, will make themselves partakers in other men's sins. 3. We must keep ourselves pure, if we will be pure ; the grace of God makes and keeps us pure, but it is by our own endeavours.

IV. Concerning absolution, to which *v.* 24, 25, seem to refer : *Some men's sins are open beforehand, going before to judgment, and some follow after,* &c. Observe, Ministers have need of a great deal of wisdom, to know how to accommodate themselves to the variety of offences and offenders that they have occasion to deal with. Some men's sins are so plain and obvious, and not found by secret search, that there is no dispute concern-ing the bringing of them under the censures of the church ; they *go before to judgment,* to lead them to censure.—*Others they follow after ;* that is, their wickedness does not presently appear, nor till after a due search has been made concerning it. Or, as some understand it. some men's sins con-tinue after they are censured ; they are not reformed by the censure, and in that case there must be no absolution. So, also, as to the evidences of repentance : *The good works of some are manifest beforehand. And those that are otherwise,* whose good works do not appear, their wickedness *can-not be hid,* and so it will be easy to discern who are to be absolved, and who are not. Observe, 1. There are secret, and there are open sins ; some men's sins are open beforehand, and going before unto judgment, and some they follow after. 2. Sinners must be differently dealt with by the church. 3. The effects of church-censures are very different ; some are thereby humbled and brought to repentance, so that their good works are manifest beforehand, while it is quite otherwise with others. 4. The incorrigible cannot be hid ; for God will bring to light the hidden things of darkness, and make manifest the counsels of all hearts.

V. Concerning Timothy himself. 1. Here is a charge to him to be care-ful of his office ; and a solemn charge it is : *I charge thee before God, as thou wilt answer it to God before the holy and elect angels, observe these things without partiality, v.* 21. Observe, It ill becomes ministers to be partial, and to have respect of persons, and to prefer one before another upon any secular account. He charges him, by all that is dear, *before God, and the Lord Jesus Christ, and the elect angels,* to guard against partiality. Ministers must give an account to God and the Lord Jesus Christ, whether, and how, they have observed all things given them in charge : and woe to them if they have been partial in their ministrations, out of any worldly politic view. 2. He charges him to take care of his health : *Drink no longer water,* &c. It seems Timothy was a mortified man to the plea-sures of sense ; he drank water, and he was a man of no strong constitu-tion of body, and for this reason Paul advises him to use wine for the helping of his stomach and the recruiting of his nature. Observe, It is a little wine, for ministers must not be given to much wine ; so much as may be for the health of the body, not so as to distemper it, for God has made wine to rejoice man's heart. Note, (1.) It is the will of God that people should take all due care of their bodies. As we are not to make them our masters, so neither our slaves ; but to use them so that they may be most fit and helpful to us in the service of God. (2.) Wine is most proper for sickly and weak people, whose stomachs are often out of order, and who labour under infirmities. *Give strong drink to him that is ready to perish, and wine to those that are of heavy hearts*, Prov. xxxi. 6. (3.) Wine should be used as a help, and not a hindrance, to our work and usefulness.

CHAPTER VI

I. He treats of the duty of servants, ver. 1, 2. II. Of false teachers, ver. 3-5. III. Of godliness and covetousness, ver. 6-10. IV. What Timothy was to flee, and what to follow, ver. 11, 12. V. A solemn charge, ver. 13-16. VI. A charge for the rich, ver. 17-19. And lastly, A charge to Timothy, ver. 20, 21.

LET as many servants as are under the yoke count their own masters worthy of all honour, that the name of God and *his* doctrine be not blasphemed. ² And they that have believing masters, let them not despise *them*, because they are brethren ; but rather do *them* service, because they are faithful and beloved, partakers of the benefit [they that partake of the benefit are believing and beloved]. These things teach and exhort. ³ If any man teach otherwise, and consent not to wholesome words, *even* the words of our Lord Jesus Christ, and to the doctrine which is according to godliness ; ⁴ He is proud [puffed up], knowing nothing, but doting about questions and strifes of words, whereof cometh envy, strife, railings, evil surmisings, ⁵ Perverse disputings [wranglings] of men of corrupt minds, and destitute of the truth, supposing that gain is godliness [that godliness is a way of gain] : from such withdraw thyself.

I. Here is the duty of servants. The apostle had spoken before of church-relations, here of our family-relations. Servants are here said to be *under the yoke*, which denotes both subjection and labour ; they are yoked to work, not to be idle. If Christianity finds servants under the yoke, it continues them under it ; for the gospel does not cancel the obligations any lie under either by the law of nature or by mutual consent. They must respect their masters, *count them worthy of all honour* (because they are their masters), of all the respect, observance, compliance, and obedience, that are justly expected from servants to their masters. Not that they were to think that of them which they were not ; but as their masters they must count them worthy of all that honour which was fit for them to receive, *that the name of God be not blasphemed.* If servants that embraced the Christian religion should grow insolent and disobedient to their masters, the doctrine of Christ would be reflected on for their sakes, as if it had made men worse livers than they had been before they received the gospel. Observe, If the professors of religion misbehave themselves, *the name of God and his doctrine* are in danger of being blasphemed by those who seek occasion *to speak evil of that worthy name by which we are called.* And this is a good reason why we should all conduct ourselves well, that we may prevent the occasion which many seek, and will be very apt to lay hold of, to speak ill of religion for our sakes. Or suppose the master were a Christian, and a believer too, and the servant a believer too, would not this excuse him, because *in Christ there is neither bond nor free?* No, by no means, for Jesus Christ did not come to dissolve the bond of civil relation, but to strengthen it: *Those that have believing masters, let them not despise them because they are brethren;* for this brotherhood relates only to spiritual privileges, not to any outward dignity or advantage (those misunderstand and abuse their religion who make it a pretence for deny-ing the duties that they owe to their relations) ; nay, *rather do them service, because they are faithful and beloved.* They must think themselves the more obliged to serve them because the faith and love that bespeak men Christians oblige them to do good ; and that is all wherein their service consists. Observe, It is a great encouragement to us in doing our duty to our relations if we have reason to think they are faithful and beloved, *and partakers of the benefit,* that is, of the benefit of Christianity. Again, Believing masters and servants are brethren, and partakers of the benefit; for in Christ Jesus there is neither bond nor free, for you are all one in Christ Jesus, Gal. iii. 28. Timothy is appointed *to teach and exhort these things.* Ministers must preach not only the general duties of all, but the duties of particular relations.

II. Paul here warns Timothy to withdraw from those who corrupted the doctrine of Christ, and made it the subject of strife, debate, and con-troversy : *If any man teach otherwise* (v. 3-5), do not preach practically, do not teach and exhort that which is for the promoting of serious godliness—if he will not consent to wholesome words, words that have a direct tendency to heal the soul—if he will *not consent* to these, even the *words of our Lord Jesus Christ.* Observe, We are not required to consent to any words as wholesome words except the words of our Lord Jesus Christ ; but to those we must give our unfeigned assent and consent, and *to the doctrine which is according to godliness.* Observe, The doctrine of our Lord Jesus is a doctrine according to godliness ; it has a direct tendency to make people godly. But he that does not consent to the words of Christ *is proud* (v. 4) and contentious, ignorant, and does a great deal of mischief to the church, knowing nothing. Observe, Commonly those are most proud who know least; for with all their knowledge they do not know them-selves.—*But doting about questions.* Those who fall off from the plain practical doctrines of Christianity fall in with controversies, which eat out the life and power of religion ; they dote about questions *and strifes of words,* which do a great deal of mischief in the church, are the occasion of *envy, strife, railings, evil surmisings.* When men are not content with the words of the Lord Jesus Christ, and the doctrine which is according to godliness, but will frame notions of their own and impose them, and that too in their own words, which man's wisdom teaches, and not in the words which the Holy Ghost teaches (1 Cor. ii. 13), they sow the seeds of all mischief in the church. Hence come *perverse disputings of men of corrupt minds* (*v.* 5), disputes that are all subtlety, and no solidity. Observe, Men of corrupt minds are *destitute of the truth.* The reason why men's minds are corrupt is because they do not stick to *the truth as it is in Jesus: supposing that gain is godliness,* making religion truckle to their secular interest. From such as these Timothy is warned to withdraw himself. We observe, 1. The words of our Lord Jesus Christ are wholesome words, they are the fittest to prevent or heal the church's wounds, as well as to heal a wounded conscience; for Christ has the tongue of the learned, to speak a word in season to him that is weary, Isa. l. 4. The words of Christ are the best to prevent ruptures in the church; for none who profess faith in him will dispute the aptness or authority of his words who is their Lord and teacher, and it has never gone well with the church since the words of men have claimed a regard equal to his words, and in some cases a much greater. 2. Whoever teaches otherwise, and does not consent to these wholesome words, he is proud, knowing nothing; for pride and ignorance commonly go together. 3. Paul sets a brand only on those who consent not to the words of our Lord Jesus Christ, and the doctrine which is according to godliness; they are proud, knowing nothing: other words more wholesome he knew not. 4. We learn the sad effects of doting about questions and strifes of words; of such doting about questions comes envy, strife, evil surmisings, and perverse disputings; when men leave the wholesome words of our Lord Jesus Christ, they will never agree in other words, either of their own or other men's invention, but will perpetually wrangle and quarrel about them; and this will produce envy, when they see the words of others preferred to those they have adopted for their own; and this will be attended with jealousies and suspicions of one another, called here *evil surmisings;* then they will proceed to perverse disputings. 5. Such persons as are given to perverse disputings appear to be men of corrupt minds, and destitute of the truth; especially such as act in this manner for the sake of gain, which is all their godliness, supposing gain to be godliness, contrary to the apostle's judgment, who reckoned godliness great gain. 6. Good ministers and Christians will withdraw themselves from such. "Come out from among them, my people, and be ye separate," says the Lord: *from such withdraw thyself.*

6 But godliness with contentment is great gain. 7 For we brought nothing into *this* world, *and it is* certain we can carry nothing out. 8 And having food and raiment [**covering**] let us be therewith content. 9 But they that will [**desire to**] be rich fall into temptation and a snare, and *into* many foolish and hurtful lusts, which drown men in destruction and perdition. 10 For the love of money is the [**a**] root of all [**all kinds of**] evil ; which while some coveted after, they have erred from the faith, and pierced themselves through with many sorrows. 11 But thou, O man of God, flee these things; and follow after righteousness, godliness, faith, love, patience, meekness. 12 Fight the good fight of [**of the**] faith, lay hold on eternal life [**the life eternal**], whereunto thou art also called, and hast professed a good profession before [**didst confess the good confession in the sight of**] many witnesses.

From the mention of the abuse which some put upon religion, making it to serve their secular advantages, the apostle,

I. Takes occasion to show the excellency of contentment and the evil of covetousness.

1. The excellency of contentment, *v.* 6–8. Some account Christianity an advantageous profession for this world. In the sense they mean this is false; yet it is undoubtedly true that, though Christianity is the worst trade, it is the best calling in the world. Those that make a trade of it, merely to serve their turn for this world, will be disappointed, and find it a sorry trade; but those that mind it as their calling, and make a business of it, will find it a gainful calling, for it has the promise of the life that now is, as well as of that which is to come.

(1.) The truth he lays down is that *godliness with contentment is great gain.* Some read it, *godliness with a competency;* that is, if a man have but a little in this world, yet, if he have but enough to carry him through it, he needs desire no more, his godliness with that will be his great gain. *For a little which a righteous man has is better than the riches of many wicked,* Ps. xxxvii. 16. We read it, *godliness with contentment;* godliness is itself great gain, it is profitable to all things; and, wherever there is true godliness, there will be contentment; but those that have arrived at the highest pitch of contentment with their godliness are certainly the easiest, happiest people in this world. *Godliness with contentment,* that is, Christian contentment (content must come from principles of godliness) is great gain; it is all the wealth in the world. He that is godly is sure to be happy in another world; and if withal he do by contentment accommodate himself to his condition in this world he has enough. Here we have, [1]. A Christian's gain; it is godliness with contentment, this is the true way to gain, yea, it is gain itself. [2.] A Christian's gain is great: it is not like the little gain of worldlings, who are so fond of a little worldly advantage. [3.] Godliness is ever accompanied with contentment in a greater or less degree; all truly godly people have learned with Paul, in whatever state they are, to be therewith content, Phil. iv. 11. They are content with what God allots for them, well knowing that this is best for them. Let us all then endeavour after godliness with contentment.

(2.) The reason he gives for it is, *For we brought nothing with us into this world, and it is certain we can carry nothing out, v.* 7. This is a reason why we should be content with a little. [1.] Because we can challenge nothing as a debt that is due to us, for we came naked into the world. Whatever we have had since, we are obliged to the providence of God for it; but he that gave may take what and when he pleases. We had our beings, our bodies, our lives (which are more than meat, and which are more than raiment), when we came into the world, though we came naked, and brought nothing with us; may we not then be content while our beings and lives are continued to us, though we have not every thing we would have? We brought nothing with us into this world, and yet God provided for us, care was taken of us, we have been fed all our lives long unto this day; and therefore, when we are reduced to the greatest straits, we cannot be poorer than when we came into this world, and yet then we were provided for; therefore let us trust in God for the remaining part of our pilgrimage. [2.] We shall carry nothing with us out of this world. A shroud, a coffin, and a grave, are all that the richest man in the world can have from his thousands. Therefore why should we covet much? Why should we not be content with a little, because, how much soever we have, we must leave it behind us? Eccl. v. 15, 16.

(3.) Hence he infers, *having food and raiment, let us be therewith content, v.* 8. Food and a *covering*, including habitation as well as raiment. Observe, If God give us the necessary supports of life, we ought to be content therewith, though we have not the ornaments and delights of it. If nature should be content with a little, grace should be content with less; though we have not dainty food, though we have not costly raiment, if we have but food and raiment convenient for us we ought to be content. This was Agur's prayer: *Give me neither poverty nor riches; feed me with food convenient for me*, Prov. xxx. 8. Here we see, [1.] The folly of placing our happiness in these things, when we did not bring any thing into this world with us, and we can carry nothing out. What will worldlings do when death shall strip them of their happiness and portion, and they must take an everlasting farewell of all these things, on which they have so much doted? They may say with poor Micah, *You have taken away my gods; and what have I more?* Jud. xviii. 24. [2.] The necessaries of life are the bounds of a true Christian's desire, and with these he will endeavour to be content; his desires are not insatiable; no, a little, a few comforts of this life, will serve him, and these he may hope to enjoy: *Having food and raiment*.

2. The evil of covetousness. *Those that will be rich* (that set their hearts upon the wealth of this world, and are resolved, right or wrong, they will have it) *fall into temptation and a snare, v.* 9. It is not said, those that are rich, but those that will be rich, that is, that place their happiness in worldly wealth, that covet it inordinately, and are eager and violent in the pursuit of it. Those that are such *fall into temptation and a snare*, unavoidably; for, when the devil sees which way their lusts carry them, he will soon bait his hook accordingly. He knew how fond Achan would be of a wedge of gold, and therefore laid that before him. They fall into *many foolish and hurtful lusts*. Observe,

(1.) The apostle supposes that, [1.] Some will be rich; that is, they are resolved upon it, nothing short of a great abundance will satisfy. [2]. Such will not be safe nor innocent, for they will be in danger of ruining themselves for ever; they fall into temptation, and a snare, &c. [3.] Worldly lusts are foolish and hurtful, for they drown men in destruction and perdition. [4.] It is good for us to consider the mischievousness of worldly fleshly lusts. They are foolish, and therefore we should be ashamed of them, hurtful, and therefore we should be afraid of them, especially considering to what degree they are hurtful, for they *drown men in destruction and perdition*.

(2.) The apostle affirms that *the love of money is the root of all evil, v.* 10. What sins will not men be drawn to by the love of money? Particularly this was at the bottom of the apostasy of many from the faith of Christ: while they coveted money, they *erred from the faith*, they quitted their Christianity, and *pierced themselves through with many sorrows*. Observe, [1.] What is the root of all evil; the love of money: people may have money, and yet not love it: but, if they love it inordinately, it will push them on to all evil. [2.] Covetous persons will quit the faith, if that be the way to get money: *Which while some coveted after, they have erred from the faith. Demas hath forsaken me, having loved this present world*, 2 Tim. iv. 10. For the world was dearer to him than Christianity. Observe, Those that err from the faith pierce themselves with many sorrows; those that depart from God do but treasure up sorrows for themselves.

II. Hence he takes occasion to caution Timothy, and to counsel him to keep in the way of God and his duty, and particularly to fulfil the trust reposed in him as a minister.   He addresses himself to him as *a man of God.* Ministers are men of God, and ought to conduct themselves accordingly in every thing ; they are men employed for God, devoted to his honour more immediately.   The prophets under the Old Testament were called men of God.   1. He charges Timothy to take heed of the love of money, which had been so pernicious to many : *Flee these things.*   It ill becomes any men, but especially men of God, to set their hearts upon the things of this world ; men of God should be taken up with the things of God.   2. To arm him against the love of the world, he directs him to follow that which is good : *Follow after righteousness, godliness, faith, love, patience, meekness :* righteousness in his conversation towards men, godliness towards God, faith and love as living principles, to support him and carry him on in the practice both of righteousness and godliness.   Those that follow after righteousness and godliness, from a principle of faith and love, have need to put on patience and meekness—patience to bear both the rebukes of Providence and the reproaches of men, and meekness wherewith to instruct gainsayers and pass by the affronts and injuries that are done us.   Observe, It is not enough that men of God flee these things, but they must follow after what is directly contrary thereto.   Further, What excellent persons men of God are, who follow after righteousness !   They are the excellent of the earth, and, being acceptable to God, they should be approved of men.   3. He exhorts him to do the part of a soldier : *Fight the good fight of faith.*   Note, Those who will get to heaven must fight their way thither. Their must be a conflict with corruption and temptations, and the opposition of the powers of darkness.   Observe, It is a good fight, it is a good cause, and it will have a good issue.   It is the fight of faith ; we do not war after the flesh, for the weapons of our warfare are not carnal, 2 Cor. x. 3, 4.   4. He exhorts him to *lay hold on eternal life.*   Observe, (1.) Eternal life is the crown proposed to us, for our encouragement to war, and to fight the good fight of faith, the good warfare.   (2.) This we must lay hold on, as those that are afraid of coming short of it and losing it. Lay hold, and take heed of losing your hold.   *Hold fast that which thou hast, that no man take thy crown,* Rev. iii. 11.   (3.) We are called to the fight, and to lay hold on eternal life.   (4.) The profession Timothy and all faithful ministers make before many witnesses is a good profession ; for they profess and engage to fight the good fight of faith and to lay hold on eternal life ; their calling and their own profession oblige them to this.

13 I give thee charge in the sight of God, who quickeneth all things, and *before* Christ Jesus, who before Pontius Pilate witnessed a [**the**] good confession ; 14 That thou keep *this* commandment without spot, unrebukeable [**without reproach**], until the appearing of our Lord Jesus Christ : 15 Which in his times he shall show, *who is* the blessed and only Potentate, the King of kings, and Lord of lords ; 16 Who only hath immortality, dwelling in the light which no man can approach unto ; whom no man hath seen, nor can see : to whom *be* honour and power everlasting.   Amen.   17 Charge them that are rich in this world, that they be not highminded, nor trust in uncertain [**nor**

have their hope rest on the uncertainty of] riches, but in the living God, who giveth us richly all things to enjoy ; [18] That they do good, that they be rich in good works, ready to distribute, willing to communicate ; [19] Laying up in store for themselves a good foundation against the time to come, that they may lay hold on eternal life **[the life which is** *life* **indeed]**. [20] O Timothy, keep that which is committed to thy trust, avoiding profane *and* vain babblings, and oppositions of science **[the knowledge which is**] falsely so called : [21] Which some professing have erred concerning the faith.   Grace *be* with thee. Amen.

The apostle here charges Timothy *to keep this commandment* (that is, the whole work of his ministry, all the trust reposed in him, all the service expected from him) *without spot, unrebukable ;* he must conduct himself so in his ministry that he might not lay himself open to any blame nor incur any blemish.   What are the motives to move him to this ?

I. He gives him a solemn charge : *I give thee charge in the sight of God that thou do this.*   He charges him as he will answer it at the great day to that God whose eyes are upon us all, who sees what we are and what we do : *God, who quickens all things,* who has life in himself, and is the fountain of life.   This should quicken us to the service of God that we serve a God who quickens all things.   He charges him before Christ Jesus, to whom in a peculiar manner he stood related as a minister of his gospel : *Who before Pontius Pilate witnessed a good confession.*   Observe, Christ died not only as a sacrifice, but as a martyr ; and he witnessed a good confession when he was arraigned before Pilate, saying (John xviii. 36, 37), *My kingdom is not of this world : I am come to bear witness unto the truth.*   That good confession of his before Pilate, *My kingdom is not of this world,* should be effectual to draw off all his followers, both ministers and people, from the love of this world.

II. He reminds him of the confession that he himself had made : *Thou hast professed a good profession before many witnesses (v.* 12), namely, when he was ordained by the laying on of the hands of the presbytery.   The obligation of that was still upon him, and he must live up to that, and be quickened by that, to do the work of his ministry.

III. He reminds him of Christ's second coming : " *Keep this commandment——until the appearing of our Lord Jesus Christ ;* keep it as long as thou live, till Christ come at death to give thee a discharge.   Keep it with an eye to his second coming, when we must all give an account of the talents we have been entrusted with," Luke xvi. 2.   Observe, The Lord Jesus Christ will appear, and it will be a glorious appearing, not like his first appearing in the days of his humiliation.   Ministers should have an eye to this appearing of the Lord Jesus Christ in all their ministrations and, till his appearing, they are to keep this commandment without spot, unrebukable.   Mentioning the appearing of Christ, as one that loved it, Paul loves to speak of it, and loves to speak of him who shall then appear.   The appearing of Christ is certain (*he shall show it*), but it is not for us to know the time and season of it, which the Father has kept in his own power : let this suffice us, that in time he will show it, in the time that he thinks fit for it.   Observe,

1. Concerning Christ and God the Father the apostle here speaks great things. (1.) That God is the only Potentate; the powers of earthly princes are all derived from him, and depend upon him. The powers that exist are ordained of God, Rom. xiii. 1. He is the only Potentate that is absolute and sovereign, and perfectly independent. (2.) He is the blessed and the only Potentate, infinitely happy, and nothing can in the least impair his happiness. (3.) He is King of kings, and Lord of lords. All the kings of the earth derive their power from him; he gave them their crowns, they hold them under him, and he has a sovereign dominion over them. This is Christ's title (Rev. xix. 16), *upon his vesture and his thigh;* for he has a name higher than the kings of the earth. (4.) He only has immortality. He only is immortal in himself, and has immortality, as he is the fountain of it, for the immortality of angels and spirits is derived from him. (5.) He dwells in inaccessible light, *light which no man can approach unto:* no man can get to heaven but those whom he is pleased to bring thither, and admit into his kingdom. (6.) He is invisible: *Whom no man hath seen, nor can see.* It is impossible that mortal eyes should bear the brightness of the divine glory. No man can see God and live.

2. Having mentioned these glorious attributes, he concludes with a doxology: *To him be honour and power everlasting. Amen.* God having all power and honour to himself, it is our duty to ascribe all power and honour to him. (1.) What an evil is sin, when committed against such a God, the blessed and only Potentate! The evil of it rises in proportion to the dignity of him against whom it is committed. (2.) Great is his condescension, to take notice of such mean and vile creatures as we are. What are we then, that the blessed God, the King of kings and Lord of lords, should seek after us? (3.) Blessed are those who are admitted to dwell with this great and blessed Potentate. *Happy are thy men* (says the queen of Sheba to king Solomon), *happy are these thy servants, who stand continually before thee,* 1 Kings x. 8. Much more happy are those who are allowed to stand before the King of kings. (4.) Let us love, adore, and praise, the great God; for *who shall not fear thee, O Lord, and glorify thy name? For thou only art holy,* Rev. xv. 4.

IV. The apostle adds, by way of postscript, a lesson for rich people, v. 17-19.

1. Timothy must charge those that are rich to beware of the temptations, and improve the opportunities, of their prosperous estate. (1.) He must caution them to take heed of pride. This is a sin that easily besets rich people, upon whom the world smiles. Charge them *that they be not high-minded,* or think of themselves above what is meet, or be puffed up with their wealth. (2.) He must caution them against vain confidence in their wealth. Charge them that they *trust not in uncertain riches.* Nothing is more uncertain than the wealth of this world; many have had much of it one day and been stripped of all the next. Riches make themselves wings, and fly away as an eagle, &c., Prov. xxiii. 5. (3.) He must charge them to *trust in God, the living God,* to make him their hope, *who giveth us richly all things to enjoy.* Those who are rich must see God giving them their riches, and giving them to enjoy them richly; for many have riches, but enjoy them poorly, not having a heart to use them. (4.) He must charge them to do good with what they have (for what is the best estate worth, any more than as it gives a man an opportunity of doing so much the more good?): *That they be rich in good works.* Those are truly rich who are rich in good works. That they be *ready to distribute, willing to communi-*

cate : not only to do it, but to do it willingly, for *God loves a cheerful giver.* (5.) He must charge them to think of another world, and prepare for that which is to come by works of charity : *Laying up in store a good foundaton against the time to come,* that they may take hold on eternal life.

2. Hence we may observe, (1.) Ministers must not be afraid of the rich ; be they ever so rich, they must speak to them, and charge them. (2.) They must caution them against pride and vain confidence in their riches : *That they be not high-minded, nor trust in uncertain riches.* Stir them up to works of piety and charity : *That they do good,* &c. (3.) This is the way for the rich to lay up in store for themselves for the time to come, that they may lay hold on eternal life ; in the way of well-doing we are to seek for glory, honour, and immortality, *and eternal life will be the end of all,* Rom. ii. 7. (4.) Here is a lesson for ministers in the charge given to Timothy : *Keep that which is committed to thy trust.* Every minister is a trustee, and it is a treasure committed to his trust, which he has to keep. The truths of God, the ordinances of God, keep these, *avoiding profane and vain babblings ;* not affecting human eloquence, which the apostle calls vain babbling, or human learning, which often opposes the truths of God, but keep close to the written word, for that is committed to our trust. Some who have been very proud of their learning, their *science, which is falsely so called,* have by that been debauched in their principles and been drawn away from the faith of Christ, which is a good reason why we should keep to the plain word of the gospel, and resolve to live and die by that. Observe, [1.] Ministers cannot be too earnestly exhorted to keep what is committed to their trust, because it is a great trust lodged with them : *O Timothy, keep that which is committed to thy trust !* as if he had said, "I cannot conclude without charging thee again ; whatever thou doest, be sure to keep this trust, for it is too great a trust to be betrayed." [2.] Ministers are to avoid babblings, if they would keep what is committed to them, because they are vain and profane. [3.] That science which opposes the truth of the gospel is falsely so called ; it is not true science, for if it were it would approve of the gospel and consent to it. [4.] Those who are so fond of such science are in great danger of erring concerning the faith ; those who are for advancing reason above faith are in danger of leaving faith.

V. Our apostle concludes with a solemn prayer and benediction : *Grace be with thee. Amen.* Observe, this is a short, yet comprehensive prayer for our friends, for grace comprehends in it all that is good, and grace is an earnest, yea, a beginning, of glory ; for, wherever God gives grace, he will give glory, and will not withhold any good thing from him who walketh uprightly. Grace be with you all. Amen.

EXPOSITION OF THE SECOND EPISTLE OF ST. PAUL TO TIMOTHY

THIS second epistle Paul wrote to Timothy from Rome, when he was a prisoner there and in danger of his life; this is evident from these words, *I am now ready to be offered, and the time of my departure is at hand,* ch. iv. 6. It appears that his removal out of this world, in his own apprehension, was not far off, especially considering the rage and malice of his persecutors: and that he had been brought before the empero Nero, which he calls *his first answer, when no man stood with him, but all men forsook him,* ch. iv. 16. And interpreters agree that this was the last epistle he wrote. Where Timothy now was is not certain. The scope of this epistle somewhat differs from that of the former, not so much relating to his office as an evangelist as to his personal conduct and behaviour.

CHAPTER I

After the introduction (ver. 1, 2) we have, I. Paul's sincere love to Timothy, ver. 3-5. II. Divers exhortations given to him, ver. 6-14. III. He speaks of Phygellus and Hermogenes, with others, and closes with Onesiphorus, ver. 15, to the end.

PAUL, an apostle of Jesus Christ by the will of God, according to the promise of life which is in Christ Jesus. ² To Timothy, *my* dearly beloved son: Grace, mercy, *and* peace, from God the Father, and Christ Jesus our Lord. ³ I thank God, whom I serve from *my* forefathers with pure conscience, that without ceasing I have remembrance of thee in my prayers night and day; ⁴ Greatly desiring to see thee, being mindful of thy tears, that I may be filled with joy; ⁵ When I call to remembrance the unfeigned faith that is in thee, which dwelt first in thy grandmother Lois, and thy mother Eunice; and I am persuaded that in thee also.

Here is, I. The inscription of the epistle. Paul calls himself *an apostle by the will of God*, merely by the good pleasure of God, and by his grace, which he professes himself unworthy of. *According to the promise of life which is in Christ Jesus*, or according to the gospel. The gospel is the promise of life in Christ Jesus; life is the end, and Christ the way, John xiv. 6. The life is put into the promise, and both are sure in Christ Jesus, the faithful witness; *for all the promises of God in Christ Jesus are yea, and all amen*, 2 Cor. i. 20. He calls Timothy his *beloved son*. Paul felt the warmest affection for him both because he had been an instrument of his conversion and because as a son with his father he had served with him in the gospel. Observe, 1. Paul was an apostle of Jesus Christ by the will of God; as he did not receive the gospel of man, nor was taught it, but had it by the revelation of Jesus Christ (Gal. i. 13), so his commission to be an apostle was not by the will of man, but of God: in the former epistle he says it was *by the commandment of God our Saviour*, and here *by the will of God*. God called him to be an apostle. 2. We have the promise of life, blessed be God for it: *In hope of eternal life, which God, who cannot lie, promised before the world began*, Tit. i. 2. It is a promise to discover the freeness and certainty of it. 3. This, as well as all other promises, is in and through Jesus Christ; they all take their rise from the mercy of God in Christ, and they are sure, so that we may safely depend on them. 4. The grace, mercy, and peace, which even Paul's dearly beloved son Timothy wanted, comes from God the Father and Christ Jesus our Lord; and therefore the one as well as the other is the giver of these blessings, and ought to be applied to for them. 5. The best want these blessings, and they are the best we can ask for our dearly-beloved friends, that they may have grace to help them in the time of need, and mercy to pardon what is amiss, and so may have peace with God the Father and Christ Jesus our Lord.

II. Paul's thanksgiving to God for Timothy's faith and holiness: he thanks God that he remembered Timothy in his prayers. Observe, Whatever good we do, and whatever good office we perform for our friends, God must have the glory of it, and we must give him thanks. It is he who puts it into our hearts to remember such and such in our prayers. Paul was much in prayer, he prayed night and day; in all his prayers he was mindful of his friends, he particularly prayed for good ministers, he prayed for Timothy, and *had remembrance of him in his prayers night and day;* he did this without ceasing; prayer was his constant business, and he never forgot his friends in his prayers, as we often do. Paul served God from his forefathers with a pure conscience. It was a comfort to him that he was born in God's house, and was of the seed of those that served God; as likewise that he had served him with a pure conscience, according to the best of his light; he had kept a conscience void of offence, and made it his daily exercise to do so, Acts xxiv. 16. *He greatly desired to see Timothy*, out of the affection he had for him, that he might have some conversation with him, *being mindful of his tears* at their last parting. Timothy was sorry to part with Paul, he wept at parting, and therefore Paul desired to see him again, because he had perceived by that what a true affection he had for him. He thanks God that Timothy kept up the religion of his ancestors, *v.* 5. Observe, The entail of religion descended upon Timothy by the mother's side; he had a good mother, and a good grandmother; they believed, though his father did not, Acts xvi. 1. It is a comfortable thing when children imitate the faith and holiness of their godly parents, and tread in their steps, 3 John 4.—*Dwelt in thy grand-mother and thy mother, and I am persuaded that in thee also.* Paul had a very charitable opinion of his friends, was very willing to hope the best concerning them ; indeed he had a great deal of reason to believe well of Timothy, for he had *no man like-minded,* Phil. ii. 20. Observe, 1. We are, according to St. Paul, to serve God with a pure conscience, so did his and our pious forefathers ; this is to draw *near with a true heart, in full assur-ance of faith, having our heart sprinkled from an evil conscience,* Heb. x. 22. 2. In our prayers we are to remember without ceasing our friends, espe-cially the faithful ministers of Christ. Paul had remembrance of his dearly beloved son Timothy in his prayers night and day.   3. The faith that dwells in real believers is unfeigned ; it is without hypocrisy, it is a faith that will stand the trial, and it dwells in them as a living principle.   It was the matter of Paul's thanksgiving that Timothy inherited the faith of his mother Eunice and his grandmother Lois, and ought to be ours when-ever we see the like ; we should rejoice wherever we see the grace of God ; so did Barnabas, Acts xi. 23, 24.   *I rejoiced greatly that I found of thy children walking in the truth,* 2 John 4.

⁶ Wherefore I put thee in remembrance that thou stir up the gift of God, which is in thee by the putting on of my hands. ⁷ For God hath not given us the spirit of fear [**fearfulness**] ; but of power, and of love, and of a sound mind [**of discipline**]. ⁸ Be not thou therefore ashamed of the testimony of our Lord, nor of me his prisoner : but be thou partaker of the afflictions of [**suffer hardship with**] the gospel according to the power of God ; ⁹ Who hath saved us, and called *us* with a holy calling, not according to our works, but according to his own purpose and grace, which was given us in Christ Jesus before the world began [**before times eternal**] ; ¹⁰ But is now made manifest by the appearing of our Saviour Jesus Christ, who hath abolished death, and hath brought life and immortality [**incorruption**] to light through the gospel : ¹¹ Whereunto I am appointed a preacher, and an apostle, and a teacher of the Gentiles.   ¹² For the which cause I also suffer these things : nevertheless I am not ashamed : for I know whom I have believed, and am persuaded that he is able to keep [**guard**] that which I have committed unto him against that day.   ¹³ Hold fast the form [**pattern**] of sound words, which thou hast heard of me, in faith and love which is in Christ Jesus.   ¹⁴ That good thing which was committed unto thee keep by the Holy Ghost which dwelleth in us.

Here is an exhortation and excitation of Timothy to his duty (*v.* 6) : *I put thee in remembrance.*   The best men need remembrancers ; what we know we should be reminded of.   2 Pet. iii. 1, I write this, *to stir up your pure minds by way of remembrance.*

I. He exhorts him to stir *up the gift of God* that was *in him.*   Stir it up as fire under the embers. It is meant of all the gifts and graces that God had given him, to qualify him for the work of an evangelist, the gifts of the Holy Ghost, the extraordinary gifts that were conferred by the imposition of the apostle's hands. These he must stir up ; he must exercise them, and so increase them : use gifts, and have gifts. *To him that hath shall be given,* Matt. xxv. 29. He must take all opportunities to use these gifts, and so stir them up, for that is the best way of increasing them. Whether the gift of God in Timothy was ordinary or extraordinary (though I incline to the latter), he must stir it up, otherwise it would decay. Further, you see that this gift was in him by the putting on of the apostle's hands, which I take to be distinct from his ordination, for that was performed by the hands of the presbytery, 1 Tim. iv. 14. It is probable that Timothy had the Holy Ghost, in his extraordinary gifts and graces, conferred on him by the laying on of the apostle's hands (for I reckon that none but the apostles had the power of giving the Holy Ghost), and afterwards, being thus richly furnished for the work of the ministry, was ordained by the presbytery. Observe, 1. The great hindrance of usefulness in the increase of our gifts is slavish fear. Paul therefore warns Timothy against this. *God hath not given us the spirit of fear, v.* 7. It was through base fear that the evil servant buried his talent, and did not trade with it, Matt. xxv. 25. Now God hath therefore armed us against the spirit of fear, by often bidding us fear not. "Fear not the face of man ; fear not the dangers you may meet with in the way of your duty." God hath delivered us from the spirit of fear, and hath given us the spirit *of power, and of love, and of a sound mind.* The spirit of power, or of courage and resolution to encounter difficulties and dangers ;—the spirit of love to God, which will carry us through the opposition we may meet with, as Jacob made nothing of the hard service he was to endure for Rachel : the spirit of love to God will set us above the fear of man, and all the hurt that man can do us ;—and the spirit of a sound mind, or quietness of mind, a peaceable enjoyment of ourselves, for we are oftentimes discouraged in our way and work by the creatures of our own fancy and imagination, which a sober, solid, thinking mind would obviate, and would easily answer. 2. The spirit God gives to his ministers is not a fearful, but a courageous spirit ; it is a spirit of power, for they speak in his name who has all power, both in heaven and earth ; and it is a spirit of love, for love to God and the souls of men must inflame ministers in all their service ; and it is a spirit of a sound mind, for they speak the words of truth and soberness.

II. He exhorts him to count upon afflictions, and get ready for them : "*Be not thou therefore ashamed of the testimony of our Lord, nor of me his prisoner.* Be not thou ashamed of the gospel, of the testimony thou hast borne to it." Observe,

1. The gospel of Christ is what we have none of us reason to be ashamed of. We must not be ashamed of those who are suffering for the gospel of Christ. Timothy must not be ashamed of good old Paul, though he was now in bonds. As he must not himself be afraid of suffering, so he must not be afraid of owning those who were sufferers for the cause of Christ. (1.) The gospel is the testimony of our Lord ; in and by this he bears testimony of himself to us, and by professing our adherence to it we bear testimony of him and for him. (2.) Paul was the Lord's prisoner, his prisoner, Eph. iv. 1. For his sake he was bound with a chain. (3.) We have no reason to be ashamed either of the testimony of our Lord or of

his prisoners; if we are ashamed of either now, Christ will be ashamed of us hereafter. *"But be thou partaker of the afflictions of the gospel, according to the power of God,* that is, expect *afflictions* for the gospel's sake, prepare for them, count upon them, be willing to take thy lot with the suffering saints in this world. *Be partaker of the afflictions of the gospel;"* or, as it may be read, *Do thou suffer with the gospel;* "not only sympathise with those who suffer for it, but be ready to suffer with them and suffer like them." If at any time the gospel be in distress, he who hopes for life and salvation by it will be content to suffer with it. Observe, [1.] Then we are likely to bear afflictions well, when we fetch strength and power from God to enable us to bear them: *Be thou partaker of the afflictions of the gospel, according to the power of God.* [2.] All Christians, but especially ministers, must expect afflictions and persecutions for the sake of the gospel. [3.] These shall be proportioned, according to the power of God (1 Cor. x. 13) resting upon us.

2. Mentioning God and the gospel, he takes notice what great things God has done for us by the gospel, *v.* 9, 10. To encourage him to suffer, he urges two considerations:—

(1.) The nature of that gospel which he was called to suffer for, and the glorious and gracious designs and purposes of it. It is usual with Paul, when he mentions Christ, and the gospel of Christ, to digress from his subject, and enlarge upon them; so full was he of that which is all our salvation, and ought to be all our desire. Observe, [1.] The gospel aims at our salvation: *He has saved us,* and we must not think much to suffer for that which we hope to be saved by. He has begun to save us, and will complete it in due time; for God calls those things that are not (that are not yet completed) as though they were (Rom. iv. 17); therefore he says, who *has* saved us. [2.] It is designed for our sanctification: *And called us with a holy calling,* called us to holiness. Christianity is a calling, a holy calling; it is the calling wherewith we are called, the calling to which we are called, to labour in it. Observe, All who shall be saved hereafter are sanctified now. Wherever the call of the gospel is an effectual call, it is found to be a holy call, making those holy who are effectually called. [3.] The origin of it is the free grace and eternal purpose of God in Christ Jesus. If we had merited it, it had been hard to suffer for it; but our salvation by it is of free grace, and not according to our works, and therefore we must not think much to suffer for it. This grace is said to be given us *before the world began,* that is, in the purpose and designs of God from all eternity; *in Christ Jesus,* for all the gifts that come from God to sinful man come in and through Christ Jesus. [4.] The gospel is the manifestation of this purpose and grace: *By the appearing of our Saviour Jesus Christ,* who had lain in the bosom of the Father from eternity, and was perfectly apprised of all his gracious purposes. By his appearing this gracious purpose was made manifest to us. Did Jesus Christ suffer for it, and shall we think much to suffer for it? [5.] By the gospel of Christ death is abolished: *He has abolished death,* not only weakened it, but taken it out of the way, has broken the power of death over us; by taking away sin he has abolished death (for the sting of death is sin, 1 Cor. xv. 56), in altering the property of it, and breaking the power of it. Death now of an enemy has become a friend; it is the gate by which we pass out of a troublesome, vexatious, sinful world, into a world of perfect peace and purity; and the power thereof is broken, for death does not triumph over those who believe the gospel, but they triumph over it. *O death! where is thy sting? O grave! where is thy victory?* 1 Cor. xv. 55. [6.] He has *brought life and immortality to light by the gospel;* he has shown us another world more clearly than it was before discovered under any former dispensation, and the happiness of that world, the certain recompense of our obedience by faith : we all with open face, as in a glass, behold the glory of God. He has brought it to light, not only set it before us, but offered it to us, by the gospel. Let us value the gospel more than ever, as it is that whereby life and immortality are brought to light, for herein it has the pre-eminence above all former discoveries : so that it is the gospel of life and immortality, as it discovers them to us, and directs us in the ready way that leads thereto, as well as proposes the most weighty motives to excite our endeavours in seeking after glory, honour, and immortality.

(2.) Consider the example of blessed Paul, *v.* 11, 12. He was appointed to preach the gospel, and particularly appointed to teach the Gentiles. He thought it a cause worth suffering for, and why should not Timothy think so too? No man needs to be afraid nor ashamed to suffer for the cause of the gospel : *I am not ashamed,* says Paul, *for I know whom I have believed, and am persuaded that he is able to keep that which I have committed unto him against that day.* Observe, [1.] Good men often suffer many things for the best cause in the world : *For which cause I suffer these things;* that is, "for my preaching, and adhering to the gospel." [2.] They need not be ashamed, the cause will bear them out ; but those who oppose it shall be clothed with shame. [3.] Those who trust in Christ know whom they have trusted. The apostle speaks with a holy triumph and exultation, as much as to say, "I stand on firm ground. I know I have lodged the great trust in the hands of the best trustee." *And am persuaded,* &c. What must we commit to Christ? The salvation of our souls, and their preservation to the heavenly kingdom ; and what we so commit to him he will keep. There is a day coming when our souls will be enquired after : "Man ! Woman ! thou hadst a soul committed to thee, what hast thou done with it? To whom was it offered, to God or Satan? How was it employed, in the service of sin or in the service of Christ?" There is a day coming, and it will be a very solemn and awful day, when we must give an account of our stewardship (Luke xvi. 2), give an account of our souls : now, if by an active obedient faith we commit it to Jesus Christ we may be sure he is able to keep it, and it shall be forthcoming to our comfort in that day.

III. He exhorts him to *hold fast the form of sound words, v.* 13. 1. "*Have* a form of sound words" (so it may be read), "a short form, a catechism, an abstract of the first principles of religion, according to the scriptures, a scheme of sound words, a brief summary of the Christian faith, in a proper method, drawn out by thyself from the holy scriptures for thy own use ;" or, rather, by the form of sound words I understand the holy scriptures themselves. 2. "Having, it *hold it fast,* remember it, retain it, adhere to it. Adhere to it in opposition to all heresies and false doctrine, which corrupt the Christian faith. Hold that fast *which thou hast heard of me.*" Paul was divinely inspired. It is good to adhere to those forms of sound words which we have in the scriptures ; for these, we are sure, were divinely inspired. That is sound speech, which cannot be condemned, Tit. ii. 8. But how must it be held fast? *In faith and love;* that is, we must assent to it as *a faithful saying,* and bid it welcome as *worthy of all acceptation.* Hold it fast in a good heart, this is the ark of the covenant, in which the tables both of law and gospel are most safely and profitably deposited, Ps. cxix. 11. Faith and love must go together; it is not enough to believe the sound words, and to give an assent to them, but we must love them, believe their truth and love their goodness, and we must propagate the form of sound words in love, speaking the truth in love, Eph. iv. 15. *Faith and love which are in Christ Jesus;* it must be Christian faith and love, faith and love fastening upon Jesus Christ, in and by whom God speaks to us and we to him. Timothy, as a minister, must *hold fast the form of sound words,* for the benefit of others. *Of healing words,* so it may read; there is a healing virtue in the word of God; *he sent his word, and healed them.* To the same purport is that (*v.* 14), *That good thing which was committed unto thee keep by the Holy Ghost, which dwelleth in us.* That good thing was the form of sound words, the Christian doctrine, which was committed to Timothy in his baptism and education as he was a Christian, and in his ordination as he was a minister. Observe, (1). The Christian doctrine is a trust committed to us. It is committed to Christians in general, but to ministers in particular. It is a good thing, of unspeakable value in itself, and which will be of unspeakable advantage to us; it is a good thing indeed, it is an inestimable jewel, for it discovers to us the unsearchable riches of Christ, Eph. iii. 8. It is committed to us to be preserved pure and entire, and to be transmitted to those who shall come after us, and we must keep it, and not contribute anything to the corrupting of its purity, the weakening of its power, or the diminishing of its perfection: *Keep it by the Holy Ghost that dwelleth in us.* Observe, even those who are ever so well taught cannot keep what they have learned any more than they could at first learn it, without the assistance of the Holy Spirit. We must not think to keep it by our own strength, but keep it by the Holy Ghost. (2.) The Holy Ghost dwells in all good ministers and Christians; they are his temples, and he enables them to keep the gospel pure and uncorrupt; and yet they must use their best endeavours to keep this good thing, for the assistance and indwelling of the Holy Ghost do not exclude men's endeavours, but they very well consist together.

¹⁵ This thou knowest, that all they which are in Asia be turned away from me; of whom are Phygellus and Hermogenes. ¹⁶ The Lord give mercy unto the house of Onesiphorus: for he oft refreshed me, and was not ashamed of my chain: ¹⁷ But, when he was in Rome, he sought me out very diligently, and found *me.* ¹⁸ The Lord grant unto him that he may find mercy of the Lord in that day: and in how many things he ministered unto me at Ephesus, thou knowest very well.

Having (*v.* 13, 14) exhorted Timothy to hold fast,

I. He mentions the apostasy of many from the doctrine of Christ, *v.* 15. It seems, in the best and purest ages of the church, there were those that had embraced the Christian faith, and yet afterwards revolted from it, nay, there were many such. He does not say that they had turned away from the doctrine of Christ (though it should seem they had), but they had turned away from him, they had turned their backs upon him, and disowned him in the time of his distress. And should we wonder at it, when many turned their backs on a much better than Paul? I mean the Lord Jesus Christ, John vi. 66.

II. He mentions the constancy of one that adhered to him, namely, Onesiphorus : *For he often refreshed me, and was not ashamed of my chain,* c. 16. Observe, 1. What kindness Onesiphorus had shown to Paul: he refreshed him, he often refreshed him with his letters, and counsels, and comforts, and he was not ashamed of his chains. He was not ashamed of him, notwithstanding the disgrace he was now under. He was kind to him not once or twice, but often ; not only when he was at Ephesus among his own friends, but when Onesiphorus was at Rome ; he took care to seek Paul *out very diligently, and found him, v.* 17. Observe, A good man will seek opportunities of doing good, and will not shun any that offer. At Ephesus he had ministered to him, and been very kind to him : Timothy knew it. 2. How Paul returns his kindness, *v.* 16-18. He that receives a prophet shall have a prophet's reward. He repays him with his prayers : *The Lord give mercy to Onesiphorus.* It is probable that Onesiphorus was now absent from home, and in company with Paul ; Paul therefore prays that his house might be kept during his absence. Though the papists will have it that he was now dead ; and, from Paul's praying for him that he might find mercy, they conclude the warrantableness of praying for the dead ; but who told them that Onesiphorus was dead ? And can it be safe to ground a doctrine and practice of such importance on a mere supposition and very great uncertainty ?

III. He prays for Onesiphorus himself, as well as for his house : *That he may find mercy in that day,* in the day of death and of judgment, when Christ will account all the good offices done to his poor members as done to himself. Observe, 1. The day of death and judgment is an awful day, and may be emphatically called *that day.* 2. We need desire no more to make us happy than to find mercy of the Lord in that day, when those that have shown no mercy will have judgment without mercy. 3. The best Christians will want mercy in that day ; *looking for the mercy of our Lord Jesus Christ,* Jude 21. 4. If you would have mercy then, you must seek for it now of the Lord. 5. It is of and from the Lord that we must have mercy ; for, unless the Lord has mercy on us, in vain will be the pity and compassion of men or angels. 6. We are to seek and ask for mercy of the Lord, who is the giver and bestower of it ; for the Lord Jesus Christ has satisfied justice, that mercy might be displayed. We are to come to a throne of grace, that we may obtain mercy, and find grace to help in the time of need. 7. The best thing we can ask, either for ourselves or our friends, is that the Lord will grant to them that they may find mercy of the Lord in that day, when they must pass out of time into eternity, and exchange this world for the other, and appear before the judgment-seat of Christ : the Lord then grant unto all of us that we may find mercy of the Lord in that day.

CHAPTER II

In this chapter our apostle gives Timothy many exhortations and directions, which may be of great use to others, both ministers and Christians, for whom they were designed as well as for him. I. He encourages him in his work, showing him whence he must fetch help, ver. 1. II. He must take care of a succession in the ministry, that the office might not die with him, ver. 2. III. He exhorts him to constancy and perseverance in this work, as a soldier and as a husbandman, considering what would be the end of all his sufferings, &c. ver. 3.–15. IV. He must shun profane and vain babblings (ver. 16-18), for they will be pernicious and mischievous. V. He speaks of the foundation of God, which standeth sure, ver. 19-21. VI. What he is to avoid—youthful lusts, and foolish and unlearned questions ; and what to do, ver. 22, to the end.

THOU therefore, my son, be strong [**strengthened**] in the grace that is in Christ Jesus. ² And the things that thou hast heard of me among many witnesses, the same commit thou to faithful men, who shall be able to teach others also. ³ Thou therefore endure hardness [**suffer hardship with me**], as a good soldier of Jesus Christ. ⁴ No man that warreth [**soldier on service**] entangleth himself with the affairs of *this* life ; that he may please him who hath chosen him to be [**enrolled him as**] a soldier. ⁵ And if a man also strive for masteries [**contend in the games**], *yet* is he not crowned, except he strive lawfully. ⁶ The husbandman that laboureth must be first partaker [**the first to partake**] of the fruits. ⁷ Consider what I say ; and the Lord give thee understanding in all things.

Here Paul encourages Timothy to constancy and perseverance in his work : *Be strong in the grace that is in Christ Jesus, v.* 1. Observe, Those who have work to do for God must stir up themselves to do it, and strengthen themselves for it. Being strong in the grace that is in Christ Jesus may be understood in opposition to the weakness of grace. Where there is the truth of grace there must be a labouring after the strength of grace. As our trials increase, we have need to grow stronger and stronger in that which is good ; our faith stronger, our resolution stronger, our love to God and Christ stronger. Or it may be understood in opposition to our being strong in our own strength : "Be strong, not confiding in thy own sufficiency, but in the grace that is in Jesus Christ." Compare Eph. vi. 10, *Be strong in the Lord, and in the power of his might.* When Peter promised rather to die for Christ than to deny him he was strong in his own strength ; had he been strong in the grace that is in Christ Jesus, he would have kept his standing better. Observe. 1. There is grace in Christ Jesus ; for the law was given by Moses, but grace and truth came by Jesus Christ, John i. 17. There is grace enough in him for all of us. 2. We must be strong in this grace ; not in ourselves, in our own strength, or in the grace we have already received, but in the grace that is in him, and that is the way to be strong in grace. 3. As a father exhorts his son, so does Paul exhort Timothy, with great tenderness and affection : *Thou, therefore, my son, be strong,* &c. Observe,

I. Timothy must count upon sufferings, even unto blood, and therefore he must train up others to succeed him in the ministry of the gospel, *v.* 2. He must instruct others, and train them up for the ministry, and so commit to them the things which he had heard ; and he must also ordain them to the ministry, lodge the gospel as a trust in their hands, and so commit to them the things which he had heard. Two things he must have an eye to in ordaining ministers :—Their fidelity or integrity ("Commit them to *faithful men,* who will sincerely aim at the glory of God, the honour of Christ, the welfare of souls, and the advancement of the kingdom of the Redeemer among men,") and also their ministerial ability. They must not only be knowing themselves, but be able to teach others also, and be apt to teach. Here we have, 1. The things Timothy was to commit to others—what he had heard of the apostle among many witnesses ; he must not deliver any thing besides, and what Paul delivered to him and others he had received of the Lord Jesus Christ. 2. He was to commit them as a trust, as a sacred deposit, which they were to keep, and to transmit pure and uncorrupt unto others. 3. Those to whom he was to commit these things must be faithful, that is, trusty men, and who were skilful to teach others. 4. Though men were both faithful and able to teach others, yet these things must be committed to them by Timothy, a minister, a man in office ; for none must intrude themselves into the ministry, but must have these things committed to them by those already in that office.

II. He must *endure hardness* (*v.* 3) : *Thou therefore,* &c. 1. All Christians, but especially ministers, *are soldiers of Jesus Christ ;* they fight under his banner, in his cause, and against his enemies, for he is the captain of our salvation, Heb. ii. 10. 2. The soldiers of Jesus Christ must approve themselves good soldiers, faithful to their captain, resolute in his cause, and must not give over fighting till *they are made more than conquerors, through him that loved them,* Rom. viii. 37. 3. Those who would approve themselves good soldiers of Jesus Christ must endure hardness ; that is, we must expect it and count upon it in this world, must endure and accustom ourselves to it, and bear it patiently when it comes, and not be moved by it from our integrity.

III. He must not entangle himself in the affairs of this world, *v.* 4. A soldier, when he has enlisted, leaves his calling, and all the business of it, that he may attend his captain's orders. If we have given up ourselves to be Christ's soldiers, we must sit loose to this world ; and though there is no remedy, but we must employ ourselves in the affairs of this life while we are here (we have something to do here), we must not entangle ourselves with those affairs, so as by them to be diverted and drawn aside from our duty to God and the great concerns of our Christianity. Those who will war the good warfare must sit loose to this world. *That we may please him who hath chosen us to be soldiers.* Observe, 1. The great care of a soldier should be to please his general ; so the great care of a Christian should be to please Christ, to approve ourselves to him. The way to please him who hath chosen us to be soldiers is not to entangle ourselves with the affairs of this life, but to be free from such entanglements as would hinder us in our holy warfare.

IV. He must see to it that in carrying on the spiritual warfare he went by rule, that he observed the laws of war (*v.* 5) : *If a man strive for masteries, yet is he not crowned, except he strive lawfully.* We are striving for mastery, to get the mastery of our lusts and corruptions, to excel in that which is good, but we cannot expect the prize unless we observe the laws. In doing

that which is good we must take care that we do it in a right manner, that
our good may not be evil spoken of. Observe here, 1. A Christian is to
strive for masteries; he must aim at mastering his own lusts and corruptions. 2. Yet he must strive according to the laws given to him; he
must strive lawfully. 3. Those who do so shall be crowned at last, after
a complete victory is obtained.

V. He must be willing to wait for a recompense (*v.* 6): *The husbandman
that laboureth must be first partaker of the fruits.* Or, as it should be read,
The husbandman labouring first must partake of the fruits, as appears by
comparing it with Jam. v. 7. If we would be partakers of the fruits, we
must labour; if we would gain the prize, we must run the race. And,
further, we must first labour as the husbandman does, with diligence and
patience, before we are partakers of the fruit; we must do the will of God,
before we receive the promises, for which reason we have need of patience,
Heb. x. 36.

The apostle further commends what he had said to the attention of
Timothy, and expresses his desire and hope respecting him: *Consider what
I say, and the Lord give thee understanding in all things, v.* 7. Here, 1. Paul
exhorts Timothy to consider those things about which he admonished him.
Timothy must be reminded to use his considering faculties about the things
of God. Consideration is as necessary to a good conversation as to a sound
conversion. 2. He prays for him: *The Lord give thee understanding in all
things.* Observe, It is God who gives understanding. The most intelligent
man needs more and more of this gift. If he who gave the revelation in
the word does not give the understanding in the heart, we are nothing.
Together with our prayers for others, that the Lord would give them
understanding in all things, we must exhort and stir them up to consider
what we say, for consideration is the way to understand, remember, and
practise, what we hear or read.

⁸ Remember that Jesus Christ of the seed of David was
raised from the dead according to my gospel: ⁹ Wherein I
suffer trouble, as an evil doer, *even* unto bonds; but the word
of God is not bound. ¹⁰ Therefore I endure all things for the
elect's sakes, that they may also obtain the salvation which is
in Christ Jesus with eternal glory. ¹¹ *It is* a faithful saying:
For if we be dead with *him,* we shall also live with *him :* ¹² If
we suffer, we shall also reign with *him :* if we deny *him,* he
also will deny us: ¹³ If we believe not [**are faithless**], *yet* he
abideth faithful : he cannot deny himself.

I. To encourage Timothy in suffering, the apostle puts him in mind of
the resurrection of Christ (*v.* 8): *Remember that Jesus Christ, of the seed of
David, was raised from the dead, according to my gospel.* This is the great
proof of his divine mission, and therefore a great confirmation of the truth
of the Christian religion; and the consideration of it should make us faithful to our Christian profession, and should particularly encourage us in
suffering for it. Let suffering saints remember this. Observe, 1. We are
to look to Jesus, the author and finisher of our faith, who, for the joy that
was set before him, endured the cross, despised the shame, and has now
sat down at the right hand of the throne of God, Heb. xii. 2. 2. The in-

carnation and resurrection of Jesus Christ, heartily believed and rightly considered, will support a Christian under all sufferings in the present life.

II. Another thing to encourage him in suffering was that he had Paul for an example. Observe,

1. How the apostle suffered (*v.* 9) : *Wherein I suffer as an evil-doer ;* and let not Timothy the son expect any better treatment than Paul the father. Paul was a man who did good, and yet suffered as an evil-doer : we must not think it strange if those who do well fare ill in this world, and if the best of men meet with the worst of treatment ; but this was his comfort, *that the word of God was not bound.* Persecuting powers may silence ministers and restrain them, but they cannot hinder the operation of the word of God upon men's hearts and consciences ; that cannot be bound by any human force. This might encourage Timothy not to be afraid of bonds for the testimony of Jesus ; for the word of Christ, which ought to be dearer to him than liberty, or life itself, should in the issue suffer nothing by these bonds. Here we see, (1.) The good apostle's treatment in the world : *I suffer trouble ;* to this he was called and appointed. (2.) The pretence and colour under which he suffered : *I suffer as an evil-doer ;* so the Jews said to Pilate concerning Christ, *If he were not a malefactor, we would not have delivered him up to thee,* John xviii. 30. (3.) The real and true cause of his suffering trouble as an evil-doer : *Wherein ;* that is, in or for the sake of the gospel. The apostle suffered trouble unto bonds, and afterwards he resisted unto blood, striving against sin, Heb. xii. 4. Though the preachers of the word are often bound, yet the word is never bound.

2. Why he suffered cheerfully : *I endure all things for the elect's sake, v.* 10. Observe (1.) Good ministers may and should encourage themselves in the hardest services and the hardest sufferings, with this, that God will certainly bring good to his church, and benefit to his elect, out of them.— *That they may obtain the salvation which is in Christ Jesus.* Next to the salvation of our own souls we should be willing to do and suffer anything to promote the salvation of the souls of others. (2.) The elect are designed to obtain salvation : *God hath not appointed us to wrath but to obtain salvation,* 1 Thess. v. 9. (3.) This salvation is in Christ Jesus, in him as the fountain, the purchaser, and the giver of it ; and it is accompanied with eternal glory : there is no salvation in Christ Jesus without it. (4.) The sufferings of our apostle were for the elect's sake, for their confirmation and encouragement.

III. Another thing with which he encourages Timothy is the prospect of a future state.

1. Those who faithfully adhere to Christ and to his truths and ways, whatever it cost them, will certainly have the advantage of it in another world : *If we be dead with him, we shall live with him, v.* 11. If, in conformity to Christ, we be dead to this world, its pleasures, profits, and honours, we shall go to live with him in a better world, to be for ever with him. Nay, though we be called out to suffer for him, we shall not lose by that, *Those who suffer for Christ* on earth shall reign with Christ in heaven, *v.* 12. Those who suffered with David in his humiliation were preferred with him in his exaltation : so it will be with those who suffer with the Son of David.

2. It is at our peril if we prove unfaithful to him : *If we deny him, he also will deny us.* If we deny him before man, he will deny us before his Father, Matt. x. 33. And that man must needs be for ever miserable whom Christ disowns at last. This will certainly be the issue, whether we believe

it or no (v. 13): *If we believe not, yet he abideth faithful; he cannot deny himself.* He is faithful to his threatenings, faithful to his promises: neither one nor the other shall fall to the ground, no, not the least jot or tittle of them. If we be faithful to Christ, he will certainly be faithful to us. If we be false to him, he will be faithful to his threatenings: *he cannot deny himself,* cannot recede from any word that he hath spoken, for he is yea, and amen, the faithful witness. Observe, (1.) Our being dead with Christ precedes our living with him, and is connected with it: the one is in order to the other; so our suffering for him is the way to reign with him. *You that have followed me in the regeneration, when the Son of man shall sit on the throne of his glory, you also shall sit upon twelve thrones, judging the twelve tribes of Israel,* Matt. xix. 28. (2.) This is a faithful saying, and may be depended on and ought to be believed. But, (3.) If we deny him, out of fear, or shame, or for the sake of some temporal advantage, he will deny and disown us, and will not deny himself, but will continue faithful to his word when he threatens as well as when he promises.

¹⁴ Of these things put *them* in remembrance, charging *them* before the Lord that they strive not about words to no profit, *but* to the subverting of the hearers. ¹⁵ Study to show thyself approved unto God, a workman that needeth not to be ashamed, rightly dividing [handling aright] the word of truth. ¹⁶ But shun profane *and* vain babblings: for they will increase unto more ungodliness. ¹⁷ And their word will eat as doth a canker: of whom is Hymenæus and Philetus; ¹⁸ Who concerning the truth have erred, saying that the resurrection is past already; and overthrow the faith of some.

Having thus encouraged Timothy to suffer, he comes in the next place to direct him in his work.

1. He must make it his business to edify those who were under his charge, *to put them in remembrance* of those things which they did already know; for this is the work of ministers; not to tell people that which they never knew before, but to put them in mind of that which they do know, *charging them that they strive not about words.* Observe, Those that are disposed to strive commonly strive about matters of very small moment. Strifes of words are very destructive to the things of God. That they strive not about words *to no profit.* If people did but consider of what little use most of the controversies in religion are, they would not be so zealous in their strifes of words, *to the subverting of the hearers,* to the drawing of them away from the great things of God, and occasioning unchristian heats and animosities, by which truth is often in danger of being lost. Observe, People are very prone to strive about words, and such strifes never answer any other ends than to shake some and subvert others; they are not only useless, but they are very hurtful, and therefore ministers are to charge the people that they do not strive about words, and they are most likely to be regarded when they charge them before the Lord, that is, in his name and from his word; when they produce their warrant for what they say.—*Study to show thyself approved unto God,* v. 15. Observe, the care of ministers must be to approve themselves unto God, to be accepted of him, and to show that they are so approved unto God. In order thereunto, there must

be constant care and industry : *Study to show thyself* such a one, *a workman that needs not be ashamed.* Ministers must be workmen ; they have work to do, and they must take pains in it. Workmen that are unskilful, or unfaithful, or lazy, have need to be ashamed ; but those who mind their business, and keep to their work, are workmen that need not be ashamed. And what is their work ? It is *rightly to divide the word of truth.* Not to invent a new gospel, but rightly to divide the gospel that is committed to their trust. To speak terror to those to whom terror belongs, comfort to whom comfort ; to give every one *his portion in due season,* Matt. xxiv. 45. Observe here, 1. The word which ministers preach is the word of truth, for the author of it is the God of truth. 2. It requires great wisdom, study, and care, to divide this word of truth rightly ; Timothy must study in order to do this well.

II. He must take heed of that which would be a hindrance to him in his work, *v.* 16. He must take heed of error : *Shun profane and vain babblings.* The heretics, who boasted of their notions and their arguments, thought their performances such as might recommend them ; but the apostle calls them *profane and vain babblings :* when once men become fond of those *they will increase unto more ungodliness.* The way of error is down-hill ; one absurdity being granted or contended for, a thousand follow : *Their word will eat as doth a canker, or gangrene ;* when errors or heresies come into the church, the infecting of one often proves the infecting of many, or the infecting of the same person with one error often proves the infecting of him with many errors. Upon this occasion the apostle mentions some who had lately advanced erroneous doctrines : *Hymeneus and Philetus.* He names these corrupt teachers, by which he sets a brand upon them, to their perpetual infamy, and warns all people against hearkening to them. They have *erred concerning the truth,* or concerning one of the fundamental articles of the Christian religion, which is truth. The resurrection of the dead is one of the great doctrines of Christ. Now see the subtlety of the serpent and the serpent's seed. They did not deny the resurrection (for that had been boldly and avowedly to confront the word of Christ), but they put a corrupt interpretation upon that true doctrine, saying that the resurrection was past already, that what Christ spoke concerning the resurrection was *to be understood mystically* and by way of allegory, that it must be meant of a spiritual resurrection only. It is true, there is a spiritual resurrection, but to infer thence that there will not be a true and real resurrection of the body at the last day is to dash one truth of Christ in pieces against another. By this they *overthrew the faith of some,* took them off from the belief of the resurrection of the dead ; and if there be no resurrection of the dead, no future state, no recompense of our services and sufferings in another world, we are of all men the most miserable, 1 Cor. xv. 19. Whatever takes away the doctrine of a future state overthrows the faith of Christians. The apostle had largely disproved this error (1 Cor. xv.), and therefore does not here enter into the arguments against it. Observe, 1. The babblings Timothy was to shun were profane and vain ; they were empty shadows, and led to profaneness : *For they will increase unto more ungodliness.* 2. Error is very productive, and on that account the more dangerous : it *will eat like a gangrene.* 3. When men err concerning the truth, they always endeavour to have some plausible pretence for it. Hymeneus and Philetus did not deny a resurrection, but pretended it was already past. 4. Error, especially that which affects the foundation, will overthrow the faith of some.

¹⁹ Nevertheless the foundation of God standeth sure, having this seal, The Lord knoweth them that are his. And, Let every one that nameth the name of Christ depart from iniquity. ²⁰ But in a great house there are not only vessels of gold and silver, but also of wood and earth ; and some to honour, and some to dishonour. ²¹ If a man therefore purge himself from these, he shall be a vessel unto honour, sanctified, and meet for the master's use, *and* prepared unto every good work.

Here we see what we may comfort ourselves with, in reference to this, and the little errors and heresies that both infect and infest the church, and do mischief.

I. It may be a great comfort to us that the unbelief of men cannot make the promise of God of no effect. Though the faith of some particular persons be overthrown, yet *the foundation of God standeth sure* (*v.* 19) ; it is not possible that they should deceive the elect. Or it may be meant of the truth itself, which they impugn. All the attacks which the powers of darkness have made upon the doctrine of Christ cannot shake it ; it stands firm, and weathers all the storms which have been raised against it. The prophets and apostles, that is, the doctrines of the Old and New Testament, are still firm ; and they have a seal with two mottoes upon it, one on the one side, and the other on the other, as is usual in a broad seal. 1. One expresses our comfort—that *the Lord knows those that are his*, and those that are not ; knows them, that is, he owns them, so knows them that he will never lose them. Though the faith of some be overthrown, yet the Lord is said to know the ways of the righteous, Ps. i. 6. None can overthrow the faith of any whom God hath chosen. 2. Another declares our duty—that every one who names the name of Christ must depart from iniquity. Those who would have the comfort of the privilege must make conscience of the duty. If the name of Christ be called upon us, we must depart from iniquity, else he will not own us ; he will say in the great day (Matt. vii. 23), *Depart from me, I never knew you, you workers of iniquity.* Observe, (1.) Whatever errors are introduced into the church, the foundation of God standeth sure, his purpose can never be defeated. (2.) God hath some in the church who are his and whom he knows to be his. (3.) Professing Christians name the name of Christ, are called by his name, and therefore are bound to depart from iniquity ; for Christ *gave himself for us, that he might redeem us from all iniquity*, Tit. ii. 14.

II. Another thing that may comfort us is that though there are some whose faith is overthrown, yet there are others who keep their integrity, and hold it fast (*v.* 20) : *In a great house there are not only vessels of gold,* &c. The church of Christ is a great house, a well-furnished house : now some of the furniture of this house is of great value, as the plate in a house ; some of small value, and put to mean uses, as the vessels of wood and earth ; so it is in the church of God. There are some professors of religion that are like the vessels of wood and earth, they are vessels of dishonour. But at the same time all are not vessels of dishonour ; there are *vessels of gold and silver*, vessels of honour, *that are sanctified and meet for the Master's use.* When we are discouraged by the badness of some, we must encourage ourselves by the consideration of the goodness of others. Now we should see to it that we be vessels of honour : we must *purge ourselves from these corrupt opinions*, that we may be sanctified for our Master's use. Observe, I. In the church there are some vessels of honour and some of dishonour ; there are some vessels of mercy and other vessels of wrath, Rom. ix. 22, 23. Some dishonour the church by their corrupt opinions and wicked lives ; and others honour and credit it by their exemplary conversation. 2. A man must purge himself from these before he can be a vessel of honour, or meet for his Master's use. 3. Every vessel must be fit for its Master's use ; every one in the church whom God approves must be devoted to his Master's service and meet for his use. 4. Sanctification in the heart is our preparation for every good work. The tree must be made good, and then the fruit will be good.

²² Flee also youthful lusts : but follow righteousness, faith, charity [**love**], peace, with them that call on the Lord out of a pure heart. ²³ But foolish and unlearned questions avoid [**refuse**], knowing that they do gender strifes. ²⁴ And the servant of the Lord must not strive ; but be gentle unto all *men*, apt to teach, patient. ²⁵ In meekness instructing [**correcting**] those that oppose themselves ; if God peradventure will give them repentance to the acknowledging [**unto the knowledge**] of the truth ; ²⁶ And *that* they may recover themselves out of the snare of the devil, who are taken captive by him at his will [**having been taken captive by the Lord's servant unto the will of God**].

I. Paul here exhorts Timothy to beware of *youthful lusts, v. 22.* Though he was a holy good man, very much mortified to the world, yet Paul thought it necessary to caution him against youthful lusts : "*Flee* them, take all possible care and pains to keep thyself pure from them." The lusts of the flesh are youthful lusts, which young people must carefully watch against, and the best must not be secure. He prescribes an excellent remedy against youthful lusts : *Follow righteousness, faith, charity, peace,* &c. Observe, I. Youthful lusts are very dangerous, for which reason even hopeful young people should be warned of them, for they war against the soul, I Pet. ii. II. 2. The exciting of our graces will be the extinguishing of our corruptions ; the more we follow that which is good the faster and the further we shall flee from that which is evil. Righteousness, and faith, and love, will be excellent antidotes against youthful lusts. Holy love will cure impure lust.—*Follow peace with those that call on the Lord.* The keeping up of the communion of saints will take us off from all fellowship with unfruitful works of darkness. See the character of Christians : they are such as *call on the Lord Jesus Christ out of a pure heart.* Observe, Christ is to be prayed to. It is the character of all Christians that they call upon him ; but our prayers to God and Christ are not acceptable nor successful except they come out of a pure heart.

II. He cautions him against contention, and, to prevent this (*v. 23*), cautions him against *foolish and unlearned questions,* that tend to no benefit, strifes of words. Those who advanced them, and doted upon them, thought themselves wise and learned ; but Paul calls them foolish and unlearned. The mischief of these is that they *gender strifes,* that they breed debates and quarrels among Christians and ministers. It is very remarkable how often, and with what seriousness, the apostle cautions Timothy against disputes in religion, which surely was not without some such design as this, to show us that religion consists more in believing and practising what God requires than in subtle disputes.—*The servant of the Lord must not strive, v.* 24. Nothing worse becomes the servant of the Lord Jesus, who himself did not strive nor cry (Matt. xii. 19), but was a pattern of meekness, and mildness, and gentleness to all, than strife and contention. The servant of the Lord must be *gentle to all men,* and thereby show that he is himself subject to the commanding power of that holy religion which he is employed in preaching and propagating.—*Apt to teach.* Those are unapt to teach who are apt to strive, and are fierce and forward. Ministers must be patient, bearing with evil, and *in meekness instructing (v.* 25) not only those who subject themselves, but those who oppose themselves. Observe, 1. Those who opposeth emselves to the truth are to be instructed ; for instruction is the scripture method of dealing with the erroneous, which is more likely to convince them of their errors than fire and faggot : he does not bid us kill their bodies, under pretence of saving their souls. 2. Such as oppose themselves are to be instructed in meekness, for our Lord is meek and lowly (Matt. xi. 29), and this agrees·well with the character of the servant of the Lord (*v.* 24): *He must not strive, but be gentle to all men, apt to teach, patient.* This is the way to convey truth in its light and power, and to overcome evil with good, Rom. xii. 21. 3. That which ministers must have in their eyes, in instructing those who oppose themselves, must be their recovery : *If God, peradventure, will give them repentance to the acknowledging of the truth.* Observe, (1.) Repentance is God's gift. (2.) It is a gift with a *peradventure* in the case of those who oppose themselves ; and therefore, though we are not to despair of the grace of God, yet we must take heed of presuming upon it. *To the acknowledging of the truth.* (3.) The same God who gives us the discovery of the truth does by his grace bring us to the acknowledging of it, otherwise our hearts would continue in rebellion against it, for we are to confess with our mouths as well as to believe with our hearts, Rom. x. 9, 10. And thus sinners recover themselves out of the snare of the devil ; see here, [1.] The misery of sinners : they are in the *snare of the devil, and are led captive by him at his will, v.* 26. They are slaves to the worst of task-masters : he is the spirit that now worketh in the children of disobedience, Eph. ii. 2. They are taken in a snare, and in the worst snare, because it is the devil's ; they are as fishes that are taken in an evil net, and as the birds that are caught in the snare. Further, They are under Ham's curse (*a servant of servants shall he be,* Gen. ix. 25), they are slaves to him who is but a slave and vassal. [2.] The happiness of those who repent : they recover themselves out of this snare, as a bird out of the snare of the fowler ; the snare is broken, and they have escaped ; and the greater the danger the greater the deliverance. When sinners repent, those who before were led captive by the devil at his will come to be led into the glorious liberty of the children of God, and have their wills melted into the will of the Lord Jesus. The good Lord recover us all out of the snare.

CHAPTER III

I. The apostle forewarns Timothy what the last days would be, with the reasons thereof, ver. 1-9. II. Prescribes various remedies against them (ver. 10, to the end), particularly his own example ("But thou hast fully known my doctrine," &c.) and the knowledge of the holy scriptures, which are able to make us wise unto salvation, and will be the best antidote against the corruptions of the times we live in. In this chapter Paul tells Timothy how bad others would be, and therefore how good he should be; and this use we should make of the badness of others, thereby to engage us to hold our own integrity so much the firmer.

THIS know also, that in the last days perilous [grievous] times shall come. ² For men shall be lovers of their own selves, covetous [lovers of money], boasters, proud, blasphemers [railers], disobedient to parents, unthankful, unholy, ³ Without natural affection, trucebreakers, false accusers, incontinent [implacable, slanderers, without self-control], fierce, despisers of those that are good [no lovers of good], ⁴ Traitors, heady, highminded, lovers of pleasures more than lovers of God; ⁵ Having a form of godliness, but denying the power thereof: from such turn away. ⁶ For of this sort are they which creep into houses, and lead captive silly women laden with sins, led away with divers lusts, ⁷ Ever learning, and never able to come to the knowledge of the truth. ⁸ Now as Jannes and Jambres withstood Moses, so do these also resist the truth: men of corrupt minds, reprobate concerning the faith. ⁹ But they shall proceed no further: for their folly shall be manifest unto all *men*, as theirs also was.

Timothy must not think it strange if there were in the church bad men; for the net of the gospel was to enclose both good fish and bad, Matt. xiii. 47, 48. Jesus Christ had foretold (Matt. xxiv.) that there would come seducers, and therefore we must not be offended at it, nor think the worse of religion or the church for it. Even in gold ore there will be dross, and a great deal of chaff among the wheat when it lies on the floor.

I. Timothy must know that in the *last days* (v. 1), in gospel times, there would *come perilous times*. Though gospel times were times of reformation in many respects, let him know that even in gospel times there would be perilous times; not so much on account of persecutions from without as on account of corruptions within. These would be difficult times, wherein it would be difficult for a man to keep a good conscience. He does not say, "Perilous times shall come, for both Jews and Gentiles shall be combined to root out Christianity;" but "perilous times shall come, for such as have *the form of godliness* (v. 5) shall be corrupt and wicked, and do a great deal of damage to the church." Two traitors within the garrison may do more hurt to it than two thousand besiegers without. Perilous times shall come, for men shall be wicked. Note, 1. Sin makes the times perilous. When there is a general corruption of manners, and of the tempers of men, this makes the times dangerous to live in; for it is hard to keep our integrity in the midst of general corruption. 2. The coming of perilous times is an evidence of the truth of scripture-predictions; if the event in this respect did not answer to the prophecy, we might be tempted to question the Divinity of the Bible. 3. We are all concerned to know this, to believe and consider it, that we may not be surprised when we see the times perilous : *This know also.*

II. Paul tells Timothy what would be the occasion of making these times perilous, or what shall be the marks and signs whereby these times may be known, *v.* 2, &c. 1. Self-love will make the times perilous. Who is there who does not love himself? But this is meant of an irregular sinful self love. Men love their carnal selves better than their spiritual selves. Men love to gratify their own lusts, and make provision for them, more than to please God and do their duty. Instead of Christian charity, which takes care for the good of others, they will mind themselves only, and prefer their own gratification before the church's edification. 2. Covetousness. Observe, Self-love brings in a long train of sins and mischiefs. When men are lovers of themselves, no good can be expected from them, as all good may be expected from those who love God with all their hearts. When covetousness generally prevails, when every man is for what he can get and for keeping what he has, this makes men dangerous to one another, and obliges every man to stand on his guard against his neighbour. 3. Pride and vain-glory. The times are perilous when men, being proud of themselves, are *boasters and blasphemers,* boasters before men whom they despise and look upon with scorn, and blasphemers of God and of his name. When men do not fear God they will not regard man, and so *vice versâ.* 4. When children are disobedient to their parents, and break through the obligations which they lie under to them both in duty and gratitude, and frequently in interest, having their dependence upon them and their expectation from them, they make the times perilous ; for what wickedness will those stick at who will be abusive to their own parents and rebel against them? 5. Unthankfulness and unholiness make the times perilous, and these two commonly go together. What is the reason that men are unholy and without the fear of God, but that they are unthankful for the mercies of God? Ingratitude and impiety go together ; for call a man ungrateful, and you can call him by no worse name. Unthankful, and impure, defiled with fleshly lusts, which is an instance of great ingratitude to that God who has provided so well for the support of the body ; we abuse his gifts, if we make them the food and fuel of our lusts. 6. The times are perilous when men will not be held by the bonds either of nature or common honesty, when they are *without natural affection,* and *truce-breakers, v.* 3. There is a natural affection due to all. Wherever there is the human nature, there should be humanity towards those of the same nature, but especially between relations. Times are perilous when children are disobedient to their parents (*v.* 2) and when parents are without natural affection to their children, *v.* 3. See what a corruption of nature sin is, how it deprives men even of that which nature has implanted in them for the support of their own kind ; for the natural affection of parents to their children is that which contributes very much to the keeping up of mankind upon the earth. And those who will not be bound by natural affection, no marvel that they will not be bound by the most solemn leagues and covenants. *They are truce-breakers,* that make no conscience of the engagements they have laid themselves under. 7.

The times are perilous when men are *false accusers* one of another, διάβολοι—*devils* one to another, having no regard to the good name of others, or to the religious obligations of an oath, but thinking themselves at liberty to say and do what they please, Ps. xii. 4. 8. When men have no government of themselves and their own appetites : not of their own appetites, for they are *incontinent;* not of their own passions, for they are *fierce;* when they have no rule over their own spirits, and therefore are like a city that is broken down, and has no walls; they are soon fired, upon the least provocation. 9. When that which is good and ought to be honoured is generally despised and looked upon with contempt. It is the pride of persecutors that they look with contempt upon good people, though they are more excellent than their neighbours. 10. When men are generally treacherous, wilful, and haughty, the times are perilous (*v.* 4)—when men are *traitors, heady, high-minded.* Our Saviour has foretold that the brother shall betray the brother to death and the father the child (Matt. x. 21), and those are the worst sort of traitors : those who delivered up their Bibles to persecutors were called *traditores,* for they betrayed the trust committed to them. When men are petulant and puffed up, behaving scornfully to all about them, and when this temper generally prevails, then the times are perilous. 11. When men are generally *lovers of pleasure more than lovers of God.* When there are more epicures than true Christians, then the times are bad indeed. God is to be loved above all. That is a carnal mind, and is full of enmity against him, which prefers anything before him, especially such a sordid thing as carnal pleasure is. 12. When, notwithstanding all this, they *have the form of godliness* (*v.* 5), are called by the Christian name, baptized into the Christian faith and make a show of religion ; but how plausible soever their form of godliness is, they deny the power of it. When they take upon them the form which should and would bring along with it the power thereof, they will put asunder what God hath joined together : they will assume the form of godliness, to take away their reproach ; but they will not submit to the power of it, to take away their sin. Observe here, (1.) Men may be very bad and wicked under a profession of religion ; they may be lovers of themselves, &c., yet have a form of godliness. (2.) A form of godliness is a very different thing from the power of it ; men may have the one and be wholly destitute of the other ; yea, they deny it, at least practically in their lives. (3.) From such good Christians must withdraw themselves.

III. Here Paul warns Timothy to take heed of certain seducers, not only that he might not be drawn away by them himself, but that he might arm those who were under his charge against their seduction. 1. He shows how industrious they were to make proselytes (*v.* 6) : they applied themselves to particular persons, visited them in their houses, not daring to appear openly ; for those that do evil hate the light, John iii. 20. They were not forced into houses, as good Christians often were by persecutions ; but they of choice crept into houses, to insinuate themselves into the affections and good opinion of people, and so to draw them over to their party. And see what sort of people those were that they gained, and made proselytes of ; they were such as were weak, *silly women;* and such as were wicked, *laden with sins, and led away with divers lusts.* A foolish head and a filthy heart make persons, especially women, an easy prey to seducers. 2. He shows how far they were from coming to the knowledge of the truth, though they pretended to be *ever learning, v.* 7. In one sense we must all be ever learning, that is, growing in knowledge, following on to know the Lord, pressing forward ; but these were sceptics, giddy and unstable, who were forward to imbibe every new notion, under pretence of advancement in knowledge, but never came to a right understanding of the truth as it is in Jesus.   3. He foretells the certain stop that should be put to their progress (*v.* 8, 9), comparing them to the Egyptian magicians who withstood Moses, and who are here named, *Jannes* and *Jambres;* though the names are not to be met with in the story of the Old Testament, yet they are found in some old Jewish writers.   When Moses came with a divine command to fetch Israel out of Egypt, these magicians opposed him.   Thus those heretics *resisted the truth* and like them were men of *corrupt minds*, men who had their understandings perverted, biassed and prejudiced against the truth, and *reprobate concerning the faith*, or very far from being true Christians ; *but they shall proceed no further*, or not much further, as some read it.   Observe, (1.) Seducers seek for corners, and love obscurity ; for they are afraid to appear in public, and therefore creep into houses.   Further, They attack those who are the least able to defend themselves, silly and wicked women.   (2.) Seducers in all ages are much alike.   Their characters are the same—namely, *Men of corrupt minds*, &c. ; their conduct is much the same—they resist the truth, as Jannes and Jambres withstood Moses ; and they will be alike in their disappointment.   (3.) Those who resist the truth are guilty of folly, yea, of egregious folly ; for *magna est veritas, et prævalebit—Great is the truth, and shall prevail.*   (4.) Though the spirit of error may be let loose for a time, God has it in a chain.   Satan can deceive the nations and the churches no further and no longer than God will permit him : *Their folly shall be manifest*, it shall appear that they are impostors, and every man shall abandon them.

¹⁰ But thou hast fully known my doctrine, manner of life [**But thou didst follow my teaching, conduct**], purpose, faith, longsuffering, charity [**love**], patience, ¹¹ Persecutions, afflictions, which came unto me at Antioch, at Iconium, at Lystra ; what persecutions I endured : but out of *them* all the Lord delivered me.   ¹² Yea, and all that will live godly in Christ Jesus, shall suffer persecution.   ¹³ But evil men and seducers [**impostors**] shall wax worse and worse, deceiving, and being deceived.   ¹⁴ But continue thou in the things which thou hast learned and hast been assured of, knowing of whom thou hast learned *them ;*   ¹⁵ And that from a child thou hast known the holy scriptures, which are able to make thee wise unto salvation through faith which is in Christ Jesus.   ¹⁶ All scripture *is* given by inspiration of God, and [**every scripture inspired of God**] *is* profitable for doctrine, for reproof, for correction, for instruction in righteousness :   ¹⁷ That the man of God may be perfect [**complete**], thoroughly furnished unto all good works.

Here the apostle, to confirm Timothy in that way wherein he walked,

I. Sets before him his own example, which Timothy had been an eye-witness of, having long attended Paul (*v.* 10) : *Thou hast fully known my doctrine.*   The more fully we know the doctrine of Christ and the apostles, the more closely we shall cleave to it ; the reason why many sit loose to it is because they do not fully know it. Christ's apostles had no enemies but those who did not know them, or not know them fully ; those who knew them best loved and honoured them the most. Now what is it that Timothy had so fully known in Paul ? 1. The doctrine that he preached. Paul kept back nothing from his hearers, but declared to them the whole counsel of God (Acts xx. 27), so that if it were not their own fault they might fully know it. Timothy had a great advantage in being trained up under such a tutor, and being apprised of the doctrine he preached. 2. He had fully known his conversation. *Thou hast fully known my doctrine, and manner of life ;* his manner of life was of a piece with his doctrine, and did not contradict it. He did not pull down by his living what he built up by his preaching. Those ministers are likely to do good, and leave lasting fruits of their labours, whose manner of life agrees with their doctrine ; as, on the contrary, those cannot expect to profit the people at all that preach well and live ill. 3. Timothy fully knew what was the great thing that Paul had in view, both in his preaching and in his conversation : "Thou hast known *my purpose,* what I drive at, how far it is from any worldly, carnal, secular design, and how sincerely I aim at the glory of God and the good of the souls of men." 4. Timothy fully knew Paul's good character, which he might gather from his doctrine, manner of life, and purpose ; for he gave proofs of his *faith* (that is, of his integrity and fidelity, or his faith in Christ, his faith concerning another world, by which Paul lived) his *long-suffering* towards the churches to which he preached and over which he presided, his *charity* towards all men, and his *patience.* These were graces that Paul was eminent for, and Timothy knew it. 5. He knew that he had suffered ill for doing well (*v.* 11) : "Thou hast fully known the *persecutions and afflictions that came unto me* " (he mentions those only which happened to him while Timothy was with him, *at Antioch, at Iconium, at Lystra*) ; "and therefore let it be no surprise to thee if thou suffer hard things, it is no more than I have endured before." 6. He knew what care God had taken of him : *Notwithstanding out of them all the Lord delivered me ;* as he never failed his cause, so his God never failed him. Thou hast fully known my *afflictions.* When we know the afflictions of good people but in part, they are a temptation to us to decline that cause which they suffer for ; when we know only the hardships they undergo for Christ, we may be ready to say, "We will renounce that cause that is likely to cost us so dear in the owning of it ; " but when we *fully* know the afflictions, not only how they suffer, but how they are supported and comforted under their sufferings, then, instead of being discouraged, we shall be animated by them, especially considering that we are told before that we must count upon such things (*v.* 12) : *All that will live godly in Christ Jesus shall suffer persecution ;* not always alike ; at that time those who professed the faith of Christ were more exposed to persecution than at other times ; but at all times, more or less, those who will live godly in Christ Jesus shall suffer persecution. They must expect to be despised, and that their religion will stand in the way of their preferment ; those who will live godly must expect it, especially those who will live godly *in Christ Jesus,* that is, according to the strict rules of the Christian religion, those who will wear the livery and bear the name of the crucified Redeemer. All who will show their religion in their conversation, who will not only be godly, but live godly, let them expect persecution, especially when they are resolute in it. Observe, (1.) The apostle's life was very exemplary for three things :

for his *doctrine*, which was according to the will of God ; for his *life*, which was agreeable to his doctrine ; and for his *persecutions and sufferings*. (2.) Though his life was a life of great usefulness, yet it was a life of great sufferings ; and none, I believe, came nearer to their great Master for eminent services and great sufferings than Paul : he suffered almost in every place; the Holy Ghost witnessed that bonds and afflictions did abide him, Acts xx. 23. Here he mentions his persecutions and afflictions at *Antioch*, at *Iconium*, at *Lystra*, besides what he suffered elsewhere. (3.) The apostle mentions the Lord's delivering him out of them all, for Timothy's and our encouragement under sufferings. (4.) We have the practice and treatment of true Christians : they live godly in Jesus Christ—this is their practice ; and they shall suffer persecution—this is the usage they must expect in this world.

II. He warns Timothy of the fatal end of seducers, as a reason why he should stick closely to the truth as it is in Jesus : *But evil men and seducers shall wax worse and worse*, &c., *v.* 13. Observe, As good men, by the grace of God, grow better and better, so bad men, through the subtlety of Satan and the power of their own corruptions, grow worse and worse. The way of sin is down-hill ; for such proceed from bad to worse, *deceiving and being deceived*. Those who deceive others do but deceive themselves ; those who draw others into error run themselves into more and more mistakes, and they will find it so at last, to their cost.

III. He directs him to keep close to a good education, and particularly to what he had learned out of the holy scriptures (*v.* 14, 15) : *Continue thou in the things which thou hast learned*. Note, It is not enough to learn that which is good, but we must continue in it, and persevere in it unto the end. Then are we Christ's disciples indeed, John viii. 31. We should not be any more *children, tossed to and fro, and carried about with every wind of doctrine, by the sleight of men and cunning craftiness, whereby they lie in wait to deceive*, Eph. iv. 14. *Be not carried about with divers and strange doctrines ; for it is a good thing that the heart be established with grace*, Heb. xiii. 9. And for this reason we should continue in the things we have learned from the holy scriptures ; not that we ought to continue in any errors and mistakes which we may have been led into, in the time of our childhood and youth (for these, upon an impartial inquiry and full conviction, we should forsake) ; but this makes nothing against our continuing in those things which the holy scriptures plainly assert, and which he that runs may read. If Timothy would adhere to the truth as he had been taught it, this would arm him against the snares and insinuations of seducers. Observe, Timothy must *continue in the things which he had learned and had been assured of*.

1. It is a great happiness to know the certainty of the things wherein we have been instructed (Luke i. 4) ; not only to know what the truths are, but to know that they are of undoubted certainty. What we have learned we must labour to be more and more assured of, that, being grounded in the truth, we may be guarded against error, for certainty in religion is of great importance and advantage : *Knowing*, (1.) "That thou hast had good teachers. Consider of *whom thou hast learned them ;* not of evil men and seducers, but good men, who had themselves experienced the power of the truths they taught thee, and been ready to suffer for them, and thereby would give the fullest evidence of their belief of these truths." (2.) "Knowing especially the firm foundation upon which thou hast built, namely, that of the scripture (*v.* 15) : *That from a child thou hast known the holy scriptures*.

2. Those who would acquaint themselves with the things of God, and be assured of them, must know the holy scriptures, for these are the summary of divine revelation.

3. It is a great happiness to know the holy scriptures from our childhood : and children should betimes get the knowledge of the scriptures. The age of children is the learning age ; and those who would get true learning must get it out of the scriptures.

4. The scriptures we are to know are the holy scriptures ; they come from the holy God, were delivered by holy men, contain holy precepts, treat of holy things, and were designed to make us holy and to lead us in the way of holiness to happiness ; being called the *holy scriptures*, they are by this distinguished from profane writings of all sorts, and from those that only treat of morality, and common justice and honesty, but do not meddle with holiness. If we would know the holy scriptures, we must read and search them daily, as the noble Bereans did, Acts xvii. 11. They must not lie by us neglected, and seldom or never looked into. Now here observe,

(1.) What is the excellency of the scripture. It is *given by inspiration of God* (*v.* 16), and therefore is his word. It is a divine revelation, which we may depend upon as infallibly true. The same Spirit that breathed reason into us breathes revelation among us : *For the prophecy came not in old time by the will of man, but holy men spoke as they were moved or carried forth by the Holy Ghost*, 2 Pet. i. 21. The prophets and apostles did not speak from themselves, but what they received of the Lord that they delivered unto us. That the scripture was given by inspiration of God appears from the majesty of its style,—from the truth, purity, and sublimity of the doctrines contained in it—from the harmony of its several parts,—from its power and efficacy on the minds of multitudes that converse with it,—from the accomplishment of many prophecies relating to things beyond all human foresight,—and from the uncontrollable miracles that were wrought in proof of its divine original : *God also bearing them witness, both with signs and wonders, and with divers miracles and gifts of the Holy Ghost, according to his own will*, Heb. ii. 4.

(2.) What use it will be of to us. [1.] *It is able to make us wise to salvation ;* that is, it is a sure guide in our way to eternal life. Note, Those are wise indeed who are wise to salvation. The scriptures are able to make us truly wise, wise for our souls and another world. "To make thee wise to salvation *through faith.*" Observe, The scriptures will make us wise to salvation, if they be mixed with faith, and not otherwise, Heb. iv. 2. For, if we do not believe their truth and goodness, they will do us no good. [2.] It is *profitable* to us for all the purposes of the Christian life, *for doctrine, for reproof, for correction, for instruction in righteousness.* It answers all the ends of divine revelation. It instructs us in that which is true, reproves us for that which is amiss, directs us in that which is good. It is of use to all, for we all need to be instructed, corrected, and reproved : it is of special use to ministers, who are to give instruction, correction, and reproof ; and whence can they fetch it better than from the scripture ? [3.] *That the man of God may be perfect, v.* 17. The Christian, the minister, is the man of God. That which finishes a man of God in this world is the scripture. By it we are *thoroughly furnished for every good work.* There is that in the scripture which suits every case. Whatever duty we have to do, whatever service is required from us, we may find enough in the scriptures to furnish us for it.

(3.) On the whole we here see, [1.] That the scripture has various uses, and answers divers ends and purposes : *It is profitable for doctrine, for reproof, for correction* of all errors in judgment and practice, and *for instruction in righteousness.* [2.] The scripture is a perfect rule of faith and practice, and was designed for the man of God, the minister as well as the Christian who is devoted to God, for it is *profitable for doctrine,* &c. [3.] If we consult the scripture, which was given by inspiration of God, and follow its directions, we shall be made men of God, *perfect and thoroughly furnished to every good work.* [4.] There is no occasion for the writings of the philosopher, nor for rabbinical fables, nor popish legends, nor unwritten traditions, to make us perfect men of God, since the scripture answers all these ends and purposes. O that we may love our Bibles more, and keep closer to them than ever ! and then shall we find the benefit and advantage designed thereby, and shall at last attain the happiness therein promised and assured to us.

CHAPTER IV

In this chapter, I. Paul with great solemnity and earnestness presses Timothy to the diligent and conscientious discharge of his work and office as an evangelist; and the charge given to him all gospel ministers are to take to themselves, ver. 1-5. II. The reason of his concern in this case, Why must Timothy now be instant in season, &c., in a particular manner? Because the church was likely to be deprived of the apostle's labours, for his departure was at hand, ver. 6-8. III. Divers particular matters, with a hint and caution, about Alexander the coppersmith, ver. 9-15. IV. He informs him of what befell him at his first answer; though men forsook him, the Lord stood by him, and this encouraged him to hope for future deliverance, ver. 16-18. And then he concludes with salutations and a benediction, ver. 19, to the end.

I CHARGE *thee* therefore before God, and the Lord Jesus Christ, who shall judge the quick and the dead at [and by] his appearing and his kingdom; ² Preach the word; be instant in season, out of season; reprove, rebuke, exhort with all longsuffering and doctrine. ³ For the time will come when they will not endure sound doctrine; but after their own lusts shall they heap to themselves teachers, having itching ears; ⁴ And they shall turn away *their* ears from the truth, and shall be turned unto fables. ⁵ But watch thou [be thou sober] in all things, endure afflictions, do the work of an evangelist, make full proof of [fulfil] thy ministry. ⁶ For I am now ready to be [am already being] offered, and the time of my departure is at hand. ⁷ I have fought a [the] good fight, I have finished *my* course, I have kept the faith : ⁸ Henceforth there is laid up for me a crown of righteousness, which the Lord, the righteous judge, shall give me at that day : and not to me only, but unto all them also that love his appearing.

2 TIMOTHY IV. 1-8   161

Observe, I. How awfully this charge is introduced (*v.* 1) : *I charge thee before God and the Lord Jesus Christ, who shall judge the quick and the dead at his appearing and his kingdom.* Observe, The best of men have need to be awed into the discharge of their duty. The work of a minister is not an indifferent thing, but absolutely necessary. Woe be to him if he preach not the gospel, 1 Cor. ix. 16. To induce him to faithfulness, he must consider, 1. That the eye of God and Jesus Christ was upon him : *I charge thee before God and the Lord Jesus Christ;* that is, "as thou tenderest the favour of God and Jesus Christ; as thou wilt approve thyself to God and Jesus Christ, by the obligations both of natural and revealed religion ; as thou wilt make due returns to the God who made thee and the Lord Jesus Christ who redeemed thee." 2. He charges him as he will answer it at the great day, reminding him of the judgment to come, which is committed to the Lord Jesus. He shall judge the quick and the dead *at his appearing and his kingdom,* that is, when he appears in his kingdom. It concerns all, both ministers and people, seriously to consider the account that they must shortly give to Jesus Christ of all the trusts reposed in them. Christ shall *judge the quick and the dead,* that is, those that at the last day shall be found alive, and those who shall be raised to life out of the grave. Note, (1.) The Lord Jesus Christ shall judge the quick and dead. *God hath committed all judgment unto the Son,* and hath appointed him the Judge of quick and dead, Acts x. 42. (2.) He will appear ; he will come the second time, and it will be a glorious appearance, as the word ἐπιφανεία signifies. (3.) Then his kingdom shall appear in its glory : *At his appearing and kingdom;* for he will then appear in his kingdom, sitting on a throne, to judge the world.

II. What is the matter of the charge, *v.* 2-5. He is charged,

1. To *preach the word.* This is ministers' business ; a dispensation is committed to them. It is not their own notions and fancies that they are to preach, but the pure plain word of God ; and they must not corrupt it, but as of sincerity, but as of God, in the sight of God, they speak in Christ, 2 Cor. ii. 17.

2. To urge what he preached, and to press it with all earnestness upon his hearers : "*Be instant in season and out of season, reprove, rebuke, exhort;* do this work with all fervency of spirit. Call upon those under thy charge to take heed of sin, to do their duty : call upon them to repent, and believe, and live a holy life, and this both in season and out of season. *In season,* when they are at leisure to hear thee, when some special opportunity offers itself of speaking to them with advantage. Nay, do it *out of season,* even when there is not that apparent probability of fastening something upon them, because thou dost not know but the Spirit of God may fasten upon them ; for the wind bloweth where it listeth ; and *in the morning we must sow our seed, and in the evening not withhold our hand,*" Eccl. xi. 6. We must do it in season, that is, let slip no opportunity ; and do it out of season, that is, not shift off the duty, under pretence that it is out of season.

3. He must tell people of their faults : "*Reprove them, rebuke them.* Convince wicked people of the evil and danger of their wicked courses. Endeavour, by dealing plainly with them, to bring them to repentance. Rebuke them with gravity and authority, in Christ's name, that they may take thy displeasure against them as an indication of God's displeasure.

4. He must direct, encourage, and quicken those who began well. "*Exhort them* (persuade them to hold on, and endure to the end) and this

with all long-suffering and doctrine." (1.) He must do it very patiently: *With all long-suffering.* "If thou do not see the effect of thy labours presently, yet do not therefore give up the cause; be not weary of speaking to them." While God shows to them all long-suffering, let ministers exhort with all long-suffering. (2.) He must do it rationally, not with passion, but *with doctrine,* that is, "In order to the reducing of them to good practices, instil into them good principles. Teach them the truth as it is in Jesus, reduce them to a firm belief of it, and this will be a means both to reclaim them from evil and to bring them to good." Observe, [1.] A minister's work has various parts: he is to *preach the word,* to *reprove, rebuke,* and *exhort.* [2.] He is to be very diligent and careful; he must be *instant in season and out of season;* he must spare no pains nor labour, but must be urgent with them to take care of their souls and their eternal concerns.

5. He must *watch in all things.* "Seek an opportunity of doing them a kindness; let no fair occasion slip, through thy negligence. Watch to thy work; watch against the temptations of Satan, by which thou mayest be diverted from it; watch over the souls of those who are committed to thy charge."

6. He must count upon afflictions, and endure them, make the best of them. Κακοπάθησον, endure *patiently.* "Be not discouraged by the difficulties thou meetest with, but bear them with an evenness of spirit. Inure thyself to hardships."

7. He must remember his office, and discharge its duties: *Do the work of an evangelist.* The office of the evangelist was, as the apostles' deputies, to water the churches that they planted. They were not settled pastors, but for some time resided in, and presided over, the churches that the apostles had planted, till they were settled under a standing ministry. This was Timothy's work.

8. He must fulfil his ministry: *Make full proof of it.* It was a great trust that was reposed in him, and therefore he must answer it, and perform all the parts of his office with diligence and care. Observe, (1.) A minister must expect afflictions in the faithful discharge of his duty. (2.) He must endure them patiently, like a Christian hero. (3.) These must not discourage him in his work, for he must do his work, and fulfil his ministry. (4.) The best way to make full proof of our ministry is to fulfil it, to fill it up in all its parts with proper work.

III. The reasons to enforce the charge.

1. Because errors and heresies were likely to creep into the church, by which the minds of many professing Christians would be corrupted (*v.* 3, 4): "*For the time will come when they will not endure sound doctrine.* Therefore improve the present time, when they will endure it. Be busy now, for it is seed-time; when the fields are white unto the harvest, put in the sickle, for the present gale of opportunity will be soon over. *They will not endure sound doctrine.* There will be those who will *heap to themselves corrupt teachers, and will turn away their ears from the truth;* and therefore secure as many as thou canst, that, when these storms and tempests do arise, they may be well fixed, and their apostasy may be prevented." People must hear, and ministers must preach, for the time to come, and guard against the mischiefs that are likely to arise hereafter, though they do not yet arise. They will *turn away their ears from the truth;* they will grow weary of the old plain gospel of Christ, and then they will be greedy of fables, and take pleasure in them, and God will give them up to those strong delusions,

because they received not the truth in the love of it, 2 Thess. ii. 11, 12. Observe, (1.) These teachers were of their own heaping up, and not of God's sending; but they chose them, to gratify their lusts, and to please their itching ears. (2.) People do so when they will not endure sound doctrine, that preaching which is searching, plain, and to the purpose; then they will have teachers of their own. (3.) There is a wide difference between the word of God and the word of such teachers; the one is sound doctrine, the word of truth, the other is only fables. (4.) Those that are turned unto fables first turn away their ears from the truth, for they cannot hear and mind both, any more than they can serve two masters. Nay, further, it is said, *They shall be turned unto fables.* God justly suffers those to turn to fables who grow weary of the truth, and gives them up to be led aside from the truth by fables.

2. Because Paul for his part had almost done his work: *Do thou make full proof of thy ministry, for I am now ready to be offered, v. 6.* And,

(1.) "Therefore there will be the more occasion for thee." When labourers are removed out of the vineyard, it is no time for those to loiter that are left behind, but to double their diligence. The fewer hands there are to work the more industrious those hands must be that are at work.

(2.) "I have done the work of my day and generation; do thou in like manner do the work of thy day and generation."

(3.) The comfort and cheerfulness of Paul, in the prospect of his approaching departure, might encourage Timothy to the utmost industry, and diligence, and seriousness in his work. Paul was an old soldier of Jesus Christ, Timothy was but newly enlisted. "Come," says Paul, "I have found our Master kind and the cause good; I can look back upon my warfare with a great deal of pleasure and satisfaction; and therefore be not afraid of the difficulties thou must meet with. The crown of life is as sure to thee as if it were already upon thy head; and therefore endure afflictions, and make full proof of thy ministry." The courage and comfort of dying saints and ministers, and especially dying martyrs, are a great confirmation of the truth of the Christian religion, and a great encouragement to living saints and ministers in their work. Here the apostle looks forward, upon his death approaching: *I am now ready to be offered.* The Holy Ghost witnessed in every city that bonds and afflictions did abide him, Acts xx. 23. He was now at Rome, and it is probable that he had particular intimations from the Spirit that there he should seal the truth with his blood; and he looks upon it now as near at hand: I am *already poured out;* so it is in the original, ἤδη σπένδομαι· that is, I am already a martyr in affection. It alludes to the pouring out of the drink offerings; for the blood of the martyrs, though it was not a sacrifice of atonement, was a sacrifice of acknowledgment to the honour of the grace of God and his truth. Observe,

[1.] With what pleasure he speaks of dying. He calls it his departure; though it is probable that he foresaw he must die a violent bloody death, yet he calls it his departure, or his release. Death to a good man is his release from the imprisonment of this world and his departure to the enjoyments of another world; he does not cease to be, but is only removed from one world to another.

[2.] With what pleasure he looks back upon the life he had lived (*v.* 7): *I have fought a good fight, I have finished my course,* &c. He did not fear death, because he had the testimony of his conscience that by the grace of God he had in some measure answered the ends of living. As a Christian, as a minister, he had fought a good fight. He had done the service, gone through the difficulties of his warfare, and had been instrumental in carrying on the glorious victories of the exalted Redeemer over the powers of darkness. His life was a course, and he had now finished it ; as his warfare was accomplished, so his race was run. *"I have kept the faith.* I have kept the doctrines of the gospel, and never betrayed any of them. Note, *First,* The life of a Christian, but especially of a minister, is a warfare and a race, sometimes compared to the one in the scripture, and sometimes to the other. *Secondly,* It is a good fight, a good warfare ; the cause is good, and the victory is sure, if we continue faithful and courageous. *Thirdly,* We must fight this good fight ; we must fight it out, and finish our course ; we must not give over till we are made more than conquerors through him who hath loved us, Rom. viii. 37. *Fourthly,* It is a great comfort to a dying saint, when he can look back upon his past life and say with our apostle, *"I have fought,* &c. I have kept the faith, the doctrine of faith and the grace of faith." Towards the end of our days to be able to speak in this manner, what comfort, unspeakable comfort, will it afford ! Let it then be our constant endeavour, by the grace of God, that we may finish our course with joy, Acts xx. 24.

[3.] With what pleasure he looks forward to the life he was to live hereafter (*v.* 8) : *Henceforth there is laid up for me a crown of righteousness,* &c. He had lost for Christ, but he was sure he should not lose by him, Phil. iii. 8. Let this encourage Timothy to endure hardness as a good soldier of Jesus Christ that there is a crown of life before us, the glory and joy of which will abundantly recompense all the hardships and toils of our present warfare. Observe, it is called *a crown of righteousness,* because it will be the recompense of our services, which *God is not unrighteous to forget ;* and because our holiness and righteousness will there be perfected, and will be our crown. God will give it as *a righteous Judge,* who will let none lose by him. And yet this crown of righteousness was not peculiar to Paul, as if it belonged only to apostles and eminent ministers and martyrs, but *to all those also that love his appearing.* Observe, It is the character of all the saints that they love the appearing of Jesus Christ : they loved his first appearing, when he appeared to take away sin by the sacrifice of himself (Heb. ix. 26) ; they love to think of it ; they love his second appearing at the great day ; love it, and long for it : and, with respect to those who love the appearing of Jesus Christ, he shall appear to their joy ; there is a crown of righteousness reserved for them, which shall then be given them, Heb. ix. 28. We learn hence, *First,* The Lord is the righteous Judge, for his judgment is according to truth. *Secondly,* The crown of believers is a crown of righteousness, purchased by the righteousness of Christ, and bestowed as the reward of the saints' righteousness. *Thirdly,* This crown, which believers shall wear, is laid up for them ; they have it not at present, for here they are but heirs ; they have it not in possession, and yet it is sure, for it is laid up for them. *Fourthly,* The righteous Judge will give it to all who love, prepare, and long for his appearing, *Surely I come quickly. Amen, even so come, Lord Jesus.*

⁹ Do thy diligence to come shortly unto me : ¹⁰ For Demas hath forsaken me, having loved this present world, and is departed unto Thessalonica ; Crescens to Galatia, Titus unto Dalmatia. ¹¹ Only Luke is with me. Take Mark, and bring

him with thee: for he is profitable to me for the ministry.
¹² And Tychicus have I sent to Ephesus. ¹³ The cloak that I
left at Troas with Carpus, when thou comest, bring *with thee*,
and the books, *but* especially the parchments. ¹⁴ Alexander the
coppersmith did me much evil: the Lord reward him according
to his works: ¹⁵ Of whom be thou ware also; for he hath greatly
withstood our words.

Here are divers particular matters which Paul mentions to Timothy,
now at the closing of the epistle. 1. He bids him hasten to him, if possible
(*v.* 9): *Do thy diligence to come shortly to me.* For Timothy was an evangelist, one who was not a fixed pastor of any one place, but attended the
motions of the apostles, to build upon their foundation. Paul wanted
Timothy's company and help; and the reason he gives is because several
had left him (*v.* 10); one from an ill principle, namely *Demas*, who abides
under an ill name for it: *Demas hath forsaken me, having loved this present
world.* He quitted Paul and his interest, either for fear of suffering
(because Paul was now a prisoner, and he was afraid of coming into trouble
upon his account) or being called off from his ministry by secular affairs,
in which he entangled himself; his first love to Christ and his gospel was
forsaken and forgotten, and he fell in love with the world. Note, Love to
this present world is often the cause of apostasy from the truths and ways
of Jesus Christ. He has gone off, has *departed to Thessalonica*, called
thither perhaps by trade, or by some other worldly business. *Crescens* had
gone one way and *Titus* another way. *Luke* however remained with Paul
(*v.* 11, 12), and was not this enough? Paul did not think it so; he loved
the company of his friends. 2. He speaks respectfully concerning *Mark:
He is profitable to me for the ministry.* It is supposed that this Mark was
he about whom Paul and Barnabas had contended, Acts xv. 39. Paul
would not take him with him to the work, because he had once flinched
and drawn back: but now, says he, *Take Mark, and bring him with thee.*
By this it appears that Paul was now reconciled to Mark, and had a better
opinion of him than he had had formerly. This teaches us to be of a forgiving spirit; we must not therefore disclaim for ever making use of those
that are profitable and useful, though they may have done amiss. 3. Paul
orders Timothy to come to him, bids him as he came through Troas to
bring with him thence those things which he had left behind him there
(*v.* 13), the cloak he had left there, which it may be, Paul had the more
occasion for in a cold prison. It is probable that it was the habit Paul
usually wore, a plain dress. Some read it, the *roll of parchment I left at
Troas;* others, the *desk* that I left. Paul was guided by divine inspiration,
and yet he would have his books with him. Whereas he had exhorted
Timothy to give attendance to reading, so he did himself, though he was
now ready to be offered. As long as we live, we must be still learning.
But especially the parchments, which some think were the originals of his
epistles; others think they were the skins of which he made his tents,
whereby he obtained a livelihood, working with his own hands. 4. He
mentions *Alexander,* and the mischief that he had done him, *v.* 14, 15.
This is he who is spoken of Acts xix. 33. It should seem, he had been a
professor of the Christian religion, a forward professor, for he was there
particularly maligned by the worshippers of Diana, and yet he did Paul
much evil. Paul was in as much danger from false brethren (2 Cor. xi. 26)

as from open enemies. Paul foretells that God would reckon with him. **It is a prophetical denunciation** of the just judgment of God that would befall him: The Lord *will reward him according to his works.* He cautions Timothy to take heed of him: " *Of whom be thou aware also,* that he do not, under pretence of friendship, betray thee to mischief." It is dangerous having anything to do with those who would be enemies to such a man as Paul. Observe, (1.) Some who were once Paul's hearers and admirers did not give him reason to remember them with much pleasure; for one forsook him, and another did him much evil, and greatly withstood his words. Yet, (2.) At the same time he mentions some with pleasure; the badness of some did not make him forget the goodness of others; such as *Timothy, Titus, Mark,* and *Luke.* (3.) The apostle has left a brand on the names and memory of two persons; the one is *Demas,* who forsook him, having loved the present world, and the other is *Alexander,* who greatly withstood his words. (4.) God will reward evil-doers, particularly apostates, according to their works. (5.) Of such as are of Alexander's spirit and temper we should beware; for they will do us no good, but all the mischief that is in their power.

¹⁶ At my first answer [**defence**] no man stood with me, but all *men* forsook me: *I pray God* that it may not be laid to their charge. ¹⁷ Notwithstanding the Lord stood with me, and strengthened me; that by me the preaching might be fully known, and *that* all the Gentiles might hear: and I was delivered out of the mouth of the lion. ¹⁸ And the Lord shall deliver me from every evil work, and will preserve [**save**] *me* unto his heavenly kingdom: to whom *be* glory for ever and ever. Amen. ¹⁹ Salute Prisca and Aquila, and the household of Onesiphorus. ²⁰ Erastus abode at Corinth: but Trophimus have I left at Miletum sick. ²¹ Do thy diligence to come before winter. Eubulus greeteth thee, and Pudens, and Linus, and Claudia, and all the brethren. ²² The Lord Jesus Christ *be* with thy spirit. Grace *be* with you. Amen.

Here, I. He gives Timothy an account of his own present circumstances.

1. He had lately been called to appear before the emperor, upon his appeal to Cæsar; and then *no man stood with him* (v. 16), to plead his cause, to bear testimony for him, or so much as to keep him in countenance, but *all men forsook him.* This was strange, that so good a man as Paul should have nobody to own him, even at Rome, where there were many Christians, whose faith was spoken of throughout the world, Rom. i. 8. But men are but men. The Christians at Rome were forward to go and meet him (Acts xxviii.); but when it came to the pinch, and they would be in danger of suffering with him, then they all forsook him. He prays that God would not lay it to their charge, intimating that it was a great fault, and God might justly be angry with them, but he prays God to forgive them. See what a distinction is put between sins of presumption and sins of infirmity. Alexander the copper-smith, who maliciously withstood Paul, he prays against: *The Lord reward him according to his works;* but respecting these Christians, who through weakness shrunk from Paul in

time of trial, he says, *The Lord lay it not to their charge.* Observe, (1.) Paul had his trials in his friends' forsaking him in a time of danger as well as in the opposition made by enemies : all forsook him. (2.) It was their sin not to appear for the good apostle, especially at his first answer ; but it was a sin of weakness, and therefore the more excusable. Yet, (3.) God might lay it to their charge, but Paul endeavours to prevent it by his earnest prayers : *Let it not be laid to their charge.*

2. *Notwithstanding this God stood by him (v.* 17), gave him extraordinary wisdom and courage, to enable him to speak so much the better himself. When he had nobody to keep him in countenance, God made his face to shine.—*That by me the preaching might be fully known,* that is, " God brought me out from that difficulty that I might preach the gospel, which is my business." Nay, it should seem, that he might preach the gospel at that time ; for Paul knew how to preach at the bar as well as in the pulpit. *And that all the Gentiles might hear ;* the emperor himself and the great men who would never have heard Paul preach if he had not been brought before them. *And I was delivered out of the mouth of the lion,* that is, of Nero (as some think) or some other judge. Some understand it only as a proverbial form of speech, to signify that he was in imminent danger. *And the Lord shall deliver me from every evil work.* See how Paul improved his experiences : "*He that hath delivered doth deliver, and we trust He will yet deliver,* will deliver me *from every evil work,* from any ill done to me by others. *And shall preserve me to his heavenly kingdom.*" And for this he gives glory to God, rejoicing in hope of the glory of God. Observe, (1.) If the Lord stand by us, he will strengthen us, in a time of difficulty and danger, and his presence will more than supply every one's absence. (2.) When the Lord preserves his servants from great and imminent danger, it is for eminent work and service. Paul was preserved that by him the preaching might be fully known, &c. (3.) Former deliverances should encourage future hopes. (4.) There is a heavenly kingdom, to which the Lord will preserve his faithful witnessing or suffering servants. (5.) We ought to give God the glory of all past, present, and future deliverances : *To whom be glory for ever and ever. Amen.*

II. He sends salutations to *Aquila, and Priscilla, and the household of Onesiphorus, v.* 19. He mentions his leaving *Trophimus sick at Miletum (v.* 20), by which it appears that though the apostles healed all manner of diseases miraculously, for the confirmation of their doctrine, yet they did not exert that power upon their own friends, lest it should have looked like a collusion.

III. He hastens Timothy to *come to him before winter (v.* 21), because he longed to see him, and because in the winter the journey or voyage would be more dangerous.

IV. He sends commendations to him from *Eubulus, Pudens, Linus, Claudia,* and all the *brethren.* One of the heathen writers at this time mentions one Pudens and his wife Claudia, and says that Claudia was a Briton, whence some have gathered that it was this Pudens, and that Claudia here was his wife, and that they were eminent Christians at Rome.

V. He concludes with a prayer, that the *Lord Jesus would be with his spirit.* We need no more to make us happy than to have the Lord Jesus Christ with our spirits ; for in him all spiritual blessings are summed up. And it is the best prayer we can put up for our friends, that the Lord Jesus Christ may be with their spirits, to sanctify and save them, and at last to receive them to himself ; as Stephen the proto-martyr prayed,

Lord Jesus, receive my spirit, Acts vii. 59. "Lord Jesus, receive that spirit which thou hast been with while it was united to the body ; do not now leave it in its separate state." *Grace be with you. Amen.* This was our apostle's token in every epistle ; so he wrote. *The grace of our Lord Jesus Christ be with you all. Amen,* 2 Thess. iii. 17, 18. And if grace be with us here to convert and change us, to make us holy, to keep us humble, and to enable us to persevere to the end, glory will crown us hereafter : *for the Lord is a sun, and a shield ; the Lord will give grace and glory, and no good thing will He withhold from those that walk uprightly. O Lord of hosts, blessed is the man that trusteth in Thee,* Ps. xxxiv. 11, 12. *Now unto the King eternal, immortal, invisible, the only wise God our Saviour, be honour and glory for ever and ever. Amen.*

EXPOSITION OF THE EPISTLE OF
ST. PAUL TO TITUS

THIS Epistle of Paul to Titus is much of the same nature with those to Timothy. Both were converts of Paul, and his companions in labours and sufferings; both were in the office of evangelists, whose work was to water the churches planted by the apostles, and to set in order the things that were wanting in them: they were vice-apostles, as it were, *working the work of the Lord, as they did*, and mostly under their direction, though not despotic and arbitrary, but with the concurring exercise of their own prudence and judgment, 1 Cor. xvi. 10, 12. We read much of this Titus, his titles, character, and active usefulness, in many places: he was a Greek, Gal. ii. 3. Paul called him *his son* (Tit. i. 4), *his brother* (2 Cor. ii. 13), *his partner and fellow-helper* (2 Cor. viii. 23), *one that walked in the same spirit and in the same steps with himself.* He went up with the apostles to the church at Jerusalem (Gal. ii. 1), was much conversant at Corinth, for which church he had *an earnest care,* 2 Cor. viii. 16. Paul's second epistle to them, and probably his first also, was sent by his hand, 2 Cor. viii. 16-18, 23; ix. 2-4; xii. 18. He was with the apostle at Rome, and thence went into Dalmatia (2 Tim. iv. 10), after which no more occurs of him in the scriptures. So that by them he appears not to have been a fixed bishop; if such he were, and in those times, the church of Corinth, where he most laboured, had the best title to him. In Crete (now called *Candia,* formerly *Hecatompolis,* from the hundred cities that were in it), a large island at the mouth of the Ægean Sea, the gospel had got some footing; and here were Paul and Titus in one of their travels, cultivating this plantation; but the apostle of the Gentiles, having on him the care of all the churches, could not himself tarry long at this place. He therefore left Titus some time there, to carry on the work which had been begun, wherein, probably, meeting with more difficulty than ordinary, Paul wrote this epistle to him; and yet perhaps not so much for his own sake as for the people's, that the endeavours of Titus, strengthened with apostolic advice and authority, might be more significant and effectual among them. He was to see all the cities furnished with good pastors, to reject and keep out the unmeet and unworthy, to teach sound doctrine, and instruct all sorts in their duties, to set forth the free grace of God in man's salvation by Christ, and withal to show the necessity of maintaining good works by those who have believed in God and hope for eternal life from him.

CHAPTER I

In this chapter we have, I. The preface or introduction to the epistle, showing from and to whom it was written, with the apostle's salutation and prayer for Titus, wishing all blessings to him, ver. 1-4. II. Entrance into the matter, by signifying the end of Titus's being left at Crete, ver. 5. III. And how the same should be pursued in reference both to good and bad ministers, ver. 6, to the end.

PAUL, a servant of God, and an apostle of Jesus Christ, according to the faith of God's elect, and the acknowledging of the truth which is after godliness; ² In hope of eternal life, which God, that cannot lie, promised before the world began [before times eternal]; ³ But hath in due times manifested his word through preaching [in the message], which is committed unto me according to the commandment of God our Saviour; ⁴ To Titus, *mine* own son after the common faith: Grace, mercy, *and* peace, from God the Father and the Lord Jesus Christ our Saviour.

Here is the preface to the epistle, showing,

I. The writer. *Paul*, a Gentile name taken by the apostle of the Gentiles, Acts xiii. 9, 46, 47. Ministers will accommodate even smaller matters, so that they may be any furthering of acceptance in their work. When the Jews rejected the gospel, and the Gentiles received it, we read no more of this apostle by his Jewish name *Saul*, but by his Roman one, *Paul. A servant of God, and an apostle of Jesus Christ.* Here he is described by his relation and office : *A servant of God,* not in the general sense only, as a man and a Christian, but especially as a minister, *serving God in the gospel of his Son,* Rom. i. 9. This is a high honour; it is the glory of angels that they are *ministering spirits, and sent forth to minister for those who shall be heirs of salvation,* Heb. i. 14. Paul is described more especially as a chief minister, *an apostle of Jesus Christ;* one who had seen the Lord, and was immediately called and commissioned by him, and had his doctrine from him. Observe, The highest officers in the church are but servants. (Much divinity and devotion are comprehended in the inscriptions of the epistles.) The apostles of Jesus Christ, who were employed to spread and propagate his religion, were therein also the servants of God; they did not set up anything inconsistent with the truths and duties of natural religion. Christianity, which they preached, was in order to clear and enforce those natural principles, as well as to advance them, and to superadd what was fit and necessary in man's degenerate and revolted state : therefore the apostles of Jesus Christ were the servants of God, *according to the faith of*

God's elect. Their doctrine agreed with the faith of all the elect from the beginning of the world, and was for propagating and promoting the same. Observe, There are elect of God (1 Pet. i. 2), and in these the Holy Spirit works precious divine faith, proper to those who are chosen to eternal life (2 Thess. ii. 13, 14): *God hath from the beginning chosen you to salvation, through sanctification of the Spirit and belief of the truth, whereunto he called you by our gospel.* Faith is the first principle of sanctification. *And the acknowledging of the truth which is after goodness.* The gospel is truth; the great, sure, and saving truth (Col. i. 5), *the word of the truth of the gospel.* Divine faith rests not on fallible reasonings and probable opinions, but on the infallible word, the truth itself, *which is after godliness,* of a godly nature and tendency, pure, and purifying the heart of the believer. By this mark judge of doctrines and of spirits—whether they be of God or not; what is impure, and prejudicial to true piety and practical religion, cannot be of divine origin. All gospel truth is after godliness, teaching and nourishing reverence and fear of God, and obedience to him; it is truth not only to be known, but acknowledged; it must be held forth in word and practice, Phil. ii. 15, 16. *With the heart man believes to righteousness, and with the mouth confession is made unto salvation,* Rom. x. 10. Such as retain the truth in unrighteousness neither know nor believe as they ought. To bring to this knowledge and faith, and to the acknowledging and professing of the truth which is after godliness, is the great end of the gospel ministry, even of the highest degree and order in it; their teachings should have this chief aim, to beget faith and confirm in it. *In* (or *for*) *hope of eternal life, v. 2.* This is the further intent of the gospel, to beget hope as well as faith; to take off the mind and heart from the world, and to raise them to heaven and the things above. The faith and godliness of Christians lead to eternal life, and give hope and well-grounded expectation of it; for *God, that cannot lie, hath promised it.* It is the honour of God that he cannot lie or deceive: and this is the comfort of believers, whose treasure is laid up in his faithful promises. But how is he said to promise before the world began? *Answer,* By promise some understand his decree: he purposed it in his eternal counsels, which were as it were his promise in *embryo:* or rather, say some, πρὸ χρόνων αἰωνίων is *before ancient times,* or many years ago, referring to the promise darkly delivered, Gen. iii. 15. Here is the stability and antiquity of the promise of eternal life to the saints. God, who cannot lie, hath promised before the world began, that is, many ages since. How excellent then is the gospel, which was the matter of divine promise so early! how much to be esteemed by us, and what thanks due for our privilege beyond those before us! *Blessed are your eyes for they see,* &c. No wonder if the contempt of it be punished severely, since he has not only promised it of old, *but (v. 3) has in due times manifested his word through preaching;* that is, made that his promise, so darkly delivered of old, *in due time* (the proper season before appointed) more plain *by preaching;* that which some called *foolishness of preaching* has been thus honoured. *Faith comes by hearing, and hearing by the word of God,* by the word preached. *Which is committed unto me.* The ministry is a trust; none taketh this honour, but he who is thereunto appointed; and whoso is appointed and called must preach the word. 1 Cor. ix. 16, *Woe is unto me if I preach not the gospel.* Non-preaching ministers are none of the apostle's successors. *According to the commandment of God our Saviour.* Preaching is a work appointed by God as a Saviour. See a proof here of Christ's deity, for by him was the gospel committed to Paul when he was converted (Acts ix. 15, 17, and *ch.* xxii. 10, 14, 15), and again when Christ appeared to him, *v.* 17-21. He therefore is this Saviour ; not but that the whole Trinity concur therein : the Father saves by the Son through the Spirit, and all concur in sending ministers. Let none rest therefore in men's calling, without God's ; he furnishes, inclines, authorises, and gives opportunity for the work.

II. The person written to, who is described, 1. By his name, *Titus,* a Gentile Greek, yet called both to the faith and ministry. Observe, the grace of God is free and powerful. What worthiness or preparation was there in one of heathen stock and education ? 2. By his spiritual relation to the apostle : *My own* (or *my genuine*) *son,* not by natural generation, but by supernatural regeneration. *I have begotten you through the gospel,* said he to the Corinthians, 1 Cor. iv. 15. Ministers are spiritual fathers to those whom they are the means of converting, and will tenderly affect and care for them, and must be answerably regarded by them. "*My own son after the common faith,* that faith which is common to all the regenerate, and which thou hast in truth, and expressest to the life." This might be said to distinguish Titus from hypocrites and false teachers, and to recommend him to the regard of the Cretans, as being among them a lively image of the apostle himself, in faith, and life, and heavenly doctrine. To this Titus, deservedly so dear to the apostle, is,

III. The salutation and prayer, wishing all blessings to him : *Grace, mercy, and peace, from God the Father, and the Lord Jesus Christ, our Saviour.* Here are, 1. The blessings wished : *Grace, mercy, and peace. Grace,* the free favour of God, and acceptance with him. *Mercy,* the fruits of that favour, in pardon of sins, and freedom from all miseries by it, both here and hereafter. And *peace,* the positive effect and fruit of mercy. Peace with God through Christ who is our peace, and with the creatures and ourselves ; outward and inward peace, comprehending all good whatsoever, that makes for our happiness in time and to eternity. Observe, Grace is the fountain of all blessings. Mercy, and peace, and all good, spring out of this. Get into God's favour, and all must be well ; for, 2. These are the persons from whom blessings are wished : *From God the Father,* the fountain of all good. Every blessing, every comfort, comes to us from God as a Father ; he is the Father of all by creation, but of the good by adoption and regeneration. *And the Lord Jesus Christ our Saviour,* as the way and means of procurement and conveyance. All is from the Father by the Son, who is Lord by nature, heir of all things, and our Lord, Redeemer, and head, ordering and ruling his members. All are put under him ; we hold of him, as *in capite,* and owe subjection and obedience to him, who is also Jesus and Christ, the anointed Saviour, and especially our Saviour, who believe in him, delivering us from sin and hell, and bringing us to heaven and happiness.

Thus far is the preface to the epistle ; then follows the entrance into the matter, by signifying the end of Titus's being left in Crete.

⁵ For this cause left I thee in Crete, that thou shouldest set in order the things that are wanting, and ordain elders in every city as I had appointed thee.

Here is the end expressed,

I. More generally : *For this cause left I thee in Crete, that thou shouldst set in order the things that are wanting.* This was the business of evangelists (in which office Titus was), to water where the apostles had planted, (1 Cor. iii. 6), furthering and finishing what they had begun ; so much ἐπιδιορθουν imports, *to order after another.* Titus was to go on in settling what the apostle himself had not time for, in his short stay there. Observe, 1. The apostle's great diligence in the gospel ; when he had set things on foot in one place, he hastened away to another. He was debtor to the Greeks and to the barbarians, and laboured to spread the gospel as far as he could among them all. And, 2. His faithfulness and prudence. He neglected not the places that he went from ; but left some to cultivate the young plantation, and carry on what was begun. 3. His humility ; he disdained not to be helped in his work, and that by such as were not of so high a rank in the ministry, nor of so great gifts and furniture, as himself ; so that the gospel might be furthered and the good of souls promoted he willingly used the hands of others in it ; a fit example for exciting zeal and industry, and engaging to faithfulness and care of the flock, and present or absent, living and dying, for ministers, as much as in them lies, to provide for the spiritual edification and comfort of their people. We may here also observe, 4. That Titus, though inferior to an apostle, was yet above the ordinary fixed pastors or bishops, who were to tend particular churches as their peculiar stated charge ; but Titus was in a higher sphere, to ordain such ordinary pastors where wanting, and settle things in their first state and form and then to pass to other places for like service as there might be need. Titus was not only a minister of the catholic church (as all others also are), but a catholic minister. Others had power habitual, and in *actu primo,* to minister anywhere, upon call and opportunity ; but evangelists, such as Titus was, had power in *actu secundo et exercito,* and could exercise their ministry wherever they came, and claim maintenance of the churches. They were everywhere actually in their diocese or province, and had a right to direct, and preside among the ordinary pastors and ministers. Where an apostle could act as an apostle an evangelist could act as an evangelist ; for *they worked the work of the Lord as they did* (1 Cor. xvi. 10), in a like unfixed and itinerant manner. Here at Crete Titus was but occasionally, and for a short time ; Paul willed him to despatch the business he was left for, and come to him at Nicopolis, where he purposed to winter ; after this he was sent to Corinth, was with the apostle at Rome, and was sent thence into Dalmatia, which is the last we read of him in scripture, so that from scripture no fixed episcopacy in him does appear ; he left Crete, and we find not that he returned thither any more. But what power had either Paul or Titus here ? Was not what they did an encroachment on the rights of civil rulers ? In no sort ; they came not to meddle with the civil rights of any. Luke xii. 14, *Who made me a judge or a divider over you ?* Their work was spiritual, to be carried on by conviction and persuasion, no way interfering with, or prejudicing, or weakening, the power of magistrates, but rather securing and strengthening it ; the *things wanting* were not such as civil magistrates are the fountains or authors of, but divine and spiritual ordinances, and appointments for spiritual ends derived from Christ the king and head of the church : for settling these was Titus left. And observe, No easy thing is it to raise churches, and bring them to perfection. Paul had himself been here labouring, and yet were there things wanting ; materials are out of square, need much hewing and fitting, to bring them into right form, and, when they are set therein, to hold and keep them so. The best are apt to decay and to go out of order. Ministers are to help against this, to get what is amiss rectified, and what is wanting supplied. This in general was Titus's work in Crete: and,

II. In special: *To ordain elders in every city*, that is, ministers, who were mostly out of the elder and most understanding and experienced Christians; or, if younger in years, yet such as were grave and solid in their deportment and manners. These were to be set where there was any fit number of Christians, as in larger towns and cities was usually the case; though villages, too, might have them where there were Christians enough for it. These presbyters or elders were to have the ordinary and stated care and charge of the churches; to feed and govern them, and perform all pastoral work and duty in and towards them. The word is used sometimes more largely for any who bear ecclesiastical function in the church, and so the apostles were *presbyters* or *elders* (1 Pet. v. 1); but here it is meant of ordinary fixed pastors, who *laboured in the word and doctrine*, and were *over the churches in the Lord;* such as are described here throughout the chapter. This word *presbyter* some use in the same sense as *sacerdos*, and translate it *priest*, a term not given to gospel ministers, unless in a figurative or allusive way, as all God's people are said to be made *kings and priests unto God* (ἱερεῖς, not πρεσβυτέρους), to offer up spiritual sacrifices of prayers, praises, and alms. But properly we have no priests under the gospel, except Christ alone, *the high priest of our profession* (Heb. iii. 1), who offered up himself a sacrifice to God for us, and ever lives, in virtue thereof, to make intercession in our behalf. Presbyters here therefore are not proper priests, to offer sacrifices, either typical or real; but only gospel ministers, to dispense Christ's ordinances, and to *feed the church of God over which the Holy Ghost has made them overseers.* Observe, 1. A church without a fixed and standing ministry in it is imperfect and wanting. 2. Where a fit number of believers is, presbyters or elders must be set; their continuance in churches is as necessary as their first appointment, *for perfecting the saints, and edifying the body of Christ, till all come to a perfect man in Christ,* till the whole number of God's chosen be called and united to Christ in one body, and brought to their full stature and strength, and that measure of grace that is proper and designed for them. Eph. iv. 12, 13. This is work that must and will be doing to the world's end, to which therefore the necessary and appointed means for it must last. What praise is due to God for such an institution! What thankfulness from those that enjoy the benefits of it! What pity and prayer for such as want it! *Pray the Lord of the harvest that he will send forth labourers into his harvest.* Faith comes by hearing, and is preserved, maintained, and made fruitful, through it also. Ignorance and corruption, decays of good and increase of all evil, come by want of a teaching and quickening ministry. On such accounts therefore was *Titus left in Crete, to set in order the things that were wanting, and to ordain elders in every city;* but this he was to do, not *ad libitum,* or according to his own will or fancy, but according to apostolic direction.

III. The rule of his proceeding: *As I had appointed thee,* probably when he was going from him, and in the presence and hearing of others, to which he may now refer, not so much for Titus's own sake as for the people's, that they might the more readily yield obedience to Titus, knowing and observing that in what he did he was warranted and supported by apostolic injunction and authority. As under the law all things were to be made according to the pattern shown to Moses in the mount; so under the gospel all must be ordered and managed according to the direction of

Christ, and of his chief ministers, who were infallibly guided by him.
Human traditions and inventions may not be brought into the church of
God. Prudent disposals for carrying on the ends of Christ's appointments,
according to the general rules of the word, there may, yea, must be ; but
none may alter anything in the substance of the faith or worship, or
order and discipline, of the churches. If an evangelist might not do
anything but by appointment, much less may others. The church is the
house of God, and to him it belongs to appoint the officers and orders
of it, as he pleases : the *as* here refers to the qualifications and character
of the elders that he was to ordain : " *Ordain elders in every city, as I
appointed thee,* such as I then described and shall now again more particularly point out to thee," which he does from the sixth verse to the
ninth inclusive.

6 If any be blameless, the husband of one wife, having faithful
children [**children that believe**], not accused of riot, or unruly.
7 For a bishop must be blameless, as the steward of God ; not
selfwilled, not soon angry, not given to wine [**no brawler**], no
striker, not given to filthy lucre ; 8 But a lover of hospitality,
a lover of good men, sober, just, holy, temperate ; 9 Holding
fast the faithful word as he hath been taught, that he may be
able by sound doctrine both to exhort and to convince the gainsayers. 10 For there are many unruly and vain talkers and
deceivers, especially they of the circumcision : 11 Whose mouths
must be stopped, who subvert whole houses, teaching things
which they ought not, for filthy lucre's sake. 12 One of themselves, *even* a prophet of their own, said, The Cretians *are*
always liars, evil beasts, slow bellies [**idle gluttons**]. 13 This
witness is true. Wherefore rebuke them sharply, that they
may be sound in the faith ; 14 Not giving heed to Jewish fables,
and commandments of men, that turn from the truth. 15 Unto
the pure all things *are* pure : but unto them that are defiled
and unbelieving *is* nothing pure ; but even their mind and conscience is defiled. 16 They profess that they know God ; but
in works they deny *him*, being abominable, and disobedient,
and unto every good work reprobate.

The apostle here gives Titus directions about ordination, showing whom
he should ordain, and whom not.

I. Of those whom he should ordain. He points out their qualifications
and virtues ; such as respect their life and manners, and such as relate to
their doctrine : the former in the sixth, seventh, and eighth verses, and
the latter in the ninth.

1. Their qualifications respecting their life and manners are,

(1.) More general : *If any be blameless ;* not absolutely without fault, so
none are, for *there is none that liveth and sinneth not ;* nor altogether un-
blamed, this is rare and difficult. Christ himself and his apostles were
blamed, though not worthy of it. In Christ there was certainly nothing

blamable ; and his apostles were not such as their enemies charged them to be. But the meaning is, He must be one who lies not under an ill character; but rather must have a good report, even *from those that are without ;* not grossly or scandalously guilty, so as would bring reproach upon the holy function ; he must not be such a one.

(2.) More particularly.

[1.] There is his relative character. In his own person, he must be of conjugal chastity : *The husband of one wife.* The church of Rome says the husband of *no* wife, but from the beginning it was not so ; marriage is an ordinance from which no profession nor calling is a bar. 1 Cor. ix. 5, *Have I not power,* says Paul, *to lead about a sister, a wife, as well as other apostles ? Forbidding to marry* is one of the erroneous doctrines of the antichristian church, 1 Tim. iv. 3. Not that ministers *must* be married ; this is not meant ; but *the husband of one wife* may be either not having divorced his wife and married another (as was too common among those of the circumcision, even for slight causes), or *the husband of one wife,* that is, at one and the same time, no bigamist ; not that he might not be married to more than one wife successively, but, being married, he must have but one wife at once, not two or more, according to the too common sinful practice of those times, by a perverse imitation of the patriarchs, from which evil custom our Lord taught a reformation. Polygamy is scandalous in any, as also having a harlot or concubine with his lawful wife ; such sin, or any wanton libidinous demeanour, must be very remote from such as would enter into so sacred a function. And, as to his children, *having faithful children,* obedient and good, brought up in the true Christian faith, and living according to it, at least as far as the endeavours of the parents can avail. It is for the honour of ministers that their children be faithful and pious, and such as become their religion. *Not accused of riot, nor unruly,* not justly so accused, as having given ground and occasion for it, for otherwise the most innocent may be falsely so charged ; they must look to it therefore that there be no colour for such censure. Children so faithful, and obedient, and temperate, will be a good sign of faithfulness and diligence in the parent who has so educated and instructed them ; and, from his faithfulness in the less, there may be encouragement to commit to him the greater, the rule and government of the church of God. The ground of this qualification is shown from the nature of his office (*v.* 7) : *For a bishop must be blameless, as the steward of God.* Those before termed presbyters, or elders, are in this verse styled bishops ; and such they were, having no ordinary fixed and standing officers above them. Titus's business here, it is plain, was but occasional, and his stay short, as was before noted. Having ordained elders, and settled things in their due form, he went and left all (for aught that appears in scripture) in the hands of those elders whom the apostle here calls bishops and stewards of God. We read not in the sacred writings of any successor he had in Crete ; but to those elders or bishops was committed the full charge of feeding, ruling, and watching over their flock ; they wanted not any powers necessary for carrying on religion and the ministry of it among them, and committing it down to succeeding ages. Now, being such bishops and overseers of the flock, who were to be examples to them, and God's stewards to take care of the affairs of his house. to provide for and dispense to them things needful, there is great reason that their character should be clear and good, that they should be blameless. How else could it be but that religion must suffer, their work be hindered, and souls prejudiced and endangered, whom they were set to save ? These are the relative qualifications with the ground of them.

[2.] The more absolute ones are expressed, *First*, Negatively, showing what an elder or bishop must not be : *Not self-willed.* The prohibition is of large extent, excluding self-opinion, or overweening conceit of parts and abilities, and abounding in one's own sense—self-love, and self-seeking, making self the centre of all,—also self-confidence and trust, and self-pleasing, little regarding or setting by others,—being proud, stubborn, froward, inflexible, set on one's own will and way, or churlish as Nabal : such is the sense expositors have affixed to the term. A great honour it is to a minister not to be thus affected, to be ready to ask and to take advice, to be ready to defer as much as reasonably may be to the mind and will of others, becoming all things to all men, that they may gain some. *Not soon angry, μὴ ὀργίλον, not one of a hasty angry temper,* soon and easily provoked and inflamed. How unfit are those to govern a church who cannot govern themselves, or their own turbulent and unruly passions ! The minister must be meek and gentle, and patient towards all men. *Not given to wine ;* there is no greater reproach on a minister than to be a wine-bibber, one who loves it, and gives himself undue liberty this way, who *continues at the wine or strong drink till it inflames him.* Seasonable and moderate use of this, as of the other good creatures of God, is not unlawful. *Use a little wine for thy stomach's sake, and thine often infirmities,* said Paul to Timothy, 1 Tim. v. 23. But excess therein is shameful in all, especially in a minister. *Wine takes away the heart,* turns the man into a brute : here most proper is that exhortation of the apostle (Eph. v. 18), *Be not drunk with wine, wherein is excess ; but be filled with the Spirit.* Here is no exceeding, but in the former too easily there may : take heed therefore of going too near the brink. *No striker,* in any quarrelsome or contentious manner, not injuriously nor out of revenge, with cruelty or unnecessary roughness. *Not given to filthy lucre ;* not greedy of it (as 1 Tim. iii. 3), whereby is not meant refusing a just return for their labours, in order to their necessary support and comfort ; but not making gain their first or chief end, not entering into the ministry nor managing it with base worldly views. Nothing is more unbecoming a minister, who is to direct his own and others' eyes to another world, than to be too intent upon this. It is called *filthy lucre,* from its defiling the soul that inordinately affects or greedily looks after it, as if it were any otherwise desirable than for the good and lawful uses of it. Thus of the negative part of the bishop's character. But, *Secondly,* Positively : he must be (*v.* 8) *a lover of hospitality,* as an evidence that he is not given to filthy lucre, but is willing to use what he has to the best purposes, not laying up for himself, so as to hinder charitable laying out for the good of others ; *receiving and entertaining strangers* (as the word imports), a great and necessary office of love, especially in those times of affliction and distress, when Christians were made to fly and wander for safety from persecution and enemies, or in travelling to and fro where there were not such public houses for reception as in our days, nor, it may be, had many poor saints sufficiency of their own for such uses—then to receive and entertain them was good and pleasing to God. And such a spirit and practice, according to ability and occasion, are very becoming such as should be examples of good works. *A lover of good men,* or *of good things ;* ministers should be exemplary in both ; this will evince their open piety, and likeness to God and their Master Jesus Christ : *Do good to all, but especially to those of the household of faith,* those who are the excellent of the earth, in whom should be all our delight. *Sober*, or *prudent*, as the word signifies ; a needful grace in a minister both for his ministerial and personal carriage and management. He should be a wise steward, and one who is not rash, or foolish, or heady ; but who can govern well his passions and affections. *Just* in things belonging to civil life, and moral righteousness, and equity in dealings, giving to all their due. *Holy* in what concerns religion ; one who reverences and worships God, and is of a spiritual and heavenly conversation. *Temperate ;* it comes from a word that signifies *strength*, and denotes one who has power over his appetite and affections, or, in things lawful, can, for good ends, restrain and hold them in. Nothing is more becoming a minister than such things as these, *sobriety, temperance, justice,* and *holiness*—sober in respect of himself, just and righteous towards all men, and holy towards God. And thus of the qualifications respecting the minister's life and manners, relative and absolute, negative and positive, what he must not, and what he must, be and do.

2. As to doctrine,

(1.) Here is his duty : *Holding fast the faithful word, as he has been taught,* keeping close to the doctrine of Christ, *the word of his grace,* adhering thereto according to the instructions he has received—holding it fast in his own belief and profession, and in teaching others. Observe, [1.] The word of God, revealed in the scripture, is a true and infallible word ; the word of him that *is the amen, the true and faithful witness,* and whose Spirit guided the penmen of it. *Holy men of God spoke as they were moved by the Holy Ghost.* [2.] Ministers must hold fast, and hold forth, the faithful word in their teaching and life. *I have kept the faith,* was Paul's comfort (2 Tim. iv. 7), and *not shunned to declare the whole counsel of God ;* there was his faithfulness, Acts xx. 27.

(2.) Here is the end : *That he may be able, by sound doctrine, both to exhort, and to convince the gainsayers,* to persuade and draw others to the true faith, and to convince the contrary-minded. How should he do this if he himself were uncertain or unsteady, not holding fast that *faithful word and sound doctrine* which should be the matter of this teaching, and the means and ground of convincing those that oppose the truth ? We see here summarily the great work of the ministry—to exhort those who are willing to know and do their duty, and to convince those that contradict, both which are to be done by *sound doctrine,* that is, in a rational instructive way, by scripture-arguments and testimonies, which are the infallible words of truth, what all may and should rest and be satisfied in and determined by. And thus of the qualifications of the elders whom Titus was to ordain.

II. The apostle's directory shows whom he snould reject or avoid—men of another character, the mention of whom is brought in as a reason of the care he had recommended about the qualifications of ministers, why they should be such, and only such, as he had described. The reasons he takes both from bad teachers and hearers among them, *v.* 10, to the end.

1. From bad teachers. (1.) Those false teachers are described. They were *unruly,* headstrong and ambitious of power, refractory and untractable (as some render it), and such as would not bear nor submit themselves to the discipline and necessary order in the church, impatient of good government and of sound doctrine. *And vain talkers and deceivers,* conceiting themselves to be wise, but really foolish, and thence great talkers, falling into errors and mistakes, and fond of them, and studious and industrious

to draw others into the same. Many such there were, *especially those of the circumcision*, converts as they pretended, at least, from the Jews, who yet were for mingling Judaism and Christianity together, and so making a corrupt medley. These were the false teachers. (2.) Here is the apostle's direction how to deal with them (*v.* 11): *Their mouths must be stopped ;* not by outward force (Titus had no such power, nor was this the gospel method), but by confutation and conviction,‸ showing them their error, *not giving place to them even for an hour.* In case of obstinacy indeed, breaking the peace of the church, and corrupting other churches, censures are to have place, the last means for recovering the faulty and preventing the hurt of many. Observe, Faithful ministers must oppose seducers in good time, *that, their folly being made manifest, they may proceed no further.* (3.) The reasons are given for this. [1.] From the pernicious effects of their errors : *They subvert whole houses, teaching things which they ought not* (namely, the necessity of circumcision, and of keeping the law of Moses, &c.), so subverting the gospel and the souls of men ; not some few only, but whole families. It was unjustly charged on the apostles *that they turned the world upside down ;* but justly on these false teachers that they drew many from the true faith to their ruin : the mouths of such should be stopped, especially considering, [2.] Their base end in what they do : *For filthy lucre's sake,* serving a worldly interest under pretence of religion. *Love of money is the root of all evil.* Most fit it is that such should be resisted, confuted, and put to shame, by sound doctrine, and reasons from the scriptures. Thus of the grounds respecting the bad teachers.

III. In reference to their people or hearers, who are described from ancient testimony given of them.

1. Here is the witness (*v.* 12): *One of themselves, even a prophet of their own*, that is, one of the Cretans, not of the Jews, Epimenides a Greek poet, likely to know and unlikely to slander them. *A prophet of their own ;* so their poets were accounted, writers of divine oracles ; these often witnessed against the vices of the people : Aratus, Epimenides, and others among the Greeks ; Horace, Juvenal, and Persius, among the Latins : much smartness did they use against divers vices.

2. Here is the matter of his testimony : Κρῆτες ἀεὶ ψεῦσται, κακὰ θηρία, γαστέρες ἀργαί—*The Cretans are always liars, evil beasts, slow bellies.* Even to a proverb, they were infamous for falsehood and lying ; κρετίζειν, to play the *Cretan*, or to lie, is the same ; and they were compared to evil beasts for their sly hurtfulness and savage nature, and called slow bellies for their laziness and sensuality, more inclined to eat than to work and live by some honest employment. Observe, Such scandalous vices as were the reproach of heathens should be far from Christians : falsehood and lying, invidious craft and cruelty, all beastly and sensual practices, with idleness and sloth, are sins condemned by the light of nature. For these were the Cretans taxed by their own poets.

3. Here is the verification of this by the apostle himself : *v.* 13. This witness is true, The apostle saw too much ground for that character. The temper of some nations is more inclined to some vices than others. The Cretans were too generally such as here described, slothful and ill-natured, false and perfidious, as the apostle himself vouches. And thence,

4. He instructs Titus how to deal with them : *Wherefore rebuke them sharply.* When Paul wrote to Timothy he bade him instruct with meekness ; but now, when he writes to Titus, he bids him rebuke them sharply. The reason of the difference may be taken from the different temper of

Timothy and Titus ; the former might have more keenness in his disposition, and be apt to be warm in reproving, whom therefore he bids to rebuke with meekness ; and the latter might be one of more mildness, therefore he quickens him, and bids him rebuke sharply. Or rather it was from the difference of the case and people : Timothy had a more polite people to deal with, and therefore he must rebuke them with meekness ; and Titus had to do with those who were more rough and uncultivated, and therefore he must rebuke them sharply ; their corruptions were many and gross, and committed without shame or modesty, and therefore should be dealt with accordingly. There must in reproving be a distinguishing between sins and sins ; some are more gross and heinous in their nature, or in the manner of their commission, with openness and boldness, to the greater dishonour of God and danger and hurt to men : and between sinners and sinners ; some are of a more tender and tractable temper, apter to be wrought on by gentleness, and to be sunk and discouraged, by too much roughness and severity ; others are more hardy and stubborn, and need more cutting language to beget in them remorse and shame. Wisdom therefore is requisite to temper and manage reproofs aright, as may be most likely to do good. Jude 22, 23, *Of some have compassion making a difference ; and others save with fear, pulling them out of the fire.* The Cretans' sins and corruptions were many, great and habitual ; therefore they must be rebuked sharply. But that such direction might not be misconstrued.

5. Here is the end of it noted : *That they may be sound in the faith* (*v.* 14), *not giving heed to Jewish fables, and commandments of men, that turn from the truth ;* that is, that they may be and show themselves truly and effectually changed from such evil tempers and manners as those Cretans in their natural state lived in, and may not adhere to nor regard (as some who were converted might be too ready to do) the Jewish traditions and the superstitions of the Pharisees, which would be apt to make them disrelish the gospel, and the sound and wholesome truths of it. Observe, (1.) The sharpest reproofs must aim at the good of the reproved ; they must not be of malice, not hatred, nor ill-will, but of love ; not to gratify pride, passion, nor any evil affection in the reprover, but to reclaim and reform the erroneous and the guilty. (2.) Soundness in the faith is most desirable and necessary. This is the soul's health and vigour, pleasing to God, comfortable to the Christian, and what makes ready to be cheerful and constant in duty. (3.) A special means to soundness in the faith is to turn away the ear from fables and the fancies of men (1 Tim. i. 4) : *Neither give heed to fables and endless genealogies, that minister questions rather than godly edifying, which is in faith.* So *ch.* iv. 7, *Refuse profane and old wives' fables, and exercise thyself rather to godliness.* Fancies and devices of men in the worship of God are contrary to truth and piety. Jewish ceremonies and rites, that were at first divine appointments, the substance having come and their season and use being over, are now but unwarranted commands of men, which not only stand not with, but turn from, the truth, the pure gospel truth and spiritual worship, set up by Christ instead of that bodily service under the law. (4.) A fearful judgment it is to be turned away from the truth, to leave Christ for Moses, the spiritual worship of the gospel for the carnal ordinances of the law, or the true divine institutions and precepts for human inventions and appointments. *Who hath bewitched you* (said Paul to the Galatians, *ch.* iii. 1, 3) *that you should not obey the truth ? Having begun in the Spirit, are you made perfect*

by the flesh? Thus having shown the end of sharply reproving the corrupt and vicious Cretans, that they might be sound in the faith, and not heed Jewish fables and commands of men.

6. He gives the reasons of this, from the liberty we have by the gospel from legal observances, and the evil and mischief of a Jewish spirit under the Christian dispensation in the last two verses. To good Christians, that are sound in the faith and thereby purified, *all things are pure.* Meats and drinks, and such things as were forbidden under the law (the observances of which some still maintain), in these there is now no such distinction, *all are pure* (lawful and free in their use,) *but to those that are defiled and unbelieving nothing is pure;* things lawful and good they abuse and turn to sin; they suck poison out of that from which others draw sweetness; their mind and conscience, those leading faculties, being defiled, a taint is communicated to all they do. *The sacrifice of the wicked is an abomination to the Lord,* Prov. xv. 8. And *ch.* xxi. 4, *The ploughing of the wicked is sin,* not in itself, but as done by him; the carnality of the mind and heart mars all the labour of the hand.

Objection. But are not these judaizers (as you call them) men who profess religion, and speak well of God, and Christ, and righteousness of life, and should they be so severely taxed? *Answer,* They *profess that they know God; but in works they deny him, being abominable, and disobedient, and to every good work reprobate, v.* 16. There are many who in word and tongue profess to know God, and yet in their lives and conversations deny and reject him; their practice is a contradiction to their profession. *They come unto thee as the people cometh, and they sit before thee as my people, and they hear thy words, but they will not do them : with their mouth they show much love, but their heart goeth after their covetousness,* Ezek. xxxiii. 31. *Being abominable, and disobedient, and to every good work reprobate.* The apostle, instructing Titus to rebuke sharply, does himself rebuke sharply ; he gives them very hard words, yet doubtless no harder than their case warranted and their need required. *Being abominable—*βδελυκτοὶ, deserving that God and good men should turn away their eyes from them as nauseous and offensive. *And disobedient—*ἀπειθεῖς, *unpersuadable* and *unbelieving.* They might do divers things ; but it was not the obedience of faith, nor what was commanded, or short of the command. *To every good work reprobate,* without skill or judgment to do anything aright. See the miserable condition of hypocrites, such as have a form of godliness, but without the power ; yet let us not be so ready to fix this charge on others as careful that it agree not to ourselves, that there be not in us *an evil heart of unbelief, in departing from the living God ;* but that we be *sincere and without offence till the day of Christ, being filled with the fruits of righteousness, which are by Jesus Christ unto the glory and praise of God,* Phil. i. 10, 11.

CHAPTER II

The apostle here directs Titus about the faithful discharge of his own office generally
(ver. 1), and particularly as to several sorts of persons (ver. 2-10), and gives the grounds
of these and of other following directions (ver. 11-14), with a summary direction in the
close, ver. 15.

BUT speak thou the things which become sound doctrine:
² That the aged men be sober, grave, temperate, sound in
faith, in charity, in patience. ³ The aged women likewise, that
they be in behaviour as becometh holiness [**reverent in demeanour**], not false accusers, not given to much wine, teachers of
good things; ⁴ That they may teach the young women to be
sober, to love their husbands, to love their children, ⁵ *To be* discreet, chaste, keepers [**workers**] at home, good, obedient to
their own husbands, that the word of God be not blasphemed.
⁶ Young men likewise exhort to be sober minded. ⁷ In all things
showing thyself a pattern of good works : in doctrine *showing*
uncorruptness, gravity, sincerity, ⁸ Sound speech, that cannot
be condemned; that he that is of the contrary part may be
ashamed, having no evil thing to say of you. ⁹ *Exhort* servants
to be obedient unto their own masters, *and* to please *them* well
in all *things;* not answering again; ¹⁰ Not purloining, but showing all good fidelity ; that they may adorn the doctrine of God
our Saviour in all things.

Here is the third thing in the matter of the epistle. In the chapter
foregoing, the apostle had directed Titus about matters of government,
and to set in order the things that were wanting in the churches. Now
here he exhorts him,

I. Generally, to a faithful discharge of his own office. His ordaining
others to preach would not excuse himself from preaching, nor might he
take care of ministers and elders only, but he must instruct private Christians also in their duty. The adversative particle (*but*) here points back
to the corrupt teachers, who vented *fables*, things vain and unprofitable :
in opposition to them, says he, " *But speak thou the things that become sound
doctrine,* what is agreeable to the word, which is pure and uncorrupt,
healthful and nourishing to eternal life." Observe, (1.) The true doctrines
of the gospel are *sound doctrines*, formally and effectively ; they are in
themselves good and holy, and make the believers so ; they make them fit
for, and vigorous in, the service of God. (2.) Ministers must be careful
to teach only such truths. If the common talk of Christians must *be uncorrupt, to the use of edifying, such as may minister grace to the hearers*
(Eph. iv. 29), much more must ministers' preaching be such. Thus the
apostle exhorts Titus generally : and then,

II. Specially and particularly, he instructs him to apply this sound
doctrine to several sorts of persons, from *v.* 2-10. Ministers must not stay
in generals, but must divide to every one his portion, what belongs to his

age, or place, or condition of life; they must be particular as well as practical in their preaching; they must teach men their duty, and must teach all and each his duty. Here is an excellent Christian directory, accommodated to the old and to the young; to men and women; to the preacher himself and to servants.

1. *To the aged men.* By aged men some understand elders by office, including deacons, &c. But it is rather to be taken of the aged in point of years. Old disciples of Christ must conduct themselves in everything agreeably to the Christian doctrine. *That the aged men be sober,* not thinking that the decays of nature, which they feel in old age, will justify them in any inordinacy or intemperance, whereby they conceit to repair them; they must keep measure in things, both for health and for fitness, for counsel and example to the younger. *Grave :* levity is unbecoming in any, but especially in the aged; they should be composed and stayed, grave in habit, speech, and behaviour; gaudiness in dress, levity and vanity in the behaviour, how unbeseeming in their years! *Temperate,* moderate and prudent, one who governs well his passions and affections, so as not to be hurried away by them to anything that is evil or indecent. *Sound in the faith,* sincere and stedfast, constantly adhering to the truth of the gospel, not fond of novelties, nor ready to run into corrupt opinions or parties, nor to be taken with Jewish fables or traditions, or the dotages of their rabbin. Those who are full of years should be full of grace and goodness, the inner man renewing more and more as the outer decays. *In charity,* or love; this is fitly joined with *faith,* which works by, and must be seen in, love, love to God and men, and soundness therein. It must be sincere love, without dissimulation : love of God for himself, and of men for God's sake. The duties of the second table must be done in virtue of those of the first; love to men as men, and to the saints as the excellent of the earth, in whom must be special delight; and love at all times, in adversity as well as prosperity. Thus must there be soundness in charity or love. And *in patience.* Aged persons are apt to be peevish, fretful, and passionate; and therefore need to be on their guard against such infirmities and temptations. Faith, love, and patience, are three main Christian graces, and soundness in these is much of gospel perfection. There is *enduring patience* and *waiting patience,* both of which must be looked after; to *bear evils* becomingly, and contentedly to *want the good* till we are fit for it and it for us, being *followers of those who through faith and patience inherit the promises.* Thus as to the aged men.

2. *To the aged women.* These also must be instructed and warned. Some by these aged women understand the deaconesses, who were mostly employed in looking after the poor and attending the sick; but it is rather to be taken (as we render it) of all aged women professing religion. They must *be in behaviour as becometh holiness :* both men and women must accommodate their behaviour to their profession. Those virtues before mentioned (*sobriety, gravity, temperance, soundness in the faith, charity, and patience*), recommended to aged men, are not proper to them only but applicable to both sexes, and to be looked to by aged women as well as men. Women are to hear and learn their duty from the word, as well as the men : there is not one way of salvation for one sex or sort, and another for another; but both must learn and practise the same things both as aged and as Christians; the virtues and duties are common. *That the aged women likewise* (as well as the men) *be in behaviour as becometh holiness ;* or as beseems and is proper for holy persons, such as they profess to be and

should be, keeping a pious decency and decorum in clothing and gesture, in looks and speech, and all their deportment, and this from an inward principle and habit of holiness, influencing and ordering the outward conduct at all times. Observe, Though express scripture do not occur, or be not brought, for every word, or look, or fashion in particular, yet general rules there are according to which all must be ordered; as 1 Cor. x. 31, *Whatever you do, do all to the glory of God.* And Phil. iv. 8, *Whatsoever things are true, whatsoever things are honest, whatsoever things are just, whatsoever things are pure, whatsoever things are lovely, whatsoever things are of good report, if there be any virtue, and if there be any praise, think on these things.* And here, whatsoever things are beseeming or unbeseeming holiness form a measure and rule of conduct to be looked to. *Not false accusers—*μὴ διαβόλους, no calumniators or sowers of discord, slandering, and backbiting their neighbours, a great and too common fault; not only loving to speak, but to speak ill, of people, and to separate very friends. A slanderer is one *whose tongue is set on fire of hell*; so much, and so directly, do these do the devil's work, that for it the devil's name is given to such. This is a sin contrary to the great duties of love, justice, and equity between one another; it springs often from malice and hatred, or envy, and such like evil causes, to be shunned as well as the effect. *Not given to much wine;* the word denotes such addictedness thereto as to be under the power and mastery of it. This is unseemly and evil in any, but especially in this sex and age, and was too much to be found among the Greeks of that time and place. How immodest and shameful, corrupting and destroying purity both of body and mind! Of what evil example and tendency, unfitting for the next thing, which is a positive duty of aged matrons, namely, to be *teachers of good things!* Not public preachers, that is forbidden (1 Cor. xiv. 34, *I permit not a woman to speak in the church*), but otherwise teach they may and should, that is, by example and good life. Hence observe, Those whose actions and behaviour become holiness are thereby teachers of good things; and, besides this, they may and should also teach by doctrinal instruction at home, and in a private way. *The words of king Lemuel, the prophecy his mother taught him.* Such a woman is praised, *She openeth her mouth with wisdom, and in her tongue is the law of kindness,* Prov. xxxi. 1, 26. *Teachers of good things* are opposed to teachers of things corrupt, or to what is trifling and vain, of no good use or tendency, old wives' fables or superstitious sayings and observances; in opposition to these, their business is, and they may be called on to it, to be teachers of good things.

3. There are lessons for young women also, whom the aged women must teach, instructing and advising them in the duties of religion according to their years. For teaching such things aged women have often better access than the men, even than ministers have, which therefore they must improve in instructing the young women, especially the young wives; for he speaks of their duty to their husbands and children. These young women the more aged must teach, (1.) To bear a good personal character: *To be sober and discreet,* contrary to the vanity and rashness which younger years are subject to: discreet in their judgments and sober in their affections and behaviour. *Discreet* and *chaste* stand well together; many expose themselves to fatal temptations by that which at first might be but indiscretion. Prov. ii. 11, *Discretion shall preserve thee, understanding shall keep thee from the evil way. Chaste,* and *keepers at home,* are well joined too. Dinah, when she went to see the daughters of the land, lost her chastity. Those whose home is their prison, it is to be feared, feel

that their chastity is their fetters. Not but there are occasions, and will be, of going abroad : but a gadding temper for merriment and company sake, to the neglect of domestic affairs, or from uneasiness at being in her place, is the opposite evil intended, which is commonly accompanied with, or draws after it, other evils. 1 Tim. v. 13, 14, *They learn to be idle, wandering from house to house ; and not only idle, but tatlers also and busybodies, speaking things which they ought not.* Their business is *to guide the house,* and they should give no occasion to the enemy to speak reproachfully. *Good,* generally, in opposition to all vice ; and specially, in her place, kind, helpful, and charitable ; as Dorcas, *full of good works and alms-deeds.* It may also have, as some think, a more particular sense ; one of a meek and yet cheerful spirit and temper, not sullen nor bitter ; not taunting nor fretting and galling any ; not of a troublesome or jarring disposition, uneasy in herself and to those about her ; but of a good nature and pleasing conversation, and likewise helpful by her advice and pains : thus *building her house and doing her husband good, and not evil, all her days.* Thus in her personal character *sober, discreet, chaste, keepers at home,* and *good :* and, (2.) In their relative capacities : *To love their husbands, and to be obedient to them :* and where there is true love this will be no difficult command. God, in nature, and by his will, hath made this subordination : *I suffer not a woman to usurp authority over the man* (1 Tim. ii. 12) ; and the reason is added : *For Adam was first formed, then Eve. Adam was not deceived, but the woman, being deceived, was in the transgression, v.* 13, 14. She fell first, and was the means of seducing the husband. She was given to be a helper, but proved a most grievous hinderer, even the instrument of his fall and ruin, on which the bond of subjection was confirmed, and tied faster on her (Gen. iii. 16): *Thy desire shall be to thy husband, and he shall rule over thee,* with less easiness, it may be, than before, It is therefore doubly enjoined : *first in innocency,* when was settled a subordination of nature, Adam being first formed and then Eve, and the woman being taken out of the man ; *and then upon the fall,* the woman being first in the transgression, and seducing the man ; here now began to be a subjection not so easy and comfortable, being a part of the penalty in her case ; yet through Christ is this nevertheless a sanctified state, Eph. v. 22, 23, *Wives submit yourselves unto your own husbands, as unto the Lord,* as owning Christ's authority in them, whose image they bear ; *for the husband is the head of the wife, even as Christ is the head of the church : and he is the saviour of the body.* God would have a resemblance of Christ's authority over the church held forth in the husband's over the wife. Christ is the head of the church, to protect and save it, to supply it with all good, and secure or deliver it from evil ; and so is the husband over the wife, to keep her from injuries, and to provide comfortably for her, according to his ability. Therefore, as the church is subject unto Christ, so let the *wives be unto their own husbands, as is fit in the Lord* (Col. iii. 18), as comports with the law of Christ, and is for his and the Father's glory. It is not then an absolute, or unlimited, nor a slavish subjection that is required ; but a loving subordination, to prevent disorder or confusion, and to further all the ends of the relation. Thus, in reference to the husbands, wives must be instructed in their duties of love and subjection to them. *And to love their children,* not with a natural affection only, but a spiritual, a love springing from a holy sanctified heart and regulated by the word ; not a fond foolish love, indulging them in evil, neglecting due reproof and correction where necessary, but a regular Christian love, showing itself in their pious education, forming their life and manners aright, taking care of their souls as well as of their bodies, of their spiritual welfare as well as of their temporal, of the former chiefly and in the first place. The reason is added : *That the word of God may not be blasphemed.* Failures in such relative duties would be greatly to the reproach of Christianity. "What are these the better for this their new religion ?" would the infidels be ready to say. The word of God and the gospel of Christ are pure, excellent, and glorious, in themselves ; and their excellency should be expressed and shown in the lives and conduct of their professors, especially in relative duties ; failures here being disgrace. Rom. ii. 24, *The name of God is blasphemed among the Gentiles through you.* "Judge what a God he is," would they be ready to say, "by these his servants ; and what his word, and doctrine, and religion, are by these his followers." Thus would Christ *be wounded in the house of his friends.* Thus of the duties of the younger women.

4. Here is the duty of young men. They are apt to be eager and hot, thoughtless and precipitant ; therefore they must be earnestly called upon and exhorted to be considerate, not rash ; advisable and submissive, not wilful and head-strong ; humble and mild, not haughty and proud ; for there are more young people ruined by pride than by any other sin. The young should be grave and solid in their deportment and manners, joining the seriousness of age with the liveliness and vigour of youth. This will make even those younger years to pass to good purpose, and yield matter of comfortable reflection when the evil days come ; it will be preventive of much sin and sorrow, and lay the foundation for doing and enjoying much good. Such shall not *mourn at the last*, but have peace and comfort in death, and after it a glorious crown of life.

5. With these instructions to Titus, respecting what he should teach others—the aged men and women, and the younger of both sexes (Titus himself probably at this time being a young man also), the apostle inserts some directions to himself. He could not expect so successfully to teach others, if he did not conduct himself well both in his conversation and preaching. (1.) Here is direction for his conversation : *In all things showing thyself a pattern of good works, v.* 7. Without this, he would pull down with one hand what he built with the other. Observe, Preachers of good works must be patterns of them also ; good doctrine and good life must go together. *Thou that teachest another, teachest thou not thyself ?* A defect here is a great blemish and a great hindrance. *In all things ;* some read, *above all things,* or *above all men.* Instructing others in the particulars of their duty is necessary, and, above all things, example, especially that of the teacher himself, is needful ; hereby both light and influence are more likely to go together. "Let them see a lively image of those virtues and graces in thy life which must be in theirs. Example may both teach and impress the things taught ; when they see purity and gravity, sobriety and all good life, in thee, they may be more easily won and brought thereto themselves ; they may become pious and holy, sober and righteous, as thou art." Ministers must be examples to the flock, and the people followers of them, as they are of Christ. And here is direction, (2.) For his teaching and doctrine, as well as for his life. *In doctrine showing uncorruptness, gravity, sincerity, sound speech, that cannot be condemned, v.* 7, 8. They must make it appear that the design of their preaching is purely to advance the honour of God, the interest of Christ and his kingdom, and the welfare and happiness of souls ; that this office was not entered into nor used with

secular views, not from ambition nor covetousness, but a pure aim at the spiritual ends of its institution. In their preaching, therefore, the display of wit or parts, or of human learning or oratory, is not to be affected ; but sound speech must be used, which cannot be *condemned;* scripture-language, as far as well may be, in expressing scripture-truths. This is sound speech, that cannot be condemned. We have more than once these duties of a minister set together, I Tim. iv. 16, *Take heed to thyself, and to the doctrine :* and, *v.* 12 of the same chapter, *" Let no man despise thy youth, but be thou an example of believers in word*—in thy speech, as a Christian, being grave, serious, and to the use of edifying ; and in thy preaching, that it be the pure word of God, or what is agreeable to it and founded on it. Thus be an example *in word :* and *in conversation,* the life corresponding with the doctrine. In doing this *thou shalt both save thyself and those that hear thee."* In 2 Tim. iii. 10, *Thou hast fully known my doctrine and manner of life* (says the same apostle), how agreeable these have been. And so must it be with others ; their teaching must be agreeable to the word, and their life with their teaching. This is the true and good minister. I Thess. ii. 9, 10, *Labouring night and day, we preached to you the gospel of God ; and you are witnesses, and God also, how holily, and justly, and unblamably, we behaved ourselves among you.* This must be looked to, as the next words show, which are, (3.) The reason both for the strictness of the minister's life and the gravity and soundness of his preaching : *That he who is of the contrary part may be ashamed, having no evil thing to say of you.* Adversaries would be seeking occasion to reflect, and would do so could they find anything amiss in doctrine or life ; but, if both were right and good, such ministers might set calumny itself at defiance ; they would have no evil thing to say justly, and so must be ashamed of their opposition. Observe, Faithful ministers will have enemies watching for their halting, such as will endeavour to find or pick holes in their teaching or behaviour ; the more need therefore for them to look to themselves, that no just occasion be found against them. Opposition and calumny perhaps may not be escaped ; men of corrupt minds will resist the truth, and often reproach the preachers and professors of it ; but let them see that *with well-doing they put to silence the ignorance of foolish men ; that, when they speak evil of them as evil-doers, those may be ashamed who falsely accuse their good conversation in Christ.* This is the direction to Titus himself, and so of the duties of free persons, male and female, old and young. Then follow,

6. The directions respecting servants. Servants must not think that their mean and low state puts them beneath God's notice or the obligations of his laws—that, because they are servants of men, they are thereby discharged from serving God. No ; servants must know and do their duty to their earthly masters, but with an eye to their heavenly one : and Titus must not only instruct and warn earthly masters of their duties, but servants also of theirs, both in his public preaching and private admonitions. Servants must attend the ordinances of God for their instruction and comfort, as well as the masters themselves. In this direction to Titus there are the duties themselves, to which he must exhort servants, and a weighty consideration wherewith he was to enforce them.

(1.) The duties themselves are these :—

[1.] *To be obedient to their own masters, v.* 9. This is the prime duty, that by which they are characterized. Rom. vi. 16, *His servants you are whom you obey.* There must be inward subjection and dutiful respect and reverence in the mind and thoughts. *"If I be a master, where is my fear,* the

dutiful affection you show to me, together with the suitable outward
significations and expressions of it, in doing what I command you?" This
must be in servants; their will must be subject to their master's will, and
their time and labour at their master's disposal and command. I Pet. ii.
18, *Servants, be subject to your masters with all fear, not only to the good and
gentle, but also to the froward.* The duty results from the will of God, and
the relation in which, by his providence, he has put such; not from the
quality of the person. If he be a master, the duties of a servant are to be
paid to him as such. Servants therefore are to be exhorted to be obedient
to their own masters. And,

[2.] *To please them well in all things,* in all lawful things, and such as belong to them to command, or at least as are not contrary to the will of their
great and superior Lord. We are not to understand it either of obeying or
pleasing them absolutely, without any limitation; but always with a reserve
of God's right, which may in no case be entrenched upon. If his command
and the earthly master's come in competition, we are instructed to obey
God rather than man; but then servants must be upon good grounds in
this, that there is an inconsistency, else are they not held to be excused.
And not only must the will of God be the measure of the servant's
obedience, but the reason of it also. All must be done with a respect to
him, in virtue of his authority, and for pleasing him primarily and chiefly,
Col. iii. 22–24. In serving the earthly master according to Christ's will,
he is served; and such shall he rewarded by him accordingly. But how are
servants to please their masters in all things, and yet not be men-pleasers?
Answer, Men-pleasers, in the faulty sense, are such as eye men alone, or
chiefly, in what they do, leaving God out, or subordinating him to man;
when the will of man shall carry it, though against God's will, or man's
pleasure is more regarded than his,—when this can content them, that the
earthly master is pleased, though God be displeased,—or when more care,
or more satisfaction, is taken in man's being pleased than in God's, this is
sinful man-pleasing, of which all must take heed. Eph. vi. 5–7, " *Servants
be obedient to those that are your masters according to the flesh, with fear and
trembling, with singleness of your heart, as unto Christ. Not with eye service,
as men pleasers* (who look at nothing but the favour or displeasure of men,
or at nothing so much as this), *but as the servants of Christ doing the will
of God from the heart; with good will doing service, as to the Lord, and not
to men;*" not to them chiefly, but to Christ, who requires, and who will
reward any good done, whether by bond or free. Observe therefore,
Christian liberty comports well with civil servitude and subjection. Persons
may serve men, and yet be the servants of Christ; these are not contrary,
but subordinate, so far as serving men is according to Christ's will and for
his sake. Christ came not to destroy or prejudice civil order and differences. " *Art thou called, being a servant? Care not for it,* I Cor. vii. 21.
Let not this trouble thee, as if it were a condition unworthy of a Christian,
or wherein the person so called is less pleasing unto God; *for he that is
called in the Lord, being a servant, is the Lord's freeman,* not free from that
service, but free in it; free spiritually, though not in a civil sense. *Likewise also he that is called, being free, is Christ's servant;* he is bound to him,
though he be not under civil subjection to any; so that, *bond or free, all
are one in Christ.*" Servants therefore should not regret nor be troubled
at their condition, but be faithful and cheerful in the station wherein God
hath set them, striving to please their masters in all things. Hard it may be
under some churlish Nabals, but it must be aimed at as much as possible.

[3.] *Not answering again;* not contradicting them, nor disputing it with them ; not giving them any disrespectful or provoking language. Job complained of his servants, that he *called them and they gave him no answer ;* that was faulty another way : *Non respondere pro convito est— Such silence is contempt :* but here it is respect, rather to take a check or reproof with humble silence, not making any confident nor bold replies. When conscious of a fault, to palliate or stand in justification of it doubles it. Yet this not answering again excludes not turning away wrath with a soft answer, when season and circumstances admit. Good and wise masters will be ready to hear and do right ; but answering unseasonably, or in an unseemly manner, or, where the case admits not excuse, to be pert or confident, shows a want of the humility and meekness which such relation requires.

[4.] *Not purloining, but showing all good fidelity.* This is another great essential of good servants, to be *honest,* never converting that to their own use which is their master's, nor wasting the goods they are entrusted with : that is, *purloining.* They must be just and true, and do for their masters as they would or should for themselves. Prov. xxviii. 24, *Whoso robbeth his father or his mother, and saith, It is no transgression, the same is the companion of a destroyer ;* he will be ready to join with him. Thus having such light thoughts of taking beyond what is right, though it be from a parent or master, is likely to harden conscience to go further ; it is both wicked in itself, and it tends to more. Be it so that the master is hard and strait, scarcely making sufficient provision for servants ; yet they must not be their own carvers, nor go about by theft to right themselves ; they must bear their lot, committing their cause to God for righting and providing for them. I speak not of cases of extremity, for preserving life, the necessaries for which the servant has a right to. *Not purloining, but showing all good fidelity ;* he must not only not steal nor waste, but must improve his master's goods, and promote his prosperity and thriving, to his utmost. He that increased not his master's talent is accused of unfaithfulness, though he had not embezzled nor lost it. Faithfulness in a servant lies in the ready, punctual, and thorough execution of his master's orders ; keeping his secrets and counsels, despatching his affairs, and managing with frugality, and to as much just advantage for his master as he is able ; looking well to his trusts, and preventing, as far as he can, all spoil, or loss, or damage. This is a way to bring a blessing upon himself, as the contrary often brings utter ruin. *If you have not been faithful in that which is another man's, who shall give you that which is your own?* Luke xvi. 12. Thus of the duties themselves, to which servants are to be exhorted. Then,

(2.) Here is the consideration with which Titus was to enforce them : *That they may adorn the doctrine of God our Saviour in all things ;* that is, that they may recommend the gospel and Christ's holy religion to the good opinion of those that are without, by their meek, humble, obedient, and faithful conduct in all things. Even servants, though they may think that such as they, in so low and inferior a condition, can do little to bring repute to Christianity, or adorn the doctrine of Christ, and set forth the excellences of his truth and ways, yet, if they be careful to do their duty, it will redound to the glory of God and the credit of religion. The unbelieving masters would think the better of that despised way, which was everywhere spoken against, when they found that those of their servants who were Christians were better than their other servants—more obedient and submissive, more just and faithful, and more diligent in their places. True religion is an honour to the professors of it ; and they should see that they do not any dishonour to it, but adorn it rather in all that they are able. Our light must shine among men, so that they, seeing our good works, may glorify our Father who is in heaven. And thus of the apostle's directions to Titus, about the discharge of his office, in reference to several sorts of persons.

11 For the grace of God that bringeth salvation hath appeared [the grace of God hath appeared, bringing salvation] to all men, 12 Teaching us that, denying ungodliness and worldly lusts, we should live soberly, righteously, and godly, in this present world ; 13 Looking for that blessed hope, and the glorious appearing of the great God and our Saviour Jesus Christ ; 14 Who gave himself for us, that he might redeem us from all iniquity, and purify unto himself a peculiar people [a people for his own possession], zealous of good works.

Here we have the grounds or considerations upon which all the foregoing directions are urged, taken from the nature and design of the gospel, and the end of Christ's death.

I. From the nature and design of the gospel. Let young and old, men and women, masters and servants, and Titus himself, let all sorts do their respective duties, for this is the very aim and business of Christianity, to instruct, and help, and form persons, under all distinctions and relations, to a right frame and conduct. For this,

1. They are put under the dispensation of *the grace of God*, so the gospel is called, Eph. iii. 2. It is grace in respect of the spring of it—the free favour and good-will of God, not any merit or desert in the creature ; as manifesting and declaring this good-will in an eminent and signal manner ; and as it is the means of conveying and working grace in the hearts of believers. Now grace is obliging and constraining to goodness : *Let not sin reign, but yield yourselves unto God* ; *for you are not under the law, but under grace,* Rom. vi. 12–14. *The love of Christ constrains us* not to live to self, but to him (2 Cor. v. 14, 15) : without this effect, grace is received in vain.

2. This gospel grace *brings salvation* (reveals and offers it to sinners and ensures it to believers)—salvation from sin and wrath, from death and hell. Hence it is called *the word of life* ; it brings to faith, and so to life, the life of holiness now, and of happiness hereafter. The law is the ministration of death, but the gospel the ministration of life and peace. This therefore must be received as salvation (its rules minded, its commands obeyed), that the end of it may be obtained, *the salvation of the soul.* And more inexcusable will the neglecters of this grace of God bringing salvation now be, since,

3. *It hath appeared,* or shone out more clearly and illustriously than ever before. The old dispensation was comparatively dark and shadowy ; this is a clear and shining light ; and, as it is now more bright, so more diffused and extensive also. For,

4. It hath appeared *to all men ;* not to the Jews only, as the glory of God appeared at mount Sinai to that particular people, and out of the view

of all others; but gospel grace is open to all, and all are invited to come and partake of the benefit of it, Gentiles as well as Jews. The publication of it is free and general: *Disciple all nations: Preach the gospel to every creature.* The pale is broken down; there is no such enclosure now as formerly. *The preaching of Jesus Christ, which was kept secret since the world began, now is made manifest, and by the scriptures of the prophets, according to the commandment of the everlasting God, made known to all nations for the obedience of faith,* Rom. xvi. 25, 26. The doctrine of grace and salvation by the gospel is for all ranks and conditions of men (slaves and servants, as well as masters), therefore engaging and encouraging all to receive and believe it, and walk suitably to it, adorning it in all things

5. This gospel revelation is to *teach,* and not by way of information and instruction only, as a schoolmaster does his scholars, but by way of precept and command, as a sovereign who gives laws to his subjects. It directs what to shun and what to follow, what to avoid and what to do. The gospel is not for speculation only or chiefly, but for practice and right ordering of life: for it teaches us,

(1.) To abandon sin: *Denying ungodliness and worldly lusts;* to renounce and have no more to do with these, as we have had: *Put off, concerning the former conversation, the old man which is corrupt;* that is, the whole body of sins, here distributed into *ungodliness* and *worldly lusts.* "Put away ungodliness and irreligion, all unbelief, neglect or disesteem of the divine Being, not loving, nor fearing, nor trusting in him, nor obeying him as we should, neglecting his ordinances, slighting his worship, profaning his name or day. Thus deny ungodliness (hate and put it away); *and worldly lusts,* all corrupt and vicious desires and affections that prevail in worldly men, and carry out to worldly things: *the lusts of the flesh also, and of the eye, and the pride of life,* all sensuality and filthiness, covetous desires and ambition, seeking and valuing more the praise of men than of God; put away all these." An earthly sensual conversation suits not a heavenly calling. *Those that are Christ's have crucified the flesh with the affections and lusts.* They have done it by covenant-engagement and promise, and have initially and prevailingly done it in act; they are going on in the work, cleansing themselves more and more from all filthiness of flesh and spirit. Thus the gospel first unteaches that which is evil, to abandon sin; and then,

(2.) To make conscience of that which is good: *To live soberly, righteously, and godly,* &c. Religion is not made up of negatives only; there must be doing good as well as eschewing evil; in these conjunctly is sincerity proved and the gospel adorned. We should live soberly with respect to ourselves, in the due government of our appetites and passions, keeping the limits of moderation and temperance, avoiding all inordinate excesses; and righteously towards all men, rendering to all their due, and injuring none, but rather doing good to others, according to our ability and their need: this seems a part of justice and righteousness, for we are not born for ourselves alone, and therefore may not live to ourselves only. *We are members one of another,* and *must seek every man another's wealth,* 1 Cor. x. 24; xii. 25. The public, especially, which includes the interests of all, must have the regards of all. Selfishness is a sort of unrighteousness; it robs others of that share in us which is their due. How amiable then will a just and righteous conduct be! It secures and promotes all interests, not particular only, but general and public, and so contributes to the peace and happiness of the world. Live righteously therefore as well as soberly. And godly towards God, in the duties of his worship and service. Regards to him indeed should run through all. *Whether you eat, or drink, or whatsoever you do, do all to the glory of God,* 1 Cor. x. 31. Personal and relative duties must be done in obedience to his commands, with due aim at pleasing and honouring him, from principles of holy love and fear of him. But there is an express and direct duty also that we owe to God, namely, belief and acknowledgment of his being and perfections, paying him internal and external worship and homage,—loving, fearing, and trusting in him,— depending on him, and devoting ourselves to him,—observing all those religious duties and ordinances that he has appointed,—praying to him, praising him, and meditating on his word and works. This is godliness, looking and coming to God, as our state now is, not immediately, but as he has manifested himself in Christ ; so does the gospel direct and require. To go to God in any other way, namely, by saints or angels, is unsuitable, yea, contrary to the gospel rule and warrant. All communications from God to us are through his Son, and our returns must also be by him. God in Christ we must look at as the object of our hope and worship. Thus must we exercise ourselves to godliness, without which there can be no adorning of that gospel which is according to it, which teaches and requires such a deportment. A gospel conversation must needs be a godly conversation, expressing our love and fear and reverence of God, our hope and trust and confidence in him, as manifested in his Son. *We are the circumcision* (who have in truth what was signified by that sacrament), *who worship God in the Spirit, and rejoice in Christ Jesus, and have no confidence in the flesh.* See in how small a compass our duty is comprised ; it is put into few words, *denying ungodliness and worldly lusts, and living soberly, righteously, and godly, in this present world.* The gospel teaches us not only how to believe and hope well, but also to live well, as becomes that faith and hope in this present world, and as expectants of another and better. There is the world that now is, and that which is to come ; the present is the time and place of our trial, and the gospel teaches us to live well here, not, however, as our final state, but with an eye chiefly to a future : for it teaches us in all,

(3.) To look for the glories of another world, to which a sober, righteous, and godly life in this is preparative : *Looking for that blessed hope, and the glorious appearing of the great God and our Saviour Jesus Christ.* Hope, by a metonymy, is put for the thing hoped for, namely, heaven and the felicities thereof, called emphatically *that hope,* because it is the great thing we look and long and wait for ; and a *blessed hope,* because, when attained, we shall be completely happy for ever. *And the glorious appearing of the great God and our Saviour Jesus Christ.* This denotes both the time of the accomplishing of our hope and the sureness and greatness of it : it will be at the second appearing of Christ, when he shall come *in his own glory, and in his Father's, and of the holy angels,* Luke ix. 26. His own glory which he had before the world was ; and his Father's, being *the express image of his person,* and as God-man, his delegated ruler and Judge ; and of the holy angels, as his ministers and glorious attendants. His first coming was in meanness, to satisfy justice and purchase happiness ; his second will be in majesty, to bestow and instate his people in it. *Christ was once offered to bear the sins of many ; and unto those that look for him will he appear the second time, without sin, unto salvation,* Heb. ix. 28. *The great God and our Saviour* (or *even our Saviour*) *Jesus Christ;* for they are not two subjects, but one only, as appears by the single article, τοῦ μεγάλου Θεοῦ καὶ Σωτῆρος, not καὶ τοῦ Σωτῆρος, and so is καὶ rendered 1 Cor. xv. 24,

When he shall have delivered up the kingdom to God, even the Father; τῷ Θεῷ καὶ Πατρί. Christ then is the *great God,* not figuratively, as magistrates and others are sometimes called gods, or as appearing and acting in the name of God, but properly and absolutely, *the true God* (1 John v. 20), *the mighty God* (Isa. ix. 6), *who, being in the form of God, thought it not robbery to be equal with God,* Phil. ii. 6. In his second coming he will reward his servants, and bring them to glory with him. Observe, [1.] There is a common and blessed hope for all true Christians in the other world. If in this life only they had hope in Christ, they were of all men the most miserable, 1 Cor. xv. 19. By hope is meant the thing hoped for, namely Christ himself, who is called *our hope* (1 Tim. i. 1), and blessedness in and through him, even riches of glory (Eph. i. 18), hence fitly termed here *that blessed hope.* [2.] The design of the gospel is to stir up all to a good life by this blessed hope. *Gird up the loins of your mind, be sober, and hope to the end for the grace that is to be brought unto you at the revelation of Jesus Christ,* 1 Pet. i. 13. To the same purport here, *Denying ungodliness and worldly lusts, live soberly, righteously, and godly, in this present world, looking for the blessed hope;* not as mercenaries, but as dutiful and thankful Christians. *What manner of persons ought you to be in all holy conversation and godliness, looking for and hastening to the coming of the day of God!* 2 Pet. iii. 11, 12. Looking and hastening, that is, expecting and diligently preparing for it. [3.] At and in the glorious appearing of Christ will the blessed hope of Christians be attained ; for their felicity will be this, *To be where he is, and to behold his glory,* John xvii. 24. The glory of the great God and our Saviour will then break out as the sun. Though in the exercise of his judiciary power he will appear as the Son of man, yet will he be mightily declared to be the Son of God too. The divinity, which on earth was much veiled, will shine out then as the sun in its strength. Hence the work and design of the gospel are to raise the heart to wait for this second appearing of Christ. *We are begotten again to a lively hope of it* (1 Pet. i. 3), turned to *serve the living God, and wait for his Son from heaven,* 1 Thess. i. 9, 10. Christians are marked by this, expecting their master's coming (Luke xii. 36), *loving his appearance,* 2 Tim. iv. 8. Let us then look to this hope ; let our loins be girt, and our lights burning, and ourselves like those who wait for their Lord ; the day or hour we know not, but *he that shall come will come, and will not tarry,* Heb. x. 37. [4.] The comfort and joy of Christians are that their Saviour is the great God and will gloriously manifest himself at his second coming. Power and love, majesty and mercy, will then appear together in the highest lustre, to the terror and confusion of the wicked, but to the everlasting triumph and rejoicing of the godly. Were he not thus the great God, and not a mere creature, he could not be their Saviour, nor their hope. Thus of the considerations to enforce the directions of all sorts to their respective duties from the nature and design of the gospel. And herewith is connected another ground, namely,

II. From the end of Christ's death : *Who gave himself for us, that he might redeem us from all iniquity, and purify unto himself a peculiar people, zealous of good works, v.* 14. To bring us to holiness and happiness was the end of Christ's death, as well as the scope of his doctrine. Here we have,

1. The purchaser of salvation—Jesus Christ, *that great God and our Saviour,* who saves not simply as God, much less as man alone ; but as God-man, two natures in one person : man, that he might obey, and suffer,

and die, for man, and be meet to deal with him and for him ; and God, that he might support the manhood, and give worth and efficacy to his undertakings, and have due regard to the rights and honour of the deity, as well as the good of his creature, and bring about the latter to the glory of the former. Such a one became us ; and this was,

2. The price of our redemption : *He gave himself.* The Father gave him, but he gave himself too ; and, in the freeness and voluntariness, as well as the greatness of the offering, lay the acceptableness and merit of it. *Therefore doth my Father love me, because I lay down my life, that I might take it again. No man taketh it from me, but I lay it down of myself,* John x. 17, 18. So John xvii. 19, *" For their sakes I sanctify myself,* or separate and devote myself to this work, to be both a priest and a sacrifice to God for the sins of men." The human nature was the offering, and the divine the altar, sanctifying the gift, and the whole the act of the person. *He gave himself a ransom for all,* 1 Tim. ii. 6. *Once in the end of the world hath he appeared, to put away sin by the sacrifice of himself.* He was the priest and sacrifice too. *We are redeemed, not with silver and gold, but with the precious blood of Christ* (1 Pet. i. 18, 19), called *the blood of God* (Acts xx. 28), that is, of him who is God.

3. The persons for whom : *For us,* us poor perishing sinners, gone off from God, and turned rebels against him. He gave himself *for us,* not only for our good, but in our stead. Messiah was cut off, not for himself, but for us. *He suffered, the just for the unjust, that he might bring us to God,* 1 Pet. iii. 18. *He was made sin for us* (an offering and sacrifice for sin), *that we might be made the righteousness of God in him,* 2 Cor. v. 21. Wonderful condescension and grace ! *He loved us, and gave himself for us ;* what can we do less than love and give up ourselves to him ? Especially considering,

4. The ends of his giving himself for us, (1.) *That he might redeem us from all iniquity.* This is fitted to the first lesson, *denying ungodliness and worldly lusts.* Christ gave himself to redeem us from these, therefore put them away. To love and live in sin is to trample under foot redeeming blood, to despise and reject one of the greatest benefits of it, and to act counter to its design. But how could the short sufferings of Christ redeem us from all iniquity ? *Answer,* Through the infinite dignity of his person. He who was God suffered, though not as God. The acts and properties of either nature are attributed to the person. God purchased his church *with his own blood,* Acts xx. 28. Could payment be made at once, no need of suffering for ever. A mere creature could not do this, from the finiteness of his nature ; but God-man could. *The great God and our Saviour gave himself for us :* this accounts for it. *By one offering he hath for ever perfected those that are sanctified,* Heb. ix. 25, 26 ; x. 14. He needed not to offer himself often, nor could he be holden of death, when he had once undergone it. Happy end and fruit of Christ's death, redemption from all iniquity ! Christ died for this : and, (2.) *To purify to himself a peculiar people.* This enforces the second lesson : *To live soberly, righteously, and godly, in this present world.* Christ died to purify as well as to pardon—to obtain grace, to heal the nature, as well as to free from guilt and condemnation. He gave himself for his church, *to cleanse it.* Thus does he make *to himself a peculiar people,* by purifying them. Thus are they distinguished from the world that lies in wickedness ; they are born of God, and assimilated to him, bear his image, are holy as their heavenly Father is holy. Observe, Redemption from sin and sancti-

fication of the nature go together, and both make a peculiar people unto God : freedom from guilt and condemnation, freedom from the power of lusts, and purification of soul by the Spirit. These are *a chosen generation, a royal priesthood, a holy nation,* and so *a peculiar people.* And, (3.) *Zealous of good works.* This peculiar people, as they are made so by grace purifying them, so must they be seen to be so by doing good, and a zeal therein. Observe, The gospel is not a doctrine of licentiousness, but of holiness and good life. We are redeemed from our vain conversation, to serve God *in holiness and righteousness all the days of our life.* Let us see then that we do good, and have zeal in it ; only looking that zeal be guided by knowledge and spirited with love, directed to the glory of God, and always in some good thing. And thus of the motive to the duties directed, from the end of Christ's death.

¹⁵ These things speak, and exhort, and rebuke with all authority. Let no man despise thee.

The apostle closes the chapter (as he began it) with a summary direction to Titus upon the whole, in which we have the matter and manner of ministers' teaching, and a special instruction to Titus in reference to himself.

I. The matter of ministers' teaching : *these things,* namely, those before mentioned : not Jewish fables and traditions, but the truths and duties of the gospel, of avoiding sin, and living soberly, righteously, and godly, in this present world. Observe, Ministers in their preaching must keep close to the word of God. *If any man speak, let him speak as the oracles of God,* 1 Pet. iv. 11, and not the figments and inventions of his own brain.

II. The manner ; by doctrine, and exhortation, and reproof with all authority. 2 Tim. iii. 16, *All scripture is given by inspiration of God, and is profitable for doctrine, for reproof, for correction, and for instruction in righteousness ;* that is, to teach sound doctrine, to convince of sin and refute error, to reform the life, and to carry forward in what is just and good ; *that the man of God* (the Christian or minister) *may be perfect, thoroughly furnished to all good works* that are to be practised by himself or to be taught to others. Here is what will furnish for all parts of his duty, and the right discharge of them. " *These things speak,* or teach ; shun not to declare the whole counsel of God." The great and necessary truths and duties of the gospel, especially, these *speak and exhort,* παρακάλει, *press with much earnestness.* Ministers must not be cold and lifeless in de-livering heavenly doctrine and precepts, as if they were indifferent things or of little concern ; but they must urge them with earnestness suitable to their nature and importance ; they must call upon persons to mind and heed, and not be *hearers only, deceiving themselves ; but doers of the word, that they may be blessed therein. And rebuke ;* convince and reprove such as contradict or gainsay, or neglect and do not receive the truth as they should or retain it in unrighteousness—those who hear it not with such a believing and obedient mind and heart as they ought, but, instead of this (it may be) live in contrary practices, showing themselves stubborn and disobedient, and to every good work reprobate. *Rebuke with all authority,* as coming in the name of God, and armed with his threatenings and discipline, whoever make light of which will do it at their peril. Ministers are reprovers in the gate.

III. Here is a special instruction to Titus in reference to himself : " *Let no man despise thee*; that is, give no occasion to do so, nor suffer it without reproof, considering that *he who despiseth despiseth not man, but God.*" Or thus, "*Speak and exhort these things,* press them upon all, as they may respectively be concerned ; with boldness and faithfulness reprove sin, and carefully look to thyself and thy own conduct, and then none will despise thee." The most effectual way for ministers to secure themselves from contempt is to keep close to the doctrine of Christ, and imitate his example—to preach and live well, and do their duty with prudence and courage ; this will best preserve both their reputation and their comfort.

Perhaps, too, an admonition might be here intended to the people—that Titus, though young, and but a substitute of the apostle, yet should not be contemned by them, but considered and respected as a faithful minister of Christ, and encouraged and supported in his work and office. "*Know those that labour among you, and are over you in the Lord, and admonish you ; and esteem them very highly in love for their work's sake,* I Thess. v. 12, 13. Mind their teaching, respect their persons, support them in their function, and, what in you lies, further their endeavours for the honour of God and the salvation of souls.*"

CHAPTER III

Of duties which concern Christians more in common, and the reasons of them, ver. 1-3. What Titus in teaching should avoid, and how he should deal with a heretic, with some other directions (ver 9-14), and salutations in the close, ver. 15.

PUT them in mind to be subject to principalities and powers, to obey magistrates [to rulers, to authorities, to be obedient], to be ready to every good work, 2 To speak evil of no man, to be no brawlers, *but* gentle, showing all meekness unto all men. 3 For we ourselves also were sometimes foolish, disobedient, deceived, serving divers lusts and pleasures, living in malice and envy, hateful, *and* hating one another. 4 But after that the kindness and love of God our Saviour toward man appeared, 5 Not by works of righteousness which we have done, but according to his mercy he saved us, by the washing of regeneration, and renewing of the Holy Ghost; 6 Which he shed on us abundantly through Jesus Christ our Saviour; 7 That being justified by his grace, we should be made heirs according to the hope of eternal life. 8 *This is* a faithful saying, and these things I will that thou affirm constantly [confidently], that they which have believed in God might be careful to maintain good works. These things are good and profitable unto men.

Here is the fourth thing in the matter of the epistle. The apostle had directed Titus in reference to the particular and special duties of several sorts of persons ; now he bids him exhort to what concerned them more in common, namely, to quietness and submission to rulers, and readiness to do good, and to equitable and gentle behaviour towards all men—things comely and ornamental of religion ; he must therefore put them in mind of such things. Ministers are people's remembrancers of their duty. As they are remembrancers for the people to God in prayers (Isa. lxii. 6), so are they from God to them in preaching : *I will not be negligent to put you always in remembrance,* 2 Pet. i. 12. Forgetfulness of duty is a common frailty ; there is need therefore of reminding and quickening them thereto. Here are the duties themselves, and the reasons of them.

I. The duties themselves, which they were to be reminded of. 1. *Put them in mind to be subject to principalities and powers, to obey magistrates.* Magistracy is God's ordinance for the good of all, and therefore must be regarded and submitted to by all ; not for wrath and by force only, but willingly and for conscience' sake. *Principalities,* and *powers,* and *magistrates,* that is, all civil rulers, whether supreme and chief or subordinate, in the government under which they live, of whatever form it be ; that they be subject to them and obey them in things lawful and honest, and which it belongs to their office to require. The Christian religion was misrepresented by its adversaries as prejudicial to the rights of princes and civil powers, and tending to faction and sedition, and to rebellion against lawful authority ; therefore *to put to silence the ignorance of foolish men,* and stop the mouths of malicious enemies, Christians must be reminded to show themselves examples rather of all due subjection and obedience to the government that is over them. Natural desire of liberty must be guided and bounded by reason and scripture. Spiritual privileges do not make void or weaken, but confirm and strengthen, their obligations to civil duties : "Remind them therefore *to be subject to principalities and powers and to obey magistrates.*" And, 2. *To be ready to every good work.* Some refer this to such good works as are required by magistrates and within their sphere : "Whatever tends to good order, and to promote and secure public tranquillity and peace, be not backward, but ready, to promote such things." But, though this be included, if not first intended, yet is it not to be hereto restrained. The precept regards doing good in all kinds, and on every occasion that may offer, whether respecting God, ourselves, or our neighbour—what may bring credit to religion in the world. *Whatsoever things are true, honest, just, pure, lovely, of good report; if there be any virtue, if there be any praise, think on these things* (Phil. iv. 8), to do and follow and further them. Mere harmlessness, or good words and good meanings only, are not enough without good works. *Pure religion and undefiled before God and the Father is this, to visit the fatherless and the widow in their affliction, and keep unspotted from the world.* "Not only take, but seek, occasion for doing good, keep fitness and readiness that way, put it not off to others, but embrace and lay hold on it thyself, delight and rejoice therein, put all in mind of this." And, 3. *To speak evil of no man :* μηδένα βλασφημεῖν, *to revile,* or *curse,* or *blaspheme none :* or (as our translation more generally) *to speak evil of none,* unjustly and falsely, or unnecessarily, without call, and when it may do hurt but no good to the person himself or any other. If no good can be spoken, rather than speak evil unnecessarily, say nothing. We must never take pleasure in speaking ill of others, nor make the worst of anything, but the best that we can. We must not go up and down as tale-bearers, carrying ill-natured stories, to the prejudice of our neighbour's good name and the destruction of brotherly love. Misrepresentations, or insinuations of bad intentions, or of hypocrisy in what is done, things out of our reach or cognizance, these come within the reach of this prohibition. As this evil is too common, so it is of great malignity. *If any man seemeth to be religious and bridleth not his tongue, that man's religion is vain,* Jam. i. 26. Such loose uncharitable talk is displeasing to God, and hurtful among men. Prov. xvii. 9, *He that covereth a transgression seeketh love* (that is, to himself by this tenderness and charity, or rather to the transgressor) ; *but he that repeateth a matter* (that blazes and tells the faults of another abroad) *separateth very friends;* he raises dissensions and alienates his friend from himself, and perhaps from others. This is among the sins to be put off (Eph. iv. 31) ; for, if indulged, it unfits for Christian communion here and the society of the blessed in heaven, 1 Cor. vi. 10. Remind them therefore to avoid this. And, 4. *To be no brawlers ; ἀμάχους εἶναι—no fighters,* either with hand or tongue, no quarrelsome contentious persons, apt to give or return ill and provoking language. A holy contending there is for matters good and important, and in a manner suitable and becoming, not with wrath nor injurious violence. Christians must follow the things that are conducive to peace, and that in a peaceful, not a rough and boisterous and hurtful way, but as becomes the servants of the God of peace and love (Rom. xii. 19), *Dearly beloved, avenge not yourselves, but rather give place unto wrath* ; this is the Christian's wisdom and duty. *The glory of a man is to pass over a transgression ;* it is the duty of a reasonable, and therefore certainly of a Christian man, whose reason is improved and advanced by religion ; such may not, and will not, presently fall foul on one who has offended him, but like God, will be *slow to anger, and ready to forgive.* Contention and strife arise from men's lusts, and exorbitant unruly passions, which must be curbed and moderated, not indulged ; and Christians need to be reminded of these things, that they do not by a wrathful contentious spirit and behaviour displease and dishonour God and discredit religion, promoting feuds in the places where they live. *He that is slow to anger is better than the mighty,* and he *that ruleth his spirit than he that taketh a city.* Wherefore it follows, 5. *But gentle ; ἐπιεικεῖς, equitable and just,* or candid and fair in constructions of things, not taking words or actions in the worst sense ; and for peace sometimes yielding somewhat of strict right. And, 6. *Showing all meekness to all men.* We must be of a mild disposition, and not only have meekness in our hearts, but show it in our speech and conduct. *All meekness*—meekness in all instances and occasions, not towards friends only, but to *all men,* though still with wisdom, as James admonishes, Jam. iii. 13. "Distinguish the person and the sin : pity the one and hate the other. Distinguish between sin and sin ; look not on all alike, there are *motes and beams.* Distinguish also between sinner and sinner : *of some have compassion, others save with fear, pulling them out of the fire, thus making a difference,* Jude 22, 23. Mind these things ; *the wisdom that is from above is pure and peaceable, gentle and easy to be entreated.*" Meekness of spirit and demeanour renders religion amiable ; it is a commanded imitation of Christ the grand exemplar, and what brings its own reward with it, in the ease and comfort of the disposition itself and the blessings accompanying it. These shall be glad and rejoice, shall be taught and guided in their way, and satisfied with bread, and beautified with salvation. Thus of the duties themselves, which Titus was to put people in mind of : for which,

II. He adds the reasons, which are derived.

1. From their own past condition. Consideration of men's natural condition is a great means and ground of equity and gentleness, and all meekness, towards those who are yet in such a state. This has a tendency to abate pride and work pity and hope in reference to those who are yet unconverted : "We ourselves also were so and so, corrupt and sinful, therefore we should not be impatient and bitter, hard and severe, towards those who are but as ourselves once were. Should we then have been willing to be contemned, and proudly and rigorously dealt with ? No, but treated with gentleness and humanity ; and therefore we should now so treat those who are unconverted, according to that rule of equity : *Quod tibi non vis fieri, alteri ne feceris—What you would not have done to you that do not you to another.*" Their past natural condition is set forth in divers particulars. *We ourselves also were sometimes,* (1.) *Foolish* ; without true spiritual understanding and knowledge, ignorant of heavenly things. Observe, Those should be most disposed to bear with others' follies who may remember many of their own ; those should be meek and gentle, and patient towards others who once needed and doubtless then expected the same. *We ourselves also were sometimes foolish.* And, (2) *Disobedient* ; heady and unpersuadable, resisting the word and rebellious even againgst the natural laws of God, and those which human society requires. Well are these set to gether, *foolish* and *disobedient.* For what folly like this, to disobey God and his laws, natural or revealed ? This is contrary to right reason, and men's true and greatest interests ; and what so foolish as to violate and go counter to these ? (3) *Deceived,* or wandering ; namely, out of the ways of truth and holiness. Man in this his degenerate state is of a straying nature, thence compared to a lost sheep ; this must be sought and brought back, and guided in the right way, Ps. cxix. 176. He is weak, and ready to be imposed upon by the wiles and subtleties of Satan, and of men lying in wait to seduce and mislead. (4) *Serving divers lusts and pleasures* ; namely, as vassals and slaves under them. Observe, Men deceived are easily entangled and ensnared ; they would not serve divers lusts and pleasures as they do, were they not blinded and beguiled into them. See here too what a different notion the word gives of a sensual and fleshly life from what the world generally has of it. Carnal people think they enjoy their pleasures ; the word calls it servitude and vassalage : they are very drudges and bond slaves under them ; so far are they from freedom and felicity in them that they are captivated by them, and serve them as taskmasters and tyrants. Observe further, It is the misery of the servants of sin that they have many masters, one lust hurrying them one way, and another another ; pride commands one thing, covetousness another, and often a contrary. What vile slaves are sinners, while they conceit themselves free ! the lusts that tempt them promise them liberty, but in yielding they become the servants of corruption ; for *of whom a man is overcome of the same is he brought into bondage.* (5.) *Living in malice,* one of those lusts that bear rule in them. Malice desires hurt to another and rejoices in it. (6.) *And envy,* which grudges and repines at another's good, frets at his prosperity and success in any thing : both are roots of bitterness, whence many evils spring : evil thoughts and speeches, tongues *set on fire of hell,* detracting from and impairing the just and due praises of others. *Their words are swords,* wherewith they slay the good name and honour of their neighbour. This was the sin of Satan, and of Cain who was of that evil one, and slew his brother ; for wherefore slew he him, but of this envy and malice, *because his own works were evil, and his brother's righteous?* These were some of the sins in

which we lived in our natural state. And, (7.) *Hateful*, or odious—deserving to be hated. (8.) *And hating one another.* Observe, Those that are sinful, living and allowing themselves in sin, are hateful to God and all good men. Their temper and ways are so, though not simply their persons. It is the misery of sinners that they hate one another, as it is the duty and happiness of saints to love one another. What contentions and quarrels flow from men's corruptions, such as were in the nature of those who by conversion are now good, but in their unconverted state made them ready to run like furious wild beasts one upon another ! The consideration of its having been thus with us should moderate our spirits, and dispose us to be more equal and gentle, meek and tender-hearted, towards those who are such. This is the argument from their own past condition here described. And he reasons,

2. From their present state. " We are delivered out of that our miserable condition by no merit nor strength of our own ; but only by the mercy and free grace of ,God, and merit of Christ, and operation of his Spirit. Therefore we have no ground, in respect of ourselves, to contemn those who are yet unconverted, but rather to pity them, and cherish hope concerning them, that they, though in themselves as unworthy and unmeet as we were, yet may obtain mercy, as we have : and so upon this occasion the apostle again opens the causes of our salvation, *v.* 4–7.

(1.) We have here the prime author of our salvation—God the Father, therefore termed here *God our Saviour. All things are of God, who hath reconciled us to himself by Jesus Christ,* 2 Cor. v. 18. All things belonging to the new creation, and recovery of fallen man to life and happiness, of which the apostle is there speaking, all these things are of God the Father as contriver and beginner of this work. There is an order in acting, as in subsisting. The Father begins, the Son manages, and the Holy Spirit works and perfects all. God (namely, *the Father*) is a Saviour by Christ, through the Spirit. John iii. 16, *God so loved the world as to give his only begotten Son, that whoever believes in him might not perish, but have everlasting life.* He is the father of Christ, and through him the Father of mercies ; all spiritual blessings are by Christ from him, Eph. i. 3. *We joy in God through Jesus Christ,* Rom. v. 11. *And with one mind, and one mouth, glorify God, even the Father of our Lord Jesus Christ,* Rom. xv. 5.

(2.) The Spring and rise of it—the divine *philanthropy,* or *kindness and love of God to man.* By grace we are saved from first to last. This is the ground and motive. God's pity and mercy to man in misery were the first wheel, or rather the Spirit in the wheels, that sets and keeps them all in motion. God is not, cannot be, moved by any thing out of himself. The occasion is in man, namely, his misery and wretchedness. Sin bringing that misery, wrath might have issued out rather than compassion ; but God, knowing how to adjust all with his own honour and perfections, would pity and save rather than destroy. He delights in mercy. *Where sin abounded, grace did much more abound.* We read of *riches of goodness and mercy,* Rom. ii. 4 ; Eph. ii. 7. Let us acknowledge this, and give him the glory of it, not turning it to wantonness, but to thankfulness and obedience.

(3.) Here is the means, or instrumental cause—the shining out of this love and grace of God in the gospel, *after it appeared,* that is, in the word. The appearing of love and grace has, through the Spirit, great virtue to soften and change and turn to God, and so is *the power of God to salvation to every one that believeth.* Thus having asserted God to be the author, his free grace the spring, and the manifestation of this in the gospel the means of salvation, that the honour of all still may be the better secured to him.

(4.) False grounds and motives are here removed : *Not by works of right-eousness which we have done, but according to his mercy, he saved us ;* not for foreseen works of ours, but his own free grace and mercy alone. Works must be in the saved (where there is room for it), but not among the causes of his salvation ; they are the way to the kingdom, not the meriting price of it ; all is upon the principle of undeserved favour and mercy from first to last. Election is of grace : we are chosen *to be* holy, not because it was antecedently seen that we should be so, Eph. i. 4. It is the fruit, not the cause, of election : *God hath from the beginning chosen you to salvation through sanctification of the Spirit and belief of the truth,* 2 Thess. ii. 13. So effectual calling, in which election breaks out, and is first seen : *He hath saved us, and called us with a holy calling ; not according to our works, but according to his own purpose and grace, which was given us in Christ Jesus before the world began,* 2 Tim. i. 9. We *are justified freely by grace* (Rom. iii. 24), and sanctified and saved by grace : *By grace you are saved, through faith ; and that not of yourselves, it is the gift of God,* Eph. ii. 8. Faith and all saving graces are God's free gift and his work ; the beginning, increase, and perfection of them in glory, all are from him. In building men up to be a holy temple unto God, from the foundation to the top-stone, we must cry nothing but *Grace, grace* unto it. It is *not of works, lest any man should boast ; but of grace, that he who glorieth should glory only in the Lord.* Thus the true cause is shown, and the false removed.

(5.) Here is the formal cause of salvation, or that wherein it lies, the beginnings of it at least—in regeneration or spiritual renewing, as it is here called. *Old things pass away, and all things become new,* in a moral and spiritual, not in a physical and natural, sense. It is the same man, but with other dispositions and habits ; evil ones are done away, as to the prevalency of them at present ; and all remains of them in due time will be so, when the work shall be perfected in heaven. A new prevailing principle of grace and holiness is wrought, which inclines, and sways, and governs, and makes the man a new man, a new creature, having new thoughts, desires, and affections, a new and holy turn of life and actions ; the life of God in man, not only from God in a special manner, but con-formed and tending to him. Here is salvation begun, and which will be growing and increasing to perfection ; therefore it is said, *He saved us.* What is so begun, as sure to be perfected in time, is expressed as if it already were so. Let us look to this therefore without delay ; we must be initially saved now, by regeneration, if on good ground we would expect complete salvation in heaven. The change then will be but in degree, not in kind. Grace is glory begun, as glory is but grace in its perfection. How few mind this ! Most act as if they were afraid to be happy before the time ; they would have heaven, they pretend, at last, yet care not for holiness now ; that is, they would have the end without the beginning ; so absurd are sinners. But without regeneration, that is, the first resur-rection, there is no attaining the second glorious one, the resurrection of the just. Here then is formal salvation, in the new divine life wrought by the gospel.

(6.) Here is the outward sign and seal thereof in baptism, called there-fore *the washing of regeneration.* The work itself is inward and spiritual ; but it is outwardly signified and sealed in this ordinance. Water is of a cleansing and purifying nature, does away the filth of the flesh, and so was apt to signify the doing away of the guilt and defilement of sin by the blood and Spirit of Christ, though that aptness alone, without Christ's institution, would not have been sufficient. This it is that makes it of this signification on God's part, a seal of righteousness by faith, as circumcision was, in the place of which it succeeds; and on ours an engagement to be the Lord's. Thus baptism saves figuratively and sacramentally, where it is rightly used. *Arise, and be baptized, and wash away thy sins, calling upon the name of the Lord,* Acts xxii. 16. So Eph. v. 26, *That he might sanctify and cleanse us by the washing of water by the word.* Slight not this outward sign and seal, where it may be had according to Christ's appointment; yet rest not in the outward washing, but look to the *answer of a good conscience,* without which the external washing will avail nothing. The covenant sealed in baptism binds to duties, as well as exhibits and conveys benefits and privileges; if the former be not minded, in vain are the latter expected. Sever not what God has joined; in both the outer and inner part is baptism complete; as he that was circumcised became debtor to the whole law (Gal. v. 3), so is he that is baptized to the gospel, to observe all the commands and ordinances thereof, as Christ appointed. *Disciple all nations, baptizing them in the name of the Father, and of the Son, and of the Holy Ghost; teaching them to observe all things whatsoever I have commanded you,* Matt. xxviii. 19, 20. This is the outward sign and seal of salvation, baptism, called here *the washing of regeneration.*

(7.) Here is the principal efficient, namely, the Spirit of God; it is the *renewing of the Holy Ghost;* not excluding the Father and the Son, who in all works without themselves are concurring; nor the use of means, the word and sacraments, by which the Spirit works; through his operation it is that they have their saving effect. In the economy of our salvation, the applying and effecting part is especially attributed to the Holy Spirit. We are said to be born of the Spirit, to be quickened and sanctified by the Spirit, to be led and guided, strengthened and helped, by the Spirit. Through him we mortify sin, perform duty, walk in God's ways; all the acts and operations of the divine life in us, the works and fruits of righteousness without us, all are through this blessed and Holy Spirit, who is therefore called the Spirit of life, and of grace and holiness; all grace is from him. Earnestly therefore is he to be sought, and greatly to be heeded by us, that we quench not his holy motions, nor resist and oppose him in his workings. *Res delicatula est Spiritus—The Spirit is a tender thing.* As we act towards him, so may we expect he will to us; if we slight, and resist, and oppose his workings, he will slacken them; if we continue to vex him, he will retire. *Grieve not therefore the Holy Spirit of God, whereby you are sealed to the day of redemption,* Eph. iv. 30. The Spirit seals by his renewing and sanctifying, his witnessing and assuring work; he distinguishes and marks out for salvation, and fits for it; it is his work: we could not turn to God by any strength of our own, any more than we can be justified by any righteousness of our own.

(8.) Here is the manner of God's communicating this Spirit in the gifts and graces of it; not with a scanty and niggardly hand, but most freely and plentifully: *Which he shed on us abundantly.* More of the Spirit in its gifts and graces is poured out under the gospel than was under the law, whence it is eminently styled *the ministration of the Spirit,* 2 Cor. iii. 8. A measure of the Spirit the church has had in all ages, but more in gospel times, since the coming of Christ, than before. *The law came by Moses, but grace and truth by Jesus Christ;* that is, a more plentiful effusion of grace, fulfilling the promises and prophecies of old. Isa. xliv. 3, *I will pour water upon him that is thirsty, and floods upon the dry ground. I will pour my Spirit upon thy seed, and my blessing upon thy offspring:* this greatest and best of blessings, an effusion of grace, and of the sanctifying gifts of the Spirit. Joel. ii. 28, *I will pour out my Spirit upon all flesh;* not on Jews only, but Gentiles also. This was to be in gospel times; and accordingly (Acts ii. 17, 18, 33), speaking of Christ risen and ascended, *having received of the Father the promise of the Holy Ghost, he hath shed forth* (says Peter) *this that you now see and hear:* and *ch.* x. 44, 45, *The Holy Ghost fell on all those that heard the word,* Gentiles as well as Jews. This indeed was, in a great measure, in the miraculous gifts of the Holy Ghost, but not without his sanctifying graces also accompanying many if not all of them. There was then great abundance of common gifts of illumination, outward calling and profession, and general faith, and of more special gifts of sanctification too, such as faith, and hope, and love, and other graces of the Spirit. Let us get a share in these. What will it signify if much be shed forth and we remain dry? Our condemnation will but be aggravated the more if under such a dispensation of grace we remain void of grace. *Be filled with the Spirit,* says the Apostle; it is duty as well as privilege, because of the means which God in the gospel is ready to bless and make effectual; this is the manner of God's communicating grace and all spiritual blessings under the gospel—*plentifully;* he is not straitened towards us, but we towards him and in ourselves.

(9.) Here is the procuring cause of all, namely, Christ: *Through Jesus Christ our Saviour.* He it is who purchased the Spirit and his saving gifts and graces. All come through him, and through him as a Saviour, whose undertaking and work it is to bring to grace and glory; he is our righteousness and peace, and our head, from whom we have all spiritual life and influences. *He is made of God to us wisdom, righteousness, sanctification, and redemption.* Let us praise God for him above all; let us go to the Father by him, and improve him to all sanctifying and saving purposes. Have we grace? Let us thank him with the Father and Spirit for it: *account all things but loss and dung for the excellency of the knowledge of him,* and grow and increase therein more and more.

(10.) Here are the ends why we are brought into this new spiritual condition, namely, justification, and heirship, and hope of eternal life: *That, being justified by his grace, we should be made heirs according to the hope of eternal life.* Justification in the gospel sense is the free remission of a sinner, and accepting him as righteous through the righteousness of Christ received by faith. In it there is the removing of guilt that bound to punishment, and the accepting and dealing with the person as one that now is righteous in God's sight. This God does freely as to us, yet through the intervention of Christ's sacrifice and righteousness, laid hold on by faith (Rom. iii. 20, &c.): *By the deeds of the law shall no flesh be justified;* but through *the righteousness of God, which is by faith of Jesus Christ unto all and upon all those that believe,* whence (*v.* 24) we are said to be *justified freely by his grace, through the redemption that is in Jesus Christ, whom God hath set forth to be a propitiation through faith in his blood, to declare his righteousness for the remission of sins, that he might be just, and the justifier of him that believeth in Jesus.* God, in justifying a sinner in the way of the gospel, is gracious to him, and yet just to himself and his law, forgiveness being through a perfect righteousness, and satisfaction made to justice by Christ, who is the propitiation for sin, and not merited by the sinner himself. So it is here: *Not by works of righteousness which we have done, but according to his mercy he saved us, that, being justified by his grace, we should be made heirs according to the hope of eternal life.* It is by grace, as the spring and rise (as was said), though *through the redemption that is in Christ* as making the way, God's law and justice being thereby satisfied, and by faith applying that redemption. *By him* (by Christ) *all that believe are justified from all things from which they could not be justified by the law of Moses,* Acts xiii. 39. Hence the apostle desires *to be found in him, not having his own righteousness, which was of the law, but that which is through the faith of Christ, the righteousness which is of God by faith.* Let us not trust therefore in our own righteousness or merit of good works, but in Christ's righteousness alone, received by faith for justification and acceptance with God. Inherent righteousness we must have, and the fruits of it in works of obedience ; not however as our justifying righteousness before God, but as fruits of our justification, and evidences of our interest in Christ and qualification for life and happiness, and the very beginning and part of it ; but the procuring of all this is by Christ, that, *being justified by his grace, we should be made heirs.* Observe, Our justification is *by the grace of God,* and our justification by that grace is necessary in order to our being made *heirs of eternal life ;* without such justification there can be no adoption and sonship, and so no right of inheritance. John i. 12, *Whoever received him* (namely, Christ), *to them gave he power to become the sons of God, even to those that believed on his name.* Eternal life is set before us in the promise, the Spirit works faith in us and hope of that life, and so are we made heirs of it and have a kind of possession of it even now ; faith and hope bring it near, and fill with joy in the well-grounded expectation of it. The meanest believer is a great heir. Though he has not his portion in hand, he has good hope through grace, and may bear up under all difficulties. There is a better state in view. He is waiting for *an inheritance incorruptible, undefiled, and that fadeth not away, reserved in heaven for him.* How well may such comfort themselves with these words ! And now all this gives good reason why we should *show all meekness to all men,* because we have experienced so much benefit by the kindness and love of God to us, and may hope that they, in God's time, may be partakers of the like grace as we are. And thus of the reasons of equal and gentle, meek and tender behaviour towards others, from their own bad condition in time past, and the present more happy state into which they are brought, without any merit or deservings of their own, and whereinto by the same grace others may be brought also.

III. The apostle, having opened the duties of Christians in common, with the reasons respecting themselves, adds another from their goodness and usefulness to men. Observe, When he has opened the grace of God towards us, he immediately presses the necessity of good works ; for we must not expect the benefit of God's mercy, unless we make conscience of our duty (*v.* 8) : *This is a faithful saying, and these things I will that thou affirm constantly* (this is a true Christian doctrine of highest importance, and which ministers must most earnestly and constantly press and inculcate), *that those who have believed in God* do not think that a bare naked faith will save them ; but it must be an operative working faith, bringing forth the fruit of righteousness ; they must make it their care *to maintain good works,* not to do them occasionally only, and when opportunities come in their way, but to seek opportunities for doing them. *These things are good and profitable unto men :* these *good works,* say some, or *the teaching of these things* rather than idle questions, as follows. These things are good in themselves, and the teaching of them useful to mankind, making persons a common good in their places. Note, Ministers, in teaching, must see that they deliver what is sound and good in itself, and profitable to those that hear : all must be to the use of edifying both of persons and societies.

⁹ But avoid foolish questions and genealogies, and contentions, and strivings about the law; for they are unprofitable and vain. ¹⁰ A man that is a heretic after the first and second admonition reject; ¹¹ Knowing that he that is such is subverted, and sinneth, being condemned of himself. ¹² When I shall send Artemas unto thee, or Tychicus, be diligent to come unto me to Nicopolis : for I have determined there to winter. ¹³ Bring Zenas the lawyer and Apollos on their journey diligently, that nothing be wanting unto them. ¹⁴ And let our's [our people] also learn to maintain good works for necessary uses, that they be not unfruitful. ¹⁵ All that are with me salute thee. Greet them that love us in the faith. Grace *be* with you all. Amen

Here is the fifth and last thing in the matter of the epistle : what Titus should avoid in teaching ; how he should deal with a heretic : with some other directions. Observe,

I. That the apostle's meaning might be more clear and full, and especially fitted to the time and state of things in Crete, and the many judaizers among them, he tells Titus what, in teaching, he should shun, *v. 9.* There are needful questions to be discussed and cleared, such as make for improvement in useful knowledge ; but idle and foolish inquiries, tending neither to God's glory nor the edification of men, must be shunned. Some may have a show of wisdom, but are vain, as many among the Jewish doctors, as well as of later schoolmen, who abound with questions of no moment or use to faith or practice ; avoid these.—*And genealogies* (of the gods, say some, that the heathen poets made such noise about ; or rather those that the Jews were so curious in) : some lawful and useful enquiries might be made into these things, to see the fulfilling of the scriptures in some cases, and especially in the descent of Christ the Messiah ; but all that served to pomp only, and to feed vanity, in boasting of a long pedigree, and much more such as the Jewish teachers were ready to busy themselves in and trouble their hearers with, even since Christ had come, and that distinction of families and tribes had been taken away, as if they would build again that policy which now is abolished, these Titus must withstand as foolish and vain.—*And contentions, and strivings about the law.* There were those who were for the Mosaic rites and ceremonies, and would have them continued in the church, though by the gospel and the coming of Christ they were superseded and done away. Titus must give no countenance to these, but avoid and oppose them ; *for they are unprofitable and vain :* this is to be referred to all those *foolish questions and genealogies,* as well as those *strivings about the law.* They are so far from instructing and building up in godliness, that they are hindrances of it rather : the Christian religion and good works, which are to be maintained, will hereby be weakened and prejudiced, the peace of the church disturbed, and the progress of the gospel hindered. Observe, Ministers must not only teach things good and useful, but shun and oppose the contrary, what would corrupt the faith,

and hinder godliness and good works ; nor should people have itching ears,
but love and embrace sound doctrine, which tends most to the use of
edifying.

II. But because, after all, there will be *heresies* and *heretics* in the
church, the apostle next directs Titus what to do in such a case, and how
to deal with such, *v.* 10. He who forsakes the truth as it is in Christ
Jesus, who broaches false doctrines and propagates them to the corrupting
of the faith in weighty and momentous points, and breaks the peace of the
church about them, after due means used to reclaim him, must be rejected.
" Admonish him once and again, that, if possible, he may be brought back,
and thou mayest gain thy brother ; but, if this will not reduce him, that
others be not hurt, cast him out of the communion and warn all Christians
to avoid him.—*Knowing that he that is such is subverted* (turned off from
the foundation) *and sinneth* grievously, being *self-condemned.* Those who
will not be reclaimed by admonitions, but are obstinate in their sins and
errors, *are subverted and self-condemned* ; they inflict that punishment upon
themselves which the governors of the church should inflict upon them :
they throw themselves out of the church, and throw off its communion, and
so are self-condemned. Observe, 1. How great an evil real heresy is, not
lightly therefore to be charged upon any, though greatly to be taken heed
of by all. Such a one is *subverted* or perverted—a metaphor from a
building so ruined as to render it difficult if not impossible to repair and
raise it up again. Real heretics have seldom been recovered to the true
faith : not so much defect of judgment, as perverseness of the will, being
in the case, through pride, or ambition, or self-willedness, or covetousness,
or such like corruption, which therefore must be taken heed of : "Be
humble, love the truth and practise it, and damning heresy will be escaped."
2. Pains and patience must be used about those that err most grievously.
They are not easily and soon to be given up and cast off, but competent
time and means must be tried for their recovery. 3. The church's means
even with heretics are persuasive and rational. They must be admonished,
instructed, and warned ; so much νουθεσία imports. 4. Upon continued
obstinacy and irreclaimableness, the church has power, and is obliged, to
preserve its own purity, by severing such a corrupt member, which discipline
may by God's blessing become effectual to reform the offender, or if not it
will leave him the more inexcusable in his condemnation.

III. The apostle subjoins some further directions, *v.* 12, 13. Here are
two personal things enjoined :—

1. That Titus should hold himself ready to come to Paul at *Nicopolis* (a
city of Thrace, as is reckoned, on the borders of Macedonia), as soon as
Artemas or *Tychicus* should be sent to Crete, to supply his place, and take
care of the churches there when he should leave them. The apostle would
not have them in their young and weak state be without one or other of
chief sufficiency, to guide and help them. Titus, it seems, was not their
ordinary fixed bishop or pastor, but an evangelist, otherwise Paul would
not have called him so much from his charge. Of Artemas we read little,
but Tychicus is mentioned on many occasions with respect. Paul calls him
a beloved brother, and faithful minister, and fellow-servant in the Lord :
one fit therefore for the service intimated. When Paul says to Titus, *Be
diligent to come to me to Nicopolis, for I have determined there to winter,* it is
plain that the epistle was not written from Nicopolis, as the postscript
would have it, for then he would have said, I determined *here,* not *there,*
to winter.

2. The other personal charge to Titus is that he would bring two of his friends on their journey diligently, and see them furnished, so that nothing should be wanting to them. This was to be done, not as a piece of common civility only, but of Christian piety, out of respect both to them and the work they were sent about, which probably was to preach the gospel, or to be in some way serviceable to the churches. *Zenas* is styled *the lawyer*, whether in reference to the Roman or the Mosaic law, as having some time been his profession, is doubtful. *Apollos* was an eminent and faithful minister. Accompanying such persons part of their way, and accommodating them for their work and journeys, was a pious and needful service ; and to further this, and lay in for it, what the apostle had before exhorted Titus to teach (*v.* 8) he repeats here. *Let ours also learn to maintain good works, for necessary uses, that they be not unfruitful, v.* 14. Let Christians, those who have believed in God, learn to *maintain good works*, especially such as these supporting ministers in their work of preaching and spreading the gospel, hereby becoming *fellow-helpers to the truth,* 3 John, 5–8. *That they be not unfruitful.* Christianity is not a fruitless profession ; the professors of it must be *filled with the fruits of righteousness, which are by Jesus Christ, to the glory and praise of God.* It is not enough that they be harmless, but they must be profitable, doing good, as well as eschewing evil.—" *Let ours* set up and maintain some honest labour and employment, to provide for themselves and their families, that they be not unprofitable burdens on the earth ; " so some understand it. Let them not think that Christianity gives them a writ of ease ; no, it lays an obligation upon them to seek some honest work and calling, and therein *to abide with God.* This is of good report, will credit religion and be good to mankind ; they will not be unprofitable members of the body, not burdensome and chargeable to others, but enabled to be helpful to those in want. *To maintain good works for necessary uses ;* not living like drones on the labours of others, but themselves fruitful to the common benefit.

IV. The apostle concludes with salutations and benedictions, *v.* 5. Though perhaps not personally known (some of them at least), yet all by Paul testify their love and good wishes to Titus, owning him thereby in his work and stimulating him to go on therein. Great comfort and encouragement it is to have the heart and prayers of other Christians with and for us. *Greet those that love us in the faith* or *for the faith,* who are our loving fellow-Christians. Holiness, or the image of God in any, is the great endearing thing that gives strength to all other bonds, and is itself the best. *Grace be with you all. Amen.* This is the closing benediction, not to Titus alone, but to all the faithful with him, which shows that though the epistle bears the single name of Titus in the inscription, yet it was for the use of the churches there, and they were in the eye, and upon the heart, of the apostle, in the writing of it. " *Grace be with you all,* the love and favour of God, with the fruits and effects thereof, according to need, spiritual ones especially, and the increase and feeling of them more and more in your souls." This is the apostle's wish and prayer, showing his affection to them, his desire of their good, and a means of obtaining for them, and bringing down upon them, the thing requested. Observe, Grace is the chief thing to be wished and begged for, with respect to ourselves or others ; it is, summarily, all good. *Amen* shuts up the prayer, expressing desire and hope, that so it may, and so it shall be.

EXPOSITION OF THE EPISTLE OF ST. PAUL TO PHILEMON

THIS epistle to Philemon is placed the last of those with the name of Paul to them, perhaps because the shortest, and of an argument peculiar and different from all the others ; yet such as the Spirit of God, who indited it, saw would, in its kind, be very instructive and useful in the churches. The occasion of it was this :—Philemon, one of note and probably a minister in the church of Colosse, a city of Phrygia, had a servant named *Onesimus*, who, having purloined his goods, ran away from him, and in his rambles came to Rome, where Paul was then a prisoner for the gospel, and, providentially coming under his preaching, was, by the blessing of God, converted by him, after which he ministered awhile to the apostle in bonds, and might have been further useful to him, but, understanding him to be another man's servant, Paul would not, without his consent, detain him, but sends him back with this letter-commendatory, wherein he earnestly sues for his pardon and kind reception.

Before we enter on the exposition, such general things as follow may be taken notice of from the epistle and what relates to it ; namely, I. The goodness and mercy of God to a poor wandering sinner, bringing him by his gracious providence under the means, and making them effectual to his conversion. Thus came he to be *sought of him that asked not for him, and to be found of him that sought him not*, Isa. lxv. i. II. The great and endeared affection between a true convert and him whom God used to be the instrument of his conversion. Paul regards this poor fugitive now as his son in the faith, and terms him his *own bowels ;* and Onesimus readily serves Paul in prison, and would gladly have continued to do so, would duty have permitted ; but being another's servant, he must return and submit himself to his master, and be at his disposal. III. The tender and good spirit of this blessed apostle Paul. With what earnestness does he concern himself for the poor slave ! Being now, through his preaching, reconciled to God, he labours for reconciliation between him and his master. How pathetic a letter does he here write in his behalf ! Scarcely any argument is forgotten that could possibly be used in the case ; and all are pressed with such force that, had it been the greatest favour to himself that he was asking, he could not have used more. IV. The remarkable providence of God in preserving such a short writing as this, that might be thought of little concern to the church, being not only a letter to a particular person (as those to Timothy, and Titus, and Gaius, and the elect lady, likewise were), but of a private personal matter, namely, the receiving of a poor fugitive servant into the favour and family of his injured master. What in this is there that concerns the common salvation? And yet over this has there been a special divine care, it being given (as the other scriptures were) by *inspiration of God*, and in some sort, as they are, *profitable for doctrine, for reproof, for correction, and for instruction in righteousness*. God would have extant a proof and instance of his rich and free grace for the encouragement and comfort of the meanest and vilest of sinners, looking to him for mercy and forgiveness; and for instruction to ministers and others not to despise any, much less to judge them as to their final state, as if they were utter castaways, but rather to attempt their conversion, hoping they may be saved; likewise how to behave towards them. Joy must be on earth, as well as there is in heaven, over one sinner who repenteth. Such must now be loved, and helped, and confirmed in good, and furthered in it; and in their outward concerns, their comfort and welfare must be consulted and promoted as much as possible. And, on their part, they must be humble and grateful, acknowledging God and his instruments in what good they have received, ready to all suitable returns, making what reparation they can in case of injuries, and living a life of thankfulness and obedience. To such purposes may this epistle have been written and preserved. And perhaps, V. There may be something further in all this; at least, by way of allusion, it is applicable to the mediation and intercession of Christ for poor sinners. We, like Onesimus, were revolters from God's service, and had injured him in his rights. Jesus Christ finds us, and by his grace works a change in us, and then intercedes for us with the Father, that we may be received into his favour and family again, and past offences may be forgiven; and we are sure that the *Father heareth him always*. There is no reason to doubt but Paul prevailed with Philemon to forgive and receive Onesimus: and more reason have we to be confident that the intercession of Christ with the Father is prevalent for the acceptance of all whose case he takes in hand and recommends to him. From these general observations, we come to the epistle itself.

In this epistle we have, I. The preface, ver. 1-7. II. The substance and body of it, ver. 8-21. And then the conclusion, ver. 22, to the end.

PAUL, a prisoner of Jesus Christ, and Timothy *our* brother, unto Philemon our dearly beloved, and fellowlabourer,
2 And to *our* beloved Apphia, and Archippus our fellowsoldier,

and to the church in thy house: ³ Grace to you, and peace, from God our Father and the Lord Jesus Christ. ⁴ I thank my God, making mention of thee always in my prayers, ⁵ Hearing of thy love and faith, which thou hast toward the Lord Jesus, and toward all saints; ⁶ That the communication [fellowship] of thy faith may become effectual by the acknowledging [in the knowledge] of every good thing which is in you in [unto] Christ Jesus. ⁷ For we have great joy and consolation in thy love, because the bowels [hearts] of the saints are refreshed by thee, brother.

I. In the first two verses of the preface we have the persons from and to whom it is written, with some annexed note or title, implying somewhat of argument to the purpose of the letter.

1. The persons writing : Paul, the principal, who calls himself *a prisoner of Jesus Christ*, that is, for Jesus Christ. To be a prisoner simply is no comfort nor honour : but such as Paul was, *for the faith and preaching of the gospel*, this was true glory and proper to move Philemon upon the request made to him by such a one. A petition from one suffering for Christ and his gospel would surely be tenderly regarded by a believer and minister of Christ, especially when strengthened too with the concurrence of Timothy, one eminent in the church, sometimes called by Paul *his son in the faith*, but now, it is likely, grown more in years, he styles him *his brother*. What could be denied to two such petitioners? Paul is not slight in serving a poor convert ; he gets all the additional help he can in it.

2. The persons written to are *Philemon and Apphia*, and with them Archippus, and the church in Philemon's house. Philemon, the master of Onesimus, was the principal, to whom the letter is inscribed, the head of the family, in whom were the authority and power of taking in or shutting out, and whose property Onesimus was : with him therefore chiefly lay the business. *To Philemon our dearly beloved, and fellow-labourer ;* a good man he was, and probably a minister, and on both accounts dearly beloved by Paul. *A lover of good men* is one property of a good minister (Tit. i. 8), and especially must such love those who labour with them in the work of the gospel, and who are faithful therein. The general calling as Christians knits those together who are Christians ; but, when conjunction in the special calling as ministers is added, this will be further endearing. Paul, in the highest degree of ministry, not only calls Timothy, an evangelist, his brother, but Philemon, an ordinary pastor, his dearly beloved fellow-labourer—an example of humility and condescension, and of all affectionate regards, even in those that are highest in the church, towards others that are labourers in the same special heavenly calling. With Philemon Apphia is joined, probably his yoke-fellow ; and, having a concern in the domestic affairs, the apostle directs to her likewise. She was a party offended and injured by Onesimus, and therefore proper to be taken notice of in a letter for reconciliation and forgiveness. Justice and prudence would direct Paul to this express notice of her, who might be helpful in furthering the good ends of his writing. She is set before Archippus, as more concerned and having more interest. A kind conjunction there is in domestic matters between husband and wife whose interests

are one, and whose affections and actings must correspond. These are the principal parties written to. The less principal are, *Archippus, and the church in Philemon's house.* Archippus was a minister in the church of Colosse, Philemon's friend, and probably co-pastor with him ; Paul might think him one whom Philemon would advise with, and who might be capable of furthering the good work of peace-making and forgiveness, and therefore might judge fit to put him in the inscription of the letter, with the adjunct of *fellow-soldier.* He had called Philemon his *fellow-labourer.* Ministers must look on themselves as labourers and soldiers, who must therefore take pains, and endure hardship ; they must stand on their guard, and make good their post ; must look on one another as fellow-labourers, and fellow-soldiers, who must stand together, and strengthen one another's hands and hearts in any work of their holy function and calling : they need see to it that they be provided with spiritual weapons, and skill to use them ; as labourers they must minister the word, and sacraments, and discipline, and watch over souls, *as those that must give an account of them ;* and, as soldiers, they must fight the Lord's battles, and not entangle themselves in the things of this life, but attend to the pleasing of him who hath chosen them to be soldiers, 2 Tim. ii. 4. To these it is added, *And to the church in thy house,* his whole family, in which the worship of God was kept up, so that he had, as it were, a church in his house. Observe, (1.) Families which generally may be most pious and orderly may yet have one or other in them impious and wicked. This was the aggravation of Onesimus's sin, that it was where he might and should have learned better ; it is likely that he was secret in his misconduct, till his flight discovered him. Hearts are unknown but to God, till overt acts discover them. (2.) This one evil servant did not hinder Philemon's house from being called and counted a church for the religious worship and order that were kept up in it ; and such should all families be—nurseries of religion, societies where God is called on, his word is read, his sabbaths are observed, and the members are instructed in the knowledge of him and of their duty to him, neglect of which is followed with ignorance and all corruption. Wicked families are nurseries for hell, as good ones are for heaven. (3.) Masters and others of the family may not think it enough to be good, singly and severally in their personal capacities, but they must be socially so ; as here Philemon's house was a church ; and Paul, for some concern that all might have in this matter of Onesimus, directs to them all, that their affection as well as Philemon's might return to him, and that in their way and place they might further, and not hinder, the reconciliation wished and sought. Desirable it is that all in a family be well affected towards one another, for furthering their particular welfare and for the common good and benefit of all. On such accounts might it be that Paul inscribed his letter here so generally, that all might be the more ready to own and receive this poor convert, and to behave affectionately towards him. Next to this inscription is,

II. The apostle's salutation of those named by him (*v.* 3) : *Grace to you and peace from God our Father and the Lord Jesus Christ.* This is the token in every epistle ; so the apostle writes. He is a hearty well-wisher to all his friends, and wishes for them the best things ; not gold, nor silver, nor any earthly good, in the first or chief place, but *grace and peace from God in Christ ;* he cannot give them himself, but he prays for them from him who can bestow them. *Grace,* the free favour and good-will of God, the spring and fountain of all blessings ; *and peace,* all good, as the fruit

and effect of that grace. *To you*, that is, be bestowed on you, and continued to you, with the comfortable feeling and sense of it in yourselves. *From God our Father and the Lord Jesus Christ.* The Holy Spirit also is understood, though not named ; for all acts towards the creatures are of the whole Trinity : from the Father, who is our Father in Christ, the first in order of acting as of subsisting ; and from Christ, his favour and good-will as God, and the fruits of it through him as Mediator, God-man. It is in the beloved that we are accepted, and through him we have peace and all good things, who is, with the Father and Spirit, to be looked to and blessed and praised for all, and to be owned, not only as Jesus and Christ, but as Lord also. In 2 Cor. xiii. 14 the apostle's benediction is full : *The grace of the Lord Jesus Christ, and the love of God, and the communion of the Holy Ghost, be with you all, Amen.* Observe, Spiritual blessings are first and especially to be sought for ourselves and others. The favour of God and peace with him, as in itself it is the best and most desirable good, so is it the cause of all other, and what puts sweetness into every mercy and can make happy even in the want of all earthly things. *Though there be no herd in the stall, and the labour of the olive fail,* yet may such *rejoice in the Lord, and joy in the God of their salvation,* Hab. iii. 17, 18. *There are many that say, Who will show us any good ?* But, if God *lift up the light of his countenance,* this will put more joy and gladness into the heart than all worldly increase, Ps. iv. 6, 7. And Num. vi. 26, *The Lord lift up the light of his conutenance upon thee, and give thee peace.* In this is summarily all good, and from this one fountain, God the *Father, Son,* and *Spirit,* all comes. After this salutation of the apostle to Philemon, and his friends and family, for better making way still for his suit to him,

III. He expresses the singular affection he had for him, by thanksgiving and prayer to God in his behalf, and the great joy for the many good things he knew and heard to be in him, *v.* 4–7. The apostle's thanksgiving and prayer for Philemon are here set forth by the object, circumstance, and matter of them, with the way whereby much of the knowledge of Philemon's goodness came to him.

1. Here is the object of Paul's praises and prayers for Philemon : *I thank my God, making mention of thee in my prayers, v.* 4. Observe. (1.) God is the author of all the good that is in any, or that is done by them. *From me is thy fruit found,* Hos. xiv. 8. To him therefore is all the praise due. 1 Chron. xxix. 13, 14, *But* [or *for*] *who am I and what is my people, that we should be able to offer so willingly after this sort ? For all things come of thee,* both wherewith to offer, and the will and heart to do it. On this account (says he) *we thank thee our God, and praise thy glorious name.* (2.) It is the privilege of good men that in their praises and prayers they come to God as their God : *Our God, we thank thee,* said David ; and *I thank my God,* said Paul. (3.) Our prayers and praises should be offered up to God, not for ourselves only, but for others also. Private addresses should not be altogether with a private spirit, minding our own things only, but others must be remembered by us. We must be affected with joy and thankfulness for any good in them, or done by them, or bestowed on them, as far as is known to us, and seek for them what they need. In this lies no little part of the communion of saints. Paul in his private thanksgivings and prayers, was often particular in remembering his friends : *I thank my God, making mention of thee in my prayers ;* sometimes it may be by name, or at least having them particularly in his thoughts ; and

God knows who is meant, though not named. This is a means of exercising love, and obtaining good for others. *Strive with me, by your prayers to God for me*, said the apostle : and what he desired for himself he surely practised on behalf of others ; so should all. *Pray one for another*, says James, v. 16.

2. Here is the circumstance : *Always making mention of thee. Always* —usually not once or twice only, but frequently. So must we remember Christian friends much and often, as their case may need, bearing them in our thoughts and upon our hearts before our God.

3. Here is the matter both of his praises and prayers, in reference to Philemon.

(1.) Of his praises. [1.] He thanks God for the love which he heard Philemon had towards the Lord Jesus. He is to be loved as God super-latively, as his divine perfections require ; and as related to us, the Lord, and our Lord, our Maker, Redeemer, and Saviour, who loved us, and gave himself for us. Paul thanks God for what he heard of this, the signal marks and expressions of it in Philemon. [2.] For his faith in Christ also. Love to Christ, and faith in him, are prime Christian graces, for which there is great ground of praise to God, where he has blessed any with them, as Rom. i. 8, *I thank my God* because *your faith is published throughout the world ;* and, in reference to the Colossians (*ch.* I. 3, 4), *We give thanks to God since we heard of your faith in Christ Jesus.* This is a saving grace, and the very principle of Christian life and of all good works. [3.] He praises God likewise for Philemon's love to all the saints. These two must go together ; for he who *loveth him that begat must and* will *love those also that are begotten of him.* The apostle joins them in that (Col. i. 3, 4), *We give thanks to God since we heard of your faith in Christ Jesus, and of the love which you have to all the saints.* These bear the image of Christ, which will be loved by every Christian. Different sentiments and ways in what is not essential will not make a difference of affection as to the truth, though difference in the degrees of love will be according as more or less of that image is discerned. Mere external differences are nothing here. Paul calls a poor converted slave *his bowels.* We must love, as God does, all saints. Paul thanked God for the good that was not only in the churches, but in the particular persons he wrote to, and though this too was known to him merely by report : *Hearing of thy love and faith which thou hast towards the Lord Jesus, and towards all saints.* This was what he enquired after concerning his friends, the truth, and growth, and fruitfulness of their graces, their faith in Christ, and love to him and to all the saints. Love to saints, if it be sincere, will be catholic and universal love towards all saints ; but faith and love, though in the heart they are hidden things, are known by the effects of them. There-fore,

(2.) The apostle joins prayer with his praises, that the fruits of Philemon's faith and love might be more and more conspicuous, so as that the com-munication of them might constrain others to the acknowledgment of all the good things that were in him and in his house towards Christ Jesus ; that their *light might so shine before men that they, seeing their good works, might* be stirred up to imitate them, and to *glorify their Father who is in heaven.* Good works must be done, not of vain-glory to be seen, yet such as may be seen to God's glory and the good of men.

4. He adds a reason, both of his prayer and his praises (*v.* 7) : *For " we have great joy and consolation in thy love, because the bowels of the saints are*

refreshed by thee, brother. The good thou hast done and still doest is abundant matter of joy and comfort to me and others, who therefore desire you may continue and abound in such good fruits more and more, to God's honour and the credit of religion. *The administration of this service not only supplieth the want of the saints, but is abundant also by many thanksgivings unto God,"* 2 Cor. ix. 12.

8 Wherefore, though I might be much bold in Christ to enjoin thee that which is convenient [**befitting**], 9 Yet for love's sake I rather beseech *thee*, being such a one as Paul the aged, and now also a prisoner of Jesus Christ. 10 I beseech thee for my son Onesimus, whom I have begotten in my bonds : 11 Which in time past was to thee unprofitable, but now profitable to thee and to me : 12 Whom I have sent again : thou therefore receive him, that is, mine own bowels [**Whom I have sent back to thee in his own person, that is, my very heart**] : 13 Whom I would have retained with me, that in thy stead [**behalf**] he might have ministered unto me in the bonds of the gospel : 14 But without thy mind would I do nothing; that thy benefit [**goodness**] should not be as it were of necessity, but willingly. 15 For perhaps he therefore departed for a season, that thou shouldst receive him for ever; 16 Not now as a servant, but above a servant, a brother beloved, specially to me, but how much more unto thee, both in the flesh, and in the Lord ? 17 If thou count me therefore a partner, receive him as myself. 18 If he hath wronged thee, or oweth *thee* ought, put that on mine account ; 19 I Paul have written *it* with mine own hand, I will repay *it :* albeit I do not say to thee how thou owest unto me even thine own self besides. 20 Yea, brother, let me have joy of thee in the Lord : refresh my bowels in the Lord. 21 Having confidence in thy obedience I wrote unto thee, knowing that thou wilt also do more than I say. 22 But withal prepare me also a lodging : for I trust that through your prayers I shall be given unto you. 23 There salute thee Epaphras, my fellow-prisoner in Christ Jesus ; 24 Marcus, Aristarchus, Demas, Lucas, my fellowlabourers. 25 The grace of our Lord Jesus Christ *be* with your spirit. Amen.

We have here,

I. The main business of the epistle, which was to plead with Philemon on behalf of Onesimus, that he would receive him and be reconciled to him. Many arguments Paul urges for this purpose, *v.* 8–21. The

1*st Argument* is taken from what was before noted, and is carried in the illative *wherefore ;* "Seeing so much good is reported of thee and found in thee, especially thy love to all saints, now let me see it on a fresh and further occasion ; *refresh the bowels of Onesimus and mine also,* in forgiving and receiving him, who is now a convert, and so a saint indeed, and meet for thy favour and love." Observe, A disposition to do good, together with past instances and expressions of it, is a good handle to take hold of for pressing to more. "*Be not weary of well-doing,* go on as thou art able, and as new objects and occasions occur, to do the same still." The

2d Argument is from the authority of him that was now making this request to him : *I might be very bold in Christ to enjoin thee that which is convenient, v.* 8. The apostles had under Christ great power in the church over the ordinary ministers, as well as the members of it, for edification ; they might require of them what was fit, and were therein to be obeyed, which Philemon should consider. This was a matter within the compass of the apostle's power to require, though he would not in this instance act up to it. Observe, Ministers, whatever their power be in the church, are to use prudence in the exercise of it ; they may not unseasonably, nor further than is requisite, put it forth ; in all they must use godly wisdom and discretion. Wherefore this may be a

3d Argument, Waiving the authority which yet he had to require, he chooses to entreat it of him (*v.* 9) : *Yet for love's sake I rather beseech thee.* Observe, It is no disparagement for those who have power to be conde- scending, and sometimes even to beseech, where, in strictness of right, they might command ; so does Paul here, though an apostle : he entreats where he might enjoin, he argues from love rather than authority, which doubt- less must carry engaging influence with it. And especially, which may be a

4th Argument, When any circumstance of the person pleading gives addi- tional force to his petition, as here : *Being such a one as Paul the aged, and now also a prisoner of Jesus Christ.* Years bespeak respect ; and the motions of such, in things lawful and fit, should be received with regard. The request of an aged apostle, and now suffering for Christ and his gospel, should be tenderly considered. "If thou wilt do any thing for a poor aged prisoner, to comfort me in my bonds, and make my chain lighter, grant me this which I desire : hereby in a manner you will do honour to Christ in the person of an aged suffering servant of his, which doubtless he will take as done to himself." He makes also a

5th Argument, From the spiritual relation now between Onesimus and himself : *I beseech thee for my son Onesimus, whom I have begotten in my bonds, v.* 10. "Though of right and in a civil respect he be thy servant, yet in a spiritual sense he is now a son to me, God having made me the instrument of his conversion, even here, where I am a prisoner for Christ's sake." Thus does God sometimes honour and comfort his suffering servants, not only working good in themselves by their sufferings, exercising and improving thereby their own graces, but making them a means of much spiritual good to others, either of their conversion, as of Onesimus here, or of their confirmation and strengthening, as Phil. i. 14, *Many brethren, wax- ing confident by my bonds, are much more bold to speak the word of the Lord without fear.* When God's servants are bound, yet his word and Spirit are not bound ; spiritual children may then be born to them. The apostle lays an emphasis here : *My son, whom I have begotten in my bonds ;* he was dear to him, and he hoped would be so to Philemon, under this considera- tion. Prison-mercies are sweet and much set by. Paul makes an argument to Philemon from this dear relation that now was between Onesimus and him, his son begotten in his bonds. And a

6th Argument is from Philemon's own interest : *Who in time past was*

to thee unprofitable, but now profitable to thee and to me, v. 11. Observe, (1.) Unsanctified persons are unprofitable persons; they answer not the great end of their being and relations. Grace makes good for somewhat: *"In time past unprofitable, but now profitable,* inclined and fitted to be so, and will be so to thee, his master, if thou receive him, as he has since his conversion been here to me, ministering to me in my confinement." There seems an allusion to the name Onesimus, which signifies *profitable.* Now he will answer to his name. It may be noted also how the apostle speaks in this matter, not as Onesimus's former case and conduct might warrant; he had wronged his master, and ran away from him, and lived as if he were his own and not his; yet as God covers the sins of penitents, forgives and does not upbraid, so should men. How tenderly does Paul here speak! Not that Onesimus's sin was small, nor that he would have any, much less himself, to take it so; but having been humbled for it, and doubtless taken shame to himself on account thereof, the apostle now would not sink his spirit by continuing to load and burden him therewith, but speaks thus tenderly when he is pleading with Philemon not to make severe reflections on his servant's misconduct, but to forgive. (2.) What happy changes conversion makes—of evil good! of unprofitable useful! Religious servants are a treasure in a family. Such will make conscience of their time and trusts, promoting the interests of those whom they serve, and managing all they can for the best. This then is the argument here urged: "It will now be for thy advantage to receive him: thus changed, as he is, thou mayest expect him to be a dutiful and faithful servant, though in time past he was not so." Whereupon,

7th Argument, He urges Philemon from the strong affection that he had to Onesimus. He had mentioned the spiritual relation before, *My son begotten in my bonds;* and now he signifies how dear he was to him: *Thou therefore receive him, that is my own bowels, v.* 12. "I love him as I do myself, and have sent him back to thee for this end, that thou shouldst receive him; do it therefore for my sake, receive him as one thus dear to me." Observe, Even good men may sometimes need great earnestness and entreaty to lay their passions, let go their resentments, and forgive those who have injured and offended them. Some have thought it to look this way, when Paul is so pathetic and earnest, mustering up so many pleas and arguments to gain what he requests. Philemon, a Phrygian, might perhaps be naturally of a rough and difficult temper, and thence need no little pains in touching all the springs that might move him to forgiveness and reconciliation; but rather should we strive to be like God, who is *slow to anger, ready to forgive, and abundant in pardons.* And again, an

8th Argument is from the apostle's denying himself in sending back Onesimus: though he might have presumed upon Philemon's leave to detain him longer, yet he would not, *v.* 13, 14. Paul was now in prison, and wanted a friend or servant to act for him, and assist him, for which he found Onesimus fit and ready, and therefore would have detained him to minister to him, instead of Philemon himself, whom if he had requested to have come to him in person for such purpose, he might have presumed he would not have refused; much less might he have reckoned that he would be unwilling his servant should do this in his stead; yet he would not take this liberty, though his circumstances needed it: *I have sent him back* to thee, that any good office of thine to me might not be *of necessity, but willingly.* Observe, Good deeds are most acceptable to God and man when done with most freedom. And Paul herein notwithstanding his apostolical power,

would show what regard he had to civil rights, which Christianity does by
no means supersede or weaken, but rather confirm and strengthen. Onesimus, he knew, was Philemon's servant, and therefore without his consent
not to be detained from him. In his unconverted state he had violated
that right, and withdrawn himself, to his master's injury ; but, now that
he had seen his sin and repented, he was willing and desirous to return to
his duty, and Paul would not hinder this, but rather further it. He
might indeed have presumed on Philemon's willingness ; but, notwithstanding his need, he would deny himself rather than take that way. And
he further urges,

9th Argument, that such a change was now wrought in Onesimus that
Philemon needed not fear his ever running from him, or injuring him any
more : *For perhaps he therefore departed for a season, that thou shouldst
receive him for ever, v.* 15. There are those of whom Solomon says, *If thou
deliver them, thou must do it again* (Prov. xix. 19) ; but the change wrought
in Onesimus was such that he would never again need one thus to intercede
for him. Charity would so hope and judge, yea, so it would be ; yet the
apostle speaks cautiously, that none might be bold to make another such
experiment in expectation of a like gracious issue. Observe, (1.) In matters
that may be wrested to ill, ministers must speak warily, that kind providences of God towards sinners be not abused to encouragements to sin, or
abatements of just abhorrence of it : *Perhaps he therefore departed from thee
for a season*, &c. (2.) How tenderly still the sins of penitents are spoken
of ; he calls it a *departure for a season*, instead of giving it the term that
it deserved. As overruled and ordered by God, it was *a departure ;* but
in itself, and in respect of the disposition and manner of the act, it was a
criminal going away. When we speak of the nature of any sin or offence
against God, the evil of it is not to be lessened ; but in the person of a
penitent sinner, as God covers it, so must we : " *He departed for a season,
that thou shouldst receive him for ever*, that upon conversion he may return,
and be a faithful and useful servant to thee as long as he lives." *Bray a
fool in a mortar, yet will not his folly depart from him.* But it is not so
with true penitents : they will not return to folly. (3.) Observe the
wisdom, and goodness, and power of God, in causing that to end so happily
which was begun and carried on for some time so wickedly, thus regarding
a poor vassal, one of such low rank and condition and so little regarded by
men, working so good and great a change in him who was so far gone in
evil ways, who had wronged a master so good, had run from a family so
pious, from the means of grace, the church in his house, that he should be
led into the way of salvation who had fled from it, and find means made
effectual at Rome who had been hardened under them at Colosse. What
riches are here of divine grace ! None so low, nor mean, nor vile, as utterly
to be despaired of. God can meet with them when running from him ;
can make means effectual at one time and place, which have not been so
at another. So was it in this instance of Onesimus ; having returned to
God, he now returns to his master, who will have more service and better
hold of him than ever—by conscience of his duty and faithfulness in it to
his life's end ; his interest therefore it will be now to receive him. So
God often brings gain to his people out of their losses. And, besides
interest, a

10th Argument is taken from the capacity under which Onesimus now
would return, and must be received by Philemon (*v.* 16) : " *Not now as a
servant* (that is, not merely or so much), *but above a servant* (in a spiritual

respect), *a brother beloved,* one to be owned as a brother in Christ, and to be beloved as such, upon account of this holy change that is wrought in him, and one therefore who will be useful unto thee upon better principles and in a better manner than before, who will love and promote the best things in thy family, be a blessing in it, and help to keep up the church that is in thy house." Observe, (1.) There is a spiritual brotherhood between all true believers, however distinguished in civil and outward respects; they are all children of the same heavenly Father, have a right to the same spiritual privileges and benefits, must love and do all good offices to and for one another as brethren, though still in the same rank, and degree, and station, wherein they were called. Christianity does not annul nor confound the respective civil duties, but strengthens the obligation to them, and directs to a right discharge of them. (2.) Religious servants are more than mere ordinary servants; they have grace in their hearts, and have found grace in God's sight, and so will in the sight of religious masters. Ps. ci. 6, *Mine eyes are upon the faithful of the land, that they may dwell with me. He that walketh in a perfect way, he shall serve me.* "Onesimus having now become such, receive and regard him as one that is partaker of the same common faith, and so *a brother beloved, specially to me* who have been the instrument of his conversion." Good ministers love not so much according to the outward good which they receive as the spiritual good which they do. Paul called Onesimus his *own bowels,* and other converts his *joy and crown.* "*A brother beloved, specially to me, but how much more to thee, both in the flesh and in the Lord;* by a double tie therefore (both civil and religious) thy servant: thy property, one of thy house and family, and now, in a spiritual respect, thy brother in Christ, which heightens the engagement. He is God's servant and thine too; here are more ties than he is under to me. How readily therefore should he be received and loved by thee, as one of thy family and one of the true faith, one of thy house and one of the church in thy house!" This argument is strengthened by another, the

11*th Argument,* From the communion of saints: *If thou count me therefore a partner, receive him as myself, v.* 17. There is a fellowship among saints; they have interest one in another, and must love and act accordingly. "Now show thy love to me, and the interest I have in thee, by loving and receiving one so near and dear to me, even as myself; own and treat him as thou wouldst me, with a like ready and true, though perhaps not equal, affection." But why such concern and earnestness for a servant. a slave, and such a one as had misbehaved? *Answer,* Onesimus being now penitent, it was doubtless to encourage him, and to support him against the fears he might have in returning to a master whom he had so much abused and wronged, to keep him from sinking into despondency and dejection, and encourage him to his duty. Wise and good ministers will have great and tender care of young converts, to encourage and hearten them what they can to and in their duty. *Objection,* But Onesimus had wronged as well as offended his master. The answer to this makes a

12*th Argument,* A promise of satisfaction to Philemon: *If he hath wronged thee, or oweth thee aught,* &c., *v.* 18, 19. Here are three things:

(1.) A confession of Onesimus's debt to Philemon: *If he hath wronged thee, or oweth thee aught.* It is not an *if* of doubting, but of illation and concession; *seeing he hath wronged thee,* and thereby has become indebted to thee; such an *if* as Col. iii. 1, and 2 Pet. ii. 4, &c. Observe, True penitents will be ingenuous in owning their faults, as doubtless Onesimus had been to Paul, upon his being awakened and being brought to repentance ; and especially is this to be done in cases of injury to others. Onesimus by Paul owns the wrong. And,

(2.) Paul here engages for satisfaction : *Put that on my account ; I Paul have written it with my own hand, I will repay it.* Observe, [1.] The communion of saints does not destroy distinction of property : Onesimus, now converted, and become a brother beloved, is yet Philemon's servant still, and indebted to him for wrongs that he had done, and not to be discharged but by free and voluntary remission, or on reparation made by himself, or some other in his behalf, which part, rather than fail, the apostle undertakes for him. [2.] Suretyship is not in all cases unlawful, but in some is a good and merciful undertaking. Only know the person and case, be not *surety for a stranger* (Prov. xi. 15), and go not beyond ability ; help thy friend thou mayest, as far as will comport with justice and prudence. And how happy for us that Christ would be made the surety of a better covenant (Heb. vii. 22), that he would be made *sin for us who knew no sin, that we might be made the righteousness of God in him.* And, [3.] Formal securities by writing, as well as by word and promise, may be required and given. Persons die, and words may be forgotten or mistaken ; writing better preserves right and peace, and has been in use with good persons, as well as others, in all ages, Jer. xxxii. 9, &c. ; Luke xvi. 5-7. It was much that Paul, who lived on contributions himself, would undertake to make good all loss by an evil servant to his master ; but hereby he expresses his real and great affection for Onesimus, and his full belief of the sincerity of his conversion : and he might have hope that, notwithstanding this generous offer, Philemon would not insist on it, but freely remit all, considering,

(3.) The reason of things between him and Philemon : "*Albeit, I do not say to thee how thou owest unto me even thy own self besides ;* thou wilt remember, without my reminding thee, that thou art on other accounts more in debt to me than this comes to." Modesty in self-praises is true praise. The apostle glances at the benefits he had conferred on Philemon : "That thou art any thing in grace and acceptation with God, or enjoyest any thing in a right and comfortable manner, it is, under God, owing to my ministry. I have been the instrument in his hand of all that spiritual good to thee ; and what thy obligation to me on this account is I leave to thee to consider. Thy forgiving a pecuniary debt to a poor penitent for my sake and at my request, and which, however, I now take upon myself to answer, thy remitting it to him, or to me, now his surety, thou wilt confess, is not so great a thing ; here is more *per contra: Thou owest to me even thy ownself besides.*" Observe, How great the endearments are between ministers and those towards whom their endeavours have been blessed to their conversion or spiritual edification ! *If it had been possible* (said Paul to the Galatians), *you would have plucked out your own eyes, and have given them to me,* Gal. iv. 15. On the other hand he calls them his *children, of whom he travailed again, till Christ was formed in them,* that is, the likeness of Christ more fully. So 1 Thess. ii. 8, *We were willing to have imparted to you not the gospel of God only, but also our own souls, because you were dear unto us.* By way of allusion, this may illustrate Christ's undertaking for us. We had revolted from God, and by sin had wronged him, but Christ undertakes to make satisfaction, *the just for the unjust, that he might bring us unto God.* "If the sinner owes thee aught, put it upon my account, I will pay the debt ; let his iniquity be laid on me, I will bear the penalty." Further, a

13*th Argument* is from the joy and comfort the apostle hereby would have on Philemon's own account, as well as on Onesimus's in such a seasonable and acceptable fruit of Philemon's faith and obedience : *Yea, brother, let me have joy of thee in the Lord : refresh my bowels in the Lord, v.* 20. Philemon was Paul's son in the faith, yet he entreats him as a brother ; Onesimus a poor slave, yet he solicits for him as if he were seeking some great thing for himself. How pathetic is he ! " *Yea, brother, or O my brother* (it is an adverb of wishing or desiring), *let me have joy of thee in the Lord.* Thou knowest that I am now a prisoner of the Lord, for his sake and cause, and need all the comfort and support that my friends in Christ can give me : now this will be a joy to me, I shall *have joy of thee in the Lord,* as seeing such an evidence and fruit of thy own Christian faith and love, and on Onesimus's account, who hereby will be relieved and encouraged." Observe, (1.) Christians should do the things that may rejoice the hearts of one another, both people and minister reciprocally, and ministers of their brethren. From the world they expect trouble ; and where may they look for comfort and joy but in one another ? (2.) Fruits of faith and obedience in people are the minister's greatest joy, especially the more of love appears in them to Christ and his members, forgiving injuries, showing compassion, being merciful as their heavenly Father is merciful. " *Refresh my bowels in the Lord.* It is not any carnal selfish respect I am actuated by, but what is pleasing to Christ, and that he may have honour therein. Observe, [1.] The Lord's honour and service are a Christian's chief aim in all things. And, [2.] It is meat and drink to a good minister to see people ready and zealous in what is good, especially in acts of charity and beneficence, as occasions occur, forgiving injuries, remitting somewhat of their right, and the like. And, once more, his last, which is the

14*th Argument,* Lies in the good hope and opinion which he expresses of Philemon : *Having confidence in thy obedience, I wrote unto thee, knowing that thou wilt also do more than I say, v.* 21. Good thoughts and expectations of us more strongly move and engage us to do the things expected from us. The apostle knew Philemon to be a good man, and was thence persuaded of his readiness to do good, and that not in a scanty and niggardly manner, but with a free and liberal hand. Observe, Good persons will be ready for good works, and not narrow and pinching, but abundant in them. Isa. xxxii. 8, *The liberal deviseth liberal things.* The Macedonians first gave themselves to the Lord, and then to his apostles by the will of God, to do what good they could with what they had, according as occasions offered.

Thus far is the substance and body of the epistle. We have,

II. The conclusion, where,

1. He signifies his good hope of deliverance, through their prayers, and that shortly he might see them, desiring Philemon to make provision for him : *But withal prepare me also a lodging ; for I trust that through your prayers I shall be given unto you, v.* 22. *But withal,* or *moreover.* He comes to another thing, yet, as may seem, not without some eye to the matter which he had been upon, that might be furthered by this intimation that he hoped he should himself soon follow, and know the effect of his epistle, which Philemon would therefore be the more stirred up to see might be to his satisfaction. Now here is,

(1.) The thing requested : *Prepare me also a lodging ;* under this all necessaries for a stranger are included. He wills Philemon to do it, intending to be his guest, as most to his purpose. Observe, Hospitality is a great Christian duty, especially in ministers, and towards ministers, such as the apostle was, coming out of such dangers and sufferings for Christ and his gospel. Who would not show the utmost of affectionate regards to such a one? It is an honourable title that he gives Gaius (Rom. xvi. 23), *My host, and of the whole church.* Onesiphorus is also affectionately remembered by the apostle on this account (2 Tim. i. 16, 18), *The Lord give mercy to the house of Onesiphorus; for he oft refreshed me and was not ashamed of my chain ; and in how many things he ministered to me at Ephesus, thou knowest.*

(2.) Here is the ground of the apostle's request : *For I trust that through your prayers I shall be given unto you.* He did not know how God might deal with him, but the benefit of prayer he had often found, and hoped he should again, for deliverance, and liberty to come to them. Observe, [1.] Our dependence is on God for life and liberty and opportunity of service ; all is by divine pleasure. [2.] When abridged of these or any other mercies, our trust and hope must be in God, without fainting or succumbing, while our case is depending. But yet, [3.] Trust must be with the use of means, prayer especially, though no other should be at hand : this hath unlocked heaven and opened prison-doors. *The fervent effectual prayer of the righteous availeth much.* [4.] Prayer of people for ministers, especially when they are in distress and danger, is their great duty ; ministers need and request it. Paul, though an apostle, did so with much earnestness, Rom. xv. 30 ; 2 Cor. i. 11 ; Eph. vi. 18, 19 ; 1 Thess. v. 25. The least may in this way be helpful to the greatest. Yet, [5.] Though prayer obtains, yet it does not merit the things obtained : they are God's gift, and Christ's purchase. *I trust that through your prayers, χαρισθήσομαι ὑμῖν—I shall be freely bestowed on you.* What God gives, he will yet be sought to for, that mercies may be valued the more, and known whence they come, and God may have the praise. Ministers' lives and labours are for the people's good ; the office was set up for them ; *he gave gifts for men, apostles,* &c. Eph. iv. 8, 11, 12. Their gifts, and labours, and lives, all are for their benefit. 1 Cor. iii. 21, 22, *All things are yours, Apollos, Cephas,* &c. [6.] In praying for faithful ministers, people in effect pray for themselves : " *I trust I shall be given unto you,* for your service, and comfort, and edification in Christ." See 2 Cor. iv. 15. [7.] Observe the humility of the apostle ; his liberty, should he have it, he would own to be through their prayers, as well as, or more than, his own ; he mentions them only through the high thoughts he had of the prayers of many, and the regard God would show to his praying people. Thus of the first thing in the apostle's conclusion.

2. He sends salutations from one who was his fellow-prisoner, and four more who were his fellow-labourers, *v.* 23, 24. Saluting is wishing health and peace. Christianity is no enemy to courtesy, but enjoins it, 1 Pet. iii. 8. It is a mere expression of love and respect, and a means of preserving and nourishing them. *There salute thee Epaphras, my fellow-prisoner in Christ Jesus.* He was of Colosse, and so countryman and fellow-citizen with Philemon ; by office he seems to have been an evangelist, who laboured among the Colossians (if he was not the first converter of them), for whom he had special affection. *Our dear fellow-servant* (said St. Paul), *and for you a faithful minister of Christ* (Col. i. 7), and (*ch.* iv. 12, 13). *A servant of Christ, always labouring for you in prayers. I bear him record that he hath a great zeal for you,* &c. A very eminent person therefore this was, who, being at Rome, perhaps accompanying Paul, and labouring in the same work of preaching and propagating the gospel, was confined in the same prison, and for the same cause ; both termed *prisoners in Christ Jesus,*

intimating the ground of their imprisonment, not any crime or wickedness, but for the faith of Christ and their service to him. An honour it is to suffer shame for Christ's name. *My fellow-prisoner in Christ Jesus* is mentioned as his glory and the apostle's comfort ; not that he was a prisoner and so hindered from his work (this was matter of affliction), but that, seeing God thus permitted and called him to suffer, his providence so ordered it that they suffered together, and so had the benefit and comfort of one another's prayers, and help, it may be, in some things ; this was a mercy. So God sometimes lightens the sufferings of his servants by the communion of saints, the sweet fellowship they have one with another in their bonds. Never more enjoyment of God have they found than when suffering together for God. So Paul and Silas, when their feet were fast in the stocks, had their tongues set at liberty, and their hearts tuned for the praises of God.—*Marcus, Aristarchus, Demas, Lucas, my fellow-labourers.* The mention of these seems in a manner to interest them in the business of the latter. How ill would it look by denial of the request of it to slight so many worthy names as most of these, at least, were ! *Marcus,* cousin of Barnabas, and son of Mary, who was so hospitable to the saints at Jerusalem (Col. iv. 10, Acts xii. 12), and whose house was the place of meeting for prayer and the worship of God. Though some failing seems to have been in him when Paul and he parted, yet in conjunction with Barnabas he went on with his work, and here Paul and he, we perceive, were reconciled, and differences forgotten, 2 Tim. iv. 11. He bids Mark to be brought to him, *for he is profitable to me for the ministry,* that is, of an evangelist. *Aristarchus* is mentioned with Marcus (Col. iv. 10), and called there by Paul his fellow-prisoner ; and speaking there of Marcus, sister's son to Barnabas, he adds, *Touching whom you received commandments ; if he come unto you, receive him :* an evidence that he himself had received him, and was reconciled to him. Next is *Demas,* who hitherto, it seems, appeared not faulty, though he is censured (2 Tim. iv. 10) as having forsaken Paul, from *love of this present world.* But how far his forsaking was, whether total from his work and profession, or partial only, and whether he repented and returned to his duty, scripture is silent, and so must we be : no mark of disgrace lay on him here, but he is joined with others who were faithful, as he is also in Col. iv. 14. *Lucas* is the last, that *beloved physician* and evangelist, who came to Rome, companion with Paul, Col. iv. 14 ; 2 Tim. iv 11. He was Paul's associate in his greatest dangers, and his fellow-labourer. The ministry is not a matter of carnal ease nor pleasure, but of pains ; if any are idle in it, they answer not their calling. Christ bids his disciples *pray the Lord of the harvest to send forth labourers,* not loiterers, *into his harvest,* Matt. ix. 38. And the people are exhorted to *know those that labour among them, and are over them in the Lord, and to esteem them very highly in love for their work's sake,* 1 Thess v. 12, 13. *My fellow-labourers,* says the apostle : ministers must be helpers together of the truth ; they serve the same Lord, in the same holy work and function, and are expectants of the same glorious reward ; therefore they must be assistants to each other in furthering the interest of their great and common Master. Thus of the salutations, and then,

3. Here is the apostle's closing prayer and benediction, *v.* 25. Observe, (1.) What is wished and prayed for : *Grace,* the free favour and love of God, together with the fruits and effects of it in all good things, for soul and body, for time and eternity. Observe, Grace is the best wish for ourselves and others ; with this the apostle begins and ends. (2.) From

whom : *Our Lord Jesus Christ,* the Son of God, second Person in the
Trinity, Lord by natural right, *by whom, and for whom, all things were
created* (Col. i. 16, John i. 1–3), *and who is heir of all things,* and, as God-
man and Mediator, who purchased us, and to whom we are given by the
Father *Jesus,* the Saviour, Matt. i. 21. We were lost and undone ; he
recovers us, and repairs the ruin. He saves by merit, procuring pardon
and life for us ; and by power, rescuing us from sin, and Satan, and hell,
and renewing us to the likeness, and bringing us to the enjoyment, of God :
thus is he Jesus ; and Christ the Messiah or anointed, consecrated and fitted
to be king, priest, and prophet, to his church. To all those offices
were there anointings under the law with oil, and to them was the Saviour
spiritually anointed with the Holy Ghost, Acts x. 38. In none but him
were all these together and in such eminence. *He was anointed with the oil
of gladness above his fellows,* Ps. xlv. 7. This Lord Jesus Christ is ours by
original title to us, and by gospel offers and gifts, his purchase of us, and
our own acceptance of him, resignation to him, and mystical union with
him : *Our Lord Jesus Christ.* Observe, All grace to us is from Christ ;
he purchased, and he bestows it. *Of his fulness we all receive, and grace
for grace,* John i. 16. *He filleth all in all,* Eph. i. 23. (3.) To whom :
Your spirit, μετὰ τοῦ πνεύματος ὑμῶν, not of Philemon only, but of all who
were named in the inscription. *With your spirit,* that is, with you, the
soul or spirit being the immediate seat of grace, whence it influences the
whole man, and flows out in gracious and holy actings. All the house
saluted are here joined in the closing benediction, the more to remind and
quicken all to further the end of the epistle.

Amen is added, not only for strong and affectionate summing up the prayer
and wish, *so let it be ;* but as an expression of faith that it will be heard, *so
shall it be.* And what need we more to make us happy than to have *the
grace of our Lord Jesus Christ with our spirit ?* This is the usual benediction, but it may be taken here to have some special respect also to the
occasion ; the grace of Christ with their spirits, Philemon's especially,
would sweeten and mollify them, take off too deep and keen resentments of
injuries, and dispose to forgive others as God for Christ's sake hath forgiven us.

EXPOSITION OF THE EPISTLE TO THE HEBREWS

CONCERNING this epistle we must enquire, I. Into the divine authority of it; for this has been questioned by some, whose distempered eyes could not bear the light of it, or whose errors have been confuted by it; such as the Arians, who deny the Godhead and self-existence of Christ; and the Socinians, who deny his satisfaction; but, after all the attempts of such men to disparage this epistle, the divine original of it shines forth with such strong and unclouded rays that he who runs may read it as an eminent part of the canon of scripture. The divinity of the matter, the sublimity of the style, the excellency of the design, the harmony of this with other parts of scripture, and its general reception in the church of God in all ages—these are the evidences of its divine authority. II. As to the divine amanuensis or penman of this epistle, we are not so certain; it does not bear the name of any in the front of it, as the rest of the epistles do, and there has been some dispute among the learned to whom they should ascribe it. Some have assigned it to Clemens of Rome; others to Luke; and many to Barnabas, thinking that the style and manner of expression is very agreeable to the zealous, authoritative, affectionate temper that Barnabas appears to be of, in the account we have of him in the Acts of the Apostles; and one ancient Father quotes an expression out of this epistle as the words of Barnabas. But it is generally assigned to the apostle Paul; and some later copies and translations have put Paul's name in the title. In the primitive times it was generally ascribed to him, and the style and scope of it very well agree with his spirit, who was a person of a clear head and a warm heart, whose main end and endeavour it was to exalt Christ. Some think that the apostle Peter refers to this epistle, and proves Paul to be the penman of it, by telling the Hebrews, to whom he wrote, of Paul's having written to them, 2 Pet. iii. 15. We read of no other epistle that he ever wrote to them but this. And though it has been objected that, since Paul put his name to all his other epistles, he would not have omitted it here; yet others have well answered that he, being the apostle of the Gentiles, who were odious to the Jews, might think fit to conceal his name, lest their prejudices against him might hinder them from reading and weighing it as they ought to do.   III. As to the scope and design of this epistle, it is very evident that it was clearly to inform the minds, and strongly to confirm the judgment, of the Hebrews in the transcendent excellency of the gospel above the law, and so to take them off from the ceremonies of the law, to which they were so wedded, of which they were so fond, that they even doted on them, and those of them who were Christians retained too much of the old leaven, and needed to be purged from it.   The design of this epistle was to persuade and press the believing Hebrews to a constant adherence to the Christian faith, and perseverance in it, notwithstanding all the sufferings they might meet with in so doing.   In order to this, the apostle speaks much of the excellency of the author of the gospel, the glorious Jesus, whose honour he advances, and whom he justly prefers before all others, showing him to be all in all, and this in lofty strains of holy rhetoric. It must be acknowledged that there are many things in this epistle hard to be understood, but the sweetness we shall find therein will make us abundant amends for all the pains we take to understand it.   And indeed, if we compare all the epistles of the New Testament, we shall not find any of them more replenished with divine, heavenly matter than this to the Hebrews.

CHAPTER I

In this chapter we have a twofold comparison stated : I. Between the evangelical and legal dispensation ; and the excellency of the gospel above that of the law is asserted and proved, ver. 1-3. II. Between the glory of Christ and that of the highest creatures, the angels ; where the pre-eminence is justly given to the Lord Jesus Christ, and clearly demonstrated to belong to him, ver. 4, to the end.

GOD, who at sundry times [**by divers portions**] and in divers manners spake in time past unto the fathers by the prophets, ² Hath in these last days spoken unto us by *his* Son, whom he hath appointed heir of all things, by whom also he made the worlds ; ³ Who being the brightness of *his* glory, and the express image of his person [*substance*], and upholding all things by the word of his power, when he had by himself purged our sins, sat down on the right hand of the Majesty on high ;

Here the apostle begins with a general declaration of the excellency of the gospel dispensation above that of the law, which he demonstrates from the different way and manner of God's communicating himself and his mind and will to men in the one and in the other : both these dispensations were of God, and both of them very good, but there is a great difference in the way of their coming from God.   Observe,

I. The way wherein God communicated himself and his will to men under the Old Testament. We have here an account, 1. Of the persons by whom God delivered his mind under the Old Testament ; they were *the prophets*, that is, persons chosen of God, and qualified by him, for that office of revealing the will of God to men. No man takes this honour to himself, unless called ; and whoever are called of God are qualified by him. 2. The persons to whom God spoke by the prophets : *To the fathers*, to all the Old Testament saints who were under that dispensation. God favoured and honoured them with much clearer light than that of nature, under which the rest of the world were left. 3. The order in which God spoke to men in those times that went before the gospel, those past times : he spoke to his ancient people *at sundry times and in divers manners*. (1.) *At sundry times*, or *by several parts*, as the word signifies, which may refer either to the several ages of the Old Testament dispensation—the patriarchal, the Mosaic, and the prophetic ; or to the several gradual openings of his mind concerning the Redeemer : to Adam, that the Messiah should come of the seed of the woman,—to Abraham, that he should spring from his loins,—to Jacob, that he should be of the tribe of Judah,—to David, that he should be of his house,—to Micah, that he should be born at Bethlehem,—to Isaiah, that he should be born of a virgin. (2.) *In divers manners*, according to the different ways in which God thought fit to communicate his mind to his prophets ; sometimes by the *illapses* of his Spirit, sometimes by *dreams*, sometimes by visions, sometimes by an audible voice, sometimes by legible characters under his own hand, as when he wrote the ten commandments on tables of stone. Of some of these different ways God himself gave an account in Num. xii. 6–8, *If there be a prophet among you, I the Lord will make myself known to him in a vision, and will speak to him in a dream. Not so with my servant Moses : with him I will speak mouth to mouth, even apparently, and not in dark speeches.*

II. God's method of communicating his mind and will under the New-Testament dispensation, these last days as they are called, that is, either towards the end of the world, or the end of the Jewish state. The times of the gospel are the last times, the gospel revelation is the last we are to expect from God. There was first the natural revelation ; then the patriarchal, by dreams, visions, and voices ; then the Mosaic, in the law given forth and written down ; then the prophetic, in explaining the law, and giving clearer discoveries of Christ : but now we must expect no new revelation, but only more of the Spirit of Christ to help us better to understand what is already revealed. Now the excellency of the gospel revelation above the former consists in two things :—

1. It is the final, the finishing revelation, given forth in the last days of divine revelation, to which nothing is to be added, but the canon of scripture is to be settled and sealed : so that now the minds of men are no longer kept in suspense by the expectation of new discoveries, but they rejoice in a complete revelation of the will of God, both preceptive and providential, so far as is necessary for them to know in order to their direction and comfort. For the gospel includes a discovery of the great events that shall befall the church of God to the end of the world.

2. It is a revelation which God has made by his Son, the most excellent messenger that was ever sent into the world, far superior to all the ancient patriarchs and prophets, by whom God communicated his will to his people in former times. And here we have an excellent account of the glory of our Lord Jesus Christ.

(1.) The glory of his office, and that in three respects :—[1.] God hath appointed him to be heir of all things. As God, he was equal to the Father ; but, as God-man and Mediator, he was appointed by the Father to be the heir of all things, the sovereign Lord of all, the absolute disposer, director, and governor of all persons and of all things, Ps. ii. 6, 7. *All power in heaven and earth is given to him ; all judgment is committed to him,* Matt. xxviii. 18 ; John v. 22. [2.] By him God made the worlds, both visible and invisible, the heavens and the earth ; not as an instrumental cause, but as his essential word and wisdom. By him he made the old creation, by him he makes the new creature, and by him he rules and governs both. [3.] He upholds all things by the word of his power : he keeps the world from dissolving. *By him all things consist.* The weight of the whole creation is laid upon Christ : he supports the whole and all the parts. When, upon the apostasy, the world was breaking to pieces under the wrath and curse of God, the Son of God, undertaking the work of redemption, bound it up again, and established it by his almighty power and goodness. None of the ancient prophets sustained such an office as this, none was sufficient for it.

(2.) Hence the apostle passes to the glory of the person of Christ, who was able to execute such an office : *He was the brightness of his Father's glory, and the express image of his person, v.* 3. This is a high and lofty description of the glorious Redeemer, this is an account of his personal excellency. [1.] He is, in person, the Son of God, the only-begotten Son of God, and as such he must have the same nature. This personal distinct-tion always supposes one and the same nature. Every son of man is man ; were not the nature the same, the generation would be monstrous. [2.] The person of the Son is the glory of the Father, shining forth with a truly divine splendour. As the beams are effulgent emanations of the sun, the father and fountain of light, Jesus Christ in his person is God manifest in the flesh, he is light of light, the true Shechinah. [3.] The person of the Son is the true image and character of the person of the Father ; being of the same nature, he must bear the same image and likeness. In beholding the power, wisdom, and goodness, of the Lord Jesus Christ, we behold the power, wisdom, and goodness, of the Father ; for he hath the nature and perfections of God in him. *He that hath seen the Son hath seen the Father ;* that is, he hath seen the same Being. He that hath known the Son hath known the Father, John xiv. 7–9. For the Son is in the Father, and the Father in the Son ; the personal distinction is no other than will consist with essential union. This is the glory of the person of Christ ; the fulness of the Godhead dwells, not typically, but really, in him.

(3.) From the glory of the person of Christ he proceeds to mention the glory of his grace ; his condescension itself was truly glorious. The sufferings of Christ had this great honour in them, to be a full satisfaction for the sins of his people : *By himself he purged away our sins,* that is, by the proper innate merit of his death and bloodshed, by their infinite intrinsic value ; as they were the sufferings of himself, he has made atonement for sin. Himself, the glory of his person and nature, gave to his sufferings such merit as was a sufficient reparation of honour to God, who had suffered an infinite injury and affront by the sins of men.

(4.) From the glory of his sufferings we are at length led to consider the glory of his exaltation : *When by himself he had purged away our sins, he sat down at the right hand of the Majesty on high,* at his Father's right hand. As Mediator and Redeemer, he is invested with the highest honour, authority, and activity, for the good of his people; the Father now does all things by him, and receives all the services of his people from him. Having assumed our nature, and suffered in it on earth, he has taken it up with him to heaven, and there it has the high honour to be next to God, and this was the reward of his humiliation.

Now it was by no less a person than this that God in these last days spoke to men; and, since the dignity of the messenger gives authority and excellency to the message, the dispensations of the gospel must therefore exceed, very far exceed, the dispensation of the law.

⁴ Being made so much better than the angels, as he hath by inheritance obtained a more excellent name than they. ⁵ For unto which of the angels said he at any time, Thou art my Son, this day have I begotten thee? And again, I will be to him a Father, and he shall be to me a Son? ⁶ And again, when he bringeth in the first-begotten into the world, he saith, And let all the angels of God worship him. ⁷ And of the angels he saith, Who maketh his angels spirits [**winds**] and his ministers a flame of fire. ⁸ But unto the Son *he saith,* Thy throne, O God, *is* for ever and ever: a sceptre of righteousness *is* the sceptre of thy kingdom. ⁹ Thou hast loved righteousness, and hated iniquity; therefore God, *even* thy God, hath anointed thee with the oil of gladness above thy fellows. ¹⁰ And, Thou, Lord, in the beginning hast laid the foundation of the earth; and the heavens are the works of thine hands: ¹¹ They shall perish; but thou remainest; and they all shall wax old as doth a garment; ¹² And as a vesture shalt thou fold them up, and they shall be changed: but thou art the same, and thy years shall not fail. ¹³ But to which of the angels said he at any time, Sit on my right hand, until I make thine enemies thy footstool? ¹⁴ Are they not all ministering spirits, sent forth to minister for [**to do service for the sake of**] them who shall be heirs of salvation?

The apostle, having proved the pre-eminence of the gospel above the law from the pre-eminence of the Lord Jesus Christ above the prophets, now proceeds to show that he is much superior not only to the prophets, but to the angels themselves. In this he obviates an objection that the Jewish zealots would be ready to make, that the law was not only delivered by men, *but ordained by angels* (Gal. iii. 19), who attended at the giving forth of the law, the hosts of heaven being drawn forth to attend the Lord Jehovah on that awful occasion. Now the angels are very glorious beings, far more glorious and excellent than men; the scripture always represents them as the most excellent of all creatures, and we know of no being but God himself that is higher than the angels; and therefore that law that was ordained by angels ought to be held in great esteem. To take off the force of this argument, the penman of this epistle proceeds to state the comparison between Jesus Christ and the holy angels, both in nature and office, and to prove that Christ is vastly superior to the angels themselves : *Being made so much better than the angels, as he hath by inheritance obtained a more excellent name than they.* Here observe,

I. The superior nature of Christ is proved from his superior name. The scripture does not give high and glorious titles without a real foundation and reason in nature ; nor would such great things have been said of our Lord Jesus Christ if he had not been as great and excellent as those words import. When it is said that Christ was made so much better than the angels, we are not to imagine that he was a mere creature, as the angels are ; the word γενόμενος, when joined with an adjective, is nowhere to be rendered *created*, and here may very well be read, *being more excellent*, as the *Syriac version* hath it. We read γινέσθω ὁ Θεὸς ἀληθής—*let God be true*, not made so, but acknowledged to be so.

II. The superiority of the name and nature of Christ above the angels is declared in the holy scriptures, and to be deduced thence. We should have known little or nothing either of Christ or of the angels, without the scriptures ; and we must therefore be determined by them in our conceptions of the one and the other. Now here are several passages of scripture cited, in which those things are said of Christ that were never said of the angels.

1. It was said of Christ, *Thou art my Son, this day have I begotten thee* (Ps. ii. 7), which may refer to his eternal generation, or to his resurrection, or to his solemn inauguration into his glorious kingdom at his ascension and session at the right hand of the Father. Now this was never said concerning the angels, and therefore by inheritance he has a more excellent nature and name than they.

2. It is said concerning Christ, but never concerning the angels, *I will be to him a Father, and he shall be to me a Son ;* taken from 2 Sam. vii. 14. Not only, " I am his Father, and he is my Son, by nature and eternal promanation ; " but, " I will be his Father, and he shall be my Son, by wonderful conception, and this his son-ship shall be the fountain and foundation of every gracious relation between me and fallen man."

3. It is said of Christ, *When God bringeth his First-begotten into the world, let all the angels of God worship him ;* that is, when he is brought into this lower world, at his nativity, let the angels attend and honour him ; or when he is brought into the world above, at his ascension, to enter upon his mediatorial kingdom, or when he shall bring him again into the world, to judge the world, then let the highest creatures worship him. God will not suffer an angel to continue in heaven who will not be in subjection to Christ, and pay adoration to him ; and he will at last make the fallen angels and wicked men to confess his divine power and authority and to fall before him. Those who would not have him to reign must then be brought forth and slain before him. The proof of this is taken out of Ps. xcvii. 7, *Worship him, all you gods,* that is, " All you that are superior to men, own yourselves to be inferior to Christ in nature and power."

4. God has said concerning Christ, *Thy throne, O God, is for ever and ever,* &c., v. 8-12. But of the angels he has only said that *he hath made them spirits, and his ministers a flame of fire, v.* 7. Now, upon comparing what he here says of the angels with what he says to Christ, the vast inferiority of the angels to Christ will plainly appear.

(1.) What does God say here of the angels? *He maketh his angels spirits, and his ministers a flame of fire.* This we have in Ps. civ. 4, where it seems to be more immediately spoken of the winds and lightning, but is here applied to the angels, whose agency the divine Providence makes use of in the winds, and in thunder and lightnings. Observe, [1.] The office of the angels ; they are God's ministers, or *servants, to do his pleasure.* It is the glory of God that he has such servants ; it is yet more so that he does not need them. [2.] How the angels are qualified for this service ; he makes them spirits and a flame of fire, that is, he endows them with light and zeal, with activity and ability, readiness and resolution to do his pleasure : they are no more than what God has made them to be, and they are servants to the Son as well as to the Father. But observe,

(2.) How much greater things are said of Christ by the Father. Here two passages of scripture are quoted.

[1.] One of these is out of Ps. xlv. 6, 7, where God declares of Christ, *First,* His true and real divinity, and that with much pleasure and affection, not grudging him that glory : *Thy throne, O God.* Here one person calls another person God, *O God.* And, if God the Father declares him to be so, he must be really and truly so ; for God calls persons and things as they are. And now let who will deny him to be essentially God at their peril, but let us own and honour him as God ; for, if he had not been God, he had never been fit to have done the Mediator's work nor to have worn the Mediator's crown. *Secondly,* God declares his dignity and dominion, as having a throne, a kingdom, and a sceptre of that kingdom. He has all right, rule, authority, and power, both as the God of nature, grace, and glory, and as Mediator ; and so he is fully adequate to all the intents and purposes of his mediatorial kingdom. *Thirdly,* God declares the eternal duration of the dominion and dignity of Christ, founded upon the divinity of his person : *Thy throne, O God, is for ever and ever,* from everlasting to everlasting, through all the ages of time, maugre all the attempts of earth and hell to undermine and overthrow it, and through all the endless ages of eternity, when time shall be no more. This distinguishes Christ's throne from all earthly thrones, which are tottering, and will at length tumble down ; but the throne of Christ shall be as the days of heaven. *Fourthly,* God declares of Christ the perfect equity of his administration, and of the execution of his power, through all the parts of his government : *A sceptre of righteousness is the sceptre of thy kingdom, v.* 8. He came righteously to the sceptre, and he uses it in perfect righteousness ; the righteousness of his government proceeds from the righteousness of his person, from an essential eternal love of righteousness and hatred of iniquity, not merely from considerations of prudence or interest, but from an inward and immovable principle : *Thou lovest righteousness and hatest iniquity, v.* 9. Christ came to fulfil all righteousness, to bring in an everlasting righteousness ; and he was righteous in all his ways and holy in all his works. He has recommended righteousness to men, and restored it among them, as a most excellent and amiable thing. He came to finish transgression, and to make an end of sin as a hateful as well as hurtful thing. *Fifthly,* God declares of Christ how he was qualified for the office of Mediator, and how he was installed and confirmed in it (*v.* 9) : *Therefore God, even thy God, hath anointed thee with the oil of gladness above thy fellows.* 1. Christ has the name Messiah from his being anointed. God's anointing of Christ signifies both his qualifying him for the office of the Mediator with the Holy Spirit and all his graces, and likewise his inauguration of him into the office, as prophets, priests, and kings, were by anointing. *God, even thy God,* imports the confirmation of Christ in the office of Mediator by the covenant of redemption and peace, that was between the Father and the Son. God is the God of Christ, as Christ is man and Mediator. 2. This anointing of Christ was *with the oil of gladness,* which signifies both the gladness and cheerfulness with which Christ undertook and went through the office of Mediator (finding himself so absolutely sufficient for it), and also that joy which was set before him as the reward of his service and sufferings, that crown of glory and gladness which he should wear for ever after the suffering of death. 3. This anointing of Christ was above the anointing of his fellows : *God, even thy God, hath anointed thee with the oil of gladness above thy fellows.* Who are Christ's fellows ? Has he any equals ? Not as God, except the Father and Spirit, but these are not here meant. As man, however, he has his fellows, and as an anointed person ; but his unction is beyond all theirs. (1.) Above the angels, who may be said to be his fellows, as they are the sons of God by creation, and God's messengers, whom he employs in his service. (2.) Above all prophets, priests, and kings, that ever were anointed with oil, to be employed in the service of God on earth. (3.) Above all the saints, who are his brethren, children of the same father, as he was a partaker with them of flesh and blood. (4.) Above all those who were related to him as man, above all the house of David, all the tribe of Judah, all his brethren and kinsmen in the flesh. All God's other anointed ones had only the Spirit in a certain measure ; Christ had the Spirit above measure, without any limitation. None therefore goes through his work as Christ did, none takes so much pleasure in it as Christ does ; for he was anointed with the oil of gladness above his fellows.

[2.] The other passage of scripture in which is the superior excellence of Christ to the angels is taken out of Ps. cii. 25–27, and is recited in *v.* 10–12, where the omnipotence of the Lord Jesus Christ is declared as it appears both in creating the world and in changing it.

First, In creating the world (*v.* 10) : *And thou, Lord, in the beginning hast laid the foundation of the earth, and the heavens are the work of thy hands.* The Lord Christ had the original right to govern the world, because he made the world in the beginning. His right, as Mediator, was by commission from the Father. His right, as God with the Father, was absolute, resulting from his creating power. This power he had before the beginning of the world, and he exerted it in giving a beginning and being to the world. He must therefore be no part of the world himself, for then he must give himself a beginning. He was πρὸ πάντων—*before all things,* and *by him all things consist,* Col. i. 17. He was not only above all things in condition, but before all things in existence ; and therefore must be God, and self-existent. He laid the foundations of the earth, did not only introduce new forms into pre-existent matter, but made out of nothing the foundations of the earth, the *primordia rerum—the first principles of things;* he not only founded the earth, but the heavens too are the work of his hands, both the habitation and the inhabitants, the hosts of heaven, the angels themselves ; and therefore he must needs be infinitely superior to them.

Secondly, In changing the world that he has made ; and here the mutability of this world is brought in to illustrate the immutability of Christ. Observe, 1. This world is mutable, all created nature is so ; this world has passed through many changes, and shall pass through more ; all these changes are by the permission and under the direction of Christ, who made the world (*v.* 11, 12) : *They shall perish, they shall all wax old as doth a*

garment; as a vesture shalt thou fold them up, and they shall be changed.
This our visible world (both the earth and visible heavens) is growing old.
Not only men and beasts and trees grow old, but this world itself grows
old, and is hastening to its dissolution ; it changes like a garment, has lost
much of its beauty and strength ; it grew old betimes on the first apostasy,
and it has been waxing older and growing weaker ever since ; it bears the
symptoms of a dying world.   But then its dissolution will not be its utter
destruction, but its change.   Christ will fold up this world as a garment
not to be abused any longer, not to be any longer so used as it has been.
Let us not then set our hearts upon that which is not what we take it to
be, and will not be what it now is.   Sin has made a great change in the
world for the worse, and Christ will make a great change in it for the
better.   *We look for new heavens and a new earth, wherein dwelleth righteousness.*   Let the consideration of this wean us from the present world, and
make us watchful, diligent, and desirous of that better world, and let us
wait on Christ to change us into a meetness for that new world that is
approaching ; we cannot enter into it till we be new creatures.   2. Christ
is immutable.   Thus the Father testifies of him, *Thou remainest, thy years
shall not fail.*   Christ is the same in himself, the same yesterday, and to-
day, and for ever, and the same to his people in all the changes of time.
This may well support all who have an interest in Christ under all the
changes they meet with in the world, and under all they feel in themselves.
Christ is immutable and immortal : his years shall not fail.   This may
comfort us under all decays of nature that we may observe in ourselves or
in our friends, though our flesh and heart fail and our days are hastening
to an end.   Christ lives to take care of us while we live, and of ours when
we are gone, and this should quicken us all to make our interest in him
clear and sure, that our spiritual and eternal life may be hid with Christ
in God.

III. The superiority of Christ to the angels appears in this that God
never said to the angels what he has said to Christ, *v.* 13, 14.

1. What has God said to Christ ?   He has said, " *Sit thou at my right
hand, till I make thy enemies thy footstool,* Ps. cx. 1.   Receive thou glory,
dominion, and rest ; and remain in the administration of thy mediatorial
kingdom until all thy enemies shall either be made thy friends by conversion or thy footstool."   Note, (1.) Christ Jesus has his enemies (would one
think it ?), enemies even among men—enemies to his sovereignty, to his
cause, to his people ; such as will not have him to reign over them.   Let
us not think it strange then if we have our enemies.   Christ never did any
thing to make men his enemies ; he has done a great deal to make them
all his friends and his Father's friends, and yet he has his enemies.   (2.)
All the enemies of Christ shall be made his footstool, either by humble
submission and entire subjection to his will casting themselves down at
his feet, or by utter destruction ; he shall trample upon those who continue obstinate, and shall triumph over them.   (3.) God the Father has
undertaken for this, and he will see it done, yea, he will himself do it ;
and, though it be not done presently, it shall certainly be done, and Christ
waits for it ; and so must Christians wait till God has wrought all their
works in them, for them, and by them.   (4.) Christ shall go on to rule and
reign till this be done ; he shall not leave any of his great designs un-
finished, he shall go on conquering and to conquer.   And it becomes his
people to go on in their duty, being what he would have them to be, doing
what he would have them to do, avoiding what he would have them to

avoid, bearing what he would have them to bear, till he make them conquerors and more than conquerors over all their spiritual enemies.

2. What has God said to the angels? He never said to them, as he said to Christ, *Sit you at my right hand;* but he has said of them here that *they are ministering spirits, sent forth to minister for those who shall be the heirs of salvation.* Note, (1.) What the angels are as to their nature : they are spirits, without bodies or inclination to bodies, and yet they can assume bodies, and appear in them, when God pleases. They are spirits, incorporeal, intelligent, active substances ; they excel in wisdom and strength. (2.) What the angels are as to their office : they are ministering spirits. Christ, as Mediator, is the great minister of God in the great work of redemption. The Holy Spirit is the great minister of God and Christ in the application of this redemption. Angels are ministering spirits under the blessed Trinity, to execute the divine will and pleasure ; they are the ministers of divine Providence. (3.) The angels are sent forth for this end—to minister to those who shall be the heirs of salvation. Here observe, [1.] The description given of the saints—they are *heirs of salvation;* at present they are under age, heirs, not inheritors. They are heirs because they are children of God ; *if children, then heirs.* Let us make sure that we are children by adoption and regeneration, having made a covenant-resignation of ourselves to God, and walking before him in a gospel-conversation, and then we are heirs of God, and joint-heirs with Christ. [2.] The dignity and privilege of the saints—the angels are sent forth to minister for them. Thus they have done in attending and acting at the giving forth of the law, in fighting the battles of the saints, in destroying their enemies. They still minister for them in opposing the malice and power of evil spirits, in protecting and keeping their bodies, pitching their tents about theirs, instructing, quickening, and comforting their souls under Christ and the Holy Ghost ; and thus they shall do in gathering all the saints together at the last day. Bless God for the ministration of angels, keep in God's way, and take the comfort of this promise, that he will *give his angels charge over you, to keep you in all your ways. They shall bear you up in their hands, lest you dash your feet against a stone,* Ps. xci. 11, 12.

CHAPTER II

In this chapter the apostle, I. Makes some application of the doctrine laid down in the chapter foregoing concerning the excellency of the person of Christ, both by way of exhortation and argument, ver. 1-4. II. Enlarges further upon the pre-eminence of Christ above the angels, ver. 5-9. III. Proceeds to remove the scandal of the cross, ver. 10-15. IV. Asserts the incarnation of Christ, taking upon him not the nature of angels, but the seed of Abraham, and assigns the reason of his so doing, ver. 16, to the end.

THEREFORE we ought to give the more earnest heed to the things which we have heard, lest at any time we should let *them* slip [lest haply we drift away *from them*]. ² For if the word spoken by angels was stedfast, and every transgression and disobedience received a just recompence of reward ; ³ How shall we escape, if we neglect so great salvation; which at the first began to be spoken by the Lord, and was confirmed unto us by them that heard *him;* ⁴ God also bearing *them* witness, both with signs and wonders, and with divers miracles [**manifold powers**], and gifts of the Holy Ghost, according to his own will?

The apostle proceeds in the plain profitable method of doctrine, reason, and use, through this epistle. Here we have the application of the truths before asserted and proved; this is brought in by the illative particle *therefore,* with which this chapter begins, and which shows its connection with the former, where the apostle having proved Christ to be superior to the angels by whose ministry the law was given, and therefore that the gospel dispensation must be more excellent than the legal, he now comes to apply this doctrine both by way of exhortation and argument.

I. By way of exhortation : *Therefore we ought to give the more diligent heed to the things which we have heard, v.* 1. This is the first way by which we are to show our esteem of Christ and of the gospel. It is the great concern of every one under the gospel to give the most earnest heed to all gospel discoveries and directions, to prize them highly in his judgment as matters of the greatest importance, to hearken to them diligently in all the opportunities he has for that purpose, to read them frequently, to meditate on them closely, and to mix faith with them. We must embrace them in our hearts and affections, retain them in our memories, and finally regulate our words and actions according to them.

II. By way of argument, he adds strong motives to enforce the exhortation.

1. From the great loss we shall sustain if we do not take this earnest heed to the things which we have heard : *We shall let them slip.* They will leak, and run out of our heads, lips, and lives, and we shall be great losers by our neglect. Learn, (1.) When we have received gospel truths into our minds, we are in danger of letting them slip. Our minds and memories are like a leaky vessel, they do not without much care retain what is poured into them ; this proceeds from the corruption of our natures, the enmity and subtlety of Satan (he steals away the word), from the entanglements and snares of the world, the thorns that choke the good seed. (2.) Those meet with an inconceivable loss who let gospel truths, which they had received, slip out of their minds ; they have lost a treasure far better than thousands of gold and silver ; the seed is lost, their time and pains in hearing lost, and their hopes of a good harvest lost ; all is lost, if the gospel be lost. (3.) This consideration should be a strong motive both to our attention to the gospel and our retention of it ; and indeed, if we do not well attend, we shall not long retain the word of God ; inattentive hearers will soon be forgetful hearers.

2. Another argument is taken from the dreadful punishment we shall incur if we do not do this duty, a more dreadful punishment than those fell under who neglected and disobeyed the law, *v.* 2, 3. Here observe, (1.) How the law is described : it was the *word spoken by angels, and declared to be stedfast.* It was the word spoken by angels, because given by the ministration of angels, they sounding the trumpet, and perhaps forming the words according to God's direction ; and God, as judge, will make use of the angels to sound the trumpet a second time, and gather all

to his tribunal, to receive their sentence, as they have conformed or not conformed to the law. *And this law is declared to be stedfast;* it is like the promise, *yea and amen;* it is truth and faithfulness, and it will abide and have its force whether men obey it or no, *for every transgression and disobedience will receive a just recompense of reward.* If men trifle with the law of God, the law will not trifle with them; it has taken hold of the sinners of former ages, and will take hold of sinners in all ages. God, as a righteous governor and judge, when he had given forth the law, would not let the contempt and breach of it go unpunished; but he has from time to time reckoned with the transgressors of it, and recompensed them according to the nature and aggravation of their disobedience. Observe, The severest punishment God ever inflicted upon sinners is no more than what sin deserves: it is *a just recompense of reward,* punishments are as just, and as much due to sin as rewards are to obedience, yea, more due than rewards are to imperfect obedience. (2.) How the gospel is described. It is salvation, a great salvation; so great salvation that no other salvation can compare with it; so great that none can fully express, no, nor yet conceive, how great it is. It is a great salvation that the gospel discovers, for it discovers a great Saviour, one who has manifested God to be reconciled to our nature, and reconcilable to our persons; it shows how we may be saved from so great sin and so great misery, and be restored to so great holiness and so great happiness. The gospel discovers to us a great sanctifier, to qualify us for salvation and to bring us to the Saviour. The gospel unfolds a great and excellent dispensation of grace, a new covenant; the great charter-deed and instrument is settled and secured to all those who come into the bond of the covenant. (3.) How sinning against the gospel is described: it is declared to be a *neglect of this great salvation;* it is a contempt put upon the saving grace of God in Christ, making light of it, not caring for it, not thinking it worth their while to acquaint themselves with it, not regarding either the worth of gospel grace or their own want of it, and undone state without it; not using their endeavours to discern the truth of it, and assent to it, nor to discern the goodness of it, so as to approve of it, or apply it to themselves. In these things they discover a plain neglect of this great salvation. Let us all take heed that we be not found among those wicked wretched sinners who neglect the grace of the gospel. (4.) How the misery of such sinners is described: it is declared to be unavoidable (*v.* 3): *How shall we escape?* This intimates, [1.] That the despisers of this salvation are condemned already, under arrest and in the hands of justice already. So they were by the sin of Adam: and they have strengthened their bonds by their personal transgression. *He that believeth not is condemned already,* John iii. 18. [2.] There is no escaping out of this condemned state but by accepting the great salvation discovered in the gospel: as for those who neglect it, the wrath of God is upon them, and it abides upon them; they cannot disengage themselves, they cannot emerge, they cannot get from under the curse. [3.] That there is a yet more aggravated curse and condemnation waiting for all those who despise the grace of God in Christ, and that this most heavy curse they cannot escape; they cannot conceal their persons at the great day, nor deny the fact nor bribe the judge, nor break the prison. There is no door of mercy left open for them; there will be no more sacrifice for sin: they are irrecoverably lost. The unavoidableness of the misery of such is here expressed by way of question: *How shall we escape?* It is an appeal to universal reason, to the consciences of sinners themselves; it is a challenge to all their power and policy, to all their interest and alliances, whether they, or any for them, can find out, or can force out, a way of escape from the vindictive justice and wrath of God. It intimates that the neglecters of this great salvation will be left not only without power, but without plea and excuse, at the judgment-day ; if they be asked what they have to say that the sentence should not be executed upon them, they will be speechless, and self-condemned by their own consciences, even to a greater degree of misery than those fell under who neglected the authority of the law, or sinned without the law.

3. Another argument to enforce the exhortation is taken from the dignity and excellency of the person by whom the gospel began to be spoken (*v.* 3) : *It began at first to be spoken by the Lord,* that is, the Lord Jesus Christ, who is Jehovah, the Lord of life and glory, Lord of all, and as such possessed of unerring and infallible wisdom, infinite and inexhaustible goodness, unquestionable and unchangeable veracity and faithfulness, absolute sovereignty and authority, and irresistible power. This great Lord of all was the first who began to speak it plainly and clearly, without types and shadows as it was before he came. Now surely it may be expected that all will reverence this Lord, and take heed to a gospel that began to be spoken by one who spoke so as never *man spoke.*

4. Another argument is taken from the character of those who were witnesses to Christ and the gospel (*v.* 3, 4) : *It was confirmed to us by those that heard him, God also bearing them witness.* Observe, (1.) The promulgation of the gospel was continued and confirmed by those who heard Christ, by the evangelists and apostles, who were eye and ear-witnesses of what Jesus Christ began both to do and to teach, Acts i. 1. These witnesses could have no worldly end or interest of their own to serve hereby. Nothing could induce them to give in their evidence but the Redeemer's glory, and their own and others' salvation ; they exposed themselves by their testimony to the loss of all that was dear to them in this life, and many of them sealed it with their blood. (2.) *God himself bore witness* to those who were witnesses for Christ ; he testified that they were authorised and sent by him to preach Christ and salvation by him to the world. And how did he bear them witness? Not only by giving them great peace in their own minds, great patience under all their sufferings, and unspeakable courage and joy (though these were witnesses to themselves), but he bore them witness *by signs, and wonders, and divers miracles, and gifts of the Holy Ghost, according to his will.* [1.] With *signs,* signs of his gracious presence with them, and of his power working by them. [2.] *Wonders,* works quite beyond the power of nature, and out of the course of nature, filling the spectators with wonder and admiration, stirring them up to attend to the doctrine preached, and to enquire into it. [3.] *Divers miracles,* or mighty works, in which an almighty agency appeared beyond all reasonable controversy. [4.] *Gifts of the Holy Ghost,* qualifying, enabling, and exciting them to do the work to which they were called—*divisions or distributions of the Holy Ghost, diversities of gifts,* 1 Cor. xii. 4, &c. And all this *according to God's own will.* It was the will of God that we should have sure footing for our faith, and a strong foundation for our hope in receiving the gospel. As at the giving forth of the law there were signs and wonders, by which God testified the authority and excellency of it, so he witnessed to the gospel by more and greater miracles, as to a more excellent and abiding dispensation.

⁵ For unto the angels hath he not put in subjection the world to come, whereof we speak. ⁶ But one in a certain place testified, saying, What is man, that thou art mindful of him? or the son of man, that thou visitest him? ⁷ Thou madest him a little lower than the angels; thou crownedst him with glory and honour, and didst set him over the works of thy hands: ⁸ Thou hast put all things in subjection under his feet. For in that he put all in subjection under him, he left nothing *that is* not put under him. But now we see not yet all things put under him. ⁹ But we see Jesus, who was made a little lower than the angels [,] for the suffering of death, crowned with glory and honour [**because of the suffering of death crowned with glory and honour**]; that he by the grace of God should taste death for every man.

The apostle, having made this serious application of the doctrine of the personal excellency of Christ above the angels, now returns to that pleasant subject again, and pursues it further (*v.* 5): *For to the angels hath he not put in subjection the world to come, whereof we speak.*

I. Here the apostle lays down a negative proposition, including a positive one—That the state of the gospel-church, which is here called *the world to come,* is *not subjected to the angels,* but under the special care and direction of the Redeemer himself. Neither the state in which the church is at present, nor that more completely restored state at which it shall arrive when the prince of this world is cast out and the kingdoms of the earth shall become the kingdom of Christ, is left to the government of the angels; but Jesus Christ will take to him his great power, and will reign. He does not make that use of the ministration of angels to give the gospel as he did to give the law, which was the state of the old or antiquated world. This new world is committed to Christ, and put in absolute subjection to him only, in all spiritual and eternal concerns. Christ has the administration of the gospel church, which at once bespeaks Christ's honour and the church's happiness and safety. It is certain that neither the first creation of the gospel church nor its after-edification or administration, nor its final judgment and perfection, is committed to the angels, but to Christ. God would not put so great a trust in his holy ones; his angels were too weak for such a charge.

II. We have a scripture-account of that blessed Jesus to whom the gospel world is put into subjection. It is taken from Ps. viii. 4–6, *But one in a certain place testified, saying, What is man, that thou art mindful of him? or the Son of man, that thou visitest him?* &c. These words are to be considered both as applicable to mankind in general, and as applied here to the Lord Jesus Christ.

1. As applicable to mankind in general, in which sense we have an affectionate thankful expostulation with the great God concerning his wonderful condescension and kindness to the sons of men. (1.) In remembering them, or being mindful of them, when yet they had no being but in the counsels of divine love. The favours of God to men all spring up out of his eternal thoughts and purposes of mercy for them; as all our dutiful regards to God spring forth from our remembrance of him. God is always

mindful of us, let us never be forgetful of him. (2.) In visiting them. God's purpose of favours for men is productive of gracious visits to them ; he comes to see us, how it is with us, what we ail, what we want, what dangers we are exposed to, what difficulties we have to encounter ; and by his visitation our spirit is preserved. Let us so remember God as daily to approach him in a way of duty. (3.) In making man the head of all the creatures in this lower world, the top-stone of this building, the chief of the ways of God on earth, and only a little lower than the angels in place, and respect to the body, while here, and to be made like the angels, and equal to the angels, at the resurrection of the just, Luke xx. 36. (4.) In crowning him with glory and honour, the honour of having noble powers and faculties of soul, excellent organs and parts of body, whereby he is allied to both worlds, capable of serving the interests of both worlds, and of enjoying the happiness of both. (5.) In giving him right to and dominion over the inferior creatures, which did continue so long as he continued in his allegiance and duty to God.

2. As applied to the Lord Jesus Christ, and the whole that is here said can be applied only to him, v. 8, 9. And here you may observe, (1.) What is the moving cause of all the kindness God shows to men in giving Christ for them and to them ; and that is the grace of God. For *what is man ?* (2.) What are the fruits of this free grace of God with respect to the gift of Christ for us and to us, as related in this scripture-testimony. [1.] That God was mindful of Christ for us in the covenant of redemption. [2.] That God visited Christ on our account ; and it was concluded between them that in the fulness of time Christ should come into the world, as the great archetypal sacrifice. [3.] That God had made him a little lower than the angels, in his being made man, that he might suffer and humble himself to death. [4.] That God crowned the human nature of Christ with glory and honour, in his being perfectly holy, and having the Spirit without measure, and by an ineffable union with the divine nature in the second person of the Trinity, the fulness of the Godhead dwelling in him bodily ; that by his sufferings he might make satisfaction, tasting death for every man, sensibly feeling and undergoing the bitter agonies of that shameful, painful, and cursed death of the cross, hereby putting all mankind into a new state of trial. [5.] That, as a reward of his humiliation in suffering death, he was crowned with glory and honour, advanced to the highest dignity in heaven, and having absolute dominion over all things, thus accomplishing that ancient scripture in Christ, which never was so accomplished or fulfilled in any mere man that ever was upon earth.

[10] For it became him, for whom *are* all things, and by whom *are* all things, in bringing many sons unto glory, to make the captain [**author**] of their salvation perfect through sufferings. [11] For both he that sanctifieth and they who are sanctified *are* all of one : for which cause he is not ashamed to call them brethren, [12] Saying, I will declare thy name unto my brethren, in the midst of the church will I sing praise unto thee. [13] And again, I will put my trust in him. And again, Behold I and the children which God hath given me.

Having mentioned the death of Christ, the apostle here proceeds to prevent and remove the scandal of the cross ; and this he does by showing both how it became God that Christ should suffer and how much man should be benefited by those sufferings.

I. How it became God that Christ should suffer : *For it became him for whom are all things, and by whom are all things, in bringing many sons to glory, to make the captain of their salvation perfect through sufferings, v.* 10. Here,

1. God is described as the final end and first cause of all things, and as such it became him to secure his own glory in all that he did, not only to act so that he might in nothing dishonour himself, but so that he might from every thing have a revenue of glory.

2. He is declared to have acted up to this glorious character in the work of redemption, as to the choice both of the end and of the means.

(1.) In the choice of the end ; and that was to bring many sons to glory, to present glory in enjoying the glorious privileges of the gospel, and to future glory in heaven, which will be glory indeed, an exceeding eternal weight of glory. Here observe, [1.] We must be the sons of God both by adoption and regeneration, before we can be brought to the glory of heaven. Heaven is the inheritance ; and only those that are the children are heirs of that inheritance. [2.] All true believers are the children of God : to *those that receive Christ he has granted the power and privilege of being the children of God, even to as many as believe on his name,* John i. 12. [3.] Though the sons of God are but a few in one place and at one time, yet when they shall be all brought together it will appear that they are many. Christ is the first-born among many brethren. [4.] All the sons of God, how many soever they are, or however dispersed and divided, shall at length be brought together to glory.

(2.) In the choice of the means. [1.] In finding out such a person as should be the captain of our salvation ; those that are saved must come to that salvation under the guidance of a captain and leader sufficient for that purpose ; and they must be all enlisted under the banner of this captain ; they must endure hardship as good soldiers of Christ ; they must follow their captain, and those that do so shall be brought safely off, and shall inherit great glory and honour. [2.] In making this captain of our salvation perfect through sufferings. God the Father made the Lord Jesus Christ the captain of our salvation (that is, he consecrated, he appointed him to that office, he gave him a commission for it), and he made him a perfect captain : he had perfection of wisdom, and courage, and strength, by the Spirit of the Lord, which he had without measure ; he was made perfect through sufferings ; that is, he perfected the work of our redemption by shedding his blood, and was thereby perfectly qualified to be a Mediator between God and man. He found his way to the crown by the cross, and so must his people too. The excellent Dr. Owen observes that the Lord Jesus Christ, being consecrated and perfected through suffering, has consecrated the way of suffering for all his followers to pass through unto glory ; and hereby their sufferings are made necessary and unavoidable, they are hereby made honourable, useful, and profitable.

II. He shows how much they would be benefited by the cross and sufferings of Christ ; as there was nothing unbecoming God and Christ, so there was that which would be very beneficial to men, in these sufferings. Hereby they are brought into a near union with Christ, and into a very endearing relation.

1. Into a near union (*v.* 11): *Both he that sanctifieth and those that are sanctified are all of one.* Observe, Christ is he that sanctifieth; he has purchased and sent the sanctifying Spirit; he is the head of all sanctifying influences. The Spirit sanctifieth as the Spirit of Christ. True believers are those who are sanctified, endowed with holy principles and powers, separated and set apart from mean and vile uses to high and holy uses and purposes; for so they must be before they can be brought to glory. Now Christ, who is the agent in this work of sanctification, and Christians, who are the recipient subjects, are all of one. How? Why, (1.) They are all of one heavenly Father, and that is God. God is the Father of Christ by eternal generation and by miraculous conception, of Christians by adoption and regeneration. (2.) They are of one earthly father, Adam. Christ and believers have the same human nature. (3.) Of one spirit, one holy and heavenly disposition; the same mind is in them that was in Christ, though not in the same measure; the same Spirit informs and actuates the head and all the members.

2. Into an endearing relation. This results from the union. And here first he declares what this relation is, and then he quotes three texts out of the Old Testament to illustrate and prove it.

(1.) He declares what this relation is: he and believers being all of one, he therefore is not ashamed to call them *brethren.* Observe, [1.] Christ and believers are brethren; not only bone of his bone and flesh of his flesh, but spirit of his spirit—brethren by the whole blood, in what is heavenly as well as in what is earthly. [2.] Christ is not ashamed to own this relation; he is not ashamed to call them brethren, which is wonderful goodness and condescension in him, considering their meanness by nature and vileness by sin; but he will never be ashamed of any who are not ashamed of him, and who take care not to be a shame and reproach to him and to themselves.

(2.) He illustrates this from three texts of scripture.

[1.] The first is out of Ps. xxii. 22, *I will declare thy name unto my brethren; in the midst of the church will I sing praise unto thee.* This psalm was an eminent prophecy of Christ; it begins with his words on the cross, *My God, my God, why hast thou forsaken me?* Now here it is foretold, *First,* That Christ should have a church or *congregation* in the world, a company of volunteers, freely willing to follow him. *Secondly,* That these should not only be brethren to one another, but to Christ himself. *Thirdly,* That he would declare his Father's name to them, that is, his nature and attributes, his mind and will: this he did in his own person, while he dwelt among us, and by his Spirit poured out upon his disciples, enabling them to spread the knowledge of God in the world from one generation to another, to the end of the world. *Fourthly,* That Christ would sing praise to his Father in the church. The glory of the Father was what Christ had in his eye; his heart was set upon it, he laid out himself for it, and he would have his people to join with him in it.

[2.] The second scripture is quoted from Ps. xviii. 2, *And again, I will put my trust in him.* That psalm sets forth the troubles that David, as a type of Christ, met with, and how he in all his troubles put his trust in God. Now this shows that besides his divine nature, which needed no supports, he was to take another nature upon him, that would want those supports which none but God could give. He suffered and trusted as our head and president. *Owen in locum.* His brethren must suffer and trust too.

[3.] The third scripture is taken from Isa. viii. 18, *Behold, I and the children which God hath given me.* This proves Christ really and truly man, for parents and children are of the same nature. Christ's children were given him of the Father, in the counsel of his eternal love, and that covenant of peace which was between them. And they are given to Christ at their conversion. When they take hold of his covenant, then Christ receives them, rules over them, rejoices in them, perfects all their affairs, takes them up to heaven, and there presents them to his Father, *Behold, I and the children which thou hast given me.*

14 Forasmuch then as the children are partakers of [sharers in] flesh and blood, he also himself likewise took part [in like manner partook] of the same; that through death he might destroy him that had the power of death, that is, the devil; 15 And deliver them who through fear of death were all their lifetime subject to bondage. 16 For verily he took not on *him the nature of* angels [not of angels doth he take hold]; but he took on *him* [taketh hold of] the seed of Abraham. 17 Wherefore in all things it behoved him to be made like unto *his* brethren, that he might be a merciful and faithful high priest in things *pertaining* to God, to make reconciliation [propitiation] for the sins of the people. 18 For in that he himself hath suffered being tempted, he *is* able to succour them that are tempted.

Here the apostle proceeds to assert the incarnation of Christ, as taking upon him not the nature of angels, but the seed of Abraham; and he shows the reason and design of his so doing.

I. The incarnation of Christ is asserted (*v.* 16): *Verily he took not upon aim the nature of angels, but he took upon him the seed of Abraham.* He took part of flesh and blood. Though as God he pre-existed from all eternity, yet in the fulness of time he took our nature into union with his divine nature, and became really and truly man. He did not lay hold of angels, but he laid hold of the seed of Abraham. The angels fell, and he let them go, and lie under the desert, defilement, and dominion of their sin, without hope or help. Christ never designed to be the Saviour of the fallen angels; as their tree fell, so it lies, and must lie to eternity, and therefore he did not assume their nature. The nature of angels could not be an atoning sacrifice for the sin of man. Now Christ resolving to recover the seed of Abraham and raise them up from their fallen state, he took upon him the human nature from one descended from the loins of Abraham, that the same nature that had sinned might suffer, to restore human nature to a state of hope and trial, and all that accepted of mercy to a state of special favour and salvation. Now there is hope and help for the chief of sinners in and through Christ. Here is a price paid sufficient for all, and suitable to all, for it was in our nature. Let us all then know the day of our gracious visitation, and improve that distinguishing mercy which has been shown to fallen men, not to the fallen angels.

II. The reasons and designs of the incarnation of Christ are declared.

1. *Because the children were partakers of flesh and blood, he must take part of the same, and be made like his brethren, v.* 14, 15. For no higher

nor lower nature than man's that had sinned could so suffer for the sin of man as to satisfy the justice of God, and raise man up to a state of hope, and make believers the children of God, and so brethren to Christ.

2. He became man that he might die; as God he could not die, and therefore he assumed another nature and state. Here the wonderful love of God appeared, that, when Christ knew what he must suffer in our nature, and how he must die in it, yet he so readily took it upon him. The legal sacrifices and offerings God could not accept as a propitiation. A body was prepared for Christ, and he said, *Lo! I come, I delight to do thy will.*

3. That *through death he might destroy him that had the power of death, that is, the devil, v.* 14. The devil was the first sinner, and the first tempter to sin, and sin was the procuring cause of death; and he may be said to have the power of death, as he draws men into sin, the ways where-of are death, as he is often permitted to terrify the consciences of men with the fear of death, and as he is the executioner of divine justice, haling their souls from their bodies to the tribunal of God, there to receive their doom, and then being their tormentor, as he was before their tempter. In these respects he may be said to have had the power of death. But now Christ has so far destroyed him who had the power of death that he can keep none under the power of spiritual death; nor can he draw any into sin (the procuring cause of death), nor require the soul of any from the body, nor execute the sentence upon any but those who choose and continue to be his willing slaves, and persist in their enmity to God.

4. That he might deliver his own people from the slavish fear of death to which they are often subject. This may refer to the Old-Testament saints, who were more under a spirit of bondage, because life and immortality were not so fully brought to light as now they are by the gospel. Or it may refer to all the people of God, whether under the Old Testament or the New, whose minds are often in perplexing fears about death and eternity. Christ became man, and died, to deliver them from those perplexities of soul, by letting them know that death is not only a conquered enemy, but a reconciled friend, not sent to hurt the soul, or separate it from the love of God, but to put an end to all their grievances and complaints, and to give them a passage to eternal life and blessedness; so that to them death is not now in the hand of Satan, but in the hand of Christ —not Satan's servant, but Christ's servant—has not hell following it, but heaven to all who are in Christ.

5. Christ must be made like unto his brethren, that he might be a merciful and faithful high priest in things pertaining to the justice and honour of God and to the support and comfort of his people. He must be faithful to God and merciful to men. (1.) In things pertaining to God, to his justice, and to his honour—to make reconciliation for the sins of the people, to make all the attributes of the divine nature, and all the persons subsisting therein, harmonise in man's recovery, and fully to reconcile God and man. Observe, There was a great breach and quarrel between God and man, by reason of sin; but Christ, by becoming man and dying, has taken up the quarrel, and made reconciliation so far that God is ready to receive all into favour and friendship who come to him through Christ. (2.) In things pertaining to his people to their support and comfort: *In that he suffered, being tempted, he is able to succour those that are tempted, v.* 18. Here observe, [1.] Christ's passion: *He suffered, being tempted;* and his temptations were not the least part of his sufferings. *He was in all*

things tempted as we are, yet without sin, ch. iv. 15. [2.] Christ's compassion : *He is able to succour those that are tempted.* He is touched with a feeling of our infirmities, a sympathising physician, tender and skilful ; he knows how to deal with tempted sorrowful souls, because he has been himself sick of the same disease, not of sin, but of temptation and trouble of soul. The remembrance of his own sorrows and temptations makes him mindful of the trials of his people, and ready to help them. Here observe, *First,* The best of Christians are subject to temptations, to many temptations, while in this world ; let us never count upon an absolute freedom from temptations in this world. *Secondly,* Temptations bring our souls into such distress and danger that they need support and succour. *Thirdly,* Christ is ready and willing to succour those who under their temptations apply to him ; and he became man, and was tempted, that he might be every way qualified to succour his people.

CHAPTER III

In this chapter the apostle applies what he had said in the chapter foregoing concerning the priesthood of Christ, I. In a serious, pathetic exhortation that this great high priest, who was discovered to them, might be seriously considered by them, ver. 1-6. II. He then adds many weighty counsels and cautions from ver. 7, to the end.

WHEREFORE, holy brethren, partakers of the heavenly calling, consider the Apostle and High Priest of our profession [confession], Christ Jesus ; 2 Who was faithful to him that appointed him, as also Moses *was faithful* in all his house. 3 For this *man* was counted worthy of more glory than Moses, inasmuch as he who hath builded the house hath more honour than the house. 4 For every house is builded by some *man ;* but he that built all things *is* God. 5 And Moses verily *was* faithful in all his house, as a servant, for the testimony of those things which were to be spoken after ; 6 But Christ as a son over his own house ; whose house are we, if we hold fast the confidence and the rejoicing [boldness and glorying] of the hope firm unto the end.

In these verses we have the application of the doctrine laid down in the close of the last chapter concerning the priesthood of our Lord Jesus Christ. And observe,

I. In how fervent and affectionate a manner the apostle exhorts Christians to have this high priest much in their thoughts, and to make him the object of their close and serious consideration ; and surely no one in earth or heaven deserves our consideration more than he. That this exhortation might be made the more effectual, observe,

1. The honourable compellation used towards those to whom he wrote : *Holy brethren, partakers of the heavenly calling.* (1.) Brethren, not only

my brethren, but the brethren of Christ, and in him brethren to all the saints   All the people of God are brethren, and should love and live like brethren. (2.) Holy brethren ; holy not only in profession and title, but in principle and practice, in heart and life. This has been turned by some into scorn : " These," say they, " are the holy brethren ; " but it is dangerous jesting with such edge-tools : *be not mockers, lest your bands be made strong.* Let those that are thus despised and scorned labour to be holy brethren indeed, and approve themselves so to God ; and they need not be ashamed of the title nor dread the scoffs of the profane. The day is coming when those that make this a term of reproach would count it their greatest honour and happiness to be taken into this sacred brotherhood. (3.) *Partakers of the heavenly calling*—partakers of the means of grace, and of the Spirit of grace, that came from heaven, and by which Christians are effectually called out of darkness into marvellous light, that calling which brings down heaven into the souls of men, raises them up to a heavenly temper and conversation, and prepares them to live for ever with God in heaven.

2. The titles he gives to Christ, whom he would have them consider, (1.) As the apostle of our profession, the prime-minister of the gospel church, a messenger and a principal messenger sent of God to men, upon the most important errand, the great revealer of that faith which we profess to hold and of that hope which we profess to have. (2.) Not only the apostle, but the high priest too, of our profession, the chief officer of the Old Testament as well as the New, the head of the church in every state, and under each dispensation, upon whose satisfaction and intercession we profess to depend for pardon of sin, and acceptance with God. (3.) As Christ, the Messiah, anointed and every way qualified for the office both of apostle and high priest. (4.) As Jesus, our Saviour, our healer, the great physician of souls, typified by the brazen serpent that Moses lifted up in the wilderness, that those who were stung by the fiery serpents might look to him, and be saved.

II. We have the duty we owe to him who bears all these high and honourable titles, and that is to consider him as thus characterised. Consider what he is in himself, what he is to us, and what he will be to us hereafter and for ever ; consider him, fix your thoughts upon him with the greatest attention, and act towards him accordingly ; look unto Jesus, the author and finisher of your faith. Here observe, 1. Many that profess faith in Christ have not a due consideration for him ; he is not so much thought of as he deserves to be, and desires to be, by those that expect salvation from him. 2. Close and serious consideration of Christ would be of great advantage to us to increase our acquaintance with him, and to engage our love and our obedience to him, and reliance on him. 3. Even those that are holy brethren, and partakers of the heavenly calling, have need to stir up one another to think more of Christ than they do, to have him more in their minds ; the best of his people think too seldom and too slightly of him. 4. We must consider Christ as he is described to us in the scriptures, and form our apprehensions of him thence, not from any vain conceptions and fancies of our own.

III. We have several arguments drawn up to enforce this duty of considering Christ the apostle and high priest of our profession.

1. The first is taken from his fidelity, *v.* 2. He was faithful to him that appointed him, as Moses was in all his house. (1.) Christ is an appointed Mediator; God the Father has sent and sealed him to that office, and

therefore his mediation is acceptable to the Father. (2.) He is faithful to that appointment, punctually observing all the rules and orders of his mediation, and fully executing the trust reposed in him by his Father and by his people. (3.) That he is as faithful to him that appointed him as Moses was in all his house. Moses was faithful in the discharge of his office to the Jewish church in the Old Testament, and so is Christ under the New ; this was a proper argument to urge upon the Jews, who had so high an opinion of the faithfulness of Moses, and yet his faithfulness was but typical of Christ's.

2. Another argument is taken from the superior glory and excellence of Christ above Moses (v. 3-6) ; therefore they were more obliged to consider Christ. (1.) Christ was a maker of the house, Moses but a member in it. By the house we are to understand the church of God, the people of God incorporated together under Christ their maker and head, and under subordinate officers, according to his law, observing his institutions. Christ is the maker of this house of the church in all ages : Moses was a minister in the house, he was instrumental under Christ in governing and edifying the house, but Christ is the maker of all things ; for he is God, and no one less than God could build the church, either lay the foundation or carry on the superstructure. No less power was requisite to make the church than to make the world ; the world was made out of nothing, the church made out of materials altogether unfit for such a building. Christ, who is God, drew the ground-plan of the church, provided the materials, and by almighty power disposed them to receive the form ; he has compacted and united this his house, has settled the orders of it, and crowned all with his own presence, which is the true glory of this house of God. (2.) Christ was the master of this house, as well as the maker, v. 5, 6. This house is styled his house, as the Son of God. Moses was only a faithful servant, for a testimony of those things that were afterwards to be revealed. Christ, as the eternal Son of God, is the rightful owner and sovereign ruler of the church. Moses was only a typical governor, for a testimony of all those things relating to the church which would be more clearly, completely, and comfortably revealed in the gospel by the Spirit of Christ ; and therefore Christ is worthy of more glory than Moses, and of greater regard and consideration. This argument the apostle concludes, [1.] With a comfortable accommodation of it to himself and all true believers (v. 6) : *Whose house we are* : each of us personally, as we are the temples of the Holy Ghost, and Christ dwells in us by faith ; all of us jointly, as we are united by the bonds of graces, truths, ordinances, gospel discipline, and devotions. [2.] With a characteristic description of those persons who constitute this house : "*If we hold fast the confidence, and the rejoicing of the hope, firmly to the end ;* that is, if we maintain a bold and open profession of the truths of the gospel, upon which our hopes of grace and glory are built, and live upon and up to those hopes, so as to have a holy rejoicing in them, which shall abide firm to the end, notwithstanding all that we may meet with in so doing." So that you see there must not only be a setting out well in the ways of Christ, but a stedfastness and perseverance therein unto the end. We have here a direction what those must do who would partake of the dignity and privileges of the household of Christ. *First*, They must take the truths of the gospel into their heads and hearts. *Secondly*, They must build their hopes of happiness upon those truths. *Thirdly*, They must make an open profession of those truths. *Fourthly*, They must live so up to them as to keep their evidences clear, that they may rejoice in hope, and

then they must in all persevere to the end. In a word, they must walk closely, consistently, courageously, and constantly, in the faith and practice of the gospel, that their Master, when he comes, may own and approve them.

7 Wherefore (as the Holy Ghost saith, To-day if ye will hear his voice, 8 Harden not your hearts, as in the provocation, in the day of temptation in the wilderness: 9 When your fathers tempted me, proved me [tempted *me* by proving *me*], and saw my works forty years. 10 Wherefore I was grieved with that generation, and said, They do alway err in *their* heart; and they have not known [but they did not know] my ways. 11 So [as] I sware in my wrath, They shall not enter into my rest.) 12 Take heed, brethren, lest there be in any of you an evil heart of unbelief, in departing from the living God. 13 But exhort one another daily, while it is called To-day; lest any of you be hardened through the deceitfulness of sin. 14 For we are made partakers of Christ, if we hold the beginning of our confidence stedfast unto the end; 15 While it is said, To-day if ye will hear his voice, harden not your hearts, as in the provocation. 16 For some, when they ·had heard, did provoke: howbeit not all that came [For who, when they heard, did provoke? Nay, did not all they that came] out of Egypt by Moses. 17 But with whom was he grieved forty years? *was it* not with them that had sinned, whose carcases fell in the wilderness? 18 And to whom sware he that they should not enter into his rest, but to them that believed not [were disobedient]? 19 So we see they could not enter in because of unbelief.

Here the apostle proceeds in pressing upon them serious counsels and cautions to the close of the chapter; and he recites a passage out of Ps. xcv. 7, &c., where observe,

I. What he counsels them to do—to give a speedy and present attention to the call of Christ. "Hear his voice, assent to, approve of, and consider, what God in Christ speaks unto you; apply it to yourselves with suitable affections and endeavours, and set about it this very day, for to-morrow it may be too late."

II. What he cautions them against—hardening their hearts, turning the deaf ear to the calls and counsels of Christ: "When he tells you of the evil of sin, the excellency of holiness, the necessity of receiving him by faith as your Saviour, do not shut your ear and heart against such a voice as this." Observe, The hardening of our hearts is the spring of all our other sins.

III. Whose example he warns them by—that of ·the Israelites their fathers in the wilderness: *As in the provocation and day of temptation;* this refers to that remarkable passage at Massah Meribah, Exod. xvii. 2-7. Observe,

1. Days of temptation are often days of provocation.

2. To provoke God, when he is trying us, and letting us see that we entirely depend and live immediately upon him, is a provocation with a witness.

3. The sins of others, especially our relations, should be a warning to us. Our fathers' sins and punishments should be remembered by us, to deter us from following their evil examples. Now as to the sin of the fathers of the Jews, here reflected upon, observe,

(1.) The state in which these fathers were, when they thus sinned : they were in the wilderness, brought out of Egypt, but not got into Canaan, the thoughts whereof should have restrained them from sin.

(2.) The sin they were guilty of : they tempted and provoked God ; they distrusted God, murmured against Moses, and would not attend to the voice of God.

(3.) The aggravations of their sin : they sinned in the wilderness, where they had a more immediate dependence upon God : they sinned when God was trying them ; they sinned when they saw his works—works of wonder wrought for their deliverance out of Egypt, and their support and supply in the wilderness from day to day. They continued thus to sin against God for forty years. These were heinous aggravations.

(4.) The source and spring of such aggravated sins, which were, [1.] They erred in their hearts ; and these heart-errors produced many other errors in their lips and live. [2.] They did not know God's ways, though he had walked before them. They did not know his ways ; neither those ways of his providence in which he had walked towards them, nor those ways of his precept in which they ought to have walked towards God ; they did not observe either his providences or his ordinances in a right manner.

(5.) The just and great resentment God had at their sins, and yet the great patience he exercised towards them (v. 10) : *Wherefore I was grieved with that generation.* Note, [1.] All sin, especially sin committed by God's professing privileged people, does not only anger and affront God, but it grieves him. [2.] God is loth to destroy his people in or for their sin, he waits long to be gracious to them. [3.] God keeps an exact account of the time that people go on in sinning against him, and in grieving him by their sins ; but at length, if they by their sins continue to grieve the Spirit of God, their sins shall be made grievous to their own spirits, either in a way of judgment or mercy.

(6.) The irreversible doom passed upon them at last for their sins. God swore in his wrath that they should not enter into his rest, the rest either of an earthly or of a heavenly Canaan. Observe, [1.] Sin, long continued in, will kindle the divine wrath, and make it flame out against sinners. [2.] God's wrath will discover itself in its righteous resolution to destroy the impenitent ; he will swear in his wrath, not rashly, but righteously, and his wrath will make their condition a restless condition ; there is no resting under the wrath of God.

IV. What use the apostle makes of their awful example, *v.* 12, 13, &c. He gives the Hebrews a proper caution, and enforces it with an affectionate compellation.

1. He gives the Hebrews a proper caution ; the word is, *Take heed,* βλέπετε—*look to it.* "Look about you ; be upon your guard against enemies both within and without ; be circumspect. You see what kept many of your forefathers out of Canaan, and made their carcases fall in the wilderness ; take heed lest you fall into the same sin and snare and dreadful sentence. For you see Christ is head of the church, a much greater person

than Moses, and your contempt of him must be a greater sin than their contempt of Moses; and so you are in danger of falling under a severer sentence than they." Observe, The ruin of others should be a warning to us to take heed of the rock they split upon. Israel's fall should for ever be a warning to all who came after them ; for *all these things happened to them for ensamples* (1 Cor. x. 11), and should be remembered by us. Take heed ; all who would get safely to heaven must look about them.

2. He enforces the admonition with an affectionate compellation : "*Brethren*, not only in the flesh, but in the Lord ; brethren whom I love, and for whose welfare I labour and long." And here he enlarges upon the matter of the admonition : *Take heed, brethren, lest there be in any of you an evil heart of unbelief in departing from the living God.* Here observe, (1.) A heart of unbelief is an evil heart. Unbelief is a great sin, it vitiates the heart of man. (2.) An evil heart of unbelief is at the bottom of all our sinful departures from God ; it is a leading step to apostasy ; if once we allow ourselves to distrust God, we may soon desert him. (3.) Christian brethren have need to be cautioned against apostasy. *Let those that think they stand take heed lest they fall.*

3. He subjoins good counsel to the caution, and advises them to that which would be a remedy against this evil heart of unbelief—that they should *exhort one another daily, while it is called to-day, v. 13.* Observe, (1.) We should be doing all the good we can to one another while we are together, which will be but a short and uncertain time. (2.) Since to-morrow is none of ours, we must make the best improvement of to-day. (3.) If Christians do not exhort one another daily, they will be in danger of being hardened through the deceitfulness of sin. Note, [1.] There is a great deal of deceitfulness in sin ; it appears fair, but is filthy ; it appears pleasant, but is pernicious ; it promises much, but performs nothing. [2.] The deceitfulness of sin is of a hardening nature to the soul ; one sin allowed prepares for another ; every act of sin confirms the habit ; sinning against conscience is the way to sear the conscience ; and therefore it should be the great concern of every one to exhort himself and others to beware of sin.

4. He comforts those who not only set out well, but hold on well, and hold out to the end (*v.* 14): *We are made partakers of Christ if we hold the beginning of our confidence stedfast to the end.* Here observe, (1.) The saints' privilege : they are made partakers of Christ, that is, of the Spirit, nature, graces, righteousness, and life of Christ ; they are interested in all that is Christ's, in all that he is, in all that he has done, or can do. (2.) The condition on which they hold that privilege, namely, their perseverance in the bold and open profession and practice of Christ and Christianity unto the end. Not but they shall persevere, being kept by the mighty power of God through faith to salvation, but to be pressed thus to it is one means by which Christ helps his people to persevere. This tends to make them watchful and diligent, and so keeps them from apostasy. Here observe, [1.] The same spirit with which Christians set out in the ways of God they should maintain and evidence to the end. Those who begin seriously, and with lively affections and holy resolutions and humble reliance, should go on in the same spirit. But, [2.] There are a great many who in the beginning of their profession show a great deal of courage and confidence, but do not hold them fast to the end. [3.] Perseverance in faith is the best evidence of the sincerity of our faith.

5. The apostle resumes what he had quoted before from Ps. xcv. 7, &c., and he applies it closely to those of that generation, *v.* 15, 16, &c. While

it is said, *To-day if you will hear*, &c. ; as if he should say, "What was recited before from that scripture belonged not only to former ages, but to you now, And to all who shall come after you ; that you take heed you fall not into the same sins, lest you fall under the same condemnation." The apostle tells them that though some who had heard the voice of God did prov.ke him, yet all did not so. Observe, (1.) Though the majority of hearers provoked God by unbelief, yet some there were who believed the report. (2.) Though the hearing of the word be the ordinary means of salvation, yet, if it be not hearkened to, it will expose men more to the anger of God. (3.) God will have a remnant that shall be obedient to his voice, and he will take care of such and make mention of them with honour. (4.) If these should fall in a common calamity, yet they shall partake of eternal salvation, while disobedient hearers perish for ever.

6. The apostle puts some queries upon what had been before mentioned, and gives proper answers to them (*v*. 17-19) : *But with whom was he grieved forty years ? With those that sinned. And to whom did he swear ?* &c. Whence observe, (1.) God is grieved only with those of his people who sin against him, and continue in sin. (2.) God is grieved and provoked most by sins publicly committed by the generality of a nation ; when sin becomes epidemic, it is most provoking. (3.) Though God grieves long, and bears long, when pressed with the weight of general and prevailing wickedness, yet he will at length ease himself of public offenders by public judgments. (4.) Unbelief (with rebellion which is the consequent of it) is the great damning sin of the world, especially of those who have a revelation of the mind and will of God. This sin shuts up the heart of God, and shuts up the gate of heaven, against them ; it lays them under the wrath and curse of God, and leaves them there ; so that in truth and justice to himself he is obliged to cast them off for ever.

CHAPTER IV

The apostle having in the foregoing chapter set forth the sin and punishment of the ancient Jews, proceeds in this, I. To declare that our privileges by Christ under the gospel exceed the privileges of the Jewish Church under Moses, as a reason why we should make a right improvement of them, ver. 1-4. II. He assigns the cause why the ancient Hebrews did not profit by their religious privileges, ver. 2. Then, III. Confirms the privileges of those who believe, and the misery of those who continue in unbelief, 3-10. IV. Concludes with proper and powerful arguments and motives to faith and obedience.

LET us therefore fear, lest, a promise being left *us* of entering into his rest, any of you should seem to come short of it. ² For unto us was the gospel preached [indeed we have had good tidings preached unto us], as well as unto them : but the word preached [word of hearing] did not profit them, not being mixed with faith in them that heard *it* [because they were not united by faith with them that heard]. ³ For we which have believed do enter into rest [that rest], as he said, As I have sworn in my wrath, if they shall enter into my rest: although the works were finished from the foundation of the world. ⁴ For he spake in a certain place of the seventh *day* on this wise, And God did rest the seventh day from all his works. ⁵ And in this *place* again, If they shall enter into my rest. ⁶ Seeing therefore it remaineth that some must enter therein, and they to whom it was first preached entered not in because of unbelief [**disobedience**]: ⁷ (Again, he limiteth a certain day, saying in David, To-day, after so long a time; as it is said, To-day if ye will hear his voice, harden not your hearts. ⁸ For if Jesus [**Joshua**] had given them rest, then would he not afterward have spoken of another day. ⁹ There remaineth therefore a rest [**a sabbath rest**] to the people of God. ¹⁰ For he that is entered into his rest, he also hath ceased from his own works [**rested from his works**], as God *did* from his.)

Here, I. The apostle declares that our privileges by Christ under the gospel are not only as great, but greater than those enjoyed under the Mosaic law. He specifies this, that we have a promise left us of entering into his rest; that is, of entering into a covenant-relation to Christ, and a state of communion with God through Christ, and of growing up therein, till we are made perfect in glory. We have discoveries of this rest, and proposals, and the best directions how we may attain unto it. This promise of spiritual rest is a promise left us by the Lord Jesus Christ in his last will and testament, as a precious legacy. Our business is to see to it that we be the legatees, that we lay our claim to that rest and freedom from the dominion of sin, Satan, and the flesh, by which the souls of men are kept in servitude and deprived of the true rest of the soul, and may be also set free from the yoke of the law and all the toilsome ceremonies and services of it, and may enjoy peace with God in his ordinances and providences, and in our own consciences, and so have the prospect and earnest of perfect and everlasting rest in heaven.

II. He demonstrates the truth of his assertion, that we have as great advantages as they. For says he (*v.* 2), *To us was the gospel preached as well as unto them;* the same gospel for substance was preached under both Testaments, though not so clearly; not in so comfortable a manner under the Old as under the New. The best privileges the ancient Jews had were their gospel privileges; the sacrifices and ceremonies of the Old Testament were the gospel of that dispensation; and, whatever was excellent in it, was the respect it had to Christ. Now, if this was their highest privilege, we are not inferior to them; for we have the gospel as well as they, and in greater purity and perspicuity than they had.

III. He again assigns the reason why so few of the ancient Jews profited by that dispensation of the gospel which they enjoyed, and that was their want of faith : *The word preached did not profit them because it was not mixed with faith in those that heard him, v.* 2. Observe, 1. The word is preached to us that we may profit by it, that we may gain spiritual riches by it; it is a price put into our hands to get wisdom, the rich endowment of the soul. 2. There have been in all ages a great many unprofitable hearers; many who seem to deal much in sermons, in hearing the word of

God, but gain nothing to their souls thereby ; and those who are not gainers by hearing are great losers. 3. That which is at the bottom of all our unprofitableness under the word is our unbelief. We do not mix faith with what we hear ; it is faith in the hearer that is the life of the word. Though the preacher believes the gospel, and endeavours to mix faith with his preaching, and to speak as one who has believed and so spoken, yet, if the hearers have not faith in their souls to mix with the word, they will be never the better for it. This faith must mingle with every word, and be in act and exercise while we are hearing ; and, when we have heard the word, assenting to the truth of it, approving of it, accepting the mercy offered, applying the word to ourselves with suitable affections, then we shall find great profit and gain by the word preached.

IV. On these considerations the apostle grounds his repeated and earnest caution and counsel that those who enjoy the gospel should maintain a holy fear and.jealousy over themselves, lest latent unbelief should rob them of the benefit of the word, and of that spiritual rest which is discovered and tendered in the gospel : *Let us fear lest, a promise being left us of entering into his rest, any of you should seem to come short of it, v.* 1. Observe, 1. Grace and glory are attainable by all under the gospel : there is an offer, and a promise to those who shall accept the offer. 2. Those who may attain them may also fall short. Those who might have attained salvation by faith may fall short by unbelief. 3. It is a dreadful thing so much as to seem to fall short of the gospel salvation, to seem so to themselves, to lose their comfortable hope ; and to seem so to others, so losing the honour of their holy profession. But, if it be so dreadful to seem to fall short of this rest, it is much more dreadful really to fall short. Such a disappoint-ment must be fatal. 4. One good means to prevent either our real falling short or seeming to fall short is to maintain a holy and religious fear lest we should fall short. This will make us vigilant and diligent, sincere and serious ; this fear will put us upon examining our faith and exercising it ; whereas presumption is the high road to ruin.

V. The apostle confirms the happiness of all those who truly believe the gospel ; and this he does,

1. By asserting so positively the truth of it, from the experience of himself and others : " *We, who have believed, do enter into rest, v.* 3. We enter into a blessed union with Christ, and into a communion with God through Christ ; in this state we actually enjoy many sweet communications of pardon of sin, peace of conscience, joy in the Holy Ghost, increase of grace, and earnests of glory, resting from the servitude of sin, and reposing ourselves in God till we are prepared to rest with him in heaven."

2. He illustrates and confirms it that those who believe are thus happy, and do enter into rest. (1.) From God's finishing his work of creation, and so entering into his rest (v. 3, 4), appointing our first parents to rest the seventh day, to rest in God. Now as God finished his work, and then rested from it, and acquiesced in it, so he will cause those who believe to finish their work, and then to enjoy their rest. (2.) From God's con-tinuing the observance of the sabbath after the fall, and the revelation of a Redeemer. They were to keep the seventh day a holy sabbath to the Lord, therein praising him who had raised them up out of nothing by creating power, and praying to him that he would create them anew by his Spirit of grace, and direct their faith to the promised Redeemer and restorer of all things, by which faith they find rest in their souls. (3.) From God's proposing Canaan as a typical rest for the Jews who believed :

and as those who did believe, Caleb and Joshua, did actually enter into Canaan ; so those who now believe shall enter into rest. (4.) From the certainty of another rest besides that seventh day of rest instituted and observed both before and after the fall, and besides that typical Canaan-rest which most of the Jews fell short of by unbelief ; for the Psalmist has spoken of another day and another rest, whence it is evident that there is a more spiritual and excellent sabbath remaining for the people of God than that into which Joshua led the Jews (v. 6–9), and this rest remaining is, [I.] A rest of grace, and comfort, and holiness, in the gospel state. This is the rest wherewith the Lord Jesus, our Joshua, causes weary souls and awakened consciences to rest, and this is the refreshing. [2.] A rest in glory, the everlasting sabbatism of heaven, which is the repose and per-fection of nature and grace too, where the people of God shall enjoy the end of their faith and the object of all their desires. (5.) This is furthur proved from the glorious forerunners who have actually taken possession of this rest—God and Christ. It is certain that God, after the creating of the world in six days, entered into his rest ; and it is certain that Christ, when he had finished the work of our redemption, entered into his rest ; and these were not only examples, but earnests, that believers shall enter into their rest : *He that hath entered into rest hath also ceased from his own works, as God did from his, v.* 10. Every true believer hath ceased from his own works of sin, from relying on his own works of righteousness, and from the burdensome works of the law, as God and Christ have ceased from their works of creation and redemption.

VI. The apostle confirms the misery of those who do not believe ; they shall never enter into this spiritual rest, either of grace here or glory hereafter. This is as certain as the word and oath of God can make it. As sure as God has entered into his rest, so sure it is that obstinate unbelievers shall be excluded. As sure as the unbelieving Jews fell in the wilderness, and never reached the promised land, so sure it is that unbelievers shall fall into destruction, and never reach heaven. As sure as Joshua, the great captain of the Jews, could not give them possession of Canaan because of their unbelief, notwithstanding his eminent valour and conduct, so sure it is that even Jesus himself, the captain of our salvation, notwithstanding all that fulness of grace and strength that dwells in him, will not, cannot, give to final unbelievers either spiritual or eternal rest : it remains only for the people of God ; others by their sin abandon them-selves to eternal restlessness.

[11] Let us labour [give diligence] therefore to enter into that rest, lest any man fall after the same example of unbelief [disobedience]. [12] For the word of God *is* quick [living] and powerful [active], and sharper than any two-edged sword, pierc-ing even to the dividing asunder of soul and spirit, and of the joints and marrow, and *is* a discerner of the thoughts and intents of the heart. [13] Neither is there any creature that is not manifest in his sight : but all things *are* naked and opened unto the eyes of him with whom we have to do. [14] Seeing then that we have a great high priest, that is passed into [through] the heavens, Jesus the Son of God, let us hold fast *our* profession. [15] For

we have not a high priest which cannot be touched with the
feeling of our infirmities; but was in all points tempted like as
we are, yet without sin. ¹⁶ Let us therefore come boldly unto
the throne of grace, that we may obtain mercy, and find grace
to help in time of need.

In this latter part of the chapter the apostle concludes, first, with a
serious repeated exhortation, and then with proper and powerful motives.

I. Here we have a serious exhortation. *Let us labour therefore to enter
into that rest, v.* 11. Observe, 1. The end proposed—rest spiritual and
eternal, the rest of grace here and glory hereafter—in Christ on earth,
with Christ in heaven. 2. The way to this end prescribed—labour, diligent
labour ; this is the only way to rest ; those who will not work now shall
not rest hereafter. After due and diligent labour, sweet and satisfying
rest shall follow ; and labour now will make that rest more pleasant
when it comes. *The sleep of the labouring man is sweet,* Eccl. v. 12. Let
us therefore labour, let us all agree and be unanimous in this, and let us
quicken one another, and call upon one another to this diligence. It is
the truest act of friendship, when we see our fellow-Christians loiter, to
call upon them to mind their business and labour at it in earnest. "Come,
Sirs, let us all go to work ; why do we sit still? Why do we loiter ?
Come, let us labour ; now is our working time, our rest remains." Thus
should Christians call upon themselves and one another to be diligent in
duty ; and so much the more as we see the day approaching.

II. Here we have proper and powerful motives to make the advice
effectual, which are drawn,

1. From the dreadful example of those who have already perished by
unbelief : *Lest any man fall after the same example of unbelief.* To have
seen so many fall before us will be a great aggravation of our sin, if we
will not take warning by them : their ruin calls loudly upon us ; their
lost and restless souls cry to us from their torments, that we do not, by
sinning as they did, make ourselves miserable as they are.

2. From the great help and advantage we may have from the word of
God to strengthen our faith and excite our diligence, that we may obtain
this rest : *The word of God is quick and powerful, v.* 12. By the word of
God we may understand either the essential or the written word : the
essential *Word,* that in *the beginning was with God and was God* (John i. 1),
the Lord Jesus Christ, and indeed what is said in this verse is true concerning him ; but most understand it of the written word, the Holy
Scriptures, which are the word of God. Now of this word it is said, (1.)
That it is *quick ;* it is very lively and active, in all its efforts, in seizing
the conscience of the sinner, in cutting him to the heart, and in comforting
him and binding up the wounds of the soul. Those know not the word of
God who call it a dead letter ; it is quick, compared to the light, and
nothing quicker than the light ; it is not only quick, but quickening ; it is
a vital light ; it is a living word, ζῶν. Saints die, and sinners die ; but
the word of God lives. *All flesh is grass, and all the glory thereof as
the flower of grass. The grass withereth, and the flower thereof falleth
away, but the word of the Lord endureth for ever,* 1 Pet. i. 24, 25. *Your
fathers, where are they ? And the prophets, do they live for ever ? But my
words, which I commanded the prophets, did they not take hold of your fathers ?*
Zech. i. 5, 6. (2.) It is *powerful.* When God sets it home by his Spirit,

it convinces powerfully, converts powerfully, and comforts powerfully. It is so powerful as to pull down strongholds (2 Cor. x. 4, 5), to raise the dead, to make the deaf to hear, the blind to see, the dumb to speak, and the lame to walk. It is powerful to batter down Satan's kingdom, and to set up the kingdom of Christ upon the ruins thereof. (3.) It is *sharper than any two-edged sword ;* it cuts both ways ; it is *the sword of the Spirit,* Eph. vi. 17. It is the two-edged sword that cometh out of the mouth of Christ, Rev. i. 16. It is sharper than any two-edged sword, for it will enter where no other sword can, and make a more critical dissection : it *pierces to the dividing asunder of the soul and the spirit,* the soul and its habitual prevailing temper ; it makes a soul that has been a long time of a proud spirit to be humble, of a perverse spirit to be meek and obedient. Those sinful habits that have become as it were natural to the soul, and rooted deeply in it, and become in a manner one with it, are separated and cut off by this sword. It cuts off ignorance from the understanding, rebellion from the will, and enmity from the mind, which, when carnal, is enmity itself against God. This sword divides between *the joints and the marrow,* the most secret, close, and intimate parts of the body; this sword can cut off the lusts of the flesh as well as the lusts of the mind, and make men willing to undergo the sharpest operation for the mortifying of sin. (4.) It is *a discerner of the thoughts and intents of the heart,* even the most secret and remote thoughts and designs. It will discover to men the variety of their thoughts and purposes, the vileness of them, the bad principles they are actuated by, the sinister and sinful ends they act to. The word will turn the inside of a sinner out, and let him see all that is in his heart. Now such a word as this must needs be a great help to our faith and obedience.

3. From the perfections of the Lord Jesus Christ, both of his person and office.

(1.) His person, particularly his omniscience : *Neither is there any creature that is not manifest in his sight, v.* 13. This is agreeable to what Christ speaks of himself : *All the churches shall know that I am he that searches the reins and hearts,* Rev. ii. 23. None of the creatures can be concealed from Christ ; none of the creatures of God, for Christ is the Creator of them all ; and there are none of the motions and workings of our heads and hearts (which may be called creatures of our own) but what are open and manifest to him with whom we have to do as the object of our worship, and the high priest of our profession. He, by his omniscience, cuts up the sacrifice we bring to him, that it may be presented to the Father. Now as the high priest inspected the sacrificed beasts, cut them up to the back-bone to see whether they were sound at heart, so all things are thus dissected, and lie open to the piercing eye of our great high priest. And he who now tries our sacrifices will at length, as Judge, try our state. We shall have to do with him as one who will determine our everlasting state. Some read the words, *to whom with us there is an account or reckoning.* Christ has an exact account of us all. He has accounted for all who believe on him ; and he will account with all : our accounts are before us. This omniscience of Christ, and the account we owe of ourselves to him, should engage us to persevere in faith and obedience till he has perfected all our affairs.

(2.) We have an account of the excellency and perfection of Christ, as to his office, and this particular office of our high priest. The apostle first instructs Christians in the knowledge of their high priest, what kind of high priest he is, and then puts them in mind of the duty they owe on this account.

[1.] What kind of high priest Christ is (*v.* 14): *Seeing we have such a high priest ;* that is, *First,* A great high priest, much greater than Aaron, or any of the priests of his order. The high priests under the law were accounted great and venerable persons ; but they were but faint types and shadows of Christ. The greatness of our high priest is set forth, 1. By his having passed into the heavens. The high priest under the law, once a year, went out of the people's sight within the veil, into the holiest of all, where were the sacred signals of the presence of God ; but Christ once for all has passed into the heavens, to take the government of all upon him, to send the Spirit to prepare a place for his people, and to make intercession for them. Christ executed one part of his priesthood on earth, in dying for us ; the other he executes in heaven, by pleading the cause, and presenting the offerings, of his people. 2. The greatness of Christ is set forth by his name, *Jesus*—a physician and a Saviour, and one of a divine nature, the Son of God by eternal generation ; and therefore having divine perfection, able to save to the uttermost all who come to God by him. *Secondly,* He is not only a great, but a gracious high priest, merciful, compassionate, and sympathising with his people : *We have not a high priest who cannot be touched with the feeling of our infirmities, v.* 15. Though he is so great, and so far above us, yet he is very kind, and tenderly concerned for us. He is touched with the feeling of our infirmities in such a manner as none else can be ; for he was himself tried with all the afflictions and troubles that are incident to our nature in its fallen state : and this not only that he might be able to satisfy for us, but to sympathize with us. But then, *Thirdly,* He is a sinless high priest : *He was in all things tempted as we are, yet without sin.* He was tempted by Satan, but he came off without sin. We seldom meet with temptations but they give us some shock. We are apt to give back, though we do not yield ; but our great high priest came off clear in his encounter with the devil, who could neither find any sin in him nor fix any stain upon him. He was tried severely by the Father. It pleased the Lord to bruise him ; and yet he sinned not, either in thought, word, or deed. He had done no violence, neither was there any deceit in his mouth. He was holy, harmless, and undefiled ; and such a high priest became us. Having thus told us what a one our high priest is, the apostle proceeds to show us,

[2.] How we should demean ourselves towards him. *First,* Let us hold fast our profession of faith in him, *v.* 14. Let us never deny him, never be ashamed of him before men. Let us hold fast the enlightening doctrines of Christianity in our heads, the enlivening principles of it in our hearts, the open profession of it in our lips, and our practical and universal subjection to it in our lives. Observe here, 1. We ought to be possessed of the doctrines, principles, and practice of the Christian life. 2. When we are so, we may be in danger of losing our hold, from the corruption of our hearts, the temptations of Satan, and the allurements of this evil world. 3. The excellency of the high priest of our profession would make our apostasy from him most heinous and inexcusable ; it would be the greatest folly and the basest ingratitude. 4. Christians must not only set out well, but they must hold out : those who endure to the end will be saved, and none but they. *Secondly,* We should encourage ourselves, by the excellency of our high priest, to come boldly to the throne of grace, *v.* 16. Here observe, 1. There is a throne of grace set up, a way of worship instituted, in which God may with honour meet poor sinners, and treat with them, and they may with hope draw nigh to him, repenting and believing.

God might have set up a tribunal of strict and inexorable justice, dispensing death, the wages of sin, to all who were convened before it; but he has chosen to set up a throne of grace. A throne speaks authority, and bespeaks awe and reverence. A throne of grace speaks great encouragement even to the chief of sinners. There grace reigns, and acts with sovereign freedom, power, and bounty. 2. It is our duty and interest to be often found before this throne of grace, waiting on the Lord in all the duties of his worship, private and public. It is good for us to be there. 3. Our business and errand at the throne of grace should be that we *may obtain mercy and find grace to help in time of need.* Mercy and grace are the things we want, mercy to pardon all our sins and grace to purify our souls. 4. Besides the daily dependence we have upon God for present supplies, there are some seasons in which we shall most sensibly need the mercy and grace of God, and we should lay up prayers against such seasons—times of temptation, either by adversity or prosperity, and especially a dying time : we should every day put up a petition for mercy in our last day. The Lord grant unto us that we may find mercy of the Lord at that day, 2 Tim. i. 18. 5. In all our approaches to this throne of grace for mercy, we should come with a humble freedom and boldness, with a liberty of spirit and a liberty of speech; we should ask in faith, nothing doubting; we should come with a spirit of adoption, as children to a reconciled God and Father. We are indeed to come with reverence and godly fear, but not with terror and amazement; not as if we were dragged before the tribunal of justice, but kindly invited to the mercy-seat, where grace reigns, and loves to exert and exalt itself towards us. 6. The office of Christ, as being our high priest, and such a high priest, should be the ground of our confidence in all our approaches to the throne of grace. Had we not a Mediator, we could have no boldness in coming to God; for we are guilty and polluted creatures. All we do is polluted; we cannot go into the presence of God alone; we must either go in the hand of a Mediator or our hearts and our hopes will fail us. We have boldness to enter into the holiest by the blood of Jesus. He is our Advocate, and, while he pleads for his people, he pleads with the price in his hand, by which he purchased all that our souls want or can desire.

CHAPTER V

In this chapter the apostle continues his discourse upon the priesthood of Christ, a sweet subject, which he would not too soon dismiss. And here, I. He explains the nature of the priestly office in general, ver. 1-3. II. The proper and regular call there must be to this office, ver. 4-6. III. The requisite qualifications for the work, ver. 7-9. IV. The peculiar order of the priesthood of Christ; it was not after the order of Aaron, but of Melchisedec, ver. 6, 7, 10. V. He reproves the Hebrews, that they had not made those improvements in knowledge which might have made them capable of looking into the more abstruse and mysterious parts of scripture, ver. 11-14.

FOR every high priest taken from among men is ordained for men in things *pertaining* to God, that he may offer both gifts and sacrifices for sins : ² Who can have compassion on the ignorant, and on them that are out of the way: for that he himself also is compassed with infirmity. ³ And by reason hereof he ought, as for the people, so also for himself, to offer for sins. ⁴ And no man taketh this honour unto himself, but he that is called of God, as *was* Aaron. ⁵ So also Christ glorified not himself to be made a high priest; but he that said unto him, Thou art my Son, to-day have I begotten thee. ⁶ As he saith also in another *place*, Thou *art* a priest for ever after the order of Melchisedec. ⁷ Who in the days of his flesh, when he had offered up prayers and supplications with strong crying and tears unto him that was able to save him from death, and was heard in that he feared [**for his godly fear**]; ⁸ Though he were a Son, yet learned he obedience by the things which he suffered; ⁹ And being made perfect, he became the author of eternal salvation unto all them that obey him.

We have here an account of the nature of the priestly office in general, though with an accommodation to the Lord Jesus Christ. We are told,

I. Of what kind of beings the high priest must be. He must be taken from among men ; he must be a man, one of ourselves, bone of our bone, flesh of our flesh, and spirit of our spirits, a partaker of our nature, and a standard-bearer among ten thousand. This implies, 1. That man had sinned. 2. That God would not admit sinful man to come to him immediately and alone, without a high priest, who must be taken from among men. 3. That God was pleased to take one from among men, by whom they might approach God in hope, and he might receive them with honour. 4. That every one shall now be welcome to God that comes to him by this his priest.

II. For whom every high priest is ordained : *For men in things pertaining to God*, for the glory of God and the good of men, that he might come between God and man. So Christ did ; and therefore let us never attempt to go to God but through Christ, nor expect any favour from God but through Christ.

III. For what purpose every high priest was ordained : *That he might offer both gifts and sacrifices for sin.*

1. That he might offer gifts or free-will offerings, brought to the high priest, so offered for the glory of God, and as an acknowledgment that our all is of him and from him ; we have nothing but what he is pleased to give us, and of his own we offer to him an oblation of acknowledgment. This intimates, (1.) That all we bring to God must be free and not forced ; it must be a gift ; it must be given and not taken away again. (2.) That all we bring to God must go through the high priest's hands, as the great agent between God and man.

2. That he might offer sacrifices for sin : that is, the offerings that were appointed to make atonement, that sin might be pardoned and sinners accepted. Thus Christ is constituted a high priest for both these ends. Our good deeds must be presented by Christ, to render ourselves and them acceptable ; and our evil deeds must be expiated by the sacrifice of himself, that they may not condemn and destroy us. And now, as we value acceptance with God and pardon, we must apply ourselves by faith to this our great high priest,

IV. How this high priest must be qualified, *v.* 2.

1. He must be one that can have compassion on two sorts of persons :—
(1.) *On the ignorant,* or those that are guilty of sins of ignorance. He must be one who can find in his heart to pity them, and intercede with God for them, one that is willing to instruct those that are dull of understanding. (2.) *On those that are out of the way,* out of the way of truth, duty, and happiness ; and he must be one who has tenderness enough to lead them back from the by-paths of error, sin, and misery, into the right way : this will require great patience and compassion, even the compassion of a God.

2. He must also be compassed with infirmity ; and so be able from himself feelingly to consider óur frame, and to sympathize with us. Thus Christ was qualified. He took upon him our sinless infirmities ; and this gives us great encouragement to apply ourselves to him under every affliction ; for in all the afflictions of his people he is afflicted.

V. How the high priest was to be called of God. He must have both an internal and external call to his office : *For no man taketh this honour to himself* (*v.* 4), that is, no man ought to do it, no man can do it legally ; if any does it, he must be reckoned a usurper, and treated accordingly. Here observe, 1. The office of the priesthood was a very great honour. To be employed to stand between God and man, one while representing God and his will to men, at another time representing man and his case to God, and dealing between them about matters of the highest importance—entrusted on both sides with the honour of God and the happiness of man—must render the office very honourable. 2. The priesthood is an office and honour that no man ought to take to himself ; if he does, he can expect no success in it, nor any reward for it, only from himself. He is an intruder who is not called of God, as was Aaron. Observe, (1.) God is the fountain of all honour, especially true spiritual honour. He is the fountain of true authority, whether he calls any to the priesthood in an extraordinary way, as he did Aaron, or in an ordinary way, as he called his successors. (2.) Those only can expect assistance from God, and acceptance with him, and his presence and blessing on them and their administrations, that are called of God ; others may expect a blast instead of a blessing.

VI. How this is brought home and applied to Christ : *So Christ glorified not himself, v.* 5. Observe here, Though Christ reckoned it his glory to be made a high priest, yet he would not assume that glory to himself. He could truly say, *I seek not my own glory,* John viii. 50. Considered as God, he was not capable of any additional glory, but as man and Mediator he did not run without being sent ; and, if he did not, surely others should be afraid to do it.

▸ VII. The apostle prefers Christ before Aaron, both in the manner of his call and in the holiness of his person. 1. In the manner of his call, in which God said unto him, *Thou art my Son, this day have I begotten thee* (quoted from Ps. ii. 7), referring to his eternal generation as God, his wonderful conception as man, and his perfect qualification as Mediator. Thus God solemnly declared his dear affection to Christ, his authoritative appointment of him to the office of a Mediator, his instalment and approbation of him in that office, his acceptance of him, and of all he had done or should do in the discharge of it. Now God never said thus to Aaron. Another expression that God used in the call of Christ we have in Ps. cx. 4. *Thou art a priest for ever, after the order of Melchisedec, v.* 6. God the Father appointed him a priest of a higher order than that of Aaron. The priesthood of Aaron was to be but temporary; the priesthood of Christ was to be perpetual: the priesthood of Aaron was to be successive, descending from the fathers to the children; the priesthood of Christ, after the order of Melchisedec, was to be personal, and the high priest immortal as to his office, without descent, having neither beginning of days nor end of life, as it is more largely described in the seventh chapter, and will be opened there. 2. Christ is here preferred to Aaron in the holiness of his person. Other priests were to offer up sacrifices, as for the *sins of others, so for themselves, v.* 3. But Christ needed not to offer for sins for himself, *for he had done no violence,* neither was there *any deceit in his mouth,* Isa. liii. 9. And such a high priest became us.

VIII. We have an account of Christ's discharge of this his office, and of the consequences of that discharge, *v.* 7-9.

1. The discharge of his office of the priesthood (*v.* 7): *Who in the days of his flesh, when he had offered up prayers and supplications,* &c. Here observe, (1.) He took to him flesh, and for some days tabernacled therein; he became a mortal man, and reckoned his life by days, herein setting us an example how we should reckon ours. Were we to reckon our lives by days, it would be a means to quicken us to do the work of every day in its day. (2.) Christ in the days of his flesh, subjected himself to death; he hungered, he was a tempted, bleeding, dying Jesus! His body is now in heaven, but it is a spiritual glorious body. (3.) God the Father was able to save him from death. He could have prevented his dying, but he would not; for then the great design of his wisdom and grace must have been defeated. What would have become of us if God had saved Christ from dying? The Jews reproachfully said, *Let him deliver him now, if he will have him,* Matt. xxvii. 43. But it was in kindness to us that the Father would not suffer that bitter cup to pass away from him; for then we must have drunk the dregs of it, and been miserable for ever. (4.) Christ, in the days of his flesh, offered up prayers and supplications to his Father, as an earnest of his intercession in heaven. A great many instances we have of Christ's praying. This refers to his prayer in his agony (Matthew xxvi. 39, and *ch.* xxvii. 46), and to that before his agony (John xvii.) which he put up for his disciples, and all who should believe on his name. (5.) The prayers and supplications that Christ offered up were joined with strong cries and tears, herein setting us an example not only to pray, but to be fervent and importunate in prayer. How many dry prayers, how few wet ones, do we offer up to God! (6.) Christ was heard in that he feared. How? Why he was answered by present supports in and under his agonies, and in being carried well through death, and delivered from it by a glorious resurrection: *He was heard in that he feared.* He had an awful sense of the wrath of God, of the weight of sin. His human nature was ready to sink under the heavy load, and would have sunk, had he been quite forsaken in point of help and comfort from God; but he was heard in this, he was supported under the agonies of death. He was carried through death; and there is no real deliverance from death but to be carried well through it. We may have many recoveries from sickness, but we are never saved from death till we are carried well through it. And those that are thus saved from death will be fully delivered at last by a glorious resurrection, of which the resurrection of Christ was the earnest and first-fruits.

2. The consequences of this discharge of his office, *v.* 8, 9, &c.

(1.) By these his sufferings *he learned obedience, though he was a Son, v.* 8.

Here observe, [1.] The privilege of Christ : *He was a Son;* the only-be-gotten of the father. One would have thought this might have exempted him from suffering, but it did not. Let none then who are the children of God by adoption expect an absolute freedom from suffering. *What Son is he whom the Father chasteneth not?* [2.] Christ made improvement by his sufferings. By his passive obedience, he learned active obedience ; that is, he practised that great lesson, and made it appear that he was well and perfectly learned in it ; though he never was disobedient, yet he never performed such an act of obedience as when he became obedient to death, even to the death of the cross. Here he has left us an example, that we should learn by all our afflictions a humble obedience to the will of God. We need affliction, to teach us submission.

(2.) By these his sufferings he was made perfect, and became the author of eternal salvation to all who obey him, *v.* 9. [1.] Christ by his sufferings was consecrated to his office, consecrated by his own blood. [2.] By his sufferings he consummated that part of his office which was to be performed on earth, making reconciliation for iniquity ; and in this sense he is said to be *made perfect,* a perfect propitiation. [3.] Hereby he has become the author of eternal salvation to men ; he has by his sufferings purchased a full deliverance from sin and misery, and a full fruition of holiness and happiness for his people. Of this salvation he has given notice in the gospel ; he has made a tender of it in the new covenant, and has sent the Spirit to enable men to accept this salvation. [4.] This salvation is actually bestowed on none but those who obey Christ. It is not sufficient that we have some doctrinal knowledge of Christ, or that we make a pro-fession of faith in him, but we must hearken to his word, and obey him. He is exalted to be a prince to rule us, as well as a Saviour to deliver us ; and he will be a Saviour to none but to those to whom he is a prince, and who are willing that he should reign over them ; the rest he will account his enemies, and treat them accordingly. But to those who obey him, devoting themselves to him, denying themselves, and taking up their cross, and following him, he will be the author, αἴτιος—the grand cause of their salvation, and they shall own him as such for ever.

10 Called of God a high priest after the order of Melchisedec. 11 Of whom we have many things to say, and hard to be uttered [of interpretation], seeing ye are dull of hearing. 12 For when for the time [by reason of the time] ye ought to be teachers, ye have need that one teach you again which *be* the first prin-ciples of the oracles of God ; and are become such as have need of milk, and not of strong meat. 13 For every one that useth milk *is* unskilful in the word of righteousness : for he is a babe. 14 But strong meat belongeth to them that are of full age, *even* those who by reason of use have their senses exercised to dis-cern both good and evil.

Here the apostle returns to what he had in *v.* 6, cited out of Ps. cx., concerning the peculiar order of the priesthood of Christ, that is, the order of Melchisedec. And here,

I. He declares he had many things which he could say to them concern-ing this mysterious person called Melchisedec, whose priesthood was eternal,.

and therefore the salvation procured thereby should be eternal also. We have a more particular account of this Melchisedec in *ch.* vii. Some think the things which the apostle means, that were hard to be uttered, were not so much concerning Melchisedec himself as concerning Christ, of whom Melchisedec was the type. And doubtless this apostle had many things to say concerning Christ that were very mysterious, hard to be uttered; there are great mysteries in the person and offices of the Redeemer; Christianity is the great mystery of godliness.

II. He assigns the reason why he did not say all those things concerning Christ, our Melchisedec, that he had to say, and what it was that made it so difficult for him to utter them, namely, the dulness of the Hebrews to whom he wrote : *You are dull of hearing.* There is a difficulty in the things themselves, and there may be a weakness in the ministers of the gospel to speak clearly about these things ; but generally the fault is in the hearers. Dull hearers make the preaching of the gospel a difficult thing, and even many who have some faith are but dull hearers, dull of understanding and slow to believe ; the understanding is weak, and does not apprehend these spiritual things ; the memory is weak, and does not retain them.

III. He insists upon the faultiness of this infirmity of theirs. It was not a mere natural infirmity, but it was a sinful infirmity, and more in them than others, by reason of the singular advantages they had enjoyed for improving in the knowledge of Christ: *For when, for the time, you ought to be teachers, you have need that one teach you again, which are the first principles of the oracles of God, v.* 12. Here observe,

1. What proficiency might have been reasonably expected from these Hebrews—that they might have been so well instructed in the doctrine of the gospel as to have been teachers of others. Hence learn, (1.) God takes notice of the time and helps we have for gaining scripture-knowledge. (2.) From those to whom much is given much is expected. (3.) Those who have a good understanding in the gospel should be teachers of others, if not in a public, yet in a private station. (4.) None should take upon them to be teachers of others, but those who have made a good improvement in spiritual knowledge themselves.

2. Observe the sad disappointment of those just expectations : *You have need that one should teach you again,* &c. Here note, (1.) In the oracles of God there are some first principles, plain to be understood and necessary to be learned. (2.) There are also deep and sublime mysteries, which those should search into who have learned the first principles, that so they may stand complete in the whole will of God. (3.) Some persons, instead of going forward in Christian knowledge, forget the very first principles that they had learned long ago ; and indeed those that are not improving under the means of grace will be losing. (4.) It is a sin and shame for persons that are men for their age and standing in the church to be children and babes in understanding.

IV. The apostle shows how the various doctrines of the gospel must be dispensed to different persons. There are in the church babes and persons of full age (*v.* 12-14), and there are in the gospel milk and strong meat. Observe, 1. Those that are babes, unskilful in the word of righteousness, must be fed with milk ; they must be entertained with the plainest truths, and these delivered in the plainest manner ; *there must be line upon line, precept upon precept, here a little, and there a little,* Isa. xxviii. 10. Christ despises not his babes ; he has provided suitable food for them. It is good to be babes in Christ, but not always to continue in that childish state; we should endeavour to pass the infant state; we should always remain in malice children, but in understanding we should grow up to a manly maturity.   2. There is strong meat for those that are of full age, *v.* 14. The deeper mysteries of religion belong to those that are of a higher class in the school of Christ, who have learned the first principles and well improved them; so that by reason of use they have their senses exercised to discern both good and evil, duty and sin, truth and error.   Observe, (1.) There have been always in the Christian state children, young men, and fathers.   (2.) Every true Christian, having received a principle of spiritual life from God, stands in need of nourishment to preserve that life.   (3.) The word of God is food and nourishment to the life of grace : *As new-born babes desire the sincere milk of the word that you may grow thereby.* (4.) It is the wisdom of ministers rightly to divide the word of truth, and to give to every one his portion—milk to babes, and strong meat to those of full age.   (5.) There are spiritual senses as well as those that are natural. There is a spiritual eye, a spiritual appetite, a spiritual taste ; the soul has its sensations as well as the body ; these are much depraved and lost by sin, but they are recovered by grace.   (6.) It is by use and exercise that these senses are improved, made more quick and strong to taste the sweetness of what is good and true, and the bitterness of what is false and evil. Not only reason and faith, but spiritual sense, will teach men to distinguish between what is pleasing and what is provoking to God, between what is helpful and what is hurtful to our own souls.

CHAPTER VI

In this chapter the apostle proceeds to persuade the Hebrews to make a better proficiency in religion than they had done, as the best way to prevent apostasy, the dreadful nature and consequences of which sin he sets forth in a serious manner (ver. 1-8), and then expresses his good hopes concerning them, that they would persevere in faith and holiness, to which he exhorts them, and sets before them the great encouragement they had from God, both with respect to their duty and happiness, from ver. 9, to the end.

THEREFORE leaving the principles of the doctrine [**Wherefore let us cease to speak of the first principles**] of Christ, let us go on unto perfection ; not laying again the foundation of repentance from dead works, and of faith toward God, 2 Of the doctrine of baptisms, and of laying on of hands, and of resurrection of the dead, and of eternal judgment.   3 And this will we do, if God permit.   4 For *it is* impossible for those who were once enlightened, and have tasted of the heavenly gift, and were made partakers of the Holy Ghost, 5 And have tasted the good word of God, and the powers of the world to come, 6 If they shall fall away, to renew them again unto repentance ; seeing they crucify to themselves the Son of God

afresh, and put *him* to an open shame. ⁷For the earth which
drinketh in the rain that cometh oft upon it, and bringeth forth
herbs meet for them by whom it is dressed, receiveth blessing
from God: ⁸But that which beareth thorns and briers *is* rejected, and *is* nigh unto cursing; whose end *is* to be burned.

We have here the apostle's advice to the Hebrews—that they would grow
up from a state of childhood to the fulness of the stature of the new man
in Christ. He declares his readiness to assist them all he could in their
spiritual progress ; and, for their greater encouragement, he puts himself
with them : *Let us go on.* Here observe, In order to their growth, Christians must leave the principles of the doctrine of Christ. How must they
leave them ? They must not lose them, they must not despise them, they
must not forget them. They must lay them up in their hearts, and lay
them as the foundation of all their profession and expectation ; but they
must not rest and stay in them, they must not be always laying the foundation, they must go on, and build upon it. There must be a superstructure ;
for the foundation is laid on purpose to support the building. Here it may
be inquired, Why did the apostle resolve to set strong meat before the
Hebrews, when he knew they were but babes ? *Answer.* 1. Though some
of them were but weak, yet others of them had gained more strength ; and
they must be provided for suitably. And, as those who are grown Christians must be willing to hear the plainest truths preached for the sake of
the weak, so the weak must be willing to hear the more difficult and
mysterious truths preached for the sake of those who are strong. 2. He
hoped they would be growing in their spiritual strength and stature, and
so be able to digest stronger meat.

I. The apostle mentions several foundation-principles, which must be
well laid at first, and then built upon ; neither his time nor theirs must be
spent in laying these foundations over and over again. These foundations
are six :—

1. Repentance from dead works, that is, conversion and regeneration,
repentance from a spiritually dead state and course ; as if he had said,
"Beware of destroying the life of grace in your souls ; your minds were
changed by conversion, and so were your lives. Take care that you return
not to sin again, for then you must have the foundation to lay again ; there
must be a second conversion, a repenting not only of, but from, dead works."
Observe here, (1.) The sins of persons unconverted are dead works ; they
proceed from persons spiritually dead, and they tend to death eternal. (2.)
Repentance for dead works, if it be right, is repentance from dead works,
a universal change of heart and life. (3.) Repentance for and from dead
works is a foundation-principle, which must not be laid again, though we
must renew our repentance daily.

2. Faith towards God, a firm belief of the existence of God, of his nature,
attributes, and perfections, the trinity of persons in the unity of essence,
the whole mind and will of God as revealed in his word, particularly what
relates to the Lord Jesus Christ. We must by faith acquaint ourselves
with these things ; we must assent to them, we must approve of them, and
apply all to ourselves with suitable affections and actions. Observe, (1.)
Repentance from dead works, and faith towards God, are connected, and
always go together ; they are inseparable twins, the one cannot live without
the other. (2.) Both of these are foundation-principles, which should be

once well laid, but never pulled up, so as to need to be laid over again ; we must not relapse into infidelity.

3. The doctrine of baptisms, that is, of being baptized by a minister of Christ with water, in the name of the Father, and of the Son, and of the Holy Ghost, as the initiating sign or seal of the covenant of grace, strongly engaging the person so baptized to get acquainted with the new covenant, to adhere to it, and prepare to renew it at the table of the Lord and sincerely to regulate himself according to it, relying upon the truth and faithfulness of God for the blessings contained in it. And the doctrine of an inward baptism, that of the Spirit sprinkling the blood of Christ upon the soul, for justification, and the graces of the Spirit for sanctification. This ordinance of baptism is a foundation to be rightly laid, and daily remembered, but not repeated.

4. Laying on of hands, on persons passing solemnly from their initiated state by baptism to the confirmed state, by returning the answer of a good conscience towards God, and sitting down at the Lord's table. This passing from incomplete to complete church-membership was performed by laying on of hands which the extraordinary conveyance of the gift of the Holy Ghost continued. This, once done, all are obliged to abide by, and not to need another solemn admission, as at first, but to go on, and grow up, in Christ. Or by this may be meant ordination of persons to the ministerial office, who are duly qualified for it and inclined to it ; and this by fasting and prayer, with laying on of the hands of the presbytery : and this is to be done but once.

5. The resurrection of the dead, that is, of dead bodies ; and their reunion with their souls, to be eternal companions together in weal or woe, according as their state was towards God when they died, and the course of life they led in this world.

6. Eternal judgment, determining the soul of every one, when it leaves the body at death, and both soul and body at the last day, to their eternal state, every one to his proper society and employment to which they were entitled and fitted here on earth ; the wicked to everlasting punishment, the righteous to life eternal.

These are the great foundation-principles which ministers should clearly and convincingly unfold, and closely apply. In these the people should be well instructed and established, and from these they must never depart ; without these, the other parts of religion have no foundation to support them.

II. The apostle declares his readiness and resolution to assist the Hebrews in building themselves up on these foundations till they arrive at perfection : *And this we will do, if God permit, v. 3.* And thereby he teaches them, 1. That right resolution is very necessary in order to progress and proficiency in religion. 2. That that resolution is right which is not only made in the sincerity of our hearts, but in a humble dependence upon God for strength, for assistance and righteousness, for acceptance, and for time and opportunity. 3. That ministers should not only teach people what to do, but go before them, and along with them, in the way of duty.

III. He shows that this spiritual growth is the surest way to prevent that dreadful sin of apostasy from the faith. And here,

1. He shows how far persons may go in religion, and, after all, fall away, and perish for ever, *v. 4, 5.* (1.) They may be *enlightened.* Some of the ancients understand this of their being baptized ; but it is rather to be understood of notional knowledge and common illumination, of which

persons may have a great deal, and yet come short of heaven. *Balaam was the man whose eyes were opened* (Num. xxiv. 3), and yet with his eyes opened he went down to utter darkness. (2.) They may *taste of the heavenly gift*, feel something of the efficacy of the Holy Spirit in his operations upon their souls, causing them to taste something of religion, and yet be like persons in the market, who taste of what they will not come up to the price of, and so but take a taste, and leave it. Persons may taste religion, and seem to like it, if they could have it upon easier terms than denying themselves, and taking up their cross, and following Christ. (3.) They may be *made partakers of the Holy Ghost,* that is, of his extraordinary and miraculous gifts; they may have cast out devils, in the name of Christ, and done many other mighty works. Such gifts in the apostolic age were sometimes bestowed upon those who had no true saving grace. (4.) They may *taste of the good word of God;* they may have some relish of gospel doctrines, may hear the word with pleasure, may remember much of it, and talk well of it, and yet never be cast into the form and mould of it, nor have it dwelling richly in them. (5.) They may have *tasted of the powers of the world to come;* they may have been under strong impressions concerning heaven and hell, may have felt some desires of heaven, and dread of going to hell. These lengths hypocrites may go, and, after all, turn apostates. Now hence observe, [1.] These great things are spoken here of those who may fall away; yet it is not here said of them that they were truly converted, or that they were justified; there is more in true saving grace than in all that is here said of apostates. [2.] This therefore is no proof of the final apostasy of true saints. These indeed may fall frequently and foully, but yet they will not totally nor finally from God; the purpose and the power of God, the purchase and the prayer of Christ, the promise of the gospel, the everlasting covenant that God has made with them, ordered in all things and sure, the indwelling of the Spirit, and the immortal seed of the word, these are their security. But the tree that has not these roots will not stand.

2. The apostle describes the dreadful case of such as fall away after having gone so far in the profession of religion. (1.) The greatness of the sin of apostasy. It is *crucifying the Son of God afresh, and putting him to open shame.* They declare that they approve of what the Jews did in crucifying Christ, and that they would be glad to do the same thing again if it were in their power. They pour the greatest contempt upon the Son of God, and therefore upon God himself, who expects all should reverence his Son, and honour him as they honour the Father. They do what in them lies to represent Christ and Christianity as a shameful thing, and would have him to be a public shame and reproach. This is the nature of apostasy. (2.) The great misery of apostates. [1.] It is impossible to renew them again unto repentance. It is extremely hazardous. Very few instances can be given of those who have gone so far and fallen away, and yet ever have been brought to true repentance, such a repentance as is indeed a renovation of the soul. Some have thought this is the sin against the Holy Ghost, but without ground. The sin here mentioned is plainly apostasy both from the truth and the ways of Christ. God can renew them to repentance, but he seldom does it: and with men themselves it is impossible. [2.] Their misery is exemplified by a proper similitude, taken from the ground that after much cultivation brings forth nothing but briars and thorns; *and therefore is nigh unto cursing, and its end is to be burned, v.* 8. To give this the greater force, here is observed the difference

that there is between the good ground and the bad, that these contraries, being set one over against the other, may illustrate each other. *First,* Here is a description of the good ground. It *drinketh in the rain that cometh often upon it.* Believers do not only taste of the word of God, but they drink it in ; and this good ground bringeth forth fruit answerable to the cost laid out, for the honour of Christ and the comfort of his faithful ministers, who are, under Christ, dressers of the ground. And this fruit-field or garden receives the blessing. God declares fruitful Christians blessed, and all wise and good men account them blessed : they are blessed with increase of grace, and with further establishment and glory at last. *Secondly,* Here is the different case of the bad ground : It *bears briars and thorns ;* it is not only barren of good fruit, but fruitful in that which is bad, briars and thorns, fruitful in sin and wickedness, which are trouble-some and hurtful to all about them, and will be most so to sinners them-selves at last ; and then such ground is rejected. God will concern himself no more about such wicked apostates ; he will let them alone, and cast them out of his care ; he will command the clouds that they rain no more upon them. Divine influences shall be restrained ; and that is not all, but such ground *is nigh unto cursing ;* so far is it from receiving the blessing, that a dreadful curse hangs over it, though as yet, through the patience of God, the curse is not fully executed. *Lastly,* Its end is to be burned. Apostasy will be punished with everlasting burnings, the fire that shall never be quenched. This is the sad end to which apostasy leads, and therefore Christians should go on and grow in grace, lest, if they do not go forward, they should go backward, till they bring matters to this woeful extremity of sin and misery.

⁹ But, beloved, we are persuaded better things of you, and things that accompany salvation, though we thus speak.   ¹⁰ For God *is* not unrighteous to forget your work and labour of love, which ye have showed toward his name, in that ye have minis-tered to the saints, and do minister.   ¹¹ And we desire that every one of you do show the same diligence to the full assur-ance of hope unto the end : ¹² That ye be not slothful, but followers of them who through faith and patience inherit the promises.   ¹³ For when God made promise to Abraham, because he could swear by no greater, he sware by himself, ¹⁴ Saying, Surely blessing I will bless thee, and multiplying I will multiply thee.   ¹⁵ And so, after he had patiently endured, he obtained the promise.   ¹⁶ For men verily swear by the greater : and an oath for confirmation *is* to them an end of all strife [and in every dispute of theirs the oath is final for confirmation]. ¹⁷ Wherein God, willing more abundantly to show unto the heirs of promise the immutability of his counsel, confirmed *it* by [interposed with] an oath : ¹⁸ That by two immutable things, in which *it was* impossible for God to lie, we might have a strong consolation [encouragement] who have fled for refuge to lay hold upon the hope set before us : ¹⁹ Which *hope* we have

as an anchor of the soul, both sure and stedfast, and which entereth into that within the veil ; [20] Whither the forerunner is for us entered, *even* Jesus, made a high priest for ever after the order of Melchisedec.

The apostle, having applied himself to the fears of the Hebrews, in order to excite their diligence and prevent their apostasy, now proceeds to apply himself to their hopes, and candidly declares the good hope he had concerning them, that they would persevere ; and proposes to them the great encouragements they had in the way of their duty.

I. He freely and openly declares the good hope he had concerning them, that they would endure to the end : *But beloved, we are persuaded better things of you, v.* 9. Observe, 1. There are things that accompany salvation, things that are never separated from salvation, things that show the person to be in a state of salvation, and will issue in eternal salvation. 2. The things that accompany salvation are better things than ever any hypocrite or apostate enjoyed. They are better in their nature and in their issue. 3. It is our duty to hope well of those in whom nothing appears to the contrary. 4. Ministers must sometimes speak by way of caution to those of whose salvation they have good hopes. And those who have in themselves good hopes, as to their eternal salvation, should yet consider seriously how fatal a disappointment it would be if they should fall short. Thus they are to work out their salvation with fear and trembling.

II. He proposes arguments and encouragements to them to go on in the way of their duty. 1. That God had wrought a principle of holy love and charity in them, which had discovered itself in suitable works that would not be forgotten of God : *God is not unrighteous to forget your labour of love, v.* 10. Good works and labour proceeding from love to God are commendable ; and what is done to any in the name of God shall not go unrewarded. What is done to the saints, as such, God takes as done to himself. 2. Those who expect a gracious reward for the labour of love must continue in it as long as they have ability and opportunity : *You have ministered to the saints, and you do minister ; and we desire that every one of you do show the same diligence.* 3. Those who persevere in a diligent discharge of their duty shall attain to the full assurance of hope in the end. Observe, (1.) Full assurance is a higher degree of hope, is full assurance of hope ; they differ not in nature, but only in degree. (2.) Full assurance is attainable by great diligence and perseverance to the end.

III. He proceeds to set before them caution and counsel how to attain this full assurance of hope to the end. 1. That they should not be slothful. Slothfulness will clothe a man with rags : they must not love their ease, nor lose their opportunities. 2. That they would follow the good examples of those who had gone before, *v.* 12. Here learn, (1.) There are some who from assurance have gone to inherit the promises. They believed them before, now they inherit them ; they have got safely to heaven. (2.) The way by which they came to the inheritance was that of faith and patience. These graces were implanted in their souls, and drawn forth into act and exercise in their lives. If we ever expect to inherit as they do, we must follow them in the way of faith and patience ; and those who do thus follow them in the way shall overtake them at the end, and be partakers of the same blessedness.

IV. The apostle closes the chapter with a clear and full account of the assured truth of the promises of God, *v.* 13, *to the end.* They are all confirmed by the oath of God, and they are all founded in the eternal counsel of God, and therefore may be depended upon.

1. They are all confirmed by the oath of God. He has not only given his people his word, and his hand and seal, but his oath. And here, you will observe, he specifies the oath of God to Abraham, which, being sworn to him as the father of the faithful, remains in full force and virtue to all true believers : *When God made a promise unto Abraham, because he could swear by no greater, he swore by himself.* Observe, (1.) What was the promise : *Surely, blessing I will bless thee, and multiplying I will multiply thee.* The blessing of God is the blessedness of his people ; and those whom he has blessed indeed he will go on to bless, and will multiply blessings, till he has brought them to perfect blessedness. (2.) What was the oath by which this promise was ratified : *He swore by himself.* He staked down his own being and his own blessedness upon it ; no greater security can be given or desired. (3.) How was that oath accomplished. Abraham, in due time, obtained the promise. It was made good to him after he had patiently endured. [1.] There is always an interval, and sometimes a long one, between the promise and the performance. [2.] That interval is a trying time to believers, whether they have patience to endure to the end. [3.] Those who patiently endure shall assuredly obtain the blessedness promised, as sure as Abraham did. [4.] The end and design of an oath is to make the promise sure, and to encourage those to whom it is made to wait with patience till the time for performance comes, *v.* 16. An oath with men is for confirmation, and is an end of all strife. This is the nature and design of an oath, in which men swear by the greater, not by creatures, but by the Lord himself ; and it is to put an end to all dispute about the matter, both to disputes within our own breasts (doubts and distrusts), and disputes with others, especially with the promiser. Now, if God would condescend to take an oath to his people, he will surely remember the nature and design of it.

2. The promises of God are all founded in his eternal counsel ; and this counsel of his is an immutable counsel. (1.) The promise of blessedness which God has made to believers is not a rash and hasty thing, but the result of God's eternal purpose. (2.) This purpose of God was agreed upon in counsel, and settled there between the eternal Father, Son, and Spirit. (3.) These counsels of God can never be altered ; they are immutable. God never needs to change his counsels ; for nothing new can arise to him who sees the end from the beginning.

3. The promises of God, which are founded upon these immutable counsels of God, and confirmed by the oath of God, may safely be depended upon ; for here we have two immutable things, the counsel and the oath of God, in which it is impossible for God to lie, contrary to his nature as well as to his will. Here observe,

(1.) Who they are to whom God has given such full security of happiness. [1.] They are the heirs of the promise : such as have a title to the promises by inheritance, by virtue of their new birth, and union with Christ. We are all by nature children of wrath. The curse is the inheritance we are born to : it is by a new and heavenly birth that any are born heirs to the promise. [2.] They are such as have fled for refuge to the hope set before them. Under the law there were cities of refuge provided for those who were pursued by the avenger of blood. Here is a much better refuge prepared by the gospel, a refuge for all sinners who shall have the heart to flee to it ; yea, though they have been the chief of sinners.

(2.) What God's design towards them is, in giving them such securities —that they might have strong consolation. Observe, [1.] God is concerned for the consolation of believers, as well as for their sanctification ; he would have his children walk in the fear of the Lord, and in the comforts of the Holy Ghost. [2.] The consolations of God are strong enough to support his people under their strongest trials. The comforts of this world are too weak to bear up the soul under temptation, persecution, and death ; but the consolations of the Lord are neither few nor small.

(3.) What use the people of God should make of their hope and comfort, that most refreshing and comfortable hope of eternal blessedness that God has given them. This is, and must be, unto them, for *an anchor to the soul, sure and stedfast*, &c., *v.* 19. Here, [1.] We are in this world as a ship at sea, liable to be tossed up and down, and in danger of being cast away. Our souls are the vessels. The comforts, expectations, graces, and happiness of our souls are the precious cargo with which these vessels are loaded. Heaven is the harbour to which we sail. The temptations, persecutions, and afflictions that we encounter are the winds and waves that threaten our shipwreck. [2.] We have need of an anchor to keep us sure and steady, or we are in continual danger. [3.] Gospel hope is our anchor ; as in our day of battle it is our helmet, so in our stormy passage through this world it is our anchor. [4.] It is sure and stedfast, or else it could not keep us so. *First*, It is sure in its own nature ; for it is the special work of God in the soul. It is a good hope through grace ; it is not a flattering hope made out of the spider's web, but it is a true work of God, it is a strong and substantial thing. *Secondly*, It is stedfast as to its object ; it is an anchor that has taken good hold, it enters that which is within the veil ; it is an anchor that is cast upon the rock, the Rock of ages. It does not seek to fasten in the sands, but enters within the veil, and fixes there upon Christ ; he is the object, he is the anchor-hold of the believer's hope. As an unseen glory within the veil is what the believer is hoping for, so an unseen Jesus within the veil is the foundation of his hope ; the free grace of God, the merits and mediation of Christ, and the powerful influences of his Spirit, are the grounds of his hope, and so it is a stedfast hope. Jesus Christ is the object and ground of the believer's hope in several respects. 1. As he has entered within the veil, to intercede with God, in virtue of that sacrifice which he offered up without the veil : hope fastens upon his sacrifice and intercession. 2. As he is the forerunner of his people, gone within the veil to prepare a place for them, and to assure them that they shall follow him ; he is the earnest and first-fruits of believers, both in his resurrection and in his ascension. 3. And he abides there, a high priest after the order of Melchisedec, a priest for ever, whose priesthood shall never cease, never fail, till he has acomplished its whole work and design, which is the full and final happiness of all who have believed on Christ. Now this should engage us to clear up our interest in Christ, that we may fix our hopes in him as our forerunner, that has entered thither for us, for our sakes, for our safety, to watch over our highest interest and concerns. Let us then love heaven the more on his account, and long to be there with him, where we shall be for ever safe, and for ever satisfied.

CHAPTER VII

The doctrine of the priestly office of Christ is so excellent in itself, and so essential a part of the Christian faith, that the apostle loves to dwell upon it. Nothing made the Jews so fond of the Levitical dispensation as the high esteem they had of their priesthood, and it was doubtless a sacred and most excellent institution; it was a very severe threatening denounced against the Jews (Hos. iii. 4), that the children of Israel should abide many days without a prince or priest, and without a sacrifice, and without an ephod, and without teraphim. Now the apostle assures them that by receiving the Lord Jesus they would have a much better high priest, a priesthood of a higher order, and consequently a better dispensation or covenant, a better law and testament; this he shows in this chapter, where, I. We have a more particular account of Melchisedec, ver. 1-3. II. The superiority of his priesthood to that of Aaron, ver. 4-10. III. An accommodation of all to Christ, to show the superior excellency of his person, office, and covenant, ver. 11, to the end.

FOR this Melchisedec, king of Salem, priest of the most high God, who met Abraham returning from the slaughter of the kings, and blessed him; ² To whom also Abraham gave a tenth part of all; first being by interpretation King of right-eousness, and after that also King of Salem, which is, King of peace, ³ Without father, without mother, without descent, having neither beginning of days, nor end of life; but made like unto the Son of God; abideth a priest continually. ⁴ Now consider how great this man *was*, unto whom even the Patriarch Abraham gave the tenth of the spoils. ⁵ And verily they that are of the sons of Levi, who receive the office of the priesthood, have a commandment to take tithes of the people according to the law, that is, of their brethren, though they come out of the loins of Abraham : ⁶ But he whose descent is not counted from them received tithes of Abraham, and blessed him that had the promises. ⁷ And without all contradiction [**without any dispute**], the less is blessed of the better. ⁸ And here men that die receive tithes; but there he *receiveth them*, of whom it is witnessed that he liveth. ⁹ And as I may so say, Levi also, who receiveth tithes, paid tithes in Abraham. ¹⁰ For he was yet in the loins of his father, when Melchisedec met him.

The foregoing chapter ended with a repetition of what had been cited once and again before out of Ps. cx. 4, *Jesus, a high priest for ever, after the order of Melchisedec.* Now this chapter is as a sermon upon that text; here the apostle sets before them some of the strong meat he had spoken of before, hoping they would by greater diligence be better prepared to digest it.

I. The great question that first offers itself is, Who was this Melchisedec ? All the account we have of him in the Old Testament is in Gen. xiv. 18, &c., and in Ps. cx. 4. Indeed we are much in the dark about him; God has thought fit to leave us so, that this Melchisedec might be a more lively

type of him whose generation none can declare. If men will not be satisfied with what is revealed, they must rove about in the dark in endless
conjectures, some fancying him to have been an angel, others the Holy
Ghost ; but,

1. The opinions concerning him that are best worthy our consideration
are these three :—(1.) The rabbin, and most of the Jewish writers, think
he was Shem the son of Noah, who was king and priest to their ancestors,
after the manner of the other patriarchs ; but it is not probable that he
should thus change his name. Besides, we have no account of his settling
in the land of Canaan. (2.) Many Christian writers have thought him to
be Jesus Christ himself, appearing by a special dispensation and privilege
to Abraham in the flesh, and who was known to Abraham by the name
Melchisedec, which agrees very well to Christ, and to what is said, John
viii. 56, *Abraham saw his day and rejoiced*. Much may be said for this
opinion, and what is said in *v*. 3 does not seem to agree with any mere
man ; but then it seems strange to make Christ a type of himself. (3.)
The most general opinion is that he was a Canaanite king, who reigned in
Salem, and kept up religion and the worship of the true God ; that he was
raised to be a type of Christ, and was honoured by Abraham as such.

2. But we shall leave these conjectures, and labour to understand, as far
as we can, what is here said of him by the apostle, and how Christ is
represented thereby, *v*. 1-3. (1.) Melchisedec was a king, and so is
the Lord Jesus—a king of God's anointing ; the government is laid upon
his shoulders, and he rules over all for the good of his people. (2.) That
he was *king of righteousness :* his names signifies *the righteous king*. Jesus
Christ is a rightful and a righteous king—rightful in his title, righteous
in his government. He is the Lord our righteousness ; he has fulfilled
all righteousness, and brought in an everlasting righteousness, and he loves
righteousness and righteous persons, and hates iniquity. (3.) He was
king of Salem, that is, king of peace ; first king of righteousness, and
after that king of peace. So is our Lord Jesus ; he by his righteousness
made peace, the fruit of righteousness is peace. Christ speaks peace,
creates peace, is our peace-maker. (4.) He was *priest of the most high God*,
qualified and anointed in an extraordinary manner to be his priest among the
Gentiles. So is the Lord Jesus ; he is the priest of the most high God,
and the Gentiles must come. to God by him ; it is only through his priesthood that we can obtain reconciliation and remission of sin. (5.) He was
*without father, without mother, without descent, having neither beginning of
days nor end of life, v*. 3. This must not be understood according to the
letter ; but the scripture has chosen to set him forth as an extraordinary
person, without giving us his genealogy, that he might be a fitter type of
Christ, who as man was without father, as God without mother ; whose
priesthood is without descent, did not descend to him from another, nor from
him to another, but is personal and perpetual. (6.) That he *met Abraham
returning from the slaughter of the kings, and blessed him*. The incident
is recorded Gen. xiv. 18, &c. He brought forth bread and wine to refresh
Abraham and his servants when they were weary ; he gave as a king,
and blessed as a priest. Thus our Lord Jesus meets his people in their
spiritual conflicts, refreshes them, renews their strength, and blesses them.
(7.) That *Abraham gave him a tenth part of all* (*v*. 2), that is, as the
apostle explains it, of all *the spoils ;* and this Abraham did as an expression of his gratitude for what Melchisedec had done for him, or as a testimony of his homage and subjection to him as a king, or as an offering

vowed and dedicated to God, to be presented by his priest. And thus are we obliged to make all possible returns of love and gratitude to the Lord Jesus for all the rich and royal favours we receive from him, to pay our homage and subjection to him as our King, and to put all our offerings into his hands, to be presented by him to the Father in the incense of his own sacrifice. (8.) That this Melchisedec was *made like unto the Son of God, and abideth a priest continually.* He bore the image of God in his piety and authority, and stands upon record as an immortal high priest ; the ancient type of him who is the eternal and only-begotten of the Father, who abideth a priest for ever.

II. Let us now consider (as the apostle advises) how great this Melchisedec was, and how far his priesthood was above that of the order of Aaron (*v.* 4, 5, &c.) : *Now consider how great this man was,* &c. The greatness of this man and his priesthood appears, 1. From Abraham's paying the tenth of the spoils unto him ; and it is well observed that Levi paid tithes to Melchisedec in Abraham, *v.* 9. Now Levi received the office of the priesthood from God, and was to take tithes of the people, yet even Levi paid tithes to Melchisedec, as to a greater and higher priest than himself ; therefore that high priest who should afterwards appear, of 'whom Melchisedec was a type, must be much superior to any of the Levitical priests, who paid tithes, in Abraham, to Melchisedec. And now by this argument of persons doing things that are matters of right or injury in the loins of their predecessors we have an illustration how we may be said to have sinned in Adam, and fallen with him in his first transgression. We were in Adam's loins when he sinned, and the guilt and depravity contracted by the human nature when it was in our first parents are equitably imputed and derived to the same nature as it is in all other persons naturally descended from them. They justly adhere to the nature, and it must be by an act of grace if ever they be taken away. 2. From Melchisedec's blessing of Abraham, *who had the promises ; and, without contradiction, the less is blessed of the greater, v.* 6, 7. Here observe, (1.) Abraham's great dignity and felicity—that he had the promises. He was one in covenant with God, to whom God had given exceedingly great and precious promises. That man is rich and happy indeed who has an estate in bills and bonds under God's own hand and seal. These promises are both of the life that now is and of that which is to come ; this honour have all those who receive the Lord Jesus, in whom all the promises are yea and amen. (2.) Melchisedec's greater honour—in that it was his place and privilege to bless Abraham ; and it is an incontested maxim *that the less is blessed of the greater, v.* 7. He who gives the blessing is greater than he who receives it ; and therefore Christ, the antitype of Melchisedec, the meriter and Mediator of all blessings to the children of men, must be greater than all the priests of the order of Aaron.

11 If therefore perfection were by the Levitical priesthood, (for under it the people received the law,) what further need *was there* that another priest should rise after the order of Melchisedec, and not be called after the order of Aaron ? 12 For the priesthood being changed, there is made of necessity a change also of the law. 13 For he of whom these things are spoken pertaineth to another tribe, of which no man gave

attendance at the altar. ¹⁴ For *it is* evident that our Lord sprang out of Juda; of which tribe Moses spake nothing concerning priesthood. ¹⁵ And it is yet far more evident: for that [**And** *what we say* **is yet more abundantly evident, if**] after the similitude of Melchisedec there ariseth another priest, ¹⁶ Who is made, not after the law of a carnal commandment, but after the power of an endless life. ¹⁷ For he testifieth, Thou *art* a priest for ever after the order of Melchisedec. ¹⁸ For there is verily a disannulling of the commandment going before for the weakness and unprofitableness thereof. ¹⁹ For the law made nothing perfect, but the bringing in of a better hope *did* [(**for the law made nothing perfect**), **and a bringing in thereupon of a better hope**]; by the which we draw nigh unto God. ²⁰ And inasmuch as not without an oath *he was made priest:* ²¹ (For those priests were made without an oath; but this with an oath by him that said unto him, The Lord sware and will not repent, Thou *art* a priest for ever after the order of Melchisedec:) ²² By so much was Jesus made a surety of a better testament [**covenant**]. ²³ And they truly were many priests, because they were not suffered to continue by reason of death: ²⁴ But this *man*, because he continueth ever, hath an unchangeable priesthood. ²⁵ Wherefore he is able also to save them to the uttermost that come unto God by him, seeing he ever liveth to make intercession for them. ²⁶ For such an high priest became us, *who is* holy, harmless, undefiled, separate from sinners, and made higher than the heavens; ²⁷ Who needeth not daily, as those high priests, to offer up sacrifice, first for his own sins, and then for the people's: for this he did once, when he offered up himself. ²⁸ For the law maketh men high priests which have infirmity; but the word of the oath, which was since the law, *maketh* the Son, who is consecrated [**perfected**] for evermore.

Observe the necessity there was of raising up another priest, after the order of Melchisedec and not after the order of Aaron, by whom that perfection should come which could not come by the Levitical priesthood, which therefore must be changed, and the whole economy with it, *v.* 11, 12, &c. Here,

I. It is asserted that perfection could not come by the Levitical priesthood and the law. They could not put those who came to them into the perfect enjoyment of the good things they pointed out to them; they could only show them the way.

II. That therefore another priest must be raised up, after the order of Melchisedec, by whom, and his law of faith, perfection might come to all who obey him; and, blessed be God, that we may have perfect holiness and perfect happiness by Christ in the covenant of grace, according to the gospel, for we are complete in him.

III. It is asserted that the priesthood being changed there must of necessity be a change of the law; there being so near a relation between the priesthood and the law, the dispensation could not be the same under another priesthood; a new priesthood must be under a new regulation, managed in another way, and by rules proper to its nature and order.

IV. It is not only asserted, but proved, that the priesthood and law are changed, *v.* 13, 14. The priesthood and law by which perfection could not come are abolished, and a priest has arisen, and a dispensation is now set up, by which true believers may be made perfect. Now that there is such a change is obvious.

1. There is a change in the tribe of which the priesthood comes. Before, it was the tribe of Levi; but our great high priest sprang out of Judah, of which tribe Moses spoke nothing concerning the priesthood, *v.* 14. This change of the family shows a real change of the law of priesthood.

2. There is a change in the form and order of making the priests. Before, in the Levitical priesthood, they were made after the law of a carnal commandment; but our great high priest was made after the power of an endless life. The former law appointed that the office should descend, upon the death of the father, to his eldest son, according to the order of carnal or natural generation; for none of the high priests under that law were without father or mother, or without descent: they had not life and immortality in themselves. They had both beginning of days and end of life; and so the carnal commandment, or law of primogeniture, directed their succession, as it did in matters of civil right and inheritance. But the law by which Christ was constituted a priest, after the order of Melchisedec, was the power of an endless life. The life and immortality which he had in himself were his right and title to the priesthood, not his descent from former priests. This makes a great difference in the priesthood, and in the economy too, and gives the preference infinitely to Christ and the gospel. The very law which constituted the Levitical priesthood supposed the priests to be weak, frail, dying, creatures, not able to preserve their own natural lives, but who must be content and glad to survive in their posterity after the flesh; much less could they, by any power or authority they had, convey spiritual life and blessedness to those who came to them. But the high priest of our profession holds his office by that innate power of endless life which he has in himself, not only to preserve himself alive, but to communicate spiritual and eternal life to all those who duly rely upon his sacrifice and intercession. Some think *the law of the carnal commandment* refers to the external rites of consecration, and the carnal offerings that were made; but *the power of an endless life* to the spiritual living sacrifices proper to the gospel, and the spiritual and eternal privileges purchased by Christ, who was consecrated by the eternal Spirit of life that he received without measure.

3. There is a change in the efficacy of the priesthood. The former was weak and unprofitable, made nothing perfect; the latter brought in a better hope, by which we draw near to God, *v.* 18, 19. The Levitical priesthood brought nothing to perfection: it could not justify men's persons from guilt; it could not sanctify them from inward pollution; it could not cleanse the consciences of the worshippers from dead works; all it could do was to lead them to the antitype. But the priesthood of Christ carries in it, and brings along with it, a better hope; it shows us the true foundation of all the hope we have towards God for pardon and salvation; it more clearly discovers the great objects of our hope; and so

it tends to work in us a more strong and lively hope of acceptance with God. By this hope we are encouraged to draw nigh unto God, to enter into a covenant-union with him, to live a life of converse and communion with him. We may now draw near with a true heart, and with the full assurance of faith, having our minds sprinkled from an evil conscience. The former priesthood rather kept men at a distance, and under a spirit of bondage.

4. There is a change in God's way of acting in this priesthood. He has taken an oath to Christ, which he never did to any of the order of Aaron. God never gave them any such assurance of their continuance, never engaged himself by oath or promise that theirs should be an everlasting priesthood, and therefore gave them no reason to expect the perpetuity of it, but rather to look upon it as a temporary law. But Christ was made a priest with the oath of God: *The Lord hath sworn and will not repent, Thou art a priest for ever after the order of Melchisedec, v. 21.* Here God has upon oath declared the immutability, excellency, efficacy, and eternity, of the priesthood of Christ.

5. There is a change in that covenant of which the priesthood was a security and the priest a surety; that is, a change in the dispensation of that covenant. The gospel dispensation is more full, free, perspicuous, spiritual, and efficacious, than that of the law. Christ is in this gospel covenant a surety for us to God and for God to us, to see that the articles be performed on both parts. He, as surety, has united the divine and human nature together in his own person, and therein given assurance of reconciliation; and he has, as surety, united God and man together in the bond of the everlasting covenant. He pleads with men to keep their covenant with God, and he pleads with God that he will fulfil his promises to men, which he is always ready to do in a way suitable to his majesty and glory, that is, through a Mediator.

6. There is a remarkable change in the number of the priests under these different orders. In that of Aaron there was a multitude of priests, of high priests, not at once, but successively; but in this of Christ there is but one and the same. The reason is plain, The Levitical priests were many, because *they were not suffered to continue by reason of death.* Their office, how high and honourable soever, could not secure them from dying; and, as one died, another must succeed, and after awhile must give place to a third, till the number had become very great. But this our high priest continues for ever, and his priesthood is ἀπαράβατον—*an unchangeable one*, that does not pass from one to another, as the former did; it is always in the same hand. There can be no vacancy in this priesthood, no hour nor moment in which the people are without a priest to negociate their spiritual concerns in heaven. Such a vacancy might be very dangerous and prejudical to them; but this is their safety and happiness, that this ever-living high priest is able to save to the utmost—in all times, in all cases, in every juncture—all who come to God by him, *v. 25.* So that here is a manifest alteration much for the better.

7. There is a remarkable difference in the moral qualifications of the priests. Those who were of the order of Aaron were not only mortal men, but sinful men, who had their sinful as well as natural infirmities; they needed to offer up sacrifices first for their own sins and then for the people. But our high priest, who was consecrated by the word of the oath, needed only to offer up once for the people, never at all for himself; for he has not only an immutable consecration to his office, but an immutable sanctity

in his person. He is *such a high priest as became us, holy, harmless, and undefiled*, &c., *v.* 26-28. Here observe, (1.) Our case, as sinners, needed a high priest to make satisfaction and intercession for us. (2.) No priest could be suitable or sufficient for our reconciliation to God but one who was perfectly righteous in his own person ; he must be righteous in himself, or he could not be a propitiation for our sin, or our advocate with the Father. (3.) The Lord Jesus was exactly such a high priest as we wanted, for he has a personal holiness, absolutely perfect. Observe the description we have of the personal holiness of Christ expressed in various terms, all of which some learned divines consider as relating to his perfect purity. [1.] He is holy, perfectly free from all the habits or principles of sin, not having the least disposition to it in his nature ; no sin dwells in him, though it does in the best of Christians, not the least sinful inclination. [2.] He is harmless, perfectly free from all actual transgression, has done no violence, nor is there any deceit in his mouth, never did the least wrong to God or man. [3.] He is undefiled, he was never accessory to other men's sins. The best of Christians have need to pray that God would forgive them their other men's sins. It is a difficult thing to keep ourselves pure, so as not to partake in the guilt of other men's sins, by contributing in some way towards them, or not doing what we ought to prevent them. Christ was undefiled ; though he took upon him the guilt of our sins, yet he never involved himself in the fact and fault of them. [4.] He is separate from sinners, not only in his present state (having entered as our high priest into the holiest of all, into which nothing defiled can enter), but in his personal purity : he has no such union with sinners, either natural or federal, as can devolve upon him original sin. This comes upon us by virtue of our natural and federal union with the first Adam, we descending from him in the ordinary way. But Christ was, by his ineffable conception in the virgin, separate from sinners ; though he took a true human nature, yet the miraculous way in which it was conceived set him upon a separate footing from all the rest of mankind. [5.] He is made higher than the heavens. Most expositors understand this concerning his state of exaltation in heaven, at the right hand of God, to perfect the design of his priesthood. But Dr. Goodwin thinks this may be very justly referred to the personal holiness of Christ, which is greater and more perfect than the holiness of the hosts of heaven, that is, the holy angels themselves, who, though they are free from sin, yet are not in themselves free from all possibility of sinning. And therefore we read, *God putteth no trust in his holy ones, and he chargeth his angels with folly* (Job. iv. 18), that is, with weakness and peccability. They may be angels one hour and devils another, as many of them were ; and that the holy angels shall not now fall does not proceed from an indefectibility of nature, but from the election of God ; they are elect angels. It is very probable that this explanation of the words, *made higher than the heavens*, may be thought too much strained, and that it ought to be understood of the dignity of Christ's state, and not the perfect holiness of his person ; and the rather because it is said he was *made* higher, γενόμενος ; but it is well known that this word is used in a neutral sense, as where it is said, γενέσθη ὁ Θεὸς ἀληθὴς—*Let God be true*. The other characters in the verse plainly belong to the personal perfection of Christ in holiness, as opposed to the sinful infirmities of the Levitical priests ; and it seems congruous to think this must do so too, if it may be fairly taken in such a sense ; and it appears yet more probable, since the validity and prevalency of Christ's priesthood in *v.* 27 are placed

in the impartiality and disinterestedness of it. He needed not to offer up
for himself : it was a disinterested mediation ; he mediated for that mercy
for others which he did not need for himself ; had he needed it himself, he
had been a party, and could not have been a Mediator—a criminal, and
could not have been an advocate for sinners. Now, to render his mediation
the more impartial and disinterested, it seems requisite not only that he
had no present need of that favour for himself which he mediated for in
behalf of others, but that he never could stand in need of it. Though he
needed it not to-day, yet if he knew he might be in such circumstances as
to need it to-morrow, or at any future time, he must have been thought to
have had some eye upon his own interest, and therefore could not act with
impartial regard and pure zeal for the honour of God on one hand, and
tender pure compassion for poor sinners on the other. I pretend not here
to follow the notes of our late excellent expositor, into whose labours we
have entered, but have taken the liberty to vindicate this notion of the
learned Dr. Goodwin from the exceptions that I know have been made
to it ; and I have the rather done it because, if it will hold good, it gives
us further evidence how necessary it was that the Mediator should be God,
since no mere creature is of himself possessed of that impeccability which
will set him above all possible need of favour and mercy for himself.

CHAPTER VIII

In this chapter the apostle pursues his former subject, the priesthood of Christ. And, I.
He sums up what he had already said, ver. 1, 2. II. He sets before them the necessary
parts of the priestly office, ver. 3-5. And, III. Largely illustrates the excellency of the
priesthood of Christ, by considering the excellency of that new dispensation or covenant for which Christ is the Mediator, ver. 6, to the end.

NOW of [in] the things which we have spoken *this is* the
sum [the chief point *is this*] : We have such a high
priest, who is set on the right hand of the throne of the Majesty
in the heavens; ² A minister of the sanctuary, and of the true
tabernacle, which the Lord pitched, and not man. ³ For every
high priest is ordained to offer gifts and sacrifices : wherefore
it is of necessity that this man have somewhat also to offer.
⁴ For [how] if he were on earth, he should not be a priest,
seeing that there are priests that offer gifts according to the
law : ⁵ Who serve unto the example [serve *that which is* a
copy] and shadow of heavenly things, as Moses was admonished
of God when he was about to make the tabernacle : for, See,
saith he, *that* thou make all things according to the pattern
showed to thee in the mount.

Here is, I. A summary recital of what had been said before concerning the excellency of Christ's priesthood, showing what we have

in Christ, where he now resides, and what sanctuary he is the minister of, *v.* 1, 2. Observe, 1. What we have in Christ ; we have a high priest, and such a high priest as no other people ever had, no age of the world, or of the church, ever produced ; all others were but types and shadows of this high priest. He is adequately fitted and absolutely sufficient to all the intents and purposes of a high priest, both with respect to the honour of God and the happiness of men and himself ; the great honour of all those who have an interest in him. 2. Where he now resides : *He sits on the right hand of the throne of the Majesty on high,* that is, of the glorious God of heaven. There the Mediator is placed, and he is possessed of all authority and power both in heaven and upon earth. This is the reward of his humiliation. This authority he exercises for the glory of his Father, for his own honour, and for the happiness of all who belong to him ; and he will by his almighty power bring every one of them in their own order to the right hand of God in heaven, as members of his mystical body, that where he is they may be also. 3. What is that sanctuary of which he is a minister : *Of the true tabernacle, which the Lord hath pitched and not man, v.* 2. The tabernacle which was pitched by man, according to the appointment of God. There was an outer part, in which was the altar where they were to offer their sacrifices, which typified Christ dying ; and there was an interior part within the veil, which typified Christ interceding for the people in heaven. Now this tabernacle Christ never entered into ; but, having finished the work of satisfaction in the true tabernacle of his own body, he is now a minister of the sanctuary, the holy of holies, the true tabernacle in heaven, there taking care of his people's affairs, interceding with God for them, that their sins may be pardoned and their persons and services accepted, through the merit of his sacrifice. He is not only in heaven enjoying great dominion and dignity, but, as the high priest of his church, executing this office for them all in general, and every member of the Church in particular.

II. The apostle sets before the Hebrews the necessary parts of Christ's priesthood, or what it was that belonged to that office, in conformity to what every high priest is ordained, *v.* 3, 4. 1. *Every high priest is ordained to offer gifts and sacrifices.* Whatever was brought by the people to be presented to God, whether expiatory sacrifices, or peace-offerings, or thank-offerings, must be offered by the priest, who was to expiate their guilt by the blood of the sacrifice, and perfume their gifts and services by his holy incense, to render their persons and performances typically acceptable ; so then it necessarily belongs to the priesthood of Christ that he should have somewhat to offer ; and he, as the antitype, had himself to offer, his human nature upon the altar of his divine nature, as the great atoning sacrifice that finished transgression, and made an end of sin once for all ; and he has the incense of his own righteousness and merits too to offer with all that his people offer up to God by him, to render them acceptable. We must not dare to approach to God, or to present any thing to him, but in and through Christ, depending upon his merits and mediation ; for if we are accepted, it is in the Beloved. 2. Christ must now execute his priesthood in heaven, in the holy of holies, the true tabernacle which the Lord hath fixed. Thus the type must be fully answered ; having finished the work of sacrificing here, he must go into heaven, to present his righteousness and to make intercession there. For, (1.) *If Christ were on earth, he would not be a priest* (*v.* 4), that is, not according to the Levitical law, as not being of the line of that priesthood ; and so long as that priesthood continued there must be a strict regard paid to the divine institution in every thing. (2.) All the services of the priest, under the law, as well as every thing in that tabernacle which was framed according to the pattern in the mount, were only exemplars and shadows of heavenly things, *v.* 5. Christ is the substance and end of the law for righteousness. Something therefore there must be in Christ's priesthood that answers to the high priest's entering within the veil to make intercession, without which he could not have been a perfect priest ; and what is this but the ascension of Christ into heaven, and his appearance there in the sight of God for his people, to present their prayers, and plead their cause ? So that, if he had still continued on earth, he could not have been a perfect priest ; and an imperfect one he could not be.

⁶ But now hath he obtained a more excellent ministry, by how much also he is the mediator of a better covenant, which was established [**hath been enacted**] upon better promises. ⁷ For if that first *covenant* had been faultless, then should no place have been sought for the second. ⁸ For finding fault with them, he saith, Behold, the days come, saith the Lord, when I will make a new covenant with the house of Israel and with the house of Judah : ⁹ Not according to the covenant that I made with their fathers in the day when I took them by the hand to lead them out of the land of Egypt ; because they continued not in my covenant, and I regarded them not, saith the Lord. ¹⁰ For this *is* the covenant that I will make with the house of Israel after those days, saith the Lord ; I will put my laws into their mind, and write them in their hearts : and I will be to them a God, and they shall be to me a people : ¹¹ And they shall not teach every man his neighbour [**fellow-citizen**], and every man his brother, saying, Know the Lord : for all shall know me, from the least to the greatest. ¹² For I will be merciful to their unrighteousness, and their sins and their iniquities will I remember no more. ¹³ In that he saith, A new *covenant*, he hath made the first old. Now that which decayeth and waxeth old *is* ready to vanish away.

In this part of the chapter, the apostle illustrates and confirms the superior excellency of the priesthood of Christ above that of Aaron, from the excellency of that covenant, or that dispensation of the covenant of grace, of which Christ was the Mediator (*v.* 6): his ministry is more excellent, by how much he is the Mediator of a better covenant. The body and soul too of all divinity (as some observe) consists very much in rightly distinguishing between the two covenants—the covenant of works and the covenant of grace ; and between the two dispensations of the covenant of grace—that under the Old Testament and that under the New. Now observe,

I. What is here said of the old covenant, or rather of the old dispensation of the covenant of grace : of this it is said, 1. That it was made with the fathers of the Jewish nation at mount Sinai (*v.* 9), and Moses was the Mediator of that covenant, when God took them by the hand, to lead them out of the land of Egypt, which intimates the great affection, condescension, and tender care of God towards them. 2. That this covenant was not found faultless (*v.* 7, 8); it was a dispensation of darkness and dread, tending to bondage, and only a schoolmaster to bring us to Christ; it was perfect in its kind, and fitted to answer its end, but very imperfect in comparison of the gospel. 3. That it was not sure or stedfast; *for the Jews continued not in that covenant, and the Lord regarded them not, v.* 9. They dealt ungratefully with their God, and cruelly with themselves, and fell under God's displeasure. God will regard those who remain in his covenant, but will reject those who cast away his yoke from them. 4. That it is decayed, grown old, and vanisheth away, *v.* 13. It is antiquated, cancelled, out of date, of no more use in gospel times than candles are when the sun has risen. Some think the covenant of peculiarity did not quite decay till the destruction of Jerusalem, though it was forfeited at the death of Christ, and was made old, and was now to vanish and perish, and the Levitical priesthood vanished with it.

II. What is here said of the New-Testament dispensation, to prove the superior excellency of Christ's ministry. It is said,

1. That it is a better covenant (*v.* 6), a more clear and comfortable dispensation and discovery of the grace of God to sinners, bringing in holy light and liberty to the soul. It is without fault, well ordered in all things. It requires nothing but what it promises grace to perform. It accepts of godly sincerity, accounting it gospel perfection. Every transgression does not turn us out of covenant; all is put into a good and safe hand.

2. That it is established upon better promises, more clear and express, more spiritual, more absolute. The promises of spiritual and eternal blessings are in this covenant positive and absolute; the promises of temporal blessings are with a wise and kind proviso, as far as shall be for God's glory and his people's good. This covenant contains in it promises of assistance and acceptance in duty, promises of progress and perseverance in grace and holiness, of bliss and glory in heaven, which were more obscurely shadowed forth by the promises of the land of Canaan, a type of heaven.

3. It is a new covenant, even that new covenant that God long ago declared he would make with the house of Israel, that is, all the Israel of God; this was promised in Jer. xxxi. 31, 32, and accomplished in Christ. This will always be a new covenant, in which all who truly take hold of it shall be always found preserved by the power of God. It is God's covenant; his mercy, love, and grace moved for it; his wisdom devised it; his Son purchased it; his Spirit brings souls into it, and builds them up in it.

4. The articles of this covenant are very extraordinary, which are sealed between God and his people by baptism and the Lord's supper; whereby they bind themselves to their part, and God assures them he will do his part; and his is the main and principal part, on which his people depend for grace and strength to do theirs. Here,

(1.) God articles with his people *that he will put his laws into their minds and write them in their hearts, v.* 10. He once wrote his laws to them, now he will write his laws in them; that is, he will give them understanding to know and to believe his law; he will give them memories to retain them; he will give them hearts to love them and consciences to recognise them; he will give them courage to profess them and power to put them in practice; the whole habit and frame of their souls shall be a table and transcript of the law of God. This is the foundation of the covenant; and, when this is laid, duty will be done wisely, sincerely, readily, easily, resolutely, constantly, and comfortably.

(2.) He articles with them to take them into a near and very honourable relation to himself. [1.] He will be to them a God; that is, he will be all that to them, and do all that for them, that God can be and do. Nothing more can be said in a thousand volumes than is comprehended in these few words: *I will be a God to them.* [2.] They shall be to him a people, to love, honour, observe, and obey him in all things; complying with his cautions, conforming to his commands, comporting with his providences, copying out his example, taking complacency in his favour. This those must do and will do who have God for their God; this they are bound to do as their part of the contract; this they shall do, for God will enable them to do it, as an evidence that he is their God and that they are his people; for it is God himself who first founds the relation, and then fills it up with grace suitable and sufficient, and helps them in their measure to fill it up with love and duty; so that God engages both for himself and them.

(3.) He articles with them that they shall grow more and more acquainted with their God (v. 11): *They shall all know me from the least to the greatest,* insomuch that there shall not be so much need of one neighbour teaching another the knowledge of God. Here observe, [1.] In the want of better instruction, one neighbour should be teaching another to know the Lord, as they have ability and opportunity for it. [2.] This private instruction shall not be so necessary under the New Testament as it was under the Old. The old dispensation was shadowy, dark, ritual, and less understood; their priests preached but seldom, and but a few at a time, and the Spirit of God was more sparingly given out. But under the new dispensation there shall be such abundance of public qualified preachers of the gospel, and dispensers of ordinances statedly in the solemn assemblies, and so great a flocking to them, as doves to their windows, and such a plentiful effusion of the Spirit of God to make the ministration of the gospel effectual, that there shall be a mighty increase and spreading of Christian knowledge in persons of all sorts, of each sex, and of all ages. O that this promise might be fulfilled in our days, that the hand of God may be with his ministers, that a great number may believe and be turned to the Lord!

(4.) God articles with them about the pardon of their sins, as what always accompanies the true knowledge of God (v. 12): *For I will be merciful to their unrighteousness,* &c. Observe, [1.] The freeness of this pardon. It does not result from merit in man, but from mercy in God; he pardons for his own name's sake. [2.] The fulness of this pardon; it extends to their unrighteousness, sins, and iniquities; to all kinds of sin, to sins highly aggravated. [3.] The fixedness of this pardon. It is so final and so fixed that God will remember their sins no more; he will not recall his pardon; he will not only forgive their sins, but forget them, treat them as if he had forgotten them. This pardoning mercy is connected with all other spiritual mercies. Unpardoned sin prevents mercy, and pulls down judgments; but the pardon of sin prevents judgment, and opens a wide door to all spiritual blessings; it is the effect of that mercy that is from everlasting, and the earnest of that mercy that shall be to everlasting. This is the excellency of the new dispensation, and these are the articles of it; and therefore we have no reason to repine, but great reason to rejoice that the former dispensation is antiquated and has vanished away.

CHAPTER IX

The apostle, having declared the Old-Testament dispensation antiquated and vanishing
away, proceeds to let the Hebrews see the correspondence there was between the Old
Testament and the New; and that whatever was excellent in the Old was typical and
representative of the New, which therefore must as far excel the Old as the substance
does the shadow. The Old Testament was never intended to be rested in, but to prepare for the institutions of the gospel. And here he treats, I. Of the tabernacle, the
place of worship, ver. 1-5. II. Of the worship and services performed in the tabernacle,
ver. 6, 7. III. He delivers the spiritual sense and the main design of all, ver. 8, to the
end.

THEN verily the first *covenant* had also ordinances of divine
service, and a worldly sanctuary [and its sanctuary, *a
sanctuary* of this world]. ² For there was a tabernacle made;
the first, wherein *was* the candlestick, and the table, and the
shewbread; which is called the sanctuary [Holy place]. ³ And
after the second veil, the tabernacle which is called the Holiest
of all [Holy of holies]; ⁴ Which had the golden censer, and the
ark of the covenant overlaid round about with gold, wherein
was the golden pot that had manna, and Aaron's rod that
budded, and the tables of the covenant; ⁵ And over it the
cherubims of glory shadowing the mercy-seat; of which we cannot now speak particularly.   ⁶ Now when these things were
thus ordained, the priests went always [continually] into the
first tabernacle, accomplishing the service *of God*.   ⁷ But into
the second *went* the high priest alone once every year, not
without blood, which he offered for himself, and *for* the errors
of the people.

Here, I. The apostle gives an account of the tabernacle, that place of
worship which God appointed to be pitched on earth ; it is called *a worldly*
sanctuary, wholly of this world, as to the materials of which it was built,
and a building that must be taken down ; it is called a worldly *sanctuary*,
because it was the court and palace of the King of Israel.   God was their
King, and, as other kings, had his court or place of residence, and attendants, furniture, and provision, suitable thereto.   This tabernacle (of which
we have the model, Exod. xxv.–xxvii.) was a moving temple, shadowing
forth the unsettled state of the church militant, and the human nature of
the Lord Jesus Christ, in whom the fulness of the Godhead dwelt bodily.
Now of this tabernacle it is said that it was divided into two parts, called
a first and a second tabernacle, an inner and an outer part, representing
the two states of the church militant and triumphant and the two natures
of Christ, human and divine.   We are also told what was placed in each
part of the tabernacle.

1. In the outer part: and there were several things, of which you have
here a sort of schedule.   (1.) The candlestick; doubtless not an empty
and unlighted one, but where the lamps were always burning.   And there

was need of it, for there were no windows in the sanctuary; and this was to convince the Jews of the darkness and the mysterious nature of that dispensation. Their light was only candle-light, in comparison of the fulness of light which Christ, the Sun of righteousness, would bring along with him, and communicate to his people; for all our light is derived from him the fountain of light. (2.) The table and the showbread set upon it. This table was set directly opposite to the candlestick, which shows that by light from Christ we must have communion with him and with one another. We must not come in the dark to his table, but by light from Christ must discern the Lord's body. On this table were placed twelve loaves for the twelve tribes of Israel, a loaf for a tribe, which stood from sabbath to sabbath, and on that day were renewed. This showbread may be considered either as the provision of the palace (though the King of Israel needed it not, yet, in resemblance of the palaces of earthly kings, there must be this provision laid in weekly), or the provision made in Christ for the souls of his people, suitable to the wants and to the relief of their souls. He is the bread of life; in our Father's house there is bread enough and to spare; we may have fresh supplies from Christ, especially every Lord's day. This outer part is called *the sanctuary* or *holy*, because erected to the worship of a holy God, to represent a holy Jesus, and to entertain a holy people, for their further improvement in holiness.

2. We have an account of what was in the inner part of the sanctuary, which was within the second veil, and is called *the holiest of all.* This second veil, which divided between the holy and the most holy place, was a type of the body of Christ, by the rending whereof not only a view, but a way, was opened for us into the holiest of all, the type of heaven itself. Now in this part were, (1.) The golden censer, which was to hold the incense, or the golden altar set up to burn the incense upon; both the one and the other were typical of Christ, of his pleasing and prevailing intercession which he makes in heaven, grounded upon the merits and satisfaction of his sacrifice, upon which we are to depend for acceptance and the blessing from God. (2.) The ark of the covenant overlaid round about with pure gold, *v.* 4. This typified Christ, his perfect obedience to the law and his fulfilling of all righteousness for us. Now here we are told both what was in this ark and what was over it. [1.] What was in it. *First, The golden pot that had manna,* which, when preserved by the Israelites in their own houses, contrary to the command of God, presently putrefied; but now, being by God's appointment deposited here in his house, was kept from putrefaction, always pure and sweet; and this to teach us that it is only in Christ that our persons, our graces, our performances are kept pure. It was also a type of the bread of life we have in Christ, the true ambrosia that gives immortality. This was also a memorial of God's miraculously feeding his people in the wilderness, that they might never forget such signal favour, nor distrust God for the time to come. *Secondly, Aaron's rod that budded,* and thereby showed that God had chosen him of the tribe of Levi to minister before him of all the tribes of Israel, and so an end was put to the murmuring of the people, and to their attempt to invade the priest's office, Num. xvii. This was that rod of God with which Moses and Aaron wrought such wonders; and this was a type of Christ, who is styled *the man, the branch* (Zech. vi. 12), by whom God has wrought wonders for the spiritual deliverance, defence, and supply of his people, and for the destruction of their enemies. It was a type of divine justice, by which Christ the Rock was smitten, and from whom the

cool refreshing waters of life flow into our souls. *Thirdly, The tables of the covenant,* in which the moral law was written, signifying the regard God has to the preservation of his holy law, and the care we all ought to have that we keep the law of God—that this we can only do in and through Christ, by strength from him, nor can our obedience be accepted but through him. [2.] What was over the ark (*v.* 5): *Over it the cherubim of glory shadowing the mercy-seat. First,* The mercy-seat, which was the covering of the ark; it was called *the propitiatory,* and it was of pure gold, as long and as broad as the ark in which the tables of the law were laid. It was an eminent type of Christ, and of his perfect righteousness, ever adequate to the dimensions of the law of God, and covering all our transgressions, interposing between the Shechinah, or symbol of God's presence, and our sinful failures, and covering them. *Secondly, The cherubim of glory* shadowing the mercy-seat, representing the holy angels of God, who take pleasure in looking into the great work of our redemption by Christ, and are ready to perform every good office, under the Redeemer, for those who are the heirs of salvation. The angels attended Christ at his birth, in his temptation, under his agonies, at his resurrection, and in his ascension, and will attend his second coming. God manifest in the flesh was seen, observed, visited, by the angels.

II. From the description of the place of worship in the Old Testament dispensation, the apostle proceeds to speak of the duties and services performed in those places, *v.* 6. When the several parts and furniture of the tabernacle were thus settled, then what was to be done there?

1. The ordinary priests went always into the first tabernacle, to accomplish the service of God. Observe, (1.) None but priests were to enter into the first part of the tabernacle, and this to teach us all that persons not qualified, not called of God, must not intrude into the office and work of the ministry. (2.) The ordinary priests were only to enter into the first part of the tabernacle, it would have been fatal presumption in them to have gone into the holiest of all; and this teaches us that even ministers themselves must know and keep in their proper stations, and not presume to usurp the prerogative of Christ, by offering up incense of their own, or adding their own inventions to the ordinances of Christ, or lording it over men's consciences. (3.) These ordinary priests were to enter into the first tabernacle always; that is, they were to devote themselves and all their time to the work of their office, and not alienate themselves at any time from it; they were to be in an habitual readiness for the discharge of their office, and at all stated appointed times were actually to attend to their work. (4.) The ordinary priests must enter into the first tabernacle, that they might there accomplish the service of God. They must not do the work of God partially or by halves, but stand complete in the whole of his will and counsel; not only beginning well, but proceeding well, and persevering to the end, fulfilling the ministry they had received.

2. Into the second, the interior part, went the high priest alone, *v.* 7. This part was an emblem of heaven, and Christ's ascension thither. Here observe, (1.) None but the high priest must go into the holiest; so none but Christ could enter into heaven in his own name, by his own right, and by his own merits. (2.) In entering into the holiest, the high priest must first go through the outer sanctuary, and through the veil, signifying that Christ went to heaven through a holy life and a violent death; the veil of his flesh was rent asunder. (3.) The high priest entered but once a year into the holiest, and in this the antitype excels the type (as in every thing

else), for he has entered once for all, during the whole dispensation of the gospel. (4.) The high priest must not enter without blood, signifying that Christ, having undertaken to be our high priest, could not have been admitted into heaven without shedding his blood for us, and that none of us can enter either into God's gracious presence here or his glorious presence hereafter, but by the blood of Jesus. (5.) The high priest, under the law, entering into the holiest, offered up that blood for himself and his own errors first, and then for the errors of the people, *v.* 7. This teaches us that Christ is a more excellent person and high priest than any under the law, for he has no errors of his own to offer for. And it teaches us that ministers, when in the name of Christ they intercede for others, must first apply the blood of Christ to themselves for their pardon. (6.) When the legal high priest had offered for himself, he must not stop there, but must also offer for the errors of the people. Our high priest, though he needs not to offer for himself, yet forgets not to offer for his people : he pleads the merit of his sufferings for the benefit of his people on earth. Observe, [1.] Sins are errors, and great errors, both in judgment and practice. We greatly err when we sin against God ; and who can understand all his errors ? [2.] They are such errors as leave guilt upon the conscience, not to be washed away but by the blood of Christ ; and the sinful errors of priests and people must be all done away by the same means, the application of the blood of Christ ; we must plead this blood on earth, while he is pleading it in heaven for us.

8 The Holy Ghost this signifying, that the way into the holiest of all was not yet made manifest, while as the first tabernacle was yet standing : 9 Which *was* a figure [parable] for the time then present, in which were offered both gifts and sacrifices, that could not make him that did the service perfect, as pertaining to the conscience ; 10 *Which stood* only in meats and drinks, and divers washings, and carnal ordinances [being only (with meats and drinks and divers washings) carnal ordinances], imposed *on them* until the time of reformation. 11 But Christ being come a high priest of good things to come, by a greater and more perfect tabernacle, not made with hands, that is to say, not of this building [creation]; 12 Neither by the blood of goats and calves, but by his own blood he entered in once into the holy place, having obtained eternal redemption *for us.* 13 For if the blood of bulls and of goats, and the ashes of a heifer sprinkling the unclean, sanctifieth to the purifying of the flesh : 14 How much more shall the blood of Christ, who through the eternal Spirit offered himself without spot to God, purge your conscience from dead works to serve the living God ?

In these verses the apostle undertakes to deliver to us the mind and meaning of the Holy Ghost in all the ordinances of the tabernacle and legal economy, comprehending both place and worship. The scriptures of the Old Testament were given by inspiration of God ; holy men of old spoke and wrote as the Holy Ghost directed them. And these Old Testament records are of great use and significancy, not only to those who first received them, but even to Christians, who ought not to satisfy themselves with reading the institutes of the Levitical law, but should learn what the Holy Ghost signifies and suggests to them thereby. Now here are several things mentioned as the things that the Holy Ghost signified and certified to his people hereby.

I. That the way into the holiest of all was not yet made manifest, while the first tabernacle was standing, *v.* 8. This was one lesson the Holy Ghost would teach us by these types ; the way to heaven was not so clear and plain, nor so much frequented, under the Old Testament as under the New. It is the honour of Christ and the gospel, and the happiness of those who live under it, that now life and immortality are brought to light. There was not that free access to God then that there is now ; God has now opened a wider door, and there is room for more, yea, even for as many as are truly willing to return unto him by Christ.

II. That the first tabernacle was only a figure for the time then present, *v.* 9. It was a dark dispensation, and but of short continuance, only designed for awhile to typify the great things of Christ and the gospel, that were in due time to shine forth in their own brightness, and thereby cause all the shadows to flee away and disappear, as the stars before the rising sun.

III. That none of the gifts and sacrifices there offered could make the offerers perfect as pertaining to conscience (*v.* 9) ; that is, they could not take away the desert, or defilement, or dominion, of sin ; they could not deliver conscience from a dread of the wrath of God ; they could neither discharge the debts, nor resolve the doubts, of him who did the service. A man might run through them all in their several orders and frequent returns, and continue to do so all his days, and yet not find his conscience either pacified or purified by them ; he might thereby be saved from corporal and temporal punishments that were threatened against the non-observers, but he could not be saved by them from sin or hell, as all those are who believe in Christ.

IV. The Holy Ghost hereby signifies that the Old Testament institutions were but external carnal ordinances imposed upon them until the time of reformation, *v.* 10. Their imperfection lay in three things :—1. Their nature. They were but external and carnal meats and drinks, and divers washings. All these were bodily exercises, which profit little ; they could only satisfy the flesh, or at best sanctify to the purifying of the flesh. 2. They were not such as were left indifferent to them to use or disuse, but they were imposed upon them by grievous corporal punishments, and this was ordered on purpose to make them look more to the promised Seed, and long more for him. 3. These were never designed for a perpetuity, but only to continue till the time of reformation, till the better things provided for them were actually bestowed upon them. Gospel times are and should be times of reformation,—of clearer light as to all things necessary to be known,—of greater love, inducing us to bear ill-will to none, but good-will to all, and to have complacency in all that are like God,—of greater liberty and freedom both of spirit and speech—and of a more holy living according to the rule of the gospel. We have far greater advantages under the gospel than they had under the law ; and either we must be better or we shall be worse. A conversation becoming the gospel is an excellent way of living ; nothing mean, foolish, vain, or servile becomes the gospel.

V. The Holy Ghost signifies to us hereby that we never make the right use of types but when we apply them to the antitype ; and, whenever we do so, it will be very evident that the antitype (as in reason it should) greatly excels the type, which is the main drift and design of all that is said. And, as he writes to those who believed that Christ had come and that Jesus was the Christ, so he very justly infers that he is infinitely above all legal high priests (v. 11, 12), and he illustrates it very fully. For,

1. *Christ is a high priest of good things to come*, by which may be understood, (1.) All the good things that were to come during the Old Testament, and now have come under the New. All the spiritual and eternal blessings the Old-Testament saints had in their day and under their dispensation were owing to the Messiah to come, on whom they believed. The Old Testament set forth in shadows what was to come ; the New Testament is the accomplishment of the Old. (2.) All the good things yet to come and to be enjoyed in a gospel state, when the promises and prophecies made to the gospel church in the latter days shall be accomplished ; all these depend upon Christ and his priesthood, and shall be fulfilled. (3.) Of all the good things to come in the heavenly state, which will perfect both the Testaments ; as the state of glory will perfect the state of grace, this state will be in a much higher sense the perfection of the New Testament than the New Testament was the perfection of the Old. Observe, All things past, present, and to come, were, and are, founded upon, and flowing from, the priestly office of Christ.

2. Christ is a high priest *by a greater and more perfect tabernacle* (v. 11), *a tabernacle not made with hands, that is to say, not of this building*, but his own body, or rather human nature, conceived by the Holy Ghost, overshadowing the blessed virgin. This was a new fabric, a new order of building, infinitely superior to all earthly structures, not excepting the tabernacle of the temple itself.

3. Christ, our high priest, has entered into heaven, not as their high priest entered into the holiest, with the blood of bulls and of goats, but by his own blood, typified by theirs, and infinitely more precious. And this,

4. Not for one year only, which showed the imperfection of that priesthood, that it did but typically obtain a year's reprieve or pardon. But our high priest entered into heaven *once for all*, and has obtained not a yearly respite, but eternal redemption, and so needs not to make an annual entrance. In each of the types there was something that showed it was a type, and resembled the antitype, and something that showed it was but a type, and fell short of the antitype, and therefore ought by no means to be set up in competition with the antitype.

5. The Holy Ghost further signified and showed what was the efficacy of the blood of the Old-Testament sacrifices, and thence is inferred the much greater efficacy of the blood of Christ. (1.) The efficacy of the blood of the legal sacrifices extended to the purifying of the flesh (v. 13) : it freed the outward man from ceremonial uncleanness and from temporal punishment, and entitled him to, and fitted him for, some external privileges. (2.) He infers very justly hence the far greater efficacy of the blood of Christ (v. 14) : *How much more shall the blood of Christ*, &c. Here observe, [1.] What it was that gave such efficacy to the blood of Christ. *First*, It was his offering himself to God, the human nature upon the altar of his divine nature, he being priest, altar, and sacrifice, his divine nature serving for the two former, and his human nature for the last ; now such a priest,

altar, and sacrifice, could not but be propitiatory. *Secondly*, It was Christ's offering up himself to God through the eternal Spirit, not only as the divine nature supported the human, but the Holy Ghost, which he had without measure, helping him in all, and in this great act of obedience offering himself. *Thirdly*, It was Christ's offering himself to God without spot, without any sinful stain either in his nature or life ; this was conformable to the law of sacrifices, which required them to be without blemish.   Now further observe, [2.] What the efficacy of Christ's blood is ; it is very great. For, *First*, It is sufficient to purge the conscience from dead works, it reaches to the very soul and conscience, the defiled soul, defiled with sin, which is a dead work, proceeds from spiritual death, and tends to death eternal.   As the touching of a dead body gave a legal uncleanness, so meddling with sin, gives a moral and real defilement, fixes it in the very soul ; but the blood of Christ has efficacy to purge it out.   *Secondly*, It is sufficient to enable us to serve the living God, not only by purging away that guilt which separates between God and sinners, but by sanctifying and renewing the soul through the gracious influences of the Holy Spirit, purchased by Christ for this purpose, that we might be enabled to serve the living God in a lively manner.

15 And for this cause he is the mediator of the new testament, that by means of death, for [that a death having taken place for] the redemption of the transgressions *that were* under the first testament, they which are called might receive the promise of eternal inheritance.   16 For where a testament *is*, there must also of necessity be the death of the testator.   17 For a testament *is* of force after men are dead [where there hath been death]: otherwise it is of no strength at all while the testator liveth [for doth it ever avail while he that made it liveth ?]   18 Whereupon neither the first *testament* was dedicated without blood. 19 For when Moses had spoken every precept to all the people according to the law, he took the blood of calves and of goats, with water, and scarlet wool, and hyssop, and sprinkled both the book, and all the people, 20 Saying, This *is* the blood of the testament which God hath enjoined unto you.   21 Moreover he sprinkled with blood both the tabernacle, and all the vessels of the ministry.   22 And almost all things are by the law purged with blood [And according to the law, I may almost say, all things are cleansed with blood] ; and without shedding of blood is no remission.

In these verses the apostle considers the gospel under the notion of a will or testament, the new or last will and testament of Christ, and shows the necessity and efficacy of the blood of Christ to make this testament valid and effectual.

I. The gospel is here considered as a testament, the new and last will and testament of our Lord and Saviour Jesus Christ.   It is observable that the solemn transactions that pass between God and man are sometimes called a covenant, here a testament.   A covenant is an agreement between two or more parties about things that are in their own power, or may be so, and this either with or without a mediator; this agreement takes effect at such time and in such manner as therein declared. A testament is a voluntary act and deed of a single person, duly executed and witnessed, bestowing legacies on such legatees as are described and characterized by the testator, and which can only take effect upon his death. Now observe, Christ is the Mediator of a New Testament (*v.* 15); and he is so for several ends and purposes here mentioned. 1. To redeem persons from their transgressions committed against the law or first testament, which makes every transgression a forfeiture of liberty, and makes men debtors, and slaves or prisoners, who need to be redeemed. 2. To qualify all those that are effectually called to receive the promise of an eternal inheritance. These are the great legacies that Christ by his last will and testament has bequeathed to the truly characterized legatees.

II. To make this New Testament effectual, it was necessary that Christ should die; the legacies accrue by means of death. This he proves by two arguments:—1. From the general nature of every will or testamentary disposition, *v.* 16. Where a testament is, where it acts and operates, there must of necessity be the death of the testator; till then the property is still in the testator's hand, and he has power to revoke, cancel, or alter his will as he pleases; so that no estate, no right, is conveyed by will, till the testator's death has made it unalterable and effectual. 2. From the particular method that was taken by Moses in the ratification of the first testament, which was not done without blood, *v.* 18, 19, &c. All men by sin had become guilty before God, had forfeited their inheritance, their liberties, and their very lives, into the hands of divine justice; but God, being willing to show the greatness of his mercy, proclaimed a covenant of grace, and ordered it to be typically administered under the Old Testament, but not without the blood and life of the creature; and God accepted the blood of bulls and goats, as typifying the blood of Christ; and by these means the covenant of grace was ratified under the former dispensation. The method taken by Moses, according to the direction he had received from God, is here particularly related. (1.) Moses spoke every precept to all the people, according to the law, *v.* 19. He published to them the tenour of the covenant, the duties required, the rewards promised to those who did their duty, and the punishment threatened against the transgressors, and he called for their consent to the terms of the covenant; and this in an express manner. (2.) Then he took the blood of calves and of goats, with water, and scarlet wool, and hyssop, and applied this blood by sprinkling it. This blood and water signified the blood and water that came out of our Saviour's pierced side, for justification and sanctification, and also shadowed forth the two sacraments of the New Testament, baptism and the Lord's supper, with scarlet wool, signifying the righteousness of Christ with which we must be clothed, the hyssop signifying that faith by which we must apply all. Now with these Moses sprinkled, [1.] The book of the law and covenant, to show that the covenant of grace is confirmed by the blood of Christ and made effectual to our good. [2.] The people, intimating that the shedding of the blood of Christ will be no advantage to us if it be not applied to us. And the sprinkling of both the book and the people signified the mutual consent of both parties, God and man, and their mutual engagements to each other in this covenant through Christ, Moses at the same time using these words, *This is the blood of the testament which God hath enjoined unto you.* This blood, typifying the blood of Christ, is the

ratification of the covenant of grace to all true believers. [3.] He sprinkled
the tabernacle and all the utensils of it, intimating that all the sacrifices
offered up and services performed there were accepted only through the
the blood of Christ, which procures the remission of that iniquity that
cleaves to our holy things, which could not have been remitted but by that
atoning blood.

²³ *It was* therefore necessary that the patterns [**copies**] of
things in the heavens should be purified with these; but the
heavenly things themselves with better sacrifices than these.
²⁴ For Christ is not entered into the holy places made with
hands, *which are* the figures of the true [**like in pattern to the
true**]; but into heaven itself, now to appear in the presence of
God for us : ²⁵ Nor yet that he should offer himself often, as
the high priest entereth into the holy place every year with blood
of others [**not his own**]; ²⁶ For then must he often have suffered
since the foundation of the world : but now once in the end of
the world [**the ages**] hath he appeared to put away sin by the
sacrifice of himself. ²⁷ And as it is appointed unto men once
to die, but after this the judgment: ²⁸ So Christ was once
offered to bear the sins of many; and unto them that look for
him shall he appear the second time without sin unto salvation
[**shall appear a second time, apart from sin, to them that
wait for him, unto salvation**].

In this last part of the chapter, the apostle goes on to tell us what the
Holy Ghost has signified to us by the legal purifications of the patterns of
the things in heaven, inferring thence the necessity of better sacrifices to
consecrate the heavenly things themselves.

I. The necessity of purifying the patterns of the things in heaven, *v.* 23.
This necessity arises both from the divine appointment, which must always
be obeyed, and from the reason of that appointment, which was to preserve
a proper resemblance between the things typifying and the things typified.
It is observable here that the sanctuary of God on earth is a pattern of
heaven, and communion with God in his sanctuary is to his people a heaven
upon earth.

II. The necessity that the heavenly things themselves should be purified
with better sacrifices than of bulls and goats; the things themselves are better
than the patterns, and must therefore be consecrated with better sacrifices.
These heavenly things are the privileges of the gospel state, begun in grace,
perfected in glory. These must be ratified by a suitable sanction or consecration; and this was the blood of Christ. Now it is very evident that the
sacrifice of Christ is infinitely better than those of the law, 1. From the
places in which the sacrifices under the law, and that under the gospel,
were offered. Those under the law were the holy places made with hands,
which are but figures of the true sanctuary, *v.* 24. Christ's sacrifice, though
offered upon earth, was by himself carried up into heaven, and is there
presented in a way of daily intercession; for he appears in the presence of
God for us. He has gone to heaven, not only to enjoy the rest and receive

the honour due to him, but to appear in the presence of God for us, to present our persons and our performances, to answer and rebuke our adversary and accuser, to secure our interest, to perfect all our affairs, and to prepare a place for us. 2. From the sacrifices themselves, *v.* 26. Those under the law were the lives and blood of other creatures of a different nature from the offerers—the blood of beasts, a thing of small value, and which would have been of none at all in this matter had it not had a typical respect to the blood of Christ ; but the sacrifice of Christ was the oblation of himself ; he offered his own blood, truly called, by virtue of the hypostatical union, *the blood of God ;* and therefore of infinite value. 3. From the frequent repetition of the legal sacrifices. This showed the imperfection of that law ; but it is the honour and perfection of Christ's sacrifice that, being once offered, it was sufficient to all the ends of it ; and indeed the contrary would have been absurd, for then he must have been still dying and rising again, and ascending and then again descending and dying ; and the great work had been always *in fieri—always doing,* and always to do, but never finished, which would be as contrary to reason as it is to revelation, and to the dignity of his person : *But now once in the end of the world hath he appeared, to put away sin by the sacrifice of himself.* The gospel is the last dispensation of the grace of God to men. 4. From the inefficacy of the legal sacrifices, and the efficacy of Christ's sacrifice. The legal sacrifices could not of themselves put away sin, neither procure pardon for it nor power against it. Sin would still have lain upon us, and had dominion over us ; but Jesus Christ by one sacrifice has made an end of sin, he has destroyed the works of the devil.

III. The apostle illustrates the argument from the appointment of God concerning men (*v.* 27, 28), and observes something like it in the appointment of God concerning Christ.

1. The appointment of God concerning men contains in it two things :— (1.) That they must once die, or, at least, undergo a change equivalent to death. It is an awful thing to die, to have the vital knot loosed or cut asunder, all relations here dropped at once, an end put to our probation and preparation state, and to enter into another world. It is a great work, and it is a work that can be but once done, and therefore had need to be well done. This is matter of comfort to the godly, that they shall die well and die but once ; but it is matter of terror to the wicked, who die in their sins, that they cannot return again to do that great work better. (2.) It is appointed to men that after death they shall come to judgment, to a particular judgment immediately after death ; for the soul returns to God as to its judge, to be determined to its eternal state ; and men shall be brought to the general judgment, at the end of the world. This is the unalterable decree of God concerning men—they must die, and they must be judged. It is appointed for them, and it is to be believed and seriously considered by them.

2. The appointment of God concerning Christ, bearing some resemblance to the other. (1.) He must be once offered, to bear the sins of many, of all the Father had given to him, of all who should believe in his name. He was not offered for any sin of his own ; he was wounded for our transgressions. God laid on him the iniquity of all his people ; and these are many, though not so many as the rest of mankind ; yet, when they are all gathered to him, he will be the first-born among many brethren. (2.) It is appointed that Christ shall appear the second time without sin, to the salvation of those who look for him. [1.] He will then appear without

sin ; at his first appearance, though he had no sin of his own, yet he stood charged with the sins of many ; he was the Lamb of God that bore upon him the sins of the world, and then he appeared in the form of sinful flesh ; but his second appearance will be without any such charge upon him, he having fully discharged it before, and then his visage shall not be marred, but shall be exceedingly glorious. [2.] This will be to the salvation of all who look for him ; he will then perfect their holiness, their happiness ; their number shall then be accomplished, and their salvation completed. Observe, It is the distinguishing character of true believers that they are looking for Christ ; they look to him by faith ; they look for him by hope and holy desires. They look for him in every duty, in every ordinance, in every providence now ; and they expect his second coming, and are preparing for it ; and though it will be sudden destruction to the rest of the world, who scoff at the report of it, it will be eternal salvation to those who look for it.

CHAPTER X

The apostle knew very well that the Hebrews, to whom he wrote, were strangely fond of the Levitical dispensation, and therefore he fills his mouth with arguments to wean them from it ; and in order thereto proceeds in this chapter, I. To lay low the whole of that priesthood and sacrifice, ver. 1-6. II. He raises and exalts the priesthood of Christ very high, that he might effectually recommend him and his gospel to them, ver. 7-18. III. He shows to believers the honours and dignities of their state, and calls them to suitable duties, ver. 19, to the end.

FOR the law having a shadow of good things to come, *and* not the very image of the things, can never with those sacrifices which they offered year by year continually make the comers thereunto perfect. ² For then would they not have ceased to be offered ? because that the worshippers once purged should have had no more conscience of sins. ³ But in those *sacrifices there is* a remembrance again *made* of sins every year. ⁴ For *it is* not possible that the blood of bulls and of goats should take away sins. ⁵ Wherefore when he cometh into the world, he saith, Sacrifice and offering thou wouldest not, but a body hast thou prepared me : ⁶ In burnt offerings and *sacrifices* for sin thou hast had no pleasure.

Here the apostle, by the direction of the Spirit of God, sets himself to lay low the Levitical dispensation ; for though it was of divine appointment, and very excellent and useful in its time and place, yet, when it was set up in competition with Christ, to whom it was only designed to lead the people, it was very proper and necessary to show the weakness and imperfection of it, which the apostle does effectually, from several arguments. As,

I. That the law had a shadow, and but a shadow, of good things to come ; and who would dote upon a shadow, though of good things, especially when the substance has come? Observe, 1. The things of Christ and the gospel are good things; they are the best things; they are best in themselves, and the best for us: they are realities of an excellent nature. 2. These good things were, under the Old Testament, good things to come, not clearly discovered, nor fully enjoyed. 3. That the Jews then had but the shadow of the good things of Christ, some adumbrations of them; we under the gospel have the substance.

II. That the law was not the very image of the good things to come. An image is an exact draught of the thing represented thereby. The law did not go so far, but was only a shadow, as the image of a person in a looking-glass is a much more perfect representation than his shadow upon the wall. The law was a very rough draught of the great design of divine grace, and therefore not to be so much doted on.

III. The legal sacrifices, being offered year by year, could never make the comers thereunto perfect; for then there would have been an end of offering them, v. 1, 2. Could they have satisfied the demands of justice, and made reconciliation for iniquity,—could they have purified and pacified conscience,—then they had ceased, as being no further necessary, since the offerers would have had no more sin lying upon their consciences. But this was not the case; after one day of atonement was over, the sinner would fall again into one fault or another, and so there would be need of another day of atonement, and of one every year, besides the daily minis-trations. Whereas now, under the gospel, the atonement is perfect, and not to be repeated; and the sinner, once pardoned, is ever pardoned as to his state, and only needs to renew his repentance and faith, that he may have a comfortable sense of a continued pardon.

IV. As the legal sacrifices did not of themselves take away sin, so it was impossible they should, v. 4. There was an essential defect in them. 1. They were not of the same nature with us who sinned. 2. They were not of sufficient value to make satisfaction for the affronts offered to the justice and government of God. They were not of the same nature that offended, and so could not be suitable. Much less were they of the same nature that was offended; and nothing less than the nature that was offended could make the sacrifice a full satisfaction for the offence. 3. The beasts offered up under the law could not consent to put themselves in the sinner's room and place. The atoning sacrifice must be one capable of consenting, and must voluntarily substitute himself in the sinner's stead: Christ did so.

V. There was a time fixed and foretold by the great God, and that time had now come, when these legal sacrifices would be no longer accepted by him nor useful to men. God never did desire them for themselves, and now he abrogated them; and therefore to adhere to them now would be resisting God and rejecting him. This time of the repeal of the Levitical laws was foretold by David (Ps. xl. 6, 7), and is recited here as now come. Thus industriously does the apostle lay low the Mosaical dispensation.

⁷ Then said I, Lo, I come (in the volume [roll] of the book it is written of me,) to do thy will, O God. ⁸ Above when he said, Sacrifice and offering and burnt offerings and *offering* for sin thou wouldest not, neither hadst pleasure *therein;* which are offered by the law; ⁹ Then said he, Lo, I come to do thy will, O God. He taketh away the first, that he may establish

the second. ¹⁰ By the which will we are [have been] sanctified
through the offering of the body of Jesus Christ once *for all.*
¹¹ And every priest standeth daily ministering and offering oftentimes the same sacrifices, which can never take away sins : ¹²
But this man, after he had offered one sacrifice for sins, for ever
sat down on the right hand of God ; ¹³ From henceforth expecting till his enemies be made his footstool. ¹⁴ For by one offering
he hath perfected for ever them that are sanctified. ¹⁵ *Whereof*
the Holy Ghost also is a witness to us : for after that he had
said before, ¹⁶ This *is* the covenant that I will make with them
after those days, saith the Lord, I will put my laws into their
hearts, and in their minds will I write them ; ¹⁷ And their sins
[*Then saith he,* **and their sins**] and iniquities will I remember
no more. ¹⁸ Now where remission of these *is, there is* no more
offering for sin.

Here the apostle raises up and exalts the Lord Jesus Christ, as high as
he had laid the Levitical priesthood low.   He recommends Christ to them
as the true high priest, the true atoning sacrifice, the antitype of all the
rest : and this he illustrates,

I. From the purpose and promise of God concerning Christ, which are
frequently recorded in the volume of the book of God, *v.* 7.   God had not
only decreed, but declared by Moses and the prophets, that Christ should
come and be the great high priest of the church, and should offer up a
perfect and a perfecting sacrifice.   It was written of Christ, in the beginning of the book of God, that *the seed of the woman should break the serpent's
head ;* and the Old Testament abounds with prophecies concerning Christ.
Now since he is the person so often promised, so much spoken of, so long
expected by the people of God, he ought to be received with great honour
and gratitude.

II. From what God had done in preparing a body for Christ (that is, a
human nature), that he might be qualified to be our Redeemer and Advocate ; uniting the two natures in his own person, he was a fit Mediator to
go between God and man ; a days-man to lay his hand upon both, a peace-
maker, to reconcile them, and an everlasting band of union between God
and the creature—"*My ears hast thou opened ;* thou hast fully instructed
me, furnished and fitted me for the work, and engaged me in it," Ps. xl.
6.   Now a Saviour thus provided, and prepared by God himself in so
extraordinary a manner, ought to be received with great affection and
gladness.

III. From the readiness and willingness that Christ discovered to engage
in this work, when no other sacrifice would be accepted, *v.* 7-9.   When
no less sacrifice would be a proper satisfaction to the justice of God than
that of Christ himself, then Christ voluntarily came into it : *Lo, I come!
I delight to do thy will, O God!* Let thy curse fall upon me, but let these
go their way.   Father, I delight to fulfil thy counsels, and my covenant
with thee for them ; I delight to perform all thy promises, to fulfil all
the prophecies."   This should endear Christ and our Bibles to us, that in
Christ we have the fulfilling of the scriptures.

IV. From the errand and design upon which Christ came; and this was to do the will of God, not only as a prophet to reveal the will of God, not only as a king to give forth divine laws, but as a priest to satisfy the demands of justice, and to fulfil all righteousness. Christ came to do the will of God in two instances. 1. In taking away the first priesthood, which God had no pleasure in; not only taking away the curse of the covenant of works, and cancelling the sentence denounced against us as sinners, but taking away the insufficient typical priesthood, and blotting out the handwriting of ceremonial ordinances and nailing it to his cross. 2. In establishing the second, that is, his own priesthood and the everlasting gospel, the most pure and perfect dispensation of the covenant of grace; this is the great design upon which the heart of God was set from all eternity. The will of God centres and terminates in it; and it is not more agreeable to the will of God than it is advantageous to the souls of men; for it is by this will that *we are sanctified, through the offering of the body of Jesus Christ once for all, v.* 10. Observe, (1.) What is the fountain of all that Christ has done for his people—the sovereign will and grace of God. (2.) How we come to partake of what Christ has done for us—by being sanctified, converted, effectually called, wherein we are united to Christ, and so partake of the benefits of his redemption; and this sanctification is owing to the oblation he made of himself to God.

V. From the perfect efficacy of the priesthood of Christ (*v.* 14): *By one offering he hath for ever perfected those that are sanctified;* he has delivered and will perfectly deliver those that are brought over to him, from all the guilt, power, and punishment of sin, and will put them into the sure possession of perfect holiness and felicity. This is what the Levitical priesthood could never do; and, if we indeed are aiming at a perfect state, we must receive the Lord Jesus as the only high priest that can bring us to that state.

VI. From the place to which our Lord Jesus is now exalted, the honour he has there and the further honour he shall have: *This man after he had offered one sacrifice for sins, for ever sat down at the right hand of God, henceforth expecting till his enemies be made his footstool, v.* 12, 13. Here observe, 1. To what honour Christ, as man and Mediator, is exalted—to the right hand of God, the seat of power, interest, and activity; the giving hand; all the favours that God bestows on his people are handed to them by Christ: the receiving hand; all the duties that God accepts from men are presented by Christ: the working hand; all that pertains to the kingdoms of providence and grace is administered by Christ; and therefore this is the highest post of honour. 2. How Christ came to this honour—not merely by the purpose or donation of the Father, but by his own merit and purchase, as a reward due to his sufferings; and, as he can never be deprived of an honour so much his due, so he will never quit it, nor cease to employ it for his people's good. 3. How he enjoys this honour—with the greatest satisfaction and rest; he is for ever sitting down there. The Father acquiesces and is satisfied in him; he is satisfied in his Father's will and presence; this is his rest for ever; here he will dwell, for he has both desired and deserved it. 4. He has further expectations, which shall not be disappointed; for they are grounded upon the promise of the Father, who hath said unto him, *Sit thou at my right hand, until I make thine enemies thy footstool,* Ps. cx. 1. One would think such a person as Christ could have no enemies except in hell; but it is certain that he has enemies on earth, very many, and very inveterate ones. Let not Christians then wonder that they have enemies, though they desire to live peaceably with all men. But Christ's enemies shall be made his footstool; some by conversion, others by confusion; and, which way soever it be, Christ will be honoured. Of this Christ is assured, this he is expecting, and his people should rejoice in the expectation of it; for, when his enemies shall be subdued, their enemies, that are so for his sake, shall be subdued also.

VII. The apostle recommends Christ from the witness the Holy Ghost has given in the scriptures concerning him; this relates chiefly to what should be the happy fruit and consequence of his humiliation and sufferings, which in general is that new and gracious covenant that is founded upon his satisfaction, and sealed by his blood (v. 15): *Whereof the Holy Ghost is a witness.* The passage is cited from Jer. xxxi. 31, in which covenant God promises, 1. That he will pour out his Spirit upon his people, so as to give them wisdom, will, and power, to obey his word: he will put his laws in their hearts, and write them in their minds, v. 16. This will make their duty plain, easy, and pleasant. 2. Their sins and iniquities he will remember no more (v. 17), which will alone show the riches of divine grace, and the sufficiency of Christ's satisfaction, that it needs not be repeated, v. 18. For there shall be no more remembrance of sin against true believers, either to shame them now or to condemn them hereafter. This was much more than the Levitical priesthood and sacrifices could effect.

And now we have gone through the doctrinal part of the epistle, in which we have met with many things dark and difficult to be understood, which we must impute to the weakness and dulness of our own minds. The apostle now proceeds to apply this great doctrine, so as to influence their affections, and direct their practice, setting before them the dignities and duties of the gospel state.

19 Having therefore, brethren, boldness to enter into the holiest by the blood of Jesus, 20 By a new and living way, which he hath consecrated [dedicated] for us, through the veil, that is to say, his flesh; 21 And *having* a high [great] priest over the house of God; 22 Let us draw near with a true heart in full assurance [fulness] of faith, having our hearts sprinkled from an evil conscience, and our bodies [body] washed with pure water. 23 Let us hold fast the profession of *our* faith without wavering; (for he *is* faithful that promised;) 24 And let us consider one another to provoke unto love and to good works: 25 Not forsaking the assembling of ourselves together, as the manner of some *is;* but exhorting *one another:* and so much the more, as ye see the day approaching. 26 For if we sin wilfully after that we have received the knowledge of the truth, there remaineth no more sacrifice for sins, 27 But a certain fearful looking for of judgment and fiery indignation [fierceness of fire] which shall devour the adversaries. 28 He that despised Moses' law died without mercy under two or three witnesses. 29 Of how much sorer punishment, suppose ye, shall he be thought worthy, who hath trodden under foot the son of God, and hath

counted the blood of the covenant, wherewith he was sanctified, an unholy thing, and hath done despite unto the Spirit of grace? ³⁰ For we know him that hath said, Vengeance *belongeth* unto me, I will recompense, saith the Lord. And again, The Lord shall judge his people. ³¹ *It is* a fearful thing to fall into the hands of the living God. ³² But call to remembrance the former days, in which, after ye were illuminated, ye endured a great fight of afflictions; ³³ Partly, whilst ye were made a gazingstock both by reproaches and afflictions; and partly, whilst ye became companions of [**partakers with**] them that were so used. ³⁴ For ye had compassion of me in my [**on them that were in**] bonds, and took joyfully the spoiling of your goods, knowing in yourselves that ye have in heaven a better and an enduring substance, [**knowing that ye yourselves have a better possession and an abiding one**]. ³⁵ Cast not away therefore your confidence, which hath great recompense of reward. ³⁶ For ye have need of patience, that, after ye have done the will of God, ye might receive the promise. ³⁷ For yet a little while, and he that shall come will come, and will not tarry. ³⁸ Now the just [**But my righteous one**] shall live by faith: but if *any man* draw back [**and if he shrink back**] my soul shall have no pleasure in him. ³⁹ But we are not of them who draw back unto perdition; but of them that believe to the saving of the soul.

I. Here the apostle sets forth the dignities of the gospel state. It is fit that believers should know the honours and privileges that Christ has procured for them, that, while they take the comfort, they may give him the glory of all. The privileges are, 1. Boldness to enter into the holiest. They have access to God, light to direct them, liberty of spirit and of speech to conform to the direction; they have a right to the privilege of a readiness for it, assistance to use and improve it and assurance and acceptance and advantage. They may enter into the gracious presence of God in his holy oracles, ordinances, providences, and covenant, and so into communion with God, where they receive communications from him, till they are prepared to enter into his glorious presence in heaven. 2. A high priest over the house of God, even this blessed Jesus, who presides over the church militant, and every member thereof on earth, and over the church triumphant in heaven. God is willing to dwell with men on earth, and to have them dwell with him in heaven; but fallen man cannot dwell with God without a high priest, who is the Mediator of reconciliation here and of fruition hereafter.

II. The apostle tells us the way and means by which Christians enjoy such privileges, and, in general, declares it to be *by the blood of Jesus,* by the merit of that blood which he offered up to God as an atoning sacrifice: he has purchased for all who believe in him free access to God in the ordinances of his grace here and in the kingdom of his glory. This blood, being sprinkled on the conscience, chases away slavish fear, and gives the believer assurance both of his safety and his welcome into the divine presence. Now the apostle, having given this general account of the way by which we have access to God, enters further into the particulars of it, *v. 20.* As, 1. It is the only way ; there is no way left but this. The first way to the tree of life is, and has been, long shut up.   2. It is a new way, both in opposition to the covenant of works and to the antiquated dispensation of the Old Testament ; it is *via novissima—the last way* that will ever be opened to men. Those who will not enter in this way exclude themselves for ever. It is a way that will always be effectual.   3. It is a living way. It would be death to attempt to come to God in the way of the covenant of works ; but this way we may come to God, and live. It is by a living Saviour, who, though he was dead, is alive ; and it is a way that gives life and lively hope to those who enter into it.   4. It is a way that Christ has consecrated for us through the veil, that is, his flesh.   The veil in the tabernacle and temple signified the body of Christ ; when he died, the veil of the temple was rent in sunder, and this was at the time of the evening sacrifice, and gave the people a surprising view into the holy of holies, which they never had before. Our way to heaven is by a crucified Saviour ; his death is to us the way of life. To those who believe this he will be precious.

III. He proceeds to show the Hebrews the duties binding upon them on account of these privileges, which were conferred in such an extraordinary way, *v.* 22, 23, &c.

1. They must draw near to God, and that in a right manner. They must draw near to God. Since such a way of access and return to God is opened, it would be the greatest ingratitude and contempt of God and Christ still to keep at a distance from him. They must draw near by conversion, and by taking hold of his covenant. They must draw near in all holy conversation, like Enoch walking with God. They must draw near in humble adorations, worshipping at his footstool. They must draw near in holy dependence, and in a strict observance of the divine conduct towards them. They must draw near in conformity to God, and communion with him, living under his blessed influence, still endeavouring to get nearer and nearer, till they come to dwell in his presence ; but they must see to it that they make their approach to God after a right manner.   (1.) With a true heart, without any allowed guile or hypocrisy. God is the searcher of hearts, and he requires truth in the inward parts. Sincerity is our gospel perfection, though not our justifying righteousness.   (2.) In full assurance of faith, with a faith grown up to a full persuasion that when we come to God by Christ we shall have audience and acceptance.   We should lay aside all sinful distrust. Without faith it is impossible to please God ; and the stronger our faith is the more glory we give to God.   And, (3.) Having our hearts sprinkled from an evil conscience, by a believing application of the blood of Christ to our souls. They may be cleansed from guilt, from filth, from sinful fear and torment, from all aversion to God and duty, from ignorance, and error, and superstition, and whatever evils the consciences of men are subject to by reason of sin.   (4.) Our bodies washed with pure water, that is, with the water of baptism (by which we are recorded among the disciples of Christ, members of his mystical body), or with the sanctifying virtue of the Holy Spirit, reforming and regulating our outward conversation as well as our inward frame, cleansing from the filthiness of the flesh as well as of the spirit. The priests under the law

were to wash, before they went into the presence of the Lord to offer before him. There must be a due preparation for making our approaches to God.

2. The apostle exhorts believers to hold fast the profession of their faith, *v.* 23. Here observe, (1.) The duty itself—to hold fast the profession of our faith, to embrace all the truths and ways of the gospel, to get fast hold of them, and to keep that hold against all temptation and opposition. Our spiritual enemies will do what they can to wrest our faith, and hope, and holiness, and comfort, out of our hands, but we must hold fast our religion as our best treasure. (2.) The manner in which we must do this —without wavering, without doubting, without disputing, without dallying with temptation to apostasy. Having once settled these great things between God and our souls, we must be steadfast and immovable. Those who begin to waver in matters of Christian faith and practice are in danger of falling away. (3.) The motive or reason enforcing this duty: *He is faithful that hath promised.* God has made great and precious promises to believers, and he is a faithful God, true to his word; there is no falseness nor fickleness with him, and there should be none with us. His faithfulness should excite and encourage us to be faithful, and we must depend more upon his promises to us than upon our promises to him, and we must plead with him the promise of grace sufficient.

IV. We have the means prescribed for preventing our apostasy, and promoting our fidelity and perseverance, *v.* 24, 25, &c. He mentions several; as, 1. That we should *consider one another, to provoke to love and to good works.* Christians ought to have a tender consideration and concern for one another, they should affectionately consider what their several wants, weaknesses, and temptations are; and they should do this, not to reproach one another, to provoke one another not to anger, but to love and good works, calling upon themselves and one another to love God and Christ more, to love duty and holiness more, to love their brethren in Christ more, and to do all the good offices of Christian affection both to the bodies and the souls of each other. A good example given to others is the best and most effectual provocation to love and good works. 2. *Not to forsake the assembling of ourselves together, v.* 25. It is the will of Christ that his disciples should assemble together, sometimes more privately for conference and prayer, and in public for hearing and joining in all the ordinances of gospel worship. There were in the apostles' times, and should be in every age, Christian assemblies for the worship of God, and for mutual edification. And it seems even in those times there were some who forsook these assemblies, and so began to apostatise from religion itself. The communion of saints is a great help and privilege, and a good means of steadiness and perseverance; hereby their hearts and hands are mutually strengthened. 3. To exhort one another, to exhort ourselves and each other, to warn ourselves and one another of the sin and danger of backsliding, to put ourselves and our fellow-christians in mind of our duty, of our failures and corruptions, to watch over one another, and be jealous of ourselves and one another with a godly jealousy. This, managed with a true gospel spirit, would be the best and most cordial friendship. 4. That we should observe the approaching of times of trial, and be thereby quickened to greater diligence: *So much the more, as you see the day approaching.* Christians ought to observe the signs of the times, such as God has foretold. There was a day approaching, a terrible day to the Jewish nation, when their city should be destroyed, and the body of the people rejected of God for rejecting Christ. This would be a day of dispersion and temptation to the chosen remnant. Now the apostle puts them upon observing what signs there were of the approach of such a terrible day, and upon being the more constant in meeting together and exhorting one another, that they might be the better prepared for such a day. There is a trying day coming on us all, the day of our death, and we should observe all the signs of its approaching, and improve them to greater watchfulness and diligence in duty.

V. Having mentioned these means of establishment, the apostle proceeds, in the close of the chapter, to enforce his exhortations to perseverance, and against apostasy, by many very weighty considerations, *v.* 26, 27, &c.

1. From the description he gives of the sin of apostasy. It is *sinning wilfully after we have received the knowledge of the truth*, sinning wilfully against that truth of which we have had convincing evidence. This text has been the occasion of great distress to some gracious souls ; they have been ready to conclude that every wilful sin, after conviction and against knowledge, is the unpardonable sin : but this has been their infirmity and error. The sin here mentioned is a total and final apostasy, when men with a full and fixed will and resolution despise and reject Christ, the only Saviour,—despise and resist the Spirit, the only sanctifier,—and despise and renounce the gospel, the only way of salvation, and the words of eternal life ; and all this after they have known, owned, and professed, the Christian religion, and continue to do so obstinately and maliciously. This is the great transgression : the apostle seems to refer to the law concerning presumptuous sinners, Num. xv. 30, 31. They were to be cut off.

2. From the dreadful doom of such apostates. (1.) There remains no more sacrifice for such sins, no other Christ to come to save such sinners ; they sin against the last resort and remedy. There were some sins under the law for which no sacrifices were provided ; but yet if those who committed them did truly repent, though they might not escape temporal death, they might escape eternal destruction ; for Christ would come, and make atonement. But now those under the gospel who will not accept of Christ, that they may be saved by him, have no other refuge left them. (2.) There remains for them only a certain fearful looking for of judgment, *v.* 27. Some think this refers to the dreadful destruction of the Jewish church and state ; but certainly it refers also to the utter destruction that awaits all obstinate apostates at death and judgment, when the Judge will discover a fiery indignation against them, which will devour the adversaries ; they will be consigned to the devouring fire and to everlasting burnings. Of this destruction God gives some notorious sinners, while on earth, a fearful foreboding in their own consciences, a dreadful looking for it, with a despair of ever being able either to endure or escape it.

3. From the methods of divine justice with those who despised Moses's law, that is, sinned presumptuously, despising his authority, his threatenings and his power. These, when convicted by two or three witnesses, were put to death ; they died without mercy, a temporal death. Observe, Wise governors should be careful to keep up the credit of their government and the authority of the laws, by punishing presumptuous offenders ; but then in such cases there should be good evidence of the fact. Thus God ordained in Moses's law ; and hence the apostle infers the heavy doom that will fall upon those that apostatize from Christ. Here he refers to their own consciences, to judge how much sorer punishment the despisers

of Christ (after they have professed to know him) are likely to undergo ; and they may judge of the greatness of the punishment by the greatness of the sin. (1.) They have *trodden under foot the Son of God.* To trample upon an ordinary person shows intolerable insolence ; to treat a person of honour in that vile manner is insufferable ; but to deal thus with the Son of God, who himself is God, must be the highest provocation—to trample upon his person, denying him to be the Messiah—to trample upon his authority, and undermine his kingdom—to trample upon his members as the offscouring of all things, and not fit to live in the world ; what punishment can be too great for such men ? (2.) They have *counted the blood of the covenant, wherewith he was sanctified, an unholy thing ;* that is, the blood of Christ, with which the covenant was purchased and sealed, and wherewith Christ himself was consecrated, or wherewith the apostate was sanctified, that is, baptized, visibly initiated into the new covenant by baptism, and admitted to the Lord's supper. Observe, There is a kind of sanctification which persons may partake of and yet fall away : they may be distinguished by common gifts and graces, by an outward profession, by a form of godliness, a course of duties, and a set of privileges, and yet fall away finally. Men who have seemed before to have the blood of Christ in high esteem may come to account it an unholy thing, no better than the blood of a malefactor, though it was the world's ransom, and every drop of it of infinite value. (3.) *Those have done despite unto the Spirit of grace,* the Spirit that is graciously given to men, and that works grace wherever it is,—the Spirit of grace, that should be regarded and attended to with the greatest care,—this Spirit they have grieved, resisted, quenched, yea, done despite to him, which is the highest act of wickedness, and makes the case of the sinner desperate, refusing to have the gospel salvation applied to him. Now he leaves it to the consciences of all, appeals to universal reason and equity, whether such aggravated crimes ought not to receive a suitable punishment, a sorer punishment than those who had died without mercy ? But what punishment can be sorer than to die without mercy ? I answer, To die by mercy, by the mercy and grace which they have despised. How dreadful is the case when not only the justice of God, but his abused grace and mercy call for vengeance !

4. From the description we have in the scripture of the nature of God's vindictive justice, *v.* 30. We know that he has said, *Vengeance is mine.* This is taken out of Ps. xciv. 1, *Vengeance belongs unto me.* The terrors of the Lord are known both by revelation and reason. Vindictive justice is a glorious, though terrible attribute of God ; it belongs to him, and he will use and execute it upon the heads of such sinners as despise his grace ; he will avenge himself, and his Son, and Spirit, and covenant, upon apostates. And how dreadful then will their case be ! The other quotation is from Deut. xxxii. 36, *The Lord will judge his people ;* he will search and try his visible church, and will discover and detect those who say they are Jews, and are not, but are of the synagogue of Satan ; and he will separate the precious from the vile, and will punish the sinners in Zion with the greatest severity. Now those who know him who hath said, *Vengeance belongeth to me, I will recompense,* must needs conclude, as the apostle does (*v.* 31) : *It is a fearful thing to fall into the hands of the living God.* Those who know the joy that results from the favour of God can thereby judge of the power and dread of his vindictive wrath. Observe here, What will be the eternal misery of impenitent sinners and apostates : they shall fall into the hands of the living God ; their punishment shall come from God's

own hand. He takes them into the hand of his justice; he will deal with them himself; their greatest misery will be the immediate impressions of divine wrath on the soul. When he punishes them by creatures, the instrument abates something of the force of the blow; but, when he does it by his own hand, it is infinite misery. This they shall have at God's hand, they shall lie down in sorrow; their destruction shall come from his glorious powerful presence; when they make their woeful bed in hell, they will find that God is there, and his presence will be their greatest terror and torment. And he is a living God; he lives for ever, and will punish for ever.

5. He presses them to perseverance by putting them in mind of their former sufferings for Christ: *But call to mind the former days, in which, after you were illuminated, you endured a great fight of afflictions, v.* 32. In the early days of the gospel there was a very hot persecution raised up against the professors of the Christian religion, and the believing Hebrews had their share of it: he would have them to remember,

(1.) When they had suffered: *In former days, after* they were *illuminated;* that is, as soon as God had breathed life into their souls, and caused divine light to spring up in their minds, and taken them into his favour and covenant; then earth and hell combined all their force against them. Here observe, A natural state is a dark state, and those who continue in that state meet with no disturbance from Satan and the world; but a state of grace is a state of light, and therefore the powers of darkness will violently oppose it. Those who will live godly in Christ Jesus must suffer persecution.

(2.) What they suffered: they *endured a great fight of afflictions,* many and various afflictions united together against them, and they had a great conflict with them. Many are the troubles of the righteous. [1.] They were afflicted in themselves. In their own persons; they were made gazing-stocks, spectacles to the world, angels, and men, 1 Cor. iv. 9. In their names and reputations (*v.* 33), by many reproaches. Christians ought to value their reputation; and they do so especially because the reputation of religion is concerned: this makes reproach a great affliction. They were afflicted in their estates, by the spoiling of their goods, by fines and forfeitures. [2.] They were afflicted in the afflictions of their brethren: *Partly while you became companions of those that were so used.* The Christian spirit is a sympathising spirit, not a selfish spirit, but a compassionate spirit; it makes every Christian's suffering our own, puts us upon pitying others, visiting them, helping them, and pleading for them. Christians are one body, are animated by one spirit, have embarked in one common cause and interest, and are the children of that God who is afflicted in all the afflictions of his people. If one member of the body suffers, all the rest suffer with it. The apostle takes particular notice how they had sympathised with him (*v.* 34): *You had compassion on me in my bonds.* We must thankfully acknowledge the compassions our Christian friends have shown for us under our afflictions.

(3.) How they had suffered. They had been mightily supported under their former sufferings; they took their sufferings patiently, and not only so, but joyfully received it from God as a favour and honour conferred upon them that they should be thought worthy to suffer reproach for the name of Christ. God can strengthen his suffering people with all might in the inner man, to all patience and long-suffering, and that with joyfulness, Col. i. 11.

(4.) What it was that enabled them thus to bear up under their sufferings. They knew in themselves that they had in heaven a better and a more enduring substance. Observe, [1.] The happiness of the saints in heaven is substance, something of real weight and worth. All things here are but shadows. [2.] It is a better substance than anything they can have or lose here. [3.] It is an enduring substance, it will outlive time and run parallel with eternity; they can never spend it; their enemies can never take it from them, as they did their earthly goods. [4.] This will make a rich amends for all they can lose and suffer here. In heaven they shall have a better life, a better estate, better liberty, better society, better hearts, better work, every thing better. [5.] Christians should know this in themselves, they should get the assurance of it in themselves (the Spirit of God witnessing with their spirits), for the assured knowledge of this will help them to endure any fight of afflictions they may be encountered with in this world.

6. He presses them to persevere, from that recompense of reward that waited for all faithful Christians (v. 35) : *Cast not away therefore your confidence, which hath great recompense of reward.* Here, (1.) He exhorts them not to cast away their confidence, that is, their holy courage and boldness, but to hold fast that profession for which they had suffered so much before, and borne those sufferings so well. (2.) He encourages them to this by assuring them that the reward of their holy confidence would be very great. It carries a present reward in it, in holy peace and joy, and much of God's presence and his power resting upon them ; and it shall have a great recompense of reward hereafter. (3.) He shows them how necessary a grace the grace of patience is in our present state (v. 36) : *You have need of patience, that after you have done the will of God you might receive the promise ;* that is, this promised reward. Observe, The greatest part of the saints' happiness is in promise. They must first do the will of God before they receive the promise ; and, after they have done the will of God, they have need of patience to wait for the time when the promise shall be fulfilled ; they have need of patience to live till God calls them away. It is a trial of the patience of Christians, to be content to live after their work is done, and to stay for the reward till God's time to give it them is come. We must be God's waiting servants when we can be no longer his working servants. Those who have had and exercised much patience already must have and exercise more till they die. (4.) To help their patience, he assures them of the near approach of Christ's coming to deliver and to reward them (v. 37) : *For yet a little while, and he that shall come will come, and will not tarry.* He will soon come to them at death, and put an end to all their sufferings, and give them a crown of life. He will soon come to judgment, and put an end to the sufferings of the whole church (all his mystical body), and give them an ample and glorious reward in the most public manner. There is an appointed time for both, and beyond that time he will not tarry, Hab. ii. 3. The Christian's present conflict may be sharp, but it will be soon over.

7. He presses them to perseverance, by telling them that this is their distinguishing character and will be their happiness ; whereas apostasy is the reproach, and will be the ruin, of all who are guilty of it (v. 38, 39) : *Now the just shall live by faith,* &c. (1.) It is the honourable character of just men that in times of the greatest affliction they can live by faith ; they can live upon the assured persuasion they have of the truth of God's promises. Faith puts life and vigour into them. They can trust God, and

live upon him, and wait his time : and, as their faith maintains their
spiritual life now, it shall be crowned with eternal life hereafter. (2.)
Apostasy is the mark and the brand of those in whom God takes no
pleasure ; and it is a cause of God's severe displeasure and anger. God
never was pleased with the formal profession and external duties and
services of such as do not persevere. He saw the hypocrisy of their hearts
then ; and he is greatly provoked when their formality in religion ends in
an open apostasy from religion. He beholds them with great displeasure ;
they are an offence to him. (3.) The apostle concludes with declaring his
good hope concerning himself and these Hebrews, that they should not
forfeit the character and happiness of the just, and fall under the brand
and misery of the wicked (*v.* 39): *But we are not,* &c. ; as if he had said,
" I hope we are not of those who draw back. I hope that you and I, who
have met with great trials already, and have been supported under them
by the grace of God strengthening our faith, shall not be at any time left
to ourselves to draw back to perdition ; but that God will still keep us by
his mighty power through faith unto salvation." Observe, [1.] Professors
may go a great way, and after all draw back ; and this drawing back
from God is drawing on to perdition : the further we depart from God the
nearer we approach to ruin. [2.] Those who have been kept faithful in
great trials for the time past have reason to hope that the same grace will
be sufficient to help them still to live by faith, till they receive the end of
their faith and patience, even the salvation of their souls. If we live by
faith, and die in faith, our souls will be safe for ever.

CHAPTER XI

The apostle having, in the close of the foregoing chapter, recommended the grace of faith
and a life of faith as the best preservative against apostasy, he now enlarges upon the
nature and fruits of this excellent grace. I. The nature of it, and the honour it reflects
upon all who live in the exercise of it, ver. 1-3. II. The great examples we have in the
Old Testament of those who lived by faith, and did and suffered extraordinary things
by the strength of this grace, ver. 4-38. And, III. The advantages that we have in the
gospel for the exercise of this grace above what those had who lived in the times of
the Old Testament, ver. 39, 40.

NOW faith is the substance [**assurance**] of things hoped for,
the evidence [**proving**] of things not seen. ²For by it
the elders obtained a good report [**For therein the elders had
witness borne to them**]. ³Through faith we understand that
the worlds were framed by the word of God, so that things
which are seen were not made of things which do appear.

Here we have, I. A definition or description of the grace of faith in two
parts. I. It *is the substance of things hoped for.* Faith and hope go together ; and the same things that are the object of our hope are the object
of our faith. It is a firm persuasion and expectation that God will perform all that he has promised to us in Christ ; and this persuasion is so

strong that it gives the soul a kind of possession and present fruition of those things, gives them a subsistence in the soul, by the first-fruits and foretastes of them : so that believers in the exercise of faith *are filled with joy unspeakable and full of glory.* Christ dwells in the soul by faith, and the soul is filled with the fulness of God, as far as his present measure will admit ; he experiences a substantial reality in the objects of faith. 2. It is *the evidence of things not seen.* Faith demonstrates to the eye of the mind the reality of those things that cannot be discerned by the eye of the body. Faith is the firm assent of the soul to the divine revelation and every part of it, and sets to its seal that God is true. It is a full appro-bation of all that God has revealed as holy, just, and good ; it helps the soul to make application of all to itself with suitable affections and endeavours ; and so it is designed to serve the believer instead of sight, and to be to the soul all that the senses are to the body. That faith is but opinion or fancy which does not realise invisible things to the soul, and excite the soul to act agreeably to the nature and importance of them.

II. An account of the honour it reflects upon all those who have lived in the exercise of it (*v.* 2) : *By it the elders obtained a good report*—the ancient believers, who lived in the first ages of the world. Observe, 1. True faith is an old grace, and has the best plea to antiquity : it is not a new invention, a modern fancy ; it is a grace that has been planted in the soul of man ever since the covenant of grace was published in the world ; and it has been practised from the beginning of the revelation ; the eldest and best men that ever were in the world were believers. 2. Their faith was their honour ; it reflected honour upon them. They were an honour to their faith, and their faith was an honour to them. It put them upon doing *the things that were of good report,* and God has taken care that a record shall be kept and report made of the excellent things they did in the strength of this grace. The genuine actings of faith will bear to be reported, deserve to be reported, and will, when reported, redound to the honour of true believers.

III. We have here one of the first acts and articles of faith, which has a great influence on all the rest, and which is common to all believers in every age and part of the world, namely, the creation of the *worlds by the word of God,* not out of pre-existent matter, but out of nothing, *v.* 3. The grace of faith has a retrospect as well as prospect ; it looks not only forward to the end of the world, but back to the beginning of the world. By faith we understand much more of the formation of the world than ever could be understood by the naked eye of natural reason. Faith is not a force upon the understanding, but a friend and a help to it. Now what does faith give us to understand concerning *the worlds,* that is, the upper, middle, and lower regions of the universe? 1. *That these worlds were* not eternal, nor did they produce themselves, but they were made by another. 2. That the maker of the worlds is God ; he is the maker of all things ; and whoever is so must be God. 3. That he made the world with great exactness ; it was a *framed* work, in every thing duly adapted and disposed to answer its end, and to express the perfections of the Creator. 4. That God made the world by his word, that is, by his essential wisdom and eternal Son, and by his active will, saying, *Let it be done, and it was done,* Ps. xxxiii. 9. 5. That the world was thus framed out of nothing, out of no pre-existent matter, contrary to the received maxim, that "out of nothing nothing can be made," which, though true of created power, can have no place with God, who can call *things that are not as if they were,*

and command them into being. These things we understand by faith.
The Bible gives us the truest and most exact account of the origin of all
things, and we are to believe it, and not to wrest or run down the scripture-
account of the creation, because it does not suit with some fantastic
hypotheses of our own, which has been in some learned but conceited men
the first remarkable step towards infidelity, and has led them into many
more.

⁴ By faith Abel offered unto God a more excellent sacrifice
than Cain, by which he obtained witness that he was righteous,
God testifying of his gifts : and by it he being dead yet speaketh.
⁵ By faith Enoch was translated that he should not see death ;
and was not found, because God had translated him : for before
his translation he had this testimony, that he pleased God.
⁶ But without faith *it is* impossible to please *him :* for he that
cometh to God must believe that he is, and *that* he is a rewarder
of them that diligently seek [that seek after] him. ⁷ By faith
Noah, being warned of God of things not seen as yet, moved
with fear [godly fear] prepared an ark to the saving of his house ;
by the which he condemned the world, and became heir of the
righteousness which is by faith. ⁸ By faith Abraham, when he
was called to go [called, obeyed to go, &c.] out into a place which
he should after receive for an inheritance, obeyed ; and he went
out, not knowing whither he went. ⁹ By faith he sojourned in
the land of promise, as *in* a strange country, dwelling in tabernacles [tents] with Isaac and Jacob, the heirs with him of the
same promise : ¹⁰ For he looked for a [the] city which hath
foundations, whose builder and maker *is* God. ¹¹ Through faith
also Sara herself received strength to conceive seed, and was
delivered of a child when she was past age, because she judged
him faithful who had promised. ¹² Therefore sprang there even
of one, and him as good as dead, *so many* as the stars of the sky
in multitude, and as the sand which is by the sea shore innumerable. ¹³ These all died in faith, not having received the
promises, but having seen them afar off, and were persuaded of
them, and embraced *them* [having seen them and greeted them
from afar] and confessed that they were strangers and pilgrims
on the earth. ¹⁴ For they that say such things declare plainly
that they seek a country [a country of their own]. ¹⁵ And
truly, if they had been mindful of that *country* from whence
they came out, they might [would] have had opportunity to
have returned. ¹⁶ But now they desire a better *country*, that is,
a heavenly : wherefore God is not ashamed to be called their
God : for he hath prepared for them a city. ¹⁷ By faith Abraham,

when he was tried, offered up Isaac: and he that had received the promises offered up his only begotten *son*, [18] Of whom it was said, That in Isaac, shall thy seed be called: [19] Accounting that God *was* able to raise *him* up even from the dead; from whence also he received him in a figure [**parable**]. [20] By faith Isaac blessed Jacob and Esau concerning things to come. [21] By faith Jacob, when he was a dying, blessed both the sons of Joseph; and worshipped, *leaning* upon the top of his staff. [22] By faith Joseph, when he died, made mention of the departing of the children of Israel; and gave commandment concerning his bones. [23] By faith Moses, when he was born, was hid three months of his parents, because they saw *he was* a proper [**goodly**] child; and they were not afraid of the king's commandment. [24] By faith Moses, when he was come to years, refused to be called the son of Pharaoh's daughter; [25] Choosing rather to suffer affliction with the people of God, than to enjoy the pleasures of sin for a season; [26] Esteeming the reproach of Christ greater riches than the treasures in Egypt: for he had respect [**looked**] unto the recompence of the reward. [27] By faith he forsook Egypt, not fearing the wrath of the king: for he endured, as seeing him who is invisible. [28] Through faith he kept the passover, and the sprinkling of blood lest he that destroyed the firstborn should touch them. [29] By faith they passed through the Red sea as by dry *land:* which the Egyptians assaying to do were drowned. [30] By faith the walls of Jericho fell down, after they were compassed about seven days. [31] By faith the harlot Rahab perished not with them that believed not [**were disobedient**], when she had received the spies with peace.

The apostle, having given us a more general account of the grace of faith, now proceeds to set before us some illustrious examples of it in the Old-Testament times, and these may be divided into two classes:—1. Those whose names are mentioned, and the particular exercise and actings of whose faith are specified. 2. Those whose names are barely mentioned, and an account given in general of the exploits of their faith, which it is left to the reader to accommodate, and apply to the particular persons from what he gathers up in the sacred story. We have here those whose names are not only mentioned, but the particular trials and actings of their faith are subjoined.

I. The leading instance and example of faith here recorded is that of Abel. It is observable that the Spirit of God has not thought fit to say any thing here of the faith of our first parents; and yet the church of God has generally, by a pious charity, taken it for granted that God gave them repentance and faith in the promised seed, that he instructed them in the mystery of sacrificing, that they instructed their children in it, and that they found mercy with God, after they had ruined themselves and all their posterity. But God has left the matter still under some doubt, as a warning to all who have great talents given to them, and a great trust reposed in them, that they do not prove unfaithful, since God would not enrol our first parents among the number of believers in this blessed calendar. It begins with Abel, one of the first saints, and the first martyr for religion, of all the sons of Adam, one who lived by faith, and died for it, and therefore a fit pattern for the Hebrews to imitate. Observe,

1. What Abel did by faith : *He offered up a more acceptable sacrifice than Cain*, a more full and perfect sacrifice, πλείονα θυσίαν. Hence learn, (1.) That, after the fall, God opened a new way for the children of men to return to him in religious worship. This is one of the first instances that is upon record of fallen men going in to worship God ; and it was a wonder of mercy that all intercourse between God and man was not cut off by the fall. (2.) After the fall, God must be worshipped by sacrifices, a way of worship which carries in it a confession of sin, and of the desert of sin, and a profession of faith in a Redeemer, who was to be a ransom for the souls of men. (3.) That, from the beginning, there has been a remarkable difference between the worshippers. Here were two persons, brethren, both of whom went in to worship God, and yet there was a vast difference. Cain was the elder brother, but Abel has the preference. It is not seniority of birth, but grace, that makes men truly honourable. The difference is observable in their persons : Abel was an upright person, a righteous man, a true believer ; Cain was a formalist, had not a principle of special grace. It is observable in their principles : Abel acted under the power of faith ; Cain only from the force of education, or natural conscience. There was also a very observable difference in their offerings : Abel brought a sacrifice of atonement, *brought of the firstlings of the flock*, acknowledging himself to be a sinner who deserved to die, and only hoping for mercy through the *great sacrifice ;* Cain brought only a sacrifice of acknowledgment, a mere thank-offering, *the fruit of the ground*, which might, and perhaps must, have been offered in innocency ; here was no confession of sin, no regard to the ransom ; this was an essential defect in Cain's offering. There will always be a difference between those who worship the true God ; some will compass him about with lies, others will be faithful with the saints ; some, like the Pharisee, will lean to their own righteousness ; others, like the publican, will confess their sin, and cast themselves upon the mercy of God in Christ.

2. What Abel gained by his faith : the original record is in Gen. iv. 4, *God had respect to Abel, and to his offering ;* first to his person as gracious, then to his offering as proceeding from grace, especially from the grace of faith. In this place we are told that he obtained by his faith some special advantages ; as, (1.) *Witness that he was righteous*, a justified, sanctified, and accepted person ; this, very probably, was attested by fire from heaven, kindling and consuming his sacrifice. (2.) God gave witness to the righteousness of his person, by testifying his acceptance of his gifts. When the fire, an emblem of God's justice, consumed the offering, it was a sign that the mercy of God accepted the offerer for the sake of the great sacrifice. (3.) *By it he, being dead, yet speaketh.* He had the honour to leave behind him an instructive speaking case ; and what does it speak to us ? What should we learn from it ? [1.] That fallen man has leave to go in to worship God, with hope of acceptance. [2.] That, if our persons and offerings be accepted, it must be through faith in the Messiah. [3.] That acceptance

with God is a peculiar and distinguishing favour. [4.] That those who obtain this favour from God must expect the envy and malice of the world. [5.] That God will not suffer the injuries done to his people to remain unpunished, nor their sufferings unrewarded. These are very good and useful instructions, and yet *the blood of sprinkling speaketh better things than that of Abel.* [6.] That God would not suffer Abel's faith to die with him, but would raise up others, who should obtain like precious faith ; and so he did in a little time ; for in the next verse we read,

II. Of the faith of Enoch, *v.* 5. He is the second of those elders that through faith have a good report. Observe,

1. What is here reported of him. In this place (and in Gen. v. 22, &c.) we read, (1.) *That he walked with God,* that is, that he was really, eminently, actively, progressively, and perseveringly religious in his conformity to God, communion with God, and complacency in God. (2.) *That he was translated, that he should not see death,* nor any part of him be found upon earth ; for God took him, soul and body, into heaven, as he will do those of the saints who shall be found alive at his second coming. (3.) *That before his translation he had this testimony, that he pleased God.* He had the evidence of it in his own conscience, and the Spirit of God witnessed with his spirit. Those who by faith walk with God in a sinful world are pleasing to him, and he will give them marks of his favour, and put honour upon them.

2. What is here said of his faith, *v.* 6. It is said that *without* this *faith it is impossible to please God,* without such a faith as helps us to walk with God, an active faith, and that we cannot come to God unless we *believe that he is, and that he is a rewarder of those that diligently seek him.* (1.) He must believe that God is, and that he is what he is, what he has revealed himself to be in the scripture, a Being of infinite perfections, subsisting in three persons, Father, Son, and Holy Ghost. Observe, The practical belief of the existence of God as revealed in the word, would be a powerful awe-band upon our souls, a bridle of restraint to keep us from sin, and a spur of constraint to put us upon all manner of gospel obedience. (2.) *That he is a rewarder of those that diligently seek him.* Here observe, [1.] By the fall we have lost God ; we have lost the divine light, life, love, likeness, and communion. [2.] God is again to be found of us through Christ, the second Adam. [3.] God has prescribed means and ways wherein he may be found ; to wit, a strict attention to his oracles, attendance on his ordinances, and ministers duly discharging their office and associating with his people, observing his providential guidance, and in all things humbly waiting his gracious presence. [4.] Those who would find God in these ways of his must *seek him diligently ;* they must seek early, earnestly, and perseveringly. *Then shall they seek him, and find him, if they seek him with all their heart ;* and when once they have found him, as their reconciled God, they will never repent the pains they have spent in seeking after him.

III. The faith of Noah, *v.* 7. Observe,

1. The ground of Noah's faith—a warning he had received from God of things as yet not seen. He had a divine revelation, whether by voice or vision does not appear ; but it was such as carried in it its own evidence ; he was *forewarned of things not seen as yet,* that is, of a great and severe judgment, such as the world had never yet seen, and of which, in the course of second causes, there was not yet the least sign. This secret warning he was to communicate to the world, who would be sure to despise

both him and his message. God usually warns sinners before he strikes; and, where his warnings are slighted, the blow will fall the heavier.

2. The actings of Noah's faith, and the influence it had both upon his mind and practice. (1.) Upon his mind; it impressed his soul with a fear of God's judgment: he was *moved with fear*. Faith first influences our affections, then our actions; and faith works upon those affections that are suitable to the matter revealed. If it be some good thing, faith stirs up love and desire; if some evil thing, faith stirs up fear. (2.) His faith influenced his practice. His fear, thus excited by believing God's threaten-ing, moved him to prepare an ark, in which, no doubt, he met with the scorns and reproaches of a wicked generation. He did not dispute with God why he should make an ark, nor how it could be capable of containing what was to be lodged in it, nor how such a vessel could possibly weather out so great a storm. His faith silenced all objections, and set him to work in earnest.

3. The blessed fruits and rewards of Noah's faith. (1.) Hereby himself and his house were saved, when a whole world of sinners were perishing about them. God saved his family for his sake; it was well for them that they were Noah's sons and daughters; it was well for those women that they married into Noah's family; perhaps they might have married to great estates in other families, but then they would have been drowned. We often say, "It is good to be akin to an estate;" but surely it is good to be akin to the covenant. (2.) Hereby he judged and condemned the world; his holy fear condemned their security and vain confidence; his faith condemned their unbelief; his obedience condemned their contempt and rebellion. Good examples will either convert sinners or condemn them. There is something very convincing in a life of strict holiness and regard to God; it commends itself to every man's conscience in the sight of God, and they are judged by it. This is the best way the people of God can take to condemn the wicked; not by harsh and censorious language, but by a holy exemplary conversation. (3.) Hereby *he became an heir of the righteousness which is by faith.* [1.] He was possessed of a true justify-ing righteousness; he was *heir to it:* and, [2.] This his right of inheritance was through faith in Christ, as *a member of Christ, a child of God,* and, if a child, then an heir. His righteousness was relative, resulting from his adoption, through faith in the promised seed. As ever we expect to be justified and saved *in the great and terrible day of the Lord,* let us now pre-pare an ark, secure an interest in Christ, and in the ark of the covenant, and do it speedily, before the door be shut, for there is not salvation in any other.

IV. The faith of Abraham, the friend of God, and father of the faithful, in whom the Hebrews boasted, and from whom they derived their pedigree and privileges; and therefore the apostle, that he might both please and profit them, enlarges more upon the heroic achievements of Abraham's faith than of that of any other of the patriarchs; and in the midst of his account of the faith of Abraham he inserts the story of Sarah's faith, whose daughters those women are that continue to do well. Observe,

1. The ground of Abraham's faith, the call and promise of God, *v.* 8. (1.) This call, though it was a very trying call, was the call of God, and therefore a sufficient ground for faith and rule of obedience. The manner in which he was called Stephen relates in Acts vii. 2, 3, *The God of glory appeared to our father Abraham, when he was in Mesopotamia——And said unto him, Get thee out of thy country, and from thy kindred, and come into*

the land which I will show thee. This was an effectual call, by which he
was converted from the idolatry of his father's house, Gen. xii. 1. This
call was renewed after his father's death in Charran. Observe, [1.] The
grace of God is absolutely free, in taking some of the worst of men, and
making them the best. [2.] God must come to us before we come to him.
[3.] In calling and converting sinners, God appears as a God of glory, and
works a glorious work in the soul. [4.] This calls us not only to leave sin,
but sinful company, and whatever is inconsistent with our devotedness to
him. [5.] We need to be called, not only to set out well, but to go on
well. [6.] He will not have his people take up that rest any where short
of the heavenly Canaan. (2.) The promise of God. God promised Abraham that the place he was called to he should afterwards receive for an
inheritance, after awhile he should have the heavenly Canaan for his
inheritance, and in process of time his posterity should inherit the earthly
Canaan. Observe here, [1.] God calls his people to an inheritance: by his
effectual call he makes them children, and so heirs. [2.] This inheritance
is not immediately possessed by them; they must wait some time for it:
but the promise is sure, and shall have its seasonable accomplishment.
[3.] The faith of parents often procures blessings for their posterity.

2. The exercise of Abraham's faith: he yielded an implicit regard to
the call of God. (1.) *He went out, not knowing whither he went.* He put
himself into the hand of God, to send him whithersoever he pleased. He
subscribed to God's wisdom, as fittest to direct; and submitted to his will,
as fittest to determine everything that concerned him. Implicit faith and
obedience are due to God, and to him only. All that are effectually called
resign up their own will and wisdom to the will and wisdom of God, and it
is their wisdom to do so; though they know not always their way, yet they
know their guide, and this satisfies them. (2) *He sojourned in the land of
promise as in a strange country.* This was an exercise of his faith. Observe,
[1.] How Canaan is called the land of promise, because yet only promised,
not possessed. [2.] How Abraham lived in Canaan, not as heir and pro-
prietor, but as a sojourner only. He did not serve an ejectment, or raise a
war against the old inhabitants, to dispossess them, but contented himself to
live as a stranger, to bear their unkindnesses patiently, to receive any favours
from them thankfully, and to keep his heart fixed upon his home, the
heavenly Canaan. [3.] He dwelt in tabernacles with Isaac and Jacob,
heirs with him of the same promise. He lived there in an ambulatory
moving condition, living in a daily readiness for his removal: and thus
should we all live in this world. He had good company with him, and
they were a great comfort to him in his sojourning state. Abraham lived
till Isaac was seventy-five years old, and Jacob fifteen. Isaac and Jacob
were heirs of the same promise; for the promise was renewed to Isaac
(Gen. xxvi. 3), and to Jacob (Gen. xxviii. 13). All the saints are heirs of
the same promise. The promise is made to believers and their children,
and to as many as the Lord our God shall call. And it is pleasant to see
parents and children sojourning together in this world as heirs of the
heavenly inheritance.

3. The supports of Abraham's faith (*v.* 10): *He looked for a city that
hath foundations whose builder and maker is God.* Observe here, (1.) The
description given of heaven: it is a city, a regular society, well established,
well defended, and well supplied: it is a city that hath foundations, even
the immutable purposes and almighty power of God, the infinite merits
and mediation of the Lord Jesus Christ, the promises of an everlasting

covenant, its own purity, and the perfection of its inhabitants : and it is a city whose builder and maker is God. He contrived the model ; he accordingly made it, and he has laid open a new and living way into it, and prepared it for his people ; he puts them into possession of it, prefers them in it, and is himself the substance and felicity of it. (2.) Observe the due regard that Abraham had to this heavenly city : he looked for it : he believed there was such a state ; he waited for it, and in the meantime he conversed in it by faith ; he had exalted and rejoicing hopes, that in God's time and way he should be brought safely to it. (3.) The influence this had upon his present conversation : it was a support to him under all the trials of his sojourning state, helped him patiently to bear all the inconveniences of it, and actively to discharge all the duties of it, persevering therein unto the end.

V. In the midst of the story of Abraham, the apostle inserts an account of the faith of Sarah. Here observe,

1. The difficulties of Sarah's faith, which were very great. As, (1.) The prevalency of unbelief for a time : she laughed at the promise, as impossible to be made good. (2.) She had gone out of the way of her duty through unbelief, in putting Abraham upon taking Hagar to his bed, that he might have a posterity. Now this sin of hers would make it more difficult for her to act by faith afterwards. (3.) The great improbability of the thing promised, that she should be the mother of a child, when she was of sterile constitution naturally, and now past the prolific age.

2. The actings of her faith. Her unbelief is pardoned and forgotten, but her faith prevailed and is recorded : *She judged him faithful, who had promised, v.* 11. She received the promise as the promise of God ; and being convinced of that, she truly judged he both could and would perform it, how impossible soever it might seem to reason ; for the faithfulness of God will not suffer him to deceive his people.

3. The fruits and rewards of her faith. (1.) *She received strength to conceive seed.* The strength of nature, as well as grace, is from God : he can make the barren soul fruitful, as well as the barren womb. (2.) *She was delivered of a child,* a man-child, a child of the promise, the comfort of his parents' advanced years, and the hope of future ages. (3.) From them, by this son, sprang a numerous progeny of illustrious persons, *as the stars of the sky (v.* 12)—a great, powerful, and renowned nation, above all the rest in the world ; and a nation of saints, the peculiar church and people of God ; and, which was the highest honour and reward of all, *of these, according to the flesh, the Messiah came, who is over all, God blessed for evermore.*

VI. The apostle proceeds to make mention of the faith of the other patriarchs, Isaac and Jacob, and the rest of this happy family, *v.* 13. Here observe,

1. The trial of their faith in the imperfection of their present state. They had not received the promises, that is, they had not received the things promised, they had not yet been put into possession of Canaan, they had not yet seen their numerous issue, they had not seen Christ in the flesh. Observe, (1.) Many that are interested in the promises do not presently receive the things promised. (2.) One imperfection of the present state of the saints on earth is that their happiness lies more in promise and reversion than in actual enjoyment and possession. The gospel state is more perfect than the patriarchal, because more of the promises are now fulfilled. The heavenly state will be most perfect of all ; for there all the promises will have their full accomplishment.

2. The actings of their faith during this imperfect state of things. Though they had not received the promises, yet,

(1.) They saw them afar off. Faith has a clear and a strong eye, and can see promised mercies at a great distance. Abraham saw Christ's day when it was afar off, and rejoiced, John viii. 56.

(2.) They were persuaded of them, that they were true and should be fulfilled. Faith sets to its seal that God is true, and thereby settles and satisfies the soul.

(3.) They embraced them. Their faith was a faith of consent. Faith has a long arm, and can lay hold of blessings at a great distance, can make them present, can love them, and rejoice in them ; and thus antedate the enjoyment of them.

(4.) They *confessed that they were strangers and pilgrims on earth.* Observe, [1.] Their condition : *Strangers and pilgrims.* They are strangers as saints, whose home is heaven ; they are pilgrims as they are travelling towards their home, though often meanly and slowly. [2.] Their acknowledgment of this their condition : they were not ashamed to own it ; both their lips and their lives confessed their present condition. They expected little from the world. They cared not to engage much in it. They endeavoured to lay aside every weight, to gird up the loins of their minds to mind their way, to keep company and pace with their fellow-travellers, looking for difficulties, and bearing them, and longing to get home.

(5.) Hereby they declared plainly that they sought another country (*v.* 14), heaven, their own country. For their spiritual birth is thence, there are their best relations, and there is their inheritance. This country they seek : their designs are for it ; their desires are after it ; their discourse is about it ; they diligently endeavour to clear up their title to it, to have their temper suited to it, to have their conversation in it, and to come to the enjoyment of it.

(6.) They gave full proof of their sincerity in making such a confession. For, [1.] They were not mindful of that country whence they came, *v.* 15. They did not hanker after the plenty and pleasures of it, nor regret and repent that they had left it ; they had no desire to return to it. Note, Those that are once effectually and savingly called out of a sinful state have no mind to return into it again ; they now know better things. [2.] They did not take the opportunity that offered itself for their return. They might have had such an opportunity. They had time enough to return. They had natural strength to return. They knew the way. Those with whom they sojourned would have been willing enough to part with them. Their old friends would have been glad to receive them. They had sufficient to bear the charges of their journey ; and flesh and blood, a corrupt counsellor, would be sometimes suggesting to them a return. But they steadfastly adhered to God and duty under all discouragements and against all temptations to revolt from him. So should we all do. We shall not want opportunities to revolt from God ; but we must show the truth of our faith and profession by a steady adherence to him to the end of our days. Their sincerity appeared not only in not returning to their former country, but in desiring a better country, that is, a heavenly. Observe, *First,* The heavenly country is better than any upon earth ; it is better situated, better stored with every thing that is good, better secured from every thing that is evil; the employments, the 'enjoyments, the society, and every thing in it, are better than the best in this world. *Secondly,* All true believers desire this better country. True faith draws forth sincere and fervent desires; and the stronger faith is the more fervent those desires will be.

(7.) They died in the faith of those promises; not only lived by the faith of them, but died in the full persuasion that all the promises would be fulfilled to them and theirs, *v.* 13. That faith held out to the last. By faith, when they were dying, they received the atonement; they acquiesced in the will of God; they quenched all the fiery darts of the devil; they overcame the terrors of death, disarmed it of its sting, and bade a cheerful farewell to this world and to all the comforts and crosses of it. These were the actings of their faith. Now observe,

3. The gracious and great reward of their faith: *God is not ashamed to be their God, for he hath prepared for them a city, v.* 16. Note, (1.) God is the God of all true believers; faith gives them an interest in God, and in all his fulness. (2.) He is called their God. He calls himself so: *I am the God of Abraham, and the God of Isaac, and the God of Jacob ;* he gives them leave to call him so; and he gives them the spirit of adoption, to enable them to cry, *Abba, Father.* (3.) Notwithstanding their meanness by nature, their vileness by sin, and the poverty of their outward condition, God is not ashamed to be called *their God :* such is his condescension, such is his love to them; therefore let them never be ashamed of being called his people, nor of any of those that are truly so, how much soever despised in the world. Above all, let them take care that they be not a shame and reproach to their God, and so provoke him to be ashamed of them; but let them act so as to be to him for a name, and for a praise, and for a glory. (4.) As the proof of this, God has prepared for them a city, a happiness suitable to the relation into which he has taken them. For there is nothing in this world commensurate to the love of God in being the God of his people; and, if God neither could nor would give his people anything better than this world affords, he would be ashamed to be called their God. If he takes them into such a relation to himself, he will provide for them accordingly. If he takes to himself the title of their God, he will fully answer it, and act up to it; and he has prepared that for them in heaven which will fully answer this character and relation, so that it shall never be said, to the reproach and dishonour of God, that he has adopted a people to be his own children and then taken no care to make a suitable provision for them. The consideration of this should inflame the affections, enlarge the desires, and excite the diligent endeavours, of the people of God after this city that he has prepared for them.

VII. Now after the apostle has given this account of the faith of others, with Abraham, he returns to him again, and gives us an instance of the greatest trial and act of faith that stands upon record, either in the story of the father of the faithful or of any of his spiritual seed; and this was his offering up Isaac: *By faith Abraham, when he was tried, offered up Isaac ; and he that had received the promises offered up his only-begotten son, v.* 17. In this great example observe,

1. The trial and exercise of Abraham's faith; he was tried indeed. It is said (Gen. xxii. 1), *God in this tempted Abraham ;* not to sin, for so God tempteth no man, but only tried his faith and obedience to purpose. God had before this tempted or tried the faith of Abraham, when he called him away from his country and father's house,—when by a famine he was forced out of Canaan into Egypt,—when he was obliged to fight with five kings to rescue Lot,—when Sarah was taken from him by Abimelech, and in many other instances. But this trial was greater than all; he was

commanded to offer up his son Isaac. Read the account of it, Gen. xxii.
2. There you will find every word was a trial : " *Take now thy son, thine
only son Isaac, whom thou lovest, and get thee into the land of Moriah, and
offer him there for a burnt-offering upon one of the mountains which I will
tell thee of.* Take thy son, not one of thy beasts or slaves, thy only son by
Sarah, Isaac thy laughter, the child of thy joy and delight, whom thou
lovest as thine own soul ; take him away to a distant place, three days'
journey, the land of Moriah ; do not only leave him there, but offer him
for a burnt-offering." A greater trial was never put upon any creature.
The apostle here mentions some things that very much added to the greatness of this trial. (1.) He was put upon it after he had received the
promises, that this Isaac should build up his family, that in him his seed
should be called (*v.* 18), and that he should be one of the progenitors of
the Messiah, and all nations blessed in him ; so that, in being called to
offer up his Isaac, he seemed to be called to destroy and cut off his own
family, to cancel the promises of God, to prevent the coming of Christ, to
destroy the whole world, to sacrifice his own soul and his hopes of salvation, and to cut off the church of God at one blow : a most terrible trial !
(2.) That this Isaac was his only-begotten son by his wife Sarah, the only
one he was to have by her, and the only one that was to be the child and
heir of the promise. Ishmael was to be put off with earthly greatness.
The promises of a posterity, and of the Messiah, must either be fulfilled
by means of this son or not at all ; so that, besides his most tender affection to this his son, all his expectations were bound up in him, and, if he
perished, must perish with him. If Abraham had ever so many sons, this
was the only son who could convey to all nations the promised blessing.
A son for whom he waited so long, whom he received in so extraordinary a
manner, upon whom his heart was set—to have this son offered up as
a sacrifice, and that by his own hand ; it was a trial that would have
overset the firmest and the strongest mind that ever informed a human
body.

2. The actings of Abraham's faith in so great a trial : he obeyed ; he
offered up Isaac ; he intentionally gave him up by his submissive soul to
God, and was ready to have done it actually, according to the command of
God ; he went as far in it as to the very critical moment, and would have
gone through with it if God had not prevented him. Nothing could be
more tender and moving than those words of Isaac : *My father, here is the
wood, here is the fire; but where is the lamb for the burnt offering?* little
thinking that he was to be the lamb ; but Abraham knew it, and yet he
went on with the great design.

3. The supports of his faith. They must be very great, suitable to the
greatness of the trial : *He accounted that God was able to raise him from
the dead, v.* 19. His faith was supported by the sense he had of the mighty
power of God, who was able to raise the dead ; he reasoned thus with himself, and so he resolved all his doubts. It does not appear that he had any
expectation of being countermanded, and prevented from offering up his
son ; such an expectation would have spoiled the trial, and consequently
the triumph, of his faith ; but he knew that God was able to raise him
from the dead, and he believed that God would do so, since such great
things depended upon his son, which must have failed if Isaac had not a
further life. Observe, (1.) God is able to raise the dead, to raise dead
bodies, and to raise dead souls. (2.) The belief of this will carry us
through the greatest difficulties and trials that we can meet with. (3.) It

is our duty to be reasoning down our doubts and fears, by the consideration of the almighty power of God.

4. The reward of his faith in this great trial (v. 19) : he received his son from the dead in a figure, in a parable. (1.) He received his son. He had parted with him to God, and God gave him back again. The best way to enjoy our comforts with comfort is to resign them up to God ; he will then return them, if not in kind, yet in kindness. (2.) He received him from the dead, for he gave him up for dead ; he was as a dead child to him, and the return was to him no less than a resurrection. (3.) This was a figure or parable of something further. It was a figure of the sacri fice and resurrection of Christ, of whom Isaac was a type. It was a figure and earnest of the glorious resurrection of all true believers, whose life is not lost, but hid with Christ in God. We come now to the faith of other Old-Testament saints, mentioned by name, and by the particular trials and actings of their faith.

VIII. Of the faith of Isaac, v. 20. Something of him we had before interwoven with the story of Abraham ; here we have something of a distinct nature—that by faith he blessed his two sons, Jacob and Esau, *concerning things to come.* Here observe,

1. The actings of his faith : He *blessed Jacob and Esau concerning things to come.* He blessed them ; that is, he resigned them up to God in covenant ; he recommended God and religion to them ; he prayed for them, and prophesied concerning them, what would be the condition, and the condition of their descendants : we have the account of this in Gen. xxvii. Observe, (1.) Both Jacob and Esau were blessed as Isaac's children, at least as to temporal good things. It is a great privilege to be the offspring of good parents, and often the wicked children of good parents fare the better in this world for their parents' sake, for things present are in the covenant ; but they are not the best things, and no man knoweth love or hatred by having or wanting such things. (2.) Jacob had the precedency and the principal blessing, which shows that it is grace and the new birth that exalt persons above their fellows and qualify them for the best blessings, and that it is owing to the sovereign free grace of God that in the same family one is taken and another left, one loved and the other hated, since all the race of Adam are by nature hateful to God—that if one has his portion in this world, and the other in the better world, it is God who makes the difference ; for even the comforts of this life are more and better than any of the children of men deserve.

2. The difficulties Isaac's faith struggled with. (1.) He seemed to have forgotten how God had determined the matter at the birth of these his sons, Gen. xxv. 23. This should have been a rule to him all along, but he was rather swayed by natural affection, and by general custom, which gives the double portion of honour, affection, and advantage, to the first-born. (2.) He acted in this matter with some reluctance. When he came to pronounce the blessing, *he trembled very exceedingly* (Gen. xxvii. 33); and he charged Jacob that he had subtly taken away Esau's blessing, v. 33, 35, but, notwithstanding all this, Isaac's faith recovered itself, and he ratified the blessing : *I have blessed him, yea, and he shall be blessed.* Rebecca and Jacob are not to be justified in the indirect means they used to obtain this blessing, but God will be justified in overruling even the sins of men to serve the purposes of his glory. Now, the faith of Isaac thus prevailing over his unbelief, it has pleased the God of Isaac to pass by the weakness of his faith, to commend the sincerity of it, and record him among

the elders, *who through faith have obtained a good report.* We now go on to,

IX. The faith of Jacob (*v.* 21), who, *when he was dying, blessed both the sons of Joseph, and worshipped, leaning upon the top of his staff.* There were a great many instances of the faith of Jacob; his life was a life of faith, and his faith met with great exercise. But it has pleased God to single two instances out of many of the faith of this patriarch, besides what has been already mentioned in the account of Abraham. Here observe,

1. The actings of his faith here mentioned, and they are two :—

(1.) *He blessed both the sons of Joseph,* Ephraim and Manasseh; he adopted them into the number of his own sons, and so into the congregation of Israel, though they were born in Egypt. It is doubtless a great blessing to be joined to the visible church of God in profession and privilege, but more to be so in spirit and truth. [1.] He made them both heads of different tribes, as if they had been his own immediate sons. [2.] He prayed for them, that they might both be blessed of God. [3.] He prophesied that they should be blessed; but, as Isaac did before, so now Jacob prefers the younger, Ephraim; and though Joseph had placed them so, that the right hand of his father should be laid on Manasseh, the elder, Jacob wittingly laid it on Ephraim, and this by divine direction, for he could not see, to show that the Gentile church, the younger, should have a more abundant blessing than the Jewish church, the elder.

(2). *He worshipped leaning on his staff ;* that is, he praised God for what he had done for him, and for the prospect he had of approaching blessedness ; and he prayed for those he was leaving behind him that religion might live in his family when he was gone. He did this *leaning on the top of his staff;* not as the papists dream, that he worshipped some image of God engraven on the head of his staff, but intimating to us his great natural weakness, that he was not able to support himself so far as to sit up in his bed without a staff, and yet that he would not make this an excuse for neglecting the worshipping of God ; he would do it as well as he could with his body, as well as with his spirit, though he could not do it as well as he would. He showed thereby his dependence upon God, and testified his condition here as a pilgrim with his staff, and his weariness of the world, and willingness to be at rest.

2. The time and season when Jacob thus acted his faith : when he was dying. He lived by faith, and he died by faith and in faith. Observe, Though the grace of faith is of universal use throughout our whole lives, yet it is especially so when we come to die. Faith has its greatest work to do at last, to help believers to finish well, to die to the Lord, so as to honour him, by patience, hope, and joy—so as to leave a witness behind them of the truth of God's word and the excellency of his ways, for the conviction and establishment of all who attend them in their dying moments. The best way in which parents can finish their course is blessing their families and worshipping their God. We have now come to,

X. The faith of Joseph, *v.* 22. And here also we consider,

1. What he did by his faith : *He made mention of the departing of the children of Israel, and gave commandment concerning his bones.* The passage is out of Gen. l. 24, 25. Joseph was eminent for his faith, though he had not enjoyed the helps for it which the rest of his brethren had. He was sold into Egypt. He was tried by temptations, by sin, by persecution, for retaining his integrity. He was tried by preferment and power

in the court of Pharaoh, and yet his faith held out and carried him through to the last. (1.) He made mention by faith of the departing of the children of Israel, that the time should come when they should be delivered out of Egypt ; and he did this both that he might caution them against the thoughts of settling in Egypt, which was now a place of plenty and ease to them; and also that he might keep them from sinking under the calamities and distresses which he foresaw were coming upon them there ; and he does it to comfort himself, that though he should not live to see their deliverance, yet he could die in the faith of it. (2.) He gave commandment concerning his bones, that they should preserve them unburied in Egypt, till God should deliver them out of that house of bondage, and that then they should carry his bones along with them into Canaan and deposit them there. Though believers are chiefly concerned for their souls, yet they cannot wholly neglect their bodies, as being members of Christ and parts of themselves, which shall at length be raised up, and be the happy companions of their glorified souls to all eternity. Now Joseph gave this order, not that he thought his being buried in Egypt would either prejudice his soul or prevent the resurrection of his body (as some of the rabbis fancied that all the Jews who were buried out of Canaan must be conveyed underground to Canaan before they could rise again), but to testify, [1.] That though he had lived and died in Egypt, yet he did not live and die an Egyptian, but an Israelite. [2.] That he preferred a significant burial in Canaan before a magnificent one in Egypt. [3.] That he would go as far with his people as he could, though he could not go as far as he would. [4.] That he believed the resurrection of the body, and the communion that his soul should presently have with departed saints, as his body had with their dead bodies. [5.] To assure them that God would be with them in Egypt, and deliver them out of it in his own time and way.

2. When it was that the faith of Joseph acted after this manner ; namely, as in the case of Jacob, when he was dying. God often gives his people living comforts in dying moments ; and when he does, it is their duty, as they can, to communicate them to those about them, for the glory of God, for the honour of religion, and for the good of their brethren and friends. We go on now to,

XI. The faith of the parents of Moses, which is cited from Exod. ii. 3, &c. Here observe, 1. The acting of their faith : they hid this their son three months. Though only the mother of Moses is mentioned in the history, yet, by what is here said, it seems his father not only consented to it, but consulted about it. It is a happy thing where yoke-fellows draw together in the yoke of faith, as heirs of the grace of God ; and when they do this in a religious concern for the good of their children, to preserve them not only from those who would destroy their lives, but from those who would corrupt their minds. Observe, Moses was persecuted betimes, and forced to be concealed ; in this he was a type of Christ, who was persecuted almost as soon as he was born, and his parents were obliged to flee with him into Egypt for his preservation. It is a great mercy to be free from wicked laws and edicts ; but, when we are not, we must use all lawful means for our security. In this faith of Moses's parents there was a mixture of unbelief, but God was pleased to overlook it. 2. The reasons of their thus acting. No doubt, natural affection could not but move them ; but there was something further. They *saw he was a proper child, a goodly child* (Exod. ii. 2), *exceedingly fair*, as in Acts vii. 20, ἀστεῖος τῷ Θεῷ—

venustus Deo—fair to God. There appeared in him something uncommon ; the beauty of the Lord sat upon him, as a presage that he was born to great things, and that by conversing with God his face should shine (Exod. xxxiv. 29), what bright and illustrious actions he should do for the deliverance of Israel, and how his name should shine in the sacred records. Sometimes, not always, the countenance is the index of the mind. 3. The prevalency of their faith over their fear. They were not afraid of the king's commandment, Exod. i. 22. That was a wicked and a cruel edict, that all the males of the Israelites should be destroyed in their infancy, and so the name of Israel must be destroyed out of the earth. But they did not so fear as presently to give up their child ; they considered that, if none of the males were preserved, there would be an end and utter ruin of the church of God and the true religion, and that though in their present state of servitude and oppression one would praise the dead rather than the living, yet they believed that God would preserve his people, and that the time was coming when it would be worth while for an Israelite to live. Some must hazard their own lives to preserve their children, and they were resolved to do it ; they knew the king's commandment was evil in itself, contrary to the laws of God and nature, and therefore of no authority nor obligation. Faith is a great preservative against the sinful slavish fear of men, as it sets God before the soul, and shows the vanity of the creature and its subordination to the will and power of God. The apostle next proceeds to,

XII. The faith of Moses himself (*v.* 24, 25, &c.), here observe,

1. An instance of his faith in conquering the world.

(1.) He *refused to be called the son of Pharaoh's daughter,* whose foundling he was, and her fondling too ; she had adopted him for her son, and he refused it. Observe [1.] How great a temptation Moses was under. Pharaoh's daughter is said to have been his only child, and was herself childless ; and having found Moses, and saved him as she did, she resolved to take him and bring him up as her son ; and so he stood fair to be in time king of Egypt, and he might thereby have been serviceable to Israel. He owed his life to this princess ; and to refuse such kindness from her would look not only like ingratitude to her, but a neglect of Providence, that seemed to intend his advancement and his brethren's advantage. [2.] How glorious was the triumph of his faith in so great a trial. He *refused to be called the son of Pharaoh's daughter* lest he should undervalue the truer honour of being a son of Abraham, the father of the faithful ; *he refused to be called the son of Pharaoh's daughter* lest it should look like renouncing his religion as well as his relation to Israel ; and no doubt both these he must have done if he had accepted this honour ; he therefore nobly refused it.

(2.) He chose *rather to suffer affliction with the people of God than to enjoy the pleasures of sin for a season, v.* 25. He was willing to take his lot with the people of God here, though it was a suffering lot, that he might have his portion with them hereafter, rather than to enjoy all the sensual sinful pleasures of Pharaoh's court, which would be but for a season, and would then be punished with everlasting misery. Herein he acted rationally as well as religiously, and conquered the temptation to worldly pleasure as he had done before to worldly preferment. Here observe, [1.] The pleasures of sin are and will be but short ; they must end in speedy repentance or in speedy ruin. [2.] The pleasures of this world, and especially those of a court, are too often the pleasures of sin ; and they are always so when we cannot enjoy them without deserting God and his people. A true believer will despise them when they are offered upon such terms. [3.] Suffering is to be chosen rather than sin, there being more evil in the least sin than there can be in the greatest suffering. [4.] It greatly alleviates the evil of suffering when we suffer with the people of God, embarked in the same interest and animated by the same Spirit.

(3.) He accounted *the reproaches of Christ greater riches than the treasures of Egypt, v. 26.* See how Moses weighed matters : in one scale he put the worst of religion—*the reproaches of Christ,* in the other scale the best of the world—*the treasures of Egypt ;* and in his judgment, directed by faith, the worst of religion weighed down the best of the world. The reproaches of the church of God are *the reproaches of Christ,* who is, and has ever been, the head of the church. Now here Moses conquered the riches of the world, as before he had conquered its honours and pleasures. God's people are, and always have been, a reproached people. Christ accounts himself reproached in their reproaches ; and, while he thus interests himself in their reproaches, they become riches, and greater riches than the treasures of the richest empire in the world ; for Christ will reward them with a crown of glory that fades not away. Faith discerns this, and determines and acts accordingly.

2. The circumstance of time is taken notice of, when Moses by his faith gained this victory over the world, in all its honours, pleasures, and treasures : *When he had come to years (v. 24) ;* not only to years of discretion, but of experience, to the age of forty years—when he was great or had come to maturity. Some would take this as detracting from his victory, that he gained it so late, that he did not make this choice sooner ; but it is rather an enhancement of the honour of his self-denial and victory over the world that he made this choice when he had grown ripe for judgment and enjoyment, able to know what he did and why he did it. It was not the act of a child, that prefers counters to gold, but it proceeded from mature deliberation. It is an excellent thing for persons to be seriously religious when in the midst of worldly business and enjoyments, to despise the world when they are most capable of relishing and enjoying it.

3. What it was that supported and strengthened the faith of Moses to such a degree as to enable him to gain such a victory over the world : *He had respect unto the recompence of reward,* that is, say some, the deliverance out of Egypt ; but doubtless it means much more—the glorious reward of faith and fidelity in the other world. Observe here, (1.) Heaven is a great reward, surpassing not only all our deservings, but all our conceptions. It is a reward suitable to the price paid for it—the blood of Christ ; suitable to the perfections of God, and fully answering to all his promises. It is a recompence of reward, because given by a righteous Judge for the righteousness of Christ to righteous persons, according to the righteous rule of the covenant of grace. (2.) Believers may and ought to have respect to this recompence of reward ; they should acquaint themselves with it, approve of it, and live in the daily and delightful expectation of it. Thus it will prove a land-mark to direct their course, a load-stone to draw their hearts, a sword to conquer their enemies, a spur to quicken them to duty, and a cordial to refresh them under all the difficulties of doing and suffering work.

4. We have another instance of the faith of Moses, namely, in forsaking Egypt : *By faith he forsook Egypt, not fearing the wrath of the king, v. 27.* Observe here, (1.) The product of his faith : *He forsook Egypt,* and all its

power and pleasures, and undertook the conduct of Israel out of it. Twice Moses forsook Egypt : [1.] As a supposed criminal, when the king's wrath was incensed against him for killing the Egyptian (Exod. ii. 14, 15), where it is said he feared, not with a fear of despondency, but of discretion, to save his life. [2.] As a commander and ruler in Jeshurun, after God had employed him to humble Pharaoh and make him willing to let Israel go. (2.) The prevalency of his faith. It raised him above the fear of the king's wrath. Though he knew that it was great, and levelled at him in particular, and that it marched at the head of a numerous host to pursue him, yet he was not dismayed, and he said to Israel, *Fear not*, Exod. xiv. 13. Those who forsook Egypt must expect the wrath of men ; but they need not fear it, for they are under the conduct of that God who is able to make the wrath of man to praise him, and restrain the remainder of it. (3.) The principle upon which his faith acted in these his motions : *He endured, as seeing him that was invisible.* He bore up with invincible courage under all danger, and endured all the fatigue of his employment, which was very great ; and this by seeing the invisible God. Observe, [1.] The God with whom we have to do is an invisible God : he is so to our senses, to the eye of the body ; and this shows the folly of those who pretend to make images of God, whom no man hath seen, nor can see. [2.] By faith we may see this invisible God. We may be fully assured of his existence, of his providence, and of his gracious and powerful presence with us. [3.] Such a sight of God will enable believers to endure to the end whatever they may meet with in the way.

5. We have yet another instance of the faith of Moses, in keeping *the passover and sprinkling of blood, v.* 28. The account of this we have in Exod. xii. 13-23. Though all Israel kept this passover, yet it was by Moses that God delivered the institution of it ; and, though it was a great mystery, Moses by faith both delivered it to the people and kept it that night in the house where he lodged. The passover was one of the most solemn institutions of the Old Testament, and a very significant type of Christ. The occasion of its first observance was extraordinary : it was in the same night that God slew the first-born of the Egyptians ; but, though the Israelites lived among them, the destroying angel passed over their houses, and spared them and theirs. Now, to entitle them to this distinguishing favour, and to mark them out for it, a lamb must be slain ; the blood of it must be sprinkled with a bunch of hyssop upon the lintel of the door, and on the two side-posts ; the flesh of the lamb must be roasted with fire ; and it must be all of it eaten that very night with bitter herbs, in a travelling posture, their loins girt, their shoes on their feet, and their staff in their hand. This was accordingly done, and the destroying angel passed over them, and slew the first-born of the Egyptians. This opened a way for the return of Abraham's posterity into the land of promise. The accommodation of this type is not difficult. (1.) Christ is that Lamb, he is our Passover, he was sacrificed for us. (2.) His blood must be sprinkled ; it must be applied to those who have the saving benefit of it. (3.) It is applied effectually only to the Israelites, the chosen people of God. (4.) It is not owing to our inherent righteousness or best performances that we are saved from the wrath of God, but to the blood of Christ and his imputed righteousness. If any of the families of Israel had neglected the sprinkling of this blood upon their doors, though they should have spent all the night in prayer, the destroying angel would have broken in upon them, and slain their first-born. (5.) Wherever this blood is applied, the

soul receives a whole Christ by faith, and lives upon him. (6.) This true faith makes sin bitter to the soul, even while it receives the pardon and atonement. (7.) All our spiritual privileges on earth should quicken us to set out early, and get forward, in our way to heaven. (8.) Those who have been marked out must ever remember and acknowledge free and distinguishing grace.

XIII. The next instance of faith is that of the Israelites passing through the Red Sea under the conduct of Moses their leader, *v.* 29. The story we have in Exodus, *ch.* xiv. Observe,

1. The preservation and safe passage of the Israelites through the Red Sea, when there was no other way to escape from Pharaoh and his host, who were closely pursuing them. Here we may observe, (1.) Israel's danger was very great; an enraged enemy with chariots and horsemen behind them; steep rocks and mountains on either hand, and the Red Sea before them. (2.) Their deliverance was very glorious. By faith they passed through the Red Sea as on dry land; the grace of faith will help us through all the dangers we meet with in our way to heaven.

2. The destruction of the Egyptians. They presumptuously attempting to follow Israel through the Red Sea, being thus blinded and hardened to their ruin, were all drowned. Their rashness was great, and their ruin was grievous. When God judges, he will overcome; and it is plain that the destruction of sinners is of themselves.

XIV. The next instance of faith is that of the Israelites, under Joshua their leader, before the walls of Jericho. The story we have Josh. vi. 5, &c. Here observe, 1. The means prescribed of God to bring down the walls of Jericho. It was ordered that they should compass the walls about once a day for seven days together and seven times the last day, that the priests should carry the ark when they compassed the walls about, and should blow with trumpets made of ram's horns, and sound a longer blast than before, and then all the people should shout, and the walls of Jericho should fall before them. Here was a great trial of their faith. The method prescribed seemed very improbable to answer such an end, and would doubtless expose them to the daily contempt of their enemies; the ark of God would seem to be in danger. But this was the way God commanded them to take, and he loves to do great things by small and contemptible means, that his own arm may be made bare. 2. The powerful success of the prescribed means. The walls of Jericho fell before them. This was a frontier town in the land of Canaan, the first that stood out against the Israelites. God was pleased in this extraordinary manner to slight and dismantle it, in order to magnify himself, to terrify the Canaanites, to strengthen the faith of the Israelites, and to exclude all boasting. God can and will in his own time and way cause all the powerful opposition that is made to his interest and glory to fall down, and the grace of faith is mighty through God for the pulling down of strong-holds; he will make Babylon fall before the faith of his people, and, when he has some great thing to do for them, he raises up great and strong faith in them.

XV. The next instance is the faith of Rahab, *v.* 31. Among the noble army of believing worthies, bravely marshalled by the apostle, Rahab comes in the rear, to show *that God is no respecter of persons.* Here consider,

1. Who this Rahab was. (1.) She was a Canaanite, a *stranger to the commonwealth of Israel,* and had but little help for faith, and yet she was a believer; the power of divine grace greatly appears when it works without the usual means of grace. (2.) She was a harlot, and lived in a way

of sin ; she was not only a keeper of a public-house, but a common woman of the town, and yet she believed that the greatness of sin, if truly repented of, shall be no bar to the pardoning mercy of God. Christ has saved the chief of sinners. *Where sin has abounded, grace has superabounded.*

2. What she did by her faith : *She received the spies in peace,* the men that Joshua had sent to spy out Jericho, Josh. ii. 6, 7. She not only bade them welcome, but she concealed them from their enemies who sought to cut them off, and she made a noble confession of her faith, *v.* 9–11. She engaged them to covenant with her to show favour to her and hers, when God should show kindness to them, and that they would give her a sign, which they did, a line of scarlet, which she was to hang forth out of the window ; she sent them away with prudent and friendly advice. Learn here, (1.) True faith will show itself in good works, especially towards the people of God. (2.) Faith will venture all hazards in the cause of God and his people ; a true believer will sooner expose his own person than God's interest and people. (3.) A true believer is desirous, not only to be in covenant with God, but in communion with the people of God, and is willing to cast in his lot with them, and to fare as they fare.

3. What she gained by her faith. She escaped perishing with those that believed not. Observe, (1.) The generality of her neighbours, friends, and fellow-citizens, perished ; it was an utter destruction that befell that city : man and beast were cut off. (2.) The cause of the people of Jericho's destruction—unbelief. They believed not that Israel's God was the true God, and that Israel was the peculiar people of God, though they had evidence sufficient of it. (3.) The signal preservation of Rahab. Joshua gave a strict charge that she should be spared, and none but she and hers ; and she taking care that the sign, the scarlet thread, should be hung out, her family were marked out for mercy, and perished not. Singular faith, when the generality are not only unbelievers, but against believers, will be rewarded with singular favours in times of common calamity.

32 And what shall I more say ? for the time would fail me to tell of Gedeon, and *of* Barak, and *of* Samson, and *of* Jephthae ; *of* David also, and Samuel, and *of* the prophets : 33 Who through faith subdued kingdoms, wrought righteousness, obtained promises, stopped the mouths of lions, 34 Quenched the violence [power] of fire, escaped the edge of the sword, out of weakness were made strong, waxed valiant in fight, turned to flight the armies of the aliens. 35 Women received their dead raised to life again [by a resurrection] : and others were tortured, not accepting deliverance ; that they might obtain a better resurrection : 36 And others had trial of *cruel* mockings and scourgings, yea, moreover of bonds and imprisonment : 37 They were stoned, they were sawn asunder, were tempted, were slain with the sword : they wandered about in sheepskins and goatskins ; being destitute, afflicted, tormented [evil entreated] ; 38 (Of whom the world was not worthy :) they wandered in deserts, and *in* mountains, and *in* dens, and caves of the earth. 39 And

these all, having obtained a good report through faith [**having had witness borne to them through their faith**], received not the promise : [40] God having provided some better thing for us, that they without [**apart from**] us should not be made perfect.

The apostle having given us a classis of many eminent believers, whose names are mentioned and the particular trials and actings of their faith recorded, now concludes his narrative with a more summary account of another set of believers, where the particular acts are not ascribed to particular persons by name, but left to be applied by those who are well acquainted with the sacred story ; and, like a divine orator, he prefaces this part of the narrative with an elegant expostulation : *What shall I say more? Time would fail me ;* as if he had said, "It is in vain to attempt to exhaust this subject ; should I not restrain my pen, it would soon run beyond the bounds of an epistle ; and therefore I shall but just mention a few more, and leave you to enlarge upon them." Observe, 1. After all our researches into the scripture, there is still more to be learned from them. 2. We must well consider in divine matters what we should say, and suit it as well as we can to the time. 3. We should be pleased to think how great the number of believers was under the Old Testament, and how strong their faith, though the objects thereof were not then so fully revealed. And, 4. We should lament it, that now, in gospel times, when the rule of faith is more clear and perfect, the number of believers should be so small and their faith so weak.

I. In this summary account the apostle mentions,

1. Gideon, whose story we have in Judges vi. 11, &c. He was an eminent instrument raised up of God to deliver his people from the oppression of the Midianites ; he was a person of mean tribe and family, called from a mean employment (threshing wheat), and saluted by an angel of God in this surprising manner. *The Lord is with thee, thou mighty man of war.* Gideon could not at first receive such honours, but humbly expostulates with the angel about their low and distressed state. The angel of the Lord delivers him his commission, and assures him of success, confirming the assurance by fire out of the rock. Gideon is directed to offer sacrifice, and, instructed in his duty, goes forth against the Midianites, when his army is reduced from thirty-two thousand to three hundred ; yet by these, with their lamps and pitchers, God put the whole army of the Midianites to confusion and ruin : and the same faith that gave Gideon so much courage and honour enabled him to act with great meekness and modesty towards his brethren afterwards. It is the excellency of the grace of faith that, while it helps men to do great things, it keeps them from having high and great thoughts of themselves.

2. Barak, another instrument raised up to deliver Israel out of the hand of Jabin, king of Canaan, Jud. iv., where we read, (1.) Though he was a soldier, yet he received his commission and instructions from Deborah, a *prophetess of the Lord;* and he insisted upon having this divine oracle with him in his expedition. (2.) He obtained a great victory by his faith over all the host of Sisera. (3.) His faith taught him to return all the praise and glory to God : this is the nature of faith ; it has recourse unto God in all dangers and difficulties, and then makes grateful returns to God for all mercies and deliverances.

3. Samson, another instrument that God raised up to deliver Israel from

the Philistines : his story we have in Judges xiii., xiv., xv., and xvi., and from it we learn that the grace of faith is the strength of the soul for great service. If Samson had not had a strong faith as well as a strong arm, he had never performed such exploits. Observe, (1.) By faith the servants of God shall overcome even the roaring lion. (2.) True faith is acknowledged and accepted, even when mingled with many failings. (3.) The believer's faith endures to the end, and, in dying, gives him victory over death and all his deadly enemies ; his greatest conquest he gains by dying.

4. Jephthah, whose story we have, Jud. xi., before that of Samson. He was raised up to deliver Israel from the Ammonites. As various and new enemies rise up against the people of God, various and new deliverers are raised up for them. In the story of Jephthah observe, (1.) The grace of God often finds out, and fastens upon, the most undeserving and ill-deserving persons, to do great things for them and by them. Jephthah was the son of a harlot. (2.) The grace of faith, wherever it is, will put men upon acknowledging God in all their ways (ch. xi. 11): *Jephthah rehearsed all his words before the Lord in Mizpeh.* (3.) The grace of faith will make men bold and venturous in a good cause. (4.) Faith will not only put men upon making their vows to God, but paying their vows after the mercy received ; yea, though they have vowed to their own great grief, hurt, and loss, as in the case of Jephthah and his daughter.

5. David, that great man after God's own heart. Few ever met with greater trials, and few ever discovered a more lively faith. His first appearance on the stage of the world was a great evidence of his faith. Having, when young, slain *the lion and the bear,* his faith in God encouraged him to encounter the great Goliath, and helped him to triumph over him. The same faith enabled him to bear patiently the ungrateful malice of Saul and his favourites and to wait till God should put him into possession of the promised power and dignity. The same faith made him a very successful and victorious prince, and, after a long life of virtue and honour (though not without some foul stains of sin), he died in faith, relying upon the everlasting covenant that God had made with him and his, ordered in all things and sure ; and he has left behind him such excellent memoirs of the trials and acts of faith in the book of Psalms as will ever be of great esteem and use, among the people of God.

6. Samuel, raised up to be a most eminent prophet of the Lord to Israel, as well as a ruler over them. God revealed himself to Samuel when he was but a child, and continued to do so till his death. In his story observe, (1.) Those are likely to grow up to some eminency in faith who begin betimes in the exercise of it. (2.) Those whose business it is to reveal the mind and will of God to others had need to be well established in the belief of it themselves.

7. To Samuel he adds *and of the prophets,* who were extraordinary ministers of the Old Testament church, employed of God sometimes to denounce judgment, sometimes to promise mercy, always to reprove sin ; sometimes to foretell remarkable events, known only to God, and chiefly to give notice of the Messiah, his coming, person, and offices ; for in him the prophets as well as the law centre. Now a true and strong faith was very requisite for the right discharge of such an office as this.

II. Having done naming particular persons, he proceeds to tell us what things were done by their faith. He mentions some things that easily apply themselves to one or other of the persons named ; but he mentions other things that are not so easy to be accommodated to any here named, but must be left to general conjecture or accommodation.

1 *By faith they subdued kingdoms, v.* 33. Thus did David, Joshua, and many of the judges. Learn hence, (1.) The interests and powers of kings and kingdoms are often set up in opposition to God and his people. (2.) God can easily subdue all those kings and kingdoms that set themselves to oppose him. (3.) Faith is a suitable and excellent qualification of those who fight in the wars of the Lord ; it makes them just, bold, and wise.

2. They *wrought righteousness,* both in their public and personal capacities ; they turned many from idolatry to the ways of righteousness ; they believed God, and it was imputed to them for righteousness ; they walked and acted righteously towards God and man. It is a greater honour and happiness to work righteousness than to work miracles ; faith is an active principle of universal righteousness.

3. They *obtained promises,* both general and special. It is faith that gives us an interest in the promises ; it is by faith that we have the comfort of the promises : and it is by faith that we are prepared to wait for the promises, and in due time to receive them.

4. They *stopped the mouths of lions;* so did Samson, Judg. xiv. 5, 6, and David, 1 Sam. xvii. 34, 35, and Daniel, vi. 22. Here learn, (1.) The power of God is above the power of the creature. (2.) Faith engages the power of God for his people, whenever it shall be for his glory, to overcome brute beasts and brutish men.

5. They *quenched the violence of the fire, v.* 34. So Moses by the prayer of faith quenched the fire of God's wrath that was kindled against the people of Israel, Num. xi. 1, 2. So did the three children, or rather mighty champions, Dan. iii. 17–27. Their faith in God, refusing to worship the golden image, exposed them to the fiery furnace which Nebuchadnezzar had prepared for them, and their faith engaged for them that power and presence of God in the furnace which quenched the violence of the fire, so that not so much as the smell thereof passed on them. Never was the grace of faith more severely tried, never more nobly exerted, nor ever more gloriously rewarded, than theirs was.

6. They *escaped the edge of the sword.* Thus David escaped the sword of Goliath and of Saul ; and Mordecai and the Jews escaped the sword of Haman. The swords of men are held in the hand of God, and he can blunt the edge of the sword, and turn it away from his people against their enemies when he pleases. Faith takes hold of that hand of God which has hold of the swords of men ; and God has often suffered himself to be prevailed upon by the faith of his people.

7. *Out of weakness they were made strong.* From national weakness, into which the Jews often fell by their unbelief ; upon the revival of their faith, all their interest and affairs revived and flourished. From bodily weakness ; thus Hezekiah, believing the word of God, recovered out of a mortal distemper, and he ascribed his recovery to the promise and power of God (Isa. xxxviii. 15, 16), *What shall I say ? He hath spoken it, and he hath also done it. Lord, by these things men live, and in these is the life of my spirit.* And it is the same grace of faith that from spiritual weakness helps men to recover and renew their strength.

8. They *grew valiant in fight.* So did Joshua, the judges, and David. True faith gives truest courage and patience, as it discerns the strength of God, and thereby the weakness of all his enemies. And they were not only valiant, but successful. God, as a reward and encouragement of their

faith, *put to flight the armies of the aliens,* of those who were aliens to their commonwealth, and enemies to their religion : God made them flee and fall before his faithful servants. Believing and praying commanders, at the head of believing and praying armies, have been so owned and honoured of God that nothing could stand before them.

9. *Women received their dead raised to life again,* v. 35. So did the widow of Zarepath (1 Kings xvii. 23), and the Shunamite, 2 Kings iv. 36. (1.) *In Christ there is neither male nor female;* many of the weaker sex have been strong in faith. (2.) Though the covenant of grace takes in the children of believers, yet it leaves them subject to natural death. (3.) Poor mothers are loath to resign up their interest in their children, though death has taken them away. (4.) God has sometimes yielded so far to the tender affections of sorrowful women as to restore their dead children to life again. Thus Christ had compassion on the widow of Nain, Luke vii. 12, &c. (5.) This should confirm our faith in the general resurrection.

III. The apostle tells us what these believers endured by faith. 1. They *were tortured, not accepting deliverance,* v. 35. They were put upon the rack, to make them renounce their God, their Saviour, and their religion. They bore the torture, and would not accept of deliverance upon such vile terms ; and that which animated them thus to suffer was the hope they had of *obtaining a better resurrection,* and deliverance upon more honourable terms. This is thought to refer to that memorable story, 2 Macc. *ch.* vii. &c. 2. They endured *trials of cruel mockings and scourgings, and bonds and imprisonment,* v. 36. They were persecuted in their reputation by *mockings,* which are cruel to an ingenuous mind ; in their persons by *scourging,* the punishment of slaves ; in their liberty by *bonds and imprisonment.* Observe how inveterate is the malice that wicked men have towards the righteous, how far it will go, and what a variety of cruelties it will invent and exercise upon those against whom they have no cause of quarrel, except in the matters of their God. 3. They were put to death in the most cruel manner ; some *were stoned,* as Zechariah (2 Chron. xxiv. 21), *sawn asunder,* as Isaiah by Manasseh. *They were tempted;* some read it, *burnt,* 2 Macc. vii. 5. *They were slain with the sword.* All sorts of deaths were prepared for them ; their enemies clothed death in all the array of cruelty and terror, and yet they boldly met it and endured it. 4. Those who escaped death were used so ill that death might seem more eligible than such a life. Their enemies spared them, only to prolong their misery, and wear out all their patience ; for they were forced to *wander about in sheep-skins and goat-skins, being destitute, afflicted, and tormented; they wandered about in deserts, and on mountains, and in dens and caves of the earth,* v. 37, 38. They were stripped of the conveniences of life, and turned out of house and harbour. They had not raiment to put on, but were forced to cover themselves with the skins of slain beasts. They were driven out of all human society, and forced to converse with the beasts of the field, to hide themselves in dens and caves, and make their complaint to rocks and rivers, not more obdurate than their enemies. Such sufferings as these they endured then for their faith ; and such they endured through the power of the grace of faith : and which shall we most admire, the wickedness of human nature, that is capable of perpetrating such cruelties on fellow-creatures, or the excellency of divine grace, that is able to bear up the faithful under such cruelties, and to carry them safely through all ?

IV. What they obtained by their faith. 1. A most honourable character and commendation from God, the true Judge and fountain of honour—that *the world was not worthy* of such men ; the world did not deserve such blessings ; they did not know how to value them, nor how to use them. Wicked men ! The righteous are not worthy to live in the world, and God declares the world is not worthy of them ; and, though they widely differ in their judgment, they agree in this, that it is not fit that good men should have their rest in this world ; and therefore God receives them out of it, to that world that is suitable to them, and yet far beyond the merit of all their services and sufferings. 2. They *obtained a good report* (v. 39) of all good men, and of the truth itself, and have the honour to be enrolled in this sacred calendar of the Old-Testament worthies, God's witnesses ; yea, they had a witness for them in the consciences of their enemies, who, while they thus abused them, were condemned by their own consciences, as persecuting those who were more righteous than themselves. 3. They obtained an interest in the promises, though not the full possession of them. They had a title to the promises, though they received not the great things promised. This is not meant of the felicity of the heavenly state, for this they did receive, when they died, in the measure of a part, in one constituent part of their persons, and the much better part ; but it is meant of the felicity of the gospel state : they had types, but not the antitype ; they had shadows, but had not seen the substance ; and yet, under this imperfect dispensation, they discovered this precious faith. This the apostle insists upon to render their faith mere illustrious, and to provoke Christians to a holy jealousy and emulation ; that they should not suffer themselves to be outdone in the exercise of faith by those who came so short of them in all the helps and advantages for believing. He tells the Hebrews that God had *provided some better things for* them (v. 40), and therefore they might be assured that he expected at least as good things from them ; and that since the gospel is the end and perfection of the Old Testament, which had no excellency but in its reference to Christ and the gospel, it was expected that their faith should be as much more perfect than the faith of the Old-Testament saints ; for their state and dispensation were more perfect than the former, and were indeed the perfection and completion of the former, for without the gospel-church the Jewish church must have remained in an incomplete and imperfect state. This reasoning is strong, and should be effectually prevalent with us all.

CHAPTER XII

The apostle, in this chapter, applies what he has collected in the chapter foregoing, and makes use of it as a great motive to patience and perseverance in the Christian faith and state, pressing home the argument, I. From a greater example than he had yet mentioned, and that is Christ himself, ver. 1-3. II. From the gentle and gracious nature of the afflictions they endured in their Christian course, ver. 4-17. III. From the communion and conformity between the state of the gospel-church on earth and the triumphant church in heaven, ver. 18, to the end.

WHEREFORE seeing we also are compassed about with so great a cloud of witnesses, let us lay aside every weight, and the sin which doth so easily beset *us*, and let us run with patience the race that is set before us, ² Looking unto Jesus the author and finisher [**perfecter**] of *our* faith; who for the joy that was set before him, endured the cross, despising the shame, and is set [**hath sat**] down at the right hand of the throne of God. ³ For consider him that endured such contradiction [**gainsaying**] of sinners against himself [**themselves**], lest ye be wearied and faint in your minds.

Here observe what is the great duty which the apostle urges upon the Hebrews, and which he so much desires they would comply with, and that is, to *lay aside every weight, and the sin that did so easily beset them, and run with patience the race set before them.* The duty consists of two parts, the one preparatory, the other perfective.

I. Preparatory: *Lay aside every weight, and the sin,* &c. 1. *Every weight,* that is, all inordinate affection and concern for the body, and the present life and world. Inordinate care for the present life, or fondness for it, is a dead weight upon the soul, that pulls it down when it should ascend upwards, and pulls it back when it should press forward: it makes duty and difficulties harder and heavier than they would be. 2. *The sin that doth so easily beset us;* the sin that has the greatest advantage against us, by the circumstances we are in, our constitution, our company. This may mean either the damning sin of unbelief or rather the darling sin of the Jews, an over-fondness for their own dispensation. *Let us lay aside* all external and internal hindrances.

II. Perfective: *Run with patience the race that is set before us.* The apostle speaks in the gymnastic style, taken from the Olympic and other exercises.

1. Christians have a race to run, a race of service and a race of sufferings, a course of active and passive obedience.

2. This race is set before them; it is marked out unto them, both by the word of God and the examples of the faithful servants of God, that cloud of witnesses with which they are compassed about. It is set out by proper limits and directions; the mark they run to, and the prize they run for, are set before them.

3. This race must be run with patience and perseverance. There will be need of patience to encounter the difficulties that lie in our way, of perseverance to resist all temptations to desist or turn aside. Faith and

patience are the conquering graces, and therefore must be always cultivated and kept in lively exercise.

4. Christians have a greater example to animate and encourage them in their Christian course than any or all who have been mentioned before, and that is the Lord Jesus Christ: *Looking unto Jesus, the author and finisher of our faith, v. 2.* Here observe,

(1.) What our Lord Jesus is to his people : he is *the author and finisher of their faith*—the beginning, perfecter, and rewarder of it. [1.] He is the author of their faith ; not only the object, but the author. He is the great leader and precedent of our faith, *he trusted in God ;* he is the purchaser of the Spirit of faith, the publisher of the rule of faith, the efficient cause of the grace of faith, and in all respects the author of our faith. [2.] He is *the finisher of our faith ;* he is the fulfiller and the fulfilling of all scripture-promises and prophecies ; he is the perfecter of the canon of scripture ; he is the finisher of grace, and of the work of faith with power in the souls of his people ; and he is the judge and the rewarder of their faith ; he determines who they are that reach the mark, and from him, and in him, they have the prize.

(2.) What trials Christ met with in his race and course. [1.] He *endured the contradiction of sinners against himself* (*v.* 3) ; he bore the opposition that they made to him, both in their words and behaviour. They were continually contradicting him, and crossing in upon his great designs ; and though he could easily have both confuted and confounded them, and sometimes gave them a specimen of his power, yet he endured their evil manners with great patience. Their contradictions were levelled against Christ himself, against his person as God-man, against his authority, against his preaching, and yet he endured all. [2.] He *endured the cross*—all those sufferings that he met with in the world ; for he took up his cross betimes, and was at length nailed to it, and endured a painful, ignominious and accursed death, in which he was numbered with the transgressors, the vilest malefactors ; yet all this he endured with invincible patience and resolution. [3.] He *despised the shame.* All the reproaches that were cast upon him, both in his life and at his death, he despised ; he was infinitely above them ; he knew his own innocency and excellency, and despised the ignorance and malice of his despisers.

(3.) What it was that supported the human soul of Christ under these unparalleled sufferings ; and that was *the joy that was set before him.* He had something in view under all his sufferings, which was pleasant to him ; he rejoiced to see that by his sufferings he should make satisfaction to the injured justice of God and give security to his honour and government, that he should make peace between God and man, that he should seal the covenant of grace and be the Mediator of it, that he should open a way of salvation to the chief of sinners, and that he should effectually save all those whom the Father had given him, and himself be the first-born among many brethren. This was the joy that was set before him.

(4.) The reward of his suffering : he *has sat down at the right hand of the throne of God.* Christ, as Mediator, is exalted to a station of the highest honour, of the greatest power and influence ; he is at the right hand of the Father. Nothing passes between heaven and earth but by him ; he does all that is done ; *he ever lives to make intercession for* his people.

(5.) What is our duty with respect to this Jesus. We must, [1.] Look unto him ; that is, we must set him continually before us as our example, and our great encouragement ; we must look to him for direction, for assistance, and for acceptance, in all our sufferings. [2.] We must consider him, meditate much upon him, and reason with ourselves from his case to our own. We must *analogize*, as the word is; compare Christ's sufferings and ours ; and we shall find that as his sufferings far exceeded ours, in the nature and measure of them, so his patience far excels ours, and is a perfect pattern for us to imitate.

(6.) The advantage we shall reap by thus doing : it will be a means to prevent our weariness and fainting (*v.* 3) : *Lest you be weary and faint in your minds.* Observe, [1.] There is a proneness in the best to grow weary and to faint under their trials and afflictions, especially when they prove heavy and of long continuance : this proceeds from the imperfections of grace and the remains of corruption, [2.] The best way to prevent this is to look unto Jesus, and to consider him. Faith and meditation will fetch in fresh supplies of strength, comfort, and courage, for he has assured them if *they suffer with him they shall also reign with him :* and this hope will be their helmet.

⁴ Ye have not yet resisted unto blood, striving against sin. ⁵ And ye have forgotten the exhortation which speaketh unto [reasoneth with] you as unto children, My son, despise not thou the chastening of the Lord, nor faint when thou art rebuked of him : ⁶ For whom the Lord loveth he chasteneth, and scourgeth every son whom he receiveth. ⁷ If ye endure chastening, [It is for chastening that ye endure ;] God dealeth with you as with sons ; for what son is he whom the father chasteneth not ? ⁸ But if ye be without chastisement, whereof all are partakers, then are ye bastards, and not sons. ⁹ Furthermore we have had fathers of our flesh which corrected [to chasten] *us*, and we gave *them* reverence : shall we not much rather be in subjection unto the Father of spirits, and live ? ¹⁰ For they verily for a few days chastened *us* after their own pleasure [as seemed good to them], but he for *our* profit, that *we* might be partakers of his holiness. ¹¹ Now no chastening for the present seemeth to be joyous, but grievous : nevertheless afterward it yieldeth the peaceable fruit of righteousness unto them which are exercised thereby. ¹² Wherefore lift up the hands which hang down, and the feeble [palsied] knees ; ¹³ And make straight paths for your feet, lest that which is lame be turned out of the way ; but let it rather be healed. ¹⁴ Follow peace with all *men*, and holiness, without which [and the sanctification without which] no man shall see the Lord : ¹⁵ Looking diligently lest any man fail [falleth short] of the grace of God ; lest any root of bitterness springing up trouble *you*, and thereby many be defiled ; ¹⁶ Lest there *be* any fornicator, or profane person, as Esau, who for one morsel of meat sold his birthright. ¹⁷ For ye know how that afterward, when he would have [desired to] inherited the

blessing, he was rejected : for he found no place of repentance, though he [(for he found no place of repentance), though he] sought it carefully with tears.

Here the apostle presses the exhortation to patience and perseverance by an argument taken from the gentle measure and gracious nature of those sufferings which the believing Hebrews endured in their Christian course.

I. From the gentle and moderate degree and measure of their sufferings : *You have not yet resisted unto blood, striving against sin, v. 4.* Observe,

1. He owns that they had suffered much, they had been striving to an agony against sin. Here, (1.) The cause of the conflict was sin, and to be engaged against sin is to fight in a good cause, for sin is the worst enemy both to God and man. Our spiritual warfare is both honourable and necessary ; for we are only defending ourselves against that which would destroy us, if it should get the victory over us ; we fight for ourselves, for our lives, and therefore ought to be patient and resolute. (2.) Every Christian is enlisted under Christ's banner, to strive against sin, against sinful doctrines, sinful practices, and sinful habits and customs, both in himself and in others.

2. He puts them in mind that they might have suffered more, that they had not suffered as much as others ; for they had *not yet resisted unto blood*, they had not been called to martyrdom as yet, though they knew not how soon they might be. Learn here, (1.) Our Lord Jesus, *the captain of our salvation*, does not call his people out to the hardest trials at first, but wisely trains them up by less sufferings to be prepared for greater. He will not put new wine into weak vessels, he is *the gentle shepherd*, who will not overdrive *the young ones of the flock.* (2.) It becomes Christians to take notice of the gentleness of Christ in accommodating their trial to their strength. They should not magnify their afflictions, but should take notice of the mercy that is mixed with them, and should pity those who are called to the fiery trial to *resist to blood ;* not to shed the blood of their enemies, but to seal their testimony with their own blood. (3.) Christians should be ashamed to faint under less trials, when they see others bear up under greater, and do not know how soon they may meet with greater themselves. If we have run with the footmen and they have wearied us, how shall we contend with horses ? if we be wearied in a land of peace, what shall we do in the swellings of Jordan ? Jer. xii. 5.

II. He argues from the peculiar and gracious nature of those sufferings that befall the people of God. Though their enemies and persecutors may be the instruments of inflicting such sufferings on them, yet they are divine chastisements ; their heavenly Father has his hand in all, and his wise end to serve by all ; of this he has given them due notice, and they should not forget it, *v. 5.* Observe,

1. Those afflictions which may be truly persecution as far as men are concerned in them are fatherly rebukes and chastisements as far as God is concerned in them. Persecution for religion is sometimes a correction and rebuke for the sins of professors of religion. Men persecute them because they are religious ; God chastises them because they are not more so : men persecute them because they will not give up their profession ; God chastises them because they have not lived up to their profession.

2. God has directed his people how they ought to behave themselves under all their afflictions ; they must avoid the extremes that many run

into. (1.) They must not despise the chastening of the Lord ; they must not make light of afflictions, and be stupid and insensible under them, for they are the hand and rod of God, and his rebukes for sin. Those who make light of affliction make light of God and make light of sin. (2.) They must not faint when they are rebuked ; they must not despond and sink under their trial, nor fret and repine, but bear up with faith and patience. (3.) If they run into either of these extremes, it is a sign they have forgotten their heavenly Father's advice and exhortation, which he has given them in true and tender affection.

3. Afflictions, rightly endured, though they may be the fruits of God's displeasure, are yet proofs of his paternal love to his people and care for them (v. 6, 7) : *Whom the Lord loveth he chasteneth, and scourgeth every son whom he receiveth.* Observe, (1.) The best of God's children need chastisement. They have their faults and follies, which need to be corrected. (2.) Though God may let others alone in their sins, he will correct sin in his own children ; they are of his family, and shall not escape his rebukes when they want them. (3.) In this he acts as becomes a father, and treats them like children ; no wise and good father will wink at faults in his own children as he would in others ; his relation and his affections oblige him to take more notice of the faults of his own children than those of others. (4.) To be suffered to go on in sin without a rebuke is a sad sign of alienation from God ; such are bastards, not sons. They may call him Father, because born in the pale of the church ; but they are the spurious offspring of another father, not of God, v. 7, 8.

4. Those that are impatient under the discipline of their heavenly Father behave worse towards him than they would do towards earthly parents, v. 9, 10. Here, (1.) The apostle commends a dutiful and submissive behaviour in children towards their earthly parents. *We gave them reverence,* even when they corrected us. It is the duty of children to give the reverence of obedience to the just commands of their parents, and the reverence of submission to their correction when they have been disobedient. Parents have not only authority, but a charge from God, to give their children correction when it is due, and he has commanded children to take such correction well : to be stubborn and discontented under due correction is a double fault ; for the correction supposes there has been a fault already committed against the parent's commanding power, and superadds a further fault against his chastening power. Hence, (2.) He recommends humble and submissive behaviour towards our heavenly Father, when under his correction ; and this he does by an argument from the less to the greater. [1.] Our earthly fathers are but *the fathers of our flesh,* but God is *the Father of our spirits.* Our fathers on earth were instrumental in the production of our bodies, which are but flesh, a mean, mortal, vile thing, formed out of the dust of the earth, as the bodies of the beasts are ; and yet as they are curiously wrought, and made parts of our persons, a proper tabernacle for the soul to dwell in and an organ for it to act by, we owe reverence and affection to those who were instrumental in their procreation ; but then we must owe much more to him who is the Father of our spirits. Our souls are not of a material substance, not of the most refined sort ; they are not *ex traduce—by traduction ;* to affirm it is bad philosophy, and worse divinity : they are the immediate offspring of God, who, after he had formed the body of man out of the earth, breathed into him a vital spirit, and so he became a living soul. [2.] Our earthly parents *chastened us for their own pleasure.* Sometimes they did it to gratify their passion rather

than to reform our manners. This is a weakness the fathers of our flesh are subject to, and this they should carefully watch against; for hereby they dishonour that parental authority which God has put upon them and very much hinder the efficacy of their chastisements. But the Father of our spirits never grieves willingly, nor afflicts the children of men, much less his own children. It is always *for our profit ;* and the advantage he intends us thereby is no less than our being partakers of his holiness; it is to correct and cure those sinful disorders which make us unlike to God, and to improve and to increase those graces which are the image of God in us, that we may be and act more like our heavenly Father. God loves his children so that he would have them to be as like himself as can be, and for this end he chastises them when they need it. [3.] The fathers of our flesh corrected us for *a few days,* in our state of childhood, when minors ; and, though we were in that weak and peevish state, we owed them reverence, and when we came to maturity we loved and honoured them the more for it. Our whole life here is a state of childhood, minority, and imperfection, and therefore we must submit to the discipline of such a state ; when we come to a state of perfection we shall be fully reconciled to all the measures of God's discipline over us now. [4.] God's correction is no condemnation. His children may at first fear lest affliction should come upon that dreadful errand, and we cry, *Do not condemn me,* but *show me wherefore thou contendest with me,* Job. x. 2. But this is so far from being the design of God to his own people that he therefore chastens them now, *that they may not be condemned with the world,* 1 Cor. xi. 32. He does it to prevent the death and destruction of their souls, that they may live to God, and be like God, and for ever with him.

5. The children of God, under their afflictions, ought not to judge of his dealings with them by present sense, but by reason, and faith, and experience : *No chastening for the present seemeth to be joyous, but grievous ; nevertheless afterwards it yieldeth the peaceable fruits of righteousness, v.* 11. Here observe,

(1.) The judgment of sense in this case—Afflictions are not grateful to the sense, but grievous ; the flesh will feel them, and be grieved by them, and groan under them.

(2.) The judgment of faith, which corrects that of sense, and declares that a sanctified affliction produces the fruits of righteousness ; these fruits are peaceable, and tend to the quieting and comforting of the soul. Affliction produces peace, by producing more righteousness ; for the fruit of righteousness is peace. And if the pain of the body contribute thus to the peace of the mind, and short present affliction produce blessed fruits of a long continuance, they have no reason to fret or faint under it ; but their great concern is that the chastening they are under may be endured by them with patience, and improved to a greater degree of holiness. [1.] That their affliction may be endured with patience, which is the main drift of the apostle's discourse on this subject ; and he again returns to exhort them that for the reason before mentioned they should *lift up the hands that hang down and the feeble knees, v.* 12. A burden of affliction is apt to make the Christian's hands hang down, and his knees grow feeble, to dispirit him and discourage him ; but this he must strive against, and that for two reasons :—*First,* That he may the better run his spiritual race and course. Faith, and patience, and holy courage and resolution, will make him walk more steadily, keep a straighter path, prevent wavering and wandering. *Secondly,* That he may encourage and not dispirit others that are in

the same way with him. There are many that are in the way to heaven
who yet walk but weakly and lamely in it. Such are apt to discourage
one another, and hinder one another ; but it is their duty to take courage,
and act by faith, and so help one another forward in the way to heaven.
[2.] That their affliction may be improved to a greater degree of holiness.
Since this is God's design, it ought to be the design and concern of his
children, that with renewed strength and patience they may *follow peace
with all men, and holiness, v.* 14. If the children of God grow impatient
under affliction, they will neither walk so quietly and peaceably towards
men, nor so piously towards God, as they should do ; but faith and patience
will enable them to follow peace and holiness too, as a man follows his
calling, constantly, diligently, and with pleasure. Observe, *First,* It is the
duty of Christians, even when in a suffering state, *to follow peace with all
men,* yea, even with those who may be instrumental in their sufferings.
This is a hard lesson, and a high attainment, but it is what Christ has
called his people to. Sufferings are apt to sour the spirit and sharpen the
passions; but the children of God must follow peace with all men. *Secondly,*
Peace and holiness are connected together ; there can be no true peace
without holiness. There may be prudence and discreet forbearance, and
a show of friendship and good-will to all ; but this true Christian peaceableness is never found separate from holiness. We must not, under pretence of living peaceably with all men, leave the ways of holiness, but
cultivate peace in a way of holiness. *Thirdly, Without holiness no man
shall see the Lord.* The vision of God our Saviour in heaven is reserved
as the reward of holiness, and the stress of our salvation is laid upon our
holiness, though a placid peaceable disposition contributes much to our
meetness for heaven.

6. Where afflictions and sufferings for the sake of Christ are not considered by men as the chastisement of their heavenly Father, and improved
as such, they will be a dangerous snare and temptation to apostasy, which
every Christian should most carefully watch against (*v.* 15, 16): *Looking
diligently lest any man fail of the grace of God, &c.*

(1.) Here the apostle enters a serious caveat against apostasy, and backs
it with an awful example.

[1.] He enters a serious caveat against apostasy, *v.* 15. Here you may
observe, *First,* The nature of apostasy ; it is *failing of the grace of God ;*
it is to become bankrupts in religion, for want of a good foundation, and
suitable care and diligence ; it is *failing of the grace of God,* coming short
of a principle of true grace in the soul, notwithstanding the means of grace
and a profession of religion, and so coming short of the love and favour of God
here and hereafter. *Secondly,* The consequences of apostasy : where persons fail of having the true grace of God, a root of bitterness will spring
up, corruption will prevail and break forth. A *root of bitterness,* a bitter
root, producing bitter fruits to themselves and others. It produces to
themselves corrupt principles, which lead to apostasy and are greatly
strengthened and radicated by apostasy—damnable errors (to the corrupting
of the doctrine and worship of the Christian church) and corrupt practices.
Apostates generally grow worse and worse, and fall into the grossest
wickedness, which usually ends either in downright atheism or in despair.
It also produces bitter fruits to others, to the churches to which these men
belonged ; by their corrupt principles and practices many are troubled, the
peace of the church is broken, the peace of men's minds is disturbed, and
many are defiled, tainted with those bad principles, and drawn into defiling

practices ; so that the churches suffer both in their purity and peace. But the apostates themselves will be the greatest sufferers at last.

[2.] The apostle backs the caution with an awful example, and that is, that of Esau, who though born within the pale of the church, and having the birthright as the eldest son, and so entitled to the privilege of being prophet, priest, and king, in his family, was so profane as to despise these sacred privileges, and to sell his birthright for a morsel of meat. Where observe, *First*, Esau's sin. He profanely despised and sold the birthright, and all the advantages attending it. So do apostates, who to avoid persecution, and enjoy sensual ease and pleasure, though they bore the character of the children of God, and had a visible right to the blessing and inheritance, give up all pretensions thereto. *Secondly*, Esau's punishment, which was suitable to his sin. His conscience was convinced of his sin and folly, when it was too late : *He would afterwards have inherited the blessing*, &c. His punishment lay in two things : 1. He was condemned by his own conscience ; he now saw that the blessing he had made so light of was worth the having, worth the seeking, though with much carefulness and many tears. 2. He was rejected of God : *He found no place of repentance* in God nor in his father ; the blessing was given to another, even to him to whom he sold it for a mess of pottage. Esau, in his great wickedness, had made the bargain, and God, in his righteous judgment, ratified and confirmed it, and would not suffer Isaac to reverse it.

(2.) We may hence learn, [1.] That apostasy from Christ is the fruit of preferring the gratification of the flesh to the blessing of God and the heavenly inheritance. [2.] Sinners will not always have such mean thoughts of the divine blessing and inheritance as now they have. The time is coming when they will think no pains too great, no cares, no tears too much, to obtain the lost blessing. [3.] When the day of grace is over (as sometimes it may be in this life), they will find no place for repentance ; they cannot repent aright of their sin ; and God will not repent of the sentence he has passed upon them for their sin. And therefore, as the design of all, Christians should never give up their title, and hope of their Father's blessing and inheritance, and expose themselves to his irrevocable wrath and curse, by deserting their holy religion, to avoid suffering, which, though this may be persecution as far as wicked men are concerned in it, is only a rod of correction and chastisement in the hand of their heavenly Father, to bring them near to himself in conformity and communion. This is the force of the apostle's arguing from the nature of the sufferings of the people of God even when they suffer for righteousness' sake ; and the reasoning is very strong.

[18] For ye are not come unto the mount that might be touched, and that burned with fire, nor unto blackness, and darkness, and tempest, [19] And the sound of a trumpet, and the voice of words ; which *voice* they that heard entreated that the word should not be spoken to them any more : [20] (For they could not endure that which was commanded, And if so much as a beast touch the mountain, it shall be stoned, or thrust through with a dart : [21] And so terrible was the sight, *that* Moses said, I exceedingly fear and quake :) [22] But ye are come unto mount Sion, and unto the city of the living God, the heavenly Jerusalem,

and to an innumerable company of angels, ²³ To the general assembly and church of the firstborn, which are written [**enrolled**] in heaven, and to God the Judge of all, and to the spirits of just men made perfect, ²⁴ And to Jesus the mediator of the new covenant, and to the blood of sprinkling, that speaketh better things than *that of* Abel. ²⁵ See that ye refuse not him that speaketh. For if they escaped not who refused him that spake [**warned** *them*] on earth, much more *shall not* we *escape*, if we turn away from him that *speaketh* [*warneth*] from heaven : ²⁶ Whose voice then shook the earth : but now he hath promised, saying, Yet once more I shake [**make to tremble**] not the earth only, but also heaven. ²⁷ And this *word*, Yet once more, signifieth the removing of those things that are shaken, as of things that are made, that those things which cannot be [**are not**] shaken may remain. ²⁸ Wherefore we receiving a kingdom which cannot be moved [**shaken**] let us have grace, whereby we may serve God acceptably with reverence and godly fear ²⁹ For our God *is* a consuming fire.

Here the apostle goes on to engage the professing Hebrews to persever-ance in their Christian course and conflict, and not to relapse again into Judaism. This he does by showing them how much the state of the gospel church differs from that of the Jewish church, and how much it resembles the state of the church in heaven, and on both accounts demands and deserves our diligence, patience and perseverance in Christianity.

I. He shows how much the gospel church differs from the Jewish church, and how much it excels. And here we have a very particular description of the state of the church under the Mosaic dispensa-tion, *v.* 10–21. 1. It was a gross sensible state. Mount Sinai, on which that church-state was constituted, was a *mount that might be touched* (*v.* 18), a gross palpable place ; so was the dispensation. It was very much external and earthly, and so more heavy. The state of the gospel church on mount Zion is more spiritual, rational, and easy. 2. It was a dark dispensation. Upon that mount there were blackness and darkness, and that church-state was covered with dark shadows and types : the gospel state is much more clear and bright. 3. It was a dreadful and terrible dis-pensation ; the Jews could not bear the terror of it. The thunder and the lightning, the trumpet sounding, the voice of God himself speaking to them, struck them with such dread that they *entreated that the word might not be so spoken to them any more, v.* 19. Yea, Moses himself said, *I exceed-ingly fear and quake.* The best of men on earth are not able to converse immediately with God and his holy angels. The gospel state is mild, and kind, and condescending, suited to our weak frame. 4. It was a limited dispensation ; all might not approach to that mount, but only Moses and Aaron. Under the gospel we have all access with boldness to God. 5. It was a very dangerous dispensation. The mount burned with fire, and whatever man or beast touched the mount must *be stoned, or thrust through with a dart, v.* 20. It is true, it will be always dangerous for presump-tuous and brutish sinners to draw nigh to God ; but it is not immediate and certain death, as here it was. This was the state of the Jewish church, fitted to awe a stubborn and hard-hearted people, to set forth the strict and tremendous justice of God, to wean the people of God from that dispensation, and induce them more readily to embrace the sweet and gentle economy of the gospel church, and adhere to it.

II. He shows how much the gospel church represents the church triumphant in heaven, what communication there is between the one and the other. The gospel church is called *mount Zion, the heavenly Jerusalem, which is free*, in opposition to mount Sinai, which tendeth to bondage, Gal. iv. 24. This was the hill on which God set his king the Messiah. Now, in coming to mount Zion, believers come into heavenly places, and into a heavenly society.

1. Into heavenly places. (1.) *Unto the city of the living God.* God has taken up his gracious residence in the gospel church, which on that account is an emblem of heaven. There his people may find him ruling, guiding, sanctifying, and comforting them ; there he speaks to them by the gospel ministry ; there they speak to him by prayer, and he hears them ; there he trains them up for heaven, and gives them the earnest of their inheritance. (2.) To *the heavenly Jerusalem*, as born and bred there. as free denizens there. Here believers have clearer views of heaven, plainer evidences for heaven, and a greater meetness and more heavenly temper of soul.

2. To a heavenly society. (1.) *To an innumerable company of angels*, who are of the same family with the saints, under the same head, and in a great measure employed in the same work, ministering to believers for their good, keeping them in all their ways. and pitching their tents about them. These for number are innumerable, and for order and union are a company, and a glorious one. And those who by faith are joined to the gospel church are joined to the angels. and shall at length be like them, and equal with them. (2.) *To the general assembly and church of the first-born. that are written in heaven*, that is, to the universal church, however dispersed. By faith we come to them, have communion with them in the same head, by the same Spirit, and in the same blessed hope, and walk in the same way of holiness, grappling with the same spiritual enemies, and hasting to the same rest, victory, and glorious triumph. Here will be the general assembly of the first-born, the saints of former and earlier times, who saw the promises of the gospel state, but received them not, as well as those who first received them under the gospel, and were regenerated thereby, and so were the first-born, and the first-fruits of the gospel church ; and thereby, as the first-born, advanced to greater honours and privileges than the rest of the world. Indeed all the children of God are heirs, and every one has the privileges of the first-born. The names of these are written in heaven, in the records of the church here : they have a name in God's house, are written among the living in Jerusalem ; they have a good repute for their faith and fidelity, and are enrolled in the Lamb's book of life, as citizens are enrolled in the livery-books. (3.) *To God the judge of all*, that great God who will judge both Jew and Gentile according to the law they are under : believers come to him now by faith, make supplication to their Judge, and receive a sentence of absolution in the gospel, and in the court of their consciences now, by which they know they shall be justified hereafter. (4.) *To the spirits of just men made perfect ;* to the best sort of men, the righteous, who are more excellent than their neighbours ; to the best part of just men, their spirits, and to these in their best state, made perfect. Believers have union with

departed saints in one and the same head and Spirit, and a title to the
same inheritance, of which those on earth are heirs, those in heaven pos-
sessors. (5.) *To Jesus the Mediator of the new covenant, and to the blood of
sprinkling, that speaketh better things than that of Abel.* This is none of the
least of the many encouragements there are to perseverance in the gospel
state, since it is a state of communion with Christ the Mediator of the new
covenant, and of communication of his blood, that speaketh better things
than the blood of Abel. [1.] The gospel covenant is a new covenant, distinct from the covenant of works; and it is now under a new dispensation,
distinct from that of the Old Testament. [2.] Christ is the Mediator of
this new covenant; he is the middle person that goes between both parties,
God and man, to bring them together in this covenant, to keep them together notwithstanding the sins of the people and God's displeasure against
them for sin, to offer up our prayers to God, and to bring down the favours
of God to us, to plead with God for us and to plead with us for God, and
at length to bring God and his people together in heaven, and to be a
Mediator of fruition between them for ever, they beholding and enjoying
God in Christ and God beholding and blessing them in Christ. [3.] This
covenant is ratified by the blood of Christ sprinkled upon our consciences,
as the blood of the sacrifice was sprinkled upon the altar and the sacrifice.
This blood of Christ pacifies God and purifies the consciences of men. [4.]
This is speaking blood, and it speaks better things than that of Abel. *First,*
It speaks to God in behalf of sinners; it pleads not for vengeance, as the
blood of Abel did on him who shed it, but for mercy. *Secondly,* To sinners,
in the name of God. It speaks pardon to their sins, peace to their
souls; and bespeaks their strictest obedience and highest love and thankfulness.

III. The apostle, having thus enlarged upon the argument to perseverance taken from the heavenly nature of the gospel church state, closes the
chapter by improving the argument in a manner suitable to the weight of
it (*v.* 25, &c.): *See then that you refuse not him that speaketh*—that speaketh
by his blood; and not only speaketh after another manner than the blood
of Abel spoke from the ground, but than God spoke by the angels, and by
Moses spoke on mount Sinai; then he spoke on earth, now he speaks from
heaven. Here observe,

1. When God speaks to men in the most excellent manner he justly expects from them the most strict attention and regard. Now it is in the gospel
that God speaks to men in the most excellent manner. For, (1.) He now
speaks from a higher and more glorious seat and throne, not from mount
Sinai, which was on this earth, but from heaven. (2.) He speaks now
more immediately by his inspired word and by his Spirit, which are his
witnesses. He speaks not now any new thing to men, but by his Spirit
speaks the same word home to the conscience. (3.) He speaks now more
powerfully and effectually. Then indeed his voice shook the earth, but
now, by introducing the gospel state, he hath shaken not only the earth,
but the heavens,—not only shaken the hills and mountains, or the spirits
of men, or the civil state of the land of Canaan, to make room for his
people,—not only shaken the world, as he then did, but he hath shaken
the church, that is, the Jewish nation, and shaken them in their church-
state, which was in Old Testament times a heaven upon earth; this their
heavenly spiritual state he hath now shaken. It is by the gospel from
heaven that God shook to pieces the civil and ecclesiastical state of the
Jewish nation, and introduced a new state of the church, that cannot be

removed, shall never be changed for any other on earth, but shall remain till it be made perfect in heaven.

2. When God speaks to men in the most excellent manner, the guilt of those who refuse him is the greater, and their punishment will be more unavoidable and intolerable ; there is no escaping, no bearing it, *v.* 25. The different manner of God's dealing with men under the gospel, in a way of grace, assures us that he will deal with the despisers of the gospel after a different manner than he does with other men, in a way of judgment. The glory of the gospel, which should greatly recommend it to our regard, appears in these three things :—(1.) It was by the sound of the gospel trumpet that the former dispensation and state of the church of God were shaken and removed ; and shall we despise that voice of God that pulled down a church and state of so long standing and of God's own building ? (2.) It was by the sound of the gospel trumpet that a new kingdom was erected for God in the world, which can never be so shaken as to be removed. This was a change made once for all ; no other change shall take place *till time shall be no more.* We have now *received a kingdom that cannot be moved,* shall never be removed, never give way to any new dispensation. The canon of scripture is now perfected, *the Spirit of prophecy has ceased,* the mystery of God is finished, he has put his last hand to it. The gospel church may be made more large, more prosperous, more purified from contracted pollution, but it shall never be altered for another dispensation ; those who perish under the gospel perish without remedy. And hence the apostle justly concludes, [1.] How necessary it is for us to obtain *grace from God, to serve him acceptably :* if we be not accepted of God under this dispensation, we shall never be accepted at all ; and we lose all our labour in religion if we be not accepted of God. [2.] We cannot worship God acceptably, unless we worship him with *godly reverence and fear.* As faith, so holy fear, is necessary to acceptable worship. [3.] It is only the grace of God that enables us to worship God in a right manner : nature cannot come up to it ; it can produce neither that precious faith nor that holy fear that is necessary to acceptable worship. [4.] God is the same just and righteous God under the gospel that he appeared to be under the law. Though he be our God in Christ, and now deals with us in a more kind and gracious way, yet he is in himself a consuming fire ; that is, a God of strict justice, who will avenge himself on all the despisers of his grace and upon all apostates. Under the gospel, the justice of God is displayed in a more awful manner, though not in so sensible a manner as under the law ; for here we behold divine justice seizing upon the Lord Jesus Christ, and making him a propitiatory sacrifice, his soul and body an offering for sin, which is a display of justice far beyond what was seen and heard on mount Sinai when the law was given.

CHAPTER XIII

The apostle, having treated largely of Christ, and faith, and free grace, and gospel
privileges, and warned the Hebrews against apostasy, now, in the close of all, recommends several excellent duties to them, as the proper fruits of faith (ver. 1-17); he then
bespeaks their prayers for him, and offers up his prayers to God for them, gives them
some hope of seeing himself and Timothy, and ends with the general salutation and
benediction ver. 18, to the end.

LET brotherly love continue. ² Be not forgetful to entertain
[show love unto] strangers : for thereby some have entertained angels unawares. ³ Remember them that are in bonds,
as bound with them ; *and* them which suffer adversity, as being
yourselves also in the body. ⁴ Marriage *is* honourable in all
[*Let* marriage *be* had in honour among all], and the bed undefiled:
but whoremongers and adulterers God will judge. ⁵ *Let your*
conversation *be* without covetousness [Be ye free from the
love of money] : *and be* content with such things as ye have :
for he hath said, I will never leave [in no wise fail] thee, nor
forsake thee. ⁶ So that we may boldly say, The Lord *is* my
helper, and I will not fear what man shall do unto me. ⁷ Remember them which have the rule over you, who have spoken
unto you the word of God : whose faith follow, considering the
end of *their* conversation [and considering the issue of their
life, imitate their faith] : ⁸ Jesus Christ the [is the] same
yesterday, and to day, and for ever. ⁹ Be not carried about with
divers and strange doctrines. For *it is* a good thing that the
heart be established with grace ; not with meats, which have
not profited them that have been occupied therein. ¹⁰ We have
an altar, whereof they have no right to eat which serve the
tabernacle. ¹¹ For the bodies of those beasts, whose blood is
brought into the sanctuary by the high priest for sin, are burned
without the camp. ¹² Wherefore Jesus also, that he might
sanctify the people with his own blood, suffered without the gate.
¹³ Let us go forth therefore unto him without the camp, bearing
his reproach. ¹⁴ For here have we no continuing city, but we
seek one to come. ¹⁵ By him therefore let us offer the sacrifice
of praise to God continually, that is, the fruit of *our* lips giving
thanks [of lips which make confession] to his name. ¹⁶ But
to do good and to communicate forget not : for with such sacrifices
God is well pleased. ¹⁷ Obey them that have the rule over you,
and submit yourselves : for they watch for your souls, as they
that must give account, that they may do it with joy, and not
with grief : for that *is* unprofitable for you.

The design of Christ in giving himself for us is that he may purchase *to himself a peculiar people, zealous of good works.* Now the apostle calls the believing Hebrews to the performance of many excellent duties, in which it becomes Christians to excel.

I. To brotherly love (*v.* 1), by which he does not only mean a general affection to all men, as our brethren by nature, all made of the same blood, nor that more limited affection which is due to those who are of the same immediate parents, but that special and spiritual affection which ought to exist among the children of God. 1. It is here supposed that the Hebrews had this love one for another. Though, at this time, that nation was miserably divided and distracted among themselves, both about matters of religion and the civil state, yet there was true brotherly love left among those of them who believed on Christ ; and this appeared in a very eminent manner presently after the shedding forth of the Holy Ghost, when they had all things common, and sold their possessions to make a general fund of subsistence to their brethren. The spirit of Christianity is a spirit of love. Faith works by love. The true religion is the strongest bond of friendship ; if it be not so, it has its name for nothing. 2. This brotherly love was in danger of being lost, and that in a time of persecution, when it would be most necessary ; it was in danger of being lost by those disputes that were among them concerning the respect they ought still to have to the ceremonies of the Mosaic law. Disputes about religion too often produce a decay of Christian affection ; but this must be guarded against, and all proper means used to preserve brotherly love. Christians should always love and live as brethren, and the more they grow in devout affection to God their heavenly Father the more they will grow in love to one another for his sake.

II. To hospitality : *Be not forgetful to entertain strangers for his sake, v.* 2. We must add to brotherly kindness charity. Here observe, 1. The duty required—*to entertain strangers,* both those that are strangers to the commonwealth of Israel, and strangers to our persons, especially those who know themselves to be strangers here and are seeking another country, which is the case of the people of God, and was so at this time : the believing Jews were in a desperate and distressed condition. But he seems to speak of strangers as such ; though we know not who they are, nor whence they come, yet, seeing they are without any certain dwelling place, we should allow them room in our hearts and in our houses, as we have opportunity and ability. 2. The motive : *Thereby some have entertained angels unawares ;* so Abraham did (Gen. xviii.), and Lot (Gen. xix.), and one of those that Abraham entertained was the son of God ; and, though we cannot suppose this will ever be our case, yet what we do to strangers, in obedience to him, he will reckon and reward as done to himself. Matt. xxv. 35, *I was a stranger, and you took me in.* God has often bestowed honours and favours upon his hospitable servants, beyond all their thoughts, *unawares.*

III. To Christian sympathy : *Remember those that are in bonds, v.* 3. Here observe,

1. The duty—to *remember those that are in bonds* and in *adversity.* (1.) God often orders it so that while some Christians and churches are in adversity others enjoy peace and liberty. All are not called at the same time to resist unto blood. (2.) Those that are themselves at liberty must sympa-thise with those that are in bonds and adversity, as if they were bound with them in the same chain : they must feel the sufferings of their brethren.

2. The reason of the duty : *As being yourselves in the body;* not only in'the body natural, and so liable to the like sufferings, and you should sympathise with them now that others may sympathise with you when your time of trial comes ; but in the same mystical body, under the same head, *and if one member suffer all the rest suffer with it,* 1 Cor. xii. 26. It would be unnatural in Christians not to bear each other's burdens.

IV. To purity and chasity, *v.* 4. Here you have, 1. A recommendation of God's ordinance of marriage, that it *is honourable in all,* and ought to be so esteemed by all, and not denied to those to whom God has not denied it. It is honourable, for God instituted it for man in paradise, knowing it was not good for him to be alone. He married and blessed the first couple, the first parents of mankind, to direct all to look unto God in that great concern, and to marry in the Lord. Christ honoured marriage with his presence and first miracle. It is honourable as a means to prevent impurity and a defiled bed. It is *honourable* and happy, when persons come together pure and chaste, and preserve the marriage bed undefiled, not only from unlawful but inordinate affections. 2. A dreadful but just censure of impurity and lewdness : *Whoremongers and adulterers God will judge.* (1.) God knows who are guilty of such sins, no darkness can hide them from him. (2.) He will call such sins by their proper names, not by the names of love and gallantry, but of whoredom and adultery, whoredom in the single state and adultery in the married state. (3.) He will bring them into judgment, he will judge them, either by their own consciences here, and *set their sins in order before them* for their deep humiliation (and conscience, when awakened, will be very severe upon such sinners), or he will set them at his tribunal at death, and in the last day ; he will convict them, condemn them, and cast them out for ever, if they die under the guilt of this sin.

V. To Christian contentment, *v.* 5, 6. Here observe, 1. The sin that is contrary to this grace and duty—*covetousness,* an over eager desire of the wealth of this world, envying those who have more than we. This sin we must allow no place in our conversation ; for, though it be a secret lust lurking in the heart, if it be not subdued it will enter into our conversation, and discover itself in our manner of speaking and acting. We must take care not only to keep this sin down, but to root it out of our souls. 2. The duty and grace that is contrary to covetousness—being satisfied and pleased *with such things as we have;* present things, for past things cannot be recalled, and future things are only in the hand of God. What God gives us from day to day we must be content with, though it fall short of what we have enjoyed heretofore, and though it do not come up to our expectations for the future. We must be content with our present lot. We must bring our minds to our present condition, and this is the sure way to contentment ; and those who cannot do it would not be contented though God should raise their condition to their minds, for the mind would rise with the condition. Haman was the great court-favourite, and yet not contented —Ahab on the throne, and yet not contented—Adam in paradise, and yet not contented ; yea, the angels in heaven, and yet not contented ; but Paul, though abased and empty, had *learned in* every *state, in* any *state, therewith to be content.* 3. What reason Christians have to be contented with their lot. (1.) *God hath said, I will never leave thee, nor forsake thee, v.* 5, 6. This was said to Joshua (*ch.* i 5), but belongs to all the faithful servants of God. Old-Testament promises may be applied to New-Testament saints. This promise contains the sum and substance of all the promises. *I will never*, no, *never leave thee, nor* ever *forsake thee.* Here are no fewer than five negatives heaped together, to confirm the promise ; the true believer shall have the gracious presence of God with him in life, at death, and for ever. (2.) From this comprehensive promise they may assure themselves of help from God : *So that we may boldly say, The Lord is my helper ; I will not fear what man shall do unto me, v.* 6. Men can do nothing against God, and God can make all that men do against his people to turn to their good.

VI. To the duty Christians owe to their ministers, and that both to those that are dead and to those that are yet alive.

1. To those that are dead : *Remember those that have had the rule over you, v.* 7. Here observe,

(1.) The description given of them. They were such as had the rule over them, and had spoken to them the word of God ; their guides and governors, who had spoken to them the word of God. Here is the dignity to which they were advanced—to be rulers and leaders of the people, not according to their own will, but the will and word of God ; and this character they filled up with suitable duty : they did not rule at a distance, and rule by others, but they ruled by personal presence and instruction according to the word of God.

(2.) The duties owing to them, even when they were dead.

[1.] "*Remember them*—their preaching, their praying, their private counsel, their example."

[2.] "*Follow* their *faith ;* be steadfast in the profession of the faith they preached to you, and labour after the grace of faith by which they lived and died so well. *Consider the end of their conversation,* how quickly, how comfortably, how joyfully, they finished their course ! " Now this duty of following the same true faith in which they had been instructed the apostle enlarges much upon, and presses them earnestly to it, not only from the remembrance of their faithful, deceased guides, but from several other motives.

First, From the immutability and eternity of the Lord Jesus Christ. Though their ministers were some dead, others dying, yet the great head and high priest of the church, *the bishop of their souls,* ever lives, and is ever the same ; and they should be steadfast and immovable, in imitation of Christ, and should remember that Christ ever lives to observe and reward their faithful adherence to his truths, and to observe and punish their sinful departure from him. Christ is the same in the Old-Testament day, in the gospel day, and will be so to his people for ever.

Secondly, From the nature and tendency of those erroneous doctrines that they were in danger of falling in with.

a. They were divers and various (*v.* 9), different from what they had received from their former faithful teachers, and inconsistent with themselves.

b. They were strange doctrines : such as the gospel church was unacquainted with, foreign to the gospel.

c. They were of an unsettling, distracting nature, like the wind by which the ship is tossed, and in danger of being driven from its anchor, carried away, and split upon the rocks. They were quite contrary to that grace of God which fixes and establishes the heart, which is an excellent thing. These strange doctrines keep the heart always fluctuating and unsettled.

d. They were mean and low as to their subject. They were about external, little, perishing things, such as *meats and drinks,* &c.

e. They were unprofitable. Those who were most taken with them, and employed about them, got no real good by them to their own souls. They did not make them more holy, nor more humble, nor more thankful, nor more heavenly.

f. They would exclude those who embraced them from the privileges of the Christian altar (*v.* 10): *We have an altar.* This is an argument of great weight, and therefore the apostle insists the longer upon it. Observe,

(*a.*) The Christian church has its altar. It was objected against the primitive Christians that their assemblies were destitute of an altar; but this was not true. *We have an altar*, not a material altar, but a personal one, and that is Christ; he is both our altar, and our sacrifice; he sanctifies the gift. The altars under the law were types of Christ; the brazen altar of the sacrifice, the golden altar of his intercession.

(*b.*) This altar furnishes out a feast for true believers, a feast upon the sacrifice, a *feast of fat things*, spiritual strength and growth, and holy delight and pleasure. The Lord's table is not our altar, but it is furnished with provision from the altar. *Christ our passover is sacrificed for us* (1 Cor. v. 7), and it follows, *therefore let us keep the feast.* The Lord's supper is the feast of the gospel passover.

(*c.*) Those who adhere to the tabernacle or the Levitical dispensation, or return to it again, exclude themselves from the privileges of this altar, from the benefits purchased by Christ. If they serve the tabernacle, they are resolved to subject themselves to antiquated rites and ceremonies, to renounce their right to the Christian altar; and this part of the argument he first proves and then improves.

[*a.*] He proves that this servile adherence to the Jewish state is a bar to the privileges of the gospel altar: and he argues thus:—Under the Jewish law, no part of the sin-offering was to be eaten, but all must be burnt without the camp while they dwelt in tabernacles, and without the gates when they dwelt in cities: now, if they will still be subject to that law, they cannot eat at the gospel-altar; for that which is eaten there is furnished from Christ, who is the great sin-offering. Not that it is the very sin-offering itself, as the papists affirm; for then it was not to be eaten, but burnt; but the gospel feast is the fruit and procurement of the sacrifice, which those have no right to who do not acknowledge the sacrifice itself. And that it might appear that Christ was really the antitype of the sin-offering, and, as such, might sanctify or cleanse his people with his own blood, he conformed himself to the type, in suffering without the gate. This was a striking specimen of his humiliation, as if he had not been fit either for sacred or civil society! And this shows how sin, which was the meritorious cause of the sufferings of Christ, is a forfeiture of all sacred and civil rights, and the sinner a common plague and nuisance to all society, if God should be strict to mark iniquity. Having thus shown that adherence to the Levitical law would, even according to its own rules, debar men from the Christian altar, he proceeds,

[*b.*] To improve this argument (*v.* 13–15) in suitable advices. *First*, *Let us go forth therefore unto him without the camp;* go forth from the ceremonial law, from sin, from the world, from ourselves, our very bodies, when he calls us. *Secondly*, Let us be willing to *bear his reproach*, be willing to be accounted the offscouring of all things, not worthy to live, not worthy to die a common death. This was his reproach, and we must submit to it; and we have the more reason because, whether we go forth

from this world to Christ or no, we must necessarily go forth in a little
time by death ; for *here we have no continuing city.* Sin, sinners, death,
will not suffer us to continue long here ; and therefore we should go forth
now by faith, and seek in Christ the rest and settlement which this world
cannot afford us, *v.* 14. *Thirdly,* Let us make a right use of this altar ;
not only partake of the privileges of it, but discharge the duties of the
altar, as those whom Christ has made priests to attend on this altar.   Let
us bring our sacrifices to this altar, and to this our high priest, and offer
them up by him, *v.* 15, 16. Now what are the sacrifices which we must
bring and offer on this altar, even Christ? Not any expiatory sacrifices ;
there is no need of them. Christ has offered the great *sacrifice of atonement,* ours are only the sacrifices of acknowledgment ; and they are,
1. The sacrifice of praise to God, which we should offer up to God continually.   In this are included all adoration and prayer, as well as thanksgiving ; this is *the fruit of our lips ;* we must speak forth the praises of
God from unfeigned lips ; and this must be offered only to God, not to
angels, nor saints, nor any creature, but to the name of God alone ; and
it must be by Christ, in a dependence upon his meritorious satisfaction
and intercession.   2. The sacrifice of alms-deeds, and Christian charity :
*To do good, and to communicate, forget not ; for with such sacrifices God is
well pleased, v.* 16.   We must, according to our power, *communicate* to the
necessities of the souls and bodies of men ; not contenting ourselves to
offer the sacrifice of our lips, mere words, but the sacrifice of good deeds ;
and these we must lay down upon this altar, not depending upon the
merit of our good deeds, but of our great high priest ; and with such sacrifices as these, adoration and alms thus offered up, God is well pleased ; he
will accept the offering with pleasure, and will accept and bless the offerers
through Christ.

2. Having thus told us the duty Christians owe to their deceased
ministers, which principally consists in following their faith and not
departing from it, the apostle tells us what is the duty that people owe to
their living ministers (*v.* 17) and the reasons of that duty : (1.) The duty—
to obey them, and submit themselves to them.   It is not an implicit
obedience, or absolute submission, that is here required, but only so far as
is agreeable to the mind and will of God revealed in his word ; and yet it
is truly obedience and submission, and that not only to God, but to the
authority of the ministerial office, which is of God as certainly, in all things
belonging to that office, as the authority of parents or of civil magistrates
in the things within their sphere.   Christians must submit to be instructed
by their ministers, and not think themselves too wise, too good, or too
great, to learn from them ; and, when they find that ministerial instructions
are agreeable to the written word, they must obey them. (2.) The motives
to this duty. [1.] They have the rule over the people ; their office, though
not magisterial, yet is truly authoritative. They have no authority to lord
it over the people, but to lead them in the ways of God, by informing and
instructing them, explaining the word of God to them, and applying it to
their several cases.   They are not to make laws of their own, but to
interpret the laws of God ; nor is their interpretation to be immediately
received without examination, but the people must search the scriptures,
and so far as the instructions of their minister are according to that rule
they ought to receive them, *not as the word of men, but, as they are indeed,
the word of God, that works effectually in those that believe.* [2.] They watch
for the souls of the people, not to ensnare them, but to save them ; to gain

them, not to themselves, but to Christ; to build them up in knowledge, faith, and holiness. They are to watch against every thing that may be hurtful to the souls of men, and to give them warning of dangerous errors, of the devices of Satan, of approaching judgments; they are to watch for all opportunities of helping the souls of men forward in the way to heaven. [3.] They must give an account how they have discharged their duty, and what has become of the souls committed to their trust, whether any have been lost through their neglect, and whether any of them have been brought in and built up under their ministry. [4.] They would be glad to give a good account of themselves and their hearers. If they can then give in an account of their own fidelity and success, it will be a joyful day to them: those souls that have been converted and confirmed under their ministry *will be their joy, and their crown, in the day of the Lord Jesus.* [5.] If they give up their account with grief, it will be the people's loss as well as theirs. It is the interest of hearers that the account their ministers give of them may be with joy, and not with grief. If faithful ministers be not successful, the grief will be theirs, but the loss will be the people's. Faithful ministers have delivered their own souls, but a fruitless and faithless people's blood and ruin will be upon their own heads.

¹⁸ Pray for us: for we trust [are persuaded] we have a good conscience, in all things willing to live honestly. ¹⁹ But I beseech *you* the rather [more exceedingly] to do this, that I may be restored to you the sooner. ²⁰ Now the God of peace, that brought again from the dead our Lord Jesus, that great Shepherd of the sheep, through the blood of the everlasting covenant, ²¹ Make you perfect in every good work to do his will, working in you that which is well-pleasing in his sight, through Jesus Christ; to whom *be* glory for ever and ever. Amen. ²² And I beseech you, brethren, suffer the word of exhortation: for I have written a letter unto you in few words. ²³ Know ye that *our* brother Timothy is set at liberty; with whom, if he come shortly, I will see you. ²⁴ Salute all them that have the rule over you, and all the saints. They of Italy salute you. ²⁵ Grace *be* with you all. Amen.

Here, I. The apostle recommends himself, and his fellow-sufferers, to the prayers of the Hebrew believers (*v.* 18): "*Pray for us;* for me and Timothy" (mentioned *v.* 23), "and for all those of us who labour in the ministry of the gospel."

1. This is one part of the duty which people owe to their ministers. Ministers need the prayers of the people; and the more earnestly the people pray for their ministers the more benefit they may expect to reap from their ministry. They should pray that God would teach those who are to teach them, that he would make them vigilant, and wise, and zealous, and successful—that he would assist them in all their labours, support them under all their burdens, and strengthen them under all their temptations.

2. There are good reasons why people should pray for their ministers; he mentions two:—

(1.) *We trust we have a good conscience*, &c., *v.* 18. Many of the Jews had a bad opinion of Paul, because he, being a Hebrew of the Hebrews, had cast off the Levitical law and preached up Christ: now he here modestly asserts his own integrity: *We trust we have a good conscience, in all things willing to live honestly. We trust !* he might have said, *We know ;* but he chose to speak in a humble style, to teach us all not to be too confident of ourselves, but to maintain a godly jealousy over our own hearts. "We trust we have a *good conscience*, an enlightened and well-informed conscience, a clean and pure conscience, a tender and faithful conscience, a conscience testifying for us, not against us: a good conscience *in all things*, in the duties both of the first and second table, towards God and towards men, and especially in all things pertaining to our ministry ; we would act honestly and sincerely in all things." Observe, [1.] A good conscience has a respect to all God's commands and all our duty. [2.] Those who have this good conscience, yet need the prayers of others. [3.] Conscientious ministers are public blessings, and deserve the prayers of the people.

(2.) Another reason why he desires their prayers is that he hoped thereby to be the sooner restored to them (*v.* 19), intimating that he had been formerly among them,—that, now he was absent from them, he had a great desire and real intention to come again to them,—and that the best way to facilitate his return to them, and to make it a mercy to him and them, was to make it a matter of their prayer. When ministers come to a people as a return of prayer, they come with greater satisfaction to themselves and success to the people. We should fetch in all our mercies by prayer.

II. He offers up his prayers to God for them, being willing to do for them as he desired they should do for him : *Now the God of peace*, &c., *v.* 20. In this excellent prayer observe, 1. The title given to God—*the God of peace*, who has found out a way for peace and reconciliation between himself and sinners, and who loves peace on earth and especially in his churches. 2. The great work ascribed to him : *He hath brought again from the dead our Lord Jesus*, &c. Jesus raised himself by his own power ; and yet the Father was concerned in it, attesting thereby that justice was satisfied and the law fulfilled. He rose again for our justification ; and that divine power by which he was raised is able to do every thing for us that we stand in need of. 3. The titles given to Christ—our Lord Jesus, our sovereign, our Saviour, and the great shepherd of the sheep, promised in Isa. xl. 11, declared by himself to be so, John x. 14, 15. Ministers are under-shepherds, Christ is the great shepherd. This denotes his interest in his people. They are the flock of his pasture, and his care and concern are for them. He feeds them, and leads them, and watches over them. 4. The way and method in which God is reconciled, and Christ raised from the dead : *Through the blood of the everlasting covenant.* The blood of Christ satisfied divine justice, and so procured Christ's release from the prison of the grave, as having paid our debt, according to an eternal covenant or agreement between the Father and the Son ; and this blood is the sanction and seal of an everlasting covenant between God and his people. 5. The mercy prayed for : *Make you perfect in every good work*, &c., *v.* 21. Observe, (1.) The perfection of the saints in every good work is the great thing desired by them and for them, that they may here have a perfection of integrity, a clear mind, a clean heart, lively affections, regular and resolved wills, and suitable strength for every good work to which they are called now, and at length a perfection of degrees to fit them for the employment and felicity of heaven. (2.) The way in which God makes his people perfect ; it is by working in them always what is pleasing in his sight, and that *through Jesus Christ, to whom be glory for ever.* Observe, [1.] There is no good thing wrought in us but it is the work of God ; he works in us, before we are fit for any good work. [2.] No good thing is wrought in us by God, but through Jesus Christ, for his sake and by his Spirit. And therefore, [3.] Eternal glory is due to him, who is the cause of all the good principles wrought in us and all the good works done by us. To this every one should say, *Amen.*

III. He gives the Hebrews an account of Timothy's liberty and his hopes of seeing them with him in a little time, *v.* 23. It seems, Timothy had been a prisoner, doubtless for the gospel, but now he was set at liberty. The imprisonment of faithful ministers is an honour to them, and their enlargement is matter of joy to the people. He was pleased with the hopes of not only seeing Timothy, but seeing the Hebrews with him. Opportunities of writing to the churches of Christ are desired by the faithful ministers of Christ, and pleasant to them.

IV. Having given a brief account of this his letter, and begged their attention to it (*v.* 22), he closes with salutations, and a solemn, though short benediction.

1. The salutation. (1.) From himself to them, directed to all their ministers who had rule over them, and to all the saints ; to them all, ministers and people. (2.) From the Christians in Italy to them. It is a good thing to have the law of holy love and kindness written in the hearts of Christians one towards another. Religion teaches men the truest civility and good-breeding. It is not a sour nor morose thing.

2. The solemn, though short benediction (*v.* 25) : *Grace be with you all. Amen.* Let the favour of God be towards you, and his grace continually working in you, and with you, bringing forth the fruits of holiness, as the first-fruits of glory. When the people of God have been conversing together by word or writing, it is good to part with prayer, desiring for each other the continuance of the gracious presence of God, that they may meet together again in the world of praise.

EXPOSITION OF THE GENERAL
EPISTLE OF JAMES

THE writer of this epistle was not James the son of Zebedee; for he was put to death by Herod (Acts xii.) before Christianity had gained so much ground among the Jews of the dispersion as is here implied. But it was the other James, the son of Alpheus, who was cousin-german to Christ, and one of the twelve apostles, Matt. x. 3. He is called *a pillar* (Gal. ii. 9), and this epistle of his cannot be disputed, without loosening a foundation-stone. It is called a general epistle, because (as some think) not directed to any particular person or church, but such a one as we call a circular letter. Others think it is called general, or catholic, to distinguish it from the epistles of Ignatius, Barnabas, Polycarp, and others who were noted in the primitive times, but not generally received in the church, and on that account not canonical, as this is. Eusebius tells us that this epistle was "generally read in the churches with the other catholic epistles." Hist. Eccles. page 53. Ed. Val. Anno 1678. James, our author, was called the just, for his great piety. He was an eminent example of those graces which he presses upon others. He was so exceedingly revered for his justice, temperance, and devotion, that Josephus the Jewish historian records it as one of the causes of the destruction of Jerusalem, "that St. James was martyred in it." This is mentioned in hopes of procuring the greater regard to what is penned by so holy and excellent a man. The time when this epistle was written is uncertain. The design of it is to reprove Christians for their great degeneracy both in faith and manners, and to prevent the spreading of those libertine doctrines which threatened the destruction of all practical godliness. It was also a special intention of the author of this epistle to awaken the Jewish nation to a sense of the greatness and nearness of those judgments which were coming upon them; and to support all true Christians in the way of their duty, under the calamities and persecutions they might meet with. The truths laid down are very momentous, and necessary to be maintained; and the rules for practice, as here stated, are such as ought to be observed in our times as well as in preceding ages.

CHAPTER I

After the inscription and salutation (ver. 1) Christians are taught how to conduct themselves when under the cross. Several graces and duties are recommended; and those who endure their trials and afflictions as the apostle here directs are pronounced blessed and are assured of a glorious reward, ver. 2-12. But those sins which bring sufferings, or the weaknesses and faults men are chargeable with under them, are by no means to be imputed to God, who cannot be the author of sin, but is the author of all good, ver. 13-18. All passion, and rash anger, and vile affections, ought to be suppressed. The word of God should be made our chief study: and what we hear and know of it we must take care to practise, otherwise our religion will prove but a vain thing. To this is added an account wherein pure religion consists, ver. 19-27.

JAMES, a servant of God and of the Lord Jesus Christ, to the twelve tribes which are scattered abroad [are of the Dispersion], greeting.

We have here the inscription of this epistle, which consists of three principal parts.

I. The character by which our author desires to be known: *James, a servant of God, and of the Lord Jesus Christ.* Though he was a prime-minister in Christ's kingdom, yet he styles himself only a servant. Note hence, Those who are highest in office or attainments in the church of Christ are but servants. They should not therefore act as masters, but as ministers. Further, Though James is called by the evangelist *the brother of our Lord,* yet it was his glory to serve Christ in the spirit, rather than to boast of his being akin according to the flesh. Hence let us learn to prize this title above all others in the world—*the servants of God and of Christ.* Again, it is to be observed that James professes himself *a servant of God and of the Lord Jesus Christ,* to teach us that in all services we should have an eye to the Son as well as the Father. We cannot acceptably serve the Father, unless we are also servants of the Son. God will have *all men to honour the Son as they honour the Father* (John v. 23), looking for acceptance in Christ and assistance from him, and yielding all obedience to him, thus confessing *that Jesus Christ is Lord, to the glory of God the Father.*

II. The apostle here mentions the condition of those to whom he writes: *The twelve tribes which are scattered abroad.* Some understand this of the dispersion upon the persecution of Stephen, Acts viii. But that only reached to Judea and Samaria. Others by the Jews of the dispersion understand those who were in Assyria, Babylon, Egypt, and other kingdoms into which their wars had driven them. The greatest part indeed of ten of the twelve tribes were lost in captivity; but yet some of every tribe were preserved, and they are still honoured with the ancient style of *twelve tribes.* These however were scattered and dispersed. 1. They were dispersed in mercy. Having the scriptures of the Old Testament, the providence of God so ordered it that they were scattered in several countries for the diffusing of the light of divine revelation. 2. They began now to be scattered in wrath. The Jewish nation was crumbling into parties and factions, and many were forced to leave their own country, as having now grown too hot for them. Even good people among them shared in the common calamity. 3. These Jews of the dispersion were those who had embraced the Christian faith. They were persecuted and

forced to seek for shelter in other countries, the Gentiles being kinder to
Christians than the Jews were. Note here, It is often the lot of even
God's own tribes to be scattered abroad. The gathering day is reserved for
the end of time ; when all the dispersed children of God shall be gathered
together to Christ their head. In the meantime, while God's tribes are
scattered abroad, he will send to look after them. Here is an apostle
writing to the scattered ; an epistle from God to them, when driven away
from his temple, and seemingly neglected by him. Apply here that of the
prophet Ezekiel, *Thus saith the Lord God, Although I have cast them far off
among the heathen, and although I have scattered them among the countries,
yet will I be to them as a little sanctuary in the countries where they shall come.*
Ezek. xi. 16. God has a particular care of his outcasts. *Let my outcasts
dwell with thee, Moab,* Isa. xvi. 3, 4. God's tribes may be scattered ; therefore we should not value ourselves too much on outward privileges. And,
on the other hand, we should not despond and think ourselves rejected,
under outward calamities, because God remembers and sends comforts to
his scattered people.

III. James here shows the respect he had even for the dispersed :
greeting, saluting them, wishing peace and salvation to them. True
Christians should not be the less valued for their hardships. It was the
desire of this apostle's heart that those who were scattered might be comforted—that they might do well and fare well, and be enabled to rejoice
even in their distresses. God's people have reason to rejoice in all places,
and at all times ; as will abundantly appear from what follows.

2 My brethren, count it all joy when ye fall into divers temptations ; 3 Knowing *this,* that the trying [proof] of your faith
worketh patience. 4 But let patience have *her* perfect work,
that ye may be perfect and entire, wanting [lacking] nothing.
5 If any of you lack wisdom, let him ask of God, that giveth to
all *men* liberally, and upbraideth not ; and it shall be given him.
6 But let him ask in faith, nothing wavering [doubting]. For
he that wavereth [doubteth] is like a wave of the sea driven
with the wind and tossed. 7 For let not that man think that he
shall receive any thing of the Lord. 8 A double minded man
is unstable in all his ways. 9 Let the brother of low degree
rejoice in that he is exalted : 10 But the rich, in that he is made
low : because as the flower of the grass he shall pass away.
11 For the sun is no sooner risen with a burning heat, but it
withereth the grass, and the flower thereof falleth, and the grace
of the fashion of it perisheth : so also shall the rich man fade
away in his ways. 12 Blessed *is* the man that endureth temptation : for when he is tried [hath been approved], he shall receive
the crown of life, which the Lord hath promised to them that
love him.

We now come to consider the matter of this epistle. In this paragraph
we have the following things to be observed :—

I. The suffering state oi Christians in this world is represented, and that in a very instructive manner, if we attend to what is plainly and neces-sarily implied, together with what is fully expressed. 1. It is implied that troubles and afflictions may be the lot of the best Christians, even of those who have the most reason to think and hope well of themselves. Such as have a title to the greatest joy may yet endure very grievous afflictions. As good people are liable to be scattered, they must not think it strange if they meet with troubles. 2. These outward afflictions and troubles are temptations to them. The devil endeavours by sufferings and crosses to draw men to sin and to deter them from duty, or unfit them for it ; but, as our afflictions are in God's hand, they are intended for the trial and improvement of our graces. The gold is put into the furnace, that it may be purified. 3. These temptations may be numerous and various : *Divers temptations*, as the apostle speaks. Our trials may be of many and different kinds, and therefore we have need to put on the whole armour of God. We must be armed on every side, because temptations lie on all sides. 4. The trials of a good man are such as he does not create to himself, nor sinfully pull upon himself ; but they are such as he is said to fall into. And for this reason they are the better borne by him.

II. The graces and duties of a state of trial and affliction are here pointed out to us. Could we attend to these things, and grow in them as we should do, how good would it be for us to be afflicted !

1. One Christian grace to be exercised is joy : *Count it all joy, v.* 2. We must not sink into a sad and disconsolate frame of mind, which would make us faint under our trials ; but must endeavour to keep our spirits dilated and enlarged, the better to take in a true sense of our case, and with greater advantage to set ourselves to make the best of it. Philosophy may instruct men to be calm under their troubles ; but Christianity teaches them to be joyful, because such exercises proceed from love and not fury in God. In them we are conformable to Christ our head, and they become marks of our adoption. By suffering in the ways of righteousness, we are serving the interests of our Lord's kingdom among men, and edifying the body of Christ ; and our trials will brighten our graces now and our crown at last. Therefore there is reason to count it all joy when trials and diffi-culties become our lot in the way of our duty. And this is not purely a New-Testament paradox, but even in Job's time it was said *Behold, happy is the man whom God correcteth.* There is the more reason for joy in afflic-tions if we consider the other graces that are promoted by them.

2. Faith is a grace that one expression supposes and another expressly requires : *Knowing this, that the trial of your faith, v.* 3 ; and then in *v.* 6, *Let him ask in faith.* There must be a sound believing of the great truths of Christianity, and a resolute cleaving to them, in times of trial. That faith which is spoken of here as tried by afflictions consists in a belief of the power, and word, and promise of God, and in fidelity and constancy to the Lord Jesus.

3. There must be patience : *The trial of faith worketh patience.* The trying of one grace produces another ; and the more the suffering graces of a Christian are exercised the stronger they grow. *Tribulation worketh patience*, Rom. v. 3. Now to exercise Christian patience aright, we must, (1.) Let it work. It is not a stupid, but an active thing. Stoical apathy and Christian patience are very different : by the one men become, in some measure, insensible of their afflictions ; but by the other they become triumphant in and over them. Let us take care, in times of trial, that patience and not passion, be set at work in us ; whatever is said or done.

let patience have the saying and doing of it : let us not allow the indulging of our passions to hinder the operation and noble effects of patience ; let us give it leave to work, and it will work wonders in a time of trouble. (2.) We must let it have its perfect work. Do nothing to limit it nor to weaken it ; but let it have its full scope ; if one affliction come upon the heels of another, and a train of them are drawn upon us, yet let patience go on till its work is perfected. When we bear all that God appoints, and as long as he appoints, and with a humble obedient eye to him, and when we not only bear troubles, but rejoice in them, then patience hath its perfect work. (3.) When the work of patience is complete, then the Christian is entire, and nothing will be wanting : it will furn sh us with all that is necessary for our Christian race and warfare, and will enable us to persevere to the end, and then its work will be ended, and crowned with glory. After we have abounded in other graces, we *have need of patience*, Heb. x. 36. But *let patience have its perfect work, and we shall be perfect and entire, wanting nothing.*

4. Prayer is a duty recommended also to suffering Christians ; and here the apostle shows, (1.) What we ought more especially to pray for—wisdom : *If any lack wisdom, let him ask of God.* We should not pray so much for the removal of an affliction as for wisdom to make a right use of it. And who is there that does not want wisdom under any great trials or exercises to guide him in his judging of things, in the government of his own spirit and temper, and in the management of his affairs ? To be wise in trying times is a special gift of God, and to him we must seek for it. (2.) In what way this is to be obtained—upon our petitioning or asking for it. Let the foolish become beggars at the throne of grace, and they are in a fair way to be wise. It is not said, "Let such ask of man," no, not of any man, but, "Let him ask of God," who made him, and gave him his understanding and reasonable powers at first, of him in whom are all the treasures of wisdom and knowledge. Let us confess our want of wisdom to God and daily ask it of him. (3.) We have the greatest encouragement to do this : *he giveth to all men liberally, and upbraideth not.* Yea, it is expressly promised that *it shall be given*, v. 5. Here is something in answer to every discouraging turn of the mind, when we go to God, under a sense of our own weakness and folly, to ask for wisdom. He to whom we are sent, we are sure, has it to give : and he is of a giving disposition, inclined to bestow this upon those who ask. Nor is there any fear of his favours being limited to some in this case, so as to exclude others, or any humble petitioning soul ; for *he gives to all men.* If you should say you want a great deal of wisdom, a small portion will not serve your turn, the apostle affirms, he *gives liberally ;* and lest you should be afraid of going to him unseasonably, or being put to shame for your folly, it is added, he *upbraideth not.* Ask when you will, and as often as you will, you will meet with no upbraidings. And if, after all, any should say, "This may be the case with some, but I fear I shall not succeed so well in my seeking for wisdom as some others may," let such consider how particular and express the promise is : *It shall be given him.* Justly then must fools perish in their foolishness, if wisdom may be had for asking, and they will not pray to God for it. But, (4.) There is one thing necessary to be observed in our asking, namely, that we do it with a believing, steady mind : *Let him ask in faith, nothing wavering*, v. 6. The promise above is very sure, taking this proviso along with us ; wisdom shall be given to those who ask it of God, provided they believe that God is able to make the simple wise, and

is faithful to make good his word to those who apply to him. This was the condition Christ insisted on, in treating with those who came to him for healing : *Believest thou that I am able to do this?* There must be *no wavering*, no staggering at the promise of God through unbelief, or through a sense of any disadvantages that lie on our own part. Here therefore we see,

5. That oneness, and sincerity of intention, and a steadiness of mind, constitute another duty required under affliction: *He that wavereth is like a wave of the sea, driven with the wind, and tossed.* To be sometimes lifted up by faith, and then thrown down again by distrust—to mount sometimes towards the heavens, with an intention to secure glory, and honour, and immortality, and then to sink again in seeking the ease of the body, or the enjoyments of this world—this is very fitly and elegantly compared to a wave of the sea, that rises and falls, swells and sinks, just as the wind tosses it higher or lower, that way or this. A mind that has but one single and prevailing regard to its spiritual and eternal interest, and that keeps steady in its purposes for God, will grow wise by afflictions, will continue fervent in its devotions, and will be superior to all trials and oppositions. Now, for the cure of a wavering spirit and a weak faith, the apostle shows the ill effects of these, (1.) In that the success of prayer is spoiled hereby : *Let not that man think that he shall receive any thing of the Lord, v. 7.* Such a distrustful, shifting, unsettled person is not likely to value a favour from God as he should do, and therefore cannot expect to receive it. In asking for divine and heavenly wisdom we are never likely to prevail if we have not a heart to prize it above rubies, and the greatest things in this world. (2.) A wavering faith and spirit has a bad influence upon our conversations. *A double-minded man is unstable in all his ways, v. 8.* When our faith and spirits rise and fall with second causes, there will be great unsteadiness in all our conversation and actions. This may sometimes expose men to contempt in the world ; but it is certain that such ways cannot please God nor procure any good for us in the end. While we have but one God to trust to, we have but one God to be governed by, and this should keep us even and steady. He that is unstable as water shall not excel. Hereupon,

III. The holy humble temper of a Christian, both in advancement and debasement, is described : and both poor and rich are directed on what grounds to build their joy and comfort. *v. 9–11.* Here we may observe, 1. Those of low degree are to be looked upon as brethren : *Let the brother of low degree,* &c. Poverty does not destroy the relation among Christians. 2. Good Christians may be rich in the world, *v. 10.* Grace and wealth are not wholly inconsistent. Abraham, the father of the faithful, was rich in silver and gold. 3. Both these are allowed to rejoice. No condition of life puts us out of a capacity of rejoicing in God. If we do not rejoice in him always, it is our own fault. Those of low degree may rejoice, if they are exalted to be rich in faith and heirs of the kingdom of God (as Dr. Whitby explains this place) ; and the rich may rejoice in humbling providences, as they produce a lowly and humble disposition of mind, which is highly valuable in the sight of God. Where any are made poor for righteousness' sake, their very poverty is their exaltation. It is an honour to be dishonoured for the sake of Christ. *To you it is given to suffer,* Phil. i. 29. All who are brought low, and made lowly by grace, may rejoice in the prospect of their exaltation at the last in heaven. 4. Observe what reason rich people have, notwithstanding their riches, to be humble and low in their own eyes, because both they and their riches are passing away : *As the flower of the grass he shall pass away.* He, and his wealth with him, *v.* 11. *For the sun has no sooner risen with a burning heat than it withereth the grass.* Note hence, worldly wealth is a withering thing. Riches are too uncertain (says Mr. Baxter on this place , too inconsiderable things to make any great or just alteration in our minds. As a flower fades before the heat of the scorching sun, *so shall the rich man fade away in his ways.* His projects, counsels, and managements for this world, are called his *ways ,* in these he shall *fade away.* For this reason let him that is rich rejoice, not so much in the providence of God, that makes him rich, as in the grace of God, that makes and keeps him humble ; and in those trials and exercises that teach him to seek his felicity in and from God, and not from these perishing enjoyments.

IV. A blessing is pronounced on those who endure their exercises and trials, as here directed : *Blessed is the man that endureth temptation, v.* 12. Observe, 1. It is not the man who suffers only that is blessed, but he who endures, who with patience and constancy goes through all difficulties in the way of his duty. 2. Afflictions cannot make us miserable, if it be not our own fault. A blessing may arise from them, and we may be blessed in them. They are so far from taking away a good man's felicity that they really increase it. 3. Sufferings and temptations are the way to eternal blessedness : *When he is tried, he shall receive the crown of life,* δόκιμος γενόμενος—*when he is approved,* when his graces are found to be true and of the highest worth (so metals are tried as to their excellency by the fire), and when his integrity is manifested, and all is approved of the great Judge. Note hence, To be approved of God is the great aim of a Christian in all his trials ; and it will be his blessedness at last, when he shall receive the crown of life. The tried Christian shall be a crowned one : and the crown he shall wear will be a crown of life. It will be life and bliss to him, and will last for ever. We only bear the cross for a while, but we shall wear the crown to eternity. 4. This blessedness, involved in a crown of life, is a promised thing to the righteous sufferer. It is therefore what we may most surely depend upon ; for, when heaven and earth shall pass away, this word of God shall not fail of being fulfilled. But withal let us take notice that our future reward comes, not as a debt, but by a gracious promise. 5. Our enduring temptations must be from a principle of love to God and to our Lord Jesus Christ, otherwise we are not interested in this promise : *The Lord hath promised to those that love him.* Paul supposes that a man may for some point of religion even give *his body to be burnt,* and yet not be pleasing to God, nor regarded by him, because of his want of charity, or a prevailing sincere love to God and man, 1 Cor. xiii. 3. 6. The crown of life is promised not only to great and eminent saints, but to all those who have the love of God reigning in their hearts. Every soul that truly loves God shall have its trials in this world fully recompensed in that world above *where love is made perfect.*

13 Let no man say when he is tempted, I am tempted of God : for God cannot be tempted with evil, neither tempteth he any man : 14 But every man is tempted, when he is drawn away of his own lust, and enticed. 15 Then when lust hath conceived, it bringeth forth [**beareth**] sin : and sin, when it is finished, bringeth forth death. 16 Do not err, my beloved brethren. 17 Every good gift and every perfect gift is from above, and

cometh down from the Father of lights, with whom is no variableness, neither shadow of turning [that is cast by turning]. ¹⁸ Of his own will begat he us with the word of truth, that we should be a kind of first-fruits of his creatures.

I. We are here taught that God is not the author of any man's sin. Whoever they are who raise persecutions against men, and whatever injustice and sin they may be guilty of in proceeding against them, God is not to be charged with it. And, whatever sins good men may themselves be provoked to by their exercises and afflictions, God is not the cause of them. It seems to be here supposed that some professors might fall in the hour of temptation, that the rod resting upon them might carry some into ill courses, and make them put forth their hands unto iniquity. But though this should be the case, and though such delinquents should attempt to lay their fault on God, yet the blame of their misconduct must lie entirely upon themselves. For, 1. There is nothing in the nature of God that they can lay the blame upon: *Let no man say, when he is tempted to take any evil course, or do any evil thing, I am tempted of God; for God cannot be tempted with evil.* All moral evil is owing to some disorder in the being that is chargeable with it, to a want of wisdom, or of power, or of decorum and purity in the will. But who can impeach the holy God with the want of these, which are his very essence? No exigence of affairs can ever tempt him to dishonour or deny himself, and therefore he cannot be tempted with evil. 2. There is nothing in the providential dispensations of God that the blame of any man's sin can be laid upon (*v.* 13): *Neither tempteth he any man.* As God cannot be tempted with evil himself, so neither can he be a tempter of others. He cannot be a promoter of what is repugnant to his nature. The carnal mind is willing to charge its own sins on God. There is something hereditary in this. Our first father Adam tells God, *The woman thou gavest me* tempted me, thereby, in effect, throwing the blame upon God, for giving him the tempter. Let no man speak thus. It is very bad to sin; but it is much worse, when we have done amiss. to charge it upon God, and say it was owing to him. Those who lay the blame of their sins either upon their constitution or upon their condition in the world, or who pretend they are under a fatal necessity of sinning, wrong God, as if he were the author of sin. Afflictions, as sent by God, are designed to draw out our graces, but not our corruptions.

II. We are taught where the true cause of evil lies, and where the blame ought to be laid (*v.* 14): *Every man is tempted* (in an ill sense) *when he is drawn away of his own lust, and enticed.* In other scriptures the devil is called *the tempter,* and other things may sometimes concur to tempt us; but neither the devil nor any other person or thing is to be blamed so as to excuse ourselves; for the true original of evil and temptation is in our own hearts. The combustible matter is in us, though the flame may be blown up by some outward causes. And therefore, *if thou scornest, thou alone shalt bear it,* Prov. ix. 12. Observe here, 1. The method of sin in its proceeding. First it draws away, then entices. As holiness consists of two parts—forsaking that which is evil and cleaving to that which is good, so these two things, reversed, are the two parts of sin. The heart is carried from that which is good, and enticed to cleave to that which is evil. It is first by corrupt inclinations, or lusting after and coveting some sensual or worldly thing, estranged from the life of God, and then by degrees fixed

in a course of sin. 2. We may observe hence the power and policy of sin.
The word here rendered *drawn away* signifies a being forcibly haled or
compelled. The word translated *enticed* signifies being wheedled and
beguiled by allurements and deceitful representations of things, ἐξελκόμενος
καὶ δελεαζόμενος. There is a great deal of violence done to conscience and
to the mind by the power of corruption : and there is a great deal of
cunning and deceit and flattery in sin to gain us to its interests. The
force and power of sin could never prevail, were it not for cunning and guile.
Sinners who perish are wheedled and flattered to their own destruction.
And this will justify God for ever in their damnation, that they destroyed
themselves. Their sin lies at their own door, and therefore their blood
will lie upon their own heads. 3. The success of corruption in the heart
(*v.* 15) : *Then, when lust hath conceived, it bringeth forth sin ;* that is, sin
being allowed to excite desires in us, it will soon ripen those desires into
consent, and then it is said to have *conceived.* The sin truly exists, though
it be but in embryo. And, when it has grown to its full size in the mind,
it is then brought forth in actual execution. Stop the beginnings of sin
therefore, or else all the evils it produces must be wholly charged upon us.
4. The final issue of sin, and how it ends : *Sin, when it is finished, bringeth
forth death.* After sin is brought forth in actual commissions, the *finishing
of it* (as Dr. Manton observes) is its being strengthened by frequent acts
and settled into a habit. And, when the iniquities of men are thus filled
up, death is brought forth. There is a death upon the soul, and death
comes upon the body. And, besides death spiritual and temporal, the
wages of sin is eternal death too. Let sin therefore be repented of and
forsaken, before it be finished ; *Why will you die, O house of Israel!*
Ezek. xxxiii. 11. God has no pleasure in your death, as he has no hand
in your sin ; but both sin and misery are owing to yourselves. Your own
hearts' lusts and corruptions are your tempters ; and when by degrees they
have carried you off from God, and finished the power and dominion of
sin in you, then they will prove your destroyers.

III. We are taught yet further that, while we are the authors and pro-
curers of all sin and misery to ourselves, *God is the Father and fountain of
all good, v.* 16, 17. We should take particular care not to err in our conceptions of God : "*Do not err, my beloved brethren,* μὴ λανᾶσθε—*do not
wonder,* that is, from the word of God, and the accounts of him you have
there. Do not stray into erroneous opinions, and go off from the standard
of truth, the things which you have received from the Lord Jesus and by
the direction of his Spirit." The loose opinions of Simon, and the Nicolaitans (from whom the Gnostics, a most sensual corrupt set of people,
arose afterwards), may perhaps, by the apostle here, be more especially
cautioned against. Those who are disposed to look into these may consult the first book of Irenæus against heresies. Let corrupt men run into
what notions they will, the truth, as it is in Jesus, stands thus : that God
is not, cannot be, the author and patronizer of anything that is evil ; but
must be acknowledged as the cause and spring of every thing that is good :
*Every good and every perfect gift is from above, and cometh down from the
Father of lights, v.* 17. Here observe, 1. God is the Father of lights. The
visible light of the sun and the heavenly bodies is from him. He said,
Let there be light, and there was light. Thus God is at once represented as
the Creator of the sun and in some respects compared to it. "As the sun
in the same in its nature and influences, though the earth and clouds, oft
interposing, make it seem to us as varying, by its rising and setting, and

by its different appearances, or entire withdrawment, when the change is not in it; so God is unchangeable, and our changes and shadows are not from any mutability or shadowy alterations in him, but from ourselves."— *Baxter.* The Father of lights, *with whom there is no variableness, neither shadow of turning.* What the sun is in nature, God is in grace, providence, and glory; aye, and infinitely more. For, 2. Every good gift is from him. As the Father of lights, he gives the light of reason. *The inspiration of the Almighty giveth understanding,* Job xxxii. 8. He gives also the light of learning: Solomon's wisdom in the knowledge of nature, in the arts of government, and in all his improvements, is ascribed to God. The light of divine revelation is more immediately from above. The light of faith, purity, and all manner of consolation is from him. So that we have nothing good but what we receive from God, as there is no evil or sin in us, or done by us, but what is owing to ourselves. We must own God as the author of all the powers and perfections that are in the creature, and the giver of all the benefits which we have in and by those powers and perfections: but none of their darknesses, their imperfections, or their ill actions are to be charged on the Father of lights; from him proceeds every good and perfect gift, both pertaining to this life and that which is to come. 3. As every good gift is from God, so particularly the renovation of our natures, our regeneration, and all the holy happy consequences of it, must be ascribed to him (*v.* 18): *Of his own will begat he us with the word of truth.* Here let us take notice, (1.) A true Christian is a creature begotten anew. He becomes as different a person from what he was before the renewing influences of divine grace as if he were formed over again, and born afresh. (2.) The original of this good work is here declared: it is of God's own will; not by our skill or power; not from any good foreseen in us, or done by us, but purely from the good-will and grace of God. (3.) The means whereby this is effected are pointed out; *the word of truth,* that is, the gospel, as Paul expresses it more plainly, 1 Cor. iv. 15, *I have begotten you in Jesus Christ through the gospel.* This gospel is indeed a word of truth, or else it could never produce such real, such lasting, such great and noble effects. We may rely upon it, and venture our immortal souls upon it. And we shall find it a means of our sanctification as it is a word of truth, John xvii. 17. (4.) The end and design of God's giving renewing grace is here laid down: *That we should be a kind of first-fruits of his creatures*—that we should be God's portion and treasure, and a more peculiar property to him, as the first-fruits were; and that we should become holy to the Lord, as the first-fruits were consecrated to him. Christ is the first-fruits of Christians, Christians are the first-fruits of creatures.

19 Wherefore [ye know this], my beloved brethren, let [But let] every man be swift to hear, slow to speak, slow to wrath: 20 For the wrath of man worketh not the righteousness of God. 21 Wherefore lay apart all filthiness and superfluity of naughtiness [putting away all filthiness and overflowing of wickedness], and receive with meekness the engrafted [implanted] word, which is able to save your souls. 22 But be ye doers of the word, and not hearers only, deceiving your own selves. 23 For if any be a hearer of the word, and not a doer, he is like unto a man beholding his natural face in a glass: 24 For he

beholdeth himself, and goeth his way, and straightway forgetteth what manner of man he was.   ²⁵ But whoso looketh
into the perfect law of liberty, and continueth *therein*, he being
not a forgetful hearer, but a doer of the work [**not a hearer
that forgetteth, but a doer that worketh**], this man shall be
blessed in his deed [**doing**].   ²⁶ If any man among you seem to
be religious, and bridleth not his tongue, but deceiveth his own
heart, this man's religion *is* vain.   ²⁷ Pure religion and undefiled before God and the Father is this, To visit the fatherless
and widows in their affliction, *and* to keep himself unspotted
from the world.

In this part of the chapter we are required,

I. To restrain the workings of passion. This lesson we should learn
under afflictions ; and this we shall learn if we are indeed begotten again
by the word of truth. For thus the connection stands—An angry and
hasty spirit is soon provoked to ill things by afflictions, and errors and ill
opinions become prevalent through the workings of our own vile and vain
affections ; but the renewing grace of God and the word of the gospel teach
us to subdue these : *Wherefore, my beloved brethren, let every man be swift
to hear, slow to speak, slow to wrath, v.* 19. This may refer, 1. To the word
of truth spoken of in the verse foregoing. And so we may observe, It is
our duty rather to hear God's word, and apply our minds to understand it,
than to speak according to our own fancies or the opinions of men, and to
run into heat and passion thereupon. Let not such errors as that of God's
being the occasion of men's sin ever be hastily, much less angrily, mentioned by you (and so as to other errors) ; but be ready to hear and consider what God's word teaches in all such cases. 2. This may be applied
to the afflictions and temptations spoken of in the beginning of the chapter.
And then we may observe, It is our duty rather to hear how God explains
his providences, and what he designs by them, than to say as David did in
his haste, *I am cut off ;* or as Jonah did in his passion, *I do well to be angry.*
Instead of censuring God under our trials, let us open our ears and hearts
to hear what he will say to us. 3. This may be understood as referring
to the disputes and differences that Christians, in those times of trial, were
running into among themselves : and so this part of the chapter may be
considered without any connection with what goes before. Here we may
observe that, whenever matters of difference arise among Christians, each
side should be willing to hear the other. People are often stiff in their
own opinions because they are not willing to hear what others have to
offer against them : whereas we should be swift to hear reason and truth
on all sides, and be slow to speak any thing that should prevent this : and,
when we do speak, there should be nothing of wrath ; for a soft answer
turneth away wrath. As this epistle is designed to correct a variety of
disorders that existed among Christians, these words, *swift to hear, slow to
speak, slow to wrath,* may be very well interpreted according to this last
explication. And we may further observe from them that, if men would
govern their tongues, they must govern their passions. When Moses's
spirit was provoked, *he spoke unadvisedly with his lips.* If we would be
slow to speak, we must be slow to wrath.

II. A very good reason is given for suppressing anger : *For the wrath of man worketh not the righteousness of God, v.* 20. It is as if the apostle had said, "Whereas men often pretend zeal for God and his glory, in their heat and passion, let them know that God needs not the passions of any man; his cause is better served by mildness and meekness than by wrath and fury." Solomon says, *The words of the wise are heard in quiet, more than the cry of him that ruleth among fools,* Eccl. ix. 17. Dr. Manton here says of some assemblies, "That if we were as swift to hear as we are ready to speak there would be less of wrath, and more of profit, in our meetings. I remember when a Manichee contested with Augustine, and with importunate clamour cried, *Hear me! hear me!* the father modestly replied, *Nec ego te, nec tu me, sed ambo audiamus apostolum—Neither let me hear thee, nor do thou hear me, but let us both hear the apostle.*" The worst thing we can bring to a religious controversy is anger. This, however it may pretend to be raised by a concern for what is just and right, is not to be trusted. *Wrath* is a human thing, and the wrath of man stands opposed to the righteousness of God. Those who pretend to serve the cause of God hereby show that they are acquainted neither with God nor his cause. This passion must especially be watched against when we are hearing the word of God. See 1. Pet. ii. 1, 2.

III. We are called upon to suppress other corrupt affections, as well as rash anger: *Lay aside all filthiness and superfluity of naughtiness, v.* 21. The word here translated *filthiness* signifies those lusts which have the greatest turpitude and sensuality in them; and the words rendered *superfluity of naughtiness* may be understood of the overflowings of malice or any other spiritual wickednesses. Hereby we are taught, as Christians, to watch against, and lay aside, not only those more gross and fleshly dispositions and affections which denominate a person filthy, but all the disorders of a corrupt heart, which would prejudice it against the word and ways of God. Observe, 1. Sin is a defiling thing; it is called filthiness itself. 2. There is abundance of that which is evil in us to be watched against; there is *superfluity of naughtiness.* 3. It is not enough to restrain evil affections, but *they must be cast from us, or laid apart.* Isa. xxx. 22, *Thou shalt cast them away as a menstruous cloth; thou shalt say, Get you hence.* 4. This must extend not only to outward sins, and greater abominations, but to all sin of thought and affection as well as speech and practice; πᾶσαν ὀυπαρίαν—*all filthiness,* every thing that is corrupt and sinful. 5. Observe, from the foregoing parts of this chapter, the laying aside of all filthiness is what a time of temptation and affliction calls for, and is necessary to the avoiding of error, and the right receiving and improving of the word of truth: for,

IV. We are here fully, though briefly, instructed concerning hearing the word of God.

1. We are required to prepare ourselves for it (*v.* 21), to get rid of every corrupt affection and of every prejudice and prepossession, and to lay aside those sins which pervert the judgment and blind the mind. *All the filthiness and superfluity of naughtiness,* before explained, must, in an especial manner, be subdued and cast off, by all such as attend on the word of the gospel.

2. We are directed how to hear it: *Receive with meekness the engrafted word, which is able to save your souls.* (1.) In hearing the word of God, we are to receive it—assent to the truths of it—consent to the laws of it; receive it as the stock does the graft; so as that the fruit which is produced may be, not according to the nature of the sour stock, but according to the nature of that word of the gospel which is engrafted into our souls. (2.) We must therefore yield ourselves to the word of God, with most submissive, humble, and tractable tempers; this is *to receive it*

with meekness. Being willing to hear of our faults, and taking it not only patiently, but thankfully, desiring also to be moulded and formed by the doctrines and precepts of the gospel. (3.) In all our hearing we should aim at the salvation of our souls. It is the design of the word of God to make us wise to salvation ; and those who propose any meaner or lower ends to themselves in attending upon it dishonour the gospel and disappoint their souls. We should come to the word of God (both to read it and hear it), as those who know it is *the power of God unto salvation to every one that believeth,* Rom. i. 16.

3. We are taught what is to be done after hearing (*v.* 22): *But be you doers of the word, and not hearers only, deceiving your own selves.* Observe here, (1.) Hearing is in order to doing ; the most attentive and the most frequent hearing of the word of God will not avail us, unless we be also doers of it. If we were to hear a sermon every day of the week, and an angel from heaven were the preacher, yet, if we rested in bare hearing, it would never bring us to heaven. Therefore the apostle insists much upon it (and, without doubt, it is indispensably necessary) that we practise what we hear. " There must be inward practice by meditation, and outward practice in true obedience." *Baxter.* It is not enough to remember what we hear, and to be able to repeat it, and to give testimony to it, and commend it, and write it, and preserve what we have written ; that which all this is in order to, and which crowns the rest, is that we be doers of the word. Observe, (2.) Bare hearers are self-deceivers ; the original word, παραλογιζόμενοι, signifies men's arguing sophistically to themselves ; their reasoning is manifestly deceitful and false when they would make one part of their work discharge them from the obligation they lie under to another, or persuade themselves that filling their heads with notions is sufficient, though their hearts be empty of good affections and resolutions, and their lives fruitless of good works. Self-deceit will be found the worst deceit at last.

4. The apostle shows what is the proper use of the word of God, who they are that do not use it as they ought, and who they are that do make a right use of it, *v.* 23-25. Let us consider each of these distinctly. (1.) The use we are to make of God's word may be learnt from its being compared to a glass, in which a man may *behold his natural face.* As a looking-glass shows us the spots and defilements upon our faces, that they may be remedied and washed off, so the word of God shows us our sins, that we may repent of them and get them pardoned ; it shows us what is amiss, that it may be amended. There are glasses that will flatter people ; but that which is truly the word of God is no flattering glass. If you flatter yourselves, it is your own fault ; *the truth, as it is in Jesus,* flatters no man. Let the word of truth be carefully attended to, and it will set before you the corruption of your nature, the disorders of your hearts and lives ; it will tell you plainly what you are. Paul describes himself as insensible of the corruption of his nature till he saw himself in the glass of the law (Rom. vii. 9): "*I was alive without the law ;* that is, I took all to be right with me, and thought myself not only clean, but, compared with the generality of the world, beautiful too ; *but when the commandment came,* when the glass of the law was set before me, *then sin revived, and I died*—then I saw my spots and deformities, and discovered that amiss in myself which before I was not aware of ; and such was the power of the law, and of sin, that I then perceived myself in a state of death and condemnation." Thus, when we attend to *the word of God,* so as to see ourselves, our true state and condition, to rectify what is amiss and to form and dress ourselves anew by the glass of God's word

this is to make a proper use of it. (2.) We have here an account of those who do not use this glass of the word as they ought : *He that beholds himself, and goes his way, and straightway forgets what manner of man he was, v. 24.* This is the true description of one who hears the word of God and does it not. How many are there who, when they sit under the word, are affected with their own sinfulness, misery, and danger, acknowledge the evil of sin, and their need of Christ ; but, when their hearing is over, all is forgotten, convictions are lost, good affections vanish, and pass away like the waters of a land-flood: he *straightway forgets.* "The word of God (as Dr. Manton speaks) discovers how we may do away our sins, and deck and attire our souls with the righteousness of Jesus Christ. *Maculæ sunt peccata, quæ ostendit lex ; aqua est sanguis Christi, quem ostendit evangelium —Our sins are the spots which the law discovers ; Christ's blood is the laver which the gospel shows.*" But in vain do we hear God's word, and look into the gospel glass, if we go away, and forget our spots, instead of washing them off, and forget our remedy, instead of applying to it. This is the case of those who do not hear the word as they ought. (3.) Those also are described, and pronounced blessed, who hear aright, and who use the glass of God's word as they should do (*v.* 25) : *Whoso looketh into the perfect law of liberty, and continueth therein,* &c. Observe here, [1.] The gospel is a law of liberty, or, as Mr. Baxter expresses it, *of liberation,* giving us deliverance from the Jewish law, and from sin and guilt, and wrath and death. The ceremonial law was a yoke of bondage ; the gospel of Christ is a law of liberty. [2.] It is a perfect law ; nothing can be added to it. [3.] In hearing the word, we look into this perfect law ; we consult it for counsel and direction ; we look into it, that we may thence take our measures. [4.] Then only do we look into the law of liberty as we should when we *continue therein*—" when we dwell in the study of it, till it turn to a spiritual life, engrafted and digested in us " (*Baxter*)—when we are not forgetful of it, but practise it as our work and business, set it always before our eyes, and make it the constant rule of our conversation and behaviour, and model the temper of our minds by it. [5.] Those who thus do, and *continue in the law and word of God,* are, and *shall be, blessed in their deed ; blessed in all their ways,* according to the first psalm, to which, some think, James here alludes. *He that meditates in the law of God, and walks according to it,* the psalmist says, *shall prosper in whatsoever he does.* And *he that is not a forgetful hearer, but a doer of the work* which God's word sets him about, James says, *shall be blessed.* The papists pretend that here we have a clear text to prove we are blessed for our good deeds ; but Dr. Manton, in answer to that pretence, puts the reader upon marking the distinctness of scripture-phrase. The apostle does not say, *for* his deeds, that any man is blessed, but *in* his deed. This is a way in which we shall certainly find blessedness, but not the cause of it. This blessedness does not lie in knowing, but in doing the will of God, John xiii. 17. *If you know these things, happy are you if you do them.* It is not talking, but walking, that will bring us to heaven.

V. The apostle next informs us how we may distinguish between a vain religion and that which is pure and approved of God. Great and hot disputes there are in the world about this matter : what religion is false and vain, and what is pure and true. I wish men would agree to let the holy scripture in this place determine the question : and here it is plainly and peremptorily declared.

1. What is a vain religion : *If any man among you seemeth to be religious,*

and bridleth not his tongue, but deceives his own heart, this man's religion is vain. Here are three things to be observed :—(1.) In a vain religion there is much of show, and affecting to seem religious in the eyes of others. This, I think, is mentioned in a manner that should fix our thoughts on the word *seemeth.* When men are more concerned to seem religious than really to be so, it is a sign that their religion is but vain. Not that *religion* itself is a vain thing (those do it a great deal of injustice who say, *It is in vain to serve the Lord*), but it is possible for people to make it a vain thing, if they have only a form of godliness, and not the power. (2.) In a vain religion there is much censuring, reviling, and detracting of others. The not bridling the tongue here is chiefly meant of not abstaining from these evils of the tongue. When we hear people ready to speak of the faults of others, or to censure them as holding scandalous errors, or to lessen the wisdom and piety of those about them, that they themselves may seem the wiser and better, this is a sign that they have but a vain religion. The man who has a detracting tongue cannot have a truly humble gracious heart. He who delights to injure his neighbour in vain pretends to love God ; therefore a reviling tongue will prove a man a hypocrite. Censuring is a pleasing sin, extremely compliant with nature, and therefore evinces a man's being in a natural state. These sins of the tongue were the great sins of that age in which James wrote (as other parts of this epistle fully show) ; and it is a strong sign of a vain religion (says Dr. Manton) to be carried away with the evil of the times. This has ever been a leading sin with hypocrites, that the more ambitious they have been to seem well themselves the more free they have been in censuring and running down others ; and there is such quick intercourse between the tongue and the heart that the one may be known by the other. On these accounts it is that the apostle has made an ungoverned tongue an undoubted certain proof of a vain religion. There is no strength nor power in that religion which will not enable a man to bridle his tongue. (3.) In a vain religion a man deceives his own heart, he goes on in such a course of detracting from others, and making himself seem somebody, that at last the vanity of his religion is consummated by the deceiving of his own soul. When once religion comes to be a vain thing, how great is the vanity !

2. It is here plainly and peremptorily declared wherein true religion consists : *Pure religion and undefiled before God and the Father is this, v.* 27. Observe, (1.) It is the glory of religion to be pure and undefiled ; not mixed with the inventions of men nor with the corruptions of the world. False religions may be known by their impurity and uncharitableness ; according to that of John, *He that doeth not righteousness* is not of God, neither he that *loveth not his brother,* 1 John iii. 10. But, on the other hand, a holy life and a charitable heart show a true religion. Our religion is not (says Dr. Manton) adorned with ceremonies, but purity and charity. And it is a good observation of his that a religion which is pure should be kept undefiled. (2.) That religion is pure and undefiled which is so before God and the Father. That is right which is so in God's eye, and which chiefly aims at his approbation. True religion teaches us to do every thing as in the presence of God ; and to seek his favour, and study to please him in all our actions. (3.) Compassion and charity to the poor and distressed form a very great and necessary part of true religion : *Visiting the fatherless and widow in their affliction.* Visiting is here put for all manner of relief which we are capable of giving to others ; and fatherless and widows are here particularly mentioned, because they are generally

most apt to be neglected or oppressed : but by them we are to understand all who are proper objects of charity, all who are in affliction. It is very remarkable that if the sum of religion be drawn up in two articles this is one—to be charitable and relieve the afflicted. Observe, (4.) An unspotted life must accompany an unfeigned love and charity : *To keep himself unspotted from the world.* The world is apt to spot and blemish the soul, and it is hard to live in it, and have to do with it, and not be defiled ; but this must be our constant endeavour. Herein consists pure and undefiled religion. The very things of the world too much taint our spirit, if we are much conversant with them ; but the sins and lusts of the world deface and defile them very woefully indeed. John comprises *all that is in the world,* which we are not to love, under three heads : *the lust of the flesh, the lust of the eyes, and the pride of life ;* and to keep ourselves unspotted from all these is to keep ourselves unspotted from the world. May God by his grace keep both our hearts and lives clean from the love of the world, and from the temptations of wicked worldly men.

CHAPTER II

In this chapter the apostle condemns a sinful regarding of the rich, and despising the poor, which he imputes to partiality and injustice, and shows it to be an acting contrary to God, who has chosen the poor, and whose interest is often persecuted, and his name blasphemed, by the rich, ver. 1-7. He shows that the whole law is to be fulfilled, and that mercy should be followed, as well as justice, ver. 8-13. He exposes the error and folly of those who boast of faith without works, telling us that this is but a dead faith, and such a faith as devils have, not the faith of Abraham, or of Rahab, ver. 14, to the end.

M Y brethren, have not the faith of our Lord Jesus Christ, *the Lord* of glory, with respect of persons. ²For if there come unto your assembly a man with a gold ring, in goodly apparel, and there come in also a poor man in vile raiment ; ³And ye have respect to him that weareth the gay clothing, and say unto him, Sit thou here in a good place ; and say to the poor, Stand thou there, or sit here under my footstool : ⁴Are ye not then partial in yourselves [**divided in your own mind**] ; and are become judges of evil thoughts? ⁵Hearken, my beloved brethren, Hath not God chosen the poor of this world rich in faith [**them that are poor as to the world** *to be* **rich in faith**], and heirs of the kingdom which he hath promised to them that love him : ⁶But ye have despised the poor. Do not rich men oppress you, and draw you before the judgment seats? ⁷Do not they blaspheme that worthy name by the which ye are called?

The apostle is here reproving a very corrupt practice. He shows how much mischief there is in the sin of προσωπολημψία—*respect of persons,* which seemed to be a very growing evil in the churches of Christ even in those early ages, and which, in these after-times, has sadly corrupted and divided Christian nations and societies. Here we have,

I. A caution against this sin laid down in general : *My brethren, have not the faith of our Lord Jesus Christ, the Lord of glory, with respect of persons, v.* 1. Observe here, 1. The character of Christians fully implied : they are such as have the faith of our Lord Jesus Christ; they embrace it; they receive it; they govern themselves by it; they entertain the doctrine, and submit to the law and government of Christ; they have it as a trust ; they have it as a treasure. 2. How honourably James speaks of Jesus Christ ; he calls him *the Lord of glory ;* for he is *the brightness of his Father's glory, and the express image of his person.* 3. Christ's being the Lord of glory should teach us not to respect Christians for any thing so much as their relation and conformity to Christ. You who profess to believe the glory of our Lord Jesus Christ, which the poorest Christian shall partake of equally with the rich, and to which all worldly glory is but vanity, you should not make men's outward and worldly advantages the measure of your respect. In professing the faith of our Lord Jesus Christ, we should not show respect to men, so as to cloud or lessen the glory of our glorious Lord ; however any may think of it, this is certainly a very heinous sin.

II. We have this sin described and cautioned against, by an instance of example of it (*v.* 2, 3) : *For if there come into your assembly a man with a gold ring,* &c. *Assembly* here is meant of those meetings which were appointed for deciding matters of difference among the members of the church, or for determining when censures should be passed upon any, and what those censures should be ; therefore the Greek word here used, συναγωγὴ, signifies such an assembly as that in the Jewish synagogues, when they met to do justice. Maimonides says (as I find the passage quoted by Dr. Manton) "That it was expressly provided by the Jews' constitutions that, when a poor man and a rich plead together, the rich shall not be bidden to sit down and the poor stand, or sit in a worse place, but both sit or both stand alike." To this the phrases used by the apostle have a most plain reference, and therefore the assembly here spoken of must be some such as the synagogue-assemblies of the Jews were, when they met to hear causes and to execute justice: to these the arbitrations and censures of their Christian assemblies are compared. But we must be careful not to apply what is here said to the common assemblies for worship ; for in these certainly there may be appointed different places for persons according to their rank and circumstances, without sin. Those do not understand the apostle who fix his severity here upon this practice ; they do not consider the word judges (used in *v.* 4), nor what is said of their being convicted as transgressors of the law, if they had such a respect of persons as is here spoken of, according to *v.* 9. Thus, now put the case : " *There comes into your assembly* (when of the same nature with some of those at the synagogue) *a man* that is distinguished by his dress, and who makes a figure, *and there comes in also a poor man in vile raiment,* and you act partially, and determine wrong, merely because the one makes a better appearance, or is in better circumstances, than the other." Observe hence, 1. God has his remnant among all sorts of people, among those that wear soft and gay clothing, and among those that wear poor and vile raiment. 2. In matters of religion, rich and poor stand upon a level ; no man's riches set him in the least nearer to God, nor does any man's poverty set him at a distance from God.

With the Most High there is no respect of persons, and therefore in matters of conscience there should be none with us. 3. All undue honouring of worldly greatness and riches should especially be watched against in Christian societies. James does not here encourage rudeness or disorder. Civil respect must be paid, and some difference may be allowed in our carriage towards persons of different ranks ; but this respect must never be such as to influence the proceedings of Christian societies in disposing of the offices of the church, or in passing the censures of the church, or in any thing that is purely a matter of religion ; here we are to know no man after the flesh. It is the character of a citizen of Zion that *in his eyes a vile person is contemned, but he honoureth those that fear the Lord.* If a poor man be a good man, we must not value him a whit the less for his poverty ; and, if a rich man be a bad man (though he may have both gay clothing and a gay profession), we must not value him any whit the more for his riches. 4. Of what importance it is to take care what rule we go by in judging of men ; if we allow ourselves commonly to judge by outward appearance, this will too much influence our spirits and our conduct in religious assemblies. There is many a man, whose wickedness renders him vile and despicable, who yet makes a figure in the world ; and, on the other hand, there is many a humble, heavenly, good Christian, who is clothed meanly ; but neither should he nor his Christianity be thought the worse of on this account.

III. We have the greatness of this sin set forth, *v.* 4, 5. It is great partiality, it is injustice, and it is to set ourselves against God, who has chosen the poor, and will honour and advance them (if good), let who will despise them. 1. In this sin there is shameful partiality : *Are you not then partial in yourselves?* The question is here put, as what could not fail of being answered by every man's conscience that would put it seriously to himself. According to the strict rendering of the original, the question is, "*Have you not made a difference?* And, in that difference, do you not judge by a false rule, and go upon false measures? And does not the charge of a partiality condemned by the law lie fully against you? Does not your own conscience tell you that you are guilty?" Appeals to conscience are of great advantage, when we have to do with such as make a profession, even though they may have fallen into a very corrupt state. 2. This respect of persons is owing to the evil and injustice of the thoughts. As the temper, conduct, and proceedings, are partial, so the heart and thoughts, from which all flows, are evil : "*You have become judges of evil thoughts ;* that is, you are judges according to those unjust estimations and corrupt opinions which you have formed to yourselves. Trace your partiality till you come to those hidden thoughts which accompany and support it, and you will find those to be *exceedingly evil.* You secretly prefer outward pomp before inward grace, and the things that are seen before those which are not seen." The deformity of sin is never truly and fully discerned till the evil of our thoughts be disclosed : and it is this which highly aggravates the faults of our tempers and lives—that *the imagination of the thoughts of the heart is evil,* Gen. vi. 5. 3. This respect of persons is a heinous sin, because it is to show ourselves most directly contrary to God (*v.* 5) : "*Hath not God chosen the poor of this world rich in faith?* &c. But you have despised them, v. 6. God has made those heirs of a kingdom whom you make of no reputation, and has given very great and glorious promises to those to whom you can hardly give a good word or a respectful look. And is not this a monstrous iniquity in you who pretend to be the

children of God and conformed to him? *Hearken, my beloved brethren ;* by
all the love I have for you, and all the regards you have to me, I beg you
would consider these things. Take notice that many of the poor of this
world are the chosen of God. Their being God's chosen does not prevent
their being poor ; their being poor does not at all prejudice the evidences
of their being chosen. Matt. xi. 5, *The poor are evangelised.*" God designed
to recommend his holy religion to men's esteem and affection, not by the
external advantages of gaiety and pomp, but by its intrinsic worth and
excellency ; and therefore chose the poor of this world. Again, take
notice that many poor of the world are rich in faith ; thus the poorest may
become rich ; and this is what they ought to be especially ambitious of. It
is expected from those who have wealth and estates that they be rich in
good works, because the more they have the more they have to do good
with ; but it is expected from the poor in the world that they be rich in
faith, for the less they have here the more they may, and should, live in
the believing expectation of better things in a better world. Take notice
further, Believing Christians are rich in title, and in being heirs of a kingdom, though they may be very poor as to present possessions. What is
laid out upon them is but little ; what is laid up for them is unspeakably
rich and great. Note again, Where any are rich in faith, there will be
also divine love ; faith working by love will be in all the heirs of glory.
Note once more, under this head, Heaven is a kingdom, and a kingdom
promised to those that love God. We read of the crown promised to those
that love God, in the former chapter (*v.* 12); we here find there is a kingdom
too. And, as the crown is a crown of life, so the kingdom will be an everlasting kingdom. All these things, laid together, show how highly the poor
in this world, if rich in faith, are now honoured, and shall hereafter be advanced by God ; and consequently how very sinful a thing it was for them to
despise the poor. After such considerations as these, the charge is cutting
indeed : *But you have despised the poor, v.* 6. 4. Respecting persons, in the
sense of this place, on account of their riches or outward figure, is shown to
be a very great sin, because of the mischiefs which are owing to worldly
wealth and greatness, and the folly which there is in Christians paying undue
regards to those who had so little regard either to their God or them : "*Do
not rich men oppress you, and draw you before the judgment-seat? Do not
they blaspheme that worthy name by which you are called? v.* 7. Consider
how commonly riches are the incentives of vice and mischief, of blasphemy
and persecution : consider how many calamities you yourselves sustain, and
how great reproaches are thrown upon your religion and your God by men
of wealth, and power, and worldly greatness ; and this will make your sin
appear exceedingly sinful and foolish, in setting up that which tends to pull
you down, and to destroy all that you are building up, and to dishonour
that worthy name by which you are called." The name of Christ is a
worthy name ; it reflects honour, and gives worth to those who wear it.

[8] If ye fulfil the royal law according to the scripture, Thou
shalt love thy neighbour as thyself, ye do well : [9] But if ye have
respect to persons, ye commit sin, and are convinced of the law
as transgressors. [10] For whosoever shall keep the whole law,
and yet offend in one *point,* he is guilty of all. [11] For he that
said, Do not commit adultery, said also, Do not kill. Now if
thou commit no adultery, yet if thou kill, thou art become a

transgressor of the law. ¹² So speak ye, and so do, as they that shall be judged by the law of liberty. ¹³ For he shall have judgment without mercy, that hath showed no mercy; and mercy rejoiceth against judgment.

The apostle, having condemned the sin of those who had an undue respect of persons, and having urged what was sufficient to convict them of the greatness of this evil, now proceeds to show how the matter may be mended ; it is the work of a gospel ministry, not only to reprove and warn, but to teach and direct. Col. i. 28, *Warning every man, and teaching every man.* And here,

I. We have the law that is to guide us in all our regards to men set down in general. *If you fulfil the royal law, according to the scripture, Thou shalt love thy neighbour as thyself, you do well, v.* 8. Lest any should think James had been pleading for the poor so as to throw contempt on the rich, he now lets them know that he did not design to encourage improper conduct towards any ; they must not hate nor be rude to the rich, any more than despise the poor ; but as the scripture teaches us to love all our neighbours, be they rich or poor, as ourselves, so, in our having a steady regard to this rule, *we shall do well.* Observe hence, 1. The rule for Christians to walk by is settled in the scriptures : *If according to the scriptures,* &c. It is not great men, nor worldly wealth, nor corrupt practices among professors themselves, that must guide us, but the scriptures of truth. 2. The scripture gives us this as a law, to love our neighbour as ourselves ; it is what still remains in full force, and is rather carried higher and further by Christ than made less important to us. 3. This law is a royal law, it comes from the King of kings. Its own worth and dignity deserve it should be thus honoured ; and the state in which all Christians now are, as it is a state of liberty, and not of bondage or oppression, makes this law, by which they are to regulate all their actions to one another, a royal law. 4. A pretence of observing this royal law, when it is interpreted with partiality, will not excuse men in any unjust proceedings. It is implied here that some were ready to flatter rich men, and be partial to them, because, if they were in the like circumstances, they should expect such regards to themselves ; or they might plead that to show a distinguished respect to those whom God in his providence had distinguished by their rank and degree in the world was but doing right ; therefore the apostle allows that, so far as they were concerned to observe the duties of the second table, they *did well in giving honour to whom honour was due* ; but this fair pretence would not cover their sin in that undue *respect of persons* which they stood chargeable with ; for,

II. This general law is to be considered together with a particular law : "*If you have respect to persons, you commit sin, and are convinced of the law as transgressors, v.* 9. Notwithstanding the law of laws, *to love your neighbour as yourselves,* and to show that respect to them which you would be apt to look for yourselves if in their circumstances, yet this will not excuse your distributing either the favours or the censures of the church according to men's outward condition ; but here you must look to a particular law, which God, who gave the other, has given you together with it, and by this you will stand fully convicted of the sin I have charged you with. This law is in Lev. xix. 15, *Thou shalt do no unrighteousness in judgment ; thou shalt not respect the person of the poor nor the person of the mighty ; but in righteousness shalt thou judge thy neighbour.* Yea, the very royal law itself, rightly explained, would serve to convict them, because it teaches them to put themselves as much in the places of the poor as in those of the rich, and so to act equitably towards one as well as the other. Hence he proceeds,

III. To show the extent of the law, and how far obedience must be paid to it. They must fulfil the royal law, have a regard to one part as well as another, otherwise it would not stand them in stead, when they pretended to urge it as a reason for any particular actions: *For whosoever shall keep the whole law, and yet offend in one point, is guilty of all, v.* 10. This may be considered, 1. With reference to the case James has been upon : Do you plead for your respect to the rich, because you are to love your neighbour as yourselves ? Why then show also an equitable and due regard to the poor, because you are to love your neighbour as yourself : or else your offending in one point will spoil your pretence of observing that law at all. *Whosoever shall keep the whole law, if he offend in one point,* wilfully, avowedly, and with continuance, and so as to think he shall be excused in some matters because of his obedience in others, *he is guilty of all,* that is, he incurs the same penalty, and is liable to the same punishment, by the sentence of the law, as if he had broken it in other points as well as that he stands chargeable with. Not that all sins are equal, but that all carry the same contempt of the authority of the Lawgiver, and so bind over to such punishment as is threatened on the breach of that law. This shows us what a vanity it is to think that our good deeds will atone for our bad deeds, and plainly puts us upon looking for some other atonement. 2. This is further illustrated by putting a case different from that before mentioned (*v.* 11) : *For he that said, Do not commit adultery, said also, Do not kill. Now, if thou commit no adultery, yet, if thou kill, thou art become a transgressor of the law.* One, perhaps, is very severe in the case of adultery, or what tends to such pollutions of the flesh ; but less ready to condemn murder, or what tends to ruin the health, break the hearts, and destroy the lives, of others : another has a prodigious dread of murder, but has more easy thoughts of adultery ; whereas one who looks at the authority of the Lawgiver more than the matter of the command will see the same reason for condemning the one as the other. Obedience is then acceptable when all is done with an eye to the will of God ; and disobedience is to be condemned, in whatever instance it be, as it is a contempt of the authority of God ; and, for that reason, if we offend in one point, we contemn the authority of him who gave the whole law, and so far are guilty of all. Thus, if you look to the law of old, you stand condemned ; for *cursed is every one that continueth not in all things that are written in the book of the law to do them,* Gal. iii. 10.

IV. James directs Christians to govern and conduct themselves more especially by the law of Christ. *So speak and so do as those that shall be judged by the law of liberty, v.* 12. This will teach us, not only to be just and impartial, but very compassionate and merciful to the poor ; and it will set us perfectly free from all sordid and undue regards to the rich. Observe here, 1. The gospel is called a law. It has all the requisites of a law ; precepts with rewards and punishments annexed ; it prescribes duty, as well as administers comfort ; and Christ is a king to rule us as well as a prophet to teach us, and a priest to sacrifice and intercede for us. *We are under the law to Christ.* 2. It is a *law of liberty,* and one that we have no reason to complain of as a yoke or burden ; for the service of God, according to the gospel, is perfect freedom; it sets us at liberty from all slavish regards, either to the persons or the things of this world. 3. We must all be judged by this law of liberty. Men's eternal condition will be determined according to the gospel; this is the book that will be opened, when we shall stand before the judgment-seat; there will be no relief to those whom the gospel condemns, nor will any accusation lie against those whom the gospel justifies. 4. It concerns us therefore so to speak and act now as becomes those who must shortly be judged by this law of liberty; that is, that we come up to gospel terms, that we make conscience of gospel duties, that we be of a gospel temper, and that our conversation be a gospel conversation, because by this rule we must be judged. 5. The consideration of our being judged by the gospel should engage us more especially to be merciful in our regards to the poor (v. 13): *For he shall have judgment without mercy that hath shown no mercy; and mercy rejoiceth against judgment.* Take notice here, (1.) The doom which will be passed upon impenitent sinners at last will be judgment without mercy; there will be no mixtures or allays in the cup of wrath and of trembling, the dregs of which they must drink. (2.) Such as show no mercy now shall find no mercy in the great day. But we may note, on the other hand, (3.) That there will be such as shall become instances of the triumph of mercy, in whom mercy rejoices against judgment: all the children of men, in the last day, will be either vessels of wrath or vessels of mercy. It concerns all to consider among which they shall be found; and let us remember that *blessed are the merciful, for they shall obtain mercy.*

¹⁴ What *doth it* profit, my brethren, though a man say he hath faith, and have not works? can faith [that faith] save him? ¹⁵ If a brother or sister be naked, and destitute of daily food, ¹⁶ And one of you say unto them, Depart in peace, be *ye* warmed and filled; notwithstanding ye give them not those things which are needful to the body; what *doth it* profit? ¹⁷ Even so faith, if it hath not works, is dead, being alone [is dead in itself]. ¹⁸ Yea, a man may say, Thou hast faith, and I have works: show me thy faith without thy works, and I will show thee my faith by my works. ¹⁹ Thou believest that there is one God; thou doest well: the devils also believe and tremble. ²⁰ But wilt thou know, O vain man, that faith without works is dead [barren]? ²¹ Was not Abraham our father justified by works, when he had offered Isaac his son upon the altar? ²² Seest thou how faith wrought with his works, and by works was faith made perfect? ²³ And the scripture was fulfilled which saith, Abraham believed God, and it was imputed unto him for righteousness: and he was called the Friend of God. ²⁴ Ye see then how that by works a man is justified, and not by faith only. ²⁵ Likewise also was not Rahab the harlot justified by works, when she had received the messengers, and had sent *them* out another way? ²⁶ For as the body without the spirit is dead, so faith without works is dead also.

In this latter part of the chapter, the apostle shows the error of those who rested in a bare profession of the Christian faith, as if that would save them, while the temper of their minds and the tenour of their lives were altogether disagreeable to that holy religion which they professed. To let them see, therefore, what a wretched foundation they built their hopes upon, it is here proved at large that a man is justified, not by faith only, but by works. Now,

I. Upon this arises a very great question, namely, how to reconcile Paul and James. Paul, in his epistles to the Romans and Galatians, seems to assert the directly contrary thing to what James here lays down, saying it often, and with a great deal of emphasis, *that we are justified by faith only, and not by the works of the law. Amicæ scripturarum lites, utinam et nostræ —There is a very happy agreement between one part of scripture and another, notwithstanding seeming differences: it were well if the differences among Christians were as easily reconciled.* "Nothing," says Mr. Baxter, "but men's misunderstanding the plain drift and sense of Paul's epistles, could make so many take it for a matter of great difficulty to reconcile Paul and James." A general view of those things which are insisted on by the Antinomians may be seen in Mr. Baxter's Paraphrase: and many ways might be mentioned which have been invented among learned men to make the apostles agree; but it may be sufficient only to observe these few things following:—1. When Paul says that *a man is justified by faith, without the deeds of the law* (Rom. iii. 28), he plainly speaks of another sort of work than James does, but not of another sort of faith. Paul speaks of works wrought in obedience to the law of Moses, and before men's embracing the faith of the gospel; and he had to deal with those who valued themselves so highly upon those works that they rejected the gospel (as Rom. x., at the beginning, most expressly declares); but James speaks of works done in obedience to the gospel, and as the proper and necessary effects and fruits of sound believing in Christ Jesus. Both are concerned to magnify the faith of the gospel, as that which alone could save us and justify us; but Paul magnifies it by showing the insufficiency of any works of the law before faith, or in opposition to the doctrine of justification by Jesus Christ; James magnifies the same faith, by showing what are the genuine and necessary products and operations of it. 2. Paul not only speaks of different works from those insisted on by James, but he speaks of a quite different use that was made of good works from what is here urged and intended. Paul had to do with those who depended on the merit of their works in the sight of God, and thus he might well make them of no manner of account. James had to do with those who cried up faith, but would not allow works to be used even as evidences; they depended upon a bare profession, as sufficient to justify them; and with these he might well urge the necessity and vast importance of good works. As we must not break one table of the law, by dashing it against the other, so neither must we break in pieces the law and the gospel, by making them clash with one another: those who cry up the gospel so as to set aside the law, and those who cry up the law so as to set aside the gospel, are both in the wrong; for we must take our work before us; there must be both faith in Jesus Christ and good works the fruit of faith. 3. The justification of which Paul speaks is different from that spoken of by James; the one speaks of our persons being justified before God, the other speaks of our faith being justified before men: "*Show me thy faith by thy works,*" says James, "let thy faith be justified in the eyes of those that behold thee by thy works;" but Paul speaks of justification in the sight of God, who justifies those only that believe in Jesus, and purely on account of the redemption that is in him. Thus we see that our persons are justified before God by faith, but our faith is justified before men by works. This is so plainly the scope and design of the apostle James that he is but confirming what Paul, in other places, says of his faith, that it is a laborious faith, and a faith working by love, Gal. v. 6; 1 Thess. i. 3; Titus iii. 8; and many other places. 4. Paul may be understood as speaking of that justification which is inchoate, James of that which is complete; it is by *faith* only that we are put into a justified state, but then good works come in for the completing of our justification at the last great day; then, *Come you children of my Father——for I was hungry, and you gave me meat*, &c.

II. Having thus cleared this part of scripture from everything of a contradiction to other parts of it, let us see what is more particularly to be learnt from this excellent passage of James; we are taught,

1. That faith without works will not profit, and cannot save us. *What doth it profit, my brethren, if a man say he hath faith, and have not works? Can faith save him?* Observe here, (1.) That faith which does not save will not really profit us; a bare profession may sometimes seem to be profitable, to gain the good opinion of those who are truly good, and it may procure in some cases worldly good things; but what profit will this be, for any to gain the world and to lose their souls? *What doth it profit?—Can faith save him?* All things should be accounted profitable or unprofitable to us as they tend to forward or hinder the salvation of our souls. And, above all other things, we should take care thus to make account of faith, as that which does not profit, if it do not save, but will aggravate our condemnation and destruction at last. (2.) For a man to have faith, and to say he has faith, are two different things; the apostle does not say, *If a man have faith without works*, for that is not a supposable case; the drift of this place of scripture is plainly to show that an opinion, or speculation, or assent, without works, is not faith; but the case is put thus, *If a man say he hath faith*, &c. Men may boast of that to others, and be conceited of that in themselves, of which they are really destitute.

2. We are taught that, as love or charity is an operative principle, so is faith, and that neither of them would otherwise be good for any thing; and, by trying how it looks for a person to pretend he is very charitable who yet never does any works of charity, you may judge what sense there is in pretending to have faith without the proper and necessary fruits of it: "*If a brother or a sister be naked, and destitute of daily food, and one of you say unto them, Depart in peace, be you warmed and filled, notwithstanding you give them not those things which are needful to the body, what doth it profit? v.* 15-17. What will such a charity as this, that consists in bare words, avail either you or the poor? Will you come before God with such empty shows of charity as these? You might as well pretend that your love and charity will stand the test without acts of mercy as think that a profession of faith will bear you out before God without works of piety and obedience. *Even so faith, if it hath not works, is dead, being alone,*" *v.* 17. We are too apt to rest in a bare profession of faith, and to think that this will save us; it is a cheap and easy religion to say, "We believe the articles of the Christian faith;" but it is a great delusion to imagine that this is enough to bring us to heaven. Those who argue thus wrong God, and put a cheat upon their own souls; a mock-faith is as hateful as mock-charity, and both show a heart dead to all real godliness. You may as soon take

pleasure in a dead body, void of soul, or sense, or action, as God takes pleasure in a dead faith, where there are no works.

3. We are taught to compare a faith boasting of itself without works and a faith evidenced by works, by looking on both together, to try how this comparison will work upon our minds. *Yea, a man may say, Thou hast faith, and I have works. Show me thy faith without thy works, and I will show thee my faith by my works, v.* 18. Suppose a true believer thus pleading with a boasting hypocrite, "Thou makest a profession, and sayest thou hast faith ; I make no such boasts, but leave my works to speak for me. Now give any evidence of having the faith thou professest without works if thou canst, and I will soon let thee see how my works flow from faith and are the undoubted evidences of its existence." This is the evidence by which the scriptures all along teach men to judge both of themselves and others. And this is the evidence according to which Christ will proceed at the day of judgment. *The dead were judged according to their works,* Rev. xx. 12. How will those be exposed then who boast of that which they cannot evidence, or who go about to evidence their faith by any thing but works of piety and mercy !

4. We are taught to look upon a faith of bare speculation and knowledge as the faith of devils : *Thou believest that there is one God ; thou doest well ; the devils also believe, and tremble, v.* 19. That instance of faith which the apostle here chooses to mention is the first principle of all religion. "*Thou believest that there is a God,* against the atheists ; and that there is but one God, against the idolaters ; *thou doest well :* so far all is right. But to rest here, and take up a good opinion of thyself, or of thy state towards God, merely on account of thy believing in him, this will render thee miserable : *The devils also believe and tremble.* If thou contentest thyself with a bare assent to articles of faith, and some speculations upon them, thus far the devils go. And as their faith and knowledge only serve to excite horror, so in a little time will thine." The word tremble is commonly looked upon as denoting a good effect of faith ; but here it may rather be taken as a bad effect, when applied to the faith of devils. They tremble, not out of reverence, but hatred and opposition to that one God on whom they believe. To rehearse that article of our creed, therefore, *I believe in God the Father Almighty,* will not distinguish us from devils at last, unless we now give up ourselves to God as the gospel directs, and love him, and delight ourselves in him, and serve him, which the devils do not, cannot do.

5. We are taught that he who boasts of faith without works is to be looked upon at present as a foolish condemned person. *But wilt thou know, O vain man, that faith without works is dead ? v.* 20. The words translated *vain man—ἄνθρωπε κενὲ,* are observed to have the same signification with the word *Raca,* which must never be used to private persons, or as an effect of anger (Matt. v. 22), but may be used as here, to denote a just detestation of such a sort of men as are empty of good works, and yet boasters of their faith. And it plainly declares them fools and abjects in the sight of God. Faith without works is said to be *dead,* not only as void of all those operations which are the proofs of spiritual life, but as unavailable to eternal life : such believers as rest in a bare profession of faith *are dead while they live.*

6. We are taught that a justifying faith cannot be without works, from two examples, Abraham and Rahab.

(1.) The first instance is that of Abraham, the father of the faithful, and the prime example of justification, to whom the Jews had a special regard (*v.* 21): *Was not Abraham our father justified by works, when he had offered Isaac his son upon the altar?* Paul, on the other hand, says (in *ch.* iv. of the epistle to the Romans) that Abraham *believed, and it was counted to him for righteousness.* But these are well reconciled, by observing what is said in Heb. xi., which shows that the faith both of Abraham and Rahab was such as to produce those good works of which James speaks, and which are not to be separated from faith as justifying and saving. By what Abraham did, it appeared that he truly believed. Upon this footing, the words of God himself plainly put this matter. Gen. xxii. 16, 17, *Because thou hast done this thing, and hast not withheld thy son, thine only son; therefore in blessing I will bless thee.* Thus the faith of Abraham was a working faith (*v.* 22), *it wrought with his works, and by works was made perfect.* And by this means you come to the true sense of that scripture which saith, Abraham believed God, *and it was imputed unto him for righteousness, v.* 23. And thus he became the *friend of God.* Faith, producing such works, endeared him to the divine Being, and advanced him to very peculiar favours and intimacies with God. It is a great honour done to Abraham that he is called and counted the friend of God. You see then (*v.* 24) how that *by works a man is justified* (comes into such a state of favour and friendship with God), *and not by faith only;* not by a bare opinion, or profession, or believing without obeying, but by having such a faith as is productive of good works. Now besides the explication of this passage and example, as thus illustrating and supporting the argument James is upon, many other useful lessons may be learned by us from what is here said concerning Abraham. [1.] Those who would have Abraham's blessings must be careful to copy after his faith: to boast of being Abraham's seed will not avail any, if they do not believe as he did. [2.] Those works which evidence true faith must be works of self-denial, and such as God himself commands (as Abraham's offering up his son, his only son, was), and not such works as are pleasing to flesh and blood and may serve our interest, or are the mere fruits of our own imagination and devising. [3.] What we piously purpose and sincerely resolve to do for God is accepted as if actually performed. Thus Abraham is regarded as offering up his son, though he did not actually proceed to make a sacrifice of him. It was a done thing in the mind, and spirit, and resolution of Abraham, and God accepts it as if fully performed and accomplished. [4.] The actings of faith make it grow perfect, as the truth of faith makes it act. [5.] Such an acting faith will make others, as well as Abraham, friends of God. Thus Christ says to his disciples, *I have called you friends,* John xv. 15. All transactions between God and the truly believing soul are easy, pleasant, and delightful. There is one will and one heart, and there is a mutual complacency. *God rejoiceth over those* who truly believe, to do them good ; and they delight themselves in him.

(2.) The second example of faith's justifying itself and us with and by works is Rahab: *Likewise also was not Rahab the harlot justified by works, when she had received the messengers, and had sent them out another way? v.* 25. The former instance was of one renowned for his faith all his life long. This is of one noted for sin, whose faith was meaner and of a much lower degree ; so that the strongest faith will not do, nor the meanest be allowed to go without works. Some say that the word here rendered *harlot* was the proper name of Rahab. Others tell us that it signifies no more than a *hostess,* or one who keeps a public house, with whom therefore the spies lodged. But it is very probable that her character was infamous ;

and such an instance is mentioned to show that faith will save the worst, when evidenced by proper works ; and it will not save the best without such works as God requires. This Rahab believed the report she had heard of God's powerful presence with Israel ; but that which proved her faith sincere was, that, to the hazard of her life, she *received the messengers, and sent them out another way.* Observe here, [1.] The wonderful power of faith in transforming and changing sinners. [2.] The regard which an operative faith meets with from God, to obtain his mercy and favour. [3.] Where great sins are pardoned, there must be great acts of self-denial. Rahab must prefer the honour of God and the good of his people before the preservation of her own country. Her former acquaintance must be discarded, her former course of life entirely abandoned, and she must give signal proof and evidence of this before she can be in a justified state ; and even after she is justified, yet her former character must be remembered ; not so much to her dishonour as to glorify the rich grace and mercy of God. Though justified, she is called *Rahab the harlot.*

7. And now, upon the whole matter, the apostle draws this conclusion, *As the body without the spirit is dead, so faith without works is dead also, v. 26.* These words are read differently ; some reading them, *As the body without the breath is dead, so is faith without works :* and then they show that works are the companions of faith, as breathing is of life. Others read them, *As the body without the. soul is dead, so faith without works is dead also :* and then they show that as the body has no action, nor beauty, but becomes a loathsome carcase, when the soul is gone, so a bare profession without works is useless, yea, loathsome and offensive. Let us then take heed of running into extremes in this case. For, (1.) The best works, without faith, are dead ; they want their root and principle. It is by faith that any thing we do is really good, as done with an eye to God, in obedience to him, and so as to aim principally at his acceptance. (2.) The most plausible profession of faith, without works, is dead : as the root is dead when it produces nothing green, nothing of fruit. Faith is the root, good works are the fruits, and we must see to it that we have both. We must not think that either, without the other, will justify and save us. This is the grace of God wherein we stand, and we should stand to it.

CHAPTER III

The apostle here reproves ambition, and an arrogant magisterial tongue; and shows the duty and advantage of bridling it because of its power to do mischief. Those who profess religion ought especially to govern their tongues, ver. 1-12. True wisdom makes men meek, and avoiders of strife and envy : and hereby it may easily be distinguished from a wisdom that is earthly and hypocritical, ver. 13, to the end.

MY brethren, be not many masters, knowing that we shall receive the greater condemnation [heavier judgment]. ² For in many things we offend all [we all stumble]. If any man offend not in word, the same *is* a perfect man, *and* able also to bridle the whole body. ³ Behold, we put bits in the horses' mouths, that they may obey us; and we turn about their whole body. ⁴ Behold also the ships, which though *they be* so great, and *are* driven of fierce winds, yet are they turned about with a very small helm, whithersoever the governor listeth [whither the impulse of the steersman willeth]. ⁵ Even so the tongue is a little member, and boasteth great things. Behold, how great a matter [how much wood] a little fire kindleth! ⁶ And the tongue *is* a fire, a world of iniquity : so is the tongue among our members, that it defileth the whole body, and setteth on fire the course [wheel] of nature; and it is set on fire of hell. ⁷ For every kind of beasts, and of birds, and of serpents, and of things in the sea, is tamed, and hath been tamed of mankind : ⁸ But the tongue can no man tame; *it is* an unruly evil, full of deadly poison. ⁹ Therewith bless we God, even the Father; and therewith curse we men, which are made after the similitude of God. ¹⁰ Out of the same mouth proceedeth blessing and cursing. My brethren, these things ought not so to be. ¹¹ Doth a fountain send forth at the same place sweet *water* and bitter? ¹² Can the fig tree, my brethren, bear olive berries? either a vine, figs? so *can* no fountain both yield salt water and fresh [neither *can* salt water yield sweet].

The foregoing chapter shows how unprofitable and dead faith is without works. It is plainly intimated by what this chapter first goes upon that such a faith is, however, apt to make men conceited and magisterial in their tempers and their talk. Those who set up faith in the manner the former chapter condemns are most apt to run into those sins of the tongue which this chapter condemns. And indeed the best need to be cautioned against a dictating, censorious, mischievous use of their tongues. We are therefore taught,

I. Not to use our tongues so as to lord it over others : *My brethren, be not many masters*, &c., *v.* I. These words do not forbid doing what we can to direct and instruct others in the way of their duty or to reprove them in a Christian way for what is amiss ; but we must not affect to speak and act as those who are continually assuming the chair, we must not prescribe to one another, so as to make our own sentiments a standard by which to try all others, because God gives various gifts to men, and expects from each according to that measure of light which he gives. "Therefore be not many *masters*" (or *teachers*, as some read it) ; "do not give yourselves the air of teachers, imposers, and judges, but rather speak with the humility and spirit of learners ; do not censure one another, as if all must be brought to your standard." This is enforced by two reasons. I. Those who thus set up for judges and censurers *shall receive the greater condemnation.* Our judging others will but make our own judgment the more strict and severe, Matt. vii. I, 2. Those who are curious to spy out the faults of others, and arrogant in passing censures upon them, may expect that God will be as extreme in marking what they say and do amiss. 2. Another reason given against such acting the master is because we are all sinners : *In many things we offend all, v.* 2. Were we to think more of our own mistakes and offences, we should be less apt to judge other people. While we are severe against what we count offensive in others, we do not consider how much there is in us which is justly offensive to them. Self-justifiers are commonly self-deceivers. We are all guilty before God ; and those who vaunt it over the frailties and infirmities of others little think how many things they offend in themselves. Nay, perhaps their magisterial deportment and censorious tongues may prove worse than any faults they condemn in others. Let us learn to be severe in judging ourselves, but charitable in our judgments of other people.

II. We are taught to govern our tongue so as to prove ourselves perfect and upright men, and such as have an entire government over ourselves : *If any man offend not in word, the same is a perfect man, and able also to bridle the whole body.* It is here implied that he whose conscience is affected by tongue-sins, and who takes care to avoid them, is an upright man, and has an undoubted sign of true grace. But, on the other hand, *if a man seemeth to be religious* (as was declared in the first chapter) *and bridleth not his tongue,* whatever profession he makes, *that man's religion is vain.* Further, he that offends not in word will not only prove himself a sincere Christian, but a very much advanced and improved Christian. For the wisdom and grace which enable him to rule his tongue will enable him also to rule all his actions. This we have illustrated by two comparisons : —1. The governing and guiding of all the motions of a horse, by the bit which is put into his mouth : *Behold, we put bits into the horses' mouths, that they may obey us, and we turn about their whole body, v.* 3. There is a great deal of brutish fierceness and wantonness in us. This shows itself very much by the tongue : so that this must be bridled ; according to Ps. xxxix. 1, *I will keep my mouth with a bridle* (or, *I will bridle my mouth*) *while the wicked is before me.* The more quick and lively the tongue is, the more should we thus take care to govern it. Otherwise, as an unruly and ungovernable horse runs away with his rider, or throws him, so an unruly tongue will serve those in like manner who have no command over it. Whereas, let resolution and watchfulness, under the influence of the grace of God, bridle the tongue, and then all the motions and actions of the whole body will be easily guided and overruled. 2. The governing of a ship by the right management of the helm : *Behold also the ships, which though they are so great, and are driven of fierce winds, yet are they turned about with a very small helm whithersoever the governor listeth. Even so the tongue is a little member, and boasteth great things, v.* 4, 5. As the helm is a very small part of the ship, so is the tongue a very small part of the body : but the right governing of the helm or rudder will steer and turn the ship as the governor pleases ; and a right management of the tongue is, in a great measure, the government of the whole man. There is a wonderful beauty in these comparisons, to show how things of small bulk may yet be of vast use. And hence we should learn to make the due management of our tongues more our study, because, though they are little members, they are capable of doing a great deal of good or a great deal of hurt. Therefore,

III. We are taught to dread an unruly tongue as one of the greatest and most pernicious evils. It is compared to a little fire placed among a great deal of combustible matter, which soon raises a flame and consumes all before it : *Behold, how great a matter a little fire kindleth ! And the tongue is a fire, a world of iniquity,* &c., *v.* 5, 6. There is such an abundance of sin in the tongue that it may be called *a world of iniquity.* How many defilements does it occasion! How many and dreadful flames does it kindle! *So is the tongue among the members that it defileth the whole body.* Observe hence, There is a great pollution and defilement in sins of the tongue. Defiling passions are kindled, vented, and cherished by this unruly member. And the whole body is often drawn into sin and guilt by the tongue. Therefore Solomon says, *Suffer not thy mouth to cause thy flesh to sin,* Eccles. v. 6. The snares into which men are sometimes led by the tongue are insufferable to themselves and destructive of others. *It setteth on fire the course of nature.* The affairs of mankind and of societies are often thrown into confusion, and all is on a flame, by the tongues of men. Some read it, *all our generations are set on fire by the tongue.* There is no age of the world, nor any condition of life, private or public, but will afford examples of this. *And it is set on fire of hell.* Observe hence, Hell has more to do in promoting the fire of the tongue than men are generally aware of. It is from some diabolical temptations, and to serve some diabolical designs, that men's tongues are inflamed. The devil is expressly called a liar, a murderer, an accuser of the brethren; and, whenever men's tongues are employed in any of these ways, they are set on fire of hell. The Holy Ghost indeed once descended in *cloven tongues as of fire,* Acts ii. And where the tongue is thus guided and wrought upon by a fire from heaven, there it kindleth good thoughts, holy affections, and ardent devotions. But when it is set on fire of hell, as in all undue heats it is, there it is mischievous, producing rage and hatred, and those things which serve the purposes of the devil. As therefore you would dread fires and flames, you should dread contentions, revilings, slanders, lies, and everything that would kindle the fire of wrath in your own spirit or in the spirits of others. But,

IV. We are next taught how very difficult a thing it is to govern the tongue: *For every kind of beasts, and of birds, and of serpents, and of things in the sea is tamed, and hath been tamed, of mankind. But the tongue can no man tame, v. 7, 8.* As if the apostle had said, "Lions, and the most savage beasts, as well as horses and camels, and creatures of the greatest strength, have been tamed and governed by men: so have birds, notwithstanding their wildness and timorousness, and their wings to bear them up continually out of our reach: even serpents, notwithstanding all their venom and all their cunning, have been made familiar and harmless, and things in the sea have been taken by men, and made serviceable to them. And these creatures have not been subdued nor tamed by miracle only (as the lions crouched to Daniel, instead of devouring him, and ravens fed Elijah, and a whale carried Jonah through the depths of the sea to dry land), but what is here spoken of is something commonly done; not only hath been tamed, but is tamed of mankind. Yet the tongue is worse than these, and cannot be tamed by the power and art which serves to tame these things. No man can tame the tongue without supernatural grace and assistance." The apostle does not intend to represent it as a thing impossible, but as a thing extremely difficult, which therefore will require great watchfulness, and pains, and prayer, to keep it in due order. And sometimes all is too little; *for it is an unruly evil, full of deadly poison.* Brute creatures may be kept within certain bounds, they may be managed by certain rules, and even serpents may be so used as to do no hurt with all their poison; but the tongue is apt to break through all bounds and rules, and to spit out its poison on one occasion or other, notwithstanding the utmost care. So that not only does it need to be watched, and guarded, and governed, as much as an unruly beast, or a hurtful and poisonous creature, but much more care and pains will be needful to prevent the mischievous outbreakings and effects of the tongue. However,

V. We are taught to think of the use we make of our tongues in religion and in the service of God, and by such a consideration to keep it from cursing, censuring, and every thing that is evil on other occasions : *Therewith bless we God, even the Father ; and therewith curse we men, who are made after the similitude of God. Out of the same mouth proceed blessing and cursing. My brethren, these things ought not so to be, v. 9, 10.* How absurd is it that those who use their tongues in prayer and praise should ever use them in cursing, slandering, and the like ! If we bless God as our Father, it should teach us to speak well of, and kindly to, all who bear his image. That tongue which addresses with reverence the divine Being cannot, without the greatest inconsistency, turn upon fellow-creatures with reviling brawling language. It is said of the seraphim that praise God, they *dare not bring a railing accusation.* And for men to reproach those who have not only the image of God in their natural faculties, but are renewed after the image of God by the grace of the gospel : this is a most shameful contradiction to all their pretensions of honouring the great Original. *These things ought not so to be ;* and, if such considerations were always at hand, surely they would not be. Piety is disgraced in all the shows of it, if there be not charity. That tongue confutes itself which one while pretends to adore the perfections of God, and to refer all things to him, and another while will condemn even good men if they do not just come up to the same words or expressions used by it. Further, to fix this thought, the apostle shows that contrary effects from the same causes are monstrous, and not to be found in nature, and therefore cannot be consistent with grace : *Doth a fountain send forth at the same place sweet water and bitter ? Can the fig-tree bear olive-berries, or a vine, figs ? Or doth the same spring yield both salt water and fresh ? v.* 11, 12. True religion will not admit of contradictions ; and a truly religious man can never allow of them either in his words or his actions. How many sins would this prevent, and recover men from, to put them upon being always consistent with themselves !

[13] Who *is* a wise man and endued with knowledge among you ? let him show out of a good conversation [by his good life] his works with meekness of wisdom.   [14] But if ye have bitter envying and strife in your hearts, glory not, and lie not against the truth.   [15] This wisdom descendeth not from above, but *is* earthly, sensual, devilish.   [16] For where envying and strife *is*, there *is* confusion and every evil work.   [17] But the wisdom that is from above is first pure, then peaceable, gentle, *and* easy to be entreated, full of mercy and good fruits, without hypocrisy [without variance, without hypocrisy].   [18] And the fruit of righteousness is sown in peace of [for] them that make peace.

As the sins before condemned arise from an affectation of being thought more wise than others, and being endued with more knowledge than they, so the apostle in these verses shows the difference between men's pretending to be wise and their being really so, and between the wisdom which is from beneath (from earth or hell) and that which is from above.

I. We have some account of true wisdom, with the distinguishing marks and fruits of it : *Who is a wise man, and endued with knowledge among you ? Let him show out of a good conversation his works with meekness of wisdom,* v. 13. A truly wise man is a very knowing man : he will not set up for the reputation of being wise without laying in a good stock of knowledge ; and he will not value himself merely upon knowing things, if he has not wisdom to make a right application and use of that knowledge. These two things must be put together to make up the account of true wisdom : who is wise, and endued with knowledge ? Now where this is the happy case of any there will be these following things :—1. A good conversation. If we are wiser than others, this should be evidenced by the goodness of our conversation, not by the roughness or vanity of it. Words that inform, and heal, and do good, are the marks of wisdom ; not those that look great, and do mischief, and are the occasions of evil, either in ourselves or others. 2. True wisdom may be known by its works. The conversation here does not refer only to words, but to the whole of men's practice ; therefore it is said, Let him show out of a good conversation his works. True wisdom does not lie in good notions or speculations so much as in good and useful actions. Not he who thinks well, or he who talks well, is in the sense of the scripture allowed to be wise, if he do not live and act well. 3. True wisdom may be known by the meekness of the spirit and temper : *Let him show with meekness,* &c. It is a great instance of wisdom prudently to bridle our own anger, and patiently to bear the anger of others. And as wisdom will evidence itself in meekness, so meekness will be a great friend to wisdom ; for nothing hinders the regular apprehension, the solid judgment, and impartiality of thought, necessary to our acting wisely, so much as passion. When we are mild and calm, we are best able to hear reason, and best able to speak it. Wisdom produces meekness, and meekness increases wisdom.

II. We have the glorying of those taken away who are of a contrary character to that now mentioned, and their wisdom exposed in all its boasts and productions : " *If you have bitter envying and strife in your hearts, glory not,* &c., v. 14-16. Pretend what you will, and think yourselves ever so wise, yet you have abundance of reason to cease your glorying, if you run down love and peace, and give way to bitter envying and strife. Your zeal for truth or orthodoxy, and your boasts of knowing more than others, if you employ these only to make others hateful, and to show your own spite and heart-burnings against them, are a shame to your profession of Christianity, and a downright contradiction to it. Lie not thus against the truth." Observe, 1. Envying and strife are opposed to the meekness of wisdom. The heart is the seat of both ; but envy and wisdom cannot dwell together in the same heart. Holy zeal and bitter envying are as different as the flames of seraphim and the fire of hell. 2. The order of things here laid down. Envying is first and excites strife ; strife endeavours to excuse itself by vain-glorying and lying ; and then (v. 16) hereupon ensue confusion and every evil work. Those who live in malice, envy, and contention, live in confusion, and are liable to be provoked and hurried to any evil work. Such disorders raise many temptations, strengthen temptations, and involve men in a great deal of guilt. One sin begets another, and it cannot be imagined how much mischief is produced : *there is every evil work.* And is such wisdom as produces these effects to be gloried in? This cannot be without giving the lie to Christianity, and pretending that this wisdom is what it is not. For observe, 3. Whence such wisdom cometh : *It descendeth not from above*, but ariseth from beneath ; and, to speak plainly, it is *earthly, sensual, devilish, v.* 15. It springs from earthly principles, acts upon earthly motives, and is intent upon serving earthly purposes. It is sensual, indulging the flesh, and making provision to fulfil the lusts and desires of it. Or, according to the original word, ψυχικὴ, it is animal or human—the mere working of natural reason, without any supernatural light. And it is devilish, such wisdom being the wisdom of devils (to create uneasiness and to do hurt), and being inspired by devils, whose condemnation is pride (1 Tim. iii. 6), and who are noted in other places of scripture for their wrath, and their accusing the brethren. And therefore those who are lifted up with such wisdom as this must fall into the condemnation of the devil.

III. We have the lovely picture of that wisdom which is from above more fully drawn, and set in opposition to this which is from beneath : *But the wisdom that is from above is first pure, then peaceable,* &c., *v.* 17, 18. Observe here, True wisdom is God's gift. It is not gained by conversing with men, nor by the knowledge of the world (as some think and speak), but it comes from above. It consists of these several things :—1. It is pure, without mixture of maxims or aims that would debase it : and it is free from iniquity and defilements, not allowing of any known sin, but studious of holiness both in heart and life. 2. The wisdom that is from above is peaceable. Peace follows purity, and depends upon it. Those who are truly wise do what they can to preserve peace, that it may not be broken ; and to make peace, that where it is lost it may be restored. In kingdoms, in families, in churches, in all societies, and in all interviews and transactions, heavenly wisdom makes men peaceable. 3. It is gentle, not standing upon extreme right in matters of property ; not saying nor doing any thing rigorous in points of censure ; not being furious about opinions, urging our own beyond their weight nor theirs who oppose us beyond their intention ; not being rude and overbearing in conversation, nor harsh and cruel in temper. Gentleness may thus be opposed to all these. 4. Heavenly wisdom is *easy to be entreated*, εὐπειθής· it is very *persuadable*, either to what is good or from what is evil. There is an easiness that is weak and faulty ; but it is not a blamable easiness to yield ourselves to the persuasions of God's word, and to all just and reasonable counsels or requests of our fellow-creatures ; no, nor to give up a dispute, where there appears a good reason for it and where a good end may be answered by it. 5. Heavenly wisdom is full of mercy and good fruits, inwardly disposed to every thing that is kind and good, both to relieve those who want and to forgive those who offend, and actually to do this whenever proper occasions offer. 6. Heavenly wisdom is without partiality. The original word, ἀδιάκριτος, signifies to be without suspicion, or free from judging, making no undue surmises nor differences in our conduct towards one person more than another. The margin reads it, *without wrangling*, not acting the part of sectaries, and disputing merely for the sake of a party ; nor censuring others purely on account of their differing from us. The wisest men are least apt to be censurers. 7. That wisdom which is from above is without hypocrisy. It has no disguises nor deceits. It cannot fall in with those managements which the world counts wise, which are crafty and guileful ; but it is sincere and open, steady and uniform, and consistent with itself. O that you and I may always be guided by such wisdom as this ! that with Paul we may be able to say, *Not with fleshly wisdom, but in simplicity and godly sincerity, by the grace of God, we have our conversation.* And then, *lastly,* true wisdom will go on to sow the fruits of righteousness in peace, and thus, if it may be, to make peace in the world, *v.* 18. And that which is sown in peace will produce a harvest of joys. Let others reap the fruits of contentions, and all the advantages they can propose to themselves by them; but let us go on peaceably to sow the seeds of righteousness, and we may depend upon it our labour will not be lost. *For light is sown for the righteous, and gladness for the upright in heart; and the work of righteousness shall be peace, and the effect of righteousness quietness and assurance for ever.*

CHAPTER IV

In this chapter we are directed to consider, I. Some causes of contention, besides those mentioned in the foregoing chapter, and to watch against them, ver. 1-5. II. We are taught to abandon the friendship of this world, so as to submit and subject ourselves entirely to God, ver. 4-10. III. All detraction and rash judgment of others are to be carefully avoided, ver. 11, 12. IV. We must preserve a constant regard, and pay the utmost deference to the disposals of divine Providence, ver 13, to the end.

FROM whence *come* wars and fightings among you? *come they* not hence, *even* of your lusts [pleasures] that war in your members? ² Ye lust, and have not: ye kill, and desire to have, and cannot obtain: ye fight and war, yet ye have not, because ye ask not. ³ Ye ask, and receive not, because ye ask amiss, that ye may consume [spend] *it* upon your lusts [pleasures]. ⁴ Ye adulterers and adulteresses, know ye not that the friendship of the world is enmity with God? whosoever therefore will be a friend of the world is the enemy of God. ⁵ Do ye think that the scripture saith in vain, The spirit that dwelleth in us lusteth to envy? [Doth the spirit which he made to dwell in us long unto envying?] ⁶ But he giveth more grace. Wherefore he [the scripture] saith, God resisteth the proud, but giveth grace unto the humble. ⁷ Submit yourselves therefore to God. Resist the devil, and he will flee from you. ⁸ Draw nigh to God, and he will draw nigh to you. Cleanse *your* hands, *ye* sinners; and purify *your* hearts, *ye* double minded. ⁹ Be afflicted, and mourn, and weep: let your laughter be turned to mourning, and *your* joy to heaviness. ¹⁰ Humble yourselves in the sight of the Lord, and he shall lift you up.

The former chapter speaks of envying one another, as the great spring of strifes and contentions; this chapter speaks of a lust after worldly things, and a setting too great a value upon worldly pleasures and friendships, as that which carried their divisions to a shameful height.

I. The apostle here reproves the Jewish Christians for their wars, and for their lusts as the cause of them : *Whence come wars and fightings among you? Come they not hence, even of your lusts that war in your members? v.* 1. The Jews were a very seditious people, and had therefore frequent wars with the Romans ; and they were a very quarrelsome divided people, often fighting among themselves ; and many of those corrupt Christians against whose errors and vices this epistle was written seem to have fallen in with the common quarrels. Hereupon, our apostle informs them that the origin of their wars and fightings was not (as they pretended) a true zeal for their country, and for the honour of God, but that their prevailing lusts were the cause of all. Observe hence, What is sheltered and shrouded under a specious pretence of zeal for God and religion often comes from men's pride, malice, covetousness, ambition, and revenge. The Jews had many struggles with the Roman power before they were entirely destroyed. They often unnecessarily embroiled themselves, and then fell into parties and factions about the different methods of managing their wars with their common enemies ; and hence it came to pass that, when their cause might be supposed good, yet their engaging in it and their management of it came from a bad principle. Their worldly and fleshly lusts raised and managed their wars and fightings ; but one would think here is enough said to subdue those lusts ; for, 1. They make a war within as well as fightings without. Impetuous passions and desires first war in their members, and then raise feuds in their nation. There is war between conscience and corruption, and there is war also between one corruption and another, and from these contentions in themselves arose their quarrels with each other. Apply this to private cases, and may we not then say of fightings and strifes among relations and neighbours that they come from those lusts which war in the members? From lust of power and dominion, lust of pleasure, or lust of riches, from some one or more of these lusts arise all the broils and contentions that are in the world ; and, since all wars and fightings come from the corruptions of our own hearts, it is therefore the right method for the cure of contention to lay the axe to the root, and mortify those lusts that war in the members. 2. It should kill these lusts to think of their disappointment : " *You lust and have not ; you kill, and desire to have, and cannot obtain, v.* 2. You covet great things for yourselves, and you think to obtain them by your victories over the Romans or by suppressing this and the other party among yourselves. You think you shall secure great pleasures and happiness to yourselves, by overthrowing everything which thwarts your eager wishes : but, alas ! you are losing your labour and your blood, while you kill one another with such views as these." Inordinate desires are either totally disappointed, or they are not to be appeased and satisfied by obtaining the things desired. The words here rendered *cannot obtain* signify cannot gain the happiness sought after. Note hence, Worldly and fleshly lusts are the distemper which will not allow of contentment or satisfaction in the mind. 3. Sinful desires and affections generally exclude prayer, and the working of our desires towards God : " *You fight and war, yet you have not, because you ask not.* You fight, and do not succeed, because you do not pray, you do not consult God in your undertakings, whether he will allow of them or not ; and you do not commit your way to him, and make known your requests to him, but follow your own corrupt views and inclinations ! therefore you meet with continual disappointments ; " or else, 4. " Your lusts spoil your prayers, and make them an abomination to God, whenever you put them up to him, v. 3. *You ask, and receive not, because you ask amiss, that you may consume it upon your lusts.*" As if it had been said, "Though perhaps you may sometimes pray for success against your enemies, yet it is not your aim to improve the advantages you gain, so as to promote true piety and religion either in yourselves or others; but pride, vanity, luxury, and sensuality, are what you would serve by your successes, and by your very prayers. You want to live in great power and plenty, in voluptuousness and a sensual prosperity; and thus you disgrace devotion and dishonour God by such gross and base ends; and therefore your prayers are rejected." Let us learn hence, in the management of all our worldly affairs, and in our prayers to God for success in them, to see that our ends be right. When men follow their worldly business (suppose them tradesmen or husbandmen), and ask of God prosperity, but do not receive what they ask for, it is because they ask with wrong aims and intentions. They ask God to give them success in their callings or undertakings; not that they may glorify their heavenly Father and do good with what they have, but that they may *consume it upon their lusts*—that they may be enabled to eat better meat, and drink better drink, and wear better clothes, and so gratify their pride, vanity, and voluptuousness. But, if we thus seek the things of this world, it is just in God to deny them; whereas, if we seek any thing that we may serve God with it, we may expect he will either give us what we seek or give us hearts to be content without it, and give opportunities of serving and glorifying him some other way. Let us remember this, that when we speed not in our prayers it is *because we ask amiss;* either we do not ask for right ends or not in a right manner, not with faith or not with fervency: unbelieving and cold desires beg denials; and this we may be sure of, that, when our prayers are rather the language of our lusts than of our graces, they will return empty.

II. We have fair warning to avoid all criminal friendships with this world: *You adulterers and adulteresses, know you not that the friendship of the world is enmity with God?* v. 4. Worldly people are here called adulterers and adulteresses, because of their perfidiousness to God, while they give their best affections to the world. Covetousness is elsewhere called idolatry, and it is here called adultery; it is a forsaking of him to whom we are devoted and espoused, to cleave to other things; there is this brand put upon worldly-mindedness—that it is enmity to God. A man may have a competent portion of the good things of this life, and yet may keep himself in the love of God; but he who sets his heart upon the world, who places his happiness in it, and will conform himself to it, and do any thing rather than lose its friendship, he is an enemy to God; it is constructive treason and rebellion against God to set the world upon his throne in our hearts. *Whosoever therefore is the friend of the world is the enemy of God.* He who will act upon this principle, to keep the smiles of the world, and to have its continual friendship, cannot but show himself, in spirit, and in his actions too, an enemy to God. *You cannot serve God and mammon,* Matt. vi. 24. Hence arise wars and fightings, even from this adulterous idolatrous love of the world, and serving of it; for what peace can there be among men, so long as there is enmity towards God? or who can fight against God, and prosper? "Think seriously with yourselves what the spirit of the world is, and you will find that you cannot suit yourselves to it as friends, but it must occasion your being envious, and full of evil inclinations, as the generality of the world are. *Do you think that the scripture saith in vain, The spirit that dwelleth in us lusteth to envy?*" v. 5.

The account given in the holy scriptures of the hearts of men by nature is *that their imagination is evil, only evil, and that continually,* Gen. vi. 5. Natural corruption principally shows itself by envying, and there is a continual propensity to this. The spirit which naturally dwells in man is always producing one evil imagination or another, always emulating such as we see and converse with, and seeking those things which are possessed and enjoyed by them. Now this way of the world, affecting pomp and pleasure, and falling into strifes and quarrels for the sake of these things, is the certain consequence of being friends to the world; for there is no friendship without a oneness of spirit, and therefore Christians, to avoid contentions, must avoid the friendship of the world, and must show that they are actuated by nobler principles and that a nobler spirit dwells in them; for if we belong to God, he gives more grace than to live and act as the generality of the world do. The spirit of the world teaches men to be churls; God teaches them to be bountiful. The spirit of the world teaches us to lay up, or lay out, for ourselves, and according to our own fancies; God teaches us to be willing to communicate to the necessities and to the comfort of others, and so as to do good to all about us according to our ability. The grace of God is contrary to the spirit of the world, and therefore the friendship of the world is to be avoided, if we pretend to be friends of God; yea, the grace of God will correct and cure the spirit that naturally dwells in us; where he giveth grace, he giveth another spirit than that of the world.

III. We are taught to observe the difference God makes between pride and humility. *God resisteth the proud, but giveth grace unto the humble, v.* 6. This is represented as the language of scripture in the Old Testament; for so it is declared in the book of *Psalms, that God will save the afflicted people* (if their spirits be suited to their condition), *but will bring down high looks* (Ps. xviii. 27); and in the book of Proverbs it is said, *He scorneth the scorners, and giveth grace unto the lowly,* Prov. iii. 34. Two things are here to be observed :—1. The disgrace cast upon the proud; God resists them; the original word, ἀντιτάσσεται, signifies, God setting himself as in battle array against them; and can there be a greater disgrace than for God to proclaim a man a rebel, an enemy, a traitor to his crown and dignity, and to proceed against him as such? The proud resists God; in his understanding he resists the truths of God; in his will he resists the laws of God; in his passions he resists the providence of God; and therefore no wonder that God sets himself against the proud. Let proud spirits hear this and tremble—*God resists them.* Who can describe the wretched state of those who make God their enemy? He will certainly fill with shame (sooner or later) the faces of such as have filled their hearts with pride. We should therefore resist pride in our hearts, if we would not have God to resist us. 2. The honour and help God gives to the humble. Grace, as opposed to disgrace, is honour; this God gives to the humble; and where God gives grace to be humble, there he will give all other graces, and, as in the beginning of this sixth verse, he will *give more grace.* Wherever God gives true grace, he will give more; for to him that hath, and useth what he hath aright, more shall be given. He will especially give more grace to the humble, because they see their need of it, will pray for it, and be thankful for it; and such shall have it. For this reason,

IV. We are taught to submit ourselves entirely to God: *Submit yourselves therefore to God. Resist the devil, and he will flee from you, v.* 7. Christians should forsake the friendship of the world, and watch against that envy and pride which they see prevailing in natural men, and should by grace learn to glory in their submissions to God. "Submit yourselves to him as subjects to their prince, in duty, and as one friend to another, in love and interest. Submit your understandings to the truths of God; submit your wills to the will of God; the will of his precept, the will of his providence." We are subjects, and as such must be submissive; not only through fear, but through love; *not only for wrath, but also for conscience' sake.* "Submit yourselves to God, as considering how many ways you are bound to this, and as considering what advantage you will gain by it; for God will not hurt you by his dominion over you, but will do you good." Now, as this subjection and submission to God are what the devil most industriously strives to hinder, so we ought with great care and steadiness to resist his suggestions. If he would represent a tame yielding to the will and providence of God as what will bring calamities, and expose to contempt and misery, we must resist these suggestions of fear. If he would represent submission to God as a hindrance to our outward ease, or worldly preferments, we must resist these suggestions of pride and sloth. If he would tempt us to lay any of our miseries, and crosses, and afflictions, to the charge of Providence, so that we might avoid them by following his directions instead of God's, we must resist these provocations to anger, *not fretting ourselves in any wise to do evil.* "Let not the devil, in these or the like attempts, prevail upon you; but *resist him and he will flee from you.*" If we basely yield to temptations, the devil will continually follow us; but if we *put on the whole armour of God,* and stand it out against him, he will be gone from us. Resolution shuts and bolts the door against temptation.

V. We are directed how to act towards God, in our becoming submissive to him, *v.* 8–10. 1. *Draw nigh to God.* The heart that has rebelled must be brought to the foot of God; the spirit that was distant and estranged from a life of communion and converse with God must become acquainted with him: "*Draw nigh to God,* in his worship and institutions, and in every duty he requires of you." 2. *Cleanse your hands.* He who comes unto God must have clean hands. Paul therefore directs to *lift up holy hands without wrath and doubting* (1 Tim. ii. 8), hands free from blood, and bribes, and every thing that is unjust or cruel, and free from every defilement of sin; he is not subject to God who is a servant of sin. The hands must be cleansed by faith, repentance, and reformation, or it will be in vain for us to draw nigh to God in prayer, or in any of the exercises of devotion. 3. The hearts of the double-minded must be purified. Those who halt between God and the world are here meant by *the double-minded.* To *purify the heart* is to be sincere, and to act upon this single aim and principle, rather to please God than to seek after anything in this world: hypocrisy is heart-impurity; but those who submit themselves to God aright will purify their hearts as well as cleanse their hands. 4. *Be afflicted, and mourn, and weep.* "What afflictions God sends take them as he would have you, and be duly sensible of them. Be afflicted when afflictions are sent upon you, and do not despise them; or be afflicted in your sympathies with those who are so, and in laying to heart the calamities of the church of God. Mourn and weep for your own sins and the sins of others; times of contention and division are times to mourn in, and the sins that occasion wars and fightings should be mourned for. *Let your laughter be turned to mourning and your joy to heaviness.*" This may be taken either as a prediction of sorrow or a prescription of seriousness. Let men think to set grief at defiance, yet God can bring it upon them ; none laugh so heartily but he can turn their laughter into mourning ; and this the unconcerned Christians James wrote to are threatened should be their case. They are therefore directed, before things come to the worst, to lay aside their vain mirth and their sensual pleasures, that they might indulge godly sorrow and penitential tears. 5. "*Humble yourselves in the sight of the Lord.* Let the inward acts of the soul be suitable to all those outward expressions of grief, affliction, and sorrow, before mentioned." Humility of spirit is here required, as in the sight of him who looks principally at the spirits of men. "Let there be a thorough humiliation in bewailing every thing that is evil ; let there be great humility in doing that which is good : *Humble yourselves.*"

VI. We have great encouragement to act thus towards God : *He will draw nigh to those that draw nigh to him* (v. 8), *and he will lift up* those who humble themselves in his sight, v. 10. Those that draw nigh to God in a way of duty shall find God drawing nigh to them in a way of mercy. Draw nigh to him in faith, and trust, and obedience, and he will draw nigh to you for your deliverance. If there be not a close communion between God and us, it is our fault, and not his. *He shall lift up the humble.* Thus much our Lord himself declared, *He that shall humble himself shall be exalted,* Matt. xxiii. 12. If we be truly penitent and humble under the marks of God's displeasure, we shall in a little time know the advantages of his favour ; he will lift us up out of trouble, or he will lift us up in our spirits and comforts under trouble ; he will lift us up to honour and safety in the world, or he will lift us up in our way to heaven, so as to raise our hearts and affections above the world. *God will revive the spirit of the humble* (Isa. lvii. 15), *He will hear the desire of the humble* (Ps. x. 17), and he will at last lift them up to glory. *Before honour is humility.* The highest honour in heaven will be the reward of the greatest humility on earth.

¹¹ Speak not evil one of another [**not against another**], brethren. He that speaketh evil of [**speaketh against**] *his* brother, and judgeth his brother, speaketh evil of [**against**] the law, and judgeth the law : but if thou judge the law, thou art not a doer of the law, but a judge. ¹² There is one lawgiver, who is able to save and to destroy : who art thou that judgest another? ¹³ Go to now, ye that say, To day or to morrow we will go into such a city, and continue there a year, and buy and sell, and get gain : ¹⁴ Whereas ye know not what *shall be* on the morrow. For what *is* your life? It is even a vapour, that appeareth for a little time, and then vanisheth away. ¹⁵ For that ye *ought* to say, If the Lord will, we shall live, and do this, or that. ¹⁶ But now you rejoice in your boastings : all such rejoicing is evil. ¹⁷ Therefore to him that knoweth to do good, and doeth *it* not, to him it is sin.

In this part of the chapter,

I. We are cautioned against the sin of evil speaking : *Speak not evil one of another, brethren, v.* 11. The Greek word, καταλαλεῖτε, signifies speaking any thing that may hurt or injure another ; we must not speak evil things of others, though they be true, unless we be called to it, and there be some necessary occasion for it; much less must we report evil things when they are false, or, for aught we know, may be so. Our lips must be guided by the law of kindness, as well as truth and justice. This, which Solomon makes a necessary part of the character of his virtuous woman, *that she openeth her mouth with wisdom, and in her tongue is the law of kindness* (Prov. xxxi. 26), must needs be a part of the character of every true Christian. *Speak not evil one of another,* 1. Because you are brethren. The compellation, as used by the apostle here, carries an argument along with it. Since Christians are brethren, they should not defile nor defame one another. It is required of us that we be tender of the good name of our brethren; where we cannot speak well, we had better say nothing than speak evil; we must not take pleasure in making known the faults of others, divulging things that are secret, merely to expose them, nor in making more of their known faults than really they deserve, and, least of all, in making false stories, and spreading things concerning them of which they are altogether innocent. What is this but to raise the hatred and encourage the persecutions of the world, against those who are engaged in the same interests with ourselves, and therefore with whom we ourselves must stand or fall? "Consider, you are brethren." 2. Because this is to judge the law: *He that speaketh evil of his brother, and judgeth his brother, speaketh evil of the law, and judgeth the law.* The law of Moses says, *Thou shalt not go up and down as a tale-bearer among thy people,* Lev. xix. 16. The law of Christ is, *Judge not, that you be not judged,* Matt. vii. 1. The sum and substance of both is that men should love one another. A detracting tongue therefore condemns the law of God, and the commandment of Christ, when it is defaming its neighbour. To break God's commandments is in effect to speak evil of them, and to judge them, as if they were too strict, and laid too great a restraint upon us. The Christians to whom James wrote were apt to speak very hard things of one another, because of their differences about indifferent things (such as *the observance of meats and days,* as appears from Rom. xiv.): "Now," says the apostle, "he who censures and condemns his brother for not agreeing with him in those things which the law of God has left indifferent thereby censures and condemns the law, as if it had done ill in leaving them indifferent. He who quarrels with his brother, and condemns him for the sake of any thing not determined in the word of God, does thereby reflect on that word of God, as if it were not a perfect rule. Let us take heed of judging the law, for the law of the Lord is perfect; if men break the law, leave that to judge them; if they do not break it, let us not judge them." This is a heinous evil, because it is to forget our place, that we ought to be doers of the law, and it is to set up ourselves above it, as if we were to be judges of it. He who is guilty of the sin here cautioned against is not a doer of the law, but a judge; he assumes an office and a place that do not belong to him, and he will be sure to suffer for his presumption in the end. Those who are most ready to set up for judges of the law generally fail most in their obedience to it. 3. Because God, the lawgiver, has reserved the power of passing the final sentence on men wholly to himself: *There is one Lawgiver, who is able to save, and to destroy: who art thou that judgest another?* v. 12. Princes and states are not excluded, by what is here said, from making laws; nor are subjects at all encouraged to disobey human laws; but God is still to be acknowledged as the supreme Lawgiver, who only can give law to the conscience, and who alone is to be absolutely obeyed. His right to enact laws is incontestable, because he has such a power to enforce them. He *is able to save, and to destroy,* so as no other can. He has power fully to reward the observance of his laws, and to punish all disobedience; he can save the soul, and make it happy for ever, or he can, after he has killed, cast into hell; and therefore should be feared and obeyed as the great Lawgiver, and all judgment should be committed to him. Since there is one Lawgiver, we may infer that it is not for any man or company of men in the world to pretend to give laws immediately to bind conscience; for that is God's prerogative, which must not be invaded. As the apostle had before warned against being many masters, so here he cautions against being many judges. Let us not prescribe to our brethren, let us not censure and condemn them; it is sufficient that we have the law of God, which is a rule to us all; and therefore we should not set up other rules. Let us not presume to set up our own particular notions and opinions as a rule to all about us; for *there is one Lawgiver.*

II. We are cautioned against a presumptuous confidence of the continuance of our lives, and against forming projects thereupon with assurance of success, *v.* 13, 14. The apostle having reproved those who were judges and condemners of the law, now reproves such as were disregardful of Providence: *Go to now,* an old way of speaking, designed to engage attention; the Greek word may be rendered, *Behold now,* or "*See, and consider, you that say,* To-day or to-morrow we will go into such a city, and continue there a year, and buy and sell, and get gain. Reflect a little on this way of thinking and talking; call yourselves to account for it." Serious reflection on our words and ways would show us many evils that we are apt, through inadvertency, to run into and continue in. There were some who said of old, as too many say still, *We will go to such a city, and do this or that,* for such a term of time, while all serious regards to the disposals of Providence were neglected. Observe here, 1. How apt worldly and projecting men are to leave God out of their schemes. Where any are set upon earthly things, these have a strange power of engrossing the thoughts of the heart. We should therefore have a care of growing intent or eager in our pursuits after any thing here below. 2. How much of worldly happiness lies in the promises men make to themselves beforehand. Their heads are full of fine visions, as to what they shall do, and be, and enjoy, in some future time, when they can neither be sure of time nor of any of the advantages they promise themselves; therefore observe, 3. How vain a thing it is to look for any thing good in futurity, without the concurrence of Providence. *We will go to such a city* (say they), perhaps to Antioch, or Damascus, or Alexandria, which were then the great places for traffic; but how could they be sure, when they set out, that they should reach any of these cities? Something might possibly stop their way, or call them elsewhere, or cut the thread of life. Many who have set out on a journey have gone to their long home, and never reached their journey's end. But, suppose they should reach the city they designed, how did they know they should continue there? Something might happen to send them back, or to call them thence, and to shorten their stay. Or suppose they should stay the full time they proposed, yet they could not be certain that they should buy and sell there; perhaps they might lie sick there, or they might not meet with those to trade with them that they expected. Yea, suppose they should go to that city, and continue there a year, and should buy and sell, yet they might not get gain; getting of gain in this world is at best but an uncertain thing, and they might probably make more losing bargains then gainful ones. And then, as to all these particulars, the frailty, shortness, and uncertainty of life, ought to check the vanity and presumptuous confidence of such projectors for futurity: *What is your life? It is even a vapour that appeareth for a little time, and then vanisheth away, v. 14.* God hath wisely left us in the dark concerning future events, and even concerning the duration of life itself. We *know not what shall be on the morrow;* we may know what we intend to do and to be, but a thousand things may happen to prevent us. We are not sure of life itself, since it is but as a *vapour,* something in appearance, but nothing solid nor certain, easily scattered and gone. We can fix the hour and minute of the sun's rising and setting to-morrow, but we cannot fix the certain time of a vapour's being scattered; such is our life: *it appears but for a little time, and then vanisheth away;* it vanisheth as to this world, but there is a life that will continue in the other world; and, since this life is so uncertain, it concerns us all to prepare and lay up in store for that to come.

III. We are taught to keep up a constant sense of our dependence on the will of God for life, and all the actions and enjoyments of it: *You ought to say, If the Lord will, we shall live, and do this, or that, v. 15.* The apostle, having reproved them for what was amiss, now directs them how to be and do better: " You ought to say it in your hearts at all times, and with your tongues upon proper occasions, especially in your constant prayers and devotions, that if the Lord will give leave, and if he will own and bless you, you have such and such designs to accomplish." This must be said, not in a slight, formal, and customary way, but so as to think what we say and so as to be reverent and serious in what we say. It is good to express ourselves thus when we have to do with others, but it is indispensably requisite that we should say this to ourselves in all that we go about. Σὺν Θεῷ—*With the leave and blessing of God,* was used by the Greeks in the beginning of every undertaking. 1. *If the Lord will, we shall live.* We must remember that our times are not in our own hands, but at the disposal of God; we live as long as God appoints, and in the circumstances God appoints, and therefore must be submissive to him, even as to life itself; and then, 2. *If the Lord will, we shall do this or that.* All our actions and designs are under the control of Heaven. Our heads may be filled with cares and contrivances. This and the other thing we may propose to do for ourselves, or our families, or our friends; but Providence sometimes breaks all our measures, and throws our schemes into confusion. Therefore both our counsels for action and our conduct in action should be entirely referred to God; all we design and all we do should be with a submissive dependence on God.

IV. We are directed to avoid vain boasting, and to look upon it not only as a weak, but a very evil thing. *You rejoice in your boastings; all such rejoicing is evil, v. 16.* They promised themselves life and prosperity, and great things in the world, without any just regard to God; and then they boasted of these things. Such is the joy of worldly people, to boast of all their successes, yea, often to boast of their very projects before they know what success they shall have. How common is it for men to boast of things which they have no other title to than what arises from their own vanity and presumption! *Such rejoicing* (says the apostle) *is evil;* it is foolish and it is hurtful. For men to boast of worldly things, and of their aspiring projects, when they should be attending to the humbling duties before laid down (in *v.* 8–10), is a very evil thing. It is a great sin in God's account, it will bring great disappointment upon themselves, and it will prove their destruction in the end. If we rejoice in God that our times are in his hand, that all events are at his disposal, and that he is our God in covenant, this rejoicing is good ; the wisdom, power, and providence of God, are then concerned to make all things work together for our good : but if we rejoice in our own vain confidences and presumptuous boasts, this is evil ; it is an evil carefully to be avoided by all wise and good men.

V. We are taught, in the whole of our conduct, to act up to our own convictions, and, whether we have to do with God or men, to see that we never go contrary to our own knowledge (*v.* 17) : *To him that knoweth to do good, and doeth it not, to him it is sin ;* it is aggravated sin : it is sinning with a witness ; and it is to have the worst witness against a man that can be, when he sins against his own conscience. Observe, 1. This stands immediately connected with the plain lesson of saying, *If the Lord will, we shall do this or that :* they might be ready to say, " This is a very obvious thing ; who knows not that we all depend upon almighty God *for life, and breath, and all things ?* " Remember then, if you do know this, whenever you act unsuitably to such a dependence, that *to him that knows to do good, and does it not, to him it is sin,* the greater sin. 2. Omissions are sins which will come into judgment, as well as commissions. He that does not the good he knows should be done, as well as he who does the evil he knows should not be done, will be condemned. Let us therefore take care that conscience be rightly informed, and then that it be faithfully and constantly obeyed ; for, if *our own hearts condemn us not, then have we confidence towards God ;* but if we say, *We see,* and do not act suitably to our sight, then *our sin remaineth,* John ix. 41.

CHAPTER V

In this chapter the apostle denounces the judgments of God upon those rich men who oppress the poor, showing them how great their sin and folly are in the sight of God, and how grievous the punishments would be which should fall upon themselves, ver. 1-6. Hereupon, all the faithful are exhorted to patience under their trials and sufferings, ver. 7-11. The sin of swearing is cautioned against, ver. 12. We are directed how to act, both under affliction and in prosperity, ver. 13. Prayer for the sick, and anointing with oil, are prescribed, ver. 14, 15. Christians are directed to acknowledge their faults one to another, and to pray one for another, and the efficacy of prayer is proved ver. 16-18. And, lastly, it is recommended to us to do what we can for bringing back those that stray from the ways of truth.

GO to now, *ye* rich men, weep and howl for your miseries that shall come upon *you.* ² Your riches are corrupted, and your garments are motheaten. ³ Your gold and silver is cankered [**are rusted**] ; and the rust of them shall be a witness against you, and shall eat your flesh as it were fire. Ye have heaped treasure together for [**in**] the last days. ⁴ Behold, the hire of the labourers who have reaped down your fields, which is of you kept back by fraud, crieth : and the cries of them which have reaped are entered into the ears of the Lord of

sabaoth. ⁵ Ye have lived in pleasure on the earth, and been
wanton ; ye have nourished your hearts, as in [hearts in] a day of
slaughter. ⁶ Ye have condemned *and* killed the just [the righteous *one*]; *and* he doth not resist you. ⁷ Be patient therefore,
brethren, unto the coming of the Lord. Behold, the husbandman waiteth for the precious fruit of the earth, and hath long
patience for it, until he receive the early and latter rain. ⁸ Be
ye also patient ; stablish your hearts : for the coming of the Lord
draweth nigh. ⁹ Grudge not one against another, brethren, lest
ye be condemned [judged] : behold, the judge standeth before
the door. ¹⁰ Take, my brethren, the prophets, who have spoken
in the name of the Lord, for an example of suffering affliction,
and of patience. ¹¹ Behold, we count them happy which endure.
Ye have heard of the patience of Job, and have seen the end of
the Lord ; that the Lord is very pitiful, and of tender mercy.

The apostle is here addressing first sinners and then saints.

I. Let us consider the address to sinners ; and here we find James
seconding what his great Master had said : *Woe unto you that are rich ; for
you have received your consolation*, Luke vi. 24. The rich people to whom
this word of warning was sent were not such as professed the Christian
religion, but the worldly and unbelieving Jews, such as are here said *to
condemn and kill the just*, which the Christians had no power to do ; and
though this epistle was written for the sake of the faithful, and was sent
principally to them, yet, by an apostrophe, the infidel Jews may be well
supposed here spoken to. They would not hear the word, and therefore it
is *written*, that they might read it. It is observable, in the first inscription
of this epistle, that it is not directed, as Paul's epistles were, *to the brethren
in Christ*, but, in general, *to the twelve tribes ;* and the salutation is not,
grace and peace from Christ, but, in general, *greeting*, ch. i. 1. The poor
among the Jews received the gospel, and many of them believed ; but the
generality of the rich rejected Christianity, and were hardened in their
unbelief, and hated and persecuted those who believed on Christ. To
these oppressing, unbelieving, persecuting, rich people, the apostle addresses
himself in the first six verses.

1. He foretells the judgments of God that should come upon them, *v.* 1–3.
They should have miseries come upon them, and such dreadful miseries that
the very apprehension of them was enough to make them weep and howl—
misery that should arise from the very things in which they placed their
happiness, and misery that should be completed by these things witnessing
against them at the last, to their utter destruction ; and they are now called
to reason upon and thoroughly to weigh the matter, and to think how they
will stand before God in judgment : *Go to now, you rich men.* (1.) "You
may be assured of this, that very dreadful calamities are coming upon you,
calamities that shall carry nothing of support nor comfort in them, but all
misery, misery in time, misery to eternity, misery in your outward afflictions, misery in your inward frame and temper of mind, misery in this
world, misery in hell. You have not a single instance of misery only
coming upon you, but miseries. The ruin of your church and nation is at
hand ; and there will come a day of wrath, when riches shall not profit

men, but *all the wicked shall be destroyed.*" (2.) The very apprehension of such miseries as were coming upon them is enough to make them weep and howl. Rich men are apt to say to themselves (and others are ready to say to them), *Eat, drink, and be merry;* but God says, *Weep and howl.* It is not said, Weep and repent, for this the apostle does not expect from them (he speaks in a way of denouncing rather than admonishing); but, " *Weep and howl,* for when your doom comes there will be nothing but *weeping, and wailing, and gnashing of teeth.*" Those who live like beasts are called to howl like such. Public calamities are most grievous to rich people, who live in pleasure, and are secure and sensual . and therefore they shall weep and howl more than other people for the miseries that shall come upon them. (3.) Their misery shall arise from the very things in which they placed their happiness. "Corruption, decay, rust, and ruin, will come upon all your goodly things : *Your riches are corrupted and your garments are moth-eaten, v.* 2. Those things which you now inordinately affect will hereafter insupportably wound you: they will be of no worth, of no use to you, but, on the contrary, will *pierce you through with many sorrows; for,*" (4.) " *They will witness agains you, and they will eat your flesh as it were fire,*" *v.* 3. Things inanimate are frequently represented in scripture as witnessing against wicked men. Heaven, earth, the stones of the field, the production of the ground, and here the very rust and canker of ill-gotten and ill-kept treasures, are said to witness against impious rich men. They think to heap up treasure for their latter days, to live plentifully upon when they come to be old; but, alas! they are only heaping up treasures to become a prey to others (as the Jews had all taken from them by the Romans), and treasures that will prove at last to be only treasures of wrath, *in the day of the revelation of the righteous judgment of God.* Then shall their iniquities, in the punishment of them, *eat their flesh as it were* with *fire.* In the ruin of Jerusalem, many thousands perished by fire; in the last judgment the wicked shall be condemned to *everlasting burnings, prepared for the devil and his angels.* The Lord deliver us from the portion of wicked rich men! and, in order to this, let us take care that we do not fall into their sins, which we are next to consider.

2. The apostle shows what those sins are which should bring such miseries. To be in so deplorable a condition must doubtless be owing to some very heinous crimes. (1.) Covetousness is laid to the charge of this people; they laid by their garments till they bred moths and were eaten; they hoarded up their gold and silver till they were rusty and cankered. It is a very great disgrace to these things that they carry in them the principles of their own corruption and consumption—the garment breeds the moth that frets it, the gold and silver breeds the canker that eats it; but the disgrace falls most heavily upon those who hoard and lay up these things till they come to be thus corrupted, and cankered, and eaten. God gives us our worldly possessions that we may honour him and do good with them; but if, instead of this, we sinfully hoard them up, through an undue affection towards them, or a distrust of the providence of God for the future, this is a very heinous crime, and will be witnessed against by the very rust and corruption of the treasure thus heaped together. (2.) Another sin charged upon those against whom James writes is oppression : *Behold, the hire of the labourers, who have reaped down your fields, which is of you kept back by fraud, crieth,* &c., *v.* 4. Those who have wealth in their hands get power into their hands, and then they are tempted to abuse that power to oppress such as are under them. The rich we here find employing the

poor in their labours, and the rich have as much need of the labours of the
poor as the poor have of wages from the rich, and could as ill be without
them ; but yet, not considering this, they kept back the hire of the
labourers ; having power in their hands, it is probable that they made as
hard bargains with the poor as they could, and even after that would not
make good their bargains as they should have done. This is a crying sin,
an iniquity that cries so as to reach the ears of God ; and, in this case, God
is to be considered as *the Lord of sabaoth,* or *the Lord of hosts,* Κυρίου
σαβαὼθ, a phrase often used in the Old-Testament, when the people of God
were defenceless and wanted protection, and when their enemies were
numerous and powerful. The Lord of hosts, who has all ranks of beings
and creatures at his disposal, and who sets all in their several places, hears
the oppressed when they cry by reason of the cruelty or injustice of the
oppressor, and he will give orders to some of those hosts that are under
him (angels, devils, storms, distempers, or the like) to avenge the wrongs
done to those who are dealt with unrighteously and unmercifully. Take
heed of this sin of defrauding and oppressing, and avoid the very appearances of it. (3.) Another sin here mentioned is sensuality and voluptuousness. *You have lived in pleasure on the earth, and been wanton, v. 5.* God
does not forbid us to use pleasure ; but to live in them as if we lived for
nothing else is a very provoking sin ; and to do this on the earth, where
we are but strangers and pilgrims, where we are but to continue for a
while, and where we ought to be preparing for eternity—this, this is a
grievous aggravation of the sin of voluptuousness. Luxury makes people
wanton, as in Hos. xiii. 6, *According to their pasture, so were they filled ;
they were filled, and their heart was exalted ; therefore have they forgotten me.*
Wantonness and luxury are commonly the effects of great plenty and
abundance ; it is hard for people to have great estates, and not too much
indulge themselves in carnal, sensual pleasures : " *You have nourished your
hearts as in a day of slaughter :* you live as if it were every day a day of
sacrifices, a festival : and hereby your hearts are fattened and nourished to
stupidity, dulness, pride, and an insensibility to the wants and afflictions
of others." Some may say, "What harm is there in good cheer, provided
people do not spend above what they have ?" What ! Is it no harm for
people to make gods of their bellies, and to give all to these, instead of
abounding in acts of charity and piety ? Is it no harm for people to unfit
themselves for minding the concerns of their souls, by indulging the
appetites of their bodies ? Surely that which brought flames upon Sodom,
and would bring these miseries for which rich men are here called to weep
and howl, must be a heinous evil ! Pride, and idleness, and fulness of
bread, mean the same thing with living in pleasure, and being wanton, and
nourishing the heart as in a day of slaughter. (4.) Another sin here charged
on the rich is persecution : *You have condemned and killed the just, and he
doth not resist you, v. 6.* This fills up the measure of their iniquity. They
oppressed and acted very unjustly, to get estates ; when they had them,
they gave way to luxury and sensuality, till they had lost all sense and
feeling of the wants or afflictions of others ; and then they persecute and
kill without remorse. They pretend to act legally indeed, they condemn
before they kill ; but unjust prosecutions, whatever colour of law they may
carry in them, will come into the reckoning when God shall make inquisition for blood, as well as massacres and downright murders. Observe here,
The just may be condemned and killed : but then again observe, When
such do suffer, and yield without resistance to the unjust sentence of

oppressors, this is marked by God, to the honour of the sufferers and the infamy of their persecutors ; this commonly shows that judgments are at the door, and we may certainly conclude that a reckoning-day will come, to reward the patience of the oppressed and to break to pieces the oppressor. Thus far the address to sinners goes.

II. We have next subjoined an address to saints. Some have been ready to despise or to condemn this way of preaching, when ministers, in their application, have brought a word to sinners, and a word to saints ; but, from the apostle's here taking this method, we may conclude that this is the best way rightly to divide the word of truth. From what has been said concerning wicked and oppressing rich men, occasion is given to administer comfort to God's afflicted people : "Be patient therefore ; since God will send such miseries on the wicked, you may see what is your duty, and where your greatest encouragement lies."

1. Attend to your duty : *Be patient* (v. 7), *establish your hearts* (v. 8), *grudge not one against another, brethren, v.* 9. Consider well the meaning of these three expressions ;—(1.) "*Be patient*—bear your afflictions without murmuring, your injuries without revenge ; and, though God should not in any signal manner appear for you immediately, wait for him. *The vision is for an appointed time ; at the end it will speak, and will not lie ; therefore wait for it. It is but a little while, and he that shall come will come, and will not tarry.* Let your patience be lengthened out to long-suffering ;" so the word here used, μακροθυμήσατε, signifies. When we have done our work, we have need of patience to stay for our reward. This Christian patience is not a mere yielding to necessity, as the moral patience taught by some philosophers was, but it is a humble acquiescence in the wisdom and will of God, with an eye to a future glorious recompense : *Be patient to the coming of the Lord.* And because this is a lesson Christians must learn, though ever so hard or difficult to them, it is repeated in *v.* 8, *Be you also patient.* (2.) "*Establish your hearts*—let your faith be firm, without wavering, your practice of what is good constant and continued, without tiring, and your resolutions for God and heaven fixed, in spite of all sufferings or temptations." The prosperity of the wicked and the affliction of the righteous have in all ages been a very great trial to the faith of the people of God. David tells us *that his feet were almost gone, when he saw the prosperity of the wicked,* Ps. lxxiii. 2, 3. Some of those Christians to whom St. James wrote might probably be in the same tottering condition ; and therefore they are called upon to establish their hearts ; faith and patience will establish the heart. (3.) *Grudge not one against another ;* the words μὴ στενάζετε signify, *Groan* not one against another, that is, "Do not make one another uneasy by your murmuring groans at what befalls you, nor by your distrustful groans as to what may further come upon you, nor by your revengeful groans against the instruments of your sufferings, nor by your envious groans at those who may be free from your calamities : do not make yourselves uneasy and make one another uneasy by thus groaning to and grieving one another." "The apostle seemeth to me " (says Dr. Manton) "to be here taxing those mutual injuries and animosities wherewith the Christians of those times, having banded under the names of *circumcision* and *uncircumcision*, did grieve one another, and give each other cause to groan ; so that they did not only sigh under the oppressions of the rich persecutors, but under the injuries which they sustained from many of the brethren who, together with them, did profess the holy faith. Those who are in the midst of common enemies, and in any suffering

circumstances, should be more especially careful not to grieve nor to groan against one another, otherwise judgments will come upon them as well as others; and the more such grudgings prevail the nearer do they show judgment to be.

2. Consider what encouragement here is for Christians to be patient, to establish their hearts, and not to grudge one against another. And (1.) " Look to the example of the husbandman : *He waits for the precious fruit of the earth, and hath long patience for it, until he receive the early and latter rain.* When you sow your corn in the ground, you wait many months for the former and latter rain, and are willing to stay till harvest for the fruit of your labour ; and shall not this teach you to bear a few storms, and to be patient for a season, when you are looking for a kingdom and everlasting felicity ? Consider him that waits for a crop of corn ; and will not you wait for a crown of glory ? If you should be called to wait a little longer than the husbandman does, is it not something proportionably greater and infinitely more worth your waiting for ? But," (2.) "Think how short your waiting time may possibly be : *The coming of the Lord draweth nigh,* v. 8 ; *behold, the Judge standeth before the door,* v. 9. Do not be impatient, do not quarrel with one another ; the great Judge, who will set all to rights, who will punish the wicked and reward the good, is at hand : he should be conceived by you to stand as near as one who is just knocking at the door." *The coming of the Lord* to punish the wicked Jews was then very nigh, when James wrote this epistle ; and, whenever the patience and other graces of his people are tried in an extraordinary manner, the certainty of Christ's coming as Judge, and the nearness of it, should establish their hearts. The Judge is now a great deal nearer, in his coming to judge the world, than when this epistle was written, nearer by above seventeen hundred years ; and therefore this should have the greater effect upon us. (3.) The danger of our being condemned when the Judge appears should excite us to mind our duty as before laid down : *Grudge not, lest you be condemned.* Fretfulness and discontent expose us to the just judgment of God, and we bring more calamities upon ourselves by our murmuring, distrustful, envious groans and grudgings against one another, than we are aware of. If we avoid these evils, and be patient under our trials, God will not condemn us. Let us encourage ourselves with this. (4.) We are encouraged to be patient by the example of the prophets (v. 10) : *Take the prophets, who have spoken in the name of the Lord, for an example of suffering affliction, and of patience.* Observe here, The prophets, on whom God put the greatest honour, and for whom he had the greatest favour, were most afflicted : and when we think that the best men have had the hardest usage in this world, we should hereby be reconciled to affliction. Observe further, Those who were the greatest examples of suffering affliction were also the best and greatest examples of patience : *tribulation worketh patience.* Hereupon James gives it to us as the common sense of the faithful (v. 11) : *We count those happy who endure :* we look upon righteous and patient sufferers as the happiest people. See *ch.* i. 2–12. (5.) Job also is proposed as an example for the encouragement of the afflicted. *You have heard of the patience of Job, and have seen the end of the Lord,* &c., v. 11. In the case of Job you have an instance of a variety of miseries, and of such as were very grievous ; but under all he could bless God, and, as to the general bent of his spirit, he was patient and humble : and what came to him in the end ? Why, truly, God accomplished and brought about those things for him which plainly prove that *the Lord is very pitiful, and of*

tender mercy. The best way to bear afflictions is to look to the end of them; and the pity of God is such that he will not delay the bringing of them to an end when his purposes are once answered; and the tender mercy of God is such that he will make his people an abundant amends for all their sufferings and afflictions. His bowels are moved for them while suffering, his bounty is manifested afterwards. Let us serve our God, and endure our trials, as those who believe the end will crown all.

¹² But above all things, my brethren, swear not, neither by heaven, neither by the earth, neither by any other oath: but let your yea be yea; and *your* nay, nay; lest ye fall into condemnation [**under judgment**]. ¹³ Is any among you afflicted? let him pray. Is any merry? let him sing psalms. ¹⁴ Is any sick among you? let him call for the elders of the church; and let them pray over him, anointing him with oil in the name of the Lord: ¹⁵ And the prayer of faith shall save the sick, and the Lord shall raise him up; and if he have committed sins, they shall be forgiven him. ¹⁶ Confess *your* faults one to another, and pray one for another, that ye may be healed. The effectual fervent prayer [**The supplication**] of a righteous man availeth much [**availeth much in its working**]. ¹⁷ Elias was a man subject to like passions as we are, and he prayed earnestly that it might not rain: and it rained not on the earth by the space of three years and six months. ¹⁸ And he prayed again, and the heaven gave rain, and the earth brought forth her fruit. ¹⁹ Brethren, if any of you do err from the truth, and one convert him; ²⁰ Let him know, that he which converteth the sinner from the error of his way shall save a soul from death, and shall hide a multitude of sins.

This epistle now drawing to a close, the penman goes off very quickly from one thing to another: hence it is that matters so very different are insisted on in these few verses.

I. The sin of swearing is cautioned against: *But above all things, my brethren, swear not,* &c., *v.* 12. Some understand this too restrictedly, as if the meaning were, "Swear not at your persecutors, at *those that reproach you and say all manner of evil of you;* be not put into a passion by the injuries they do you, so as in your passion to be provoked to swear." This swearing is no doubt forbidden here: and it will not excuse those that are guilty of this sin to say they swear only when they are provoked to it, and before they are aware. But the apostle's warning extends to other occasions of swearing as well as this. Some have translated the words, πρὸ πάντων—*before all things;* and so have made the sense of this place to be that they should not, in common conversation, *before everything they say,* put an oath. All customary needless swearing is undoubtedly forbidden, and all along in scripture condemned, as a very grievous sin. Profane swearing was very customary among the Jews, and, since this epistle is directed in general *to the twelve tribes scattered abroad* (as before has been observed) we may conceive this exhortation sent to those who believed not. It is hard to suppose that swearing should be one of the spots of God's children, since Peter, when he was charged with being a disciple of Christ and would disprove the charge, cursed and swore, thereby thinking most effectually to convince them that he was no disciple of Jesus, it being well known of such that they durst not allow themselves in swearing; but possibly some of the looser sort of those who were called Christians might, among other sins here charged upon them, be guilty also of this. It is a sin that in later years has most scandalously prevailed, even among those who would be thought above all others entitled to the Christian name and privileges. It is very rare indeed to hear of a dissenter from the Church of England who is guilty of swearing, but among those who glory in their being of the established church nothing is more common; and indeed the most execrable oaths and curses now daily wound the ears and hearts of all serious Christians. James here says,

1. *Above all things, swear not;* but how many are there who mind this the least of all things, and who make light of nothing so much as common profane swearing! But why *above all things* is swearing here forbidden? (1.) Because it strikes most directly at the honour of God and most expressly throws contempt upon his name and authority. (2.) Because this sin has, of all sins, the least temptation to it: it is not gain, nor pleasure, nor reputation, that can move men to it, but a wantonness in sinning, and a needless showing an enmity to God. *Thy enemies take thy name in vain,* Ps. cxxxix. 20. This is a proof of men's being enemies to God, however they may pretend to call themselves by his name, or sometimes to compliment him in acts of worship. (3.) Because it is with most difficulty left off when once men are accustomed to it, therefore it should above all things be watched against. And, (4.) "*Above all things swear not,* for how can you expect the name of God should be a strong tower to you in your distress if you profane it and play with it at other times?" But (as Mr. Baxter observes) "all this is so far from forbidding necessary oaths that it is but to confirm them, by preserving the due reverence of them." And then he further notes that "The true nature of an oath is, by our speech, *to pawn the reputation of some certain or great thing,* for the *averring of a doubted less thing;* and not (as is commonly held) an appeal to God or other judge." Hence it was that swearing by the heavens, and by the earth, and by the other oaths the apostle refers to, came to be in use. The Jews thought if they did but omit the great oath of *Chi-Eloah,* they were safe. But they grew so profane as to swear by the creature, as if it were God; and so advanced it into the place of God; while, on the other hand, those who swear commonly and profanely by the name of God do hereby put him upon the level with every common thing.

2. *But let your yea be yea, and your nay, nay; lest you fall into condemnation;* that is, "let it suffice you to affirm or deny a thing as there is occasion, and be sure to stand to your word, and be true to it, so as to give no occasion for your being suspected of falsehood; and then you will be kept from the condemnation of backing what you say or promise by rash oaths, and from profaning the name of God to justify yourselves. It is being suspected of falsehood that leads men to swearing. Let it be known that you keep to truth, and are firm to your word, and by this means you will find there is no need to swear to what you say. Thus shall you escape the condemnation which is expressly annexed to the third commandment: *The Lord will not hold him guiltless that taketh his name in vain.*"

II. As Christians we are taught to suit ourselves to the dispensations of Providence (v. 13): *Is any among you afflicted? Let him pray. Is any merry? Let him sing psalms.* Our condition in this world is various; and our wisdom is to submit to its being so, and to behave as becomes us both in prosperity and under affliction. Sometimes we are in sadness, sometimes in mirth; God has set these one over against the other that we may the better observe the several duties he enjoins, and that the impressions made on our passions and affections may be rendered serviceable to our devotions. Afflictions should put us upon prayer, and prosperity should make us abound in praise. Not that prayer is to be confined to a time of trouble, nor singing to a time of mirth; but these several duties may be performed with special advantage, and to the happiest purposes, at such seasons. 1. In a day of affliction nothing is more seasonable than prayer. The person afflicted must pray himself, as well as engage the prayers of of others for him. Times of affliction should be praying times. To this end God sends afflictions, that we may be engaged to seek him early; and that those who at other times have neglected him may be brought to enquire after him. The spirit is then most humble, the heart is broken and tender; and prayer is most acceptable to God when it comes from a contrite humble spirit. Afflictions naturally draw out complaints; and to whom should we complain but to God in prayer? It is necessary to exercise faith and hope under afflictions; and prayer is the appointed means both for obtaining and increasing these graces in us. *Is any afflicted? Let him pray.* 2. In a day of mirth and prosperity singing psalms is very proper and seasonable. In the original it is only said *sing*, ψαλλέτω, without the addition of psalms or any other word: and we learn from the writings of several in the first ages of Christianity (particularly from a letter of Pliny's, and from some passages in Justin Martyr and Tertullian) that the Christians were accustomed to sing hymns, either taken out of scripture, or of more private composure, in their worship of God. Though some have thought that Paul's advising both the Colossians and Ephesians to *speak to one another* ψαλμοῖς καὶ ὕμνοις καὶ ᾠδαῖς πνευματικαῖς *in psalms, and hymns, and spiritual songs*, refers only to the compositions of scripture, the psalms of David being distinguished in Hebrew by *Shurim, Tehillin*, and *Mizmorim*, words that exactly answer these of the apostle. Let that be as it will, this however we are sure of, that the singing of psalms is a gospel ordinance, and that our joy should be holy joy, consecrated to God. Singing is so directed to here as to show that, if any be in circumstances of mirth and prosperity, he should turn his mirth, though alone, and by himself, into this channel. Holy mirth becomes families and retirements, as well as public assemblies. Let our singing be such as to make *melody with our hearts unto the Lord*, and God will assuredly be well pleased with this kind of devotion.

III. We have particular directions given as to sick persons, and *healing pardoning mercy promised* upon the observance of those directions. *If any be sick*, they are required, 1. To *send for the elders*, πρεσβυτέρους τῆς ἐκκλησίας—*the presbyters*, pastors, or ministers *of the church, v.* 14, 15. It lies upon sick people as a duty to send for ministers, and to desire their assistance and their prayers. 2. It is the duty of ministers to pray over the sick, when thus desired and called for. *Let them pray over him;* let their prayers be suited to his case, and their intercessions be as becomes those who are affected with his calamities. 3. In the times of miraculous healing, the *sick were to be anointed with oil in the name of the Lord.* Expositors generally confine this anointing with oil to such as had the power of working miracles ; and, when miracles ceased, this institution ceased also. In Mark's gospel we read of the apostle's anointing with oil many that were sick, and healing them, Mark vi. 13. And we have accounts of this being practised in the church two hundred years after Christ ; but then the gift of healing also accompanied it, and, when the miraculous gift ceased, this rite was laid aside. The papists indeed have made a sacrament of this, which they call *the extreme unction.* They use it, not to heal the sick, as it was used by the apostles ; but as they generally run counter to scripture, in the appointments of their church, so here they ordain that this should be administered only to such as are at the very point of death. The apostle's anointing was in order to heal the disease ; the popish anointing is for the expulsion of the relics of sin, and to enable the soul (as they pretend) the better to combat with the powers of the air. When they cannot prove, by any visible effects, that Christ owns them in the continuance of this rite, they would however have people to believe that the invisible effects are very wonderful. But it is surely much better to omit this anointing with oil than to turn it quite contrary to the purposes spoken of in scripture. Some protestants have thought that this anointing was only permitted or approved by Christ, not instituted. But it should seem, by the words of James here, that it was a thing enjoined in cases where there was faith for healing. And some protestants have argued for it with this view. It was not to be commonly used, not even in the apostolical age ; and some have thought that it should not be wholly laid aside in any age, but that where there are extraordinary measures of faith in the person anointing, and in those who are anointed, an extraordinary blessing may attend the observance of this direction for the sick. However that be, there is one thing carefully to be observed here, that the saving of the sick is not ascribed to the *anointing with oil,* but to prayer : *The prayer of faith shall save the sick,* &c., *v.* 15. So that, 4. Prayer over the sick must proceed from, and be accompanied with, a lively faith. There must be faith both in the person praying and in the person prayed for. In a time of sickness, it is not the cold and formal prayer that is effectual, but the prayer of faith. 5. We should observe the success of prayer. The Lord shall raise up ; that is, if he be a person capable and fit for deliverance, and if God have any thing further for such a person to do in the world. *And, if he have committed sins, they shall be forgiven him ;* that is, where sickness is sent as a punishment for some particular sin, that sin shall be pardoned, and in token thereof the sickness shall be removed. As when Christ said to the impotent man, *Go and sin no more, lest a worse thing come unto thee,* it is intimated that some particular sin was the cause of his sickness. The great thing therefore we should beg of God for ourselves and others in the time of sickness is the pardon of sin. Sin is both the root of sickness and the sting of it. If sin be pardoned, either affliction shall be removed in mercy or we shall see there is mercy in the continuance of it. When healing is founded upon pardon, we may say as Hezekiah did : Thou hast, in love to my soul, *delivered it from the pit of corruption,* Isa. xxxviii. 17. When you are sick and in pain, it is most common to pray and cry, *O give me ease! O restore me to health !* But your prayer should rather and chiefly be, *O that God would pardon my sins !*

IV. Christians are directed to *confess their faults one to another, and so to join in their prayers with and for one another, v.* 16. Some expositors connect this with *v.* 14. As if when sick people send for ministers to pray over them they should then confess their faults to them. Indeed, where any are conscious that their sickness is a vindictive punishment of some particular sin, and they cannot look for the removal of their sickness without particular applications to God for the pardon of such a sin, there it may be proper to acknowledge and tell his case, that those who pray over him may know how to plead rightly for him. But the confession here required is that of Christians to one another, and not, as the papists would have it, to a priest. Where persons have injured one another, acts of injustice must be confessed to those against whom they have been committed. Where persons have tempted one another to sin, or have consented in the same evil actions, there they ought mutually to blame themselves and excite each other to repentance. Where crimes are of a public nature, and have done any public mischief, there they ought to be more publicly confessed, so as may best reach to all who are concerned. And sometimes it may be well to confess our faults to some prudent minister or praying friend, that he may help us to plead with God for mercy and pardon. But then we are not to think that James puts us upon telling every thing that we are conscious is amiss in ourselves or in one another ; but so far as confession is necessary to our reconciliation with such as are at variance with us, or for reparation of wrongs done to any, or for gaining information in any point of conscience and making our own spirits quiet and easy, so far we should be ready to confess our faults. And sometimes also it may be of good use to Christians to disclose their peculiar weaknesses and infirmities to one another, where there are great intimacies and friendships, and where they may help each other by their prayers to obtain pardon of their sins and power against them. Those who make confession of their faults one to another should thereupon pray with and for one another. The 13th verse directs persons to pray for themselves : *Is any afflicted, let him pray ;* the 14th directs to seek for the prayers of ministers ; and the 16th directs private Christians to pray one for another ; so that here we have all sorts of prayer (ministerial, social, and secret) recommended.

V. The great advantage and efficacy of prayer are declared and proved : *The effectual fervent prayer of a righteous man availeth much,* whether he pray for himself or for others : witness the example of Elias, *v.* 17, 18. He who prays must be a righteous man ; not righteous in an absolute sense (for this Elias was not, who is here made a pattern to us), but righteous in a gospel sense ; not loving nor approving of any known iniquity. *If I regard iniquity in my heart, the Lord will not hear my prayer,* Ps. lxvi. 18. Further, the prayer itself must be a fervent, in-wrought, well-wrought prayer. It must be a pouring out of the heart to God ; and it must proceed from a faith unfeigned. Such prayer avails much. It is of great advantage to ourselves, it may be very beneficial to our friends, and we are assured of its being acceptable to God. It is good having those for friends whose prayers are available in the sight of God. The power of prayer is here proved from the success of Elijah. This may be encouraging to us even in common cases, if we consider that Elijah was *a man of like passions with us.* He was a zealous good man and a very great man, but he had his infirmities, and was subject to disorder in his passions as well as others. In prayer we must not look to the merit of man, but to the grace of God. Only in this we should copy after Elijah, that he prayed earnestly, or, as it is in the original, *in prayer he prayed.* It is not enough to say a prayer, but we must pray in prayer. Our thoughts must be fixed, our desires firm and ardent, and our graces in exercise; and, when we thus pray in prayer, we shall speed in prayer. Elijah *prayed that it might not rain;* and God heard him in his pleading against an idolatrous persecuting country, so that *it rained not on the earth for the space of three years and six months. Again he prayed, and the heaven gave rain,* &c. Thus you see prayer is the key which opens and shuts heaven. To this there is an allusion, Rev. xi. 6, where the two witnesses are said to have power *to shut heaven, that it rain not.* This instance of the extraordinary efficacy of prayer is recorded for encouragement even to ordinary Christians to be instant and earnest in prayer. God never says to any of the seed of Jacob, *Seek my face in vain.* If Elijah by prayer could do such great and wonderful things, surely the prayers of no righteous man shall return void. Where there may not be so much of miracle in God's answering our prayers, yet there may be as much of grace.

VI. This epistle concludes with an exhortation to do all we can in our places to promote the conversion and salvation of others, *v.* 19, 20. Some interpret these verses as an apology which the apostle is making for himself that he should so plainly and sharply reprove the Jewish Christians for their many faults and errors. And certainly James gives a very good reason why he was so much concerned to reclaim them from their errors, because in thus doing he should save souls, and hide a multitude of sins. But we are not to restrain this place to the apostle's converting such as erred from the truth; no, nor to other ministerial endeavours of the like nature, since it is said, "If any err, and one convert him, let him be who he will that does so good an office for another, he is therein an instrument of saving a soul from death." Those whom the apostle here calls brethren, he yet supposes liable to err. It is no mark of a wise or a holy man to boast of his being free from error, or to refuse to acknowledge when he is in an error. But if any do err, be they ever so great, you must not be afraid to show them their error; and, be they ever so weak and little, you must not disdain to make them wiser and better. If they err from the truth, that is, from the gospel (the great rule and standard of truth), whether it be in opinion or practice, you must endeavour to bring them again to the rule. Errors in judgment and in life generally go together. There is some doctrinal mistake at the bottom of every practical miscarriage. There is no one habitually bad, but upon some bad principle. Now to convert such is to reduce them from their error, and to reclaim them from the evils they have been led into. We are not presently to accuse and exclaim against an erring brother, and seek to bring reproaches and calamities upon him, but to convert him: and, if by all our endeavours we cannot do this, yet we are nowhere empowered to persecute and destroy him. If we are instrumental in the conversion of any, *we* are said to convert them, though this be principally and efficiently the work of God. And, if we can do no more towards the conversion of sinners, yet we may do this—pray for the grace and Spirit of God to convert and change them. And let those that are in any way serviceable to convert others know what will be the happy consequence of their doing this: they may take great comfort in it at present, and they will meet with a crown at last. He that is said to *err from the truth* in *v.* 19 is described as *erring in his way* in *v.* 20, and we cannot be said to convert any merely by altering their opinions, unless we can bring them to correct and amend their ways. This is conversion—to turn a sinner from the error of his ways, and not to turn him from one party to another, or merely from one notion and way of thinking to another. He who thus converteth a sinner from the error of his ways *shall save a soul from death.* There is a soul in the case ; and what is done towards the salvation of the soul shall certainly turn to good account. The soul being the principal part of the man, the saving of that only is mentioned, but it includes the salvation of the whole man : the spirit shall be saved from hell, the body raised from the grave, and both saved from eternal death. And then, by such conversion of heart and life, a *multitude of sins shall be hid.* A most comfortable passage of scripture is this. We learn hence that though our sins are many, even a multitude, yet they may be hid or pardoned ; and that when sin is turned from or forsaken it shall be hid, never to appear in judgment against us. Let people contrive to cover or excuse their sin as they will, there is no way effectually and finally to hide it but by forsaking it. Some make the sense of this text to be, that conversion shall *prevent* a multitude of sins ; and it is a truth beyond dispute that many sins are prevented in the party converted, many also may be prevented in others that he may have an influence upon, or may converse with. Upon the whole, how should we lay out ourselves with all possible concern for the conversion of sinners ! It will be for the happiness and salvation of the converted ; it will prevent much mischief, and the spreading and multiplying of sin in the world ; it will be for the glory and honour of God ; and it will mightily redound to our comfort and renown in the great day. *Those that turn many to righteousness,* and those who help to do so, *shall shine as the stars for ever and ever.*